First Responders

| LIST OF CONTRIBUTORS |

The authors of this book served under Presidents George W. Bush and Barack Obama at the Board of Governors of the Federal Reserve System (Federal Reserve Board), the Federal Deposit Insurance Corporation, the Federal Reserve Bank of New York, and the U.S. Department of Treasury during the crisis years.

SCOTT G. ALVAREZ (Nonbanks, Legal) was general counsel of the Federal Reserve Board.

MICHAEL BARR (Housing) was assistant secretary of the Treasury for financial institutions under Secretary Timothy F. Geithner.

THOMAS C. BAXTER, JR. (Legal) was general counsel and executive vice president of the Federal Reserve Bank of New York.

BEN S. BERNANKE (Editor; Introduction) was chairman of the Federal Reserve Board from 2006 to 2014.

TIM CLARK (Banks II) was senior adviser, Division of Banking Supervision and Regulation of the Federal Reserve Board.

BRIAN DEESE (Autos) was special assistant to President Obama for economic policy.

WILLIAM C. DUDLEY (Nonbanks) was president of the Federal Reserve Bank of New York from 2009 to 2018, and before that, system open market account manager to the Federal Open Market Committee and head of the markets group at the Federal Reserve Bank of New York.

WILLIAM B. ENGLISH (Classic Lender of Last Resort) was deputy director, Division of Monetary Affairs, Federal Reserve Board, and later became director.

JASON FURMAN (Fiscal Policy) was deputy director of the White House National Economic Council and deputy assistant to President Obama for economic policy from 2009 to 2010. He later served as chairman of Obama's Council of Economic Advisers.

TIMOTHY F. GEITHNER (Editor; Introduction) was president of the Federal Reserve Bank of New York from 2003 to 2009 and the 75th secretary of the Treasury from 2009 to 2013 under President Obama.

ROBERT F. HOYT (Legal) was general counsel of the Department of the Treasury under both Secretaries Henry M. Paulson, Jr., and Geithner.

DAN JESTER (GSEs, Banks I, Autos) was a contractor for the Department of the Treasury under Secretary Paulson.

MATTHEW KABAKER (GSEs, Banks II) was senior adviser to Treasury Secretary Geithner and deputy assistant secretary, capital markets.

NEEL T. KASHKARI (Housing, TARP) was assistant secretary of Treasury for international economics and development under Secretary Paulson and later interim assistant secretary of Treasury for financial stability under Secretaries Paulson and Geithner.

DONALD KOHN (Monetary Policy) was the vice chairman of the Federal Reserve Board from 2006 to 2010.

MICHAEL H. KRIMMINGER (Debt Guarantees) was special adviser for policy to Chairman Sheila Bair, deputy to the chairman for policy, and general counsel of the Federal Deposit Insurance Corporation.

ANDREAS LEHNERT (Housing) was chief, Household and Real Estate Finance Section, and assistant director, Division of Research and Statistics, at the Federal Reserve Board.

J. NELLIE LIANG (Editor; Nonbanks, Outcomes) was associate director, Division of Research and Statistics, at the Federal Reserve Board, and later became director of the Division of Financial Stability.

LORIE LOGAN (Novel Lender of Last Resort) was vice president and director of Treasury markets, Federal Reserve Bank of New York.

CLAY LOWERY (International) was assistant secretary of Treasury for international affairs under Secretary Paulson.

TIMOTHY G. MASSAD (TARP) was in the Office of Financial Stability from May 2009 to June 2014, first as chief counsel and then as assistant secretary of Treasury for financial stability under Secretaries Geithner and Jacob Lew.

MARGARET M. McCONNELL (Outcomes) was deputy chief of staff for policy, Federal Reserve Bank of New York.

PATRICIA C. MOSSER (Classic Lender of Last Resort) was senior vice president, markets group, Federal Reserve Bank of New York, and also the acting system open market account manager for the Federal Open Market Committee in 2009.

DAVID NASON (Banks I) was assistant secretary of Treasury for financial institutions under Secretary Paulson.

WILLIAM NELSON (Novel Lender of Last Resort) was associate director, Division of Monetary Affairs, Federal Reserve Board.

JEREMIAH NORTON (GSEs, Banks I) was deputy assistant secretary of Treasury for financial institutions under Secretary Paulson.

PATRICK PARKINSON (Novel Lender of Last Resort) was deputy director, Division of Research and Statistics, Federal Reserve Board.

HENRY M. PAULSON, JR. (Editor; Introduction) was the 74th secretary of the Treasury from 2006 to 2009 under President George W. Bush.

LEE SACHS (GSEs, Banks II) was counselor to Treasury Secretary Geithner.

BRIAN SACK (Monetary Policy) was system open market account manager for the Federal Open Market Committee and head of the markets group at the Federal Reserve Bank of New York from 2009 to 2012.

STEVEN M. SHAFRAN (Money Market Fund Guarantees, Autos) was senior adviser to Treasury Secretary Paulson.

NATHAN SHEETS (International) was director of the division of international finance at the Federal Reserve Board.

PHILLIP SWAGEL (Housing, Outcomes) was assistant secretary of Treasury for economic policy under Secretary Paulson.

EDWIN (TED) TRUMAN (International) was counselor to Treasury Secretary Geithner.

JAMES R. WIGAND (Triage & Resolution) was deputy director of the Federal Deposit Insurance Corporation Division of Resolutions and Receiverships and served as the FDIC's chief resolution strategist during the crisis.

FIRST RESPONDERS

INSIDE THE U.S. STRATEGY
FOR FIGHTING THE 2007–2009
GLOBAL FINANCIAL CRISIS

||||||||||||||||||||||||||

EDITED BY

BEN S. BERNANKE, TIMOTHY F. GEITHNER,

AND HENRY M. PAULSON, JR.,

WITH J. NELLIE LIANG

||||||||||||||||||||||||||

Yale

UNIVERSITY PRESS

NEW HAVEN AND LONDON

This book is the result of a project supported by the Brookings Institution's Hutchins Center on Fiscal & Monetary Policy, David Wessel, director, and the Yale Program on Financial Stability at the Yale School of Management, Andrew Metrick, director.

Yale University Press books may be purchased in quantity for educational, business, or promotional use. For information, please e-mail sales.press@yale.edu (U.S. office) or sales@yaleup.co.uk (U.K. office).

Designed by Sonia L. Shannon
Set in Minion Pro and Gotham Display type by Westchester Publishing Services.
Printed in the United States of America.

Library of Congress Control Number: 2019940872
ISBN 978-0-300-24444-1 (hardcover: alk. paper)

A catalogue record for this book is available from the British Library.

This paper meets the requirements of ANSI/NISO Z39.48-1992 (Permanence of Paper).

10 9 8 7 6 5 4 3 2 1

| CONTENTS |

| ILLUSTRATIONS |

| TABLES |

| ABBREVIATIONS |

13(3)/Section 13(3)	Federal Reserve Act of 1913, Section 13(3)
ABCP	asset-backed commercial paper
ABS	asset-backed securities
AGP	Asset Guarantee Program
AIFP	Automotive Industry Financing Program
AIG	American International Group
ALT-A	Alternative-A; measure of mortgage risk that falls between prime and subprime
AMLF	Asset-Backed Commercial Paper Money Market Mutual Fund Liquidity Facility
AMT	alternative minimum tax
ARRA	American Recovery and Reinvestment Act of 2009, or Recovery Act
BEA	Bureau of Economic Analysis, U.S. Department of Commerce
BHC	bank holding company
BIS	Bank for International Settlements
BNY	Bank of New York Mellon
BoA	Bank of America
BoC	Bank of Canada
BoE	Bank of England
BoJ	Bank of Japan
CAMELS	capital adequacy, asset quality, management, earnings, liquidity, and sensitivity to market risk
CAP	Capital Assistance Program
CBO	Congressional Budget Office
CDCI	Community Development Capital Initiative
CDFI	Community Development Financial Institution
CDOs	collateralized debt obligations
CDS	credit default swap(s)
CEA	Council of Economic Advisers

CMBS	commercial mortgage-backed securities
CP	commercial paper
CPFF	Commercial Paper Funding Facility
CPP	Capital Purchase Program
CY	calendar year
DFA	Dodd-Frank Wall Street Reform and Consumer and Protection Act of 2010, or Dodd-Frank
DGP	Debt Guarantee Program
DIF	Deposit Insurance Fund (under FDIC)
DTI	debt-to-income ratio
ECB	European Central Bank
EESA	Emergency Economic Stabilization Act of 2008
ESF	Exchange Stabilization Fund
Fannie Mae	Federal National Mortgage Association
FCIC	Financial Crisis Inquiry Commission
FDIC	Federal Deposit Insurance Corporation
FDICIA	Federal Deposit Insurance Corporation Improvement Act of 1991
FHA	Federal Housing Administration
FHFA	Federal Housing Finance Agency
FHLB	Federal Home Loan Bank
FinSOB	Financial Stability Oversight Board (U.S. body established under EESA)
FMAP	Federal Medical Assistance Percentage
FOMC	Federal Open Market Committee
FRA	Federal Reserve Act of 1913
FRB/US	Federal Reserve's large-scale estimated general equilibrium model of the U.S. economy
FRBNY	Federal Reserve Bank of New York, or New York Fed
FRED	Federal Reserve Economic Data, Federal Reserve Bank of St. Louis
Freddie Mac	Federal Home Loan Mortgage Corporation
FSB	Financial Stability Board (international body established by the G-20)
FSF	Financial Stability Forum
FSOC	Financial Stability Oversight Council
FSP	Financial Stability Plan

FX	foreign exchange
GAO	U.S. Government Accountability Office
GDP	gross domestic product
GE	General Electric
GECC	GE Capital Corporation
GFC	global financial crisis
GM	General Motors Company
GMAC	General Motors Acceptance Corporation (now Ally Financial)
Group of Seven (G-7)	Canada, France, Germany, Italy, Japan, the United Kingdom, and the United States
Group of Twenty (G-20)	G-7 plus Argentina, Australia, Brazil, China, India, Indonesia, Mexico, Russia, Saudi Arabia, South Africa, South Korea, Turkey, and the European Union
GSEs	government-sponsored enterprises (such as Fannie Mae, Freddie Mac)
HAMP	Home Affordable Modification Program
HARP	Home Affordable Refinance Program
HERA	Housing and Economic Recovery Act of 2008
HFA	Housing Finance Agency
HIRE	Hiring Incentives to Restore Employment
HOLC	Home Owners' Loan Corporation
HOPE NOW	alliance of lenders, counselors, investors, and other mortgage market participants formed to help homeowners avoid foreclosures
HUD	U.S. Department of Housing and Urban Development
IDB	Inter-American Development Bank
IFIs	international financial institutions
IMF	International Monetary Fund
IPC	individual, partnership, or corporation
IPO	initial public offering
IRS	Internal Revenue Service
JPMC	JPMorgan Chase
Libor	London Interbank Offered Rate
LLC	limited liability company
LLP	Legacy Loan Program
LTV	loan-to-value ratio

MBS	mortgage-backed securities
MHA	Making Home Affordable
MLEC	Master Liquidity Enhancement Conduit
MMF	money market fund
MMIFF	Money Market Investor Funding Facility
NAB	New Arrangements to Borrow, IMF
NAV	net asset value
NBER	National Bureau of Economic Research
NUMMI	New United Motor Manufacturing, Inc.
OCC	Office of the Comptroller of the Currency, U.S. Department of the Treasury
OECD	Organisation for Economic Co-operation and Development
OFHEO	Office of Federal Housing Enterprise Oversight
OFS	Office of Financial Stability, U.S. Department of the Treasury
OIG	Office of Inspector General, U.S. Department of the Treasury
OIS	overnight indexed swap
OMB	Office of Management and Budget
OMOs	open market operations
OTC	over the counter
OTS	Office of Thrift Supervision, U.S. Department of the Treasury
PDCF	Primary Dealer Credit Facility
PPIP	Public-Private Investment Program
PSPA	preferred stock purchase agreement
QE	quantitative easing
repo	repurchase agreement
RMBS	residential mortgage-backed securities
RTC	Resolution Trust Corporation
S&L	savings and loan
S&P 500	Standard & Poor's 500 index
SAAR	seasonally adjusted annual rate
SBA	Small Business Administration
SBA 7a	Small Business Administration 7(a) Securities Purchase Program
SCAP	Supervisory Capital Assistance Program
SDR	special drawing right
SEC	U.S. Securities and Exchange Commission
SFP	Supplementary Financing Program

SIGTARP	Special Inspector General for the Troubled Asset Relief Program
SIPC	Securities Investor Protection Corporation
SIV	structured investment vehicle
SNAP	Supplemental Nutrition Assistance Program
SNB	Swiss National Bank
SPSPA	Senior Preferred Stock Purchase Agreement
SPV	special purpose vehicle
TAF	Term Auction Facility
TAGP	Transaction Account Guarantee Program
TALF	Term Asset-Backed Securities Loan Facility
TARP	Troubled Assets Relief Program
TIP	Targeted Investment Program
TLAC	total loss-absorbing capacity
TLGP	Temporary Liquidity Guarantee Program
TSLF	Term Securities Lending Facility
WaMu	Washington Mutual
WTO	World Trade Organization
ZLB	zero lower bound

| CHAPTER ONE |

The Financial Crisis and Its Lessons for the Future

BEN S. BERNANKE, TIMOTHY F. GEITHNER, AND HENRY M. PAULSON, JR.

The financial crisis of 2008 was the most damaging financial event in the United States since the Great Depression. It brought down some of the nation's largest and oldest financial institutions and brought others to the brink of failure before the government intervened to rescue them. The crisis paralyzed global credit, ravaged global finance, and plunged the American economy into the most painful recession since the 1930s. But it did not result in a second Depression, even though by many measures the financial upheaval was more severe than the events that helped trigger the first Depression. Instead, following the stabilization of the financial system in 2009, the U.S. economy began a slow but sustained expansion, which (at this writing) has brought the national unemployment rate to its lowest level in half a century.

To be sure, that a new Depression was avoided isn't much consolation to those who lost homes, jobs, and incomes in the deep recession that the crisis engendered. It also has limited political salience—as Barney Frank, the Massachusetts Democratic congressman with whom we worked closely during the crisis, liked to say, you can't put a counterfactual on a bumper sticker. Still, the government response to the crisis in the United States was both forceful and effective, helping to end the crisis and mitigate the (still very severe) economic damage. The response was also very unpopular, of course, involving as it did interventions that appeared aimed at helping some of those seen as responsible for the crisis. We argue in this chapter that the unpopularity of the government response, despite its effectiveness, stems in significant part from the fact that the government entered the crisis with inadequate powers and an outdated regulatory structure, which forced a more improvised and constrained set of policies than might otherwise have been possible. Policymakers should be thinking now about how to make the response to the next crisis both more effective and more politically palatable.

The government's response to the crisis evolved in stages. It began in a conventional way, with traditional central bank lending designed to restore liquidity to the commercial banking system. But when conventional lender-of-last-resort measures failed to quell the panic, the response gradually escalated, first to unconventional central bank lending to shore up short-term funding markets and provide liquidity to nonbank firms, then to direct government rescues of failing financial giants and backstops for vital credit markets, and eventually to massive government injections of capital and guarantees of liabilities for the entire financial system. The response also included extraordinary efforts to reverse the economic free fall and jump-start a recovery through fiscal and monetary stimulus.

It wasn't a smooth or mistake-free process. As already noted, the U.S. government did not have the powers it needed to fight the panic until it was well under way, nor was there an established playbook for an emergency like this. Things got very dark before Congress agreed to provide new, essential authorities, but ultimately it did. In the end, a collaborative effort by two successive presidents of opposing parties, a politically divided Congress, the Federal Reserve, the Treasury Department, the Federal Deposit Insurance Corporation, and thousands of dedicated public servants at a variety of agencies was successful in ending the panic, preventing a new Depression, and launching a slow but steady recovery.

The three of us were among the policymakers who helped shape the national and global response to the crisis—Ben S. Bernanke as chair of the Federal Reserve; Henry M. Paulson, Jr., as secretary of the Treasury under President George W. Bush; and Timothy F. Geithner as president of the Federal Reserve Bank of New York during the Bush years and then as Treasury secretary under President Barack Obama. We have all written memoirs about our experiences, but ten years after the crisis we thought it would be valuable to be part of a more comprehensive review of the U.S. policy response—the rationale for the choices that were made, an assessment of what worked and what didn't, and some lessons for the future. The U.S. government has emergency protocols in place for responding to disasters like pandemics or terror attacks, but it lacks a basic playbook for containing the damage from financial disasters.

This is why we're so pleased that the Brookings Institution's Hutchins Center on Fiscal and Monetary Policy and the Yale School of Management's Program on Financial Stability have sponsored a thorough review of the government response to the crisis and the economic and financial outcomes. The chapters in this volume—on subjects such as the Federal Reserve's conventional and unconventional lending, the government takeover of Fannie Mae and Freddie Mac, the bank capital and guarantee programs, U.S. fiscal, monetary, and housing policies during the crisis, and many more—provide important details about and assessments of each element of that response. The final chapter summarizes the state of the evidence on the outcomes of the crisis.

Importantly, the authors of the chapters to follow have vital first-hand knowledge, in that they were among the key practitioners who devised and executed the policies about which they have written. The three of us observed their work first-hand during the crisis. We watched these patriotic public officials show remarkable creativity and integrity, exploring the best of the bad options, working tirelessly to find the most effective way to minimize the risk of economic devastation and repair the damage of the crisis. In each of the chapters that follow, the authors describe the specific challenges they confronted, the options they considered and rejected as well as those they chose, the legal, political, and economic constraints, the gritty but essential details of implementation, the outcomes of their choices, and the lessons learned. We hope their collective efforts will memorialize what was learned from the experience of 2007–2009 and help our successors and theirs better navigate future crises.

THE CRISIS AS PANIC

The crisis of 2008 was a classic financial panic, a staple of economic history at least since the Dutch tulip crisis of 1637, except this time it was rooted in a mania over dubious mortgages rather than fashionable flowers. As the housing boom went bust, investors and creditors frantically reduced their exposures to anything and anyone associated with mortgages and financial instruments backed by mortgages, triggering fire sales and margin calls. The financial panic crippled credit and shattered confidence in the broader economy, while the resulting job losses and foreclosures created more panic in financial markets, a vicious cycle that threatened to drag down the economy along with the financial system.

It's hard to overstate just how chaotic and frightening the crisis became. A one-month period starting in September 2008 included the abrupt nationalization of the mortgage giants Fannie Mae and Freddie Mac, the most aggressive financial intervention by the U.S. government since the Depression; the failure of the venerable investment bank Lehman Brothers, the largest bankruptcy in U.S. history; the collapse of the brokerage firm Merrill Lynch into the arms of Bank of America; an $85 billion rescue of the insurer AIG to prevent an even larger bankruptcy than Lehman's; the demise of Washington Mutual and Wachovia, the two largest failures of federally insured banks in U.S. history; the first-ever government guarantees for more than $3 trillion worth of money market funds; the equally unprecedented backstopping of a further $1 trillion worth of commercial paper; and congressional approval, after an initial market-crushing rejection, of a $700 billion arsenal of government support for the entire financial system. This all happened during the home stretch of a presidential campaign. History was moving at warp speed, and consequential decisions had to be made every day in the fog of uncertainty.

Importantly, the events of 2007–2009 were a panic not only in the psychological sense, although emotions certainly ran high, but also in a narrower, technical sense. For economic historians, a panic refers specifically to a broad-based run on short-term liabilities. Panics can occur because finance, a large and dynamic sector that is normally an important driver of economic growth, is also inherently fragile. The fragility stems from the fact that banks and other financial intermediaries perform two key economic functions that occasionally come into conflict. First, they give people an easily accessible place to stash their money, one that provides more safety and a higher interest rate than a mattress. Second, they use that money to make loans to households and businesses. In other words, they borrow short-term in order to lend long-term, a process known as "maturity transformation."

Maturity transformation is a vital social function, but it comes with a built-in risk: Every institution that borrows short and lends long is vulnerable to a "run on the bank," if for any reason depositors or other short-term creditors lose confidence in that institution. Even a solvent bank, with assets more valuable than its liabilities, can collapse if those assets are too illiquid to cover its immediate demands for cash. A panic is a bank run writ large: It is a situation in which creditors lose confidence in the system as a whole and run on a wide range of short-term liabilities. Historically, panics have typically led to large contractions in credit and sharp declines in asset prices, with predictably disastrous effects on the broader economy.

The United States, like most countries, has tried to reduce the danger of runs and panics with regulations that limit banks from taking excessive risks, along with government insurance for depositors that reduces their incentive to run if they fear their bank is in danger. But modern financial institutions depend on many forms of funding other than deposits that remain uninsured and potentially "runnable." And in the modern age, a run on a bank no longer requires a physical run from an actual bank, just a click of a mouse.

The more general point is that financial institutions, unlike other businesses whose success depends primarily on the cost and quality of their goods and services, depend primarily on confidence. No financial institution can function without it, but it can go at any time, for rational or irrational reasons. When it goes, it usually goes quickly, and it's hard to get back. Fear is hard-wired into the human psyche, and the herd mentality is powerful, which makes stampedes hard to predict and hard to stop. Consequently, the potential for panic can never be fully eradicated, because there's no way to eradicate overconfidence or confusion.

In other words, the world will face the threat of financial crises as long as risk-taking and maturity transformation remain central to finance, and as long as humans remain human. Unfortunately, disaster will always be possible.

So what made this particular disaster happen?

THE HOUSING BOOM AND THE MORTGAGE MANIA

This crisis began, as major crises usually do, with a credit boom. But while all crises begin with credit booms, not all credit booms end in crises, and the vulnerabilities in the system that can seem obvious in retrospect did not seem obvious at the time. In fact, the financial system seemed more stable than ever in the years before the crisis; banks were enjoying record profits, and 2005 was the first year without a U.S. bank failure since the Depression. The U.S. economy seemed strong as well, and there was widespread confidence that if it did slow, the financial system would be resilient. It had weathered a series of modest recessions in the previous decades, and banks seemed to have plenty of capital to absorb losses in case of a downturn.

However, the credit boom of the early 2000s was an unusually powerful one, which resulted in both ordinary families and many financial institutions becoming dangerously overextended. Much of the boom took place in the U.S. mortgage market. Mortgage debt per U.S. household soared 63 percent from 2001 to 2007, much faster than household incomes. And the industry's underwriting standards, especially for higher-risk subprime mortgages to lower-income borrowers, eroded dramatically. Many lenders would approve just about any applicant to borrow just about the entire cost of a new home regardless of their credit history—whether or not they had a job, provided any documents verifying their income, or demonstrated any realistic hope of making their monthly payments.

Normally, lenders have strong incentives to be careful about how much they lend and to whom, because they need to get paid back to make money. But in the years before the crisis, Wall Street firms had responded to a strong global appetite for safe-looking assets by packaging mortgages into complex mortgage-backed securities that they could sell to investors in search of higher returns. This investor demand gave those Wall Street firms an equally powerful appetite for mortgages that could serve as raw materials for these securities. And loan originators that knew they could sell their mortgages without retaining any of the risk of default had little incentive to seek creditworthy borrowers. These loans became grist for a lucrative mill that divided the payment streams from mortgages with different degrees of risk and then repackaged them into securities, a process known as securitization.

This "originate-to-distribute" mortgage model created bad incentives, and some analysts have blamed it for the entire crisis. In this view, disaster could have been averted if mortgage lenders had been required to hold more of their loans, because they wouldn't have been so reckless if they had more "skin in the game." But that can't be the whole story, since many of those lenders and their parent companies did hold many of their loans, as well as securities backed by their loans, and accepted them as solid collateral in short-term lending markets. Firms like Countrywide Financial, the nation's largest mortgage lender, had plenty of skin in the game; they ran into trouble because they didn't distribute *enough* of the risky loans they originated.

In reality, the principal driver of the mortgage boom was excessive optimism about the housing market. Rising house prices promoted easy borrowing terms, and easy terms in turn helped drive prices even higher. There was a widespread assumption that borrowers could buy more house than they could afford without significant risk, because if they had trouble making payments they could always refinance or sell at a profit—and for years that rosy assumption was often correct. Even mortgage brokers and Wall Street bankers invested their own money in real estate throughout the boom. They were just as caught up in the mania as the buyers of their mortgage-backed securities.

Low-quality mortgages ended up imperiling the entire financial system—not so much because of the direct losses on the mortgages themselves, which were significant but likely manageable, but because of the securitization boom, which carved those mortgages into securities that became a ubiquitous form of currency and collateral throughout the system. These securities often received triple-A stamps of approval from credit rating agencies that received fees from the firms that issued them, and markets often treated the securities as if they were almost as safe as Treasuries. The flawed models justifying those triple-A ratings depended in part on the optimistic belief that even if housing prices did slump in one region of the country, they would never crash all across the country at the same time. That had been true since World War II, but the assumption that securities assembled from geographically diverse mortgages would never see serious losses turned out to be wrong. Home prices would plunge more than 30 percent nationwide, and the portion of subprime mortgages in or near default would soar from 6 percent to more than 30 percent.

Again, the systemic danger was not just that mortgages were less safe than they seemed. The systemic danger was that the securities they backed had come to underpin much of modern finance, which made the health of the entire system dependent on the perceived health of the mortgage market in ways almost no one recognized at the time. That dependence would have been dangerous even if the securities had been straightforward, transparent, and traded on public exchanges. But the new products of financial engineering were often complex, opaque, and embedded with hidden leverage. These products were supposed to help reduce risk, by spreading it around and customizing it to the needs of the investor, but they made the overall system more vulnerable to a crisis of confidence and harder to stabilize after the crisis began. Once mortgages started to go bad and derivatives constructed from mortgages started to seem risky, it felt easier and safer to sell them all than to try to figure out just how risky individual securities were. Meanwhile, the market for buying and selling derivatives was an archaic mess of millions of contracts among thousands of private counterparties, where it was often nearly impossible to figure out who held what and who owed what to whom. That meant that in a crisis, investors and creditors would be uncertain what exposures they had or what was going on with their counterparties. And uncertainty promotes panic.

Still, in the years before the crisis, the subprime mortgage market did not look like a threat to take down the entire system. Less than one-seventh of all outstanding mortgages in the United States were subprime. The defaults and delinquencies that triggered the crisis were mostly concentrated in adjustable-rate subprime, which accounted for less than one-twelfth of all mortgages. Straightforward calculations suggested that even if every subprime mortgage borrower defaulted, the losses would be modest relative to the size of the economy, and easily absorbed by the capital buffers of major banks and other lenders. What such calculations missed—what almost everyone missed—was the way mortgages were poised to become a vector of panic throughout the financial system.

A VULNERABLE FINANCIAL SYSTEM

Not all bubbles and busts threaten the stability of the broader financial system. When the dot-com bubble of the late 1990s burst, investors in previously high-flying internet stocks lost money, but there wasn't much of a ripple effect. Panics happen only when bubbles are financed with borrowed money that can run. During the mortgage bubble, financial institutions borrowed heavily in short-term and even overnight credit markets—such as the repo and asset-backed commercial paper markets—in order to finance bets on mortgage-related assets. Both the borrowers and the regulators underestimated the run risk of these short-term liabilities, because many of these borrowings were collateralized with specific assets that could be claimed by lenders in the event of default. That assessment would prove wrong in the crisis, as many creditors would decide that refusing to renew their loans was preferable to the risk that they would be stuck with collateral that would be difficult to value and hard to sell. Many financial institutions also ramped up their overall leverage (including longer-term debt) before the crisis, in some cases borrowing more than $30 for every dollar of shareholder capital—leaving themselves extremely limited cushions against losses. And many of these heavily leveraged institutions had become so big, so interconnected, and so tightly woven into the fabric of modern finance that they would pose a serious danger to the system if they ever unraveled.

This buildup of leverage, especially runnable debt, helped make the financial system vulnerable to an unexpected shock. What made the situation even more explosive—and a crisis much more difficult to anticipate or head off—was that many of the highly levered institutions were not technically "banks," in that they did not hold bank charters. They behaved like banks, borrowing short and lending long, but they operated outside the commercial banking system, with neither the supervisory oversight nor the safety net our system provides for institutions with commercial bank charters. Before the crisis, more than half the leverage in U.S. finance had migrated to these "shadow banks" or "nonbanks"—investment banks such as Bear Stearns and Lehman Brothers, the mortgage giants Fannie Mae and Freddie Mac, insurance companies such as AIG, money market funds, corporate finance arms such as GE Capital and GMAC, and even nonbank affiliates of traditional commercial banks. These firms all engaged, to a greater or lesser extent, in the fragile alchemy of maturity transformation—but without the security of insured deposits that never run, without effective regulatory constraints on their leverage, and without the ability to turn to the Fed for help if their financing evaporated. In short, our financial system had outgrown a regulatory system necessary to mitigate risk. Chapter 4, by Scott G. Alvarez, William C. Dudley, and J. Nellie Liang, provides more background on nonbank financial institutions, their regulation, and their role in the intermediation of credit.

The inadequate coverage of shadow banks was just one of the weaknesses (although a major one) of the U.S. financial regulatory system on the eve of the crisis. Creaky and fragmented, the regulatory framework in large part reflected the financial system as it had existed during the Depression or earlier, when commercial banks dominated the provision of credit and were thus the focus of regulatory supervision. But even oversight of commercial banks could be incoherent, as responsibilities for supervising them were divided among the Fed, the Office of the Comptroller of the Currency (OCC), the Federal Deposit Insurance Corporation (FDIC), the Office of Thrift Supervision (OTS), foreign regulators that helped supervise U.S. affiliates of overseas banks, and various state banking commissions of varying levels of vigilance and competence. In some cases, banks effectively got to choose their own supervisors—Countrywide reorganized as a thrift in order to enjoy the lenient oversight of the OTS—and often had multiple supervisors with unclear lines of authority.

Outside the commercial banks, the regulation of risk-taking was even spottier. Fannie Mae and Freddie Mac, known as government-sponsored enterprises, or GSEs, had their own ineffectual Washington regulator. The Securities and Exchange Commission (SEC) oversaw investment banks but did not try to constrain their leverage or limit their reliance on short-term funding. The SEC mostly focused on investor protection, as did the Commodity Futures Trading Commission, whose purview included many derivatives markets. And while the Federal Trade Commission, the Fed, and a slew of other federal and state agencies had various financial consumer protection responsibilities, it wasn't anyone's top priority.

Meanwhile, none of these agencies was responsible for analyzing or protecting against systemic risk. There was no single regulator responsible for safeguarding or even monitoring the safety and soundness of the system as a whole, rather than the safety and soundness of individual institutions; no supervisor had visibility into the entire system of nonbanks and banks. Nobody was assessing the general safety of derivatives or overnight funding or other potential threats to stability that cut across institutional lines. And while the FDIC had emergency authority to wind down failing commercial banks in a swift and orderly fashion, no one had the authority to step in to avoid a chaotic bankruptcy of a major nonbank, to inject capital into a nonbank, or to guarantee its liabilities.

The gaps and weaknesses of the regulatory system certainly contributed to the vulnerability of the financial system in the run-up to the crisis. It is now evident, for example, that the government let major financial institutions take on too much risk relative to their capital. Capital is the shock absorber that can help an institution withstand losses, retain confidence, and remain solvent during a crisis—and in retrospect, America's financial institutions needed a lot more of it. But that's in retrospect. On the eve of the crisis, banks were holding more capital than their legally mandated capital requirements, and the market-based measure of risk in those institutions suggested they were still relatively strong. The New York Fed did ask the banks it oversaw to run stress tests modeling the potential impact of recessions and other types of shocks, but the economy and financial system had been relatively stable for so long that none came up with a scenario that significantly dented its capital buffer.

It would later become obvious that the backward-looking capital regime for banks, designed to protect against the kind of losses created by relatively mild recent recessions, was not nearly conservative enough. Regulators also allowed banks to count too much poor-quality capital toward their required ratios, rather than insisting on loss-absorbing common equity. Supervisors failed to recognize how much leverage banks had hidden in complex derivatives and off-balance-sheet vehicles, which made them look better capitalized than they actually were. And there were few limitations on the ability of banks to rely on uninsured, short-term funding.

But while the existing capital regime for commercial banks was too weak, it was nonetheless restrictive enough to drive trillions of dollars' worth of leverage into nonbanks that weren't constrained by those requirements. Tougher requirements on banks, without extending those requirements to other financial institutions, would have made banks safer. But they would have also pushed more risk into the rest of the financial system, beyond the scope of the bank safety net, possibly leaving the overall financial system even more fragile. That's the paradox, and the danger, of a fragmented regulatory system that sets different standards for institutions that call themselves banks and institutions that get described by some other name. The most damaging problem with America's capital regime was not that it was applied too weakly but that it was applied too narrowly. The institutions with the most marginal mortgage holdings and the least stable funding bases also had the thinnest capital buffers, but as a practical matter they were largely outside the reach of the regulatory system. In 2005, banks and thrifts under federal supervision originated only 20 percent of all subprime mortgages.

Regulations should have been stronger and more comprehensive, and the regulators more vigilant and more proactive. And the political effort to build those stronger defenses should have happened during the boom. But during the boom, if the prevailing political mood was inhospitable to stricter enforcement of existing bank regulations, it was downright hostile to reforms modernizing those regulations or extending them to nonbanks. Because the system had seemed relatively resilient, the main debate in the years before the crisis was whether there should be additional *de*regulation, not broader, tougher regulation.

Unfortunately, reform is extremely tough to achieve without a crisis to make the case for it. This was most vivid with Fannie Mae and Freddie Mac, the two massive GSEs that owned or guaranteed half the residential mortgages in the United States. Markets assumed the government, having chartered Fannie Mae and Freddie Mac, would rescue them if they ever got in trouble, so the companies felt safe piling up leverage. We all expressed concern before the crisis that they were seriously undercapitalized and underregulated. But despite a major effort by Hank to get reform legislation, Congress was not prepared to act until the firms were on the brink of collapse.

The three of us were all uncomfortable with these gaps before the crisis. We all tried to lean against the prevailing winds of overconfidence, pushing back against the notion that crises were vestiges of the past, calling for more robust risk management and humility about tail risks, establishing new risk committees and task forces within our institutions to try to focus attention on systemic threats. But we were not sufficiently forceful in acting to contain those threats, and none of us recognized how they were about to spiral out of control. For all of our experience with the theory and practice of crises and crisis management—in academia, markets, and government—we still failed to anticipate the worst crisis of our lifetimes. We were worried that something terrible could conceivably happen, but even in the months leading up to it, we didn't foresee how. It was a failure of imagination, not just institutional organization.

Of course, we were not alone in our failures. The crisis caught just about everyone by surprise. One lesson for crisis detection is that it's incredibly hard to predict a financial meltdown. Some people might be prescient about some things, but you can't count on prescience as a realistic crisis-avoidance strategy. Our analyses gave insufficient weight not only to the possibility of a nationwide decline in housing prices but also to the risk of a broader loss of confidence in the stability of financial institutions. We didn't foresee how the complexity and opacity of mortgage-backed securities would lead creditors and investors to stampede when "mortgage" became a scary word. We didn't anticipate how bad news about one segment of the housing market could create what has been called the "mad cow disease effect," in which rumors about the occurrence of the disease in a few animals frighten consumers into abandoning all purchases of beef rather than trying to figure out where or whether any risk actually exists.

Subprime and the complexities of mortgage securitization markets were a problem, but if they hadn't triggered a financial panic, the damage would have been mostly limited to a subset of subprime borrowers and lenders. More than half of the U.S. housing losses would happen *after* the height of the panic in the fall of 2008. Without the panic, the housing crisis itself would have been much less severe.

But a panic did occur. Which meant that the fate of the financial system, and the economy, would depend on the policy response.

EARLY DAYS: THE LIMITS OF A LENDER OF LAST RESORT

If we had to pick the date that the crisis began, it would be August 9, 2007, when the French bank BNP Paribas froze withdrawals from three funds that held securities backed by U.S. subprime mortgages. What made the news so unnerving was not that securities backed by subprime mortgages were losing value but that BNP Paribas had no idea how to assign them any value, because no one was buying them "regardless of their quality." That kind of inchoate fear and uncertainty is the stuff panics are made of. Banks were hoarding cash, the rates they charged each other to borrow were spiking, and skittish investors were pulling money out of other funds to make sure their cash didn't get frozen as well.

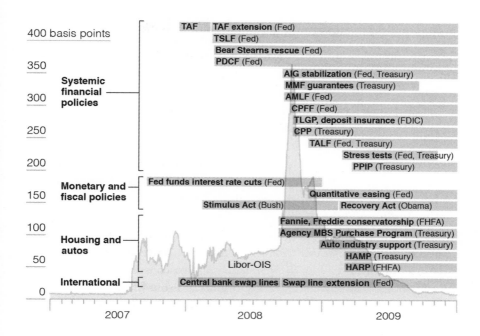

Figure 1.1 **Government Responses to the Financial Crisis**

Notes: (1) Start dates for programs reflect the date of their announcement. (2) Stress tests include the Supervisory Capital Assessment Program (SCAP), under which the Federal Reserve and other bank supervisors conducted the stress tests, and the Capital Assistance Program (CAP), a capital backstop for capital-deficient institutions. (3) Acronyms used in this figure are defined in the list of abbreviations at the front of this book. (4) Libor-OIS is the difference between the London Interbank Offered Rate (Libor) and the overnight indexed swap (OIS) rate.

Source: Three-month Libor-OIS: Bloomberg Finance L.P.

In the early phase of any crisis, policymakers have to calibrate how forcefully to respond to a situation they don't yet entirely understand. Governments that routinely ride to the rescue at the first hint of trouble can encourage reckless speculation, propping up nonviable firms and setting up the financial system to fall from a higher cliff in the future. Failure is usually a healthy phenomenon, instilling discipline in survivors. Early in a crisis, the default assumption should be that private firms face the consequences of their mistakes, even though they often clamor for help.

But it's a delicate balance as, in a serious crisis, government inaction or timidity can make things worse. When financial first responders are too slow to act, a building panic might rage out of control, with consequences for everyone, not just overleveraged speculators. Unfortunately, crises don't announce themselves as either idiosyncratic brush fires that burn themselves out or systemic upheavals that threaten the entire economy. Policymakers need to figure it out as they go along.

The early symptoms of the crisis in 2007 looked like classic liquidity problems. And the only tools available at that time were the lending and monetary policy authorities of the Fed. For these reasons, much of the initial action would have to come from the Federal Reserve. When confidence erodes and credit markets seize up, a central bank can serve as a "lender of last resort," providing liquidity to solvent firms when private lenders won't. The Federal Reserve's lender-of-last-resort function, the discount window, offers emergency loans to any commercial bank facing a cash crunch; and in the early moments of a liquidity crisis, the discount window is the natural place to start. William B. English and Patricia C. Mosser, in Chapter 2, provide a deeper discussion of the Fed's traditional lender-of-last-resort tools and strategies.

The classic playbook for this dimension of a financial crisis is *Lombard Street,* the 1873 book by the British journalist Walter Bagehot that's still considered the bible of central banking. Bagehot recognized that the only way to stop a run is to show the world there's no need to run, to make credit easily available to solvent firms until the panic subsides: "Lend freely, boldly, and so that the public may feel you mean to go on lending," he wrote. The loans should be expensive enough that they'll remain attractive only as long as the crisis lasts—Bagehot advised "a penalty rate"—and they should be secured by solid collateral to protect the central bank in case of default. But the goal should be to make public money available when private money isn't, to push back against panic and stabilize credit.

After BNP Paribas, the European Central Bank (ECB) and the Fed immediately injected enormous amounts of cash into frozen credit markets by buying Treasury securities on the open market. The Fed also issued a statement encouraging commercial banks to borrow from the discount window. The liquidity provision helped bring temporary calm to the markets, but banks did not come to the discount window; they were afraid they would look desperate if markets got wind that they had paid a penalty rate to borrow from the central bank. The Fed tried to reduce the stigma of the window by reducing the penalty, but banks remained nervous that borrowing from the discount window would be a signal of weakness.

By December, several of Wall Street's largest firms were announcing unprecedented and unexpected write-downs driven by huge mortgage exposures. The mania that had fueled the boom had long faded and sentiment was perilously close to panic, with investors and creditors running away from anything associated with the word "mortgage." The troubled mortgage securities would all be worth something someday, because not all of the underlying mortgages would default, and the ones that did would recoup some of their value in foreclosure sales. But the more people ran away from the securities, the more their prices plunged, and the more rational it became for others to run away from them. Clearly, the Fed's conventional tools were not sufficient to unclog the pipes of the credit markets. And the financial turmoil was already creating problems in the broader economy, as worried businesses and consumers reined in hiring and spending. The arbiters at the National Bureau of Economic Research would later conclude that the Great Recession began that month.

At that point, the Fed took two tentative steps beyond the standard Bagehot playbook. The first was the opening of the Term Auction Facility (TAF), a program designed to overcome the stigma of the discount window by lengthening the terms of the loans and auctioning them to eligible banks. Borrowers would pay a market rate determined by auction, not a penalty rate, so they wouldn't seem so desperate if word of their loans leaked. Within a year, the Fed would be lending five times as much through the TAF as through the discount window. The second step was the establishment of swap lines with the ECB and other foreign central banks, so they in turn could on-lend dollars to private banks in their own countries. Since the dollar is effectively the global currency, making dollars available to foreign central banks was an important step toward calming global markets. A year later, the Fed would have more than $500 billion in swaps outstanding, enshrining it as the lender of last resort to the world. Chapter 17, by Clay Lowery, Nathan Sheets, and Edwin (Ted) Truman, includes a discussion of the swaps, their rationale, and how they worked.

All these interventions were criticized at the time as overreactions that would reward the reckless and interfere with a long-overdue deleveraging process. From the very start of the crisis, there was intense political pressure on the Fed to back off and let the market adjust on its own. At the same time, there was intense market pressure on the Fed to do even more. Ben and his Fed colleagues were trying to balance the imperative of avoiding a crash with the need to maintain market discipline, and the Fed rejected several pleas for emergency loans from struggling nonbanks that lacked access to the discount window.

For example, Countrywide Financial asked the Fed for help in the early days of the crisis when its short-term creditors pulled back and it began running out of cash. But it seemed too early in the triage process to help an irresponsible real estate lender that still had options other than default; Bank of America ended up swallowing Countrywide and its troubled mortgage portfolio.

As financial conditions continued to deteriorate into 2008, we grew increasingly anxious about our lack of authority to deal with the excessive leverage and precarious financing that dominated the shadow banking system. As already noted, the government's safety net was strongest in the case of the traditional banking system—deposit insurance to discourage runs, the FDIC's tools for managing the failure of an insolvent depository institution in an orderly fashion on the back end, and the Fed's ability to lend to banks against solid collateral during an emergency. But the traditional banking system no longer dominated American finance, and it wasn't the epicenter of the crisis in its early stages. The Fed did have the power under Section 13(3) of the Federal Reserve Act to lend to nonbanks in "unusual and exigent circumstances," but it had not used that authority since the Depression.

In March, the long-standing precedent was broken, as the Fed invoked its 13(3) powers to create the Term Securities Lending Facility (TSLF), which would extend liquidity to some nonbanks, including the five major investment banks. (Rather than actually making loans, the TSLF swapped, on a temporary basis, highly liquid Treasury securities for other highly rated but less liquid assets.) Thus, the central bank moved beyond its traditional lender-of-last-resort role, focused on commercial banks, to a much wider application of its emergency lending powers. Alvarez, Thomas C. Baxter, Jr., and Robert F. Hoyt discuss the Fed's legal authorities in Chapter 5; and Lorie Logan, William Nelson, and Patrick Parkinson cover the Fed's novel lender-of-last-resort programs in Chapter 3.

But before the TSLF could even get started, the U.S. government had to engineer an unprecedented rescue of the weakest investment bank, Bear Stearns, an 85-year-old firm that was twice the size of Countrywide and far more intertwined with the rest of the financial system.

BEAR STEARNS: THE PANIC ESCALATES

Like Countrywide, Bear faced an extreme crisis of confidence; creditors had stopped rolling over its commercial paper, repo lenders were demanding more collateral, and hedge funds were closing their brokerage accounts with the firm.

And an investment bank that doesn't have the confidence of its clients or the markets doesn't have much of anything. Trading businesses depend on trust, and once people started doubting whether Bear was certain to meet its obligations, they were rushing to take their business elsewhere. Bear had 5,000 trading counterparties and 750,000 open derivatives contracts, so it was disturbing to imagine the hysteria it could unleash by defaulting on its obligations—fire sales of its collateral; frantic unwinding of its derivatives trades; a meltdown of the repo market; a likely run on Lehman Brothers, the next-weakest investment bank; perhaps even the collapse of Fannie Mae and Freddie Mac, which were propping up what was left of the U.S. mortgage market. The system had already been weakened by seven months of stress, and the failure of a firm as inextricably enmeshed in it as Bear could have torn it apart. Chapter 4, by Alvarez, Dudley, and Liang, explores in more detail the rationale for trying to save Bear.

At first, we didn't think we could prevent Bear's collapse and the ensuing blow to the system. The federal government did not have the kind of resolution powers for nonbanks that the FDIC had for winding down insolvent commercial banks, so it had no way to stand behind Bear's obligations and avoid the turmoil of default. Our emergency authorities simply weren't as broad as many people assumed. The Treasury couldn't do much without congressional authorization, while the Fed's authority was mostly limited to lending against good collateral. As we've noted, neither the Fed nor the Treasury had powers to guarantee obligations, invest government capital, or buy illiquid assets to stop a run. The Fed did have its emergency lending power under Section 13(3), but 13(3) lending could not rescue an insolvent firm or make a nonviable business viable.

In a panic, it can be difficult to tell whether a troubled firm is truly insolvent, as opposed to illiquid. Markets are not always right or rational, and it's always possible that securities nobody wants during a spasm of panic will turn out to be solid once confidence returns. Temporary illiquidity is precisely the situation that lender-of-last-resort authority is designed to address. But Bear's decline, so much faster and sharper than the declines of similar firms, suggested its weakness was real and extreme. The extent of its losses and the weakness of its core businesses meant that the Fed could not lend it enough to save it. If the Fed had lent into the run, with no further support for the firm, it would have financed the exit of a subset of the remaining creditors and damaged its own credibility without saving the firm or stabilizing the system. So we initially thought the Fed's response would have to be limited to injecting more liquidity into the markets to contain the damage from an unavoidable collapse, what Tim called "putting foam on the runway."

There was one other option that we thought might work, which was to find another financial institution strong enough to acquire Bear and take on its obligations. JPMorgan Chase agreed to do just that, provided the Fed took on the risk of $30 billion worth of Bear's worst mortgage assets. The Fed can intervene under 13(3) only if it is "secured to the satisfaction" of the Reserve Bank making the loan, but after an analysis by the investment firm BlackRock concluded there was a reasonable chance the Fed could break even on those assets, Ben and Tim decided to go forward. Hank also wrote a letter supporting the Fed loan, implicating the Treasury in the Fed's momentous decision. The rescue worked, but it required JPMorgan to guarantee most of Bear's liabilities during the pendency of the shareholder vote to stop nervous creditors from running.

At the same time, the Fed invoked 13(3) again to launch a more aggressive lending program for investment banks called the Primary Dealer Credit Facility (PDCF), which would accept collateral that was broader and shakier than what the TSLF would accept. We hoped the Bear intervention would settle the markets, but we also knew that Bear wasn't the only overleveraged investment bank relying too heavily on short-term funding that could disappear in a heartbeat. Lehman had similar problems, and it was 75 percent larger than Bear, with more real estate exposure and an even larger derivatives book. Markets were losing confidence in the entire investment bank model, which meant that Merrill Lynch, Morgan Stanley, and even Goldman Sachs might need access to emergency financing as well.

The Bear intervention did calm the markets for a time, but it also provided a searing dose of the politics of crisis response. Many politicians and pundits accused us of overreacting, arguing that the economic impact of an investment bank's failure would be modest—an argument that would be convincingly disproved by Lehman's failure six months later. The criticism with greater political impact was that our actions amounted to squandering taxpayer dollars to bail out a reckless firm, an action that not only was unfair but would incentivize firms to take greater risks in the future—a problem known as moral hazard.

Our actions did ensure that Bear's creditors and counterparties got paid in full so that they would stop running, and so that creditors and counterparties of similarly situated firms wouldn't start running. But Bear itself did not get bailed out. The firm ceased to exist. Its senior executives lost their jobs and much of their wealth. Its shareholders received 94 percent less than the firm was worth at its peak in early 2007. All interventions create moral hazard, but it was hard to see how Bear's fate would have encouraged other firms to emulate its approach. And confidence in Lehman continued to erode over the summer, suggesting that markets were not convinced the government would be willing or able to ride to the rescue again. Moreover, the taxpayer dollars were not lost; the loan that financed Bear's risky assets was fully repaid, producing a $2.5 billion return for taxpayers.

Of course, the point of the loan was not to make money but to avoid the collapse of a systemically important firm and the resulting economic damage. It's still frightening to think of the chain reaction Bear's failure might have produced at a time when the mortgage giants Fannie and Freddie had not yet been stabilized. Doing nothing was still an option when Countrywide was under pressure, but Bear really was too interconnected to fail, and after seven months of building panic, we judged that the system was too fragile to handle its failure.

Much of the commentary after Bear emphasized the immense powers of the U.S. government, but the episode actually exposed the inadequacy of those powers. We had succeeded in devising a solution this time, but we had also gotten lucky. If JPMorgan hadn't been willing to buy Bear, and to guarantee most of the firm's liabilities during the pendency of its shareholder vote, the system might have imploded that March. The U.S. government still had no way to inject capital into a struggling firm, buy its assets, or guarantee its liabilities, which meant it had no way to stop a full-blown run on a failing firm; if the firm was a nonbank, we couldn't even wind it down safely to avoid default. The combination of the Bear intervention and the Fed's new PDCF lending facility helped build expectations that we had the will and the means to prevent the failure of major firms, but in reality the government's capacity to save them was uncomfortably constrained.

After Bear's rescue, Ben and Hank told Barney Frank, chairman of the House Financial Services Committee, that, absent a buyer, the government would be powerless to stop a run on Lehman unless Congress provided the emergency powers to wind down a failing nonbank. Frank confirmed what they suspected—that it would be impossible to get Congress to act, unless they made a compelling case that a prospective Lehman failure would harm the U.S. economy. And, of course, that would have precipitated exactly what we wanted to avoid.

FANNIE AND FREDDIE: FIRING THE BAZOOKA

The next existential threats to the system were Fannie and Freddie, which together held or guaranteed more than $5 trillion worth of mortgage debt. Equally important, they were also the last major source of mortgage financing in the United States, backing three of every four new home loans. That meant their collapse would crush the already battered housing market, which would mean more foreclosures on Main Street and more panic about mortgage securities on Wall Street. At the same time, trillions of dollars' worth of their own securities, long considered safe investments, were held by governments and financial institutions throughout the world. In other words, Fannie and Freddie were undeniably systemic. They did not cause the crisis, as some critics have suggested; until late in the boom, the underwriting for the mortgages they bought and backed was relatively conservative for the industry. But by July 2008, they were suffering large losses.

The U.S. government had no standing authority to rescue Fannie and Freddie, so Hank had to persuade Congress to provide the necessary powers. We were worried that merely asking for the power to backstop the mortgage giants could accelerate the panic by confirming the magnitude of the emergency; nevertheless, Hank asked Congress for unlimited authority—his euphemism was "unspecified"—to inject capital into Fannie and Freddie. He argued that if Congress gave him broad power to act, the market's anxieties about the viability of the firms would dissipate and he would be less likely to have to use that power. "If you've got a squirt gun in your pocket, you may have to take it out," he explained. "If you've got a bazooka, and people know you've got it, you may not have to take it out." By the end of July, the Democratic-controlled Congress enacted legislation that gave the Republican administration the bazooka that Hank had requested, proving that Washington was capable of passing tough bipartisan measures when a crisis demanded it, though perhaps no earlier than that.

Unfortunately, once examiners from the Fed and the OCC got to look under the hood of Fannie and Freddie, they found that both firms were functionally insolvent, with flimsy capital cushions that were mostly accounting fictions. Hank and his team at Treasury soon agreed the only solution was to force Fannie and Freddie into conservatorship—basically, nationalization without day-to-day government control—even though he had just told Congress he didn't believe he would need to use his bazooka. His priority was avoiding a systemic meltdown, not protecting his reputation for consistency. Ben made clear that the Fed would fully support Treasury, including by making loans to Fannie and Freddie if necessary, just as Treasury had fully supported the Fed's actions earlier in the crisis.

On September 5, Hank and Ben gave the CEOs of Fannie and Freddie the news that the government was seizing control of their companies. They would lose their jobs, their shareholders would lose almost all their equity, and the Treasury would inject $100 billion into each company to avoid looming defaults on their debt and the securities they guaranteed. The run on Fannie and Freddie quickly subsided, because the companies and the mortgages they insured now had official government backing. They would also do more than any other public or private action to help stabilize the housing market and, ultimately, reduce the number of foreclosures. And again, these extraordinary interventions would end up turning a sizable profit for taxpayers. For more on the government-sponsored enterprises and the government's intervention, see Chapter 6, by Dan Jester, Matthew Kabaker, Jeremiah Norton, and Lee Sachs.

But these interventions did not quell the panic. We had hoped that our show of force would calm the markets and maybe even provide a reprieve for Lehman Brothers. Rather than breathing a sigh of relief, market participants evidently concluded that if the government was worried enough to take such extreme measures, the situation must be even worse than it looked—particularly for firms like Lehman, with large portfolios of real estate investments. We had averted another catastrophe, but within days, we would face yet another challenge, in the form of a collapsing Lehman Brothers.

LEHMAN AND AIG: THE EXPLOSION

The panic built for more than a year before it took Lehman Brothers down, but many Americans still mark the beginning of the crisis with Lehman's collapse. It eclipsed all that came before and seemed responsible for all that followed. But it was more of a symptom than a cause of the weaknesses in the system. Fannie, Freddie, AIG, and Merrill Lynch were all much larger than Lehman, and all arrived at the brink of collapse around the same time. In fact, Lehman exemplified the factors from which the crisis stemmed: It was a loosely regulated, heavily overleveraged, deeply interconnected nonbank with too much exposure to the real estate market and too much runnable short-term financing. What made the story of Lehman different was that it ended in disaster. (For more on the government's nonbank interventions, including Lehman and AIG, see Chapter 4, by Alvarez, Dudley, and Liang.)

Lehman was the nightmare we had been trying to prevent for a year, an uncontrolled failure of a systemically important firm. Since we had prevented an uncontrolled failure of Bear Stearns six months earlier, we had just saved Fannie and Freddie a week earlier, and we would go on to save AIG two days later, many observers assumed we had let Lehman fail on purpose—and quite a few praised us for doing so. But that was not the case. We did everything in our power to try to prevent Lehman's collapse. But everything in our power turned out not to be enough.

It quickly became clear that a reprise of the Bear endgame was under way for Lehman: lenders demanding more collateral, hedge funds closing accounts, ratings agencies threatening downgrades. The markets sensed imminent collapse, and the government still had no way to inject capital or guarantee the liabilities of a failing nonbank to avoid default. Our strategy for Lehman was the same as it had been for Bear: Find a buyer, or buyers.

As Lehman's failure loomed, Hank and his team put out the word that taxpayers would not subsidize a Lehman deal. This was part negotiating tactic and part just a reflection of the reality that neither the Fed nor the government had the ability to prevent the collapse of a failing investment bank. To have a chance of preventing failure, we needed to motivate the private sector to assume as many of Lehman's bad assets as possible, to increase the likelihood that a Bear Stearns–like rescue would be possible. But we all knew that if the government needed to take on some risk to get Lehman sold, we would do it to avoid a devastating collapse. We were determined to avoid disruptive failures of major institutions.

While our strategy for Lehman was the same as for Bear—find a buyer that could stand behind the firm's obligations and reassure counterparties and customers—this time the buyer didn't materialize. Bank of America, which had expressed off-and-on interest, decided instead to buy Merrill Lynch, the next-weakest investment bank. That acquisition defused a major threat to the system, as Merrill seemed likely to be the next to fail. But it left only one potential savior for Lehman, the British bank Barclays. Barclays seemed serious about acquiring Lehman, particularly if it could leave behind some bad assets, but on the Sunday morning of what would become known as Lehman weekend, British regulators scuttled the potential deal. They said they didn't want British taxpayers on the hook for Lehman's problems.

As unthinkable as it seemed, we were out of options. At that point the only authority available was the Fed's power, under Section 13(3), to lend against solid collateral. The Fed did have some discretion about what counted as acceptable collateral, and Ben and Tim were willing to take some risks in extremis. But some of the sharpest minds in government and finance had just reviewed Lehman's assets over that weekend, and the verdict had been as brutal as the market's: Lehman's real estate portfolio appeared to be worth only half what the company had claimed. The Fed would have helped finance an acquisition from a willing buyer as it had with Bear, but without a buyer it couldn't lend enough to save an insolvent firm deep into a run. By that point we had months of evidence of the company's inability to raise private capital, and a 2013 study would conclude that its capital hole might have been as big as $200 billion. A Fed loan to the disintegrating nonbank would have given some of the firm's remaining creditors a chance to escape at taxpayer expense but would not have made the firm viable or assuaged fears of systemic collapse.

After Lehman filed for the largest bankruptcy in U.S. history, editorialists in influential outlets like the *New York Times* and *Wall Street Journal* were pleased we had resisted the temptation to use public dollars to rescue a failed enterprise. For a moment, critics hailed our commitment to free-market discipline, our willingness to teach Wall Street a lesson by letting irresponsible speculators pay for their sins. But the praise was misguided, as we would have rescued Lehman if we could have. Yes, Hank had suggested before Lehman went down that the government wouldn't help, but that was a tactic to pressure the private sector to participate in a rescue that the Fed and the Treasury lacked the power to execute on their own. In the days following the collapse, Hank and Ben also noted in subsequent congressional testimony that the markets had time to prepare for Lehman's failure, which gave some critics the impression that we had been comfortable with the firm's collapse. But we had agreed among ourselves that we needed to downplay our inability to save Lehman, because we feared that such an admission would accelerate the run. Public communication during a panic is both vitally important and incredibly difficult, and we were trying to find a balance between being blunt and being reassuring. The reality was inescapable: We weren't able to prevent Lehman's collapse, and unless we got help from Congress we could be facing more Lehmans down the road.

The fall of Lehman dramatically accelerated the crisis, sending global markets into a state of shock. But a less frantic, less visible run on the financial system had been building for more than a year, and Lehman was hardly the only systemic firm whose collapse threatened the entire financial system. The next domino to fall, only hours after Lehman declared bankruptcy, was the global insurer AIG.

AIG was even bigger and more dangerous to the system than Lehman. AIG provided insurance for millions of individuals, as well as 180,000 businesses that employed two-thirds of the American workforce. Critically, AIG's Financial Products division, which resembled a hedge fund grafted onto a traditional insurance company, had $2.7 trillion worth of derivatives contracts, mostly credit default swaps insuring financial instruments held by other large firms. If AIG collapsed, the other systemic institutions would lose their disaster insurance when they needed it most. Since the exposures of other systemic firms were hard to measure, an AIG default risked triggering runs throughout the system. And default was imminent. AIG would need $85 billion to meet its obligations and remain afloat, at a time when financial institutions were hoarding whatever liquidity they could find.

Once again, no mechanism was available to wind down a teetering insurer without bankruptcy and default, and we had no power to inject capital, guarantee liabilities, or buy assets. This time, though, we did think the Fed might be able to lend to AIG in amounts sufficient to stave off its collapse. Unlike investment banks, which have nothing if they don't have the confidence of market participants, AIG had a number of relatively stable income-generating insurance businesses with independent, investment-grade ratings. The Fed could lend against good collateral, and AIG's collection of regulated insurance subsidiaries with premium-paying policyholders and mandatory reserves seemed to qualify. It was also important that, due to the value of its insurance subsidiaries, most market participants viewed AIG as a viable firm despite the enormous liquidity shortfall at its holding company.

Any loan to a failing nonbank in the throes of a run would still be risky, and we knew it might only buy the system time to prepare for a default. But to prevent an AIG bankruptcy on Tuesday, September 16, the day after Lehman's filing, the Fed gave it an $85 billion credit line. The terms were very tough and included a high penalty interest rate and claims on 79.9 percent of the firm—just below the threshold that would force the government to bring the company onto its own balance sheet, but enough to ensure taxpayers would get most of the upside if the firm survived.

We knew that saving AIG the day after Lehman failed would look like a lurch, but the circumstances of the two firms were different. Unlike Lehman, AIG had solid collateral, enough to secure the funding it needed to stay in business and to satisfy market participants that it was viable. We still drove a tough bargain, partly to maximize the protection for taxpayers, partly to minimize the moral hazard we'd create for the future. AIG's shareholders later sued because they thought we treated them too harshly, and as galling as that was, it did reflect our commitment to saving the broader system rather than everyone in it.

Critics still complained that we were rewarding failure. It's true that stopping the panic and avoiding chaotic defaults sometimes required us to protect creditors and counterparties. But, for the most part, failure was not rewarded. The CEO of AIG was ousted as part of the company's rescue, as were the leaders of Fannie and Freddie, and over the course of the crisis, the CEOs of Countrywide, Bear, Merrill, Lehman, Citigroup, and Wachovia also lost their jobs. The shareholders of virtually every financial firm saw their stock prices plunge. Many institutions would ultimately also face large fines. These were hardly attractive paths for future financiers to follow. In particular, we certainly would have let AIG fail if we had thought the pain could be limited to the company's executives and shareholders, but we knew that the collapse of a systemic firm at that juncture would have been catastrophic for the financial system and the economy.

It turned out that AIG was in even more dire straits than we thought. It continued to unravel after its initial loan, and the rescue ended up expanding to an unthinkable $185 billion, taking into account both loans and capital injections. Eventually, though, AIG paid the money back with interest, and the government made a $23 billion profit. The real payoff, though, was avoiding the broader damage that would have followed AIG's default.

THE FALLOUT

Despite our aggressive interventions, the situation continued to deteriorate. The Fed tried to apply another more powerful dose of foam on the runway by expanding its lending facilities again, providing short-term credit against just about any collateral for banks and investment banks, but markets continued to fall. Corporate bond spreads widened twice as much as they had after the crash of 1929. Yields on short-term Treasury bills actually went negative, reflecting the frenetic flight to safety; investors were so afraid of investing in any private asset that they were willing to pay the government to hold their cash. That same Tuesday saw a new disaster, when the Reserve Primary Fund, a money market fund that had invested heavily in Lehman's commercial paper, announced it could no longer pay its investors 100 cents on the dollar and was halting redemptions. Investors afraid that other money market funds would also "break the buck" and freeze their cash pulled $230 billion out of the industry that week, a scary run on institutions that operated as de facto banks but without government deposit insurance.

As money market funds hunkered down, buying even less commercial paper and lending even less in the repo markets, the liquidity squeeze for banks and nonbanks intensified further. The effects were also spilling over to the "real" economy: CEOs of such highly rated nonfinancial companies as General Electric, Ford, and even Coca-Cola warned Hank they were having trouble selling their paper, depriving them of the short-term funding they relied on to manage operations and pay their suppliers and workers. That threatened to force them to cut back inventories and delay payments to small and midsize suppliers, which would in turn have to lay off workers. The crisis was about to spread, in a more concrete and palpable way, from Wall Street to Main Street.

We were determined to stop the runs on money market funds, which invested $3.5 trillion for 30 million Americans, and the associated contraction of the commercial paper market, which provided vital day-to-day liquidity for so many real-economy companies. Hank's team came up with the idea of using Treasury's $50 billion Exchange Stabilization Fund to guarantee the money funds, analogous to the FDIC's guarantee of bank deposits. The Fed buttressed the new guarantee by launching another new lending program, the awkwardly named Asset-Backed Commercial Paper Money Market Mutual Fund Liquidity Facility (AMLF), a circuitous but effective effort to thaw the market for commercial paper by helping banks buy it from money funds. Within two weeks, the program was financing $150 billion worth of securities. Steven M. Shafran discusses the run on the money funds and the government response in Chapter 7 in this volume.

These interventions worked. Investors stopped running from money market funds now that they had government insurance; since Treasury charged the funds a premium and never had to pay any claims, taxpayers ended up turning another profit. The extra liquidity from the Fed helped as well, but the real lesson was the power of a government guarantee. When crisis managers can credibly promise protection against catastrophic outcomes, market participants don't have to act in anticipation of those outcomes, so the feared outcomes don't happen.

GOING TO CONGRESS

For some time, we had been dangerously behind the curve of the panic, because our existing arsenal of tools was too weak to contain the force of the run. We needed a way to forestall disasters for the entire financial sector, rather than trying to deal with one firm at a time, and there was no way to do that without Congress acting to give us the fiscal resources we needed to stop the panic. But for months we knew that congressional buy-in was impossible because legislators and their constituents didn't see an urgent need. We had been stuck in a catch-22: We needed substantial new authorities to stop the crisis. But we never could have gotten those authorities from Congress without a clear worsening in financial conditions. The weeks following the Lehman failure showed, unfortunately, how bad things could get.

There was still the question of what tools to ask for. Hank had hoped to bolster confidence in endangered firms by having the government buy some of the toxic, illiquid assets weighing down their balance sheets. He also hoped the purchases would revive the market for similar mortgage assets that we didn't buy, effectively recapitalizing the entire financial system. The proposal he sent to Congress was for a Troubled Assets Relief Program (TARP) to buy up to $700 billion of illiquid mortgage assets. It was not going to be an easy sell: At a series of hearings, Hank and Ben were pilloried for coddling Wall Street. And the issue quickly got entangled in the ongoing presidential campaign, which made it even harder to build a bipartisan consensus for action.

During the two weeks that Hank was negotiating with Congress over the terms of the TARP, the panic claimed another huge firm, Washington Mutual, the largest FDIC-insured bank ever to fail. (See Chapter 11, by James R. Wigand, on FDIC resolutions during the crisis.) FDIC chairman Sheila Bair worked out a deal for JPMorgan Chase to buy WaMu without government aid. But the FDIC's deal not only wiped out WaMu's shareholders, which was appropriate; it also imposed heavy losses on WaMu's senior debt holders. In other words, it allowed WaMu to default on its debts, the result we had been so desperate to avoid for other firms. This kind of "haircut" makes sense in ordinary times, forcing creditors to suffer the consequences of unwise loans, but it was counterproductive during a panic, in that it sent a message to the creditors of other financial firms that their safest course was to run.

Bair thought our rescues had created too much moral hazard and saw WaMu's failure as a teachable moment. She was also protective of her agency's Deposit Insurance Fund, often citing her legal obligation to seek the least-cost option. But there was a "systemic risk exception" to that obligation when financial stability was at stake, and haircutting WaMu seemed likely to create significant risk of more bank failures. Sure enough, the next morning there was a run on Wachovia, the fourth-largest bank in the country. The cost of insuring Wachovia's senior debt against default doubled, and the price of its ten-year bonds dropped by nearly two-thirds. Fortunately, after more tumultuous negotiations, Wells Fargo agreed to acquire Wachovia without haircuts or government help, avoiding another ugly collapse.

We wanted to reassure the markets there would be no more Lehmans or WaMus, and to make those assurances credible we needed TARP. Hank and his team hashed out a deal with congressional leaders in 12 days, and although that was lightning speed for Congress, it seemed like an eternity for us. Unfortunately, the seriousness of the situation had not completely sunk in, and on September 29 the House narrowly rejected the TARP legislation. That Congress was reluctant to act even after Lehman confirmed that no earlier effort to get new authorities or fiscal support could have been successful.

The stock market plunged 9 percent the day of the House vote, jolting some recalcitrant representatives to their senses. By the end of the week, the Democratic-controlled Congress and the Republican administration had combined to pass the TARP, slightly modified from the version the House had rejected, making the politically radioactive Wall Street rescue a bipartisan effort. The bill gave Treasury remarkably expansive power, making it clear Hank could use the Troubled Assets Relief Program to do more than just buy troubled assets. And in fact, by the time the legislation passed, the Treasury and the Fed were already focusing on an alternative plan.

DEPLOYING TARP

When we first proposed TARP, Hank believed asset purchases would be better for restoring stability than capital investments. His goal was to recapitalize the banking system; but in past crises, whenever governments had injected capital directly into banks, the terms had been so punitive that only failed or failing banks had accepted the capital. The result in many cases had been a costly nationalization of the weakest banks without much recapitalization of the banking system as a whole. Hank believed that buying distressed assets would boost the prices of assets remaining in the banks, which would strengthen their balance sheets, improve their capital positions, and shore up investor confidence. By contrast, Hank feared, government capital injections raised the specter of nationalization, which risked accelerating the flight from the major banks. In recent weeks, shareholders in Fannie, Freddie, and AIG had been nearly wiped out after the government had taken equity stakes in those enterprises, and Hank worried that other bank shareholders would flee if they thought their equity was at risk of getting diluted as well.

But the situation was deteriorating at an alarming rate. Even after Congress passed TARP, the stock market had its worst week since 1933, and the spread reflecting stress in interbank lending hit an all-time high. We needed immediate action to settle the markets. And designing a fair and effective program of asset purchases was a complex and difficult task. The bottom line was that the system needed more capital, and buying assets was an indirect and inefficient way to boost capital levels; there was also no easy way to determine which assets Treasury should buy and how much it should pay. Hank's team considered various approaches involving auctions and partnerships with private-sector investors, but it was clear that setting up a workable program would take too long. We needed a simpler, swifter, and more efficient approach to get help to the system while there was still a system to help. By the time Congress approved TARP, we all agreed that injecting capital directly into financial institutions through government purchases of newly issued shares would be a much quicker, more powerful, and more cost-effective strategy. Chapter 8, by Jester, David Nason, and Norton, discusses this stage of bank recapitalization in detail; Chapter 14, by Timothy G. Massad and Neel T. Kashkari, explains the administrative implementation of TARP.

Our challenge was to devise terms tough enough to protect taxpayers, but not so tough they would discourage participation by strong firms and stigmatize the program. We did not believe we could force firms with capital ratios above their regulatory minimums to participate in TARP, and we were worried that if only the weakest firms accepted government capital, the markets would run from those firms while the rest of the system would remain undercapitalized. So Hank's team decided to buy nonvoting preferred stock rather than common equity, which would help calm fears of a government takeover, and to do so on relatively attractive terms, so that strong as well as weak banks would accept the capital. And while we did tighten some restrictions on compensation for participating CEOs, as Congress required, we did not impose restrictions on compensation and bonuses for other bank executives. We wanted to maximize participation.

For 14 months of the crisis, our powers had been limited to the Fed's efforts to address liquidity problems. Now government capital was finally available to address the underlying solvency problems. But creditors and investors were still pulling back from strong as well as weak firms, and we feared that capital injections alone would be insufficient to break the panic.

The simplest and most powerful way to ensure that banks could attract financing was to guarantee their debts, just as Treasury had done for money market funds after the Reserve Fund broke the buck. Several European countries had already decided to provide comprehensive guarantees for the liabilities of their banks, and we wanted similar defenses so that creditors would no longer be tempted to run. It occurred to us that since the FDIC had the power to backstop banks one at a time, it could invoke its systemic risk exception to backstop all banks at once. Bair was reluctant to expose her agency's insurance fund to more risk and had criticized our whatever-it-takes approach to avoiding defaults. But she had seen the market backlash to the defaults by Lehman and WaMu, and to her credit, she agreed to consider guaranteeing some bank obligations. Chapter 9, by Michael H. Krimminger, provides a detailed analysis of the FDIC's program.

Initially, Bair pushed to impose punitive fees on the guarantees to protect the FDIC's insurance fund, and even to limit the guarantees to 90 percent of bank debts, an implicit 10 percent haircut. But we argued that taking some risk up front to protect banks against runs would reduce the risk of cascading failures that could drain her entire fund. And the FDIC could always increase fees on the financial industry to replenish its fund after the crisis was over. Ultimately, she agreed to charge fees low enough to avoid stigma, and guarantee debts in full rather than imposing haircuts—which, after all, would have defeated the purpose of the guarantees.

We wanted to throw everything we had at the crisis, so the Fed also set up a new lending program to prevent the collapse of the commercial paper market, to make sure major corporations could finance their operations for longer than a day or two. The Commercial Paper Funding Facility (CPFF) involved another novel interpretation of the Fed's emergency authority, but it would buy $242 billion worth of paper in its first week, helping to unclog important short-term credit channels for businesses. The program would earn $849 million for taxpayers, never incurring a single loss. Logan, Nelson, and Parkinson explore this and other novel lender-of-last-resort programs devised by the Fed in Chapter 3.

We needed to launch the programs quickly with a show of overwhelming force, so on Columbus Day, Hank summoned the CEOs of nine of the most systemically important firms to the Treasury. We explained that we expected all nine of them to accept a total of $125 billion worth of Treasury capital, along with FDIC guarantees of any new debt they issued. It was a package deal: no government guarantees without the government capital. A few banks that considered themselves better capitalized were concerned the program would make them look as weak as their more imperiled competitors, and all the banks were reluctant to take on the government as an investor. But we reminded them that none of them should be confident they had enough capital to survive the severe recession that lay ahead, much less the runs that would accompany a meltdown of the system. All nine firms needed the system to survive, and the best way to ensure that was for all nine firms to participate in TARP. We would then make another $125 billion available to smaller banks, which wouldn't have to worry about stigma with the nine large banks on board. That afternoon, all nine CEOs accepted the TARP capital, and the stock market posted its biggest single-day point gain in history. In the ensuing months, we would move quickly to inject capital into nearly 700 smaller banks.

TARP was a turning point, the first effort to deploy the full resources of the U.S. government to end the crisis, a big step toward restoring stability. The Europeans took a more traditional approach that fall, nationalizing failing banks and offering capital to other banks at terms so punitive that few agreed to accept it. As a consequence, their banking system would remain undercapitalized for years, hampering their economic recovery. But the very attributes that would make TARP so successful would also increase its unpopularity with the American public, who saw it as an unwarranted gift to the bankers who had just broken the economy. And although important progress had been made, the crisis was not yet over.

While we now had a more effective strategy in place to respond to the financial panic, the economic consequences of the meltdown were becoming increasingly apparent. In the fourth quarter of 2008, the U.S. economy contracted at an 8.2 percent annual rate and shed nearly 2 million jobs, as September's shocks on Wall Street began rippling through Main Street. The troubled assets on bank balance sheets grew more troubled than ever, as increased mortgage defaults and delinquencies heightened concerns about mortgage-backed securities. The worst recession since the Depression was intensifying, and the economic contraction was undermining the work we had done to stabilize the financial system.

Markets quickly began to wonder whether our new pot of money would be large enough to plug the system's remaining holes. We had already committed $250 billion to the banking sector, leaving $450 billion of TARP funds available. A New York Fed analysis found the banking sector alone would need a further $290 billion in capital in a "stress scenario," and as much as $684 billion in an "extreme stress scenario." It was a perilous time, made more perilous by the uncertainty of the presidential transition. President-elect Obama had signaled his support for our whatever-it-takes strategy by nominating Tim to succeed Hank at Treasury, but the ten-week limbo stage still felt unconscionably long, and the TARP math quickly turned ugly.

We had committed to avoiding the failure of another systemic firm, but the costs of meeting this promise were adding up. AIG was suffering historically large losses, and Treasury had to pump in a further $40 billion of TARP capital to stabilize the firm. Hank agreed to buy an additional $20 billion worth of Citigroup stock as part of a rescue plan that included government guarantees for some of the bank's worst assets. He and Ben engineered a similar rescue for Bank of America, deploying another $20 billion in TARP capital. Treasury committed another $20 billion to backstop a new Fed program designed to revive the paralyzed consumer credit markets by jump-starting the stalled markets for securities backed by consumer credit. The Term Asset-Backed Securities Loan Facility (TALF) would create demand for securities backed by credit card loans, student loans, car loans, and small business loans by accepting them as collateral for Fed loans to investors.

Outside of the financial sector, General Motors and Chrysler were also on life support. And even though TARP wasn't originally intended for industrial companies, which can usually declare bankruptcy and then restructure or liquidate in an orderly fashion, the banking system was so fragile that the debtor-in-possession financing that bankrupt firms rely on in normal times was unavailable. An uncontrolled bankruptcy of an automaker could have led to millions of layoffs across the country, so President Bush approved a total of $23.5 billion for bridge loans to the two failing automakers, as well as deals to recapitalize and restructure their financing arms. In Chapter 13, Brian Deese, Shafran, and Jester discuss the decisions to rescue and restructure GM and Chrysler.

These interventions also worked as intended. The loans to GM and Chrysler kept the companies alive through the uncertainties of the presidential transition. The TALF program helped counteract the trend of banks restricting credit on Main Street when it was needed most, and the Fed wouldn't absorb any losses on its TALF loans. The federal backstops for Citi and Bank of America helped ease runs on both firms, and neither firm would ever have to use its government guarantees or protections for ring-fenced assets.

Still, the new president could hardly feel grateful. By the time Obama took office, more than half the TARP funds had already been committed, the economy was in free fall, and the financial system—despite the massive assistance it had received—was still teetering. Doubt was spreading that we could uphold our commitment to avoid the collapse of another systemic firm without a second TARP. In fact, Obama's first budget proposal would include a $750 billion placeholder for additional financial rescues. There was a growing belief among financial experts across the ideological spectrum that the banking sector was unsalvageable and that Obama would have to nationalize some or all of it. Many of Tim's colleagues in the new administration shared that view, and persistent media leaks suggesting that nationalization looked inevitable were accelerating the panic. Bank earnings in the first quarter actually started to look a bit better, but investors in bank stocks were rushing to sell their shares before the government could dilute them or wipe them out.

The financial system and the broader economy were dragging each other down. A successful stabilization would require shoring up both simultaneously.

On the financial side, Tim and Ben wanted to avoid a broad nationalization of the banking system unless it was absolutely necessary. Even nationalizing one or two major firms risked triggering runs on the remaining firms that could lead to additional government takeovers. In February, Tim proposed a less drastic approach alternative to nationalization, a plan to restore confidence in the health of banks with a mix of unprecedented transparency and additional capital. The centerpiece would be the Supervisory Capital Assessment Program (SCAP), or "the stress test." The Fed and other bank regulators would conduct rigorous reviews to determine the size of the losses each major bank could face in a Depression-like downturn, disclose those loss estimates publicly, and give any banks that didn't have enough capital to withstand those losses six months to raise what they needed. The ones that couldn't attract the investment privately would then be forced to accept additional TARP capital—and possibly government control. See Chapter 10, by Tim Clark, Kabaker, and Sachs, for more on the Obama administration's plan to recapitalize the banks.

The strategy was a risky one. If the more pessimistic observers were right, exposing the books of the banks to the sunlight would just confirm their insolvency, TARP would run out of money trying to fill their capital holes, and large-scale nationalization would end up happening anyway. But markets were already assuming the worst, and Tim and his colleagues thought it was at least possible that perceptions of the health of the banking system were worse than reality. The stress test would provide a more accurate picture of the health of banks—and then would make sure the sick ones got the capital they needed, either voluntarily from investors or forcibly from TARP.

The market's initial reaction to the announcement of the plan was overwhelmingly negative. The downsides of the stress test were obvious: There would be excruciating uncertainty until it was done, and there was no guarantee the answers it ultimately produced would be conducive to calm. Some skeptics warned that the stress test would be a sham, subjecting the banks to a gentle scenario engineered to give them a clean bill of health. But we knew that unless it was demonstrably tough, the markets would keep assuming the worst regardless of the results. The scenario the Fed used to assess the health of the banks was quite tough, envisioning a steep rise in the unemployment rate, as well as declines in housing prices that were worse than the reality of 2009, which resulted in projected loan losses at a rate even worse than during the Great Depression.

Nevertheless, the results the Fed released in May were much better than many in the markets had expected. The Fed determined that nine of the 19 largest financial firms were already adequately capitalized to withstand the test's worst-case scenario, and the other ten needed, collectively, only about $75 billion in additional capital. The Fed also provided detailed disclosures of projected losses by firm and by type of loan that demonstrated how it had reached its conclusions, and the market considered the results credible. The cost of insuring against defaults by financial institutions quickly dropped, and the private sector regained its confidence to invest in banks. The undercapitalized firms soon raised almost all the capital they needed to comply with the stress test mandate, many within weeks of the test. The only firm that couldn't raise equity privately was GMAC, so Treasury filled the gap with a modest infusion of TARP funds; even the rescue of GMAC—now known as Ally Bank—would eventually generate a $2.4 billion profit for the Treasury. As late as April 2009, the International Monetary Fund was still predicting that the U.S. government would spend $2 trillion rescuing its banking system. But TARP's capital programs for banks and insurers would end up earning about $50 billion for the Treasury. Overall, the government's financial interventions would produce about $200 billion in profits for taxpayers.

The stress test was a somewhat anticlimactic conclusion to a 20-month ordeal, finally reassuring the markets that the financial system was solvent. There would be no more Lehmans. To be sure, the stress test was not a magic solution to the crisis but rather the culmination of a series of interventions that collectively worked to stabilize the system. The Fed's lending and liquidity programs; the rescues of Bear, Fannie, Freddie, and AIG; the Treasury's guarantee of money market funds; the FDIC's guarantees of the debt of banks and other intermediaries; and the TARP capital we pumped into the banking system (along with the private capital we pushed banks to raise throughout the crisis) were all necessary elements. If not for those earlier steps toward stability, the results of the stress test would have been much less reassuring to markets and much more expensive for taxpayers.

Critically, the actions to fix the financial system were complemented by aggressive actions to revive the broader economy, without which the former would have been insufficient. A stronger financial system in turn promoted economic recovery, which began in June 2009. The powerful array of financial and economic policies deployed by the U.S. government were all the more powerful because they were deployed in concert.

RESTARTING THE ECONOMIC ENGINE

Throughout the crisis, the Fed had loosened monetary policy to try to bolster the rapidly weakening economy. (Chapter 15, by Donald Kohn and Brian Sack, discusses crisis-era monetary policy.) In October 2008, the Fed coordinated a rate cut with other major central banks; and in December 2008, it became the first major central bank to reduce its target short-term interest rate essentially to zero, where it would remain for the next seven years. But the economy kept unraveling, so Ben and his colleagues pursued a series of unorthodox measures to counteract deflationary and recessionary pressures at the zero lower bound on rates. The Fed began its campaign in late 2008 by buying $100 billion worth of debt issued by Fannie and Freddie and $500 billion worth of mortgage-backed securities guaranteed by the two firms. This was not only an effort to revive demand for the securities and boost the sagging housing market, but also a signal that the Fed would continue to support growth in creative ways even though it could no longer cut short-term interest rates.

When the economy continued to falter in early 2009, the Fed launched an experiment in monetary stimulus known as "quantitative easing," buying mortgage securities and then Treasury bonds to try to bring down long-term interest rates and fight the Great Recession. The initial round, known as QE1, would expand to $1.75 trillion in purchases of financial assets, sending a message that the Fed would not stand by and let the economy stagnate. The Fed would pursue QE2 and QE3 in 2010 and 2012, respectively, eventually expanding its balance sheet to more than $4.5 trillion, nearly five times its precrisis peak. Studies have found that quantitative easing lowered long-term Treasury and mortgage rates and helped support the recovery; it also encouraged other central banks to adopt similar programs to support global growth. Like many other crisis-era programs, quantitative easing also proved highly profitable for the taxpayer, as the Fed remitted the interest earned on its asset purchases to the Treasury.

While the Fed pursued its creative monetary policies, the Obama administration pushed a variety of fiscal policies designed to get the economy moving again, starting with the largest fiscal stimulus bill in U.S. history. (See Chapter 16, by Jason Furman, on fiscal policy during the crisis era.) Hank had negotiated a bipartisan $150 billion stimulus package early in 2008, but that was before the crisis had had its full impact, and the American Recovery and Reinvestment Act in early 2009 was a much more ambitious effort to offset the collapse in private demand. It stoked the economy with $300 billion in temporary tax cuts along with $500 billion worth of new federal spending—including relief to victims of the recession, public works designed to provide jobs while upgrading the nation's infrastructure, and direct aid to states. Congressional Republicans almost unanimously opposed the package, but most independent economists agree that the Recovery Act helped save jobs and boost growth. State and local governments offset some of its power with tax hikes, layoffs, and spending cuts, but the program helped launch the recovery in the United States while other developed economies were still shrinking.

In retrospect, given the severity of the downturn, the economy might well have benefited from an even larger stimulus package. But there were only 60 votes in the Senate for $800 billion, and no filibuster-proof support for anything larger. Congressional Democrats did follow up with a dozen more modest stimulus measures cutting payroll taxes, expanding unemployment aid, and sending more help to states, injecting $657 billion more into the economy over several years. The Obama administration also poured more TARP money into a controversial auto rescue plan that forced General Motors and Chrysler into receivership as a prelude to restructuring. Overall, the auto industry would receive more than $80 billion from TARP, but in the end, the net cost to taxpayers would be only $9.3 billion (see Chapter 13, by Deese, Shafran, and Jester, on the auto program). Between 2008 and 2012, the overall federal fiscal expansion (including automatic countercyclical stabilizers) amounted to about 3.4 percent of GDP per year. The measures were also quite progressive in their impact; the bottom 40 percent of families were, collectively, mostly protected from reductions in overall income.

Tim and his colleagues in the Obama administration also launched a series of new programs to support the housing market, building on the recapitalization of Fannie and Freddie and the Fed's actions to lower mortgage interest rates. Michael Barr, Kashkari, Andreas Lehnert, and Phillip Swagel discuss these programs, as well as housing policies during the Bush administration, in Chapter 12. Obama housing programs included the Home Affordable Refinance Program (HARP), to help underwater homeowners refinance their mortgages, and the Home Affordable Modification Program (HAMP), to help delinquent homeowners modify their monthly payments.

Like the financial interventions, the housing programs had plenty of critics. Those on the right saw the programs as fiscally irresponsible giveaways to irresponsible homeowners; some have attributed the rise of the Tea Party movement to this perception. Those on the left felt just as strongly that the government's response to the foreclosure crisis was weak and late, and it's true that these programs were painfully slow and disappointing in their reach. In particular, HAMP was a logistical nightmare, reliant on a dysfunctional loan servicing industry that routinely lost paperwork, failed to return phone calls, and gave borrowers the runaround. It also had onerous compliance requirements and restrictive eligibility rules to protect against fraud, which further bogged down an already unwieldy process, and persuaded banks to restructure millions of mortgages privately rather than deal with the government red tape. Ultimately, HAMP would directly support only a fraction of Obama's goal of 3 million to 4 million mortgage modifications, but in the end the combination of government and private-sector modifications reached more than 8 million homeowners. After a similarly glacial start, HARP would eventually help more than 3 million homeowners refinance their mortgages, while nearly 25 million others would take advantage of low rates to refinance without government help.

In retrospect, the federal actions that had the greatest impact on housing were what ultimately became a $400 billion lifeline for Fannie and Freddie, which kept mortgage credit flowing after private capital abandoned the field, and the Fed's purchases of mortgage-backed securities, which helped keep mortgage rates low and facilitated refinancing. The programs designed to help individual homeowners refinance their homes or modify their mortgages also helped millions, despite their flaws. But Congress was never enthusiastic about a dramatically more powerful housing strategy, and Tim and most of his colleagues in the Obama administration believed that additional dollars spent on unemployment benefits, infrastructure projects, payroll tax cuts, and aid to states would have more economic bang for the buck—while raising fewer dilemmas about fairness—than programs aimed narrowly at homeowners.

Solving the economic crisis was a necessary condition for solving the housing crisis, while the reverse was not necessarily true. In the end, economic recovery turned out to be the best housing program. Home prices stabilized after the Great Recession ended, gradually lifting millions of underwater homeowners above water.

As financial markets began to function again and the effects of monetary and fiscal policies began to be felt, the economy stopped contracting and began to expand in mid-2009. U.S. auto sales had plunged to 10 million in 2009, but they were back up to precrisis levels of 17 million by 2015. The credit crunch ended for consumers as well as for financial institutions, although banks remained skittish about lending, especially to prospective homebuyers. Compared with the recoveries of other countries in this crisis or historical recoveries from past crises, the U.S. recovery began unusually quickly, and while it was not as strong as we had hoped, it has been unusually steady. An economy that was shedding more than 2 million jobs a quarter has now added some 19 million jobs over 100 consecutive months of employment growth, a record for sustained job creation. The stock market has more than tripled since bottoming out in March 2009, so retirement accounts that took a hit during the crisis have more than recovered. Median income has risen and poverty rates have declined. Liang, Margaret M. McConnell, and Swagel review the evidence on outcomes in Chapter 18.

Still, the crisis was the most damaging economic event since the Depression. It was *not* responsible for rising inequality, wage stagnation, declining labor force participation, and other adverse economic trends that have been developing for decades, although it may have worsened some of those trends. But it was the source of millions of layoffs and foreclosures and substantial hardships for millions of families. A crucial lesson of this experience is that a big financial crisis can be devastating even when it is met by an aggressive policy response, even when it benefits from the formidable financial might of the United States, and even when political leaders put politics aside. The best strategy for a financial crisis is not to have one. And the best way to limit the damage when there is one is to make sure crisis managers have the tools to control the crisis before it gets out of control.

ARE WE READY FOR THE NEXT CRISIS?

Financial crises will never be entirely preventable, because they are products of human emotions and perceptions, as well as inevitable lapses of human regulators and policymakers. But that's not an argument for passivity or inaction before a crisis hits. Even though there's no silver bullet capable of eradicating financial crises, there's a lot government officials can do to try to make crises less frequent and less likely to spiral out of control when they occur.

The U.S. government was not well prepared for the events of 2007–2009. Better preparation could have created better outcomes. If the U.S. regulatory system had been less balkanized and more capable of addressing the risks outside commercial banks, if U.S. crisis managers had been empowered all along to use overwhelming force to avoid financial collapse, and if mechanisms had been in place from the start to ensure the financial system would pay for its own rescue, the panic would have been less intense and less damaging. And, we believe, the politics would have been better.

A decade later, the vital question to ask is whether the United States is better prepared today. We believe the answer is yes and no. Because the financial system is more resilient and there are better safeguards in place, the risk of a serious panic has been reduced. But the authorities that government officials have to respond to a financial emergency are even weaker than they were a decade ago. The government's ability to respond to a collapse in economic demand with monetary and fiscal stimulus—its so-called Keynesian arsenal—has also been depleted.

Regarding crisis prevention, the news is generally good. A tougher, smarter, and more comprehensive regulatory regime, nationally and globally, is helping to constrain excessive risk-taking and leverage, increase transparency, and make the financial system less vulnerable to shocks, wherever they may arise. In particular, the Dodd-Frank Wall Street Reform and Consumer Protection Act of 2010 in the United States, along with the Basel III regulatory reforms in the international arena, has created bigger buffers and much stricter constraints on the risks firms can take with borrowed money. Chapter 17, by Lowery, Sheets, and Truman, provides more details on international cooperation in financial regulatory reform.

The strongest safeguards against panic are requirements that force firms to hold more loss-absorbing capital and to rely less on debt, especially short-term debt. The Basel III international agreement tripled the minimum capital requirements for banks and quadrupled them for the largest banks. It also required higher-quality capital, ensuring that the global system would have much hardier shock absorbers against severe shocks. The rules the Fed crafted for U.S. banks were even tougher. In response, banks have raised and retained significant amounts of new capital since the crisis.

The postcrisis reforms also established much more conservative liquidity requirements worldwide and in the United States, forcing lenders to hold more cash and other liquid assets while relying less on short-term financing that could run at the first sign of trouble. Before the crisis, uninsured short-term liabilities amounted to about one-third of the assets in the financial system; today they compose only about one-sixth. The repo market is much smaller, the assets it finances are much safer, and intraday credit, the riskiest element of repo, is down 90 percent from the precrisis peak.

These new rules would be of limited value if they applied only to the traditional banking system. As the crisis showed, risk seeks the path of least resistance, migrating to institutions and corners of financial markets where the rules are less stringent or are enforced less strictly. But the new restrictions on risk-taking are broader as well as stricter, applying not only to commercial banks but also to broker-dealers and other nonbanks that used to operate in the shadows. Before the crisis, firms holding only 42 percent of the system's assets faced significant constraints on their leverage; now that figure has risen to 88 percent. Furthermore, the reforms targeted financial instruments and funding markets as well as individual firms. For example, Dodd-Frank required most derivatives to be traded openly on public exchanges rather than negotiated in private deals, reducing the danger that uncertainty about what's in them and who's exposed to them would again stoke panic. The law also imposed more conservative margin requirements for derivatives trades, another way of discouraging excessive risk-taking.

The postcrisis reforms made the rules even tougher for the firms that would pose the greatest danger to the system if they collapsed. A "systemic surcharge" on the largest banks requires them to hold more capital than smaller institutions against a given amount of risk, reducing their incentive to take on leverage and increasing their buffers against losses. Dodd-Frank also included language barring mergers that would concentrate more than 10 percent of the system's liabilities in a single bank, empowering the Fed to break up banks it considered a serious threat to the system, and requiring the Fed to conduct annual stress tests of big banks to make sure they are prepared for worst-case scenarios.

Some have criticized the reforms for preserving too much of the status quo, instead of breaking up big banks and reinstating the Depression-era Glass-Steagall Act rules that separated commercial and investment banking. But it's far from clear that Glass-Steagall-type restrictions would have avoided the recent crisis or would limit the risk of future crises. After all, Bear Stearns, Lehman Brothers, Fannie Mae, Freddie Mac, and AIG were nonbanks unaffected by Glass-Steagall, while Wachovia and Washington Mutual were commercial banks that got into trouble the old-fashioned way, by making bad loans. Size is not always a negative; the crisis would have been much worse if JPMorgan, Bank of America, and Wells Fargo hadn't been huge enough to swallow not-quite-as-huge Bear, WaMu, Countrywide, Merrill Lynch, and Wachovia before they collapsed. And smallness is not always a positive; a cascade of failures by relatively tiny banks helped trigger the Great Depression. In any case, the nation's largest banks have performed well over their first eight years of stress testing under Dodd-Frank; in 2018, the Fed concluded they would still have more capital *after* a severe global recession that increased the unemployment rate by 6 percentage points than they had during the good times *before* the crisis. And a 2014 report by the Government Accountability Office found the biggest banks could no longer borrow at much lower rates than small banks, a sign markets are less convinced they are too big to fail.

We would have liked to see more restructuring of the antiquated financial regulatory system, but the political turf battles proved insurmountable. Dodd-Frank did create the Financial Stability Oversight Council (FSOC) of regulators led by the Treasury secretary, which made at least one government body, though not a single agency, responsible for assessing and limiting risks across the financial system. And the FSOC does have the power to act to minimize systemic risks it detects, including the power to designate any financial institution as "systemically important" and subject to stricter supervision by the Fed. Dodd-Frank also took a tentative step toward reorganization by abolishing the Office of Thrift Supervision, the perennially captured regulator of Countrywide, WaMu, and AIG. Otherwise, though, every agency in the federal organization chart survived. Dodd-Frank even added an agency to that cluttered chart: the Consumer Financial Protection Bureau, which consolidated the consumer protection divisions of all the other regulators into one powerful new cop on the financial beat. But it made sense to create a one-stop shop for consumer protection, which had often languished inside agencies with other priorities. Aggressive enforcement of fraud protections in consumer credit markets, in addition to helping ordinary Americans keep more of their money, could enhance financial stability, by cracking down on the kind of shoddy underwriting and other predatory behaviors that caused so many problems in the mortgage market.

Together, these reforms should reduce the frequency of crises. They are already forcing financial institutions, especially larger financial institutions, to hold more and higher-quality capital, accumulate less leverage, and finance themselves in safer ways—and annual stress tests are making sure they're preparing for adversity. The derivatives market is much more transparent, consumer protections have been enhanced, and there is finally a government body responsible for monitoring potential dangers to the entire system.

It is also conceivable that the world will get better at anticipating and preempting financial shocks. Central banks and international institutions have invested heavily in financial stability units that try to identify danger signs and vulnerabilities. The Federal Reserve has recently begun to issue its own regular financial stability report, complementing one put out by the FSOC. We support these efforts, but we suspect that they will not fully protect the financial system from the failures of imagination and limitations of memory that seem hard-wired in human beings. Someday we will have another crisis. That's when government responders will need a safety net, and we are afraid America is even more riddled with holes than it was before the crisis.

|||||

The story of how the crisis happened is complex, involving a variety of interlocking factors, including excessive leverage, bad mortgage underwriting, runnable funding, opaque securitization, outdated regulation, and more. The story of why the crisis got so bad, in contrast, is in large part a simple one, whose main theme is the weak and antiquated emergency weapons that we and other regulators had to fight the panic.

When the crisis began, the Fed had one principal crisis-fighting tool, its ability to lend through its discount window to commercial banks against solid collateral. It could lend to nonbanks against collateral, but only if it invoked its emergency Section 13(3) authorities, and even then only if the borrowers were near or past the point of no return. Otherwise, the Fed's authority was surprisingly crimped; for example, its power to buy financial assets was limited to Treasuries and securities issued by the government-sponsored enterprises (like Fannie and Freddie), while other central banks could buy much riskier securities and in some cases equities. And Treasury had virtually no standing authority to intervene in a crisis.

During the crisis, the Fed applied its lending authorities through an alphabet soup of programs, and its aggressive interventions helped provide essential liquidity for stressed firms and markets. But conventional and even unconventional lending by the central bank cannot magically restore confidence in deeply troubled firms or troubled assets; indeed, the entire crisis illustrated the limits of Bagehot's playbook. The Fed also reinterpreted its emergency lending authority in creative ways to avert catastrophic collapses of Bear Stearns and AIG, but those last-ditch rescues didn't restore confidence in the financial system either, because the government had no way to reassure investors and creditors that other major firms wouldn't face similar collapses. We had to go to Congress to get the authority we needed to recapitalize endangered firms and guarantee their obligations, and even then it took time to reassure the markets that there was no longer a reason to run. If we had started the crisis with greater ability to intervene when the system is at risk, we could have acted more forcefully, swiftly, and comprehensively, with less reliance on ad hoc rescues.

But the crisis produced a powerful political backlash against anything that could be construed as enabling bailouts, and the Dodd-Frank legislation curtailed rather than expanded the government's crisis-fighting tools. Treasury's authority to inject capital was not renewed. The FDIC's broad guarantee authority for bank debt was eliminated, as was the Fed's ability to lend to troubled individual nonbanks like AIG and Bear. The Fed retained the power under 13(3) to lend to broad classes of institutions, as it had done for primary dealers, and to support key funding markets, as it had done for commercial paper, but with less flexibility than before. For example, Congress limited the Fed's discretion to judge when its loans are secured to its satisfaction, making it harder for it to accept risky collateral in a future emergency.

Congress also took away the Treasury's power to use the Exchange Stabilization Fund to issue guarantees, even though that power protected the savings of ordinary Americans after the Reserve Primary Fund broke the buck, and it curtailed the executive branch's ability to take credit risk alongside the Fed, as it did to backstop consumer credit markets through the TALF. The Dodd-Frank legislation even weakened the Fed's traditional lender-of-last-resort programs, adding disclosure rules that, whatever their benefits in terms of transparency, will increase the stigma of taking loans from the Fed, making it harder for the Fed to provide liquidity to the system in a future crisis.

Dodd-Frank did create one important new power for crisis fighters, known as "orderly liquidation authority," a bankruptcy-like mechanism for failing complex firms that would allow crisis managers to wind them down in an orderly and predictable manner, as the FDIC already does for smaller and simpler banks. Our inability to do this during the crisis was a frequent source of frustration—and during Lehman weekend, a source of disaster. The goal of crisis management should not be to prevent all failures but rather to prevent chaotic failures that can trigger widespread financial instability. A well-crafted resolution authority could be an elegant way to avoid chaos while helping to ensure that no financial institution is too big to fail. The FDIC, with the Fed's support, has invested substantial resources in planning how this authority might be invoked under various scenarios.

We won't know how well this new resolution authority will work until it's used, and the three of us do not entirely agree on its promise. We don't want to dismiss the importance of the new resolution regime, or the "living wills" that systemically important firms must draw up in good times to help the government wind them down in case of disaster. But it's fair to say that the new authority is likely to be more effective in managing the failure of a Lehman-type firm in an otherwise stable environment than when the entire system is on the edge of panic.

Of course, when a crisis does arrive, Congress would have the power to undo the preemptive limitations it has placed on financial first responders. But that is easier said than done in a nonparliamentary democracy where legislative changes require support from the president, the House, and a filibuster-proof majority in the Senate. At a minimum, the crisis fighters of the future would have to follow our suboptimal path of spending time, energy, and political capital to get the tools they need while the emergency is ongoing, which would make crises deeper and longer and increase their ultimate cost to the economy and to taxpayers. And it is hard to look at the bitterly polarized politics of modern America and feel confident that a bipartisan consensus for unpopular but necessary actions would emerge when it mattered most.

IIIII

As bad as the crisis and subsequent recession were, they would have been much worse if the Federal Reserve, Congress, and the executive branch had not engineered massive monetary and fiscal stimulus to stop the contraction and boost the recovery. Another key lesson of 2008 was that measures to stabilize the financial system can't succeed if the economy is imploding, while measures to revive the economy can't succeed if the financial system is collapsing. They all have to work together, and a government's ability to limit the intensity of a financial crisis depends on its macroeconomic room for maneuver.

Before the crisis, America's Keynesian arsenal was reasonably well stocked. The Fed had plenty of capacity to lower short-term interest rates as needed to support the economy, while the rest of the government had budgetary room to undertake expansionary fiscal policies like tax cuts and increased spending. Today, the scope for Keynesian policies looks far more constrained, which could be a serious handicap in a future crisis or deep recession. And while the Fed has been slowly raising rates, which will help replenish the monetary ammunition it deployed during the last crisis, Washington's political branches are squandering their fiscal ammunition when they ought to be gathering more.

On the monetary side, Ben's successors at the Fed, Janet Yellen and Jerome Powell, have begun a gradual process of unwinding the $4.5 trillion book of securities the Fed accumulated through quantitative easing, while slowly nudging interest rates above 2 percent as we write these words. However, it appears that even once monetary policy returns to a neutral stance, the prevailing interest rates will be lower than in the past. If so, the Fed won't have as much headroom to loosen policy with rate cuts if the economy falters, although new quantitative easing might remain an option.

On the fiscal side, after ballooning above $1 trillion during the crisis, the budget deficit initially fell as the emergency subsided, the financial rescues were repaid, and the economy rebounded, while Congress raised taxes and cut the rate of growth in spending. But now the annual deficit is soaring above $1 trillion again, because of major tax cuts unaccompanied by spending restraint— and as an aging population puts additional strain on future entitlement obligations, the United States could face unsustainable long-term deficits as far as the eye can see. When the next crisis or even an ordinary downturn hits, depressing tax revenues and making the deficit even worse, policymakers will find it much harder, politically and economically, to match the aggressive response of a decade ago.

It will take a long period of less profligate policy choices and benign economic conditions to restore America's macroeconomic firepower to levels that could help end another emergency. Right now, even a modest recession could leave Washington without much fiscal leeway to respond to a crisis, or for that matter to upgrade infrastructure, tackle the opioid epidemic, address climate change, stabilize Social Security, or provide permanent tax relief for hardworking families. America was grappling with rising income inequality, middle-class insecurity, and other economic challenges well before the crisis of 2008, but the crisis made them worse, and soaring budget deficits could hobble our ability to deal with them.

WHAT IS TO BE DONE?

The United States and other major economies have made substantial financial and economic progress over the past decade. But as history has demonstrated, long periods of confidence and stability can produce overconfidence and instability. Rules that seem necessary in the aftermath of a disaster start to feel onerous in calmer times, as the traumas of the past recede into the distance.

The enemy is forgetting. The current regulatory burden has not prevented banks from enjoying record profits and expanding their lending, but the financial industry is pushing hard for regulatory relief. We believe the first rule for additional financial reform should be Hippocratic: First, do no harm. We should be careful not to allow a general weakening of the most powerful defenses against crisis. So far, virtually all of the Dodd-Frank reforms remain in place. But when times are good, the dangers of backsliding can seem negligible. As time passes and memories fade, it will be vital that the inevitable pressures to push for a softer regulatory approach do not re-create the vulnerabilities that existed before the crisis.

In fact, the costs of financial crises can be so enormous that there ought to be a serious push for even stronger measures to prevent and mitigate them. It's hard to get the political system to act without a crisis to force its hand, especially in a time of angry partisan gridlock, but the stakes are high enough that Washington ought to treat financial stability as an emergency before it becomes one.

When it comes to crisis prevention, the main challenge for reforms will be beating back the pressure to weaken the tough new capital, leverage, liquidity, and margin rules. A related challenge will be making sure that as market participants adapt to the new rules, diverting risk to areas where oversight seems looser, regulators have the discretion and the will to adapt as well. Commercial banks are still a smaller portion of the U.S. financial system than they are in other major economies, and vigilance will be required to ensure that risky leverage doesn't migrate to new shadows. It's worth remembering how much risk-taking drifted away from banks before the crisis when capital requirements were much lower; now the incentives to find new opportunities for regulatory arbitrage will be even stronger. The balkanized financial regulatory system could still use organizational reform as well, to reduce turf battles among redundant agencies with overlapping responsibilities.

Otherwise, though, the framework for crisis prevention is in decent shape. We're more worried about what happens when the next crisis nevertheless occurs. We recognize that the public is not clamoring to make it easier for our successors to rescue bankers. Still, disempowering financial rescuers will not prevent financial rescues; it will only delay them and make them much costlier. Somehow, Washington needs to muster the courage to restock the emergency arsenal with the tools that helped end the crisis of 2008—the authority for crisis managers to inject capital into banks, buy their assets, and especially to guarantee their liabilities, the most powerful weapon governments have for quelling panics.

These proposals may sound radical, but the FDIC already has most of these authorities when dealing with commercial banks, and it uses these authorities regularly, efficiently, and without political blowback. We should be investigating how to extend these authorities so they apply to any institution engaged in maturity transformation. The resolution authority in Dodd-Frank also needs to be enhanced, so that when large complex banks are on the brink of failure, the FDIC can fully stand behind their obligations while winding them down in an orderly fashion. That may create some short-term costs for taxpayers, but the FDIC can recoup any outlays from the industry after the crisis passes. A key consideration is to avoid imposing haircuts on creditors during a panic, which only accelerates the panic. The impulse to ensure that risk-takers pay a price for their risk-taking is understandable, but requiring crisis managers to extract that price during a crisis only makes it harder to end the crisis.

One feature of the FDIC model that makes it work well is that it extracts that price *before* a crisis strikes—and makes clear that even if the price turns out to be steeper than anticipated, the industry will eventually foot the bill. We would like to see Congress adopt a similar insurance model that would work for the broader financial system, so crisis managers would have the leeway to put public dollars at risk with the assurance that any shortfalls would ultimately be repaid by financial institutions. We're not so naïve as to think this would solve the political problems of financial crisis management; government efforts to calm panics will always be susceptible to attack as unwarranted bailouts for irresponsible speculators. But an up-front legal mandate that the financial industry will pay all the costs of financial crisis-fighting could help. We achieved this outcome in practice a decade ago; the financial sector paid in full for the protection we provided. But it would be better if this were automatic and clearly understood in advance.

Finally, we hope that Washington will take advantage of the improving economy to prepare for the challenges that are sure to come. This will require a new commitment to fiscal responsibility, because the current approach of slashing taxes while boosting spending in good times will make it much more difficult to provide fiscal stimulus in bad times. Most important, we should be taking steps to address long-standing structural problems, including growing disparities in income that undermine the health of our economy and our democracy. We need to find ways to have more Americans participate in the nation's economic success, and not only because it's the right thing to do. A stronger economy in which opportunity and prosperity are more widely spread will leave the country better prepared to withstand the shocks that economies are heir to, including financial shocks.

A decade ago, we watched Democrats and Republicans set aside political and ideological differences to save the country from catastrophe, reinforcing the belief that the United States, when confronted with crisis, though perhaps only when confronted with crisis, tends to do what is necessary. But that was hard to do at the time, and might be harder in a future crisis. We are certainly not optimistic it will be done before a crisis, especially now that our divided and paralyzed political system seems incapable of making thoughtful choices about the future.

Still, the current mix of constraints on the emergency policy arsenal is dangerous for the United States—and, considering the global importance of the U.S. financial system and the dollar, dangerous for the world. Over the past century, the world has made great progress in reducing the astronomical costs to governments and individuals of war, famine, and disease. But it has made virtually no progress in reducing the similarly astronomical costs of financial crises. We can do better, and the stakes are so huge that doing even a little better could save trillions of dollars and improve millions of lives. There's no time like the present to start.

| CHAPTER TWO |

The Use and Effectiveness of Conventional Liquidity Tools Early in the Financial Crisis

WILLIAM B. ENGLISH AND PATRICIA C. MOSSER

INTRODUCTION

Strains in financial markets related to the excesses in the housing and mortgage sectors began to show in the first half of 2007, with significant deterioration in residential real estate markets, stock market volatility, hedge fund failures, and rising losses on subprime mortgage loans. Despite this turmoil, the cost of bank short-term borrowing remained fairly stable. Then on August 9, BNP Paribas, the second-biggest bank in the euro area, announced it would no longer redeem shares in three investment funds with large exposures to U.S. asset-backed securities (ABS) backed by subprime mortgages (BNP Paribas 2007). The bank said that liquidity in the market for such securities had evaporated, making the valuation of the securities impossible.

The Paribas announcement was only one of several negative shocks to financial markets in the summer of 2007, but it was the straw that broke the camel's

We thank Anshu Chen, Benjamin Henken, Aidan Lawson, and David Tam of the Yale Program on Financial Stability for their excellent research assistance. Thanks also to John McGowan and Lyle Kumasaka for their assistance with the data, and to Debby Perlmutter and Susan McLaughlin for useful conversations on the implementation of the tools discussed in this chapter. We commend the many colleagues we had at the Federal Reserve Board and the Federal Reserve Bank of New York who played critical roles in the development and implementation of these tools. We have benefited from comments from Ben Bernanke, Tim Geithner, David Wessel, Nellie Liang, Bob Goetz, and other participants in a workshop held at Yale University in March 2018. All errors are ours.

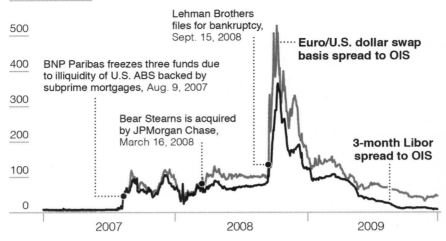

600 basis points

500   Lehman Brothers
files for bankruptcy,
Sept. 15, 2008   Euro/U.S. dollar swap
basis spread to OIS

400   BNP Paribas freezes three funds due
to illiquidity of U.S. ABS backed by
subprime mortgages, Aug. 9, 2007

300

    Bear Stearns is acquired
by JPMorgan Chase,
200   March 16, 2008   3-month Libor
spread to OIS

100

0

2007   2008   2009

Figure 2.1 **Three-Month Funding Spreads to OIS: Libor and FX Swaps**

Note: ABS are asset-backed securities; OIS is the overnight indexed swap; FX is foreign exchange.

Sources: Bloomberg Finance L.P.; authors' calculations

back and had an immediate impact on funding markets (see Figure 2.1). Funding costs for banks jumped amid uncertainty about both the valuation of mortgage-related assets and banks' exposures to them. The market for asset-backed commercial paper (ABCP), where there was considerable uncertainty about exposures to mortgage-related assets, was particularly stressed amid a pullback by money market investors. In response, the European Central Bank (ECB) injected significant reserves—the equivalent of $130 billion—into the euro-area money markets (ECB 2007). When markets opened in the United States, money markets came under strain as well, with the U.S. branches of European banks reportedly bidding up money market rates. The Federal Reserve took action, conducting open market operations (OMOs) that added $24 billion of reserves to the U.S. banking system that day (Federal Reserve Bank of New York 2019).

The financial crisis had, in effect, begun. It was left to the Fed and other central banks to provide liquidity as the lender of last resort—the traditional role for a central bank in a crisis, as Walter Bagehot outlined in *Lombard Street* in 1873.

This chapter is about the design, the use, and, ultimately, the inadequacy of the Fed's conventional lending tools during the first part of the financial crisis.

The tools we discuss—discount window lending, the Term Auction Facility (TAF), and the single-tranche repo program—were the first line of defense for the Fed in managing the largest liquidity crisis in nearly 80 years. These conventional-authority lending programs were not only implemented first, starting that August, but at the height of the panic in late 2008, they were also among the largest lending programs used by U.S. banks and particularly by branches, agencies, and subsidiaries of non-U.S. financial institutions operating in the United States.

The conventional-authority tools were innovative adaptations of long-standing lending programs used by the Fed. The innovations took several forms, but in general they were designed to address liquidity pressures in the broad financial system. In other words, they were adapted to manage a systemic financial panic rather than to provide liquidity to specific institutions or to manage policy interest rates. The Fed developed the programs on a piecemeal basis, often in short time spans and based on limited information. As a result, they had to be adjusted several times over the course of the crisis. Although the consensus view is that the conventional programs did ease liquidity and funding strains in key lending markets, their impact was limited and ultimately proved insufficient to halt the broader financial panic. As a consequence, the Fed turned to its emergency lending authorities as well.

BACKGROUND, LEGAL AUTHORITIES, AND HISTORY

Broadly speaking, the Fed has traditionally employed two types of lending. First, under Section 10 of the Federal Reserve Act (discount window authority), the Fed can lend to a restricted set of counterparties (commercial banks and other deposit-taking institutions) against a broad set of collateral.[1] Second, under Section 14 (open market authority), the Fed can use repurchase agreements (repos) to lend to a potentially broad set of counterparties against a narrow set of collateral (government and government agency securities and foreign exchange). In practice, however, the list of counterparties for open market operations was restricted to a relatively small number (about 20 at the time of the crisis) of large, global securities dealers, known as primary dealers.[2]

---

1. We refer to these counterparties as "banks." The list of eligible collateral for discount window lending and associated haircuts is determined and published by the Federal Reserve banks. In general, most sound bank assets can be pledged.
2. Primary dealers are generally large securities firms that agree to participate in Treasury auctions and Federal Reserve operations. See "Primary Dealers," Federal

Historically, discount window borrowing by banks was considered the Fed's main tool in its role as lender of last resort, although large loans were relatively rare.[3] During previous periods of financial turmoil, such as those caused by the bankruptcy of Penn Central in 1970, the failure of Continental Illinois in 1984, the 1987 stock market crash, and the September 11, 2001, attacks, the Fed made public announcements to emphasize its willingness to meet the liquidity needs of banks with discount window loans. In part, the intention behind such lending was to use the banks to allocate the funds to their customers, allowing the Fed to minimize its role in credit allocation. But as we saw during the financial crisis, banks may not effectively pass on liquidity if they are under pressure themselves. Moreover, banks accounted for only about a third of financial intermediation in the United States in 2007, so the majority of the financial system had no direct access to the discount window.[4]

In contrast, open market authority was used on an almost daily basis to implement monetary policy by the Open Market Desk at the Federal Reserve Bank of New York (the Desk) on behalf of the Federal Open Market Committee (FOMC).[5] However, open market operation tools were occasionally adapted for emergency liquidity provision as well. For example, to alleviate potential liquidity strains in the run-up to the century date change on January 1, 2000, the Desk sold options on repo operations. In times of stress, the Desk had also conducted single-tranche repo operations under which the primary dealers could deliver any type of OMO collateral—Treasury, agency debt, or agency mortgage-backed securities (MBS)—in a single repo operation to obtain (typically term) funding. Such operations were used before the century date change

---

Reserve Bank of New York, accessed May 28, 2019, https://www.newyorkfed.org/markets/primarydealers.

3. In normal times, discount window credit is divided into "primary credit," which is available on a short-term basis to generally sound banks; "secondary credit," which is available on a short-term basis to banks that do not qualify for primary credit; and "seasonal credit," which is available to smaller institutions with large seasonal fluctuations in deposits or loans. See Federal Reserve (2018).

4. See Kohn (2009) for a discussion.

5. In these normal operations, the Open Market Desk conducted repos and reverse repos with the primary dealers to adjust the supply of reserves and keep the federal funds rate close to the target rate set by the FOMC. Since 1999, the collateral for these operations has been Treasury securities, agency debt securities, and agency mortgage-backed securities (MBS). See Federal Reserve Bank of New York (2000).

and after the September 11, 2001, attacks as well as in August 2007 (Federal Reserve Bank of New York 2008).

The financial crisis, though, was different, and the Fed found new and innovative ways to put both discount window and open market tools to use. Discount window credit was provided at a lower premium to market rates and for longer terms starting in August 2007. The Fed also created a new program, the Term Auction Facility, in December 2007, under which it auctioned fixed amounts of term discount window credit to eligible borrowers. The establishment of the TAF was coordinated with central bank liquidity swap lines, which allowed foreign central banks to lend dollars to banks in their jurisdictions.[6] Finally, starting in March 2008, the Desk conducted large weekly single-tranche repo operations to provide primary dealers with term funding for their agency MBS.

THE INITIAL RESPONSE

The Fed's response to the growing stress in financial markets in the second half of 2007 and the first part of 2008 started in a traditional manner. The Desk used temporary OMOs to provide additional reserves and keep the federal funds rate trading near its target. In addition, the Fed emphasized the availability of discount window credit for banks with unusual funding needs. Policymakers then eased lending policies at the discount window to encourage its use.

As noted, the efforts began in earnest after the August 9 announcement by BNP Paribas, with both the Fed and the ECB adding substantial reserves on that day. However, the following day money market conditions deteriorated. As a consequence, the ECB injected another round of reserves into the banking system, and the Desk ultimately conducted three single-tranche repo operations to add liquidity.[7] That morning, the FOMC met by conference call and agreed that it would be appropriate to issue a statement acknowledging the market pressures and noting the Committee's intention to provide the reserves required to keep the federal funds rate trading near its target (FOMC 2007a). In addition, and consistent with previous practice in times of market stress,

---

6. See Chapter 17, on international policy coordination, for a discussion of the swap lines.
7. See William Dudley's report in FOMC (2007a).

the statement noted: "In current circumstances, depository institutions may experience unusual funding needs because of dislocations in money and credit markets. As always, the discount window is available as a source of funding" (FOMC 2007b).

Despite this announcement, virtually no primary credit was extended through the discount window in the week ending August 15 (Board of Governors 2007a), and strains in money markets increased as investors pulled back from providing funding, particularly term funding, in the markets for asset-backed commercial paper and other asset-backed securities (FOMC 2007c). The Desk continued to conduct reserve-adding operations to help keep the federal funds rate trading near target.

On the evening of August 16, the FOMC met by teleconference to discuss the situation. Members agreed to issue a short statement the following morning saying that, though there was no change in the stance of monetary policy, the downside risks to the economy had increased. At the same time, the Board announced a temporary easing of discount window lending policy, including a 50-basis-point reduction in the discount rate and a willingness to lend for terms of up to 30 days, renewable by the borrower (FOMC 2007d; Board of Governors 2007b).

Taken together, these announcements acknowledged the deterioration in markets and showed that the Fed was taking steps to address the strains. Those steps were intended to give financial firms the time to assess the appropriate valuations of the troubled assets and avoid fire sales. In addition, by providing a lower-cost backstop for term funding markets, policymakers expected these changes in lending policy to help limit the tendency for investors to shorten the term of funding they would provide to banks, reducing rollover risk and making banks more willing to provide term funding to their customers.

These decisions by the Board and the FOMC reflected a balancing of a number of factors.[8] First, policymakers wanted to emphasize the distinction between monetary policy and liquidity policy. The Committee considered going further and cutting the federal funds rate. Indeed, Richmond Fed president Jeffrey Lacker, who was concerned that easing the terms of discount window credit could slow needed adjustments in financial markets, said, "Given the choice between a rate cut and this discount window program change, I'd rather have a rate cut." But the economic outlook was little changed, so the Commit-

---

8. The material discussed in this paragraph is drawn from FOMC (2007c).

tee did not want to ease monetary policy only to support financial firms and markets, because doing so could lead to moral hazard. "I'd really prefer to avoid giving any impression of a bailout, or a put, if we can," Fed chairman Ben S. Bernanke told his fellow FOMC members. Instead, the decision was to use liquidity policy—the discount window actions—to directly address the pressures in funding markets.

Second, although policymakers wanted to provide liquidity, they also wanted to avoid overreacting, encouraging moral hazard. In normal times, discount window lending addressed this concern by following Bagehot's dictum, which calls for lending to solvent banks at a high rate against good collateral.[9] Specifically, the Fed provided collateralized loans for a short term, traditionally overnight, at a penalty rate of 100 basis points above the target federal funds rate. Such lending was available only to banks qualifying for primary credit—those judged to be in generally sound financial condition. Those firms not qualifying for primary credit could turn to secondary credit at a higher cost and with more administrative oversight.

Third, policymakers realized that there was significant stigma attached to discount window borrowing, making banks hesitant to borrow from the Fed even if they faced liquidity pressures.[10] In part, this stigma reflected the long history of the discount window as an administered facility, although the changes to the discount window announced in 2002 had been intended to make it a "no questions asked" facility (Madigan and Nelson 2002). In addition, this stigma reflected in part a concern that such borrowing could become known to creditors and counterparties and thus contribute to further liquidity problems at borrowing firms. Although the Fed kept the identities of borrowing firms confidential, the publication of weekly balance sheet information for each Reserve Bank would allow interested observers to see if there had been significant lending in a particular district.[11] Those published data, along with reports from market participants, could be used to identify, or at least speculate about, which institutions were borrowing.

---

9. See Bagehot (1873). See also Madigan (2009) and Tucker (2014) for modern applications of Bagehot's dictum.
10. See Carlson and Rose (2017) for a discussion of stigma at the discount window.
11. Under provisions of the Dodd-Frank Act, the Federal Reserve is now required to publish the names of discount window borrowers with a two-year lag. As discussed below, concern about that publication will likely increase stigma in future periods of market stress.

However, policymakers judged that the stigma would be reduced if the penalty rate at the window were cut. In addition, by emphasizing in their statement that the changes in discount window policy were being made temporarily in response to significant market strains, policymakers hoped to encourage banks to see borrowing at the discount window as appropriate given the unusual circumstances.

Some consideration was given to cutting the primary credit rate by 75 basis points, rather than 50 basis points, to further counter stigma. However, that possibility raised a fourth consideration: Since the extent of the stigma was not known, some policymakers were concerned that a 25-basis-point spread of the discount rate over the federal funds target rate could lead to large and variable draws on discount window credit that would be difficult to manage in the federal funds market, perhaps undermining the Desk's control over the federal funds rate.[12] Moreover, with primary credit available for a 30-day term, and term spreads in the federal funds market sharply higher, such a narrow spread could contribute to moral hazard, as the discount window might be an attractive funding source for some banks, particularly smaller and weaker institutions that faced higher funding costs. That being said, policymakers noted that the effectiveness of the changes in discount window lending policy was not clear, and generally agreed that the appropriate level of the primary credit spread might need to be revisited (FOMC 2007c).

Unfortunately, the stigma attached to discount window credit was more substantial than policymakers had hoped, and banks were not willing to come to the window even on the new terms. In an effort to improve the effectiveness of the discount window, policymakers reached out to a few larger banks to encourage them to borrow in hopes that such borrowing would help reduce stigma (Bernanke 2015). In the end, four large institutions did come to the window, for $500 million each, but in public statements they said that they had done so only as a demonstration, and they repaid the bulk of the loans quickly (JPMorgan Chase 2007).

12. Note that the Federal Reserve did not have the authority to pay interest on reserves at this time, so to the extent that the strains reflected a misallocation of reserves rather than a shortfall in aggregate reserves, the Desk would have to offset the effect on reserves of discount window lending and all other lending programs by undertaking redemptions and sales of Treasury securities and reverse repo (borrowing) operations. In practice, this was what the Desk did to offset the reserves impact of all lending programs until October 2008.

One reason that banks may have limited their discount window borrowing was the availability of term credit from the Federal Home Loan Banks (FHLBs).[13] In the summer and fall of 2007, the terms on FHLB advances were attractive relative to the prevailing terms in the market for many institutions, and such advances were less costly than discount window credit and available at longer maturities. As a consequence, the total volume of advances increased sharply as conditions deteriorated in the final months of 2007.

But the willingness and ability of the FHLBs to provide liquidity was undermined by subsequent market events. After the failure of Bear Stearns, the FHLBs increased the haircuts imposed on collateral provided for advances, reflecting tighter private funding conditions for high-risk mortgage assets. (By contrast, the Fed did not change its discount window haircuts during the crisis.) As the crisis deepened in the summer and fall of 2008, the distress and eventual conservatorship of Fannie Mae and Freddie Mac—two other large housing-related government-sponsored enterprises (GSEs)—was accompanied by pressures on the funding of the FHLBs. In response the Fed purchased discount notes issued by the GSEs, including the FHLBs, in September 2008. Lending by the FHLBs peaked in that month, at roughly $1 trillion, before falling back, even as lending by the Fed increased vastly as the crisis accelerated.

ADDITIONAL STEPS: THE TERM AUCTION FACILITY AND SWAP LINES

As early as August 2007, staff at the Fed began to work on alternative ways to provide discount window credit to combat stigma. In 2001–2002, as part of its work on how to implement monetary policy if the supply of Treasury securities proved insufficient for its usual operations, the Fed had examined the possibility of an "Auction Credit Facility," under which discount window credit would be auctioned to banks on a regular basis.[14] Those plans were repurposed in 2007 as a lender-of-last-resort facility, called the Term Auction Facility.

An auction approach to providing discount window credit had three significant benefits.[15] First, by auctioning credit periodically, the amount of

---

13. This paragraph and the next follow the discussion in Ashcraft, Bech, and Frame (2010) regarding the liquidity provided by the FHLBs during the crisis.
14. See the Federal Reserve System Study Group on Alternative Instruments for System Operations (2002).
15. The material discussed in this paragraph and the next is drawn from FOMC (2007e, 2007f).

discount window credit would be known in advance (assuming the auctions would be fully subscribed). As a result, the Desk could plan other operations to offset the effects of the TAF credit on aggregate reserves and thus manage the federal funds rate. Second, using an auction could help diminish stigma. Because the auction would be open to many institutions and the price would be set based on the bids, there could be safety in numbers. That is, banks would not wait for others to borrow before going to the window, but all could borrow at the same time, reducing the risk that borrowers would become known. In addition, borrowing at an auction could be seen as simply borrowing at a market-determined rate, not at a penalty rate. Perhaps more important, the auction process took some time to complete, with funds from a given auction disbursed three days later—meaning that those borrowing at an auction did not need to have immediate funds, limiting concern that creditors and counterparties might have about the financial health of such banks. Indeed, banks couldn't be sure that they would win at the auction—and if they didn't win, they needed to have an alternative source of funds. Third, the Fed could gain insight into funding pressures by observing the bidding behavior of banks at the TAF.

In addition to the TAF, the Fed considered a number of other policies. These options included a reduction in the target federal funds rate, a further reduction in the spread between the primary credit rate and the funds rate target, and the introduction of a new term lending facility independent of the primary credit program and potentially with different terms and conditions. However, all of these options had significant shortcomings. The Committee continued to view monetary policy and credit policy as distinct tools with separate objectives. A reduction in the federal funds rate would be called for to manage the real economic effects of the market strains but was not seen as an appropriate policy to address the strains directly.[16] And a further reduction in the discount rate spread was still seen as potentially causing greater and more volatile use of the window, making monetary policy implementation more difficult. It could also lead a large number of smaller banks to turn to the discount window because of its relatively low cost, potentially overwhelming discount window administration. A demand-driven term lending facility, under which banks could choose when to borrow term funds and in what volume, was also

16. See Chapter 15, on the monetary policy response, for a discussion of the gradual changes in the Fed's economic outlook as the crisis progressed.

seen as likely to raise complications for monetary policy implementation and, if the rate were not greatly reduced, as unlikely to overcome stigma as effectively as the auction format.

Another policy option first discussed in August 2007 was the establishment of liquidity swap lines with foreign central banks.[17] Much of the liquidity pressure in dollar funding markets reflected difficulties that foreign banks, in many cases in Europe, had in obtaining dollar funding for their large holdings of dollar-denominated assets, including asset-backed securities that had become relatively illiquid. Although discount window credit could assist such foreign banks so long as they had U.S. operations to borrow from the Fed, such loans raised questions about the ability of the Fed to assess the solvency of the parent institutions. Swap lines could address that issue by allowing the Fed to provide dollars to a foreign central bank, which would in turn on-lend the dollars to banks in its jurisdiction.[18]

By the time of the September FOMC meeting, market conditions had eased somewhat, and the Committee judged that additional liquidity policy was not required at that time. Over the course of the fall, though, investors continued to pull back from a range of term funding markets, particularly those for asset-backed commercial paper conduits and structured investment vehicles.[19] Term funding was increasingly shortened to overnight lending. Term funding costs for banks, which had fallen in the early fall, rebounded to new highs by late November, reflecting in part concerns about year-end funding conditions as well as the liquidity and financial strength of banking institutions.

Against that backdrop, at meetings in December 2007 the FOMC once again discussed the possibility of implementing a TAF and establishing swap lines with foreign central banks (specifically, the ECB and the Swiss National Bank).[20] As a possible alternative, the Committee considered the use of term repos with

---

17. Liquidity swap lines had been established by the Fed, the ECB, and the Bank of England (and the existing line with the Bank of Canada had been increased in size) after the September 11 terrorist attacks. The lines expired after 30 days, and only the ECB drew on its line, and for only three days. See Kos (2001).
18. See Chapter 17, on international policy coordination, for additional discussion.
19. See Covitz, Liang, and Suarez (2013) for a discussion of the collapse of the ABCP market.
20. The material discussed in this paragraph and the next is drawn from FOMC (2007f, 2007g). Logistically, the swap lines were a decision by the FOMC, whereas the TAF was a decision by the Board of Governors.

the primary dealers to support their funding and add additional reserves, at least over year-end. Such an approach would be more conventional and thus might reduce the risk that investors would become more worried about the outlook based on the highly unusual actions taken by the Fed. However, as Chairman Bernanke noted, if "there is a problem with dollar funding in Europe . . . [it] creates problems in other markets." But he also indicated that although it would be desirable for the ECB to use a swap line to lend dollars to European banks, the ECB was "unwilling to do that except in the context of some kind of broader operation." Thus, if Fed policymakers were inclined to employ the swap lines, they would likely need to implement the TAF as well.

On balance, most policymakers were inclined to go forward with the two new programs, and the bulk of the discussion focused on the specific provisions to be employed. With regard to the TAF, the key decisions were the size of the program and the minimum rate to be charged. On the one hand, the extent of stigma was uncertain, and it was possible that bidding for TAF funds would be light. On the other hand, a larger auction amount would presumably lead to a lower stop-out rate and thus reduce stigma and encourage participation. And given the large size of U.S. money markets, a small program might have only a limited effect on pricing. William Poole, president of the St. Louis Fed, expressed the concern that "at the margin, [the TAF at the proposed size] doesn't do anything to change banks' funding costs." But Chairman Bernanke responded by saying: "Well, this may not be big enough. . . . One of the advantages of this [is] that we can scale it up potentially quite a bit." In the end, policymakers chose to maintain flexibility on the size of the program by leaving the size of TAF operations up to the chairman, based on a recommendation by the Desk manager.

Regarding the minimum bid rate, policymakers noted that allowing lower minimum bid rates could encourage participation in the auctions; but some worried that when demand was weak, the resulting low stop-out rates could contribute to moral hazard. Given these cross-currents, policymakers set the minimum bid rate as the overnight indexed swap (OIS) rate over the same period, meaning that winning bidders would not get funds at a cost below what they could expect by borrowing on a daily basis in the federal funds market. There was also considerable discussion about the maximum size of bids. To ensure that the number of winning firms at each auction was not too small, and thus limit possible problems with stigma, policymakers decided that each firm could bid no more than 10 percent of the total size of the auction. In addition, the maximum TAF bid was limited to half the bidder's collateral pledged to the discount window to ensure that sufficient collateral remained for daylight overdrafts and regular discount window borrowing. At the same time, there was concern that the program be made available to smaller banks, so the minimum bid was set at $10 million (and subsequently reduced to $5 million).[21]

Policymakers also discussed whether the standards for banks to participate in TAF auctions should be tighter than the "generally sound financial condition" required for access to primary credit. A tighter standard could help limit the Fed's risk, but it could further stigmatize traditional primary credit. Moreover, judgments about the condition of financial institutions were challenging under the circumstances, so some institutions that could appropriately benefit from the TAF might not be able to use it. It was also emphasized that Reserve Banks always have the right to refuse to make loans that would not be sound, allowing them to protect themselves from riskier firms. In the end, the primary credit standard was used for the TAF as well.[22]

The first TAF operation, held on December 17, 2007, auctioned $20 billion of 28-day discount window credit (Board of Governors 2007c). The next day, the ECB allocated $20 billion drawn under the new swap line to euro-area banks at the same rate established at the TAF auction, and the Swiss National Bank auctioned $4 billion using proceeds from its swap line. In the United States, the first TAF auction suggested the TAF had succeeded in managing stigma. There were 93 bidders, with total bids of more than $60 billion. Thirty-one banks obtained funds, at a stop-out rate of 4.65 percent—40 basis points over the target federal funds rate and 48 basis points over the minimum bid rate (see Figure 2.2).[23]

Perhaps more important, the coordinated actions by multiple central banks sent a clear message that the funding pressures were global and would be jointly

21. A system for noncompetitive tenders was considered but never adopted.
22. To simplify the Desk's efforts to offset the effects of TAF funding in reserves markets, the auctions were conducted every other Monday, with funds disbursed on the following Thursday, the first day of the subsequent reserve maintenance period, and with a term of 28 days—that is, two 14-day maintenance periods.
23. For data on the TAF, see "Term Auction Facility (TAF)," Board of Governors of the Federal Reserve System, accessed May 28, 2019, https://www.federalreserve.gov /regreform/reform-taf.htm. The one-month OIS rate was low relative to the target federal funds rate at the time because market participants expected the FOMC to cut rates at its December meeting.

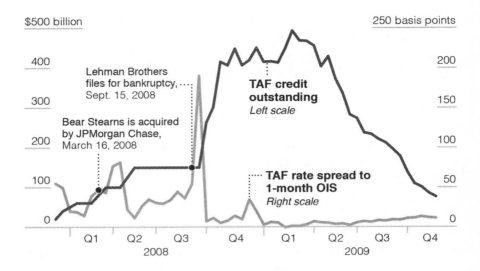

$500 billion   250 basis points

400   200

      Lehman Brothers
      files for bankruptcy,····   **TAF credit**
300   Sept. 15, 2008   **outstanding**   150
                                         Left scale
      Bear Stearns is acquired
      by JPMorgan Chase,
200   March 16, 2008   100

100   ···· **TAF rate spread to**   50
                                              1-month OIS
                                              Right scale
  0   0

            Q1   Q2   Q3   Q4   Q1   Q2   Q3   Q4
                    2008   2009

Figure 2.2 Term Auction Facility: Spread to One-Month OIS and Amount Outstanding

Note: TAF is the Term Auction Facility; OIS is the overnight indexed swap.

Sources: Bloomberg Finance L.P.; Federal Reserve Board; authors' calculations

addressed, a practice that continued throughout the crisis.[24] By the end of January 2008, the total amount of TAF funding outstanding was $60 billion, reflecting two overlapping auctions of $30 billion each.[25]

THE NEXT STEPS: EARLY 2008

Despite the central bank actions, mortgage securities, particularly those backed by high-risk mortgages, continued to impose significant losses on banks, mortgage originators, investors, dealers, and mortgage insurers. The impairment

24. See Chapter 17, on international policy coordination, for additional information on coordination across central banks.
25. To make its provisions of credit to banks more effective, the Fed provided a number of larger institutions with temporary exemptions from Section 23A of the Federal Reserve Act, which limits the ability of banks to lend funds to affiliates. In the first half of 2007, the Fed had granted only two such exemptions. However, in the second half of the year, it granted seven new exemptions and modified one; in 2008, it provided 12 more. See Chapter 4, on nonbank financial institutions, for additional discussion.

and eventual failure of several mortgage insurers caused large declines in the credit ratings of mortgage securities backed by high-risk mortgages and great uncertainty about their future valuations. As a result, high-risk mortgage securities could not be financed in repo and other secured funding markets. The largest securities firms faced both declines in the value of important assets and the loss of a key funding source for the same assets. In turn, investors became increasingly concerned about the financial strength of major securities firms, most notably Bear Stearns, which had a particularly outsize role in high-risk mortgage markets.

By early March 2008, the withdrawal of funding in repo markets—particularly the triparty repo market—became a run.[26] Although all securities firms lost some repo funding for MBS, the run was particularly intense over the next two weeks for Bear Stearns. Even agency MBS (which had explicit or implicit U.S. government backing) were increasingly difficult to fund via repo markets. The spread between one-month repo rates using agency MBS collateral and Treasury collateral, typically about 20 basis points, rose to about 75 basis points by early March 2008 and subsequently moved higher, as shown in Figure 2.3.

To address the strains in mortgage funding markets, the Fed expanded the size of TAF auctions and introduced a single-tranche repo program.[27] As noted earlier, single-tranche repo operations are a variation on standard OMOs often used in times of market stress.[28] In standard OMO, repo lending is auctioned separately for each type of eligible collateral (Treasury, agency debt, and agency mortgage-backed securities). By contrast, a single-tranche repo operation is

26. The triparty repo market is a market in which repo transactions between two counterparties are facilitated by a clearing bank that has both counterparties as customers. Broker-dealer firms use the triparty repo market to fund both their own securities holdings and those of their customers. At the time of the crisis, triparty repos totaled about $2.8 trillion, with much of the financing at short maturities. See Brickler, Copeland, and Martin (2011).
27. The program was proposed in a memo to the FOMC on the evening of March 6, 2008, and implemented the following morning. See Bernanke (2015) and Board of Governors (2008a).
28. In a standard operation, the Desk at the New York Fed offers at auction repo lending (typically with overnight maturity) against three types of collateral: Treasury securities, agency securities, and agency MBS. Bids from the primary dealers for standard repo operations are sorted into three tranches based on the type of collateral: one for Treasury securities only, a second for Treasury and agency debt securities, and a third for all three types of collateral.

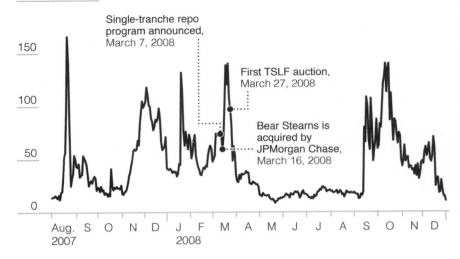

200 basis points

Single-tranche repo
program announced,
March 7, 2008

First TSLF auction,
March 27, 2008

Bear Stearns is
acquired by
JPMorgan Chase,
March 16, 2008

150

100

50

0

Aug. S O N D J F M A M J J A S O N D
2007   2008

Figure 2.3 Repo Spread: One-Month Agency MBS to U.S. Treasuries

Note: TSLF is the Term Securities Lending Facility; MBS are mortgage-backed securities.

Source: Federal Reserve Bank of New York

simply an auction of repo lending against all collateral types together, so lending is overwhelming against the least liquid and riskiest collateral allowed: agency MBS.

Though single-tranche repo operations are a traditional monetary policy implementation tool, the March 2008 single-tranche repo program used the tool in a new way. The operations were not needed to control the federal funds rate; instead, they were conducted as a lender-of-last-resort facility for the primary dealers, including some of the largest global financial intermediaries. The Desk auctioned $15 billion of single-tranche repo each week in March and expanded the program to $20 billion per week in April 2008, with the facility reaching a total size of $80 billion (see Figure 2.4).[29]

29. The original memo from the Desk to the FOMC proposed auctions of only $10 billion per week. The program's potential size was increased to $25 billion per week, or $100 billion total, at the request of Chairman Bernanke, but its maximum size never exceeded $80 billion. See Bernanke (2015).

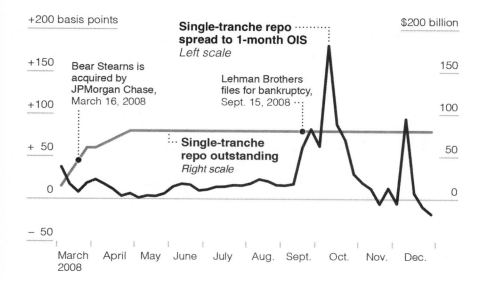

+200 basis points $200 billion

Single-tranche repo
spread to 1-month OIS
Left scale

+150   150
Bear Stearns is
acquired by   Lehman Brothers
JPMorgan Chase,   files for bankruptcy,
+100 March 16, 2008   Sept. 15, 2008   100

                             Single-tranche
+ 50   **repo outstanding**   50
                             Right scale

   0   0

− 50

     March   April   May   June   July   Aug.   Sept.   Oct.   Nov.   Dec.
     2008

Figure 2.4 **Single-Tranche Repo: Spread to One-Month OIS and Amount Outstanding**

Note: OIS is the overnight indexed swap.

Sources: Bloomberg Finance L.P.; Federal Reserve Board; authors' calculations

Like the TAF, the large increase in Fed lending through the single-tranche repo program could have significantly increased the quantity of excess reserves, making it difficult to keep the federal funds rate at the FOMC's target. To avoid that outcome, the program was expanded gradually, and the Desk redeemed and sold Treasury securities from the permanent portfolio and conducted reverse repo operations to control the size of the Fed's balance sheet and thus the federal funds rate.[30]

SUBSEQUENT DEVELOPMENTS

With the conventional tools already heavily engaged, the Fed turned to its emergency lending authority under Section 13(3) of the Federal Reserve Act as market conditions continued to deteriorate. To provide further support for

30. See FOMC (2008) for a discussion of the impact of the single-tranche repo program on the reserves market and monetary policy operations.

broker-dealers, the Fed introduced newly created programs such as the Term Securities Lending Facility (TSLF) and the Primary Dealer Credit Facility (PDCF) in March 2008, and a panoply of additional lending programs following the failure of Lehman Brothers in the fall.[31]

Use of the conventional tools continued to expand, however. As noted earlier, the spread of the primary credit rate over the funds rate target was cut to 25 basis points in March, and the term of primary credit loans was extended to 90 days (Board of Governors 2008b). The size of the TAF auctions was greatly increased, and the Fed introduced 84-day TAF operations in August in addition to the previous 28-day operations. In the fall, the size of TAF auctions was increased to such a degree that bids fell short of the auction sizes, and the rate on TAF loans fell to the minimum bid rate.[32]

By contrast, the size of the single-tranche repo program remained at $80 billion through the end of 2008. There was no need to increase the size of the program, as both the PDCF and the TSLF provided credit to the same counterparties against a broader range of collateral. The single-tranche program was phased out starting in December 2008, following the announcement that the Fed would undertake outright purchases of agency MBS for its permanent portfolio.[33]

All in all, the Fed's lending operations (including the discount window, the TAF, the single-tranche repo program, the 13(3) facilities, and the swap lines) peaked near $2 trillion at the end of 2008. Of this total, more than $600 billion was accounted for by the discount window, the TAF, and the single-tranche repo program (see Table 2.1). Thus, despite their conventional nature, these tools provided about as much liquidity as either the central bank swap lines or the 13(3) facilities.

Many of the Fed's lending programs had been priced so that they would be unattractive under normal market conditions. As market strains eased, borrowing from the Fed fell back. However, given the relatively narrow 25-basis-point spread of the primary credit rate over the target federal funds rate, discount window lending was subject to adverse selection over time as

---

31. See Chapter 3, on novel lender-of-last-resort programs, for a discussion of these programs.
32. The minimum bid rate was the OIS rate until early 2009, when it was changed to the interest rate paid on reserve balances.
33. See Chapter 15, on the monetary policy response, for a discussion of the large-scale asset purchases.

Table 2.1 Federal Reserve Assets, December 2007 and 2008

	Dec. 12, 2007 ($ in billions)	Dec. 10, 2008 ($ in billions)	Dec. 10, 2008 Non U.S.[A] (percent)
Conventional authority tools			
Repo (including single tranche)	48	80	58
Discount window	5	90	89
TAF	—	448	46
Subtotal: conventional authority direct lending	52	618	54
Liquidity swap lines[B]	—	583	100
Total conventional authority	52	1,201	76
Emergency authority tools			
13(3) liquidity programs[C]	—	584	
13(3) lending for AIG and Bear Stearns	—	104	
Total emergency authority	—	687	
Securities			
U.S. Treasuries (unencumbered)	773	286	
Agencies (discount notes only)	0	16	
Other assets	60	72	
Total assets	885	2,262	

Note: Totals may not sum due to rounding.

[A] Percentage of borrowing by institutions with ultimate corporate parents having home countries outside the United States as of December 10, 2008.

[B] Swap lines authorized by the FOMC under Section 14 of the Federal Reserve Act.

[C] Includes the Asset-Backed Commercial Paper Money Market Mutual Fund Liquidity Facility, the Commercial Paper Funding Facility, the PDCF, and the TSLF.

— Program not in place.

Sources: Federal Reserve Board, Factors Affecting Reserve Balances. Swap line data: Federal Reserve Board via Federal Reserve Economic Data (FRED). Non-U.S. amounts: authors' calculations based on data from Federal Reserve Board

some smaller and weaker institutions found the window attractive even as market functioning improved. In November 2009, the Fed announced that the maturity of primary credit loans would be shortened to 28 days in early 2010, and on February 19, 2010, the Fed increased the discount rate to 50 basis points over the rate paid on excess reserve balances and returned the term of discount window loans to overnight (Board of Governors 2010). Following these two changes, the volume of outstanding primary credit gradually fell back to near zero. Similarly, the minimum bid rate at TAF auctions represented low-cost funding for some firms, and they also continued to borrow from the Fed despite improved market conditions. The Fed gradually reduced the size of TAF auctions, and on February 18, 2010, the minimum bid rate was increased by 25 basis points, to 50 basis points. The final TAF auction, for $25 billion of 28-day credit, was held on March 8, 2010, with take-up of only $3.4 billion.

INTERNATIONAL USAGE

From the beginning of the crisis, funding market strains were particularly intense for non-U.S. financial institutions. The U.S. dollar serves as the benchmark currency for pricing of financial assets globally, as the dominant international reserve currency, and as the primary currency used in financing international trade. As a result, going into the crisis the largest non-U.S. global banks had large books of lending and investments denominated in U.S. dollars. They regularly funded their dollar assets through the commercial paper, repo, Eurodollar, and foreign exchange swap markets, but unlike U.S. banks, they typically did not have a U.S. dollar retail deposit base to rely on for relatively stable funding. Instead, they relied on U.S. banks and investors, particularly money market mutual funds, to obtain the dollars they needed.[34]

As the funding stresses accelerated over the course of the crisis, non-U.S. banks were particularly hard hit and became the largest borrowers from the Fed's conventional-authority facilities. Foreign banking organizations (including branches, agencies, and subsidiaries) accounted for about 85 percent of discount window credit from the start of the crisis through the end of 2009 (see Figure 2.5). Similarly, foreign banking organizations accounted for more than 60 percent of TAF borrowing over the life of that program, and usage of the single-tranche repo program by broker-dealer subsidiaries of foreign bank-

---

34. See Baba, Ash, and Ramaswamy (2009) for a discussion.

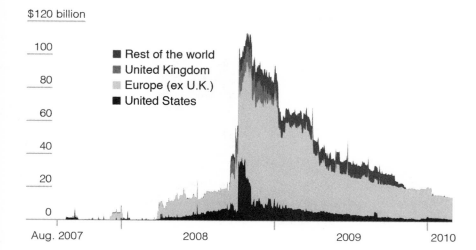

$120 billion

- Rest of the world
- United Kingdom
- Europe (ex U.K.)
- United States

100

80

60

40

20

0

Aug. 2007   2008   2009   2010

Figure 2.5 Discount Window: Amounts Outstanding by Region

Notes: (1) Transaction-level data on discount window lending during the crisis were released following court proceedings brought under the Freedom of Information Act (for more information, see "FOIA Service Center," Board of Governors of the Federal Reserve System, accessed May 28, 2019, https://www.federalreserve.gov/foia /servicecenter.htm). (2) Region refers to the home country of the corporate parent of the institution borrowing from the facility.

Sources: Federal Reserve Board; authors' calculations

ing organizations accounted for about 75 percent of the total (see Figures 2.6 and 2.7). Of course, foreign banks also borrowed dollars from foreign central banks that had been provided by the Fed through the central bank swap lines. By December 2008, direct borrowing by non-U.S. banks from the Fed through the discount window, the TAF, and the single-tranche repo program, plus indirect borrowing via the swap lines, amounted to about $900 billion, or more than 75 percent of the funds provided by the Fed through those facilities (see the final column in Table 2.1).

EVALUATING THESE TOOLS

Evaluating the effectiveness of the Fed's liquidity provision early in the crisis is difficult. Clearly, the actions taken were not sufficient to head off the much deeper financial crisis that unfolded. But given the financial system's exposures

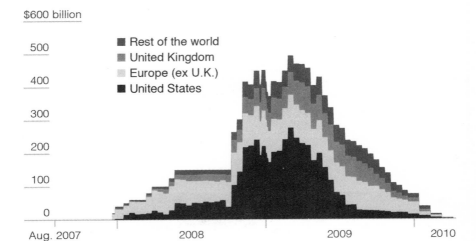

Figure 2.6 Term Auction Facility: Amounts Outstanding by Region

Note: Region refers to the home country of the corporate parent of the institution borrowing from the facility.

Sources: Federal Reserve Board; authors' calculations

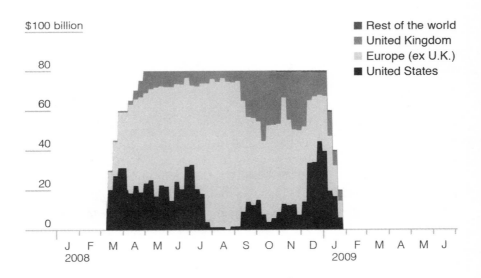

Figure 2.7 Single-Tranche Repo: Amounts Outstanding by Region

Note: Region refers to the home country of the corporate parent of the institution borrowing from the facility.

Sources: Federal Reserve Board; authors' calculations

to housing-related assets, the uncertainty about those exposures, and the ultimate size of the losses incurred, better outcomes may have been difficult to achieve given the Fed's limited authorities, short of 13(3) lending. That said, the early steps did ease strains in funding markets relative to what would otherwise have happened.

Efforts by economists to evaluate the effectiveness of the TAF program have produced mixed results. As noted above, the TAF did appear to reduce the stigma associated with discount window lending.[35] But empirical tests of the effects of TAF lending on term spreads raise difficult issues of identification. The TAF was introduced in response to mounting market strains, so any positive effects of the TAF may be hard to disentangle from the underlying deterioration in markets. For example, Taylor and Williams (2009) use simple regression tests to see if TAF auctions helped reduce term spreads, and they find no statistically significant effect of the TAF over the period from its introduction through August 2008. However, this result is fragile, depending on the details of the regression test used. McAndrews, Sarkar, and Wang (2017) employ a more flexible test, and they find that announcements about the size and duration of the TAF program did help reduce Libor-OIS spreads.

More broadly, the purpose of the discount window and the TAF was to ease strains in financial markets and thus improve the flow of credit to businesses and households. Recent work by Berger et al. (2016) suggests that discount window credit and the TAF did indeed help achieve those objectives. Using data on individual banks, they find that Fed credit was associated with a reduction in funds obtained from other sources and an increase in loans by the borrowing banks. Although it is hard to be confident about identifying the effect on aggregate lending, the results suggest that the TAF had the desired economic effects.

In short, the TAF appears to have been successful in combating stigma, encouraging banks facing funding pressures to obtain financing from the Fed. And there is evidence that the Fed's lending helped ease strains in funding markets more broadly and may have supported economic activity.

The single-tranche repo program was simple to announce and implement and was well understood by the primary dealers, with no stigma attached

---

35. See Armentier, Krieger, and McAndrews (2008) and Armentier et al. (2015) for further discussion of the TAF and its effects on stigma.

to its use. More important, given the speed with which market conditions deteriorated in early March 2008, the single-tranche repo program had the advantage of immediate implementation, in contrast to the time taken to design and implement new lending programs, such as the TAF and the 13(3) lending facilities.

Although there are no published studies of the impact of the single-tranche repo program, it was successful in providing term funding for agency MBS, a market that was impaired because of the disruptions in mortgage markets, and increasing the supply of Treasury securities in the market, which were in high demand for the same reason. Specifically, information on operations and repo spreads suggests the program had an immediate positive impact on liquidity and funding strains in some parts of the repo markets. One-month repo spreads for agency MBS collateral, which had risen in late February and early March, fell almost immediately, although they spiked higher again around the time of Bear Stearns' collapse (Federal Reserve Bank of New York 2009). As can be seen in Figure 2.3, MBS repo spreads did not stabilize until late March, when the single-tranche repo program, the TSLF, and the PDCF all had been put in place. Early demand for borrowing in the single-tranche repo program was high (up to five times the quantity auctioned), but it slowly diminished as the program grew, the 13(3) facilities were put in place, and funding market tensions eased in the spring and summer. Ultimately, the program's impact was likely quite limited because allowable OMO collateral was too narrow to provide a sufficient backstop to repo markets.

Taken together, the discount window, the TAF, and the single-tranche repo program provided important term funding to key financial intermediaries, particularly the large financial firms that made up the core of the global financial system. But policymakers judged that only limited amounts of the liquidity provided by the Fed to these firms were being passed on to their customers.[36] The lack of liquidity pass-through likely reflected concerns about capital adequacy given uncertainty around future losses on mortgage-related assets, which reduced the willingness of intermediaries to lend. For the same reasons, counterparty risk for individual firms rose sharply, increasing the uncertainty

---

36. See, for example, Bernanke (2009). The results of the effects of the TAF and the discount window on lending in Berger et al. (2016), though statistically significant, are not very large.

they faced regarding future access to funding and leading them to conserve their liquidity and not lend to others.

CONCLUSIONS AND LESSONS LEARNED

In the end, the Fed's conventional lender-of-last-resort authorities proved inadequate to manage a systemic event of the size seen in 2007–2009 and in a market-based financial system such as that of the United States. The kaleidoscope of financial markets and institutions in the U.S. financial system is inconsistent with the lender-of-last-resort framework that allows only depository institutions to borrow against a broad range of collateral and limits all others to borrowing via repo against a very narrow set of collateral. As a result, facilities based on 13(3) lending authorities had to be used to provide funds to a range of firms and markets, and ultimately government capital was required to stem the crisis. That said, the Federal Reserve's experience with its conventional lending authorities suggests some lessons for liquidity provision by central banks in the future.

Lesson 1:
Central banks have a unique role.

The U.S. experience during the crisis showed that the central bank is ultimately the only entity with the ability and the mandate to provide essentially unlimited emergency liquidity when the financial system is under extreme pressure. The experiences of the Federal Home Loan Banks, Fannie Mae, and Freddie Mac are instructive. These housing-related GSEs came under significant pressure or collapsed, and the Fed ultimately provided support by purchasing their discount notes in September 2008.

Lesson 2:
Plan in advance.

Because the central bank must stand ready to provide emergency liquidity, it should plan how it would do so. Prudent risk management, good policy design, and an assessment of a program's impact take time. The Fed should design systemic liquidity facilities in advance and test them regularly. There is precedent for such testing. The FOMC authorizes the Desk to periodically conduct tests, called "small value exercises," of policy tools that are not used currently but may be needed in the future.[37] Lender-of-last-resort facilities for systemic liquidity provision should be designed and tested in a similar way.[38]

Planning and testing should take into account a range of issues. First, they should include an assessment of the scalability of the facilities so that they can be opened up to a larger group of counterparties if needed—for example, to ensure that access does not favor any class of firms (such as larger or more complex firms). Second, planning should include interactions with monetary policy implementation to ensure that the introduction of large-scale lending programs would still allow the Fed to implement monetary policy effectively. As noted, decisions about the implementation of liquidity programs were affected by the need to control the federal funds rate, sometimes constraining the crisis response.[39] But with sufficient advance planning, management of the policy interest rate is feasible even with a large balance sheet.[40]

More broadly, the Fed should design and test emergency facilities that can be adapted so that they remain effective as the structure of the financial system evolves. For example, the Fed could consider ways to expand the range of financial firms to which it could lend under open market authority in a systemic event. This would reduce the risk of liquidity being trapped inside a particular set of counterparties and improve the Fed's ability to provide liquidity across the financial system in a crisis.[41] By planning in advance, the Fed could better manage the risks associated with additional counterparties and shorten

---

37. See, for example, Federal Reserve Bank of New York (2018).
38. For example, the Bank of England has provided information on how it would provide liquidity in a future crisis in its Sterling Monetary Framework. See "The Sterling Monetary Framework," Bank of England, accessed May 28, 2019, https://www.bankofengland.co.uk/markets/the-sterling-monetary-framework.
39. See Chapter 3, on novel lender-of-last-resort policies, for further discussion of these issues.
40. As demonstrated by the FOMC's "Normalization Principles and Plans"; see FOMC (2014).
41. Using a very large group of counterparties for traditional OMOs is unwieldy and unnecessary in normal times, but the ability to expand such operations to lend to a broad set of counterparties—for example, commercial banks, broker-dealers, asset managers, insurance companies, and finance companies—would improve the Fed's ability to provide liquidity broadly if necessary.

its response time in a crisis. In a large systemic event, however, use of 13(3) lending facilities would almost certainly be needed as well.

Lesson 3:
Plan internationally.

As noted above, much of the borrowing from the Fed during the crisis was by foreign firms. Moreover, the role of the dollar in global finance has, if anything, become more important in recent years (McCauley, McGuire, and Sushko 2015). Thus, in a future crisis, it is likely that the Fed will once again need to consider how to provide liquidity to banks based in other countries. In addition to existing central bank liquidity swap arrangements, advance discussions with foreign central banks are needed to clarify the responsibilities of home and host central banks when directly lending to internationally active banks during a crisis. The appropriate roles of home and host central banks will most likely depend on whether the problems are at a single troubled firm or are systemic, but it would be useful to reach at least a rough meeting of the minds on how different cases might be handled.

Lesson 4:
Implement early.

Early implementation of lending programs could have made them more effective. Of course, the potential benefits of responding more rapidly would need to be weighed against the possible moral hazard costs of blunting private incentives to manage risks. But the TAF and the swap facilities were implemented more than four months after the first run in the ABCP market, allowing a downward cycle of rapid deleveraging, withdrawal of short-term funding, and fire sales to build and eventually accelerate through 2008. If the TAF had been implemented earlier, it would have provided term liquidity earlier, potentially slowing the deterioration in term funding markets and allowing more time for orderly deleveraging.

Some of the delay was because of operational implementation of the TAF, but it also reflected an understandable reluctance on the part of policymakers to announce and explain an untested lending program. Moreover, the high legal hurdles required for use of 13(3) authority by the Fed will necessarily cause delay, so earlier implementation of liquidity facilities using conventional authorities may be particularly important to help slow funding withdrawals and reduce the odds that they will accelerate and become a panic. This reinforces Lesson 2.

Lesson 5:
Manage stigma.

Liquidity provision during the crisis was difficult in some cases because of the stigma associated with borrowing from the Fed. Moreover, the Dodd-Frank Act has most likely increased this stigma. The Fed is required to publish the names of borrowers with a two-year lag and to provide congressional leaders with information on recipients of emergency credit within a week. Given the widespread public criticism of borrowing from the Fed following the crisis and concerns that information provided to Congress could leak, firms will be hesitant to come to the Fed in a future crisis. The U.S. experience with the TAF and cross-country comparisons of the design of central bank lending facilities suggest a few key design features that could help minimize stigma. First, use auctions or tenders. Having all firms bid for funding at the same time provides common cover for all borrowers. Standing facilities, where firms individually decide to borrow, are more likely to have stigma. Second, familiarity with facility design and structure can reduce stigma. The fact that the single-tranche repo program was, in the view of market participants, executed "just like an OMO" appeared to reduce the stigma associated with it. (The same observation applies to the TSLF.) This is an additional rationale for Lesson 2.

Lesson 6:
Manage moral hazard.

Government backstop facilities, including lender-of-last-resort facilities, always have moral hazard costs. Broad liquidity provision in a crisis is no exception, and moral hazard is a particular concern if new counterparties without comprehensive regulation and prudential supervision are given access to central bank liquidity facilities. Access rules for central bank facilities can help address such concerns. In addition, the pricing of lending facilities as well as collateral policies, such as haircuts, are also important moral hazard mitigants.

A long-standing principle for mitigating moral hazard is that central bank lending rates and collateral haircuts should be conservative. Both should be set at levels that are high relative to those in normal market conditions, but below those demanded by private lenders in a crisis. Such policies reduce moral hazard by making borrowing from the central bank unattractive in normal times. Larger haircuts also help protect the central bank from credit risk by acknowledging that loans will often be made during times of financial market stress, when asset prices are volatile and the intrinsic value of collateral is difficult to judge.

In practice, the Fed's lending rates, eligible collateral, and haircut policies varied significantly across the facilities introduced during the crisis, potentially allowing counterparties to benefit from the differences.[42] That said, it would not be appropriate for collateral rules and lending rates to be identical for all programs given their different legal authorities, structures, counterparties, and risk profiles. But consistency on these issues should be considered as part of the planning process.

IIIII

In short, more advance planning for emergency liquidity provision is needed. Although supervisory and regulatory changes put in place after the crisis should help reduce the odds of another crisis that would require emergency liquidity provision by the Fed, it seems unlikely that these measures will be completely effective. Thus it is appropriate for the Fed and other central banks to plan now, when markets are calm, for how to best protect their economies from future periods of market turbulence and systemic crisis.

REFERENCES

Armentier, Olivier, Eric Ghysels, Asani Sarkar, and Jeffrey Shrader. 2015. "Discount Window Stigma during the 2007–2008 Financial Crisis." *Journal of Financial Economics* 118: 317–35.
Armentier, Olivier, Sandra Krieger, and James McAndrews. 2008. "The Federal Reserve's Term Auction Facility." *Current Issues in Economics and Finance* 14: 1–10.

42. For example, the dollars provided by the swap lines were typically priced at a penalty rate, whereas the TAF auctions offered a lower rate for most of the crisis period. As a result, weaker banks borrowed greater amounts for a longer period of time (into 2010) from the TAF, and usage of the swap lines naturally declined as market conditions improved. Similarly, discount window collateral policies were different from collateral requirements in open market operations and the emergency facilities.

Ashcraft, Adam B., Morton L. Bech, and W. Scott Frame. 2010. "The Federal Home Loan Bank System: The Lender of Next-to-Last Resort?" *Journal of Money, Credit and Banking* 42: 551–83.

Baba, Naohiko, Robert N. Ash, and Srichander Ramaswamy. 2009. "US Dollar Money Market Funds and Non-US Banks." *BIS Quarterly Review,* March, 65–81.

Bagehot, Walter. 1873. *Lombard Street.* London: Scribner's and Sons.

Berger, Allen N., Lamont K. Black, Christa H. S. Bouwman, and Jennifer Dlugosz. 2016. "The Federal Reserve's Discount Window and TAF Programs: 'Pushing on a String?'" Mimeo, University of South Carolina.

Bernanke, Ben S. 2009. "Federal Reserve Policies to Ease Credit and Their Implications for the Fed's Balance Sheet." Speech at the National Press Club Luncheon, Washington, D.C., February 18, 2009.

Bernanke, Ben S. 2015. *The Courage to Act: A Memoir of a Crisis and Its Aftermath.* New York: W. W. Norton.

BNP Paribas. 2007. "BNP Paribas Investment Partners Temporarily Suspends the Calculation of the Net Asset Value of the Following Funds: Parvest Dynamic ABS, BNP Paribas ABS EURIBOR and BNP Paribas ABS EONIA." Press release, August 9, 2007. https://group.bnpparibas/en/press-release/bnp-paribas-investment-partners -temporaly-suspends-calculation-net-asset-funds-parvest-dynamic-abs-bnp-paribas -abs-euribor-bnp-paribas-abs-eonia.

Board of Governors. 2007a. H.4.1 statistical release, August 30, 2007.

Board of Governors. 2007b. "Federal Reserve Board Discount Rate Action." Press release, August 17, 2007.

Board of Governors. 2007c. "Federal Reserve Announces Results of Auction of $20 Billion in 28-Day Credit Held on December 17, 2007." Press release, December 19, 2007.

Board of Governors. 2008a. "Board of Governors Announces Two Initiatives to Address Heightened Liquidity Pressures in Term Funding Markets." Press release, March 7, 2008.

Board of Governors. 2008b. "Board of Governors Announces Two Initiatives Designed to Bolster Market Liquidity and Promote Orderly Market Functioning." Press release, March 16, 2008.

Board of Governors. 2010. "Federal Reserve Approves Modifications to the Terms of Its Discount Window Lending Programs." Press release, February 18, 2010.

Brickler, Lucinda, Adam Copeland, and Antoine Martin. 2011. "Everything You Wanted to Know about the Tri-Party Repo Market, but Didn't Know to Ask," blog post, *Liberty Street Economics,* April 11, 2011. https://libertystreeteconomics.newyorkfed.org/2011/04 /everything-you-wanted-to-know-about-the-tri-party-repo-market-but-didnt-know -to-ask.html.

Carlson, Mark, and Jonathan D. Rose. 2017. "Stigma and the Discount Window." Federal Reserve FEDS Notes, December 19, 2017.

Covitz, Daniel, Nellie Liang, and Gustavo A. Suarez. 2013. "The Evolution of a Financial Crisis: Collapse of the Asset-Backed Commercial Paper Market." *Journal of Finance* 68: 815–48.

ECB (European Central Bank). 2007. *Monthly Bulletin,* September 2007.

Federal Reserve. 2018. "The Federal Reserve Discount Window." https://www.frbdiscount window.org/en/Pages/General-Information/The-Discount-Window.aspx.

Federal Reserve Bank of New York. 2000. *Domestic Open Market Operations during 1999: A Report Prepared for the FOMC by the Markets Group of the Federal Reserve Bank of New York*. New York: Federal Reserve Bank of New York, March.

Federal Reserve Bank of New York. 2008. *Domestic Open Market Operations during 2007: A Report Prepared for the FOMC by the Markets Group of the Federal Reserve Bank of New York*. New York: Federal Reserve Bank of New York, March.

Federal Reserve Bank of New York. 2009. *Domestic Open Market Operations during 2008: A Report Prepared for the FOMC by the Markets Group of the Federal Reserve Bank of New York*. New York: Federal Reserve Bank of New York, January.

Federal Reserve Bank of New York. 2018. "Statement Regarding Agency Mortgage-Backed Securities Small Value Exercise," May 15, 2018.

Federal Reserve Bank of New York. 2019. "Historical Transaction Data." Accessed May 28, 2019. https://www.newyorkfed.org/markets/omo_transaction_data.

Federal Reserve System Study Group on Alternative Instruments for System Operations. 2002. *Alternative Instruments for Open Market and Discount Window Operations*. Washington, D.C.: Board of Governors of the Federal Reserve System.

FOMC (Federal Open Market Committee). 2007a. Transcript of the FOMC conference call on August 10, 2007.

FOMC (Federal Open Market Committee). 2007b. "FOMC Statement: The Federal Reserve Is Providing Liquidity to Facilitate the Orderly Functioning of Financial Markets," August 10, 2007.

FOMC (Federal Open Market Committee). 2007c. Transcript of the FOMC conference call on August 16, 2007.

FOMC (Federal Open Market Committee). 2007d. "FOMC Statement," August 17, 2007.

FOMC (Federal Open Market Committee). 2007e. Transcript of the FOMC meeting on September 18, 2007.

FOMC (Federal Open Market Committee). 2007f. Transcript of the FOMC conference call on December 6, 2007.

FOMC (Federal Open Market Committee). 2007g. Transcript of the FOMC meeting on December 11, 2007.

FOMC (Federal Open Market Committee). 2008. Transcript of the FOMC conference call on March 10, 2008.

FOMC (Federal Open Market Committee). 2014. "Policy Normalization." https://www.federalreserve.gov/monetarypolicy/policy-normalization.htm.

JPMorgan Chase. 2007. "JPMorgan Chase, Bank of America and Wachovia Encourage Use of Fed Discount Window." Press release, August 22, 2007. https://jpmorganchaseco.gcs-web.com/news-releases/news-release-details/jpmorgan-chase-bank-america-and-wachovia-encourage-use-fed.

Kohn, Donald L. 2009. "Money Markets and Financial Stability." Speech at the Federal Reserve Bank of New York and Columbia Business School Conference on the Role of Money Markets, New York, May 29, 2009.

Kos, Dino. 2001. "Treasury and Federal Reserve Foreign Exchange Operations." *Federal Reserve Bulletin* 87: 757–62.

Madigan, Brian F. 2009. "Bagehot's Dictum in Practice: Formulating and Implementing Policies to Combat Financial Crisis." Remarks at the Federal Reserve Bank of Kansas City's Annual Economic Symposium, Jackson Hole, Wyoming, August 21, 2009.

Madigan, Brian F., and William R. Nelson. 2002. "Proposed Revision to the Federal Reserve's Discount Window Lending Programs." *Federal Reserve Bulletin* 88 (July): 313–19.

McAndrews, James, Asani Sarkar, and Zhenyu Wang. 2017. "The Effect of the Term Auction Facility on the London Interbank Offered Rate." Federal Reserve Bank of New York Staff Report No. 335.

McCauley, Robert N., Patrick McGuire, and Vladyslav Sushko. 2015. "Global Dollar Credit: Links to US Monetary Policy and Leverage." *Economic Policy* 30, no. 82 (April 1): 187–229.

Taylor, John B., and John C. Williams. 2009. "A Black Swan in the Money Market." *American Economic Journal: Macroeconomics* 1: 58–83.

Tucker, Paul. 2014. "The Lender of Last Resort and Modern Central Banking: Principles and Reconstruction." *BIS Papers* 79: 10–42.

CHAPTER THREE

The Fed's Novel Lender-of-Last-Resort Programs

LORIE LOGAN, WILLIAM NELSON, AND
PATRICK PARKINSON

SETTING THE STAGE

In March 2008, developments in financial markets were becoming increasingly ominous. Strains in the mortgage-backed-securities markets were spreading to other markets. Nervous buyers were starting to back away from a range of securities, from municipal bonds to asset-backed securities, including asset-backed commercial paper. Firms were having trouble obtaining short-term financing. The strains continued to appear even though the Federal Reserve had expanded the availability of liquidity through the discount window and open market operations.

But the Fed was reaching the limits of its conventional liquidity tools, even as it found new and creative ways to use them. In the decades before the crisis, nonbank financial firms had become an increasingly important source of credit to the U.S. economy. Nonbank financial firms, including not only well-known institutions but also more obscure but equally important components of the "shadow banking system," relied on short-term-debt instruments

The authors would like to thank James Egelhof, former assistant vice president, and Tony Baer, senior associate, Federal Reserve Bank of New York, for assistance in the preparation of this chapter. The innovative lending facilities described in this chapter reflect the expertise and dedication of staff at the Federal Reserve and U.S. Treasury, many of whom worked countless nights and weekends and made personal sacrifices to develop and implement these facilities. It is impossible to list everyone whose contributions made a difference, but we would like to express our sincerest appreciation to all those who supported a truly collaborative effort.

like asset-backed commercial paper (ABCP) or repurchase agreements for a significant portion of their funding.[1] With investors concerned about the quality of collateral backing such instruments and reluctant to roll them over as they matured, credit markets began to freeze. It was the beginning of a panic.

The issue came to a head on the evening of Sunday, March 9, when Ben S. Bernanke, chairman of the Federal Reserve Board, emailed members of the Federal Open Market Committee (FOMC) about a novel plan developed by staff at the New York Fed to lend Treasury securities to primary dealers against other, riskier collateral that had become hard to finance in private markets—a program that had been in development for months called the Term Securities Lending Facility (TSLF). There was a big condition to its adoption: It required the Fed to take an extraordinary step—to invoke a little-known provision of the Federal Reserve Act, Section 13(3), that gave Reserve Banks, with the approval of the Board of Governors, authority to lend to nonbanks in "unusual and exigent circumstances." It had not been used since the Great Depression, and even then it had been used only sparingly. "This is unusual but so are market conditions," Bernanke wrote in the email. "I strongly recommend that we proceed with this plan."[2] He needed broad support, both from all five Board members and from a majority vote of the overall committee.

The next night, he convened an unscheduled call with the FOMC and described the urgency of the situation. "We're doing things we haven't done before," he acknowledged. Put simply, the economy was in a downward spiral, where fear fed on itself. The innovative TSLF was approved by the FOMC, 9–0, and it was announced the next day.

It would be the first of these novel lender-of-last-resort Fed programs designed to stabilize the financial markets and revive the flow of lending. In this chapter we discuss the most important of these facilities in the order in which they were introduced:

- Term Securities Lending Facility (TSLF)—provided a backstop to secured lending markets;
- Primary Dealer Credit Facility (PDCF)—helped, with TSLF, ease strains in secured lending markets;

---

1. For more on the response to problems in the shadow banking system, see Chapter 4.
2. Ben S. Bernanke, *The Courage to Act: A Memoir of a Crisis and Its Aftermath* (New York: W. W. Norton, 2015), 208.

- Asset-Backed Commercial Paper Money Market Mutual Fund Liquidity Facility (AMLF)—helped end the run on money market mutual funds;
- Commercial Paper Funding Facility (CPFF)—provided a liquidity backstop to the commercial paper market;
- Term Asset-Backed Securities Loan Facility (TALF)—helped restore the flow of credit to consumers and small businesses.[3]

There was no playbook for these programs, no manual that spelled out their design and implementation. As was the case with the conventional liquidity tools used before them, the novel facilities were introduced on a piecemeal basis, in short time frames, constrained by operational and legal requirements, and based on limited information. As a result, they were refined repeatedly. But in the end, we believe, and research shows,[4] that the programs eased liquidity pressures on nonbank financial firms and thereby helped avoid an even more severe contraction of credit to businesses and households.

PROVIDING A BACKSTOP TO SECURED FINANCING MARKETS: THE TSLF AND PDCF

At the center of the growing pressures in the financial industry was the triparty repo market. This important market provided securities dealers what were in effect short-term loans backed by the dealers' inventory of securities as collateral. But many of the firms that provided those loans, like money market mutual funds and securities lenders, became increasingly risk averse as they focused on maintaining their own liquidity. At the same time, the clearing banks that facilitated these transactions and took on substantial intraday exposures were becoming concerned about the possibility of getting stuck with huge exposures to a failed dealer.

The triparty repo market needed a backstop, a way to provide liquidity to dealers, as providers of repo financing began to quickly pull away from the weaker investment banks. Repo financing, after all, supported the liquidity and continued operation of fixed-income markets, including the vital U.S.

---

3. Table 3.1 in the appendix to this chapter gives some high-level information about each of the programs, including the dates of operation and the peak amounts lent.
4. See Table 3.2 in the appendix for a summary of research on the effectiveness of these programs.

government securities and mortgage-backed-securities markets, and had grown rapidly in the years leading up to the creation of the TSLF and PDCF.

But creating such a liquidity facility was easier said than done. Dealers did not have access to the Fed's traditional lender-of-last-resort facility, the discount window, and there were no legal agreements or technical infrastructure in place for lending to dealers against riskier collateral, to price the loans, to put the money on the wire, or to keep accounts.

Also, who would receive the loans? The Fed maintained a small network of firms—the primary dealers—that it used to underwrite Treasury debt auctions and act as counterparties on the Desk's open market operations. This was never intended to be the list of important nonbank financial firms. Indeed, the New York Fed had gone to some lengths over the years to emphasize that primary dealer status was not a "Good Housekeeping Seal of Approval" for a firm. However, the primary dealers were the set of firms with which the Fed had agreements and operational arrangements already in place.

Finally, there was the fundamental issue of fairness. The regulatory compact with banks was understood: In exchange for submitting to capital and liquidity regulations, as well as reserve requirements, banks got access to programs aimed at providing a liquidity backstop that other financial firms did not get, namely FDIC insurance and the Fed's discount window. Dealers, by contrast, had elected not to adopt this business model. Was it fair that they now got that backstop from the Fed? Would this promote moral hazard?

In the end, the Fed created two main programs to support primary dealers around the same time in March 2008: the Term Securities Lending Facility, announced on Tuesday, March 11; and, before the staff could get the TSLF up and running, the Primary Dealer Credit Facility, announced on Sunday, March 16, and implemented the next day. They were closely related to the single-tranche open market operations program, another auction facility available to primary dealers implemented that month under Section 14 of the Federal Reserve Act.[5]

---

5. Through this program, the Fed conducted 28-day repos in which dealers obtained cash by delivering open market eligible collateral. These were variations on a standard open market operation and were not needed for the Desk to control the federal funds target rate. Instead, they were longer in term and intended to address liquidity pressures in term funding markets. One key difference in the TSLF from the single-tranche repos is that as bond-for-bond transactions, they had no impact on the supply of bank reserves. Additionally, the TSLF and PDCF allowed for a

The TSLF and PDCF were more alike than different, sharing a few commonalities in particular. First, both were borne out of the infrastructure of existing Fed operations: for the TSLF, a program called securities lending, and for the PDCF, a combination of discount window lending and reserve-management open market operations.

Both involved full-recourse "collateralized lending": We give you something, you give us something, and later we will put it all back with a fee on top; if you don't pay up, we can go after all your assets. It was a kludge to build this program on top of the Fed's existing infrastructure, but by doing so the staff was able to adapt this setup within short time constraints. Primary dealers would be the group of dealers eligible to participate, if for no other reason than because those firms had the legal relationships and infrastructure already established.

Second, both programs were built on top of the existing triparty secured financing infrastructure, with the clearing banks at the center. This arrangement was familiar to the Fed, as it was used for some open market operations. It also had a few important benefits. It allowed the Fed to implement the program quickly, because dealers would finance their securities on the existing platform. The clearing banks would also manage the collateral, for example, by valuing it and applying haircuts, something that would take the Fed significant time to develop. And, because a lender-of-last-resort capability was embedded in the clearing banks' platform, they could be confident that their customers would be able to settle their intraday obligations, one way or another, and therefore had no need to pull the plug on any dealer.

One important difference between the programs was in their impact on bank reserves. The TSLF was a bond-for-bond program, meaning that in exchange for dealers' less-liquid securities, the Fed gave Treasuries. These were, of course, easily convertible by the dealer into cash (because the Treasury repo market continued to work well), but the conversion was another step. The benefit was that the Fed was not adding more cash to the economy and did not have to take offsetting actions to manage the federal funds target rate. This was a key difference in the TSLF from the single-tranche repo program and from the PDCF, and meant it could be scaled up or down more quickly.

The two programs also differed in their pricing and how they allocated credit. The PDCF was a "standing facility," meaning that loans were provided on

broader set of collateral to be pledged, which is why TSLF schedule 2 and PDCF operations were implemented under Section 13(3) authority.

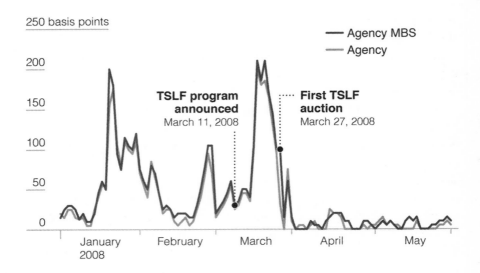

250 basis points

200

150

TSLF program announced
March 11, 2008

First TSLF auction
March 27, 2008

— Agency MBS
— Agency

100

50

0

January
2008
February
March
April
May

Figure 3.1 **Financing Spreads and the Term Securities Lending Facility**

Note: The chart plots the spread between overnight agency and agency mortgage-backed security (MBS) repo rates and the overnight Treasury general collateral repo rate.

Source: Federal Reserve Bank of New York, based on data from Bloomberg Finance L.P.

a continual basis in the amounts requested at a predetermined interest rate. The interest rate on PDCF repos equaled the relatively expensive primary credit rate plus a fee added for persistent usage. The TSLF was an "auction facility," meaning that a specific quantity was periodically auctioned off. While the PDCF was therefore a more reliable source of funds, its elevated interest rate and persistent-usage fee may have led to some stigma being associated with its use.

The programs were widely seen as providing an important backstop to primary dealers. As the private market pulled back from financing housing-related assets, primary dealers were able to finance these with the Fed, maintaining liquidity in fixed-income markets and avoiding a broad collapse of the securities industry. Clearing banks continued business, and when conditions normalized, dealers returned to private markets.

Some policymakers had hoped that the existence of the programs would be enough to promote confidence, and that their credibility as a backstop would mean they wouldn't actually need to be used. This hope went unrealized. Spreads in repo markets fell as the programs took hold in March and April 2008, as seen in Figure 3.1, but the volume of Fed lending through these programs

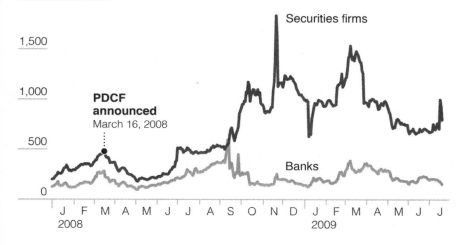

2,000 basis points

1,500

Securities firms

1,000

PDCF announced
March 16, 2008

500

Banks

0

J F M A M J J A S O N D J F M A M J J
2008   2009

Figure 3.2 Credit Default Swap Spreads

Note: PDCF is the Primary Dealer Credit Facility.

Source: Federal Reserve Bank of New York, based on data from Thomson Reuters Datastream

was significant. As the crisis continued to accelerate, the liquidity provided through the facilities served as a bridge, allowing time for other, broader actions to restore confidence in the dealers and the broader financial system.

Significantly, the success of the PDCF and TSLF in operating as bridges was due in part to a willingness among policymakers to make ad hoc changes. The original list of counterparties was supplemented with additional dealer-affiliated borrowers in September 2008. The list of eligible collateral was also repeatedly expanded to include lower-quality assets, along with other program parameters. For example, in September 2008, the PDCF's acceptable collateral set was expanded to almost all securities accepted in the repo market, and the TSLF's was similarly expanded from high-quality assets to all investment-grade debt securities.

Additionally, the programs were priced from the start so that they would be unattractive under normal market conditions. As strains eased over the course of 2009, with credit default swap spreads of dealers coming down from a peak in late 2008, as shown in Figure 3.2, borrowings from the programs unwound naturally. The programs were officially closed in 2010 to little fanfare, having reached near-zero levels of usage well beforehand, as seen in Figure 3.3.

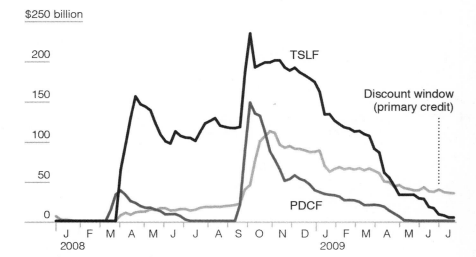

$250 billion

Figure 3.3 Crisis Facility Usage, Jan. 1, 2008–July 15, 2009

Note: TSLF is the Term Securities Lending Facility; PDCF is the Primary Dealer Credit Facility.

Source: Federal Reserve Bank of New York, based on data from Federal Reserve Board of Governors

PROVIDING LIQUIDITY TO MONEY MARKET FUNDS: THE AMLF

Even though the TSLF and the PDCF helped provide some stability in financing markets, they could only do so much, especially once Lehman Brothers declared bankruptcy on Monday, September 15, 2008.

Importantly, Lehman's bankruptcy revealed a significant fragility in the money market fund (MMF) sector. Although Lehman's vulnerability had been apparent to many, one fund, the Reserve Primary Fund, held so much Lehman commercial paper that writing down its value forced the fund to "break the buck," or fall below its mandated net asset value of $1 per share, on September 16. The response was swift and severe: In the subsequent two weeks, investors in "prime" money market funds—those whose investments included highly rated corporate debt—withdrew more than $300 billion from such funds, representing a 20 percent plunge in total assets under management at the trough seen in Figure 3.4.

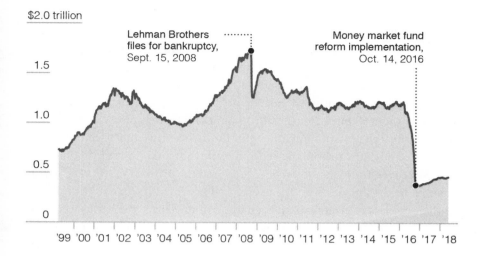

$2.0 trillion

Lehman Brothers
files for bankruptcy,
Sept. 15, 2008

Money market fund
reform implementation,
Oct. 14, 2016

1.5

1.0

0.5

0

'99 '00 '01 '02 '03 '04 '05 '06 '07 '08 '09 '10 '11 '12 '13 '14 '15 '16 '17 '18

Figure 3.4 **Prime Money Market Fund Assets under Management**

Source: Federal Reserve Bank of New York, based on data from iMoneyNet

A modern-day form of a bank run was taking place, and it was threatening to undermine financial stability. The Fed and the Treasury knew they had to avoid further strains on the markets. While Treasury devised a way to guarantee further losses on money market fund assets and halt the runs, as discussed in Chapter 7, the Fed explored how it might provide liquidity to money market funds that were still experiencing runs.

Fed vice chairman Donald Kohn asked Federal Reserve Board staff to explore potential lender-of-last-resort programs. A seemingly insurmountable problem became apparent: Even if the Fed were willing to lend to money market funds, some funds lacked the authority to borrow money, and even those that had the authority generally were extremely reluctant to use it because they feared that disclosure of their borrowing would spook investors. When staff reported this to Kohn, he told them that failure was not an option and to come up with a program that would work.

Back in their offices, the staff concluded that they needed a plan that would permit money funds to meet redemptions by selling assets at amortized cost (that is, without incurring a loss). The Fed did not have authority to buy private money market instruments, but it could lend to others for the purpose of buying such instruments. A plan was developed to lend to banks at the discount window to finance banks' purchases of asset-backed commercial paper from money market funds at amortized cost. The program also authorized lending to broker-dealers and bank holding companies on the same terms, which is why it was authorized under the emergency lending authority of Section 13(3) as well as the regular lending authority under Section 10B.

To give banks incentive to participate, the Fed offered loans at favorable terms—without recourse, for the full amount of the assets purchased (no haircut), and for the remaining maturity of the assets. This approach effectively transferred all of the risks to the Fed and made the banks' intermediation riskfree. Moreover, the loans would be extended at the primary credit rate, which was well below the yields on the assets, and provided the banks with profits on their riskless intermediation. Even under these terms, the banks were still concerned that the purchases might undermine the confidence of their creditors if their regulatory capital ratios declined. To address this concern, the Fed made temporary modifications to its capital rules to exempt assets purchased from money market funds as part of the program.

Given that its loans to the banks were nonrecourse, the Fed was relying entirely on the value of the assets that the banks had purchased from the money market funds for repayment. The assets were limited to ABCP, so that the loans were backed primarily by the collateral.[6] Furthermore, to limit credit risk to the Fed, the facility purchased ABCP with only the highest short-term ratings from the credit rating agencies. Importantly, prime money market funds as a group held about 12 percent of their assets in ABCP, so that, even with this limit, the program would provide many MMFs access to substantial liquidity.

Despite these measures, investors perceived the collateral as risky and illiquid and demanded higher spreads, as seen in Figure 3.5.

This program was announced just three days after the Reserve Primary Fund broke the buck, and the program became operational just one business

---

6. ABCP is generally seen as riskier than other types of commercial paper because it is issued by special-purpose vehicles whose only means of payment is income derived from assets contributed to the vehicle. ABCP is not backed by a general promise to pay by the bank or other financial firm that set up the vehicle or that originated the underlying assets. The Fed's choice to restrict the assets purchased under the program to ABCP can be seen as more about making it clear that the Fed's loans were backed by specific assets as collateral, in contrast to their being unsecured loans to businesses. This approach was thought to fit more clearly within the Fed's legal authority and better conform to beliefs about appropriate central bank practices.

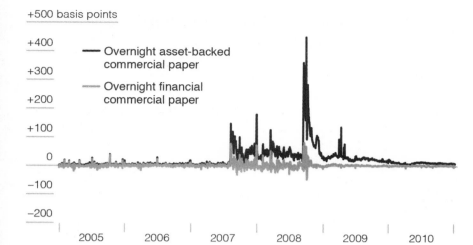

+500 basis points

+400

— Overnight asset-backed
commercial paper

+300

+200

— Overnight financial
commercial paper

+100

0

−100

−200

2005   2006   2007   2008   2009   2010

Figure 3.5   Commercial Paper Rate Spreads over the Effective Federal Funds Rate

Source: Federal Reserve Bank of New York, based on data from Bloomberg Finance L.P.

day later. While the other novel lender-of-last-resort programs were operated by the New York Fed, the AMLF was operated by the Federal Reserve Bank of Boston, which had deep expertise in the money market fund industry and was in a position to implement the program quickly.

This innovative program provided substantial liquidity to money market funds at a critical moment. Although the Treasury's guarantee, announced the same day as the AMLF, was ultimately quite effective in curtailing redemptions, during the first few weeks after the announcement (when the program details were still unclear), some funds continued to experience significant redemptions. Consequently, the AMLF was used heavily almost immediately; lending under the program reached a peak of about $150 billion after only ten days. Over the remainder of 2008, loan balances fell to about $20 billion at year-end as liquidity pressures on MMFs diminished, no doubt in part because the Treasury guarantee stabilized outflows. An upturn in AMLF lending in mid-2009 seemed to be spurred by funds' concerns about the credit quality of ABCP sponsors rather than by liquidity pressures on the money market funds. To ensure that the facility was used only for liquidity reasons, in June 2009 the Fed limited the program to ABCP purchased from money market funds that were experiencing significant redemptions. After that, balances resumed their downward path, and no further loans were made after July 2009.

PROVIDING LIQUIDITY TO THE COMMERCIAL
PAPER MARKETS: THE CPFF

Although the AMLF and the Treasury Department's guarantee stanched the run on money market funds and forestalled asset fire sales, it was not a cure-all. In the weeks following Lehman's collapse, investors remained reluctant to purchase commercial paper and asset-backed commercial paper. And those purchases they did make were of paper with very short maturities, as seen in Figure 3.6. The effect was unsettling: The volume of outstanding paper continued to shrink, spreads remained very wide, and an increasingly high percentage of outstanding paper needed to be refinanced each day.[7]

Well before the end of September, the Fed and the Treasury Department had concluded that the commercial paper markets needed a liquidity backstop. But designing it proved challenging. Unlike the AMLF, which used the discount window, this backstop required new infrastructure.

The backstop, called the Commercial Paper Funding Facility (CPFF), was not announced until October 7 and did not become operational until October 27. The CPFF involved the creation of a special purpose vehicle (SPV) to purchase commercial paper and asset-backed commercial paper directly from the issuers, with funding provided via loans from the Federal Reserve Bank of New York, authorized under Section 13(3). It was a broad market backstop, in that all U.S. issuers of commercial paper and asset-backed commercial paper, including U.S. issuers with a foreign parent, were eligible to issue paper to the special purpose vehicle, provided that the paper had earned the highest short-term ratings from the credit rating agencies. Furthermore, the SPV was allowed to purchase from each eligible issuer an amount of paper equal to the highest amount of paper it had outstanding earlier in 2008, preventing issuers from expanding their program to take further advantage of the facility.

The CPFF met the need for term funding by purchasing three-month paper at spreads that were significantly narrower than the prevailing spreads. This

---

7. Large foreign and domestic banks issued much of the outstanding commercial paper, were the sponsors of much of the outstanding ABCP, and had committed to providing backstop liquidity to many issuers of much of the paper that they themselves did not issue or sponsor. If investors stopped rolling over maturing paper, those banks would have been subject to extreme funding and balance sheet pressures that almost surely would have forced them to sharply curtail lending to businesses and households.

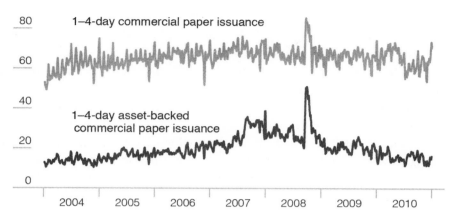

Figure 3.6 **Overnight Issuance as a Percentage of Total Commercial Paper Issuance**

Notes: The chart plots a five-day rolling average. Overnight issuance is 1–4 day.

Source: Federal Reserve Bank of New York, based on data from Federal Reserve Board of Governors "Commercial Paper Rates and Outstanding Summary" derived from data supplied by the Depository Trust & Clearing Corporation

three-month term was itself an important innovation, since it effectively reduced rollover risk among issuers that had become forced into overnight funding. Still, the spreads were significantly wider than those before the crisis, so as to provide issuers an incentive to exit the facility as spreads normalized.

By far the most difficult and contentious design issue was how to ensure that the New York Fed's credit extensions to the SPV would be "indorsed or otherwise secured to the satisfaction of the Federal Reserve Bank," as required by Section 13(3). Clearly the credit extensions would need to be made with full recourse to the SPV and secured by all the assets of the SPV. But consensus quickly emerged that relying solely on the commercial paper and asset-backed commercial paper held by the SPV would not provide satisfactory security, and hopes that TARP (Troubled Assets Relief Program) funds could be used to capitalize the SPV went unfulfilled. Instead, issuers were required to pay an upfront registration fee of 10 basis points on the maximum amount of paper that they were eligible to sell. In addition, issuers of commercial paper (other than ABCP) were required to pay an additional fee of 100 basis points per annum on paper sold to the SPV, unless the issuer posted acceptable collateral or had its paper endorsed by an acceptable endorser. Finally, because commercial paper was sold at a discount, as paper matured and the principal was repaid, earnings accrued and accumulated within the SPV, providing collateral to absorb any losses from subsequent defaults by other issuers.

From its first day of operation, the CPFF was heavily used, purchasing the overwhelming majority of new term paper. In January 2009, when the program's size peaked, the CPFF held approximately $350 billion of commercial paper and asset-backed commercial paper, which was 20 percent of total paper outstanding. The existence of the program greatly contributed to the normalization of market conditions, and as the environment stabilized, issuers had strong incentives to sell their paper in the market. Throughout 2009, CPFF use steadily declined, reaching a level of about $10 billion in December. The program was allowed to expire on February 1, 2010. Although staff involved in the development of the novel lender-of-last-resort programs generally agree that the CPFF (and the AMLF) posed somewhat greater risk to the Fed than the other programs discussed in this chapter, over its life no issuers of paper purchased by the CPFF defaulted. In addition, the SPV accumulated about $5 billion of capital through the fees and interest received from issuers. That was ultimately accounted for as income to the New York Fed and remitted to the Treasury for the benefit of taxpayers.

REVIVING THE ABS MARKETS: THE TALF

In the decades leading up to the financial crisis, securitization had become an increasingly common technique for financing a wide range of consumer and business loans.[8] For example, about one-half of credit card loans and one-third of auto loans were funded through securitization in the years preceding the crisis.[9] In 2006, gross issuance of asset-backed and private mortgage-backed securities totaled nearly $2.4 trillion.

---

8. These included subprime and other nonagency mortgages, home equity lines of credit, small business loans, auto loans, student loans, business equipment loans, and credit card loans.
9. Securitization involves pooling loans or other receivables and funding the pool with asset-backed securities (ABS). The securities are typically divided into tranches, with the senior tranche having first claim to proceeds and last responsibility for losses. In addition, the issuer of the loan typically retains some of the risk of the pool.

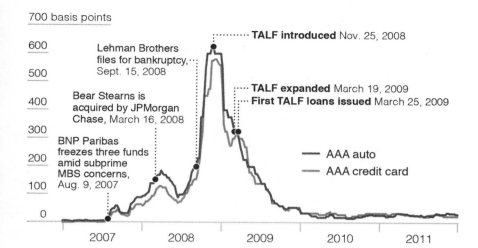

700 basis points

600 — Lehman Brothers files for bankruptcy, Sept. 15, 2008

500 —

TALF introduced Nov. 25, 2008

400 — Bear Stearns is acquired by JPMorgan Chase, March 16, 2008

TALF expanded March 19, 2009
First TALF loans issued March 25, 2009

300 —

200 — BNP Paribas freezes three funds amid subprime MBS concerns,

100 — Aug. 9, 2007

—— AAA auto
—— AAA credit card

0 —

2007 2008 2009 2010 2011

Figure 3.7 **Consumer Asset-Backed Security Spreads**

Note: MBS are mortgage-backed securities; TALF is the Term Asset-Backed Securities Loan Facility.

Source: Federal Reserve Bank of New York, based on data from JP Morgan and Bloomberg Finance L.P.

But as the financial crisis intensified in the fall of 2008, investor demand for highly rated asset-backed securities evaporated. As seen in Figures 3.7 and 3.8, spreads increased dramatically, while new ABS issuance declined to almost zero. In response, lending terms and standards were tightened by those lenders whose funding relied on securitization. For example, the average interest rate on auto loans extended by finance companies—companies that were heavily dependent on securitization—rose from 3.25 percent in July 2008 to more than 8 percent by December 2008. This sharp deterioration in credit contributed to a severe contraction in the economy.

In October 2008, staff members at the Federal Reserve Board, the New York Fed, and Treasury began discussing ways to encourage a revival of issuance of ABS using a combination of Federal Reserve lending and TARP funds. Revival of the ABS markets was not an end in itself but a means of restoring credit access to businesses and households, thereby promoting economic recovery.

Staff quickly settled on two possible models. The model favored by Board staff involved market participants forming funds that would invest in ABS to

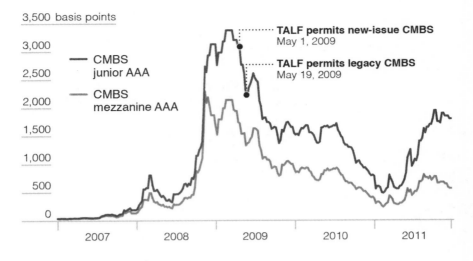

Figure 3.8 Commercial Mortgage-Backed Security Spreads

Note: CMBS are commercial mortgage-backed securities; TALF is the Term Asset-Backed Securities Loan Facility.

Source: Federal Reserve Bank of New York, based on data from JP Morgan and Bloomberg Finance L.P.

which the Fed would provide leverage, Treasury would provide mezzanine financing, and private investors would provide equity.[10] New York Fed staff favored a model under which the Federal Reserve would lend to private investors in the ABS, with Treasury providing the Federal Reserve credit protection. The latter model was adopted and became the Term Asset-Backed Securities Loan Facility, or TALF. An important advantage of the TALF model was that it would naturally sunset when credit risk spreads normalized and alternative financing became more attractive than TALF loans.

In the initial program announcement, TALF loans had maturities of one year. After further consultation with potential participants in the program, the maturities were extended to three years, then later to five years, to better match the maturities of the underlying collateral. The interest rate spreads on TALF loans were set below spreads on highly rated ABS prevailing during the finan-

10. A similar model was eventually adopted by the Treasury as the Public-Private Investment Program (PPIP), although the PPIP did not include leverage from the Fed.

cial crisis but well above spreads in more normal market conditions, providing investors an incentive to repay the loans as financial conditions normalized. TALF loans were collateralized by the ABS purchased but did not provide for further recourse to the borrower except in very limited circumstances.

The nonrecourse aspect of the loans provided investors with downside protection during a period of extraordinary economic uncertainty and risk aversion. If the collateral declined in value to less than the value of the loan, borrowers had the option of walking away from the loan, leaving the Fed and Treasury with the collateral, so the borrower could not lose more than the initial amount invested to cover the haircut.

The program was announced in November 2008 and began operations in March 2009, with the four-month gap reflecting the challenge of designing the program so that it was both safe and effective. Initially, the program accepted only newly issued, highly rated ABS backed by new or recently extended auto loans, credit card loans, student loans, and small business loans. It was reasoned that these categories of ABS all had securitization structures that had performed well in the crisis, or were backed by loans that were completely or partially guaranteed by the government, and therefore could be evaluated quickly and generally posed less risk.

The authorized size of the program was initially $200 billion, backed by $20 billion in credit protection for the Fed from the Treasury. Because of the credit protection provided by the TARP funds, the Fed was able to participate in the program in its traditional role as liquidity provider without taking on more than minimal credit risk, notwithstanding the longer terms and nonrecourse nature of the loans provided.

The program quickly expanded, as shown in Figure 3.9. On February 10, 2009, the Federal Reserve and Treasury announced that they intended to increase the program size to a potential maximum of $1 trillion backed by additional TARP funding. They also announced that they would consider expanding collateral to commercial mortgage-backed securities (CMBS), private residential mortgage-backed securities (RMBS), and other asset-backed securities.

By May, the program had been expanded to include newly issued, highly rated securities backed by business equipment loans, loans to retailers to finance their inventories, mortgage servicer advances, vehicle fleet receivables, insurance premium loans, and commercial mortgages (CMBS), as well as highly rated existing CMBS. The Fed had considered recommending accepting newly issued or existing residential mortgage-backed securities or newly

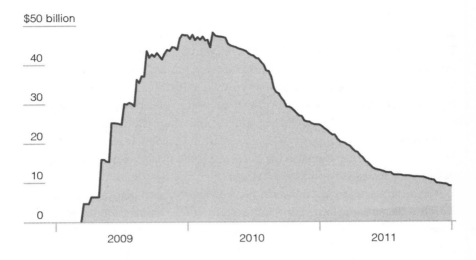

$50 billion

40

30

20

10

0

2009   2010   2011

Figure 3.9 Outstanding Term Asset-Backed Securities Loan Facility Loans (Weekly)

Source: Federal Reserve Bank of New York, based on data from Federal Reserve Board of Governors

issued or existing collateralized loan obligations but ultimately decided against this because the TALF appeared unlikely to be able to improve conditions in the markets for those securities at acceptable levels of risk to the government. For example, the team that evaluated the possibility of lending against legacy private RMBS concluded that the level of haircut needed to protect the government from losses could be as high as 100 percent.

Although the TALF was authorized to make up to $1 trillion in loans, because of the improvement in financial markets in the latter half of 2009, only about $70 billion in loans was extended. More than 2,000 loans were extended to nearly 200 borrowers, including traditional asset managers, pension funds, hedge funds, and banks, as well as many smaller financial companies. The TALF closed for new loans backed by ABS and existing CMBS in March 2010, and for new loans backed by newly issued CMBS in June 2010. In total, TALF supported the origination of nearly 3 million auto loans, more than 1 million student loans, nearly 900,000 loans to small businesses, 150,000 other business loans, and millions of credit card loans.

To protect the Fed and the Treasury, several layers of risk controls were built into the TALF program. First, TALF loans were extended only to finance purchases of securities acquired in arms-length transactions—an investor borrowing from the TALF had to be unaffiliated with the originator or seller of the ABS presented as TALF collateral, and no side payments could be made between the investor and the seller. Second, the securities were required to have triple-A ratings from two or more credit rating agencies and were subject to an additional risk assessment by the Federal Reserve. Third, the maximum allowable amount of each TALF loan was always less than the market value of the ABS purchased by a haircut that depended on the riskiness of the collateral.

Although extensive credit protections were necessary because of the complexity and variety of the underlying collateral, the program's effectiveness was diminished because of the long time it took to begin operation. In particular, there was a four-month period between initial conception and initial operation, an additional two months before the subsequent expansion was largely complete, and about five further months before the last type of TALF loan, backed by newly issued CMBS, was extended.[11] The nonrecourse nature of the lending program made it especially important that it be designed carefully, while the disparate nature of the collateral made the design challenging and time-consuming. To speed up the design, staff considered establishing only broad collateral criteria and applying a large haircut, leaving it to the borrowers to determine the specific type of ABS to pledge. However, this blanket approach was potentially subject to serious adverse selection.

The program was not without its critics. For example, the initial announcement that only a few types of ABS were acceptable—a decision meant to reduce the launch time of the program—added to the perception that the Fed

---

11. A few examples may help illustrate the many hurdles that needed to be overcome to bring the TALF to market. For primary dealers to operate as TALF agents, it was necessary for the Securities and Exchange Commission (SEC) to issue an exemption from the prohibition on broker-dealers "arranging for the extension or maintenance of credit." For closed-end funds to participate as investors in the program, it was necessary for the SEC to issue an exemption from the custody provision of the Investment Company Act of 1940. Hedge funds were unwilling to participate as investors until the Fed issued an exemption from limits it had imposed on executive compensation of companies that received Section 13(3) loans. Because the initial operations took place before the Fed had its own credit review capacity built, it relied on ratings by credit agencies. Before accepting the ratings, the Fed staff had to get comfortable with the ratings methodologies, given that the methodologies were largely discredited in other parts of structured finance. Similarly, in the legacy CMBS program, following feedback from investors and additional analysis, the Fed concluded that super senior conduit CMBS (triple A rated) was acceptable but mezzanine conduit CMBS (also triple A rated but structurally junior) was too risky.

and Treasury were engaged in "credit allocation": pursuing an industrial policy that promoted some economic sectors over others. The use of a uniform standard for evaluating ABS aimed to resolve this concern, but achieving this in practice was challenging, since ABS often follow bespoke structures to meet the idiosyncratic business situations of their issuers.

Another challenge for the TALF was the perception that it was a giveaway program for the rich because its counterparties were largely hedge funds or specialized TALF funds established by asset management companies. For example, *Rolling Stone* magazine published an article on TALF, illustrated with pigs in makeup, pointing out that some wives of Wall Street executives, which it called the "Real Housewives of Wall Street," had made money under the program (Taibbi 2011). In contrast to that perception, the Fed engaged in extensive outreach to minority- and women-owned businesses that were potential borrowers, and the New York Fed approved several additional "TALF agents," chosen to help bring in a more diverse investor base. Staff and policymakers also emphasized the objective of encouraging lending to Main Street and gave concrete examples of lending that actually occurred because of the program whenever possible.

In the end, despite the lengthy process involved in its launch, the TALF was an important contributor to a revival of ABS markets and improvements in the flow of credit to households and businesses. Following a slowing of non-mortgage ABS issuance in late 2008 to less than $1 billon per month, issuance increased to $35 billion over the first three months of TALF lending in 2009. During its initial months of operation, about half of ABS market issuance was supported by TALF lending. The level of support provided by the program then declined as market functioning improved. This is depicted in Figure 3.10, which shows how eligibility and issuance in TALF-eligible asset classes evolved over the course of the program.

POLICY ASSESSMENT

The overarching goal of these novel lender-of-last-resort programs was to mitigate potential increases in the cost and decreases in the availability of credit to U.S. businesses and households. A number of research papers, and our own experience, found that the programs contributed to a narrowing of spreads and helped slow the liquidity runs, averting a far more serious contraction in credit supply.

As these programs were announced and implemented, both policymakers and market participants perceived them to be effective. As discussed in previ-

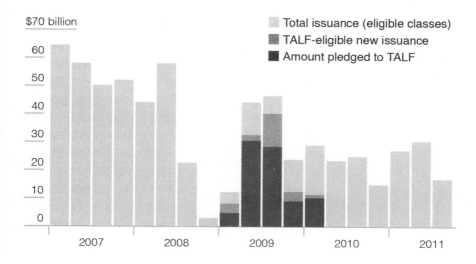

Figure 3.10 **Total Issuance in TALF-Eligible Classes and Breakdown of TALF Issuance**

Note: TALF is the Term Asset-Backed Securities Loan Facility.

Source: Federal Reserve Bank of New York, based on data from JP Morgan, Bloomberg Finance L.P., and the Federal Reserve Board of Governors

ous sections, after the launching of the TSLF and PDCF, runs on secured financing of dealers generally slowed. The AMLF helped avoid fire sales by prime money market funds until the Treasury guarantee restored confidence among money market fund investors. The CPFF allowed issuers to resume issuance of term commercial paper and asset-backed commercial paper and contributed to the narrowing of spreads that eventually enabled issuers to sell term paper to investors other than the CPFF. And the TALF helped revive the ABS markets, which had been moribund in the immediate aftermath of Lehman's failure. All of these developments headed off what surely would have been a much more severe contraction of credit.

In retrospect, though, we think that earlier introduction of broader programs and, in some cases, in larger initial size could have been more effective. The programs were not approved and implemented until it was abundantly clear that runs were seriously impairing the ability of the financial institutions affected to meet the credit needs of the economy. Furthermore, the TSLF and PDCF initially financed rather narrow ranges of collateral, which were broadened only when it became clear that the narrow parameters were limiting the effectiveness of the programs. Although we can't prove that earlier introduction of broader programs would have headed off the greater financial pressures and reductions in credit supply that later emerged, we believe it to be quite plausible. Furthermore, by getting ahead of the panic, the Fed might actually have needed to do less emergency lending than it did by enhancing confidence and encouraging firms to continue to intermediate credit.

To be sure, the earlier launch of broader programs would have posed somewhat more risk to the Fed, but potential losses to the Fed still would seem to pale in comparison with the shortfalls in economic activity that were associated with the higher costs and reduced availability of credit that occurred.

But these views not only are the product of hindsight; they also ignore the legitimate concerns that policymakers had to consider at the time. As noted earlier, in 2007 and well into 2008, the economic outlook was not so dire that policymakers could put aside worries that a dramatic expansion of the Fed's balance sheet would get in the way of the Fed's monetary policy objectives. And in setting program parameters, policymakers had to strike a balance between limiting moral hazard and credit risk and supporting the credit needs of the economy.

LESSONS LEARNED

Lesson 1:
Be prepared.

Before the financial crisis, the Fed had prepared some well-developed plans to respond to its conception of a "banking crisis." One was modeled on the failure of Continental Illinois in 1984, but that was focused on a single institution and was not designed for a systemic breakdown. The Fed also maintained a "crisis binder" that included a list of potential dire scenarios and a list of lender-of-last-resort responses as well as summaries of crisis tools. But these proved of little value in addressing the 2008 financial crisis. The Fed found itself improvising under short time and operational constraints.

Ultimately, the availability of emergency authorities under Section 13(3) allowed the Fed to take aggressive action. Yet it still took time to develop robust, operationally sound programs, especially as these required using infrastructure or practices that are not part of routine business. Even in a crisis, the Fed needs to protect its integrity with proper controls, governance, and compliance. Future crisis responses should be faster and more robust if this type of work is conducted well in advance. Indeed, the Fed now conducts operational readiness testing of a variety of types of open market operations to ensure it is prepared to implement monetary policy across a range of possible conditions. These efforts could be expanded to also incorporate readiness testing for future novel facilities, including ensuring that such facilities appropriately evolve over time along with the financial and economic environment.

Lesson 2:
Be flexible in monetary policy implementation.

During the crisis, the Fed's ability to provide an effective lender-of-last-resort function came into conflict with the monetary policy implementation framework. To maintain interest rate control, the Fed needed to keep a fairly tight control of reserve balances.

Policymakers tried, at least initially, to design the liquidity facilities in ways that would limit reserve creation and increase the predictability of reserve balances, such as capping the size of lending programs, running them only as term facilities that were offered infrequently and with a lag, or using intricate noncash structures like TSLF.[12] However, it became evident that the size of the emergency lending programs exceeded the Fed's ability to sterilize with its existing tools.

This inherent conflict eased in October 2008 when Congress gave the Fed immediate authority to pay interest on reserves, accelerating prior authorization that had not been scheduled to take effect until 2011. This adjustment makes it much less likely that the Fed will find itself caught in the artificial trade-off between interest rate control and financial stability in the future.

---

12. To improve the capacity for sterilization and achieve the necessary flexibility to provide the liquidity the system needed, the Fed and Treasury worked together to develop a novel solution: The Treasury issued a special series of Treasury bills and parked the cash raised by selling these bills in a segregated account at the Fed. The program, known as the Supplementary Financing Program (SFP) and launched two days after the failure of Lehman Brothers, proved to be much more scalable than the Fed's own draining tools. Because the Treasury deposits provided partial funding for the Fed's liquidity injections, they reduced the need for the lending to be financed by new reserves. But SFP suffered from two flaws. First, debt issued under this program was subject to the statutory "debt ceiling," and second, the program was entirely controlled by Treasury. Both concerns could be addressed if the Fed were granted the ability to issue bills.

Lesson 3:
Coordinate planning and clarify roles.

As the crisis mounted and reliance on novel lending tools increased, concerns grew that the Fed's actions were pushing the institution's boundaries in ways that risked its independence, including with respect to both monetary policy and lending decisions.[13]

The need to clearly delineate the separate roles of the Fed and Treasury was largely addressed in March 2009 with a joint statement. It came at the peak of crisis-era risk aversion and around the launch of a large expansion of the TALF. The statement promised four key things. First, the Fed and Treasury would collaborate on emergency lending, making clear that the Treasury approved of it. Second, the Fed would confine its focus to broad aggregates and avoid credit allocation. Third, the Fed would maintain its monetary independence, and the Treasury and the Fed would seek legislative authority for "additional tools the Federal Reserve can use to sterilize the effects of its lending or securities purchases on the supply of bank reserves." And fourth, the Fed and Treasury would collaborate to address the regulatory weaknesses that contributed to the crisis. This statement was followed by a comprehensive speech in April 2009 by Chairman Bernanke, "The Federal Reserve's Balance Sheet," that elaborated on these points.

After the crisis, many of the principles of the joint statement were put into action in some form.[14] Still, the underlying question of how much and what kind

13. The concerns fell along four main lines. First, since the Fed had taken on significant credit risk and faced the risk of loss, it was taking an action some saw as proximate to fiscal spending, such as through the TALF. Second, by lending to nontraditional counterparties and against nontraditional types of assets, it was seen by some as engaging in credit allocation. Third, by expanding reserves to fund this lending without full confidence in the ability to control interest rates in that environment, it for a time relied on the Treasury-operated SFP to help drain reserves in the banking system to maintain interest rate control. And finally, because the Fed was operating in close cooperation with Treasury over a prolonged period of time to resolve the crisis, some worried that this relationship would become entrenched and that Treasury would come to exert inappropriate influence over core monetary policy decisions.

14. In the Dodd-Frank Act, the Fed's authority to undertake emergency lending is now available only for broad-based programs, and then only with the secretary of the Treasury's concurrence. This served to address concerns about credit allocation and clarify that the fiscal authority would be accountable for the results of these programs. Regulatory reform also, of course, occurred. And authority to pay interest

of risk the central bank should take in a crisis was never entirely resolved. We recommend that planning together in advance around potential crisis responses is critical to work through remaining ambiguity and ultimately to prevent crucial delays from operational, process, and communication complexities to launch robust and flexible programs in the future.

Lesson 4:
Avoid stigmatizing borrowers.

Financial institutions are often reluctant to draw on lender-of-last-resort facilities because they do not want to become stigmatized or be seen as being financially troubled. Institutions are particularly sensitive to two aspects of program design: the terms at which the loans are offered and whether (and when) the identities of the borrowers are disclosed.

With respect to the terms, generations of central bankers have been taught that central bank credit should be extended at a "penalty rate," in part to discourage borrowers from excessive reliance on central bank credit. But the crisis demonstrated that charging a rate in excess of the rate that the borrower would pay in the private market dooms a lender-of-last-resort program to failure because it signals that the borrower is in trouble.

To address this concern, the novel lender-of-last-resort programs generally involved extending central bank credit at rates below the market rates prevailing during the crisis but above the rate that had prevailed under normal market conditions. Borrowers were incentivized to use the programs during the crisis but were also incentivized to curtail their use as soon as market conditions normalized.

With respect to disclosure of borrowers, the users of the novel lender-of-last-resort programs were not disclosed until well after the crisis was over. Some believe that disclosure is necessary to accommodate the public interest and to hold the Fed accountable for its actions. But contemporaneous disclosure is unnecessary for these purposes. Even the prospect of delayed public disclosure may cause financial institutions to conclude that curtailing credit or selling assets is preferable to being identified as the recipient of a bailout, all of which could defeat the purpose of the programs.

---

on reserves supplemented by the ability to conduct reverse repos proved sufficient to control rates with abundant levels of bank reserves.

Lesson 5:
Consider broadening access to the discount window.

While standing access to the discount window has historically been granted only to depository institutions in large part because the associated moral hazard is contained by stringent regulation and supervision, postcrisis many of the largest broker-dealers are in bank holding companies or intermediate holding companies subject to bank-like oversight. Accordingly, policymakers should consider extending discount window access to broker-dealers, but only those that are in bank holding companies. In this regard, the United States would be following the example of the United Kingdom. Since the crisis, broker-dealers in the United Kingdom have been granted routine access to liquidity from the Bank of England.

CONCLUSION

The Fed's novel lender-of-last-resort facilities served an important role in mitigating the effects of the crisis by extending liquidity to the crucial nonbank sector, supporting repo and securitization markets, and helping to limit the tightening of credit to businesses and households. The facilities also served as vital stopgap measures until fiscal authorities were able to take necessary action.

The range of programs created—in terms of the markets they were directed at, the types of participants they lent to, and the collateral they accepted—underscores the value of broad emergency lending authority. The programs were innovative and imaginative, but they also were fundamentally reactive, as policymakers strove to balance the need to provide necessary support to the economy with the uncertainty of the environment and desire to limit moral hazard and credit risk.

The programs also highlight a number of lessons that will be crucial in the next crisis. Broad authorities, intellectual nimbleness, and operational planning are key. Liquidity provision should not conflict with monetary policy implementation. Lending facilities should be designed to minimize stigma. The Fed must be able to expand its liquidity provision and footprint in financial markets during times of crisis. Fiscal and monetary authorities should be clear on the types of risks each will take and coordinate plans in advance. These issues will be central to the effective management of the next crisis.

Table 3.1 Summary of Novel Lender-of-Last-Resort Facilities

Facility	TSLF	PDCF	AMLF	CPFF	TALF
Full name	Term Securities Lending Facility	Primary Dealer Credit Facility	Asset-Backed Commercial Paper Money Market Mutual Fund Liquidity Facility	Commercial Paper Funding Facility	Term Asset-Backed Securities Loan Facility
Peak usage[A]	$235.5 billion (10/01/2008)	$146.6 billion (10/01/2008)	$152.1 billion (10/01/2008)	$348.2 billion (1/21/2009)	$48.2 billion (3/17/2010)
Date announced	3/11/2008	3/16/2008	9/19/2008	10/7/2008	11/25/2008
First operation	3/27/2008	3/17/2008	9/22/2008	10/27/2008	3/25/2009
Facility closed	2/1/2010	2/1/2010	2/1/2010	2/1/2010	6/30/2010
Description	Weekly loan facility that offered Treasury securities held by the system open market account (SOMA) for loan against program-eligible collateral, typically over a 28-day term	Overnight loan facility providing funding to primary dealers in exchange for triparty-eligible collateral	Program whereby the Federal Reserve provided nonrecourse loans to U.S. depository institutions, U.S. bank holding companies, U.S. broker-dealer subsidiaries of such holding companies, and U.S. branches and agencies of foreign banks. These institutions used the funding to purchase eligible ABCP from money market mutual funds	Program whereby the Federal Reserve Bank of New York provided three-month loans to the CPFF LLC, a specially created limited liability company (LLC) that used the funds to purchase commercial paper directly from eligible issuers	A funding facility that supported the issuance of ABS collateralized by loans of various types to consumers and businesses of all sizes

(continued)

Table 3.1 (continued)

Facility	TSLF	PDCF	AMLF	CPFF	TALF
Eligible borrowers/ counterparties	Primary dealers	Primary dealers	U.S. depository institutions, U.S. bank holding companies, U.S. broker-dealer subsidiaries of such holding companies, and U.S. branches and agencies of foreign banks	Only U.S. issuers of commercial paper, including U.S. issuers with a foreign parent, were eligible to sell commercial paper to the special purpose vehicle	Any U.S. company that owned eligible collateral could borrow from the TALF through an account relationship with a TALF agent
Legal authority	Only "Schedule 2" collateral required authority of Section 13(3). "Schedule 1" collateral, securities of a type eligible for open market operations, did not	Section 13(3) of the Federal Reserve Act	Section 13(3) of the Federal Reserve Act	Section 13(3) of the Federal Reserve Act	Section 13(3) of the Federal Reserve Act

^A Maximum value of outstanding loans.

Source: Federal Reserve Bank of New York, based on data from Federal Reserve Board of Governors

Table 3.2 Subsequent Analysis of the Effectiveness of the Novel Lender-of-Last-Resort Facilities

TSLF

A report by the Federal Reserve Board's Office of Inspector General (2010) notes that although it may not be possible to assess the specific, direct impact of the TSLF, there were indications of improvements in the functioning of financial markets. Fleming, Hrung, and Keane (2010, 594) found that banks had been reluctant to use the Fed's discount window because of a perceived stigma associated with banks' creditworthiness if their borrowing were to become known and that the TSLF "may have overcome this stigma because of its competitive auction format." Wiggins and Metrick (2016) found that the TSLF successfully mitigated part of the liquidity problem suffered by primary dealers. A report by Hrung and Seligman (2011) found that for every estimated $1 billion increase in Treasury collateral from TSLF, the federal funds–repo spread narrowed by roughly 1.2 basis points. By contrast, Wu (2008, 18) found that "although TAF [had] a strong effect in reducing financial strains in the interbank money market, primarily through relieving financial institutions' liquidity concerns," "the TSLF and PDCF . . . had less discernible effects in relieving financial strains in the Libor market."

PDCF

Adrian, Burke, and McAndrews (2009, 7) note that borrowing from the PDCF was widely used when, "in the wake of the Lehman Brothers failure, other primary dealers experienced severe difficulties obtaining funding in the capital markets, as lenders imposed higher haircuts on repos" and would not accept all types of securities as collateral. The PDCF fulfilled one of its purposes—namely, it was available to primary dealers when a failure of a primary dealer led to severe funding disruptions for the surviving dealers. Regarding usage, the U.S. Government Accountability Office (2011) did not find evidence of a systematic bias favoring one or more eligible institutions, although Boyson, Helwege, and Jindra (2014) found that borrowing from Fed liquidity programs remained concentrated through the crisis, and the largest loans were provided to primary dealers under the PDCF facility.

AMLF

The Fed's Office of Inspector General (2010) report found that the AMLF effectively provided liquidity to money funds to help ease redemption concerns and fostered liquidity in money markets generally. Duygan-Bump et al. (2013) reached a similar conclusion. They found that facility participation was more likely among funds that experienced larger redemptions and that had lower holdings of U.S. Treasury and U.S. agency securities. Using a difference-in-difference approach, they found that outflows were lower at funds that held higher levels of AMLF-eligible collateral and that spreads on AMLF-eligible ABCP narrowed by more than yields on similar but ineligible securities.

(continued)

Table 3.2 (continued)

CPFF

Adrian, Kimbrough, and Marchioni (2011) found that the CPFF supported the orderly functioning of the commercial paper market during the crisis. They found that the facility contributed to a material reduction in the fraction of commercial paper issued on an overnight basis and a narrowing of spreads on eligible CP. They report that the spreads on one-month AA-rated unsecured CP and ABCP declined sharply over the first few months of operation, whereas spreads on A2/P2 commercial paper, which was ineligible for the CPFF, edged up.

TALF

A number of studies have found that TALF had a beneficial impact on ABS markets, although the impact is difficult to measure precisely, in part because there was an improvement in financial market conditions generally when the program began. Agarwal et al. (2010) analyzed the role of ABS markets in generating credit and liquidity and how this role was disrupted during the financial crisis. Before the creation of TALF, spreads on two-year and three-year triple-A-rated ABS "soared to up to 600 basis points for auto ABS and 550 basis points for credit card ABS. Soon after the creation of TALF on November 28, 2008, spreads dropped by more than 200 basis points in both of these sectors" (109). The authors found that the introduction of TALF caused the ABS interest rate to narrow from its historical highs in the fourth quarter of 2018, declining progressively at each expansion; "at the completion of TALF, spreads have fallen to approximately precrisis levels."

Ashcraft, Malz, and Pozsar (2012) found that the program contributed to a sharp decline in spreads in ABS markets by improving liquidity conditions and also had a longer-term impact by encouraging improvements in the design of CMBS. Ashcraft, Gârleanu, and Pedersen (2010), moreover, found some evidence that TALF reduced the spreads on legacy CMBS that were accepted into the program. By examining the behavior of asset prices around TALF announcements, Campbell et al. (2011) found that TALF had broad positive impacts on ABS markets rather than at the security level, suggesting that the program worked by improving investor sentiment rather than by subsidizing or certifying the particular securities that were funded by the program.

REFERENCES

Adrian, Tobias, Christopher R. Burke, and James J. McAndrews. 2009. "The Federal Reserve's Primary Dealer Credit Facility." *Current Issues in Economics and Finance: Federal Reserve Bank of New York* 15, no. 4 (August).

Adrian, Tobias, Karin Kimbrough, and Dina Marchioni. 2011. "The Federal Reserve's Commercial Paper Funding Facility." *Federal Reserve Bank of New York Staff Reports,* no. 423 (January).

Agarwal, Sumkit, Jacqueline Barrett, Crystal Cun, and Mariacristina De Nardi. 2010. "The Asset-Backed Securities Markets, the Crisis and TALF." *Federal Reserve Bank of Chicago Economics Perspectives,* no. 4Q (December).

Ashcraft, Adam, Nicolae Gârleanu, and Lasse Heje Pedersen. 2010. "Two Monetary Policy Tools: Interest Rates and Haircuts." NBER Working Paper, no. 16337, September.

Ashcraft, Adam, Allan Malz, and Zoltan Pozsar. 2012. "The Federal Reserve's Term Asset-Backed Securities Loan Facility." *Federal Reserve Bank of New York Economic Policy Review* (November).

Bernanke, Ben S. 2009. "The Federal Reserve's Balance Sheet." Speech, Federal Reserve Bank of Richmond 2009 Credit Markets Symposium, Charlotte, North Carolina, April 3, 2009. https://www.federalreserve.gov/newsevents/speech/bernanke20090403a.htm.

Bernanke, Ben S. 2015. *The Courage to Act: A Memoir of a Crisis and Its Aftermath.* New York: W. W. Norton.

Boyson, Nicole M., Jean Helwege, and Jan Jindra. 2014. "Thawing Frozen Capital Markets and Backdoor Bailouts: Evidence from the Fed's Liquidity Programs." SSRN (September).

Campbell, Sean, Daniel Covitz, William Nelson, and Karen Pence. 2011. "Securitization Markets and Central Banking: An Evaluation of the Term Asset-Backed Securities Loan Facility." *Journal of Monetary Economics* 58 (5): 518–31.

Duygan-Bump, Burcu, Patrick Parkinson, Eric Rosengren, Gustavo A. Suarez, and Paul Willen. 2013. "How Effective Were the Federal Reserve Emergency Liquidity Facilities? Evidence from the Asset-Backed Commercial Paper Money Market Mutual Fund Liquidity Facility." *Journal of Finance* 68, no. 2 (April): 715–37.

Fleming, Michael J., Warren B. Hrung, and Frank M. Keane. 2010. "Repo Market Effects of the Term Securities Lending Facility." *American Economic Review* 100, no. 2 (May): 591–96.

Hrung, Warren B., and Jason S. Seligman. 2011. "Responses to the Financial Crisis, Treasury Debt, and the Impact on Short-Term Money Markets." *Federal Reserve Bank of New York Staff Reports,* no. 481 (January).

Office of Inspector General. 2010. *The Federal Reserve's Section 13(3) Lending Facilities to Support Overall Market Liquidity: Function, Status, and Risk Management.* Washington, D.C.: Board of Governors of the Federal Reserve System.

Taibbi, Matt. 2011. "The Real Housewives of Wall Street." *Rolling Stone,* April 12, 2011. https://www.rollingstone.com/politics/politics-news/the-real-housewives-of-wall-street-246430/.

U.S. Government Accountability Office. 2011. *Performance and Accountability Report: Fiscal Year 2011*. Washington, D.C.: U.S. Government Accountability Office.

Wiggins, Rosalind, and Andrew Metrick. 2016. "The Federal Reserve's Financial Crisis Response B: Lending & Credit Programs for Primary Dealers." SSRN (February).

Wu, Tao. 2008. "On the Effectiveness of the Federal Reserve's New Liquidity Facilities." Federal Reserve Bank of Dallas Working Papers, no. 0808, April.

CHAPTER FOUR

Nonbank Financial Institutions

New Vulnerabilities and Old Tools

SCOTT G. ALVAREZ, WILLIAM C. DUDLEY, AND

J. NELLIE LIANG

INTRODUCTION: WEIGHING THE ECONOMIC RISKS

By the mid-2000s, nonbank financial firms had become a critical and integral part of the financial system in the United States. Some of these firms matched the largest banking organizations in importance and interconnectedness in the intermediation and funding markets. As a result, the failure of a large nonbank firm could potentially pose the same threat to the stability of the financial system as the failure of a large banking organization.

Yet the tools available to the Treasury, the Federal Deposit Insurance Corporation (FDIC), and the Federal Reserve—the agencies charged with acting as first responders in a financial crisis—to mitigate the effects of the failure of a large and systemically integrated nonbank firm were fewer and more circumscribed than those for addressing the failure of a systemically important bank. Thus, the challenges already inherent in any government attempt to arrest a developing financial crisis were more intense than when dealing with a crisis involving only depository institutions.

The authors thank Thomas Baxter, Sarah Dahlgren, Dan Jester, and Jim Millstein for providing critical insights and comments. The authors also acknowledge the importance of "The Early Phases of the Financial Crisis: Reflections on the Lender of Last Resort" by Timothy F. Geithner, as prepared for delivery on May 15, 2018, at the Bank of International Settlements Seminar "Crisis Response: A 10-Year Retrospective" and recently published in Vol. 1, Issue 1, of the *Journal of Financial Crises,* in helping frame some of the important issues discussed in this chapter.

This chapter explains why nonbank financial firms were among the largest sources of stress during the financial crisis, and it describes the challenges that the first responders faced, given the tools they had, in dealing with the systemic threats posed by the failures of those firms. We do not recount the full sequence of events leading up to lending to some of these firms, but instead focus on a few critical economic questions that the Fed had to grapple with when deciding whether to lend by using its emergency authorities.

Specifically, would a failure likely cause material harm to the economy, would broad-based lending facilities cushion the impact, and would lending actually prevent a disruptive failure?

We view the efforts to mitigate the systemic consequences or prevent the failures of major nonbank financial firms to be only part of the broader set of responses to deal with the collapse of funding and intermediation in the sizable nonbank financial system. That broader program included the Fed's Term Securities Lending Facility (TSLF) and Primary Dealer Credit Facility (PDCF); conservatorship of Fannie Mae and Freddie Mac, the government-sponsored enterprises (GSEs); and Treasury's guarantees for money market mutual funds. It also encompassed efforts to support the asset-backed commercial paper (ABCP) and commercial paper (CP) markets through the Asset-Backed Commercial Paper Money Market Mutual Fund Liquidity Facility (AMLF) and the Commercial Paper Funding Facility (CPFF), and securitizations through the Term Asset-Backed Securities Loan Facility (TALF) and the Public-Private Investment Program (PPIP).

SETTING THE STAGE

The vulnerabilities of nonbank financial institutions contributed significantly to the severity and breadth of the financial crisis. In the decades before the crisis, the relative share of credit from banks fell, and the share of credit from a range of different types of nonbank institutions rose substantially. Investment banks grew in size and importance, as did many finance companies, funded primarily in the short-term wholesale funding markets.

Alongside the growing importance of these types of firms was a significant increase in securitization, as well as a dramatic expansion in the derivatives markets, which enabled financial firms and corporations to manage their risks in new ways. The diversity of financial institutions and financial instruments and the rise of new sources of financing for households and businesses brought significant economic benefits, but also new risks.

The relative stability of the U.S. financial system in the decades before the crisis helped mask these risks and bolster the perception that these changes had made the financial system more stable. However, once the U.S. housing bubble burst, the fragility of the system became evident.

GROWTH OF NONBANK FINANCIAL FIRMS

The significance of nonbank financial institutions at the onset of the crisis can be illustrated by the sharp rise in credit they provided to households, businesses, and government. Credit outstanding to the nonfinancial sector as a percentage of GDP had risen to more than 250 percent at the peak of the crisis, and most of that growth took place outside of depository institutions (Figure 4.1). Credit from broker-dealers, finance companies, and asset-backed securities was 72 percent of GDP in 2008, up from 15 percent in the mid-1980s, and about equal to the amount of credit provided by traditional deposit-taking institutions. Fannie Mae and Freddie Mac had also expanded rapidly by securitizing mortgages with an implicit government credit guarantee and by purchasing other securitizations for their own portfolios.

Two key developments led to nonbanks competing effectively with banks.

One development involved innovations in securitizations that allowed nonbanks to provide a broader array of credit. Residential mortgages, commercial mortgages, and auto and credit card loans could be bundled and sold as securitized products. Initially, these securitizations were relatively simple and offered a way to redistribute risk. For example, mortgages originated by banks and nonbanks were bundled into mortgage-backed securities (MBS), with the securities holder receiving the cash flows from the underlying mortgages. Later, this evolved into a much more complicated system of structured finance. The cash flows from bundles of relatively risky assets such as subprime mortgages were allocated preferentially first to higher-rated (such as, triple-A-rated) securities tranches versus lower-rated tranches in collateralized debt obligations (CDOs). These CDOs could, in turn, serve as the underlying assets in more-complex CDOs, still supported by cash flows of the subprime mortgages and other lower-quality financial assets.

A second development, the deepening of the U.S. money markets, also supported the rapid growth of credit from nonbanks. Interest rate ceilings that limited the rates that commercial banks could pay depositors contributed to the emergence of money market mutual funds in the late 1970s and early 1980s. A large repo market developed that enabled securities firms to fund their

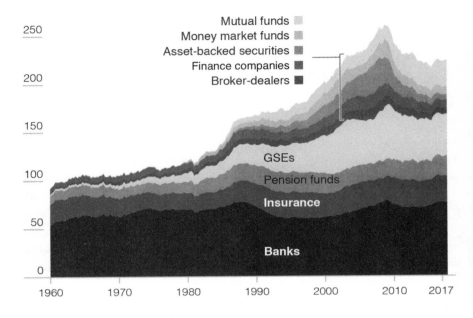

300% of GDP

250

200

150

100

50

0

Mutual funds ▨
Money market funds ▨
Asset-backed securities ▧
Finance companies ■
Broker-dealers ■

GSEs

Pension funds

Insurance

Banks

1960   1970   1980   1990   2000   2010   2017

Figure 4.1 **Nonfinancial Credit Outstanding, by Holder**

Notes: (1) GSEs are government-sponsored enterprises. (2) Excludes credit held by monetary authority.

Source: Federal Reserve Board, Financial Accounts of the United States

portfolios on a short-term basis (mostly overnight) with money market mutual funds and other short-term investors, and the development of the commercial paper market allowed nonbank finance companies to fund loan originations. Repo and commercial paper—"runnable liabilities"—grew much more rapidly than deposits at traditional depository institutions in the years preceding the financial crisis, peaking from 2007 to 2008, before investors pulled back sharply when concerns about collateral and counterparties rose (Figure 4.2).

But the reliance on short-term wholesale funding by nonbanks turned out to be a significant vulnerability in the financial system because this type of funding—unlike bank deposits that were guaranteed by deposit insurance—was very fragile. Although those that lent to securities firms were generally well secured by the repo collateral that secured the lending, during times of stress,

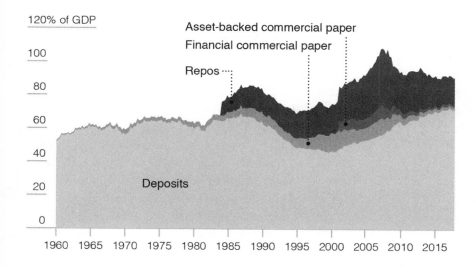

Figure 4.2 **Selected Short-Term Liabilities of Financial Firms**

Note: Data for asset-backed commercial paper not available before 2001.

Source: Federal Reserve Board, Financial Accounts of the United States

the lenders took little comfort from this because they often had no capability or appetite to take possession of the collateral and liquidate it should their counterparty fail. Instead, they pulled back from the repo market when there was a risk that a securities firm might fail. Investors in commercial paper also expect repayment of principal on demand, and generally would pull back quickly on any signs of issuer weakness.

Securities firms with these more vulnerable business models also got bigger. As securitization grew in scale, breadth, and complexity, fixed-income trading activity increased significantly. Soon securities firms were making markets on a global basis (and holding inventory) in sovereigns, corporates, and mortgages, and in products securitized from these underlying assets, and offering a suite of derivative products to help their customers manage interest rate, currency, and credit risks.

Growth of securities firms also was facilitated by deregulation in the United States and abroad, with the United Kingdom's "Big Bang" an important milestone facilitating the consolidation and rapid expansion of the securities industry in London. To support this global expansion, the major U.S. investment banks needed more capital, and they converted from private partnerships to public corporations. As public corporations, these firms had permanent capital and could use their retained earnings to fund their global expansion.

As investment banks were expanding rapidly, the largest U.S. commercial banks entered the securities business. Commercial banks initially gained a toehold in the business using Section 20 of the Glass-Steagall Act, which allowed commercial banks to have affiliates as long as those affiliates were not "engaged principally" in the underwriting and distribution of securities. This provision effectively eroded the separation of investment banking from commercial banking, long ahead of the repeal of Glass-Steagall by the Gramm-Leach-Bliley Act in 1999. The impetus for the expansion by commercial bank holding companies (BHCs) into the securities industry was both offensive, to expand into what were rapidly growing businesses, and defensive, to follow corporate clients that were increasingly raising funds directly from the capital markets rather than by borrowing from the banks.

This change was significant. Earlier, commercial banks had viewed securities firms mainly as customers. Now they saw them as rivals that were competing aggressively for their corporate business.

As intermediation activity shifted from banks to securities firms, leverage (assets divided by book equity) in the financial sector increased. Because securities firms were allowed to operate without the leverage requirements that applied to banks, they were able to operate with higher leverage than the banks during the stable economic and financial environment that prevailed before the crisis. Higher leverage was justified, in part because the firms tended to hold securities that were more liquid than loans and that were marked to market. Leverage at broker-dealers rose ahead of the crisis, spiking from about 20 in 2001 to almost 45 in 2008.[1]

At the same time, the financial intermediation process grew more complex. Rather than banks simply taking deposits and lending those deposits to households and businesses, the intermediation chains often became much longer and more intricate. For example, instead of a depository institution making a mortgage and funding it with insured deposits, a depository institution or mortgage broker might originate a mortgage and sell it to be securitized by

---

1. Tobias Adrian and Hyun Shin, "The Changing Nature of Financial Intermediation and the Financial Crisis of 2007–09," Federal Reserve Bank of New York staff report No. 439, April 2010. Changes in the net capital rule in 2004 also contributed to the increase in leverage.

Fannie Mae or Freddie Mac, or to a private-label securitization. The securitization then might be purchased by a structured investment vehicle, funded by ABCP held by a money market mutual fund. Similarly, the prepayment risk embedded in the underlying mortgage, rather than being borne by the depository institution, would be borne by the mortgage-backed security investor and might be hedged with interest rate swaps and/or options.[2]

One indication of greater complexity and interconnectedness is that while total credit to the nonfinancial sector grew quickly, total debt of the financial sector grew even faster. In the early 1980s, total debt of the nonfinancial sector was about six times as large as debt of the financial sector. By 2008, that ratio had fallen to two.[3] Also, the number and notional value of financial derivatives contracts outstanding soared. For example, the total notional value of over-the-counter interest rate swap obligations had risen to more than $300 trillion by 2008, just 27 years after the first swap transaction in 1981, and credit derivatives had risen to about $60 trillion in 2008 from near zero in the early 2000s.[4]

REGULATORY FRAMEWORK

During this transformation of the financial system, prudential regulation and supervision did not keep pace with the rapid structural changes.

Commercial banks had been operating with a well-developed prudential regime of minimum capital requirements and other constraints focused on preventing bank failures and maintaining the safety and soundness of the commercial banking industry. In essence, this was the quid pro quo for the government insurance provided for retail deposits and access to the Fed's discount window lending facility.

In contrast, the emphasis for securities firms had been on protecting customers from activities such as fraudulent sales and insider trading. Consequently, regulation and supervision of nonbank financial firms was largely

---

2. Commercial banks remained closely connected to much of the new business activity. Securities firms, Fannie Mae and Freddie Mac, and hedge funds were all major counterparties. Moreover, many of the new financial structures that were developed to hold securitized instruments, such as structured investment vehicles, were supported by backstop lines of credit from commercial banks.
3. Calculated from the Federal Reserve's flow of funds statistics.
4. "OTC Derivatives Outstanding," Bank of International Settlements, https://www.bis.org/statistics/derstats.htm?m=6|32|71.

focused on investor protection through adequate disclosure of financial and investment information, rules against fraudulent behavior, and the establishment of minimum qualifications for brokers and others in their dealings with customers. When securities firms became troubled, the goal was to ensure that the firm's investments could be segregated from those of its customers and returned to the customer if the firm were to fail and had to be liquidated; the focus was not on the consequences of failure in terms of contagion to other firms. When major securities firms had failed in the past (for example, Drexel Burnham Lambert in 1990), there typically wasn't much systemic consequence.

Moreover, supervisory and regulatory authority over the U.S. financial system was divided among a host of different federal and state regulators, with the particular charter of the institution determining the applicable regulator. This arrangement created an opportunity for firms to find less stringent regulation by the choice of charter under which they would operate their business. The result allowed situations such as the Office of Thrift Supervision (OTS) having responsibility for the Financial Products Group of American International Group (AIG), which was engaged in selling credit default swap protection against complex CDOs and interest rate and foreign exchange swaps.

In the same vein, there was no well-established lender-of-last-resort apparatus to support nondepository institutions. While commercial banks could borrow from the Federal Reserve through the discount window or from the Federal Home Loan Banks against mortgage collateral as a normal course of business, securities firms and other nonbank financial entities did not have such a backstop.

The central bank's power to lend to such firms, or to provide broad-based backstops to particular financial markets and products, was generally limited to the emergency authority contained in Section 13(3) of the Federal Reserve Act (FRA), with lending against Treasury, agency, and agency mortgage-backed securities collateral a notable exception. Under Section 13(3), the central bank could provide credit only under unusual and exigent circumstances when access to credit was judged as being unavailable elsewhere (see Chapter 5, on legal authorities, for more detail). The statutory hurdle to using the Section 13(3) authority was very high. Before the financial crisis, the Federal Reserve had last used this authority during the Great Depression. Securities firms or other nonbank financial firms could not count on this type of intervention.

As a result, on the eve of the crisis, many vulnerabilities of the financial system were not well understood by regulators or market participants. Moreover, unlike the case with a troubled depository institution, there were no effective means for preventing the failure of a large nonbank firm or resolving the failure of such a firm expeditiously and in a way that avoided contagion.

OFFICIAL RESPONSES TO DISTRESSED NONBANK FINANCIAL FIRMS

INCREASING STRESSES ON NONBANK FIRMS AND THE INITIAL RESPONSES

As house prices began falling in 2006, specialized mortgage lenders were the first firms to come under stress. Most of these lenders were independent and not affiliated with a bank, and they needed to borrow short-term funds to operate. But many lost access to funding and failed as house prices fell and mortgage delinquencies began to climb. Dozens of mortgage lenders, including such notable firms as New Century and American Home, failed in the first three quarters of 2007 as disruptions hit the ABCP market—more than a year before Fannie and Freddie were put into conservatorship and Lehman Brothers failed. Securities firms also were facing increasing losses from the effects of falling house prices as the value of private-label mortgage-backed securities declined and funding costs rose.

The Fed was concerned about the effects of a housing correction and financial firm weaknesses on the economy, and it encouraged depository institutions to make greater use of the discount window, first by cutting the primary credit rate and extending loan maturities, and in December 2007 by creating the Term Auction Facility (TAF) to reduce stigma (see Chapter 5, on legal authorities). However, TAF could provide liquidity directly only to depository institutions, which meant this lender-of-last-resort tool could not reach nonbank mortgage lenders, securities broker-dealers, insurance companies, and other nonbank financial firms. Moreover, statutory limits (Section 23A of the FRA) on the ability of a depository institution to provide funding to its nonbank parent and affiliates meant that the discount window was not a viable tool to support the nonbank parts of banking organizations, including such large ones as Citigroup and Bank of America.[5]

---

5. Section 23A of the Federal Reserve Act, among other things, generally prohibits a bank from providing funding to a nonbank parent or affiliate (through either extensions of credit or asset purchases) in an amount that exceeds 10 percent of the bank's capital and surplus. This restriction protects a bank—which collects deposits

The authorities also encouraged weaker firms to raise private capital to not only shore up their own financial positions in the event of a recession but also help avert an outcome whereby weak financial institutions were forced to restrict credit, which would then make any recession deeper. At the January 2008 meeting of the Federal Open Market Committee (FOMC), with current data showing GDP growth still positive, Federal Reserve Bank of New York (FRBNY) president Timothy F. Geithner, vice chairman of the FOMC, expressed concerns about the ability of financial firms to absorb projected credit losses if house prices were to decline 20 percent more. Announced write-downs by the largest financial firms in the second half of 2007 had already reached $100 billion, with about one-half by nonbank firms. Federal Reserve chairman Ben S. Bernanke, in his summary remarks, said, "Like others, I am most concerned about what has been called the adverse feedback loop—the interaction between a slowing economy and the credit markets."

To raise capital, firms turned to strategic investors or agreed to be acquired. Merrill Lynch raised $12.8 billion in two offerings in late 2007 and early 2008, after posting substantial losses in late 2007, and Morgan Stanley raised $5.6 billion in the fourth quarter of 2007. Banking firms, including Citigroup, Wachovia, and Washington Mutual, also raised capital, given substantial reported write-downs. Others were less successful. Countrywide, the largest mortgage lender at the time, averted failure in early 2008 by agreeing to be acquired by Bank of America for a fraction of its peak market value. Bear Stearns found in the winter of 2007 and spring of 2008 that it was unable to raise sufficient capital to remain independent. In early 2008, the financial system was looking very weak, and the prospects had significantly increased that a run on liquidity might further shock the system by precipitating the failure of large financial firms that were thinly capitalized.

insured by the FDIC and ultimately the taxpayer—by limiting the amount of risk the bank may take from funding its uninsured affiliates. At the time of the financial crisis, the Federal Reserve could provide an exception to this limit but, as a matter of practice, consulted with the FDIC in each case and generally would not grant an exception over the FDIC's objection. Although the Federal Reserve granted several 23A exceptions during the crisis, these generally involved allowing a nonbanking company to transfer to its depository institution affiliate assets that the depository institution could have originated directly; a condition of the exception was that the parent company would provide a funded guarantee to the depository institution against losses on the transferred assets.

LENDER-OF-LAST-RESORT CONSIDERATIONS

When private capital was not available, authorities had to determine whether and how to intervene under emergency authorities. The lender of last resort can help mitigate the risk that illiquidity becomes acute and the markets misperceive the underlying problem to be solvency. But the lender of last resort cannot solve the fundamental problem that capital is too thin to absorb potential losses.

Although a rigid or formal process to determine how or when to use various tools was not established before the crisis, the active consideration of several questions best describes the way in which the Federal Reserve approached deciding whether to use its lender-of-last-resort authority to provide liquidity to nonbank financial firms. First, would the failure of the institution likely cause material damage to the core of the financial system and the overall economy? In addition to the significance of a firm's role in the funding and credit markets and its linkages with other firms, the potential damage is also a function of the state of the economy at that moment in time. Failure of a large nonbank in a relatively stable world would matter less than the failure of even a modest-size institution in a very fragile world.

Second, could the broader provision of liquidity to the markets be powerful enough to contain the risk of a broader run in the event of a firm's failure? If so, then the first instinct should be not to intervene to try to prevent the failure of a specific institution.

Third, could lending prevent failure? The emergency lending authority in the Federal Reserve Act did not require a finding of solvency, and illiquidity itself cannot be disqualifying. But Federal Reserve lending authority was not designed to be used to rescue the nonviable. The emergency provisions require that the Federal Reserve be satisfactorily secured, which limits the amount of risk the Federal Reserve could take and the ability of the Federal Reserve to rescue institutions close to the point of insolvency. If the assets and businesses of the institution had enough value to support a loan large enough to prevent failure, the Federal Reserve could use its emergency lending authority to prevent that failure. In contrast, if the value of the assets held by the firm was not sufficient to support a loan large enough to allow it to continue to operate, the Federal Reserve did not have the ability to act on its own to prevent that failure. In this case, it might be able to use its lending powers to help support the acquisition of a failing firm by a willing acquirer. The point of emergency lending, however, was not simply to fund the exit of creditors without stabilizing the financial system.

These framing questions are a guide for decision-making. However, no plan survives first contact with a crisis, and translating a plan into concrete actions depends on the actual facts, the information available and amount of time available to assess that information, and the tools afforded. Ultimately, actions are determined by what is feasible in the moment.

Consideration of these questions is what led the Federal Reserve to use its emergency authorities to lend to a number of nonbank financial firms during 2008 and 2009.

SECURITIES FIRMS AND MARKET-WIDE LIQUIDITY FACILITIES

The end for Bear Stearns came quickly when it faced a run on its funding during the week of March 10, 2008. Bear had been unable to raise private capital. On that Monday, Bear Stearns had about $18 billion in cash reserves. By Thursday night, its cash reserves had fallen to approximately $2 billion, an amount that the management of Bear Stearns did not believe would be sufficient to allow Bear to survive the next day.

The potential disruption to the financial system from the abrupt failure of Bear Stearns could be avoided if a merger partner could be found quickly. The Treasury, the Federal Reserve, and the Securities and Exchange Commission (SEC) immediately set out to find an able acquirer. JPMorgan Chase was interested, and others might be found, but only if Bear Stearns could survive Friday and into the weekend to allow interested bidders to evaluate the firm. The Federal Reserve determined to use its emergency Section 13(3) lending authority on Friday morning, March 14, 2008, to provide Bear with funding to bridge to the weekend.

By the end of that weekend, only JPMC, which had extensive dealings with Bear Stearns in the triparty repo market and knew the businesses of Bear well, was interested in acquiring the firm. But JPMC was unwilling to go forward unless the Federal Reserve Bank of New York was willing to assume the risk in lending against a pool of about $30 billion of the nearly $400 billion in assets held by Bear. At that point, the Federal Reserve made a second decision to provide liquidity to assist the acquisition by providing funding for a portfolio of Bear's assets.

These two decisions were not easy and certainly would not be free from second-guessing. Leading up to both decisions, there was significant debate inside both the Federal Reserve and Treasury regarding whether the Federal Reserve should provide emergency credit. The discussions included long multi-agency phone calls on the night before and morning of the Friday credit as well as numerous calls and meetings before the second loan facilitating the acquisition.

On the one hand, Bear was the smallest of the major investment banks and significantly smaller than the large banking organizations, and it might be possible to mitigate the effect of Bear's failure on other firms and markets. Indeed, before the failure of Bear Stearns, the Federal Reserve had announced its decision to open a broad-based facility called the Term Securities Lending Facility (TSLF), which might limit the effect of the failure of Bear on other firms like it by allowing primary dealers to improve their access to liquidity by swapping a variety of illiquid assets for U.S. Treasury securities. And while it was working on finding a buyer for Bear Stearns, the Federal Reserve was developing a second liquidity facility—the Primary Dealer Credit Facility (PDCF)—to provide additional liquidity to primary dealers, which it announced on Sunday, March 16, 2008.

Moreover, it was not clear that the Fed's lending authority alone would be enough to save Bear. The market had lost confidence in Bear's ability to meet its obligations, its core businesses were bleeding away, and the value of its financial assets was declining rapidly. It was far from clear that Fed lending to Bear—the only emergency tool available to the government at the time—would stabilize the firm; instead, it could simply have facilitated the quick exit of creditors and counterparties.

On the other hand, the failure of Bear Stearns during the business day on Friday (which its own management feared) or the failure to avoid its collapse on Monday would likely be highly disruptive to markets and, even with the Federal Reserve's facilities, could set off a panic at the other large broker-dealers, possibly inflicting wide-ranging damage because of the critical role these firms had come to play in the financial system. The economy was weak and deteriorating, and Bear Stearns was very large and integrated with numerous other financial firms. The weaknesses at Bear were emblematic of the vulnerabilities at the other major investment banks. Like the other investment banks, Bear Stearns was highly leveraged and depended heavily on short-term funding from the triparty repo market. In the triparty repo market, lenders had an incentive to run at the first sign of trouble to avoid the risk that they would have to take possession of and liquidate the collateral that backstopped their triparty repo loans. If Bear's failure were to cause funds from money markets to pull back from funding the other investment banks as well, that could precipitate additional forced sales of similar mortgage securities. Fire sales at a time when financial markets were already on edge from the ongoing housing correction could lead to a downward spiral of asset prices and further losses for these firms, causing severe damage to the functioning of the financial system and the economy.

Federal Reserve lending could also calm markets and reduce further damage to the economy by showing that the Federal Reserve and Treasury were willing to use their emergency powers. Although using these emergency powers might suggest that the government believed that the economy and the financial system were more fragile than the public believed and that the government had the ability to prevent disruptive failures, waiting too long to invoke emergency powers—or not using them at all—could suggest that the Federal Reserve and Treasury were either asleep at the switch or simply willing to watch as Rome burned. And there was the prospect that Bear could be acquired and substantial equity injected into the firm, something the government could not do.

The history of panics demonstrates that the balance must tilt in favor of acting. Inaction can prolong and exacerbate the real consequences for consumers, businesses, and future economic growth from shocks that tear at the weaknesses in the system.[6]

The request for emergency credit to help finance the acquisition of Bear Stearns by JPMC raised an additional question for the Federal Reserve: Would it be possible and appropriate for the Federal Reserve to use its emergency authority to help fund a particular asset pool as a way of facilitating the acquisition of Bear Stearns by JPMC?

The Federal Reserve's lending authority was shaped by the principles of Bagehot—lend freely to solvent firms against good collateral at penalty rates when this is needed to save the financial system.[7] During the Great Depression, that was manifested in secured loans to a borrower that typically had

---

6. For example, Carmen Reinhart and Kenneth Rogoff document severe recessions and weak recoveries from financial crises. Based on 63 episodes in advanced economies, average GDP per capita losses are almost 10 percent from peak to trough, with a downturn lasting three years and a recovery of output to precrisis levels taking eight years. Carmen M. Reinhart and Kenneth S. Rogoff, "Recovery from Financial Crises: Evidence from 100 Episodes," *American Economic Review* 104, no. 5 (2014): 50–55.
7. See Brian F. Madigan, "Bagehot's Dictum in Practice: Formulating and Implementing Policies to Combat the Financial Crisis" (speech, Federal Reserve Bank of Kansas City's Annual Economic Symposium, Jackson Hole, Wyoming, Aug. 21, 2009), www.federalreserve.gov/newsevents/speech/madigan20090821a.htm.

business operations. The credit that facilitated JPMC's acquisition of Bear Stearns—while meeting the statutory requirements for emergency lending to a nonbanking firm—was asset-based lending that depended on the value of financial assets that were pledged as collateral to secure the loan, with JPMC providing subordinated debt that would absorb the first $1.15 billion in losses, if any, on the sale of the collateral.

Although this type of lending is common in the banking industry, it was new to the Federal Reserve and would expose the Federal Reserve to fluctuations in the value of the underlying collateral during a financial crisis without the protection of general recourse to JPMC.[8] Nonetheless, as the central bank, the Federal Reserve could be patient and allow the value of the assets backing the loan to recover as the financial crisis abated, thereby both enhancing the chances for repayment of the loan and avoiding the adverse effects on the economy that would accompany fire sales of those assets during the crisis. There would still be risk that the value of the assets would not recover and the loan would not be fully repaid. However, that risk appeared small, and the risk to the economy, which was fragile at the time, from the failure of Bear appeared likely to be significant.

Concern about this risk of loss to the Federal Reserve led the chairman of the Federal Reserve and the president of the FRBNY, though not legally required, to request that Treasury provide protection against that potential loss before making the final decision to extend emergency credit to facilitate the acquisition of Bear Stearns by JPMC. The Treasury did not believe it had authority to backstop the Federal Reserve against loss or to provide funds to support the emergency credit or facilitate the acquisition of Bear Stearns. However, the secretary provided the Federal Reserve with a letter that both expressed support for the decision to use extraordinary lending authority and recognized the potential risks of loss on the loan. The Fed and Treasury believed that after nine months of a crisis that had inflicted liquidity problems

8. To facilitate this credit, the Federal Reserve made its first use of a special purpose vehicle (SPV) to hold and account for the portfolio of collateral. It provided the Fed more control over the sale of the assets and greater transparency to the public. The SPV was valuable to JPMC because the capital charge associated with holding those assets would have absorbed some of the cushion remaining on both its risk-weighted and total capital ratios. A significant amount of the portfolio that was considered relatively low risk to the Federal Reserve was securities with underlying risk backed by Fannie and Freddie that would have counted against JPMC's total (non-risk-weighted) capital ratio.

and losses on financial institutions throughout the United States and Europe, a Bear bankruptcy would be a severe shock to the system and could precipitate the failures of other fragile securities firms.

After the collapse and acquisition of Bear Stearns, market confidence in all of the large investment banks eroded further. It became more difficult for investors to assess the scale of actual and expected losses of these firms and how much the failure of one firm would raise the probability of failure of the others, as the probability of a recession was increasing. Consequently, lenders pulled back from Lehman, Goldman Sachs, Merrill Lynch, and Morgan Stanley, among others.

An astounding aspect of the run on Bear Stearns was that short-term creditors had been refusing to provide funding to Bear even when collateralized by Treasury securities. This refusal stemmed from concerns that if Bear Stearns failed, the repo counterparties would have to assume and liquidate the collateral. The Federal Reserve established the PDCF to provide backup liquidity to the investment banks in the event that they experienced a situation similar to Bear's. The PDCF enabled the Fed to lend to primary dealers against most of the types of collateral that were used in the triparty repo market. The PDCF helped support the triparty repo market by assuring investors that there would be a backstop source of liquidity available to the primary dealers.

Even with the Fed's PDCF and TSLF programs in place, the financial system continued to become more fragile, which confirmed the judgment of policymakers that intervening to help prevent the abrupt failure of Bear was justified. Lehman Brothers was widely viewed as the next securities firm most vulnerable to the housing downturn and impending recession. The Treasury, the Federal Reserve, and the SEC strongly urged Lehman to raise significant capital and liquidity. A condition of access to the PDCF was that the borrowing firms provide the Federal Reserve regular information about their financial condition, providing a window into these firms that was not previously open to the Federal Reserve.

Lehman Brothers presented challenges that were similar to those of Bear Stearns but magnified in several respects. Lehman was larger and widely perceived to have substantially greater embedded losses than Bear, suggesting that negative spillovers from its failure would be even greater. A stress test conducted jointly by the Federal Reserve and the SEC in May and June 2008 showed that Lehman did not have sufficient liquidity or capital to survive even a mild version of the stresses experienced by Bear Stearns. Moreover, the risks of a deep recession and a more severe crisis had continued to increase through the summer. The market seemed to agree with this assessment: Five-year credit default swap premiums for Lehman rose through the summer and were higher than those for Merrill Lynch, Morgan Stanley, Goldman Sachs, and all of the large commercial banks.

Lehman's position was especially perilous, in part because, in its attempts to raise capital, it had opened its books to a broad universe of potential investors and partners in a process that did not increase confidence. It was viewed to have some unattractive businesses relative to its competitors. From June to September of 2008, Lehman had raised only $6 billion in additional capital (while announcing a $2.8 billion loss in early June and a $3.9 billion loss in early September). It also had raised about $20 billion in additional liquidity, but much of that was immediately encumbered as collateral for existing obligations. These meager efforts left Lehman vulnerable. Its plan to spin off $30 billion of its riskiest assets into a separate company, leaving a "clean Lehman," failed because the market was unwilling to acquire the assets at what Lehman perceived their value to be.[9]

There was some hope that placing the GSEs into conservatorship—thereby putting the U.S. government squarely behind the guarantees made by the GSEs against losses on many mortgages—would have the collateral benefit of relieving some funding pressures for Lehman. However, when Lehman's effort to obtain capital from the Korea Development Bank failed the day after the GSE conservatorship was announced, a run on Lehman began.

Going into the weekend of September 13–14, Lehman, Merrill Lynch, and AIG were all at the edge of failure. The Treasury, the Federal Reserve, and the SEC convened a consortium of the world's major financial firms with the hope—and direction—to find a private-sector solution to Lehman. The agencies facilitated the efforts of potential acquirers to review Lehman's books and made the case to the entire consortium that it was in their best interest to fund a special purpose vehicle that would take Lehman's unwanted assets either to facilitate the acquisition of Lehman or to otherwise prevent its disorderly failure. The agencies also closely monitored—and encouraged—efforts by various investors and lenders to arrange a solution for AIG, and they pushed management at Merrill Lynch to find a partner quickly.

9. Randall Smith, "Lehman's Revamp Plan Draws Doubters," *Wall Street Journal*, Sept. 11, 2008, https://www.wsj.com/articles/SB122103219388318869?mod=searchresults&page=1&pos=6.

Over the course of that weekend, it became even clearer that Lehman had been overvaluing its assets and that the economic risk in Lehman's pool of assets was substantial. Moreover, the financial institutions that were most likely to find value in Lehman's businesses did not believe that those businesses had sufficient value relative to their significant risks, and certain investors had begun to express their concerns publicly. After this initial review, only two firms showed serious interest in acquiring Lehman—Bank of America and Barclays. BoA's rough estimate, based on data from Lehman itself, was that Lehman had $60 billion to $70 billion of assets marked well above what they were likely to be worth. Barclays also estimated that at least $50 billion of Lehman's real estate and private equity assets were significantly overvalued.[10] Although these surely were opening bids in a negotiation, they indicated the depth of Lehman's losses and the relative weakness of its businesses.

By Saturday afternoon, BoA had decided that Lehman's capital hole was too deep and that the firm was more fragile and less valuable than Merrill. Barclays was then left as the only potential buyer, but on the condition that it could leave behind a substantial pool of the riskiest assets, which the private consortium had tentatively agreed to fund.

Though this felt like the makings of a solution, it was not. With every deal, there is a period of delay between announcement and consummation, and with that delay comes uncertainty that unexpected subsequent events will prevent the deal from being completed. In the case of Bear Stearns, that uncertainty was eliminated by JPMC providing a guarantee of Bear Stearns' obligations during the negotiation period. A similar guarantee would be needed were Barclays to acquire Lehman.

The British regulators refused to waive a London Stock Exchange requirement that Barclays's shareholders approve an open-ended guarantee of Lehman's trading book during the pre-closing period. That would leave a dangerous period of 30 to 60 days of delay and uncertainty. Barclays asked whether the Federal Reserve would provide a full guarantee of Lehman's trading book during this period.

10. Henry M. Paulson, Jr., *On the Brink: Inside the Race to Stop the Collapse of the Global Financial System* (New York: Business Plus, Hachette Book Group, 2010), 199, 206; Andrew Ross Sorkin, *Too Big to Fail: The Inside Story of How Wall Street and Washington Fought to Save the Financial System—and Themselves* (New York: Viking, 2009), 300, 319, 336, 340; David Wessel, *In Fed We Trust: Ben Bernanke's War on the Great Panic* (New York: Random House, 2009), 13, 17–19.

The Federal Reserve considered it but determined that it did not have the legal ability to provide an open-ended guarantee—that is, an unlimited loan for an indefinite period without reasonable certainty that sufficient collateral or a merger partner would be available to ensure repayment.[11] Although the British authorities did not say it explicitly at the time, they made it clear in accounts written after the crisis that they deemed Lehman too close to insolvency to risk burdening an already weak Barclays. They interpreted the indications that the Federal Reserve could not provide a guarantee as further indication that Lehman was too weak.[12]

It became increasingly clear that the market did not believe Lehman was viable. Without a willing buyer, without access to a resolution regime like the FDIC's for banks, and without capital to inject into the firm, there were no more options to prevent Lehman's failure and bankruptcy. The difficult question was not whether the failure of Lehman would seriously shock the economy—that seemed likely.

The difficult question for the Federal Reserve was whether it could lend sufficiently and in a way that would prevent the disorderly failure of Lehman and the shocks that would accompany that failure. The judgment of the Federal Reserve was that the combination of the fragility of Lehman's businesses and the scale of losses in its assets meant that the Federal Reserve could not provide Lehman with a loan large enough to save it. The Federal Reserve believed that lending into the ongoing run would just finance the exit of other creditors, fail to arrest the collapse in confidence in the institution, and erode the ultimate value left for the rest of the creditors, all without improving the odds that Lehman would survive or a viable buyer would emerge.

Would a loan to buy time have been helpful in limiting the damage, even if it simply delayed rather than prevented failure? That was not at all clear at the time. To lend ineffectively, without stabilizing the firm and credibly preventing failure, would not have been reassuring to a market at the edge of panic.[13]

---

11. Thomas C. Baxter, Jr., statement before the Financial Crisis Inquiry Commission, Sept. 1, 2010, http://fcic-static.law.stanford.edu/cdn_media/fcic-testimony/2010-0901 -Baxter.pdf.
12. Paulson, *On the Brink*, 209.
13. In responding to the Financial Crisis Inquiry Commission, Chairman Ben S. Bernanke expounded on this reasoning: "The credit relied on by Lehman to remain in operation was in the hundreds of billions of dollars and the lack of confidence that led counterparties to pull away from Lehman suggested that Lehman would

The Federal Reserve did lend to the Lehman broker-dealer, which would go through a Securities Investor Protection Corporation (SIPC) proceeding and was not included in the Lehman holding company bankruptcy filing, against collateral in the broker-dealer (which represented a relatively small part of the firm) in order to help limit some of the damage from a rapid liquidation and bridge the broker-dealer to an acquisition by Barclays.[14] But the Federal Reserve did not believe that Lehman's assets or businesses would provide security for a loan large enough to convince the markets that the Lehman conglomerate was viable.

After Lehman declared bankruptcy and Merrill Lynch announced it would be acquired by Bank of America, the pressure switched focus to the remaining two large independent investment banks—Goldman Sachs and Morgan Stanley. That Sunday evening, the Fed expanded the PDCF to accept any type of security that could have been used in the triparty repo market, including collateral located overseas, to provide a fuller backstop for funding for the remaining investment banks. Confidence eroded in Goldman and Morgan Stanley even after the PDCF was expanded. Both investment banks began to urgently seek strategic investors with strong balance sheets, and the Bush administration went to Congress to request emergency authorities to stabilize the financial system and prevent future disruptive failures.

---

need a credit backstop of all its obligations in order to prevent a debilitating run by its counterparties. Moreover, the value of a substantial portion of assets held by Lehman, especially its investments in residential mortgage-backed securities, loans, and real estate, was falling significantly. Derivative positions were subject to continuing collateral calls that required amounts of Lehman funding that could not easily be quantified in advance. And clearing parties were demanding collateral as a condition for serving as an intermediary in transactions with Lehman. We saw no evidence that Lehman had sufficient collateral to support these types and amounts of taxpayer support from the Federal Reserve. . . . Moreover, without a potential buyer for Lehman, the Federal Reserve could not be certain how long it would be required to fund Lehman or what the ultimate source of repayment, if any, would have been." Ben Bernanke, testimony before the Financial Crisis Inquiry Commission 2010, 11–12, http://fcic-static.law.stanford.edu/cdn_media/fcic-testimony/TBTF/Chairman%20Bernanke%20Follow%20Up.pdf.

14. The Federal Reserve coordinated with the SEC to have the Lehman broker-dealer continue to operate with funding from the Fed while it wound down its book, since, at a smaller size, an SIPC proceeding would be more orderly in the event an acquisition was not finalized.

Following the model of the JPMC–Bear Stearns merger, the agencies pushed both Goldman Sachs and Morgan Stanley to consider combining with commercial banking firms. Neither firm found the prospect of merging with a commercial bank to be attractive. No well-capitalized bank seemed to be interested. And combining one of these investment banks with a weak banking organization, such as Wachovia, might not have forestalled the failure of the combined firm.

Instead, the Federal Reserve Bank of New York returned to an idea that had been rejected earlier in the summer: encourage both firms to become bank holding companies. For the firms to gain the designation of a bank holding company, the Federal Reserve was required to find that they had sufficient financial and managerial resources to meet regulatory and supervisory requirements and to safely and soundly continue operations. An essential element of this strategy was obtaining capital from an outside investor, because a meaningful capital injection would provide a private-sector endorsement of the firm's financial health and new business plan. This strategy could be helpful if it demonstrated to markets that both firms were positioned to survive, with greater reliance on their insured bank and under the same prudential supervisory regime that applied to a large commercial banking organization. To facilitate the migration of these firms to a business strategy more like a commercial banking organization, the Federal Reserve could also grant both firms an exception from the limitations in Section 23A of the Federal Reserve Act to allow the firms to transfer bankable assets into their respective insured banks.

Both firms were approved to become federally regulated bank holding companies, on the condition they raise equity, which both firms were successful in doing. Goldman Sachs secured a commitment for a $5 billion equity investment from Warren Buffett and raised another $5 billion through a public offering. Morgan Stanley secured a commitment of about $9 billion of new equity from a large Japanese banking conglomerate, Mitsubishi UFJ Financial Group.

The combination of the equity injections and the BHC designation provided some modest relief. However, becoming a bank holding company did not give either firm material additional access to emergency funding. Although both firms already owned insured depository institutions that had direct access to the Federal Reserve's discount window before becoming bank holding companies, these banks were limited by law in the amount of funding they could pass on to their nonbank parent and affiliates (in particular their securities broker-dealers, which were very large before the conversion to BHCs and would remain so after the conversion). Ultimately, it took capital from the Troubled Assets Relief Program (TARP), which gave the Treasury the ability to purchase assets and equity from financial institutions, and guarantees of new borrowing by the holding companies from the FDIC to provide a measure of stability for both firms.

AIG

At the end of 2007, AIG was the largest insurance conglomerate in the United States, with more than $1 trillion in total assets. Its businesses included large life insurance companies and large property and casualty insurance companies with operations in more than 130 countries; one of the largest airplane leasing companies in the world; a large securities lender (securities lending outstanding of $88.4 billion in the third quarter of 2007); and a derivatives operation that provided massive credit default swap protection to banking organizations all over the world (credit default swaps with notional value of $527 billion at the end of 2007).[15] Although portions of the company were subject to supervision and regulation by various state insurance commissioners and foreign regulators, large portions of the firm were not subject to regulation, and the regulatory framework for the consolidated supervision of a firm of this size or complexity was totally inadequate.[16]

AIG controlled several profitable and viable insurance companies and had a high credit rating. Nonetheless, it was facing increasingly severe liquidity pressures going into the weekend before Lehman's failure. It was also actively seeking new sources of capital and funding, and had quickly become perceived in the markets as close to failure. AIG's sizable securities lending business involved lending assets owned by the insurance companies, with the permission of the state insurance supervisors, and investing the cash collateral obtained

15. Robert L. McDonald and Anna Paulson, "AIG in Hindsight" (NBER Working Paper, no. 21108, 2015).
16. While the OTS was nominally charged with supervising AIG because AIG owned a small savings association, the regulatory and supervisory framework established by the Savings and Loan Holding Company Act focused the OTS on ensuring that the firm had sufficient resources to operate the savings association, which was a small part of the conglomerate, and not on ensuring that the conglomerate would itself operate subject to prudential standards adequate to ensure the viability of the entire conglomerate.

into risky, illiquid mortgage-backed securities held outside the insurance companies. Counterparties in this business were refusing to roll over their positions and instead were demanding return of their cash and securities. At the same time, the financial products division of AIG, also outside the regulated insurance companies, was experiencing increasing demands for cash and collateral to support the credit protection it had sold. The regulated AIG insurance companies could not provide funding to those activities without the agreement of the appropriate state insurance supervisor, whose charge was to protect the viability of the insurance company and its policyholders. Although the New York state insurance superintendent allowed certain of the insurance subsidiaries to provide about $20 billion to help AIG meet its margin calls, that amount was not nearly enough to satisfy AIG's needs.

Going into the weekend of September 13–14, the Federal Reserve had become concerned that a disorderly failure of AIG would pose material risks to other financial firms and the economy by leading to further forced sales of mortgage securities and a substantial loss of credit protection that had been purchased from AIG by financial firms, which would increase the stress on a financial system reeling from the fragilities revealed at the GSEs and Lehman. As with the investment banks, the authorities pushed for a private-sector solution to AIG. Indeed, a number of banking firms and investors were reviewing AIG's financial statements and considering whether to invest in the firm over the same weekend that firms were considering the purchase of Lehman. But none could get comfortable with the magnitude of the risk or with the company's management, especially after AIG was downgraded after Lehman's failure, so there was no buyer for AIG.

Without a private-sector solution, there were very few options available to address the liquidity problems at AIG in order to reduce disruptions to its many counterparties and policyholders. While each state has a framework for the resolution of an insurance company chartered by that state, there was no framework other than bankruptcy for the resolution of the portions of the AIG conglomerate that were not insurance companies. Accordingly, when the derivatives operations and the securities lending operations of AIG experienced significant losses and liquidity strains, AIG was faced with the prospect of resolution in bankruptcy. Neither the markets nor the public was expecting the failure of AIG, and its bankruptcy would have been by far the largest in U.S. history. Moreover, a bankruptcy proceeding, which is designed to protect the company's creditors and counterparties, would not take account of systemic risks as it worked through the complicated unwinding of derivative and securities lending agreements. Further, it would have created tremendous disruptions in an economy and financial system already in crisis and struggling to adjust to the announcement of Lehman's failure.

At this point, the only tool available to prevent the disorderly and unexpected failure of AIG in the days following the failure of Lehman was the emergency authority available to the Federal Reserve to provide credit under Section 13(3). For the reasons discussed earlier, the failure of AIG appeared certain to cause material distress at a time when the economy was perilously weak and struggling under the weight of Lehman's unexpected bankruptcy announcement. It was unclear as yet which markets might benefit from additional broad-based lending facilities sponsored by the Federal Reserve, and neither the Federal Reserve nor the Treasury had authority to provide the capital that the financial system needed to restore confidence.

The Fed believed that AIG's insurance company subsidiaries had substantial value and would enable the company to be viable in the long term and provided adequate value to collateralize the loan. Also important, market participants believed that AIG's problems were limited to a liquidity shortfall at the holding company and that the value of its insurance companies made the company solvent and viable.

On Tuesday, September 16, 2008, with the support of the Treasury and after discussions with state insurance supervisors about the health of the insurance companies controlled by AIG, the Federal Reserve announced it would provide AIG with a revolving line of credit in an amount of $85 billion secured by all of AIG's assets, including the shares of its insurance company subsidiaries.[17] This loan was intended to be large enough to meet AIG's projected liquidity needs. But even that turned out not to be enough. All told, the Federal Reserve and Treasury needed to provide more than $180 billion in capital commitments and liquidity funding over time.

As a condition of the loan, the Federal Reserve required a tough set of terms that it believed was appropriate to protect and compensate taxpayers for the risk associated with making the loan to a failing company. These terms included a penalty interest rate, a requirement to provide substantial convert-

---

17. Excluded from this collateral were shares of certain foreign subsidiaries and previously encumbered assets. See Federal Reserve Bank of New York, Credit Agreement between AIG and the Federal Reserve Bank of New York, Sept. 22, 2008, https://www.newyorkfed.org/medialibrary/media/aboutthefed/aig/pdf/original _credit_agreement.pdf.

ible preferred stock to a trust for the benefit of the United States, a limited duration on the loan, covenants limiting the acquisitions and activities of AIG, and the replacement of the CEO and ultimately the board. These financial terms were similar to those required by private lenders to a troubled firm. Indeed, the terms of the Federal Reserve credit were modeled on terms prepared for a private-sector lender that ultimately decided not to take the risk of lending to AIG after Lehman failed.

Over the next few months, it became clear that the financial condition of AIG was worse than the Fed or the markets had anticipated. In addition, the credit rating agencies indicated that the initial terms of the emergency credit—in particular, the high interest rate, the size of the credit, the short duration of the credit, and the senior position of the Fed, as well as unexpectedly large losses embedded in AIG's derivatives and securities lending portfolios—were leading them to consider a further downgrade of the credit ratings for AIG. Lower ratings would increase the financial stress on AIG by subjecting it to higher collateral requirements and increased liquidity demands from counterparties. Fortunately, in early October, Congress enacted the Emergency Economic Stabilization Act (EESA), which empowered the Treasury to inject capital using TARP funds. EESA allowed the Federal Reserve and the Treasury to restructure the government assistance to AIG in a way that proved to be necessary to satisfy the credit rating agencies and market participants that were now questioning AIG's solvency.

Importantly, the Treasury used TARP funds to provide much-needed capital to AIG and reduce its dependence on the Federal Reserve's revolving line of credit. And because the Federal Reserve provides credit during emergencies as a way of helping stabilize the financial system and limit disruptions to the economy—not for the purpose of maximizing profits as would a private investor or lender—it was willing to restructure the AIG credit by lowering the interest rate on the credit (still, however, charging a penalty rate). The Federal Reserve also determined to extend additional emergency credit through two new special purpose vehicles that alleviated AIG's critical need for liquidity arising from its securities lending and credit default swap programs. In these transactions, AIG provided funding to the SPVs that was subordinated to the Federal Reserve's senior credit, and the Federal Reserve had the right to share in any residual value of the pledged collateral, which ultimately earned billions of dollars for the taxpayer.

The Federal Reserve and the Treasury restructured their arrangements with AIG several times more during 2009 to address potential downgrades by the credit rating agencies. The need to continually adjust the structure of support to meet the credit rating agencies' criteria was an ongoing challenge for the government and would not have been possible without the ability of Treasury to inject capital into AIG. But ultimately, all of the government funding came back with a profit of $22 billion.

GOVERNANCE ISSUES

Absent a viable alternative to bankruptcy, the Federal Reserve and Treasury provided a large amount of credit and equity to AIG, which placed them in an unusual position regarding the governance of the conglomerate. A difficult but important issue for the government when it provides emergency assistance is how much and what type of involvement the government should have in a firm's operations.

In the case of AIG, the Federal Reserve and Treasury required the company to make changes to its management and its board of directors, mandated development of a plan to repay the government from the sale of assets of the company, imposed limits on new activities and expansion, and required regular reporting and access to information. The Federal Reserve and the Treasury also closely monitored the management, activities, and financial condition of the company. These are actions that a private lender and preferred equity investor (the position obtained by the Treasury using TARP funds) in a troubled company might be expected to take.

At the same time, the Federal Reserve took steps to limit the role the government would play as a result of the government obtaining a sizable amount of the voting securities of AIG in connection with the Federal Reserve's loan by requiring AIG to place those securities into a trust overseen by trustees independent of the government. The trust was created to ensure that decisions regarding those shares—including any voting rights that might accrue—would be made by the independent trustees, not by government policymakers. This meant the independent trustees would have an important role in the governance of AIG.[18]

These various conditions were designed to ensure that the taxpayer would be repaid and that the government would not become enmeshed in trying to

18. Treasury, as the direct holder of the TARP preferred shares, coordinated with the trustees but had independent rights with respect to executive compensation, and information and observation rights.

operate AIG on a day-to-day basis. However, in late fall of 2008 and into 2009, Congress and the public began to demand more government involvement in AIG's operations and management. Congress also imposed limits on the compensation of executives and certain other employees of AIG by statute. Some of these demands were intended to incentivize AIG's management to repay its government assistance more quickly, to reduce any advantage AIG might have over other insurance companies and competitors that had not received government assistance during the financial crisis, or to advance other constituency causes. They also reflected a growing sense of unease about fairness and the justness of government interventions to support the functioning of the financial system.

Some government involvement in the operations and management of AIG was an unavoidable consequence of government assistance of the size and type provided to AIG. The amount and type of government involvement in corporate governance will likely affect the willingness of firms to accept such assistance in the future. That may be desirable; but it will also potentially have a cost in that it could lead to more disruptive failures. This makes it even more critical that a credible supervisory and regulatory framework be in place to prevent the failure of a large systemically important firm and that a workable resolution framework be available in the event that prevention is not successful.

AVAILABILITY OF TARP TO SUPPORT OTHER NONBANK FINANCIAL FIRMS

With the passage of EESA in early October and the availability of TARP funds, the authorities could respond more forcefully to reduce the fallout of financial firms' distress on the economy. Treasury used TARP to support some nonbank financial firms such as AIG and for ring-fence transactions for Citigroup and Bank of America. TARP also allowed the development of broader programs, such as the Capital Purchase Program, which injected capital widely into the banking system. Other programs supported by TARP, such as TALF and PPIP, aimed at liquefying important funding and securitization markets, helped both troubled bank and nonbank financial firms ease specific liquidity pressures. By being available broadly to all participants in particular markets, these facilities ensured that all participants in those markets—not just specific firms targeted for government assistance—had access to liquidity on the same terms and conditions. These TARP-supported programs complemented other programs deployed by the agencies, such as the FDIC's Temporary Liquidity Guarantee Program (TLGP) and the Federal Reserve's CPFF program, which allowed large nonbank financial firms such as General Electric Capital Corporation—one of the largest issuers of commercial paper—to obtain much-needed funding.

THE NONBANK FINANCIAL SECTOR AFTER THE CRISIS

The nonbank financial sector looks very different than it did on the eve of the financial crisis, as many firms failed, market participants changed their attitudes about the risks of those firms, and the firms themselves adjusted their business models. Only two of the five largest U.S. investment banks in 2007 remain as stand-alone firms, but they now operate as regulated bank holding companies. The largest foreign investment banks operating in the United States always were parts of foreign banking organizations, but they are now required by the Federal Reserve to set up an intermediate holding company for their U.S. operations. Many finance companies—nonbank financial companies that specialize in providing credit to consumers or businesses—failed or made strategic decisions to dramatically shrink their businesses. Activities that had supported the growth of nonbanks, such as securitization and short-term wholesale funding, shrank sharply and remain below precrisis levels.

Before the crisis, many large securities firms had been regulated by the SEC, with the focus on investor protection rather than on safety and soundness and financial stability. Now, as parts of bank holding companies, these firms are subject to a regulatory and supervisory regime designed to ensure their safety and soundness, to mitigate the risk that such firms might fail in the future, and to reduce the adverse consequences for the financial system and economy if they were to fail.

However, as this recent financial crisis demonstrated, financial markets and firms are always changing, and risks to the financial system and the economy may come from places that are not perceived as a threat to the system today. The Dodd-Frank Act (DFA) took an important step to address systemic risks that might emerge outside the banking industry by establishing the Financial Stability Oversight Council (FSOC). The council has the responsibility to monitor and take actions to reduce systemic risk, including the authority to designate nonbank financial firms as systemic and subject to regulation and supervision by the Federal Reserve.

The DFA also established an orderly liquidation authority that allows the FDIC (and in the case of a securities broker-dealer, the SIPC) to resolve a nonbank financial firm in the event bankruptcy is not a viable option. Unlike a case under bankruptcy, the DFA provides that the resolving agency may take actions to avoid or mitigate serious adverse effects on the financial stability or economic condition of the United States. At the same time, the DFA reduced the Federal Reserve's 13(3) lender-of-last-resort authority by prohibiting facilities designed to support individual firms and banning lending to firms that are deemed insolvent.

LESSONS LEARNED

We highlight several key lessons:

Lesson 1:
Nonbank financial firms that depend on wholesale short-term funding can pose material risks to the economy.

Aggressive actions may be needed to contain the costs of fire sales and panics. The financial system changed in fundamental ways in the decades leading up to the crisis, with more credit and risk transfer provided through financial markets and intermediated by nonbank firms. But many nonbank firms depend on wholesale short-term funding rather than stable insured deposits; thus, they are more vulnerable to decreased investor confidence, which can lead to fire sales and market contagion. While not all nonbank failures will pose material risks to the economy, systemic risk is likely greater when the rest of the financial system and economy already are weak. The history of financial panics suggests that aggressive actions are needed to reduce the severity of losses for households, businesses, and the economy as a whole.

Lesson 2:
Some current market practices are highly procyclical.

Crisis responders should try to anticipate the procyclical nature of such market practices as credit rating agency downgrades and increases in market calls by counterparties when designing their countermeasures, because their impact on the liquidity needs of an individual firm may have ripple effects, increasing the needs of other market participants. For example, AIG was downgraded after Lehman's failure, leading to a substantial increase in its liquidity needs. It was downgraded again after the Fed's liquidity funding in part because the rating agencies perceived the Fed's credit terms to be onerous.

Lesson 3:
Responses to reduce the future risk to the financial system and economy from distressed nonbank firms require coordination among regulators.

The extraordinary responses undertaken with respect to nonbank firms during the crisis required government agencies to combine their information, tools, expertise, and judgment. This collaboration is especially important if the authorities that have tools, such as the Fed or the FDIC, are not the primary regulator of a distressed firm or otherwise do not have regular access to information about the firm. Programs that supported short-term funding markets and securitization during the crisis were effective because they combined Treasury's TARP capital with FDIC guarantees and Fed lending, all in line with the provisions of each agency's legal authorities. Coordination enhances the legitimacy of actions by ensuring that various perspectives are fully considered.

Lesson 4:
Government capital for private firms in a crisis can reduce harm to the economy, but firms must be held to the same standards and business practices as other firms and the taxpayer should be compensated.

In the case of AIG, efforts were made during the crisis to avoid government control, through the creation of an independent trust to manage the government's voting securities. However, the public's perception was that the ownership stake meant that the government should be able to direct AIG's actions. In the future, regulatory agencies should very clearly communicate their strategy and actions to lawmakers and the public to prevent a similar backlash. In particular, the agencies need to explain that an intervention to prevent a firm's failure is not motivated by a desire to save the firm per se, but rather to avoid a breakdown in the financial system that could have terrible consequences for employment and other economic activity.

Lesson 5:
Keep the regulatory and supervisory regime, as well as crisis management tools, up to date with the evolving structure of the financial system.

In the decades preceding the financial crisis, the nonbank sector grew rapidly in scale, scope, and complexity, with securitization, derivatives, and money markets enabling securities firms to compete more effectively with depository institutions. But the regulatory regime did not keep pace with those changes, and risks arose outside the prudential regulatory boundaries. In addition, the tools available to help distressed nonbanks had been designed for a financial system dominated by commercial banks. We should expect that the financial sector will continue to evolve, responding to new regulations and technological developments. The regulatory and supervisory regime must evolve too, with regular updates tied to a macroprudential policy approach.

The FSOC now has the responsibility to monitor and take actions to reduce systemic risk, including designating nonbank firms as systemic and thus subject to prudential regulation and supervision. The FSOC can also assess certain activities as systemic. Reducing system risk requires having a credible resolution process when there is no capital available and when bankruptcy, the preferred approach under the DFA, is not a viable option. Title II of the DFA gives orderly liquidation authority to the FDIC, providing a way to resolve a systemic nonbank firm to forestall contagion to similar firms and to the broader economy.

Revising crisis management tools is equally important since even up-to-date regulatory regimes will not be able to prevent financial crises from ever happening again. Policymakers should consider expanding the Fed's authority as lender of last resort to nonbank financial firms on a timely basis rather than only after circumstances are judged to be unusual and exigent. Greater moral hazard risks could be mitigated by lender-of-last-resort loans that are well secured by pledged collateral at a penalty rate, and to firms with appropriate prudential standards in place. Such an expansion would improve the stability of funding for all firms by reducing the odds that liquidity stresses on one firm escalate into contagion and solvency problems for others.

| CHAPTER FIVE |

The Legal Authorities Framing the Government's Response

SCOTT G. ALVAREZ, THOMAS C. BAXTER, JR.,
AND ROBERT F. HOYT

INTRODUCTION: THE EVOLVING NEED FOR EMERGENCY TOOLS

The Federal Reserve, the Treasury Department, and the Federal Deposit Insurance Corporation (FDIC) each took strong and innovative actions to mitigate the financial crisis. These actions were well grounded in law and consistent with the direction of policymakers to do "everything possible" to address the crisis.

In some cases, the legal authority being applied was archaic or had not been used or interpreted for many years. In other cases, the law was being applied for the first time. In most cases, the legal authorities were built on the lessons of past crises involving "retail" panics and failures of depository institutions that were unlike the crisis that began in 2007.

Since many of these authorities were enacted, financial markets have evolved and changed in significant ways. By 2007, important markets, such as the repo and the commercial paper markets, and new intermediaries, like money market mutual funds and asset-backed securitization vehicles, had evolved to become critical sources of funding to businesses and consumers. Nonbanks rivaled depository institutions as intermediaries, becoming critical credit conduits to businesses, consumers, and investors.

We would like to express our appreciation to all the incredible lawyers at the Federal Reserve, the Treasury, and the Federal Deposit Insurance Corporation who worked diligently to ensure creative and responsible actions to mitigate the effects of the financial crisis while meeting the highest legal standards.

Indeed, the 2007 crisis first manifested in the shadows of a financial system that did not exist during the years of the Great Depression or the 1980s and early 1990s, when the foundation for the emergency legal authorities of the federal agencies was built and last modified. The strong interconnections that had developed between nonbank financial firms and depository institutions increased both the scope and the depth of the impact that vulnerabilities in nonbank firms could have on banks and the financial system as a whole.

The agencies responded to this new set of challenges by using the legal authorities available to them in ways that were contemplated by the authors of those authorities and in ways that, while clearly permissible, were new and innovative. And, as happened during past crises, Congress also responded by enacting new authorities to address these new problems.

An important lesson is that emergency authorities must evolve to reflect changes in the financial system. Because the system is dynamic and constantly evolving, every crisis is and will be different.

Emergency authorities must evolve or be drawn broadly enough to accommodate this inevitable evolution. Laws that are too narrow in scope or that handcuff policymakers in fashioning a measured response can dramatically reduce the ability of the government to implement an effective response, resulting in an increase in the costs and pain inflicted on citizens and the economy. The government may choose not to intervene in a particular crisis, but it should have available to it an effective arsenal of tools that gives it the option to intervene if it chooses to do so.

Although legal authorities and new emergency tools can be and have been added during a crisis, typically this is too late; it is more effective and less costly if the tools are in place before a crisis starts. Early and forceful action to address problems as they emerge allows policymakers to mitigate, and in some cases prevent, any destabilizing effects.

In the wake of the latest crisis, Washington strengthened some of the tools to enhance the resiliency of financial firms and the financial system to help prevent and limit the damage during another crisis, and it added a new power that allows the government to "resolve" (close or liquidate), rather than support, the biggest struggling financial firms using funding from the banking industry itself, not from taxpayers.

At the same time, however, Congress took away from the agencies, or diminished the scope of, some of the legal tools that were essential in restoring stability in the last crisis, giving itself greater responsibility for addressing future emergencies.

The Dodd-Frank Act (DFA), for example, took away the Fed's power to lend to failing firms or to take assets off their balance sheets. In the future, the Fed may extend emergency credit only through broad-based facilities designed to help the financial system as a whole. Congress also took away Treasury's ability to use the Exchange Stabilization Fund (ESF) to guarantee money market funds. And the FDIC has lost significant authority to provide assistance to the financial system, even if that assistance would prevent failures that pose systemic risk, without the concurrence of Congress.

AS THE CRISIS UNFOLDED: THE TOOLS AT HAND

The public often assumes that the government is subject to the same principle that applies to a private company—a company may do that which is not prohibited. But that is not correct: The government has the ability to do only what the law permits.

As the financial crisis began to unfold and deepen during the second half of 2007 and through September 2008, regulators looked closely at the tools available to address the situation. Some were antiquated and cumbersome, and taken together they amounted to a short list of narrowly circumscribed powers.

The president was authorized to declare a bank holiday that would close all banks but had no other special powers to deploy in a financial emergency. Treasury, unlike several foreign finance ministries, had no special emergency powers to address a financial crisis beyond controlling the ESF, worth about $50 billion. The Securities and Exchange Commission (SEC) could halt trading on the stock exchanges but couldn't provide emergency credit to a failing broker-dealer. And no one in the federal government had the authority to resolve players in the shadow banking system that were in trouble. Nor did any agency have the power to acquire troubled assets or to inject capital into even *traditional* financial firms, in stark contrast to some other countries—such as the United Kingdom and Switzerland—that were also being buffeted by the crisis.

The Federal Reserve's monetary policy tools were (and remain) powerful, but they could not be narrowly tailored to address the specifics of the crisis. Rather, these powers are designed and intended to address weaknesses in the broad economy.

The most robust tools available to address particular problems involved depository institutions, perhaps because their failure played such a prominent role in the Great Depression.

The Fed is authorized to make secured loans to depository institutions at any time. And the FDIC provides a strong backstop with deposit insurance—a tool designed to protect consumers and maintain confidence in depository institutions.

The FDIC is also empowered to resolve failing depository institutions. The agency is authorized not only to marshal assets to pay depositors and other creditors but also to manage the resolution in a way that minimizes the risk to the financial system. An important limitation requires the FDIC to resolve each institution in the manner least costly to the Deposit Insurance Fund. Congress wisely added a "systemic risk" exception to this limitation, permitting the FDIC, in extraordinary circumstances, to take other actions needed to address the potential effects on the system of depository institution failures. However, even this emergency exception did not extend to a nonbanking financial firm in distress, such as American International Group (AIG), Bear Stearns, or Lehman Brothers.

In fact, the dearth of tools to address nonbank financial firms was consequential in determining the government's response to the threats to the financial system and economy that emerged from this critical part of the system.

Indeed, until October 2008—deep into the crisis—the only tool available to address issues at nonbank financial firms was the Fed's emergency authority to lend on a secured basis.

Congress added two critical powers during the crisis.

The first authorized the government to place the Federal National Mortgage Association (Fannie Mae) and the Federal Home Loan Mortgage Corporation (Freddie Mac), both government-sponsored enterprises, into conservatorship to avert their disruptive failure and liquidation in bankruptcy. (For more details, see Chapter 6.)

The second, created with the enactment of the Emergency Economic Stabilization Act (EESA),[1] was the Troubled Assets Relief Program (TARP), which authorized Treasury to acquire troubled financial assets and inject capital into financial firms. (See Chapter 14.) The powers conferred by EESA were used in the ways anticipated by the proponents and in other ways that were innovative and evidenced interpretive agility. TARP contained a sunset date and is no longer available. Although not a new tool, as part of the TARP legislation Congress also increased deposit insurance, a tool created during the 1930s to decrease the likelihood of runs at depository institutions, to $250,000 from $100,000.

---

1. Public Law 110-343, 122 Stat. 3765 (Oct. 3, 2008).

THE FED'S LENDING AUTHORITY: PROVIDING CREDIT TO DEPOSITORY INSTITUTIONS AND SOME NONBANKS

CREDIT FOR DEPOSITORY INSTITUTIONS

From its inception in 1913, the Federal Reserve has been authorized under a variety of statutes to provide credit to depository institutions. The authority most used for such lending is Section 10B of the Federal Reserve Act (FRA), which permits lending during both normal and crisis times.[2]

One important requirement under Section 10B is that the credit be "secured to the satisfaction of the [lending] Reserve Bank."[3] In their lending activities, Reserve Banks have traditionally relied on collateral pledged by the borrowing depository institution, typically a first-priority perfected security interest in collateral with a value equal to, or greater than, the amount of the credit.[4]

One of the first actions taken by the Fed in the late summer of 2007 was to encourage depository institutions to take advantage of its discount window to meet liquidity stresses and to make credit available for extended periods—up to 30 days rather than overnight.[5]

---

2. The provision that became Section 10B was added to the FRA in 1932. Before 1932, the Fed could lend to a bank by discounting certain types of notes held by the borrowing bank. See, for example, Sections 4(8), 13(2), and 13(6) of the FRA.

3. See 12 USC 347b. The Fed has always viewed the language and purpose of Section 10B as authorizing extensions of credit, not grants or capital injections. Section 10B refers to "advances," which are commonly defined as extensions of credit; establishes limitations on the duration of advances, which is characteristic of extensions of credit but not of grants or capital injections; and requires "security," a common feature of credit but not of grants or capital injections. The Fed's Board of Governors may set parameters for Reserve Bank lending, including requirements regarding the types and minimum amount of collateral. See 12 USC 347b(a). However, the Board has not set such requirements except at the recommendation of a Reserve Bank. It has generally left the Reserve Bank with discretion to determine when, whether, and how it will become secured.

4. Before making a loan to a depository institution, the Fed typically perfects its first priority by taking possession of the collateral or otherwise acting to perfect its security interest in the collateral (for example, by filing a financing statement).

5. See "FOMC Statement: The Federal Reserve Is Providing Liquidity to Facilitate the Orderly Functioning of Financial Markets," Board of Governors of the Federal Reserve System, Aug. 10, 2007, www.federalreserve.gov/newsevents/pressreleases /monetary20070810a.htm; and "Federal Reserve Board Discount Rate Action," Board of Governors of the Federal Reserve System, Aug.17, 2007, www.federalreserve

However, seeking credit from the Fed carries with it a level of stigma that discourages borrowing even when it is in the bank's best interests. Particularly during periods of stress, and especially during a crisis, depository institutions depend on appearing strong, to keep the confidence, and deposits, of their customers. They develop a heightened sensitivity that borrowing from the Fed will be viewed by investors, counterparties, and customers as a sign that the institution is desperate and unable to obtain funding from other sources.

To remove this stigma, the Fed's Board of Governors authorized the establishment of the Term Auction Facility (TAF) in December 2007 to provide credit to depository institutions. One feature of the TAF was an auction format for determining the interest rate on credit it extended.

The Fed relies on Section 14(d) of the FRA to set its rate. That section authorizes the Reserve Bank to establish a rate on a periodic basis, subject to review and determination of the Board.[6] Section 14(d) also sets a substantive requirement that the rate "be fixed with a view of accommodating commerce and business."[7]

Historically, the Fed set an interest rate for credit extensions using one of two methods—by establishing a specific numerical rate or by adopting a formula to calculate the rate.[8] The legal question raised by the TAF was whether the rate could be set by auction.

An auction provided an elegant way to meet the substantive requirement of accommodating business and commerce. TAF provided depository institutions with access to a specific amount of credit to help meet the liquidity

---

.gov/newsevents/pressreleases/monetary20070817a.htm. An advance under Section 10B may not have a term longer than four months unless it is secured by mortgages on one-to-four-family residences. 12 USC 347b. Advances under Section 10B are typically made on an overnight basis and may be extended or renewed each day with the agreement of the lending Reserve Bank if the depository institution remains able to repay the credit.

6. The attorney general decided in 1919 that the requirement that the Reserve Bank establish a rate "subject to review and determination of the Board" meant that the Board had the ultimate authority to determine the rate under Section 14(d). 32 Opinions of the United States Attorney General, no. 81 (1919). This allows the Board to ensure that uniform national rates are charged on Federal Reserve credit.
7. See 12 USC 357.
8. See, for example, 12 CFR 201.51 (primary and secondary credit set at a specific rate; seasonal credit rate set using a formula that averages the target interest rate of the Federal Open Market Committee [FOMC] and the rate paid on three-month certificates of deposit).

demands of their operations, including providing credit to businesses that would facilitate commerce. An auction provided a mechanism for setting the precise rate that would make that credit available to institutions most in need.

To satisfy the procedural requirement that the Reserve Bank set the rate, subject to review and determination of the Board, the Fed analogized to its long-standing practice of setting rates for seasonal credit by formula.[9] Seasonal credit from the Fed allows banks—typically community banks—to meet the fluctuating needs of farmers and vacation areas. Because seasonal credit is episodic and typically extended for several weeks, the rate was determined by applying a set formula—recommended by the Reserve Banks and approved by the Board—to various inputs when the credit was extended. It thus dispensed with the need to have the Reserve Bank recommend, and the Board approve, a specific rate for each credit when it was requested.

The TAF auction was functionally and substantively the same—the Reserve Banks recommended that the rate be set at a specific minimum level subject to a higher rate set through an auction that had certain characteristics and inputs. Thus, the Reserve Banks recommended using a defined procedure that would lead to a specific rate at the time credit was extended. The Board approved this approach, fulfilling the procedural requirements of Section 14(d).[10]

EMERGENCY CREDIT FOR NONDEPOSITORY INSTITUTIONS

An important constraint in Section 10B is that it authorizes the Reserve Banks to extend credit only to a certain kind of borrower, the depository institution. Other constraints in the FRA (most notably, Section 23A) significantly limit the ability of a depository institution to pass on funds it borrows to its affiliates.[11] Thus, Section 10B could not be used to lend to a depository institution affiliated with a nonbanking financial firm with the expectation that the depository institution would "on-lend" a significant amount of those funds to its

---

9. See 12 CFR 201.51.
10. See "Federal Reserve and Other Central Banks Announce Measures Designed to Address Elevated Pressures in Short-Term Funding Markets," Board of Governors of the Federal Reserve System, Dec. 12, 2007, www.federalreserve.gov/newsevents /pressreleases/monetary20071212a.htm; see also minutes of the meeting of the Board of Governors, Board of Governors of the Federal Reserve System, Jan. 21, 2008, www .federalreserve.gov/newsevents/pressreleases/files/monetary20080226a1.pdf.
11. See 12 USC 371c.

affiliate. Consequently, lending by a Reserve Bank to a nonbanking firm (like Bear Stearns or AIG) or to a nonbank affiliate of a depository institution (such as the securities affiliate of Citibank or the nonbank holding company Bank of America) may be done effectively only by using the emergency lending authority provided in Section 13(3).

During the crisis, Section 13(3) authorized the Fed to extend credit to any individual, partnership, or corporation under certain specified conditions.[12] These conditions included that at least five members of the seven-member Board determine that circumstances are "unusual and exigent" and authorize the credit, and that the credit be "endorsed or otherwise secured to the satisfaction of the [lending] Reserve Bank."[13]

Before 2008, the Fed extended credit using its emergency authority only during the Great Depression.[14] During that period, it made approximately $1.5 million in loans to individuals, partnerships, and corporations secured by various types of assets. Among the borrowers were a vegetable farmer and a typewriter manufacturer.[15]

In 2008, the Fed started to extend emergency credit to a very different group of borrowers, and in amounts that would add up to hundreds of billions of dollars.

12. See 12 USC 343. The Fed is also authorized to lend to nondepository borrowers under Section 13(13) of the FRA, which allows an advance to any individual, partnership, or corporation secured by U.S. government or agency securities. 12 USC 347c.
13. See 12 USC 343. In 2008, Section 13(3) also required that the rate on the credit be set in accordance with Section 14(d) of the FRA, required the lending Reserve Bank "obtain evidence" that the borrower was "unable to secure adequate credit accommodations from other banking institutions," and provided that any credit extended under that section was subject to any limitations, restrictions, and regulations prescribed by the Board. 12 USC 343 (2008).
14. The Fed announced its willingness to use its emergency lending authority under Section 13(3) during the 1960s, when savings associations came under severe pressure from high interest rates at a time when they were prohibited by statute from paying high rates to attract deposits. However, the crisis passed and no loans were in fact extended by the Fed.
15. Howard H. Hackley, *Lending Function of the Federal Reserve Banks: A History* (Washington, D.C.: Board of Governors of the Federal Reserve System, May 1973), 130. See also Parinitha Sastry, "The Political Origins of Section 13(3) of the Federal Reserve Act," FRBNY Economic Policy Review, 27, citing Banking and Monetary Statistics, Board of Governors (1943), Table 88, Bills Discounted by Class of Paper, 340.

THE COLLAPSE OF BEAR STEARNS AND A MISSING BOARD GOVERNOR

The first extension of Section 13(3) emergency credit during the crisis came in March 2008, prompted by the rapid collapse of Bear Stearns, the smallest of Wall Street's Big Five investment firms.[16] There was no disagreement that the pressures experienced by the U.S. economy that month met the threshold requirement for invoking Section 13(3) that circumstances be unusual and exigent, and Bear had failed to find another banking firm willing to provide a credit lifeline.[17]

The novel legal issue raised by the initial Bear Stearns credit, extended on Friday, March 14, involved the requirement of approval by at least five members of the seven-member Board. At the time, the Board had two vacancies, and one of the five sitting members was traveling and unreachable.

When the Board met that Friday morning to ensure that Bear Stearns had sufficient liquidity to make it through the day and into the weekend, only four members were present in Washington or available by phone to vote. (The funding for Bear Stearns was originally conceived as a discount window loan to JPMorgan Chase Bank [JPMC Bank], which was a significant counterparty of Bear Stearns and had agreed to on-lend the funds to the firm but without recourse to itself. JPMC—the parent of JPMC Bank—ultimately acquired the firm.)[18]

16. The Fed announced that it would open a broad-based lending vehicle, the Term Securities Lending Facility (TSLF), several days before extending the Bear Stearns credit. Although the TSLF also relied on the authority provided in Section 13(3), it did not become operational until several weeks later.

17. The requirement of "unusual and exigent circumstances" was intended to ensure that this extraordinary lending authority was used only during emergencies. However, when Section 13(3) was enacted in 1932, it was not expected that the Fed would make a specific finding that the circumstances surrounding *each borrower* were "unusual and exigent," only that general economic circumstances met those requirements. Hackley, *Lending Function,* 128. Indeed, upon enactment in 1932, the congressional authors of the authority and the president declared to the Federal Reserve that economic circumstances at the time were unusual and exigent, and the president urged the Fed to invoke its new authority immediately and begin extending credit widely. See Letter from President Herbert H. Hoover to Governor Eugene Meyer, quoted in Federal Reserve Board minutes, July 26, 1932; see also Sastry, "Political Origins of Section 13(3)," footnote 199.

18. This type of on-lending arrangement ordinarily might not require invoking Section 13(3) because the credit being extended was to a bank, not a nonbank. However,

To authorize the loan with just four votes, the Fed relied on a provision of law added after the terrorist attacks on September 11, 2001, that allowed the Board to invoke Section 13(3) authority in the event that fewer than five members were in service or available at the time, so long as the vote by the Board was unanimous and the Board took certain other steps, including finding that immediate action was necessary.[19] The Board then voted 4–0 to provide funds to a nondepository institution for the first time since the 1930s.

A SECOND LEGAL ISSUE: TO "DISCOUNT" FOR ANY INDIVIDUAL, PARTNERSHIP, OR CORPORATION

A second legal issue in extending credit to a nonbank under Section 13(3) was whether the borrower could provide its own promissory note to receive the credit or had to provide a note involving a third party. The distinction was crucial: A promissory note would facilitate the process enormously.

At the time, Section 13(3) authorized the Reserve Banks to "discount for any individual, partnership, or corporation, notes, drafts and bills of exchange" (hereinafter, "notes") under certain circumstances. Section 10B, on the other hand, authorizes the Fed to "make advances" to depository institutions.

The Fed had long recognized that there was no legal distinction between an advance and a discount for purposes of Section 13(3). Both are extensions of credit.

When originally enacted, Section 13(3) authorized the Reserve Banks to "discount" only certain types of notes—specifically, notes "of the kinds . . . eligible for discount for member banks under other provisions of the [Federal Reserve] Act." In its initial authorization to Reserve Banks to exercise the lending authority under Section 13(3)—issued just five days after Congress enacted that authority—the Board recognized that the reference to notes "of the kinds . . . eligible for discount" had a practical and legal difference when the issuer of the note was considered.

The only notes that could be presented for discount under the other provisions of the FRA at the time Section 13(3) was enacted were those that, put simply,

---

in this case, all of the collateral posted as security was owned by Bear Stearns, and the loan would be made without recourse to JPMC Bank or any of its assets. For that reason, the Board determined that the loan was in principle to Bear Stearns and decided it must invoke Section 13(3).
19. See 12 USC 248(r).

were for agricultural, industrial, or commercial purposes.[20] A bank could not present its own promissory note for discount because its activities were not considered to be agricultural, industrial, or commercial. Thus, a bank could present for discount only the note of a third party that was engaged in agricultural, industrial, or commercial transactions. However, the Board reasoned that because a bank could present a third-party note for discount that had the required purpose, that same note was eligible for discount if presented by the third-party issuer itself under Section 13(3) because the third-party note was "of the kind" eligible for discount if presented by a bank.[21]

This recognition would turn out to be of critical practical and legal significance in making Section 13(3) a useful tool during emergencies. It made administration of lending under Section 13(3) as straightforward as accepting a promissory note from the nonbank individual, partnership, or corporation (IPC). It is a reading that was cemented with the repeal in 1991 of the requirement that notes be "of the kind" eligible for discount if presented by a bank.[22]

A THIRD ISSUE: ENDORSED OR OTHERWISE SECURED TO THE SATISFACTION OF THE RESERVE BANK

Another legal issue revolved around the provision that each loan extended under Section 13(3) must be endorsed or otherwise secured to the satisfaction of the lending Reserve Bank.[23]

---

20. This is often referred to as the "Real Bills Doctrine." For a detailed discussion of the history and purpose of the doctrine, see Hackley, *Lending Function*, 191.
21. See Federal Reserve Board circular dated July 26, 1932, Paragraph III, printed in 1932 Federal Reserve Bulletin 518, 519 (Aug. 1932). See also Hackley, *Lending Function*, 129; and Sastry, "Political Origins of Section 13(3)," 24.
22. In 1991, the requirement in Section 13(3) that notes be for an agricultural, industrial, or commercial purpose was repealed. This change, made in response to the 1987 stock market crash, was designed to allow the Fed to lend under Section 13(3) to securities broker-dealers and other IPCs that were not considered to be engaged in agricultural, industrial, or commercial transactions. Pub. L. 102-242, Section 473 (Dec. 19, 1991). See Remarks of Senator Chris Dodd, Congressional Record, 102nd Congress, 1st Session, p. S36131 (Nov. 27, 1991). This provision "give[s] the Federal Reserve flexibility to respond to instances in which the overall financial system threatens to collapse."
23. Originally, Section 13(3) required that credit be *both* endorsed *and* secured to the satisfaction of the lending Reserve Bank. Pub. L. 72-302, Section 210 (July 21, 1932). Congress amended that requirement in 1935 so that the note could be *either*

This provision imposes a limitation on Federal Reserve emergency credit, but with a fair degree of discretion. It authorizes credit that is both endorsed and secured—that is, credit that is with legal recourse to the borrower or a third-party endorser, with collateral to back up repayment. It also authorizes credit that is endorsed but not otherwise secured—for example, credit that is backed only by a third-party guarantee. And, importantly, it authorizes credit that is "otherwise secured" without an endorsement—that is, a secured loan that, if the borrower does not pay, leaves recourse to the pledged collateral.[24] This type of secured lending became one of the most important tools in the Fed's emergency lending arsenal.

But that raises the question, what level of security is enough?

The statute sets no specific level that must be obtained, instead leaving the determination to the Reserve Bank.[25] Indeed, the precursor of Section 13(3), which would have granted this emergency lending authority to the Reconstruction Finance Corporation, required that credit be "fully and adequately" secured, terms that do not appear in Section 13(3).

How, then, should the Reserve Bank exercise its discretion? Could the Fed extend credit with a level of security that it understood at the time would not be sufficient to provide for full repayment? In other words, could the Fed extend credit under Section 13(3) expecting to take a loss?

Every statute must be interpreted in harmony with its purpose, and the purpose of Section 13(3) (as exhibited both in its wording and in its legislative history) was to authorize the Fed to extend credit with the expectation of full repayment, not to make grants or inject capital.[26] Funds extended without the expectation of full repayment may be a credit in part, but they are a grant or

---

endorsed *or* secured. Pub. L. 74-305, Section 322 (Aug. 23, 1935); 12 USC 343. An endorsement works as a guarantee by the signer, such that if the instrument is not paid by the primary obligor, the endorser will take it up. It is, therefore, similar to collateral—both provide forms of recourse if the party extended credit does not repay.

24. Asset-based lending has long been recognized as an authorized activity for a bank. See, for example, OCC Letter from John E. Shockey, Deputy Chief Counsel, OCC (March 29, 1976); OCC Banking Circular 215; OCC Examining Circular 223; OCC Interpretive Letter 1117 (June 2009).

25. Section 10B also requires that all credit extended by the Fed to depository institutions under that section be "secured to the satisfaction of the [lending] Reserve Bank."

26. See Hackley, *Lending Function*, 129.

capital injection to the extent repayment is not reasonably expected—and are not consistent with the language or purpose of the section.

Moreover, when Congress granted the Fed lending authority under Section 13(3), the Fed was empowered to act as a bank—the central bank and lender of last resort.[27] And at that time (and since), the Fed was a regulator of banks. As a regulator, it has long criticized bank lending as unsafe and unsound if the loan is made without the expectation and reasonable belief that it would be fully repaid with interest. In the case of lending to a troubled firm during a time of economic stress, repayment depends largely on the amount and quality of the security backing the credit.

To be consistent with the purpose of the statute, the security required to satisfy the lending Reserve Bank needed to be at a level sufficient for the bank to reasonably believe it would be fully repaid.

TWO COMPLEMENTARY KEY INNOVATIONS: SPECIAL PURPOSE VEHICLES AND ASSET-BASED LENDING

In several cases, the Fed used special purpose vehicles (SPVs) to facilitate lending under Section 13(3). An SPV is a corporate entity established to own assets funded by debt without that debt becoming an obligation of the owner of the SPV if the SPV enters bankruptcy. SPVs turned out to be one of the most innovative tools used during the crisis.[28]

The Fed created one SPV, called Maiden Lane LLC, to facilitate the Bear Stearns loan and two more—Maiden Lane II LLC and Maiden Lane III LLC—to facilitate credit to AIG, the beleaguered finance and insurance giant.

In each case, JPMC and AIG provided independent capital to their respective SPV in the form of subordinated debt that functioned as the equity of the

---

27. Indeed, the Reserve Banks are chartered as banks and are empowered to engage in "the business of banking." 12 USC 341(Seventh). And Section 13(3) provides that the Fed may extend credit under that section only if it is not available from "*other* banking institutions" (emphasis added).

28. The Reserve Bank served the incidental role of establishing and administering the SPV. Conducting these duties was clearly a useful and valuable part of effectuating the lending transactions authorized under Section 13(3) and reflected use of the incidental powers conferred on the Reserve Banks by Section 4, paragraph four of the FRA. 12 USC 341 (Seventh).

SPV, and the Fed provided senior funding.[29] Like an equity investor, the subordinated debt holder wouldn't receive any repayment until the Fed was fully repaid.

In general, the use of an SPV to hold the assets allowed the Fed, as the managing member of the SPV, to better manage the collateral securing its loan, and thereby better ensure full repayment. Using SPVs avoided potential conflicts regarding the valuation of the assets and the timing of their sale that might have arisen had the collateral remained on the balance sheet of JPMC or AIG.

Importantly, the SPV also provided more transparency. SPVs allowed the Fed to make weekly reports on the collateral's value and the amount disposed during the previous week and to audit the collateral without interference. Indeed, financial statements for the SPVs used in the Fed's Section 13(3) lending were all fully audited by an independent outside accounting firm and made public along with the annual audited financial statements of the Federal Reserve System.[30]

The SPVs also allowed the Fed to maximize the advantage of asset-based lending, which was a new type of lending for the agency. While the Fed believed at the time it extended credit to each SPV that the value of the collateral was sufficient to repay the loan, that expected value was less than the precrisis value of the collateral. The Fed, as the central bank, could be patient and allow the collateral to recover its precrisis value. So the Fed negotiated—as a term of its senior loan—to receive a portion of the amount actually collected on the sale of the collateral in the event that amount exceeded what was needed to repay the Fed's loan and the investor's subordinated debt. This potential value would help compensate the Fed—and the taxpayer—for the risk of the credit and allow the taxpayer to share in a portion of the borrower's profit made possible by the Fed's loan. Indeed, that potential was realized, and the three SPVs collected billions of dollars in extra value for the taxpayer.

29. JPMC provided $1 billion in subordinated debt to Maiden Lane LLC. Similarly, AIG provided $1 billion in subordinated funding to Maiden Lane II LLC, and $5 billion in subordinated funding to Maiden Lane III LLC, with the Fed extending senior credit of about $28.8 billion to Maiden Lane LLC, $19.5 billion to Maiden Lane II LLC, and $24.3 billion to Maiden Lane III LLC.
30. See, for example, Federal Reserve System Monthly Report on Credit and Liquidity Programs and the Balance Sheet, June 2009, http://www.federalreserve.gov /monetarypolicy/files/monthlyclbsreport200906.pdf.

Although valuable innovations, SPVs and asset-based lending were not used in all of the Fed's emergency lending transactions. For example, as already noted, the Fed extended credit to depository institutions through its discount window and made other credit available to AIG and Bear Stearns directly, fully secured by collateral owned by the borrowers and retained on their balance sheets.

The availability of these different approaches adds flexibility that allows the Fed to "become secured" in various circumstances, and thereby protects the taxpayer in many types of emergencies.

THE EXCEPTION TO THE EXCEPTION: LEHMAN BROTHERS

The security requirement in Section 13(3) was central in every lending decision made by the Fed, but it was no more consequential than in the case of Lehman Brothers.

Going into the weekend of September 13–14, 2008, Barclays, a British banking organization, indicated an interest in acquiring Lehman, the fourth-largest U.S. investment firm. Had Barclays decided to acquire Lehman on that Sunday, it would have needed time to finalize documentation and obtain regulatory and shareholder approvals. To ensure that creditors did not continue their run on Lehman during that period, an open-ended guarantee of Lehman's obligations was needed, like the one provided by JPMC when it acquired Bear Stearns. But on that Sunday, Barclays said it could not issue that type of guarantee without a shareholder vote, which would produce a substantial delay and introduce uncertainty about whether Barclays could finalize the acquisition.

The question became whether the Fed could use its Section 13(3) authority to provide an open-ended guarantee of Lehman's trading obligations in the interim or, in the alternative, provide a loan to Lehman of sufficient size to allow it to continue to operate.

The answer was no. Lehman had no one willing to endorse credit extended by the Fed. Moreover, the unlimited nature of the guarantee to bridge the period until Barclays obtained the required approvals and the information from firms that had evaluated Lehman's financial statements during the weekend about the significant losses embedded in its assets (indicating far less value than Lehman's financial statements suggested) raised strong doubt whether Lehman had sufficient collateral to secure the full repayment of the size and type of credit it needed. Consequently, the Fed was not positioned to be secured to its satisfaction.

As a legal matter, this eliminated Section 13(3) as a useful tool for rescuing Lehman, and, after Barclays withdrew its interest for its own reasons, Lehman filed for bankruptcy protection on Monday, September 15. As noted, Section 13(3) authorizes the Fed to extend credit, not to make grants or provide capital.

Lehman's broker-dealer subsidiary presented a different matter. Although it was a major business of Lehman's, the broker-dealer represented less than half of Lehman's assets and held few of Lehman's troubled assets. Importantly, Lehman's broker-dealer needed a more limited amount of financing and had sufficient valuable assets to support borrowing from the Federal Reserve. This allowed the Federal Reserve to use its Section 13(3) authority to lend to Lehman's broker-dealer in the week after Lehman's announcement of its bankruptcy filing and before the acquisition of the broker-dealer by Barclays out of the Lehman bankruptcy.[31]

AIG: A LEGAL CHALLENGE

AIG required more attention and support from the Fed and Treasury than any other nonbank financial firm, and the transaction with AIG was the only one that produced a legal challenge. Circumstances were clearly unusual and exigent, and AIG faced collapse because other financial institutions and investors had determined, despite the encouragement of the Treasury and Federal Reserve, not to provide the funding AIG needed—two critical conditions for invoking Section 13(3). Importantly, unlike Lehman, AIG had substantial assets it could pledge to secure credit from the Federal Reserve, including shares of several large and viable insurance subsidiaries.

The Fed relied on Section 13(3) initially to extend a revolving line of credit to AIG and to provide additional credit using two SPVs, modeled after the SPV used for Bear Stearns. After TARP was enacted, Treasury provided capital to AIG by acquiring securities that the firm issued. Together, these actions prevented the firm's collapse and the systemic consequences.

The novel legal issue in the rescue was whether the FRA permitted the Fed to establish some of the specific loan terms. The Fed charged a penalty interest rate and a loan commitment fee on the revolving line of credit to AIG. Importantly,

---

31. This collateralized lending was not sufficient, however, to prevent Lehman—the parent company of the broker-dealer—from entering bankruptcy.

following the example of the private parties negotiating credit to AIG during the Lehman weekend, the Fed negotiated for AIG to provide consideration in the form of equity—a so-called equity kicker—for obtaining emergency credit from the Fed. Certain AIG shareholders challenged the Fed's authority to obtain some of these terms, in particular, to require AIG to provide equity as consideration for receiving the emergency credit. The challenge was unsuccessful.

Charging a penalty rate and noninterest compensation in connection with extending credit is a long-standing and common practice in banking and a proper exercise of the Fed's emergency lending authority under the FRA.[32] In previous cases, the Fed had required borrowers to pay noninterest compensation, in the form of fees and premiums, under both Sections 13(3) and 10B of the FRA. These forms of consideration were imposed to cover the expenses in extending credit, including the costs associated with negotiating and documenting the credit and valuing collateral as well as the potential costs of litigation.

The requirement that AIG provide convertible shares, amounting to approximately 79 percent of its outstanding common stock, as one of the conditions for the credit was negotiated to provide the American people with the upside potential that could result from the Fed's successful rescue of AIG—a potential that was, in fact, realized.[33] An equity kicker is a common feature of lending to a troubled debtor. It both compensates the lender for the extra risk of lending to a troubled borrower and postpones the lender's receipt of that value until a more benign time for the borrower. And it was a proper exercise of the authority granted to the Fed under the FRA, which imposes no limits on the types or amounts of interest or other consideration for lending that the Fed may charge.

In addition, Section 13(3) specifically provides that Reserve Bank lending under that section must conform to any "limitations, restrictions, and regulations as the Board . . . may prescribe." The FRA does not curb the discretion

---

32. See, for example, 12 CFR 7.4002(a) (authorizing national banks to impose noninterest fees and other charges in connection with their business activities); see also OCC Interpretive Letter 932 (Aug. 17, 2001), footnote 2 (charging noninterest fees and other premiums is inherent in the business of banking).
33. The Fed transferred these shares to the AIG Credit Facility Trust created for the benefit of Treasury. Treasury, which used TARP funds to provide capital to AIG, ultimately exchanged and sold these shares to receive repayment for those funds.

of the Board in setting those limitations, restrictions, and regulations. The Board was apprised that the Reserve Bank sought authorization to receive fair and appropriate compensation for credit it extended to AIG and made its authorization of the initial credit subject to the Reserve Bank's obtaining a form of equity as compensation.[34]

Moreover, Section 4 of the FRA authorizes the Reserve Banks "to exercise . . . such incidental powers as shall be necessary to carry on the business of banking" in connection with any authority granted by the FRA.[35] National banks (and many state banks) have long been permitted to receive an equity kicker as supplementary compensation for the risks of extending credit.[36] Charging noninterest fees and other forms of compensation that are typically collected by a bank extending a similar type of credit is clearly part of the business of banking and within the incidental powers granted by Section 4.

To interpret the FRA as permitting the Fed to receive only interest compensation for providing credit is to limit the central bank (and, by extension, the taxpayer) to what is less than fair and adequate compensation for taking on the extra risks and expenses of emergency lending.[37] This approach would also have the deleterious effect of rewarding the shareholders of the troubled debtor who did nothing to curtail the debtor's risk appetite.

GOING FORWARD

The credits extended by the Fed using Section 13(3) authority in the AIG case, like those extended in the case of Bear Stearns, were all fully repaid with interest.

34. See "Federal Reserve Board, with Full Support of the Treasury Department, Authorizes the Federal Reserve Bank of New York to Lend up to $85 Billion to American International Group (AIG)," Board of Governors of the Federal Reserve System, Sept. 16, 2008, www.federalreserve.gov/newsevents/pressreleases /other20080916a.htm.
35. 12 USC 341 (Seventh).
36. See, for example, 12 CFR 7.1006 (national banks are authorized by rule to accept warrants and other evidence of shares of profit, income, or earnings of a business in connection with lending); OCC Interpretive Letter 620 (July 15, 1992); OCC Interpretive Letter 421 (March 14, 1988); see also, for example, "Index of Activities and Investments Permissible for Illinois Banks and Their Subsidiaries," Illinois Department of Financial and Professional Regulation, Oct. 1998, www.idfpr.com /Banks/CBT/COMCL/POSB/BTSTBKPW.asp (regarding Illinois state banks).
37. See *Starr International Co., Inc.* v *United States,* No. 2015-5103, 2015-5133 (Federal Cir. 2017).

On the other hand, Section 13(3) was unavailable for extending credit to Lehman because the firm could not meet the statutory requirement of providing sufficient security or endorsement to satisfy the Fed that its loans would be fully repaid.

The fact that Bear Stearns and AIG were rescued and Lehman filed for bankruptcy has fed a debate about whether the Fed should have done more to rescue Lehman, particularly in light of the damage to the financial system that its failure caused.

Although it is true that the outcome for Lehman was stark and singular, unlike that of Bear Stearns and AIG, it is simply untrue that the Fed did not try to fashion a durable rescue. But the rescue had to be accomplished within the parameters fixed by statute, and because Lehman failed in mid-September, the statutory powers had to be evaluated before TARP existed. For the Fed, this meant reliance on Section 13(3), which authorized emergency lending only with the expectation of repayment.

Congress visited this debate in the Dodd-Frank Act and confirmed that the Fed should not take the risk of loss on credit to failing firms. To that end, Congress amended Section 13(3) to, among other things, require that collateral pledged to the Fed have a lendable value sufficient to protect taxpayers from losses, and prohibit the Fed from lending to failing firms to save them from insolvency or to take assets off their balance sheets. Rather, in future crises, it may extend emergency credit under Section 13(3) only through broad-based lending facilities designed to provide liquidity to the system as a whole.[38]

These new restrictions will prevent the Fed from extending credit as it did in the cases of Bear Stearns and AIG (and from designing ring-fencing programs for Citigroup and Bank of America). Instead, Dodd-Frank provides emergency liquidation authority that allows the government to manage the resolution of troubled financial firms.

---

38. Congress also amended Section 13(3) to require that the Treasury approve of such lending. In effect, the changes codified many aspects of the Fed's approach to extending credit during the crisis.

THE TREASURY'S EMERGENCY AUTHORITY: THE MONEY MARKET FUND GUARANTEE PROGRAM AND TARP

In the days following the failure of Lehman and the near failure of AIG, it became clear that policymakers needed additional tools to address the deepening crisis beyond the Fed's limited authority to extend credit.

USING THE EXCHANGE STABILIZATION FUND TO SUPPORT MONEY MARKET MUTUAL FUNDS

In mid-September 2008, Treasury did not have broad powers to address a financial crisis. But it did have control over the ESF, and it used that authority in an extraordinary and innovative way to stem the runs on money market mutual funds that threatened the financial system following Lehman's failure.

On September 19, the department unveiled its Temporary Guarantee Program for Money Market Funds. With this program, Treasury agreed to guarantee the share price of any publicly offered eligible money market mutual fund that agreed to participate in the program by purchasing assets from qualifying money market mutual funds at the amortized cost of the asset, plus accrued but unpaid interest. Each fund was required to pay the Treasury an insurance premium to participate.

The program would not have been successful without a credible backstop of funding. The only source of funds that Treasury could call on was the ESF. Using it to guarantee money market mutual funds was certainly novel and creative. Importantly, it was also well within the discretion of the secretary under Section 10 of the Gold Reserve Act.

The secretary reasoned that using the ESF to help stem runs on the money market industry was consistent with Congress's intent in creating it. The runs were threatening to spread the destabilizing stresses on the financial system beyond the United States. Forcing fire sales of assets by money funds to meet the demands of investors would cause a further deterioration of the U.S. economy and declines in the dollar's value.

The program was successful in stopping the industry's erosion. In October, while the program was beginning and prior to its extension by the secretary,[39]

39. The program was initially set to expire after three months but was extended until September 18, 2009.

Congress enacted legislation allowing ESF to continue to support the money fund guarantee.

At the same time, it enacted legislation prohibiting the secretary from using the ESF to provide a guarantee in the future. With this tool removed, and TARP now expired, Treasury is left with no emergency tools to address a future crisis.[40]

THE EMERGENCY ECONOMIC STABILIZATION ACT AND TARP

As delinquencies in residential mortgages increased, financial asset values continued to drop, and financial firms—both banks and nonbanks—had increasing difficulty raising capital to offset the losses from declining asset prices. It became apparent that the United States lacked certain emergency tools that were proving to be effective in other countries.

In particular, neither the Treasury nor the Federal Reserve had emergency authority to take action to stabilize asset prices or to inject capital into struggling but viable financial firms. Moreover, the resolution regime available for most nondepository institutions was bankruptcy, a court-administered process that focused on satisfying creditors without taking account of the systemic consequences of a firm's failure or the manner of its resolution.

To address these weaknesses, Congress, at the urging of the president, the Treasury, and the Federal Reserve, enacted EESA on October 3, 2008.[41] EESA, in turn, established the TARP, with potentially $700 billion available to purchase troubled financial assets.[42]

Throughout TARP's existence, Treasury developed programs designed to stabilize the financial system and alleviate the housing crisis. The most successful use of TARP injected much-needed capital into financial firms by acquiring equity stakes in the firms.

Although the wisdom of this approach was criticized by some in Congress, its legal basis was never in doubt.

Securities issued by qualifying financial firms are financial instruments. After EESA's passage, the Treasury secretary and the Fed chairman determined

---

40. See 12 USC 5236; Pub. L. 110-343, section 131 (Oct. 3, 2008); 122 Stat. 3797.
41. Public Law 110-343, 122 Stat. 3765 (Oct. 3, 2008).
42. See 12 USC 5211(a)(1). For a complete discussion of TARP's terms and conditions, see Chapter 14.

that purchases of such securities would be the most effective way to quickly promote stability by providing viable firms with capital to offset the devaluation of other assets they held.[43]

The authority to purchase troubled assets, including the capital of financial firms, to prevent disorderly failures and systemic shocks was one of the most effective tools during the crisis. It was also controversial because of the many policy issues it raised about the appropriate level of government involvement in distressed firms. It is an authority that remains in the arsenal of many foreign finance ministries and central banks. In the United States, that authority expired on October 3, 2010.

THE FEDERAL RESERVE'S CREATION OF BROAD-BASED LENDING FACILITIES

Before 2008, the Fed had provided emergency credit under Section 13(3) strictly on a firm-by-firm basis, making only a small number of loans to nondepository institutions. During the crisis, it was evident that lending to specific firms would not be sufficient to address the liquidity needs of the overall economy, which had grown more complex and interconnected since the 1930s.

The Fed responded in an innovative way: It created broad-based lending facilities that were designed to relieve pressures on liquidity felt by entire markets, not just by specific firms.[44]

The basic purpose of these facilities was the same as that of traditional emergency lending to specific borrowers—to provide liquidity to allow large numbers of borrowers to conduct sound transactions involving good assets whose value was uncertain because of financial turmoil. The innovation was that each

---

43. Under Section 3 of EESA, "troubled assets" includes "any other financial instrument that the Secretary, after consultation with the Chairman of the Board of Governors of the Federal Reserve System, determines the purchase of which is necessary to promote financial market stability. . . ." 12 USC 5202(9)(B). The purchase of securities issued by a financial institution is fully consistent with the factors the secretary is required to consider in acquiring "troubled assets." See 12 USC 5213(1) through (9).

44. These included the Primary Dealer Credit Facility (PDCF), Term Securities Lending Facility (TSLF), Asset-Backed Commercial Paper Money Market Mutual Fund Liquidity Facility (AMLF), Single-Tranche Term Repurchase Agreements, Commercial Paper Funding Facility (CPFF), Money Market Investor Funding Facility (MMIFF), and Term Asset-Backed Securities Loan Facility (TALF).

facility would allow borrowers to access central bank liquidity on the same terms and conditions so long as the funding was used to support a given market. In other words, the facility was not designed simply to provide liquidity to a single identified borrower to be used for the borrower's individual needs. Altogether, hundreds of borrowers participated in the broad-based facilities.

Because these facilities involved lending to nonbanks, they were based on the powers in Section 13(3).

The facilities raised a number of legal issues of first impression. Two related questions involved the finding of "unusual and exigent" circumstances[45] and the collection of evidence that borrowers were unable to secure adequate credit accommodations from other banking institutions.[46] In addition, as with the emergency loans to specific firms previously discussed, careful attention was paid to ensure that the borrower's promise to repay was secured to the satisfaction of the lending Reserve Bank.

The Fed approached the determination of "unusual and exigent" circumstances in the same way that Congress had in enacting Section 13(3). The required finding focused not on the borrower but on economic conditions and the role that a particular market played in the broader economy. The economy was experiencing unusual pressures and distress, greater than anything since the Depression, 75 years earlier. For each market targeted by a broad-based lending program, statistical evidence and observations of market conditions were gathered to show that it was contracting or experiencing extraordinary stresses.[47]

45. Each was authorized with the approval of a supermajority vote of the Board.
46. The rate on credit extended under each broad-based lending facility was set in accordance with Section 14(d) of the FRA, which, as noted above, requires that it be set "with a view to accommodating commerce and business." See 12 USC 357. This approach resulted in different rates for different facilities. For example, the rate most helpful for "accommodating commerce and business" with a facility designed to provide liquidity to money market funds, such as the AMLF, was one that would encourage lending to funds under stress and was not an appropriate rate to charge on a facility, like the TALF, that was intended to fund the asset-backed securities (ABS) market. Importantly, accommodating commerce and business during an emergency also allowed the Fed to establish rates that compensated it for the greater risks of lending in such a stressful economic period and were higher than would be the case during normal times, thereby discouraging borrowers from using the facilities as markets began to normalize.
47. For example, the AMLF and MMIFF were created to help stem runs on money market funds. Market evidence showed that these runs were threatening to

These statistics and anecdotes helped fulfill the requirement in Section 13(3) that the Reserve Bank "obtain evidence that [the borrowing] individual, partnership, or corporation is unable to secure adequate credit accommodations from other banking institutions." That requirement was designed to ensure that the Fed did not supplant private-sector lenders and become the lender of first resort.[48]

In the case of the broad-based facilities, evidence from participants in each targeted market indicated that credit was becoming increasingly difficult to obtain. Market data revealed that activity and liquidity were diminishing, rates and spreads were rising, and credit was either not available or less available to consumers and businesses. The Reserve Banks continued to monitor the markets throughout the life of each facility. As evidence accumulated that a particular market was becoming active and could be sustained without Fed liquidity support, a termination date was set for its facility.

As noted earlier, a central element of Section 13(3) is that credit be endorsed or otherwise secured to the satisfaction of the lending Reserve Bank.

In the case of the broad-based facilities, this requirement was generally met by having the borrower post collateral. The type of collateral was market specific. For example, collateral pledged under TALF consisted of securities backed by consumer credit-card receivables, auto loans, student loans, or small business loans.

Credit extended under CPFF, targeted to the commercial paper market, was secured in a new manner.

This market involves the issuance of highly rated short-term debt, known as commercial paper, by financial and nonfinancial companies to underwrite their lending activities or commercial operations.

CPFF was originally conceived as a vehicle that would be owned and funded by private investors or by the Treasury using TARP funds. The Treasury and/or

---

destabilize the value of assets held by the funds, reduce confidence in financial markets generally, and reduce the liquidity available to consumers and businesses that relied on the funds. TALF was created to provide liquidity to the ABS market, which had virtually ceased to function, resulting in sizable reductions in the availability of auto loans, student loans, and small business loans and similar securitized credits. CPFF was created because the commercial paper market was failing to supply credit to corporations, and the PDCF was a response to a dramatic reduction in the funding available in the triparty repo market. See Chapter 3.

48. See Hackley, *Lending Function,* 129.

investors would hold an equity or subordinated position and the vehicle would obtain credit from the Fed secured by the commercial paper held by the vehicle. However, it soon became apparent that the same stresses that were reducing liquidity in the commercial paper market were discouraging investors from funding a commercial paper vehicle, even with Fed liquidity, and the Treasury was moved to focus on other priorities.

The challenging question for CPFF was how to fulfill the "endorsed or otherwise secured" requirement. Commercial paper may be either secured or unsecured. Secured commercial paper was already supported by assets of the issuing corporation. This provided justification for its acquisition, since Section 13(3) authorized the discount of a secured note, backed by the collateral pledged by the issuer. In considering unsecured commercial paper, attorneys at the Fed focused on the fact that insurance was a form of endorsement. Indeed, credit insurance providing that the insurer will repay a debt in the event of the borrower's death, disability, or other specified event is a type of guarantee or endorsement. This concept led Fed lawyers and economists to explore the novel idea that CPFF could include a pool of assets and funds—an insurance pool—that would be available to cover losses on commercial paper that might default.

CPFF required all participants to pay fees to obtain funding for commercial paper. To create a pool of funds to protect against losses from defaults on unsecured paper, issuers of uncollateralized paper would be required to pay a special premium to CPFF. The size of the premium was tied to the amounts expected to be needed to cover any losses. The combined pool of fees paid by all participants that issued commercial paper and the special fees paid by issuers of unsecured paper would be available to absorb losses on the unsecured paper, mutualizing those losses much as an insurance fund would.

Thus, the non-asset-backed commercial paper acquired by CPFF was supported by the obligation of the commercial firm to repay, and the credit of the borrower was enhanced by the funds in the pool of premiums collected by CPFF. This enabled the lending Reserve Bank to conclude that the credit extended through CPFF was secured to its satisfaction.

CPFF and the other broad-based lending facilities were successful in restoring the functioning of their respective markets. When Congress repealed the Fed's authority to lend to specific IPCs under Section 13(3), it specifically retained the authority in that section to create this type of broad-based lending vehicle.

OTHER ACTIONS

A number of other actions were taken by the Fed, Treasury, and the FDIC to mitigate the crisis.

These included the Temporary Liquidity Guarantee Program (TLGP) implemented by the FDIC, swap lines with foreign central banks and Single-Tranche Term Repurchase Agreements established by the Fed, a number of TARP investment programs undertaken by the Treasury, and the ring-fencing facilities for Citigroup and Bank of America announced jointly by the Treasury, the FDIC, and the Fed.

Although each of these programs represented an important effort by the sponsoring agency, all of them (with the exception of TLGP) relied on relatively straightforward interpretations of the underlying legal authority.

TLGP relied on a novel review of the FDIC Act and merits its own discussion in Chapter 9.

The FDIC's authority to reinstitute a TLGP in a future crisis was significantly inhibited by Dodd-Frank, which prohibits the agency from establishing a debt guarantee program like TLGP without Congress's consent. The change essentially requires enactment of a new authorizing law.[49]

CONCLUSION

The legal authorities available to the Fed, Treasury, and the FDIC during the financial crisis shaped and constrained their responses. The authorities allowed the government to take some actions that had worked in the past. They also allowed the agencies to act in innovative ways that may not have been imagined by the authors of the empowering laws.

Policymakers were united in a view that everything "possible" should be done within the bounds of the law to mitigate the crisis (and their lawyers explored every avenue). Yet in certain situations, such as the collapse of Lehman, the law did not permit the government to take actions that it wanted to take.[50]

---

49. See sections 1104, 1105, 1106 of the Dodd-Frank Wall Street Reform and Consumer Protection Act of 2010, Pub. L 111-203 (July 21, 2010); 124 Stat. 1376.
50. For example, the government did not have authority to close or liquidate a nondepository institution in a manner that, unlike bankruptcy, allowed consideration of the impact of the resolution on financial stability.

The initial response to the crisis was to add supervisory tools—such as stress test requirements, enhanced prudential standards, swap margin requirements, and other authorities designed to improve the resiliency of the financial system—so that future crises could be avoided.

And the government also now has authority to resolve systemically important financial firms in a manner that provides funding backed by the banking industry (and not the taxpayer) and that empowers policymakers to maintain financial stability and limit damage to the economy. This authority, while untested and undoubtedly imperfect, puts a new tool in the crisis management toolbox that is an alternative to government lending or capital support.

At the same time, though, Congress imposed significant limitations on the emergency authorities used by the agencies during the last crisis, thereby making Congress more deeply responsible for developing a response to the next crisis. In the next crisis, it will be up to Congress to decide in real time during the frenzy of a crisis whether to make available some of the emergency tools that helped stem the last crisis, such as providing emergency credit to nondepository institutions outside of a broad-based market facility (as was done by the Fed), supporting the money market fund industry (as was done by Treasury), and establishing an industry-backed debt guarantee program (as was done by the FDIC). And Congress will again have to determine—in the midst of the crisis—whether to provide capital to the financial system on an emergency basis, as it did in enacting EESA.

This reservation of power may limit moral hazard and impose market discipline if Congress ensures that both large and small entities are exposed to failure during the next crisis. Still, narrow or limited emergency authority could prevent policymakers from acting quickly and effectively to help the broader economy, and result in more damage to a wider range of consumers and businesses.

An alternative approach would be to provide a wide and mighty arsenal of emergency powers subject to strong, workable governance requirements, ensuring that these tools are used only during an emergency and only to the extent necessary.

Limiting the authority to act during a financial crisis will not prevent the next crisis. But it will shape the government's response to that crisis—and fundamentally determine its cost to the nation.

| CHAPTER SIX |

Rescuing the Mortgage Giants

DAN JESTER, MATTHEW KABAKER,
JEREMIAH NORTON, AND LEE SACHS

INTRODUCTION

From the day Henry M. Paulson, Jr., was sworn in as Treasury secretary in July 2006, Fannie Mae and Freddie Mac were at the top of our list of policy priorities. We shared Secretary Paulson's concerns that these companies posed a major risk and might someday threaten the U.S. financial system and the broader economy.

Fannie Mae and Freddie Mac were known as government-sponsored enterprises (GSEs) because they were chartered by Congress, required to support the mortgage market, and called on to satisfy certain government housing policies. At the same time, they were publicly traded and managed for the benefit of their shareholders (who received significant profits over time) and their senior executives (who enjoyed Wall Street–level compensation). The government and taxpayers were not protected from the risk inherent in their business or compensated for the implicit obligation they had assumed.

The primary business of Fannie and Freddie was to buy mortgages that met defined criteria, which they then bundled into mortgage-backed securities

This chapter is a collaborative effort involving authors from two administrations—Dan Jester and Jeremiah Norton from the Bush administration, and Matt Kabaker and Lee Sachs from the Obama administration; not all the authors agree with all the views expressed in the text. It covers only the period up to December 2009, when the government-sponsored enterprise policies in response to the financial crisis were largely completed. The authors would like to recognize the many contributions from their colleagues throughout both administrations, without whom none of these policies would have been possible. In particular, the authors wish to acknowledge the efforts of two members of the Paulson Treasury, Kevin Fromer and David Nason, in helping to secure the GSE reform legislation.

(MBS) guaranteed by the GSEs and sold to investors. The mortgage companies also purchased and held their own portfolios of MBS, some that were guaranteed by the GSEs and others that were not.

All of this made the GSEs a dominant force in the secondary mortgage market. In 2008, they owned or guaranteed more than $5 trillion in residential mortgages and mortgage-backed securities, or almost half of the country's home loans. They purchased about 80 percent of all new home mortgages.[1] The GSEs were also among the biggest creditors and counterparties in the global capital markets. To finance their operations, they issued more than $1.7 trillion of debt[2]—much of it sold not only to U.S. investors but also to China, Japan, Russia, and Saudi Arabia, among other foreign governments. In the summer of 2008, foreign investors held more than $1 trillion in debt issued by the GSEs.[3]

Given the GSEs' congressional charter and government sponsorship, many investors, particularly foreign governments, viewed the GSE debt securities as if they were backed by the full faith and credit of the United States. As a consequence, the GSEs enjoyed an enormous funding advantage. They could borrow money at lower costs than similarly rated corporations without setting aside much capital to protect against losses, and they could use the proceeds to build an investment portfolio of MBS. Together, their investment portfolios totaled $1.5 trillion, adding significant interest rate and credit risk.

Fannie and Freddie were powerful institutions in Washington, with an unparalleled lobbying and political giving operation and roots that ran deep into communities across the nation. Despite the widely understood risk they posed, no legislation to reform the GSEs was able to obtain congressional approval.

But as housing prices declined and the economy weakened, the dangers of the GSEs became painfully evident. In 2007, Fannie and Freddie reported combined losses of more than $5 billion. In the first quarter of 2008, the companies reported a combined loss of more than $2 billion.

1. Henry M. Paulson, Jr., *On the Brink: Inside the Race to Stop the Collapse of the Global Financial System* (New York: Business Plus, Hachette Book Group, 2010), 3. As the housing market teetered, Fannie and Freddie's role would grow to fund three out of every four new mortgages. See U.S. Financial Crisis Inquiry Commission (FCIC), *The Financial Crisis Inquiry Report: Final Report of the National Commission on the Causes of the Financial and Economic Crisis in the United States* (2011), 312.
2. Timothy F. Geithner, *Stress Test: Reflections on Financial Crises* (New York: Crown Publishers, 2014), 169.
3. Paulson, *On the Brink,* 159.

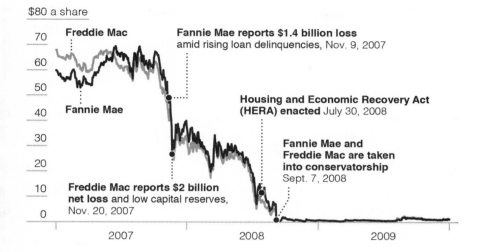

$80 a share

70 **Freddie Mac**

Fannie Mae reports $1.4 billion loss amid rising loan delinquencies, Nov. 9, 2007

60

50

40 **Fannie Mae**

Housing and Economic Recovery Act (HERA) enacted July 30, 2008

30

Fannie Mae and Freddie Mac are taken into conservatorship Sept. 7, 2008

20

10 **Freddie Mac reports $2 billion net loss** and low capital reserves, Nov. 20, 2007

0

2007　　　　2008　　　　2009

Figure 6.1 **Fannie Mae and Freddie Mac Stock Prices, 2007–2009**

Source: The Center for Research in Security Prices at Chicago Booth via Wharton Research Data Services (WRDS)

Investors began to lose confidence in both GSEs as losses ballooned. By the end of June 2008, the stock prices of both companies had declined more than 70 percent over the prior year. In the first two weeks of July, their share prices declined an additional 50 percent, reacting, in part, to a Wall Street research report that suggested they might need to raise as much as $75 billion in additional capital.

With one mortgage broker after another toppling like dominoes, Secretary Paulson believed strongly that we could not let the overall housing finance system collapse, especially given the underlying economic and market fragility. He decided to seek congressional approval for a new set of tools to prevent a destabilizing insolvency that could pose a threat not just to the housing market and the broader economy but also to the standing of the United States on the global stage and the status of the American dollar as the world's primary reserve currency.

SECURING THE LIFELINE

Rescuing Fannie Mae and Freddie Mac was always going to be a delicate operation. The GSEs themselves refused to acknowledge they were in trouble.

Although Fannie and Freddie had bipartisan support and long-standing ties to many Democrats on Capitol Hill, conservative Republicans were widely opposed to anything that smacked of a bailout. Even as we concluded that new powers were needed, we knew there were risks in approaching Congress. Secretary Paulson described the situation as the catch-22 of crisis policymaking: "There was always the chance by asking for these powers we would confirm just how fragile the GSEs were and spook investors," he wrote. "Then, if Congress failed to come through, the markets would implode."[4]

To lessen the risk of a failure, Secretary Paulson consulted with congressional leaders; the Federal Reserve; the GSEs' regulator, the Office of Federal Housing Enterprise Oversight (OFHEO); and the GSEs. With the groundwork laid, Secretary Paulson proposed a plan to Congress on July 13, 2008, that was designed to permit the GSEs to continue operating in support of the housing and mortgage markets, to ensure that the GSEs had adequate capital to continue their business, and to reduce systemic risk by strengthening regulation of the GSEs.[5]

The proposal had three key elements:

1. Providing Treasury authority to purchase GSE securities, including the ability to inject capital;
2. Creating a new regulator for the GSEs, with the power to place Fannie and Freddie in receivership, and giving the Fed a consultative role in setting new capital requirements and other prudential standards;
3. Providing a liquidity backstop for the GSEs by increasing their line of credit with the Treasury.

We knew this was a bold move, limiting the independence of the GSEs and requiring Congress to cede much of its power over Fannie and Freddie. We sought "standby authority" for the administration so that we could address liquidity problems, such as a failed auction of agency debt. We also insisted that we be given the ability to make equity investments. And instead of proposing a specific dollar amount, we characterized the authority as "unspeci-

---

4. Paulson, *On the Brink,* 147.
5. See "Paulson Announces GSE Initiatives," U.S. Department of the Treasury, July 13, 2008, https://www.treasury.gov/press-center/press-releases/Pages/hp1079.aspx.

fied," which would be constrained only by the government's debt limit.[6] The idea was that an effectively bottomless federal backstop would prevent investors from losing confidence in the GSEs, even if large losses continued.

Complicating matters, OFHEO had recently said that both Fannie and Freddie were adequately capitalized—calling into question whether our request for massive resources was necessary. There was concern at Treasury, however, that the GSEs were in serious jeopardy. Their financial performance was deteriorating, equity investors voted with their feet, the overall housing picture was bleak, and the GSEs' thin capital layers did not provide an adequate cushion to absorb the losses many were forecasting. Given this backdrop, putting a dollar cap on the request would have been counterproductive, creating its own issues. A specific request, for example, might have implied that we had identified the size of the capital hole, which we had not.

We recognized that it would be politically impossible to ask Congress for both an unlimited sum of money and an unlimited amount of time. So we set an expiration date on the authorities for the end of December 2009—a date chosen to give the next administration some breathing room to assess next steps.

But even asking for those authorities on a temporary basis was a stretch. Many lawmakers didn't believe that we needed these new powers; others were simply stunned by the sheer magnitude of the request. Even in their current state, Fannie and Freddie still held enough sway on Capitol Hill to add language to the bill requiring that the administration obtain the GSEs' prior consent for any government investment. This ultimately would become a serious constraint.

Still, Secretary Paulson insisted that the bigger and broader the government's firepower, the less likely it was to use it—and the less it would ultimately cost taxpayers. "If you have got a squirt gun in your pocket, you may have to take it out," he famously told the Senate Banking Committee. "If you have got a bazooka and people know you have got it, you may not have to take it out. . . . I just say that by having something that is unspecified, it will increase confidence. And by increasing confidence it will greatly reduce the likelihood it will ever be used."[7]

6. Paulson, *On the Brink,* 148.
7. Henry M. Paulson, Jr., "Recent Developments in U.S. Financial Markets and Responses to Them," Senate Committee on Banking, Housing, and Urban Affairs:

We also asked Congress to create a new and strengthened regulator to oversee the GSEs. OFHEO had limited authority and a reputation for lax oversight. The newly created Federal Housing Finance Agency (FHFA), while taking on the previous OFHEO staff, would have more flexibility to make judgments about the financial condition of the GSEs, just as prudential bank regulators were able to do. We also asked Congress to provide the FHFA with the ability to place the GSEs in receivership, giving it the power to facilitate the orderly resolution of a failed GSE, similar to how the Federal Deposit Insurance Corporation (FDIC) had long approached failed banks. Further, we believed permitting the Fed to act in a consultative role on capital standards would lead to a better assessment of the current capital position of the GSEs and over time lead to enhanced regulatory oversight with improved capital standards.

Our plan reflected an effort to balance a host of competing interests. We needed to cover the losses, but we sought to do so in a way that made clear to the markets that the government was fully committed to taking responsibility for and ownership of the GSE while not shocking the public into fearing that our investment would end up being a total loss to taxpayers.

A little more than two weeks after the proposal, following a series of intense negotiations, Congress approved the Housing and Economic Recovery Act (HERA) on July 30. It was, as Secretary Paulson noted, "the most expansive power to commit funds ever given to a Treasury secretary."[8]

ASSESSING THE FINANCIAL CONDITION OF THE GSEs

As soon as the legislation passed, we pulled together a "due diligence" team from across the government, led by a handful of banking examiners from the Fed working in close collaboration with colleagues from the Office of the Comptroller of the Currency (OCC) and the FDIC. None of these regulatory agencies had previously been responsible for GSE oversight or had access to the GSEs' internal records. Having been designated a "consultative" regulator, the Fed for the first time gained the same access to the information that Fannie and Freddie provided to their primary supervisor, now the FHFA. We also retained Morgan Stanley to provide an independent review and, together with

---

July 15, 2008, transcript, 19, https://www.govinfo.gov/content/pkg/CHRG
-110shrg50410/pdf/CHRG-110shrg50410.pdf.
8. Paulson, *On the Brink*, 155.

our outside counsel, Wachtell, Lipton, Rosen & Katz, offer advice on capital alternatives. The team's first task was to estimate the potential losses of the GSEs relative to their capital positions.

By law, the FHFA was confined to basing its capital adequacy determination on whether the GSEs held the minimum capital required by statute. Congress required that the GSEs hold capital equal to 2.5 percent of their balance sheet assets and 0.45 percent of off-balance-sheet guarantees, much less than the capital that banking regulators required of commercial banks. The Fed examiners were free to assess whether an institution was, or could be, operating in an unsafe or unsound manner. In reaching that determination, the Fed could take into account a GSE's current or likely future financial condition as opposed to analysis based on more dated financial and regulatory reporting.

Throughout August, the banking regulators and their mortgage experts analyzed the GSEs' mortgage holdings and guarantees to determine estimates of potential future losses. The findings were more than troubling. The Fed found that the GSEs were significantly "under-reserved" and that the combined losses of Fannie and Freddie could total between $60 billion and $70 billion,[9] suggesting that both companies were already insolvent. The OCC also found "insufficient reserves for future losses and identified significant problems in credit and risk management."[10] Additionally, a significant portion of their regulatory capital was in the form of deferred tax assets, which traditional banking regulators limit for measuring capital adequacy.[11] The analysis raised significant concerns about the viability of the GSEs as freestanding businesses; we were concerned about risking taxpayer funds in shareholder-owned companies with such dire prospects ahead.

Nonetheless, executives at Fannie and Freddie continued to tell Treasury that they were adequately capitalized and could manage through the housing downturn without breaching their required capital levels. Their loss projections were more favorable than our cross-agency team's findings in part because they had not considered the prospect of a sharp, nationwide decline in housing

9. Tim Clark (former senior adviser, Federal Reserve Board, Division of Banking Supervision and Regulation), interview with Eric Dash, April 2018.
10. FCIC, *Financial Crisis Inquiry Report*, 317.
11. W. Scott Frame, Andreas Fuster, Joseph Tracy, and James Vickery, "The Rescue of Fannie Mae and Freddie Mac," Federal Reserve Bank of New York staff reports, March 2015, 11, http://som.yale.edu/sites/default/files/Frame_W_Scott_et_al_The _Rescue_of_Fannie_Mae_and_Freddie_Mac.pdf.

prices. Tellingly, each time the GSEs' executives came in for a meeting, their prior worst-case loss projections turned into the next presentation's best-case scenario. Right up to the moment they were placed into conservatorship, both GSEs maintained that they were adequately capitalized.[12]

While maintaining that their finances were still sound, Fannie's management asked for a significant government investment to boost confidence and encourage investors to come off the sidelines with fresh capital. Given our assessment of their capital position, we viewed their idea as unworkable.

Based on the magnitude of the GSEs' expected losses relative to their capital resources, we concluded that we could not invest in Fannie and Freddie in their current form while providing adequate protection for taxpayers. Indeed, given that the boards of the GSEs had a fiduciary duty to protect their shareholders, we doubted they would accept any serious deal. And we worried that protracted negotiations, which almost certainly would leak, would only cause further market distress. Accordingly, Secretary Paulson decided the only investment he could endorse would be to stabilize the GSEs following their entry into either receivership or conservatorship.

CONSERVATORSHIP OR RECEIVERSHIP?

HERA left the decision on how to handle an insolvent GSE to the director of the FHFA, not the Treasury secretary. And the FHFA could not place Fannie or Freddie into receivership or conservatorship unless it concluded that the GSEs were critically undercapitalized or operating in an unsafe and unsound manner. As part of HERA, Congress incorporated our request to grant the FHFA a new set of legal tools that empowered it to resolve the GSEs. This process, known as receivership, effectively called for the FHFA to take over the administration of the GSEs and liquidate their assets.

Receivership, however, was fraught with peril. Resolving a financial institution through receivership requires the government to affirm or reject various contracts—everything from the leases for office space to complex financial

12. As of the second quarter of 2018, the GSEs had required a government investment totaling $191 billion. See Federal Housing Finance Agency, "Quarterly Draws on Treasury Commitments to Fannie Mae and Freddie Mac per the Senior Preferred Stock Purchase Agreements," accessed April 30, 2019, https://www.fhfa.gov/datatools/downloads/documents/market-data/table_1.pdf.

derivatives—in a couple of days. Not only would it likely create precisely the kind of chaos we were trying to quell, but we also doubted we could execute such a plan in the time required without the full cooperation of the GSEs. Based on management's assertion that the GSEs had adequate capital, and their significant support on Capitol Hill, we had no expectation that they would voluntarily and confidentially work to develop a credible plan for receivership prior to a public announcement. We were also worried that receivership could leave us tied up in a morass of litigation. Our goal was to stabilize markets and build confidence, and we feared that the uncertainty of receivership would have the opposite effect.

Moreover, the FHFA had a modest staff and no institutional experience managing a receivership. Fannie and Freddie would be two of the biggest receiverships of all time. Could the FHFA really do the job?

By contrast, conservatorship—effectively a government takeover—would allow things to pause and permit a more managed process. Treasury's commitment of capital would stabilize the GSEs, avoid a default on their debt, and permit them to keep operating, supporting the mortgage market.

Given the potential for chaos, our team moved swiftly to reach a resolution with the GSEs. We knew that markets were fragile and suspected more bad news was on the way from Lehman, Washington Mutual, and Wachovia. We feared that continued uncertainty over the status of the GSEs would lead to further difficulties for other financial institutions. We hoped announcing a solution for the GSEs would put us in the strongest possible position to deal with what lay ahead.

The GSEs could enter conservatorship either voluntarily or involuntarily by order of the FHFA. Our preference was to have the GSEs recognize the reality and volunteer. But we knew we had to build an airtight case for involuntary conservatorship so the GSEs would have no choice but to acquiesce.

As we were making our plans, we discovered a problem. On August 25, we learned that the FHFA's examiners had recently drafted and sent letters to Fannie and Freddie reviewing their second-quarter financial statements. They had concluded that both companies had ample capital, and in fact, exceeded their regulatory capital. Still, the FHFA had an out: Its regulators could use their discretionary authority to downgrade that assessment.

If we were to carry through with the conservatorship process, we would have to help the FHFA build a much stronger case. The FHFA examiners suggested arguing that the GSEs had employed unsafe and unsound practices. But we knew, and the Fed and OCC agreed, that any such case must be well supported by analysis.

Using more sophisticated models than the ones the FHFA employed, both our cross-agency team and Morgan Stanley identified significant weaknesses in the GSEs' capital positions. And unlike the FHFA's point-in-time analysis, the stress-test-like approach that our team relied on identified a range of potential losses that, once exposed, could contribute to further deterioration.[13] The findings were clear, and the Fed and OCC examiners who led the effort were persuasive. As a result of their analysis, the FHFA staff changed its assessment and concluded that the GSEs were indeed significantly under-capitalized.

STRUCTURING THE INVESTMENT

Heavily discounting managements' optimistic outlook, our team had already begun considering different ways to inject capital into the GSEs, even before receiving the estimated losses from the regulators.

Once we decided that we would invest only after Fannie and Freddie entered conservatorship, we then had to decide the form of investment. Even though the U.S. government had never explicitly guaranteed GSE debt, investors—including a significant number of foreign governments—purchased the securities with an expectation that the United States would stand behind the debt. So we knew that we would have to protect the senior debt holders to reduce systemic risk.

The next question was the treatment of subordinated debt. The subordinated debt had been introduced with the idea of increasing market discipline at the GSEs. If possible, we would have placed the government investment senior to the subordinated debt. Doing so, however, would have triggered a default on the senior debt. Committed to avoiding default on the senior debt, we had no choice but to protect the subordinated debt as well.

That meant that the government's investment would be junior to the debt but senior to the existing preferred and common stock. Concerned about any

13. Our approach essentially marked the first time that macro-based stress tests had been applied as a significant supervisory tool. Six months later, stress tests became a critical component of the Geithner Treasury's crisis response plan, when the Fed conducted a comprehensive assessment of the financial health of the nation's largest banking institutions.

potential systemic risk, we asked the banking agencies to assess the potential exposures of banks to the GSE preferred, and they concluded that only a limited number of small institutions had holdings that were significant relative to their capital. Placing the Treasury investment senior to the existing preferred and common was highly unpopular with investors, but we thought it was essential to protecting taxpayers.

CREATING THE PREFERRED STOCK PURCHASE AGREEMENT

The next question we faced was even thornier: Just how much money would we need to stabilize the GSEs? The ultimate losses were unknown, so we sought the flexibility to increase the size of the investment as needed. But we were constrained by the HERA legislation, which permitted us to invest only up until December 31, 2009.

We found the germ of a solution in the use of a "keepwell" agreement. In traditional corporate finance, a keepwell is an agreement between a parent company and a subsidiary in which the parent guarantees it will provide the required capital for the subsidiary.[14] We applied similar logic to the GSEs.

The keepwell, which became known as the preferred stock purchase agreement (PSPA), allowed us to maintain a positive net worth at the GSEs regardless of the future losses. In exchange for an initial payment from each GSE of $1 billion (in the form of preferred stock), the Treasury committed to maintain the GSEs' positive net worth. As losses mounted, the GSEs could ask for more capital from the government, and Treasury's preferred stock claim would increase accordingly. The benefit of this structure was that it met the requirements of HERA legislation to make the investment before our authority expired at the end of 2009, while providing the flexibility to increase future funding.

We also designed the preferred stock to be perpetual, meaning it did not have a stated maturity date. This provided further assurance that the GSEs would be able to continue their business without worrying about a looming maturity date for the preferred.

---

14. The discussion of Treasury's design of the keepwell agreement and eventual preferred stock purchase agreement for the GSEs is taken largely from Paulson, *On the Brink*, 167–68.

No one would care about the level of GSE capital if the GSEs were backed by a government promise to keep them solvent. The PSPAs effectively made explicit the previously implicit government guarantee of the GSEs and provided the reassurance long-term investors needed.

While the PSPAs were an elegant solution, we were concerned that some in Congress might complain about the appearance of circumventing lawmakers' intent. As it turned out, there was relatively little criticism.

In selecting the size limit of the PSPA commitment, we wanted a big number to eliminate any reasonable concern. The ultimate constraint was the debt ceiling, which had been increased by $800 billion. Initially we wanted to continue with the concept of the "unspecified" authority by not selecting a specific number. The Justice Department's Office of Legal Counsel, however, suggested that we would be on firmer ground if we set a cap. We settled on $100 billion per GSE, or $200 billion in total—a figure that was much larger than the estimated losses at the time. Importantly, we knew we were leaving the next administration with the flexibility to add to the investment if our estimates of losses and capital requirements were too low. The Obama administration later took advantage of this to double the size of the commitment.

OBTAINING OWNERSHIP IN THE GSEs

We set the dividend rate on the preferred based on a review of the market for similar securities. The preferred would pay a 10 percent cash dividend, except if a GSE failed to pay the required dividend in cash. In that case, dividends would accrue at 12 percent.

We were determined that Treasury would receive warrants to acquire common shares so that it would share in the upside if the GSEs were to return to profitability. If we could have made the taxpayer stake equivalent to 100 percent of the common shares, we would have. But that would have created an accounting issue. If the government were to have obtained an 80 percent or larger stake in the GSEs, it would have been required to consolidate the GSEs' financial results onto its own balance sheet. By acquiring warrants for 79.9 percent of total shares, just under that threshold, we avoided adding trillions of GSE debt and guarantees to the federal balance sheet. At the same time, Treasury worked with the IRS to obtain regulations that helped preserve tens of billions of dollars of future tax benefits for the GSEs.

REFORMING THE GSEs

Beyond the financial terms of our investment, we took a number of steps to begin reshaping the GSEs. Secretary Paulson had been adamant that if large sums of taxpayer money were to be spent, we would need to send a strong message of a fresh start by replacing the chief executives of these institutions. We were fortunate to find two excellent and well-qualified people to become new CEOs immediately.

To reduce the systemic risk, we limited the ability of the GSEs to increase their debt by more than 10 percent from their June 30, 2008, balances. Large debt balances had been used to finance the growth of their investment portfolios.

To maintain stability in the current mortgage market, we permitted the GSEs to increase their portfolios modestly until the end of 2009, up to $850 billion each. But to reduce systemic risk from that point on, we required the portfolios to be gradually reduced by 10 percent per year, largely through natural runoff, until they reached $250 billion.

Another important action was curbing GSE lobbying. From the 1990s on, Fannie and Freddie relied on an aggressive lobbying strategy to advance their corporate interests. They would regularly host events in the districts of influential lawmakers and court the affordable housing partners, and they built up a significant political action committee to contribute to campaigns. Now, with the companies in conservatorship and the government as the controlling investor, it was both unnecessary and inappropriate for the GSEs to lobby. Eliminating lobbying also had the effect of appeasing some of the critics of the deal.

There were other steps with less immediate financial impact but with significant policy implications. One was putting compensation restrictions on members of the senior management team, including limits on potential golden parachute payments. We also set up a separate program to help troubled homeowners, known as HOPE NOW. Given the government intervention, we believed that Fannie and Freddie needed to focus on their basic business first.

STABILIZING THE MORTGAGE MARKETS

To further support the availability of mortgage financing, we created a program for Treasury to purchase newly issued mortgage-backed securities

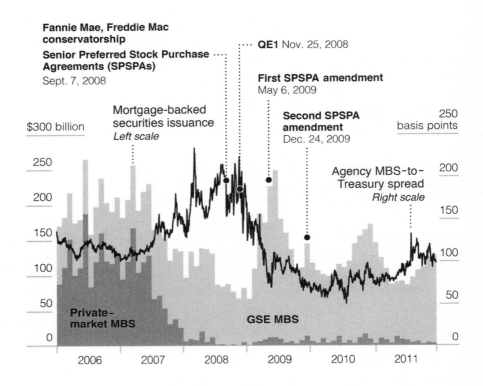

Figure 6.2 MBS Issuance and Agency MBS-to-Treasury Spread

Notes: (1) This is the spread between the 30-year Fannie Mae current coupon mortgage-backed security (MBS) and the ten-year Treasury note. (2) GSEs are government-sponsored enterprises.

Sources: MBS issuance: Securities Industry and Financial Markets Association; agency MBS spread: Bloomberg Finance L.P.; authors' calculations

guaranteed by the GSEs. The Treasury MBS purchase program launched in early September and almost immediately had a positive effect, helping send mortgage rates lower. Treasury purchases over time totaled approximately $225 billion. The Fed's quantitative easing program, initiated later, included the purchase of more than $1.25 trillion of GSE MBS between January 2009 and March 2010, providing additional support for the housing market.

On September 7, 2008, the FHFA placed the GSEs in conservatorship and Treasury announced its commitment to purchase preferred stock.

GSEs AND THE NEXT PHASE OF FINANCIAL CRISIS RESPONSE

From the perspective of those of us joining the Obama administration, the Paulson Treasury's conservatorship plan gave us breathing room to focus attention on the issues in the rest of the financial system. The preferred stock purchase agreements helped reassure investors, at least temporarily, that Fannie and Freddie would continue to have the capital they needed to operate safely. The debt purchases showed that the U.S. government believed in the GSE guarantee. And the credit facility provided additional reassurance that Fannie and Freddie would have access to the funds they needed.

We also quickly came to the same conclusion our predecessors reached. As much as we found the government takeover distasteful and the GSEs in desperate need of reform, it would be premature to start making sweeping changes. For one thing, GSE securities were embedded throughout the global financial system. At the same time, keeping the mortgage finance market functioning as smoothly as possible was a necessary element of our larger effort to revive the damaged economy.

The importance of the GSEs was only reinforced by the lack of alternative channels of mortgage finance. When President Barack Obama entered office, the private mortgage securitization market had been effectively closed for six months. And with investors concerned by a morass of litigation swirling around troubled mortgage bonds, there was little hope at the time for reviving it quickly. Nor could we expect the Federal Housing Administration to take on any more of the load than it was already bearing. Fannie and Freddie, as a result of their government support, were essentially "the only game in town."[15] If we did anything to undermine their stability, we would risk a further collapse in housing prices, which would drag the economy further into a downward spiral.

RAISING THE PSPA COMMITMENTS

For these reasons and more, we concluded that it would be unwise to start backing away from the GSEs, even as critics called for winding them down. Indeed, we would ultimately have to increase our support of the GSEs.

---

15. FCIC, *Financial Crisis Inquiry Report*, 311, citing interview with Henry M. Paulson, Jr.

By the end of the year, many Wall Street analysts were conducting their own stress tests on the potential losses at the major banks. Those of us on the Obama administration transition team were concerned Fannie and Freddie might capture their attention next. By our own projections, the results would be alarming. We feared that the GSEs might easily require more than the previous administration had committed. Just how much more, we asked ourselves, would be needed to maintain a well-functioning mortgage credit market?

Even though the Paulson Treasury had come up with an innovative way of supporting the GSEs, it capped that support at $100 billion for each GSE, suggesting that amount would be more than sufficient to cover losses. However, as the housing market continued to decline, it became clear that more support would be necessary.

We faced the same dilemma our predecessors did. How much capital should we commit? It had to be enough so that the GSEs would be stable and we wouldn't have to face the same question again and again. But if the number were too large, it might spook the markets into thinking that Fannie and Freddie were in even more dire shape than previously believed.

The result? In May 2009, we doubled the size of the PSPA commitment to $200 billion per GSE.

RAISING THE PORTFOLIO LIMITS

The other issue we had to address was what to do about the enormous mortgage bond investment portfolios that Fannie and Freddie had accumulated. Because of their implicit government guarantee, over time the GSEs had used their quasi-government status to take advantage of ultralow borrowing costs to purchase mortgage-backed securities—and then capture the spread income for their private shareholders. To critics of the GSEs, this was a far cry from supporting the American dream of homeownership; it was operating an investment fund funded by the full faith and credit of the taxpayer. If the Geithner Treasury was serious about reforming the GSEs, the argument went, it would need to force them to shrink these portfolios.

The trouble was that we once again faced Augustine's dilemma—the right answer for the future was the wrong answer for here and now. The portfolios needed to shrink, but not yet. Forcing Fannie and Freddie to reduce the size of their portfolios would likely have established two negative dynamics.

First, it would likely encourage a massive fire sale of mortgage assets at the precise time that we were rolling out program after program to avoid the type of downward pricing spiral it would have fueled. (That is why the Paulson Treasury calibrated its GSE mortgage portfolio reduction policy to the natural runoff schedule of the investments.)

Second, it might exacerbate the artificially forced selling that was already occurring in the market for nonperforming loans. In the ordinary course of making good on their guarantees of pools of mortgages, Fannie and Freddie would buy back the individual nonperforming loans from pools that they guaranteed and hold them in their mortgage investment portfolio. So as the losses in their guarantee book increased, Fannie and Freddie were forced to buy hundreds of billions of dollars of loans that became delinquent in the fall of 2008. Their portfolios—which were supposed to be shrinking—started to sharply increase for good reason. The increase was part of fulfilling their core mission as opposed to making investments in other securities for profit.

For these reasons, even though we agreed that the GSEs needed to reduce their investment portfolios over the medium term, we didn't think it was prudent to begin that process in the middle of a crisis. So, in May 2009, we lifted the cap on the portfolios by $100 billion each—a move that not only avoided a fire sale but also gave Fannie and Freddie some additional headroom to continue buying more of the distressed mortgages from their own mortgage security trusts.

RAISING THE PSPA COMMITMENTS—AGAIN

In the spring and summer of 2009, we began to see small signs of stabilization in the housing market and what some were calling "green shoots" of an economic recovery. The stress tests for the banks, along with other actions we had taken, had injected some much-needed confidence into the financial system. With interest rates low and the expansion of programs to encourage mortgage modifications, creditworthy borrowers were refinancing their home loans in droves.

With all of the focus on stress tests for the banks, it was only a matter of time before market participants and others began calling for similarly rigorous analysis of the GSEs. We wanted to get ahead of that, so we asked our colleagues at both the FHFA and the Fed to conduct informal, nonpublic stress tests to evaluate the depth of the losses on Fannie's and Freddie's books. Just as we had for the banks a few months earlier, we wanted to get a better handle on the GSEs' ability to withstand a severe recession. Neither GSE fared well.

Wall Street, meanwhile, was offering up its own projections, and some predicted that Treasury might need more than the $200 billion that we had committed to each GSE.

With hundreds of thousands of foreclosures still in the pipeline and home prices still falling, our outlook on the housing market remained negative. And we were very concerned about what might happen to Fannie's and Freddie's finances if the economy were to fail to recover in 2010, leading to still more losses.

Confronted with the very real possibility that the GSEs might need even more capital, we were faced with a difficult, if now somewhat familiar, choice. We could seek to provide unlimited capital (but the politics of this choice were as bad as they were when we considered and dismissed it in May 2009 and when our predecessors had considered and dismissed it in 2008). Or we could try to increase the limits by a finite sum just before our authority ran out (but we would run the risk of choosing a number that ultimately proved inadequate to cover the eventual losses). So we settled on what we referred to as "doing unlimited without doing unlimited."

The concept was to increase the PSPA cap by the amount of any losses the GSEs incurred. That way, definitionally, the cushion inside the cap would be a permanently fixed number and the cap could essentially increase automatically as needed. Since there was no hard-set limit, it also avoided the risk of a front-page headline: "Obama Administration Increases Cap to $400 billion." Instead, "Obama Administration Changes Formula" was a less newsworthy event.

The formula we envisioned was straightforward. Our $200 billion would increase by the amount of the net loss going forward. For example, if the GSEs lost another $10 billion on top of the $200 billion of capital we had already committed, the limit would increase to $210 billion and the draw would go up by $10 billion. There would always be enough money.

Secretary Geithner was reluctant to go that far, and he was concerned that it would not pass muster with Congress. So he advised us to put a stop date after which the mechanism would terminate, and whatever cap was in place at that date would be the permanent cap.

This seemed a sensible approach. What's more, if Fannie and Freddie were going to suffer additional losses, they would probably be front loaded because the GSEs are forced to set aside additional money in reserve if they believe they face a credible pattern of losses.

As a result, any capital needs were most likely going to come earlier rather than later, giving us confidence that we could give our "formulaic increase" device an end date of December 31, 2012. After that, the PSPAs would no longer be allowed to grow.

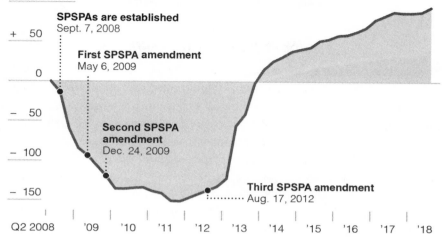

+$100 billion

SPSPAs are established
Sept. 7, 2008

First SPSPA amendment
May 6, 2009

Second SPSPA amendment
Dec. 24, 2009

Third SPSPA amendment
Aug. 17, 2012

Q2 2008 '09 '10 '11 '12 '13 '14 '15 '16 '17 '18

Figure 6.3 **Net Capital Flows from the Senior Preferred Stock Purchase Agreements**

Note: Net capital flows equal paid dividends minus capital draws under the SPSPAs for Fannie Mae and Freddie Mac.

Sources: Federal Housing Finance Agency; authors' calculations

We announced the amendment on Christmas Eve 2009, drawing little public attention. It was the one action most incongruous with all the steps we had taken to wind down the government's direct involvement in the financial sector that year. We had allowed healthier banks to start repaying their TARP funds. We were withdrawing our federal support from the liquidity that helped resuscitate important markets. Yet we were ratcheting up our involvement with the GSEs even as we vowed to wind them down.

We were convinced that it was critical to provide Fannie and Freddie with a taxpayer lifeline during the crisis. And ultimately, we thought, Congress would figure out a way to do comprehensive housing finance reform within the next three years. (In 2011, in fact, we put out a white paper outlining several options.)[16] As of this writing, Fannie Mae and Freddie Mac remain under conservatorship.

16. U.S. Department of the Treasury and U.S. Department of Housing and Urban Development, "Reforming America's Housing Finance Market: A Report to

LESSONS AND ASSESSMENT

Lesson 1:
The GSE structure was highly flawed.

The combination of a public mission with private ownership and implied government support proved toxic. The GSE guarantee was not explicit, priced, regulated, or structured in any meaningful way. Compare the original GSE implicit guarantee with a similar liability guarantee for the banking system: deposit insurance. In that case, the guarantee is well structured, explicit, priced, and regulated by an independent body. As a result of the poor design of the GSE guarantee, it became necessary at an early stage of the crisis to make the implicit guarantee explicit.

The regulatory supervision and capital standards for the GSEs were also wholly inadequate. Capital rules for financial intermediaries should be divorced from political economy and enforced by strong, independent regulatory agencies.

Lesson 2:
Maintaining the GSEs was a critical element of the crisis response.

Treasury's investment in, and commitment to, the GSEs following their conservatorship played a vital role in addressing and reducing the potential impact of the crisis. The series of actions by both administrations fulfilled their primary mission: avoiding a destabilizing failure of the GSEs and supporting the shaky housing finance market.

But they accomplished even more. Unheralded by comparison with so many other crisis-era moves, these actions also eased the path to recovery. Most homeowners never realized it, but preserving Fannie's and Freddie's operational capabilities permitted credit to continue flowing into the mortgage market, helping to stop the downward cycle in home prices and contributing to the slow but steady economic recovery.

Although profit was not the motive for the investment, and should not be the sole or primary basis for evaluating the Treasury's actions, the government

---

Congress," Feb. 2011, https://www.treasury.gov/initiatives/Documents /Reforming%20America%27s%20Housing%20Finance%20Market.pdf.

has received dividends in excess of the funds it invested. Over the past decade, Fannie and Freddie have paid total cumulative dividends of more than $285 billion compared with an aggregate investment of $191 billion under the PSPAs.[17] The positive budget impact may be a significant reason that Congress has allowed the GSEs to survive in their current form.

Lesson 3:
Conservatorship can be an effective tool in a crisis.

While conservatorship is not the best choice in all situations, it was the most effective tool here. Under the circumstances in September 2008, pursuing a receivership would not have met the policy goals of reducing systemic risk, maintaining mortgage availability, and protecting the taxpayer.

Conservatorship, on the other hand, permitted a time-out to allow the GSEs to continue guaranteeing mortgages and supporting housing finance while providing clarity of governance and duties for the board of directors and the management team. The conservatorship itself was not a permanent solution, but it eliminated the immediate systemic threat posed by the potential failures of the GSEs. The ability to execute the conservatorship depended on the substantial funding authorization obtained from Congress.

Institutionally, compared with bank holding companies as they existed before the crisis, the GSEs were also better candidates for conservatorship. They had a relatively simple operational model and a less complicated liability structure that was unlikely to deteriorate substantially under a prolonged period of government control.

17. Tabulated using the standard calculation dividends from PSPAs less draws under the PSPAs. See FHFA, "Dividends on Enterprise Draws from Treasury," https://www .fhfa.gov/DataTools/Downloads/Documents/Market-Data/Table_2.pdf; FHFA, "Quarterly Draws on Treasury Commitments to Fannie Mae and Freddie Mac per the Senior Preferred Stock Purchase Agreements," https://www.fhfa.gov/DataTools /Downloads/Documents/Market-Data/Table_1.pdf; Note: This number does not include the profit from selling the GSE MBS portfolio ($25 billion). See "Treasury Completes Wind Down of Mortgage-Backed Securities Investment, Generates $25 Billion Positive Return for Taxpayers," press release, U.S. Department of the Treasury, March 19, 2012, https://www.treasury.gov/press-center/press-releases /Pages/tg1453.aspx.

Lesson 4:
Conservatorship was not designed as a GSE reform plan.

Our primary goal was to avoid a failure of the GSEs and thus a further collapse in the housing market and the financial system. We were trying to prevent a disaster—not design a reform package. Indeed, our plans intentionally allowed the GSEs to continue to function while Congress settled on a long-term plan.

Given that the GSEs remain under what was supposed to be a temporary conservatorship a decade later, it is tempting to ask whether we should have designed a mechanism to force an ultimate resolution of their status. We believed then, and continue to believe today, that this could well have destabilized markets by creating ongoing doubt over how the situation would be resolved against a looming deadline. So while we view the overhaul of the GSEs as important to the health of the housing market and the economy, we remain convinced that the steps we took were the right ones under the circumstances.

CHAPTER SEVEN

Money Market Funds

Collapse, Run, and Guarantee

STEVEN M. SHAFRAN

SETTING THE STAGE

On the night of Sunday, September 14, 2008, word leaked that the rescue of Lehman Brothers had failed and that a bankruptcy filing was inevitable. The fallout would turn out to be vast, posing a systemic risk to the financial system. Caught up in the maelstrom was a part of the financial industry otherwise thought to be healthy: the money market fund complex. The Reserve Primary Fund, the oldest money market fund in existence, with nearly $63 billion in assets, held approximately $785 million of Lehman commercial paper, or about 1.2 percent of its net assets.[1] Commercial paper is a short-term unsecured obligation of the borrower, and the Lehman paper would, in all likelihood, be worth much less than par in the event of a bankruptcy. In the wake of the Lehman news, the management of the Reserve Primary Fund started facing substantial redemption requests on Monday morning. Despite the almost certain losses they were going to take on the Lehman investment, they let those redeeming investors out at par value of $1 a share. They didn't want to admit that their shares were going to "break the buck," which is industry

David Nason, who served in the Treasury Department as assistant secretary for financial institutions, provided critical assistance in the design and implementation of the money market fund guarantee and contributed to this chapter.

1. That summer, as other funds were unloading Lehman's commercial paper, the Reserve Primary Fund was adding to its position, Timothy F. Geithner wrote in his memoir, *Stress Test: Reflections on Financial Crises* (New York: Crown Publishers, 2014).

parlance for falling below the $1 par value that investors expect money market funds to maintain.

On Monday morning, the commercial paper new issuance market also began to seize up. In the absence of better information, investors (mostly money market funds) did not want to commit to buying newly issued paper. That afternoon, the chief executive of General Electric told Treasury secretary Henry M. Paulson, Jr., that GE was having trouble funding itself.[2]

The next morning, the run at the Reserve Primary Fund accelerated. The panic started to spread to other money market funds, which began to face unusual and heavy redemption requests. By Tuesday afternoon, the Reserve Primary Fund announced that it could no longer redeem investors at $1 a share. It had broken the buck. On Monday and Tuesday, it had received redemption requests for more than $40 billion, and more than $10 billion of those requests had been honored on Monday. By allowing some investors out at par on Monday, it concentrated the Lehman loss onto the remaining investors who had not run for the doors fast enough.

This is the root of an investor panic. In the overnight cash market, no one is rewarded for patience, and many investors sell if there is uncertainty and do their homework later. Investors fled to safety. By Wednesday, full panic had set in. Paulson learned that Ken Wilson, a senior adviser working at Treasury, was getting calls from such money market fund managers as BlackRock, Bank of New York Mellon, and Northern Trust. The message was the same: They were all facing significant redemptions even though they did not have any bad Lehman paper. Between September 10 and October 1, $439 billion would be taken out of prime funds, which invested in high-rated commercial paper and other short-term obligations with credit risk, and $362 billion would move into government-only funds, which primarily invested in U.S. Treasuries and other government securities.[3]

As money market fund managers worried about redemptions, they began to hoard cash and stopped buying new-issue paper. The commercial paper market was grinding to a halt. Meanwhile, financial and industrial firms were

---

2. Henry M. Paulson, Jr., *On the Brink: Inside the Race to Stop the Collapse of the Global Financial System* (New York: Business Plus, Hachette Book Group, 2010), 172.
3. Ben S. Bernanke, *The Courage to Act: A Memoir of a Crisis and Its Aftermath* (New York: W.W. Norton, 2015), 293.

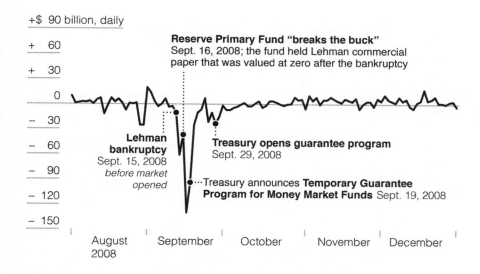

+$ 90 billion, daily

Reserve Primary Fund "breaks the buck"
Sept. 16, 2008; the fund held Lehman commercial
paper that was valued at zero after the bankruptcy

Lehman bankruptcy
Sept. 15, 2008
before market opened

Treasury opens guarantee program
Sept. 29, 2008

···Treasury announces **Temporary Guarantee Program for Money Market Funds** Sept. 19, 2008

August 2008 September October November December

Figure 7.1 **Prime Institutional Money Market Fund Flows**

Sources: iMoneyNet; author's calculations, based on Lawrence Schmidt, Allan Timmermann,
and Russ Wermers, "Runs on Money Market Mutual Funds," *American Economic Review*, 106 (9)
(2016): 2625–57

running low on cash and were not sure how they were going to fund their daily operations.

The public and political class had been watching the financial crisis unfold for at least a year. Two subprime credit funds managed by Bear Stearns had failed in July 2007. In August 2007, BNP Paribas in France surprised the market when it suspended fund redemptions at three of its liquid funds that managed $2.2 billion. As concerns mounted, money market funds dramatically withdrew from the asset-backed commercial paper market, leading to a drop of $400 billion in several weeks. Bear Stearns nearly failed in March 2008 and was acquired that month by JPMorgan Chase. Fannie Mae and Freddie Mac were nationalized in early September, and then came the failure of Lehman and American International Group (AIG) following one long weekend.

The money market fund collapse was different. It touched the common man and brought the crisis close to home for everyone, not just financiers and policymakers. Individuals' savings were at risk; nothing was more politically sensitive. Small companies that used money market funds for overnight cash to earn a little interest income were facing losses on the equivalent of money in the bank, money used to pay suppliers and make payroll.

Large corporations that lost access to the commercial paper market had similar problems. Without the cash provided from the regular sale of commercial paper to money market funds, they wouldn't be able to make vendor or employee payments.

In addition to the call from General Electric, Paulson was hearing from the chief executives of highly rated industrial and consumer products companies such as Coca-Cola and Colgate-Palmolive, which were also having trouble selling their paper. The chief executive of a triple-A-rated consumer products company warned him that it couldn't sell its commercial paper and was having severe liquidity problems.

In addition, banks and other financial institutions were losing access to a source of funds and, if called on, were required to provide liquidity to corporations with lines-of-credit facilities. Drawdowns on credit lines by corporations at this time would place extreme pressure on banks' balance sheets and could force them to liquidate assets to stay above minimum capital requirements. Distressed selling was going to lower prices for even the highest-quality assets and could quickly metastasize into a solvency problem for the banking system. A run on the money market funds could lead to a run on banks. The potential spillover damage was enormous.

This is an insider's account of why the federal government decided to backstop the entire money market fund industry and how we did it. We were conscious of the fact that the devil is in the details and that design choices would affect other markets. We needed to stop a panic in the short term, implement a program that would protect the system and taxpayers in the intermediate term, and plan for an exit that would allow the program to wind down in the longer term.

We were on the clock. We had just days to announce a program, a weekend to design it, and an additional week to stand it up. Trillions of dollars were at risk, and, as Ben S. Bernanke, chairman of the Federal Reserve, famously said, we were looking over the edge at the abyss.

MONEY MARKET FUNDS

Money market funds didn't always play such an important role in the nation's financial system. As recently as the 1970s, the industry barely existed. Consumers at the time faced a dearth of choices when it came to managing their cash. Banks could not pay interest on checking account deposits. Only savings and loans were allowed to pay interest, and those rates were set by regulators. Cash management accounts, or CMAs, hadn't been invented.

All that would change as deregulation arrived in the world of finance. One of the first benefits for the retail public investor was an ability to earn interest on cash accounts at market rates. Now, not only were bank regulators removing a prohibition but securities regulators were extending a seal of approval to a new invention: money market funds. The U.S. Securities and Exchange Commission (SEC) *required* funds to have a value of $1 per share every night, which they could report if the par value of their holdings was above $0.995 per share. What could be safer? By the fall of 2008, more than 30 million Americans had a money market fund account. The entire money market fund complex managed more than $3.5 trillion of cash for individuals and corporations. The funds were an important link between investors attracted to their low risk and high liquidity and banks and corporations that relied on them as a buyer of short-term debt. They had also become a critical source of dollar funding for European banks.

Their influence had only grown during the years before the financial crisis. By 2008, three major types of funds were available: *government funds*, which invested only in government debt like U.S. Treasuries and agency debt like securities issued by Fannie Mae and Freddie Mac; *prime funds*, like the Reserve Primary Fund, which mostly bought highly rated corporate securities; and *municipal funds* that invested in tax-exempt municipal bonds. What they all had in common were requirements set by the SEC to hold short-term securities, to have limited credit risk, and to be highly liquid.

Prime funds came into existence to meet investor demand for higher yields. These funds invested in paper other than simple U.S. government securities, and the Reserve Primary Fund was such a fund. It bought securities like highly rated commercial paper issued by industrial companies (for example, Coca-Cola) and nonbank finance companies (such as GE Capital), certificates of deposit issued by banks (both domestic and foreign), and asset-backed commercial paper (ABCP) from mortgage and finance companies, including ABCP by structured investment vehicles. Each of these issuers was highly dependent on regular access to the short-term funding markets to run their businesses and in turn was dependent on money market funds to buy the short-term paper. Although the prime funds could not invest in securities that did not have top ratings from the credit agencies, the securities nevertheless carried more risk and were less liquid than U.S. Treasuries and other securities that were backed, implicitly or explicitly, by the federal government. The requirements for highly rated securities and fixed net asset value (NAV) contributed to the appearance, particularly to retail investors, that prime funds were as low risk as government funds. Looking for higher returns, investors piled into prime funds like the Reserve Primary Fund. By the time of the crisis, the prime money market fund industry stood at $2.0 trillion in assets, and the government fund product was approximately $1.5 trillion in size. As Paulson put it, "The industry's setup was too good to be true. The idea that you could earn more than what the federal government paid for overnight liquidity and still have overnight liquidity made absolutely no sense."[4]

The deep connection among individuals, their savings, their government, and the money market fund complex that began in the 1970s is crucial to understanding why and how we did what we did in 2008 to protect this industry and its customers. To the public at large, and to many on Capitol Hill, the failure of Bear Stearns and Lehman Brothers could be thought of as Wall Street problems. When it appeared that the money market fund industry was facing panic and a run, the problems had arrived on Main Street. The politics of the crisis had changed.

INSIDE THE TREASURY

As the money market fund complex unraveled, we gathered inside the Treasury on Tuesday, September 16, and began to work on these problems. The formal assignment was to address liquidity problems in the cash markets. The real task was to arrest a panic.

Market intervention is never easy and is fraught with the potential for unintended consequences. Yet, intervention was exactly what we needed to do—even though we did not enter into government service to interfere with the private allocation of capital and investment. We needed to protect the financial system and the taxpayer, on the one hand, and intervene with expediency in a crisis, on the other. This is a necessary and difficult balancing act. The more expedient the solution, the greater the risk that the government would lose money and political support. The more structure embedded in the support, the more likely we would lose market impact.

Over the course of Tuesday and Wednesday, we considered many programs and ideas. From that list, several stood out as decent possibilities. They included

4. Paulson, *On the Brink,* 234.

proposing to the Fed that it open the discount window to money market funds; suggesting that the Fed allow commercial paper issuers to sell directly to the Fed; and creating an entity like the Federal Deposit Insurance Corporation (FDIC) for the money market fund industry. But these ideas were either too complex or too cumbersome to quickly stop the panic. Some of the potential solutions would have required the Federal Reserve to have a role, and it was tackling the problem with its own programs.[5]

Other ideas would have required us to obtain authorities, through legislation in Congress, that we did not have and, just as important, did not have the time to obtain. That left us with the most direct and impactful option available: using the Treasury-controlled Exchange Stabilization Fund to support a government guarantee of the money market funds.

On Thursday, during an all-hands call with senior leaders from Treasury, the Fed, and the Federal Reserve Bank of New York, Paulson let us know that he preferred a guarantee program. He told the team, "I want to get ahead of this panic." Our program had to be bold, simple in design, affordable to the system and taxpayer, effective, and within existing authorities. It needed to be credible to the man on the street, which we called the "*USA Today* test"; credible to Wall Street so that institutional investors would stop redeeming; and credible to the money market fund complex so that the fund managers would join and not fight.

STRUCTURING THE GUARANTEE

Once Paulson decided that the U.S. Treasury would provide a guarantee to the money market fund complex, we turned our attention to the details. At the most basic level, we knew that the power of the program would be in its simplicity. If we said that the federal government was providing a guarantee, and

---

5. The Fed announced a liquidity program called the Asset-Backed Commercial Paper Money Market Mutual Fund Liquidity Facility (AMLF) to support the short-term funding markets. See "Treasury Announces Guaranty Program for Money Market Funds," U.S. Department of the Treasury, Sept. 19, 2008, https://www.treasury.gov /press-center/press-releases/Pages/hp1147.aspx. Operationalized by the Federal Reserve Bank of Boston, the program lent to banks to help provide a market for the ABCP that money market funds were being forced to sell. (A more extended discussion of the program, along with another liquidity program from the Fed, the Commercial Paper Funding Facility, can be found in Chapter 3.)

the program was simple and credible, the panic would subside, the run would stop, and the likelihood of the guarantee ever being called on would be minimal.

We had to move quickly, before all the details were ironed out, but not until we knew we had the legal authority. Within 24 hours, our plan had gone to the White House and back. Once the White House approved, we went public. We made the announcement on Friday, September 19.

Standing between us and the desired simplicity of the guarantee program were several difficult realities that needed to be balanced. At the time, the money market fund industry had $3.5 trillion of assets and we had access to only $50 billion from the Treasury-controlled Exchange Stabilization Fund. (Congress has since taken away this authorized use of the fund.) How could we stretch that $50 billion of capital to credibly cover the entire money market fund complex?

We also grappled with the issue of fairness to the taxpayers. To address this concern, we decided that we needed to charge fund managers a fee to participate in the program. That required a work stream to determine what price would be appropriate. We wanted to design other features that would make sure benefits flowed to investors and not to the owners of the funds. We wanted to design something that would attract broad participation of the funds because it would be important to avoid stigma and adverse selection (where only the bad funds enroll). Always, in the back of our minds, we knew that if we added too many complicating factors, we would lose the power of simplicity. This was the design balancing act.

The actual "product" that we created over the next ten days was called the Temporary Guarantee Program for Money Market Funds.[6]

What follows is a discussion of seven design concepts that we considered as we sought to balance simplicity against our available pool of funds and the need to protect the taxpayer. Success for us meant that we got the balance right and that individual investors, corporate treasurers, and the fund managers would believe that the guarantee we created was credible.

1. *Cover losses and not assets.* Our first concern was stretching the $50 billion we had from the Exchange Stabilization Fund to cover a $3.5 tril-

---

6. The final policy documents can be reviewed at http://som.yale.edu/sites/default/files /files/Guarantee%20Agreement%2024Aug15%20v1.pdf.

lion industry. We needed to figure out how to make each $1 we had cover $70 of funds. While it would have been nice to place a blanket guarantee on the full $3.5 trillion, that would require a commitment that could be given only by Congress. In light of our limited resources, our first decision was to cover losses incurred by investors and not the full balance of any investor's account. The judgment of market participants was that the majority of money market fund assets were safe and money-good. The market value of Lehman's commercial paper had dropped to zero, but there wasn't a lot of similar paper in the system. Market participants that we spoke to did not believe that the money market funds were sitting on top of substantial credit problems. We were fighting a liquidity run, not a solvency problem. So, by designing a program that covered losses, we addressed the markets' need to know that someone was standing behind the system and that they would not lose money on safe assets. From our perspective, the Treasury's risk was limited to the ultimate shortfall an investor would have, not the full amount of the investment.

2. *Filing a claim should be a last resort.* We called this element of our program death insurance, as opposed to life insurance. The idea was that a fund could file for a claim under our guarantee program only if the owners of the fund were willing to close the fund and go out of business. We wanted to avoid anything that appeared to promote moral hazard. Over the more than 30 years that money market funds had been around, numerous fund parents had bailed out their own funds when they had losses and were facing the stigma of breaking the buck. In 1994, for example, sponsor firms saved about 50 funds[7] from breaking the buck because of a rout in the bond market.[8] These rescues had been done to avoid the reputational risk to the fund manager. Most money market funds were housed in large fund management firms, and the firms were keen to avoid reputational embarrassment. Historically, if a money market fund had a bad asset that was going to force a fund to break the buck, the parent would typically buy the troubled asset from the fund at par. That solved the credit problem for the fund, and the parent then

---

7. Eric Dash, "Rethinking Money Market Funds," *New York Times,* July 11, 2008, https://www.nytimes.com/2008/07/11/business/11fund.html.
8. In 2012, a study by the Federal Reserve Bank of Boston found that a sponsor firm had bailed out its ailing money market fund at least 21 times from 2007 to 2011.

worked out the troubled asset away from the daily requirement that all assets be worth par. Given this well-established history, we did not want the presence of our newly designed guarantee program to create a government-subsidized bailout for fund managers. We hoped that managers would continue to bail out their own funds to the extent they could. We believed that the death insurance strategy would decrease the use of the guarantee and create real negative outcomes for managers whose funds had bad assets. Not everyone agreed with this approach. It did "lessen" the power and simplicity of the guarantee, but we determined that this was a complication the market would accept.

3. *Cover investors and not the funds.* As part of the process of keeping the size of the government's risk down, we determined that while we would enter into the guarantee contract with the managers for each of their funds, the beneficiary would be the actual investors and not the fund itself. This provided us an opportunity to directly touch the beneficiary (the proverbial "man on the street") and not have the program appear to be a bailout of the funds themselves.

4. *Cover specific investors in specific funds on a specific date and for a specified amount.* We needed a clear understanding of the government's risk exposure. We required that every fund participating in the program supply us with a list of the individual investors in the fund and the amounts held by the investors on the day that the insurance policy went into effect. We decided to cover those investors for those amounts and nothing more. For example, if someone owned $1,000 of Fund A and that fund joined the insurance program, that investor was covered for any losses incurred on that holding. If the investor subsequently bought an additional $1,000 of the same fund, any losses on that additional investment were not covered. If the investor sold the original $1,000 investment and bought $1,000 in Fund B, even if Fund B was participating in the guarantee program, the new investment was not insured. Why did we do it this way? In addition to limiting risks, we wanted to limit any unintended consequences that could arise as a result of this program. We worried about people getting scared and moving from one fund to another, and about people taking funds from uninsured funds and moving them to those that were insured. In addition, we covered government-only funds as well as prime funds, a move that the money market fund industry supported even though government-only funds posed little risk. At the

time we were designing this, we had no idea what percentage of the funds out there would choose to participate. We believed that the approach we took would encourage more funds to participate, because those that didn't would be taking a chance with their investors' funds. Additionally, we believed that this incentive to join would ultimately make the whole system safer by encouraging broad participation. Finally, we were alerted to another issue by Sheila Bair, chairman of the Federal Deposit Insurance Corporation. If we made the guarantee too open-ended, she pointed out, it would encourage investors to move money from FDIC-insured deposits at banks (with limits, at the time, of $100,000 per account) to newly guaranteed money market funds. That would trigger a run on large deposits in the banking system. In the never-ending job of balancing the program, we came down on the side of being a little less bold and a little more controlled, with a view that we could always improve the program's scope and benefits if necessary.

5. *Pay out at the end and only if all other options have been exhausted.* The concept of death insurance meant that the only way a fund could apply for the benefits of the program was to go out of business. The actual mechanics of how a claim would be processed supported this concept, kept the Treasury's dollars at risk to a minimum, and are worth reviewing. Under the guarantee, if a fund was in a situation where its net asset value was less than 99.5 percent of par, that would technically mean that it had broken the buck, a "Triggering Event" under the guarantee program. The first line of defense was for the parent company to buy the problem assets to return the NAV to at least 99.5 percent, allowing the fund to meet its value and regulatory obligations. In the event that the parent would not or could not do so, then the fund management company could pursue protection under our guarantee program. The process we designed included the following steps: (1) within 24 hours of the Triggering Event, the fund managers had to notify the government and immediately halt any investor redemptions; (2) within five days, they needed to begin liquidating the fund and returning proceeds to all the investors; and (3) within not more than 30 days, they could make a claim to the government to cover any shortfalls. By way of example, assume a $1 billion fund had a Triggering Event and $900 million was owned by investors who were holders as of the day the program began. If the fund were wound down and liquidated for 97 percent of par, then all investors would get

97 cents per dollar invested. The insured investors would then receive an additional 3 cents from the government via the guarantee. In this case, the government would pay a total of $27 million to the underlying insured investors.

6. *Charge for insurance and structure pricing to reflect risk.* The decision to charge for the insurance was one of the more difficult and complicated judgments we made. We looked at three options: not charging at all, charging based on a forecasted expected loss, and charging what we thought the market could bear. The case for not charging was simple enough—by giving the guarantee away, we would encourage maximum enrollment in the program and would put maximum water on the fire. By doing it this way, we thought we would end the panic, end the run, and minimize the possibility of system loss. Sounds great, except it didn't feel right or fair. Our use of the Exchange Stabilization Fund money meant that while the U.S. taxpayers as a whole were shouldering risk, the universe of direct beneficiaries was narrower: people with deposits in money market funds and the managers who oversaw those funds. So, although the entire country was an indirect beneficiary of our moves, the charge-nothing option wasn't completely persuasive.

We decided we needed to go with one of the other options and charge something. The next step was to set a price. We took a top-down and bottom-up approach to the analysis. We asked for help from the New York Fed to prepare an expected-loss model that would forecast the losses we could expect the Treasury to incur as the provider of the guarantee. With only 24 hours to get something done, this was going to be a quick, high-level analysis. The other approach we considered was to look at profitability in the sector as a whole and charge something that would be meaningful as a percentage of the margins earned by most managers. We were concerned that if we charged too much, managers would be taking losses, and no one would enroll. Pricing was going to be an art; we would not be able to scientifically get to the "right" number. The key was to pick a number that would be as much as we could get to cover potential losses but not be so high that fund managers would push back. It should be in the range of what staff at the New York Fed was suggesting we needed to cover expected losses. And finally, we knew that this was a short-term program, so we thought we could err on the high side and that would motivate the industry to push to get rid of the program as soon as it was safe to do so. In the end, we settled on charging 1 basis point for three months of coverage, which works out to 4 basis points per year. At the time, we believed that industry profits ranged from 5 to 10 basis points per year on these products, so our fee was meaningful but affordable. It was also consistent with the analysis done at the Fed. In addition, for funds that had net asset values of 99.50 to 99.75 percent, we increased the fee to 1.5 basis points per quarter, or 6 basis points per year.

7. *Scrutinize participants.* Finally, we determined to do our best to keep bad actors out of the program and to exclude those who tried to participate but had "preexisting conditions" and had already broken the buck. This might go to the heart of the difference between an insurance program and a true bailout. We chose to specifically exclude from coverage any fund with a NAV of less than 99.50 percent of par. We wanted to protect investors (and the system) from a panic and run that looked as if it would cause a lot of damage. We did not want to cure losses that had already been sustained (because of credit mistakes) at the few funds that were already in trouble.

MAKING THE GUARANTEE WORK

As soon as Paulson communicated our intention to provide a guarantee, the job of selling the deal began.

Our job was to ensure maximum participation and avoid tainting participants. We needed all of the major players to agree to join the program. As we would do with the Troubled Assets Relief Program (TARP), we fought hard to avoid a situation where only the weak participated. That would be the kiss of death. Beyond the hard work and countless individual calls to money market fund industry chief executives that were required, the substance we sold relied on three basic design features. First, the fees we charged reflected industry economics and were palatable to participants. Second, we had a clear near-term program termination date of three months and an outside sunset date of 12 months. It was extremely important that everyone understand we were not looking to permanently reshape the industry; to deliver on that promise, the guarantee needed to go away by its terms. Finally, we had clear legal documents, with an open enrollment period and a firm deadline. We did not leave time for haggling and lobbyists seeking to influence the terms.

The program went live on Monday, September 29. Participation was greatest in the initial phase. At its height, 366 companies and 1,486 individual funds participated. Out of the funds holding $3.46 trillion of assets in the money market fund complex, more than $3.2 trillion, or approximately 93 percent of total assets, enrolled in the program and purchased insurance. The participation rate declined as liquidity returned to the system, money market funds held less risky paper, and fewer funds felt the need to guarantee their portfolios.

By most economic measures, the program was a success. From the day we announced the program, the run on the money market funds slowed to a halt and the panic subsided. In the two-week period after the implementation of the program on September 29, the total assets in money market funds (both taxable and tax-exempt) stabilized and then began to slowly increase. From approximately $3.4 trillion on October 1, they reached $3.9 trillion on January 14, 2009.

Ultimately, no payments were made under the program, which actually generated a surplus for the government. Thanks to the combined force of the guarantee and other programs including the Commercial Paper Funding Facility and the Asset-Backed Commercial Paper Money Market Mutual Fund Liquidity Facility (AMLF), commercial paper issuance came back to life and the number of defaults among issuers of obligations held by money market funds plunged, raising the value of all asset prices.

The guarantee program was extended two times and wound down after a 12-month life. Total premium income paid to the Treasury was $1.2 billion.

LESSONS LEARNED

Lesson 1:
Details matter.

Every response is a combination of strategy (how big and disruptive of a signal are policymakers sending) and tactics (how exactly will the intervention work). Details matter, because a big proclamation that can't be wired will fail.

Lesson 2:
Know your audience.

Every policy response has an audience. This includes market professionals, the man on the street, and political leaders. Be sure you have addressed the audience you choose with a message they will understand. Keeping the public with you will protect policymakers and the system in the long term.

Lesson 3:
Keep it simple.

The guarantee program passed the *USA Today* test; individuals and politicians understood what we were doing. Market participants, including issuers, institutional buyers, and money market fund managers, understood and accepted the intervention.

Lesson 4:
Anticipate unintended consequences.

Key features of the program minimized unintended consequences. Fair fees, definitions of eligible assets, participation cutoff dates for investors, sunset provisions, a wind-down requirement to apply for insurance—all of these worked to ensure maximum participation and minimal long-term disruption.

Lesson 5:
Protect the taxpayer.

Never forget that market participants will game the system to their benefit. The more you know and learn about how the precrisis market functioned, the better you can tailor a solution that works and protects the taxpayer.

Lesson 6:
Industry structure matters.

The final and perhaps most important lesson of all goes to the structure of the industry. Shadow banking exists all over the globe. The scare we faced in 2008 and the issues that arose as we designed our response will reemerge the next time the system sees a run on a shadow bank. Entities that are not subject to bank-like constraints—and do not have access to the bank safety net of deposit insurance and access to the Fed—should not be allowed to issue deposit-like assets with daily liquidity and give the false impression to the public that they carry no risk of loss.

CHAPTER EIGHT

Recapitalizing the Banking System

DAN JESTER, DAVID NASON, AND JEREMIAH NORTON

INTRODUCTION

In September 2008, the financial system was unraveling. Fannie Mae and Freddie Mac entered conservatorship. Lehman Brothers filed for bankruptcy. The Federal Reserve, with the support of Treasury, rescued American International Group (AIG). A major money market mutual fund "broke the buck," and credit markets were stalling out. It was clear that the problems had grown too big for Treasury and the Fed to handle without additional authorities and resources. And because it was now clear that we were facing a crisis, for the first time we believed that we could get Congress to act.

For most Americans, and especially for those who believe in the private allocation of capital and investment, it was a giant leap to have the U.S. government inject capital into the banking system. For us, it was anathema to our deeply held policy views. We did not enter government service contemplating such actions, nor were we cavalier in doing so. But the events of September and October 2008 made the decision the best choice for the stability of the banking system and the country.

What Treasury ultimately did—rescued major financial institutions without nationalizing them—had never been attempted anywhere with such speed and scale. The Treasury program applied broadly across regulated banking entities—from large, global institutions to regional lenders and community banks—to help them withstand a severe financial shock and continue lending through the depths of the crisis. Its implementation was the result of intense work, analysis, and planning over a short period measured in days, not weeks.

The authors would like to recognize the many contributions from their former colleagues, without whom these policies would not have been possible.

In our view, the program largely achieved its mission, with few losses, and rewarded taxpayers with an overall profit for the risks they took. But the policy quickly became unpopular and controversial, and to this day, it remains the subject of intense debate.

This chapter aims to provide insights into the policy decisions that led the government to invest billions of dollars in the U.S. banking system. These included the following:

- A gradual shift from a private-sector-led response to a government-led solution using funds authorized by the Troubled Assets Relief Program (TARP) legislation;
- An abrupt change from funding asset purchases to making direct equity investments in financial institutions;
- The design and structuring of the government capital investments;
- The pairing of expansive government guarantees with the capital investments to stabilize the system.

SETTING THE STAGE

Ever since Henry M. Paulson, Jr., was sworn in as Treasury secretary in July 2006, he focused his staff on preparing for a financial crisis. As chief executive of Goldman Sachs, he had seen how frothy market conditions had become and worried about a repeat of the type of financial shocks that rippled through global markets nearly a decade earlier. He was also aware that the housing market was deteriorating. But by Paulson's own account, he did not appreciate how far-reaching the problems of the mortgage securitization market could become.[1]

By the summer of 2007, it was clear that the problems of the housing market were starting to pose a threat to the broader financial system. That fall, financial institutions of all sizes—from big Wall Street banks to relatively small and obscure entities known as structured investment vehicles, or SIVs—began to report that liquidity in critical short-term funding markets was starting to dry up. Paulson was deeply concerned that if the situation deteriorated, borrowing costs would quickly escalate, causing the most vulnerable firms to sell

---

1. Henry M. Paulson, Jr., *On the Brink: Inside the Race to Stop the Collapse of the Global Financial System* (New York: Business Plus, Hachette Book Group, 2010), 64.

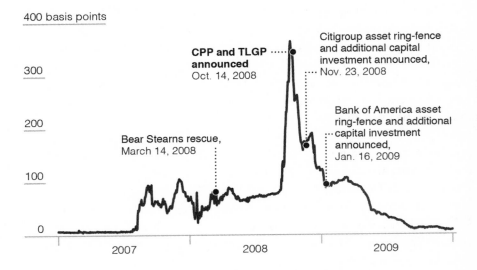

400 basis points

300

200

100

0

2007   2008   2009

Citigroup asset ring-fence
and additional capital
investment announced,
Nov. 23, 2008

CPP and TLGP
announced
Oct. 14, 2008

Bank of America asset
ring-fence and additional
capital investment
announced,
Jan. 16, 2009

Bear Stearns rescue,
March 14, 2008

Figure 8.1 **Three-Month U.S. Libor-OIS Spread, 2007–2009**

Note: CPP is the Capital Purchase Program; TLGP is the Temporary Liquidity
Guarantee Program; Libor-OIS is the difference between the London Interbank Offered
Rate (Libor) and the overnight indexed swap (OIS) rate.

Source: Bloomberg Finance L.P.

their assets at a steep discount to raise cash. Once financial institutions slipped
into such a downward spiral, it was hard to get out. (See Figure 8.1.)

Paulson urged financial institutions—privately and publicly—to raise capital and strengthen liquidity, and many of them did. During the second half of
2007, financial institutions raised more than $83 billion of equity, a more
than 20 percent increase from the same period in 2006.[2] Bear Stearns, Citigroup, Merrill Lynch, and Morgan Stanley each raised billions of dollars from
investors in Asia and the Middle East.[3]

2. Remarks by Treasury Secretary Henry M. Paulson, Jr., on Housing and Capital
   Markets before the New York Society of Securities Analysts, U.S. Treasury, Jan. 7,
   2008.
3. Bear Stearns was set to raise $1 billion from CITIC Securities in China; however,
   CITIC pulled out of negotiations after Bear was purchased by JPMorgan Chase in
   March 2008. Citigroup raised $7.50 billion from the Abu Dhabi Investment
   Authority on November 27, 2007; $6.88 billion from the Government of Singapore

These infusions of capital, though, were made on burdensome terms, and they did little to reassure the markets. In many ways, the infusions had the opposite effect. Worried that Wall Street was still behind the curve, Paulson privately urged the heads of other large financial institutions to raise additional capital. Most pushed back, maintaining that they were adequately capitalized and wanting to avoid diluting their existing shareholders. They were also concerned that raising capital would stigmatize their institutions and make them look vulnerable. After all, they could see the upheaval in the executive ranks of the banks that did raise money.

Paulson also used Treasury's convening power to urge banks to strengthen their balance sheets in other ways. One initiative was designed to address the dangers of hidden leverage in banks' off-balance-sheet SIVs. Under the proposal, Citigroup, Bank of America, and JPMorgan Chase would pool together funds upward of $75 billion[4] to form what we called the Master Liquidity Enhancement Conduit, or MLEC, which was better known as a Super-SIV. For a fee, the Super-SIV would buy assets from traditional SIVs and then hold them until market conditions improved. The plan never got off the ground. There were disagreements among the participating banks about pricing, with stronger banks viewing the plan as a bailout of weaker institutions, in addition to broader concerns about the complexity of execution. But it was a model we would revisit again and again throughout the crisis.

Ultimately, Paulson recognized the limitations of the bully pulpit and, most particularly, the limits of addressing a systemic crisis with no legal authorities and government money. And he continued to push his staff to think about developing tools to address the deteriorating financial environment. In February 2008, he asked his staff members to begin working with their colleagues at the Federal Reserve to explore various policy options. They summarized their ideas in a memo that became known as the "Break the Glass" Bank

---

Investment Corporation on January 15, 2008; and an additional $3 billion from the Kuwait Investment Authority on January 15, 2008. Merrill Lynch raised $2 billion from the Kuwait Investment Authority and another $2 billion from the Korean Investment Corporation on January 15, 2008. Merrill Lynch also raised $4.4 billion from Temasek on December 24, 2007; however, the investment increased to $5 billion after Temasek exercised a stock option of $600 million in Merrill Lynch common stock on February 1, 2008. Morgan Stanley raised $5.60 billion from the China Investment Corporation on December 19, 2007.
4. Paulson, *On the Brink*, 79.

Recapitalization Plan.[5] It contained a number of ideas: having the government buy illiquid assets, having the government guarantee or insure mortgage-related assets, having the Federal Housing Administration refinance individual mortgages, and, finally, purchasing equity stakes in banks.

All the options shifted the policy focus to the Treasury sponsoring actions to improve bank capital rather than the Federal Reserve providing liquidity. The idea that held the most sway with Paulson was the plan to buy $500 billion in illiquid mortgage-related assets from banks. By doing so, banks' balance sheets would be freed up of the bad assets, which would encourage more lending. To oversee the purchased securities, the government would rely on private-sector asset managers, and taxpayers would bear the risk and reap any returns. While the memo proposed the emergency fund, the thought of a divided Congress giving a Treasury secretary that kind of authority at that time was unimaginable. There was also concern that if we were to seek emergency powers and funding from Congress and didn't receive them, we might just precipitate the market collapse we were trying to prevent.

Paulson had strong reasons, both philosophical and practical, for favoring this plan. For one, he was opposed to just about any idea that could be characterized as nationalization. When the government acquires ownership of formerly privately held assets, the conditions are created for undesirable government influence or control. He also feared that government ownership of the banks would make it hard for them to reestablish profitability and return to private status.

So when the crisis intensified in September 2008, Paulson returned to the idea of an asset purchase plan. He believed that just by announcing that the government had a big pool of money available for an asset purchase program, asset prices would increase, and then government purchases would further boost prices. That, in turn, would create a virtuous circle where banks could re-mark their assets at higher levels, which would free up capital and increase confidence so that prices would continue to rise.

The Treasury secretary also believed that discussions of government ownership would frighten rather than reassure investors. In just the prior two weeks, Fannie Mae and Freddie Mac had entered conservatorship, and AIG had been rescued. In both cases, the government obtained rights to approximately 80 percent of total shares in the government-sponsored enterprises and

5. Paulson, *On the Brink*, 131.

AIG, substantially diluting shareholders. On September 18, three days after Lehman Brothers' collapse, Treasury sent its proposal to Congress calling for the $700 billion Troubled Assets Relief Program, asking only for the authority to purchase "mortgage-related assets" from U.S. financial institutions.

To motivate Congress to act, Paulson and Federal Reserve chairman Ben S. Bernanke had to describe the nature of the crisis and the risk of systemic failure. They also had to explain that a core element of the crisis was the vast number of highly illiquid mortgage-related assets, many of which were distressed, that were sitting on banking institution balance sheets, leading to questions of the adequacy of banking capitalization. Publicly, both Paulson and Bernanke championed the idea of setting a price and creating liquidity for these assets to provide some balance sheet relief. While Bernanke provided the academic gravitas, Paulson argued passionately that it was the most effective way to recapitalize the banking system. Recognizing the priority placed on the asset purchase plan, we nevertheless had our doubts about the plan and especially about limiting ourselves solely to asset purchases. So it was important that any legislation give Treasury broad authority.

By late evening on Saturday, September 27, Treasury negotiators reached agreement with the leadership of both parties on the $700 billion TARP legislation. But the following Monday, the House rejected the TARP bill by a margin of 228 to 205. All told, the S&P 500 would drop 8.8 percent, wiping out more than $1 trillion in value in its worst day since the October 1987 stock market crash.

As Treasury resumed negotiations with Congress, financial conditions continued to deteriorate. Depositors were on edge in the wake of the two biggest bank collapses in U.S. history—those of Washington Mutual and Wachovia. Meanwhile, funding pressure grew so intense that Goldman Sachs and Morgan Stanley, the last of the remaining large Wall Street investment banks, raised billions of dollars in additional capital in order to be granted holding company status and access to the Federal Reserve's discount window.[6] During this time,

6. To obtain the designation of a bank holding company, both firms needed to show the Fed that they had sufficient financial and managerial resources to meet regulatory and supervisory requirements and to safely and soundly continue operations. Goldman Sachs secured a commitment for a $5 billion equity investment from Warren Buffett and raised another $5 billion through a public offering. Morgan Stanley secured a commitment of about $9 billion of new equity from a large Japanese banking conglomerate, Mitsubishi UFJ Financial Group.

Bernanke and the authors of this chapter told Paulson that solving the crisis would most likely require capital injections. Paulson agreed and told President George W. Bush that he believed a capital program would probably be necessary.

On Friday, October 3, the House followed the Senate's lead and voted, 263–171, to approve the Emergency Economic Stabilization Act of 2008, giving the Treasury Department the authority and resources to address the crisis.

The final bill permitted the Treasury secretary to purchase troubled assets that were defined as "residential or commercial mortgages and any securities, obligations, or other instruments that are based on or related to such mortgages." The bill also included a second definition of troubled assets, which was "any other financial instrument that the Secretary, after consultation with the Chairman of the Board of Governors of the Federal Reserve System, determines the purchase of which is necessary to promote financial market stability." This definition provided the federal government broad flexibility to invest directly in banks, or, as Treasury did later that year, even the auto industry.

Paulson wanted to keep his options open on how to respond because of the crisis's dynamic nature. Before he left for the weekend, he urged the team to figure out how long it would take for Treasury to begin purchasing the banks' toxic assets. Then he asked us as well: "Figure out a way we can put equity into these companies."

|||||

In the days after Congress passed TARP, rather than rallying, the equity markets continued to decline at an alarming rate in the United States and Europe, with seven European nations acting to rescue banks. In a race against time, Treasury and the Fed developed a plan to stabilize the markets. We recognized the need to act forcefully—and fast.

We quickly decided that an asset purchase plan could not be executed quickly, nor would it maximize the use of TARP funds. Instead, we decided to pursue a broad-based program to make government investments directly in the banks.

We concluded that even if successful, the auctions might not be large enough or at prices high enough to provide significant benefits. Given the estimated $2 trillion of distressed assets on the banks' balance sheets, there was concern that even hundreds of billions in purchases would not deliver the desired benefit. Asset purchases can have a significant direct capital impact only if the purchaser pays a meaningful premium above the bank's carrying value. It was possible, though uncertain, that limited asset purchases might provide an additional benefit by increasing the value of distressed assets generally and thereby increase equity capital. Another consideration was the question of what would happen if the auctions were successful and established prices that implied losses greater than what investors and creditors estimated.

Designing the auction process had many practical challenges. There was a vast universe of eligible assets, including more than 20,000 mortgage-backed securities—each containing its own pool of underlying mortgages with different vintages, borrower characteristics, credit ratings, and delinquency rates. In addition, we were concerned that we might have to wait until December to run test auctions for even a few hundred million dollars of assets.

Purchasing equity stakes to recapitalize the banks was much more straightforward and had been used previously, though not always to great positive effect. And it certainly had not been executed with the structure or at the scale being proposed. The prospect of government investments in banks offended us from a policy perspective and was politically toxic; however, we needed to address the capitalization of our banking system.

A major virtue of the equity stakes program, however, was that it could be standardized so that it could apply to every type of financial institution. We knew it would be more effective too. By immediately injecting capital, banks would have more capital to absorb losses if the economy worsened. They would also have greater capacity to lend and not hunker down and hoard capital. All of this, we hoped, would restore confidence so that over time private capital would return to the banking system.

Another virtue was that it provided a far bigger impact than simply buying assets. If you purchase assets, every dollar you spend can buy only one dollar of assets. On the other hand, if you invest one dollar into a bank, that dollar can create between $8 and $12 of lending capacity depending on the overall capital adequacy of the banking institution. So if you were to invest hundreds of billions of dollars, you could significantly recapitalize the nation's banks and strengthen their capacity to lend.

DESIGNING AND IMPLEMENTING THE CAPITAL PURCHASE PROGRAM

After TARP was passed on October 3, we began working with our colleagues at the Fed and the Federal Deposit Insurance Corporation (FDIC) to design the Capital Purchase Program (CPP). Our goal was to develop a plan as quickly as possible because the financial markets were on the brink of a systemic collapse. We unveiled the program to banks on October 13, ten days after obtaining congressional approval, and announced it publicly the next day.

As we designed the CPP, we mapped out a strategy that was fundamentally different from every recapitalization plan that had been tried before. Instead of "nationalizing" only failing or weak banks, we would welcome *all* qualifying, healthy institutions. There were multiple iterations of the program. For example, the initial version called for a government matching investment for any private capital raised. This concept was quickly dismissed because the public equity markets were essentially closed for even the strongest banking institutions.

We sought to design a program to recapitalize the banks that would be understandable, easy to implement, and broadly accepted to maximize its effect. We had to address a number of issues. First, and importantly, we had no legal authority, even after the passage of TARP, to force a bank to accept an investment. To encourage broad participation, our terms had to incentivize rather than punish participation. Making the investment program attractive maximized the chances it could be implemented quickly. Second, we wanted the program to be widely adopted. The system as a whole was undercapitalized; unless we addressed the shortfall, the crisis could simply spread from relatively weak institutions to relatively strong ones. Third, an attractive program would allow us to avoid stigmatizing any specific financial institution, since healthier banks could justify participation as a way of obtaining relatively inexpensive capital. Last, we believed that the preferred investment structure was simple and easy to understand for market participants—both the banks accepting the investment and the market counterparties looking to transact with safe institutions.

A key decision was how much money to deploy. Although Congress authorized a total of $700 billion for TARP, it released only $350 billion initially and had the ability to block Treasury's request for the second $350 billion. Because we wanted to make sure funds were available in case we faced an unexpected event, we decided that we would allocate $250 billion to the CPP investments. With $250 billion as the constraint, we agreed with the Federal Reserve that each eligible and participating institution would be able to issue CPP preferred stock equal to and not less than 1 percent, but no greater than 3 percent of its risk-weighted assets, subject to a maximum of $25 billion.

We focused on preferred shares for three main reasons. First, there were legitimate concerns about the government becoming a controlling or significant shareholder. Since preferred stock was nonvoting, its use allowed us to avoid many of the governance responsibilities that come with significant equity ownership, such as voting on shareholder proposals or taking seats on the board. Second, we also thought preferred stock would be more palatable to healthier banks, which would be reluctant to take the government on as a business partner. Finally, from the government's perspective, preferred shares sat higher in the capital structure. That meant the taxpayer was more likely to get paid back.

The trade-off was that the government banking preferred shares were seen by investors as lower-quality capital than common equity, given their senior position in the capital stack. Many investors were skeptical that the preferred stock would be as effective at absorbing losses as common stock. In our view, however, preferred stock was ultimately contingent common stock. If desired and needed, the preferred shares could be converted into common equity with the government's consent. This is the approach that was used later for both Citigroup and AIG in related programs when preferred investments were exchanged for common stock.

Likewise, we came up with other ways to make these investments attractive, even to healthy institutions. One was allowing banks that accepted government capital to continue paying dividends to their existing shareholders (although they were not allowed to increase their dividends). Although the government was criticized widely for making such dividends permissible, we believed that a dividend ban would significantly discourage many institutions from accepting a government investment and frustrate a central goal in recapitalizing the system.

Another way we made these investments attractive was to set the dividend rate below current market levels. We initially planned for a 5 percent cash dividend rate, with the total effective dividend rate increasing by roughly 1 percent per year based on how long the banks kept the preferred outstanding. Paulson continued to solicit others' input, including that of Warren Buffett, who also favored preferred equity investments with favorable terms. After taking all of this into account, we then revised our initial plan so that the preferred shares would pay a 5 percent dividend in the first five years and then escalate to 9 percent in the following years. This initial 5 percent dividend rate was attractive because it was less expensive than the rate banks would have had to pay to issue preferred in the market. And the five-year period before the 9 percent dividend kicked in provided institutions a strong incentive to pay back the government while giving them a reasonable amount of time to recover from the crisis.

To reward taxpayers if things went as well as we had hoped, and to comply with the TARP law, we attached warrants to the investments. Treasury would receive warrants with a ten-year maturity that could be exercised at any time, with an aggregate market value equal to 15 percent of the total value of the preferred; the strike price on the warrants equaled the previous 20-day average stock price for each institution on the day of preliminary approval of the investment. This allowed taxpayers to participate in the upside from recovery in the financial system.

Finally, we treaded carefully around the issue of compensation. When Congress approved the TARP legislation, it called on any institution that received government funds to meet "appropriate standards for executive compensation and corporate governance." The rules put restrictions on senior executive pay packages, including banning excessive severance payments, new golden parachute payments, and contracts that encouraged unnecessary risk taking. Critics on both the left and the right pushed us to draw an even harder line on executive pay and banker compensation. However, we felt that placing additional rules would stigmatize and jeopardize the program if it looked as if the government was controlling compensation. That is what happened when banks were nationalized, and it would have discouraged and limited the broad participation needed to recapitalize the financial system.

There was one other critical issue: the treatment by regulators of the preferred investments. Our preferred shares, as originally conceived, did not actually qualify as Tier 1 capital, the primary metric that regulators use to determine whether an institution is appropriately capitalized. That was because the dividend payments on our shares were cumulative (except in limited circumstances), allowing the government to collect in the future any dividends not paid by a bank. To count as Tier 1 capital, preferred shares had to be noncumulative and nonredeemable—meaning the bank would not owe any missed dividend payments in arrears. We found this an unacceptable risk to the taxpayer. To fulfill our goal of strengthening the banks' financial position, the Fed amended its capital rules so that these new investments would qualify as Tier 1 capital. The compromise was that when a financial institution paid back the government investment, it had to replace it with qualifying Tier 1 capital.

The preferred stock was structured as a perpetual instrument without a specified maturity date. Together with cumulative dividends, this enabled the preferred to be treated as Tier 1 capital. Although the step-up in the dividend rate after the fifth anniversary was designed to incentivize repayment, we did not want banks to rush to repay the preferred investment before confidence increased that the banks were adequately capitalized. To provide additional incentive for repayment, we provided firms an opportunity to reduce the outstanding warrants by 50 percent by raising qualifying private capital before the end of 2009.

Even as we designed the CPP, the rapid succession of market events made some concerned that capital alone might not be sufficient. Timothy F. Geithner, president of the Federal Reserve Bank of New York, was particularly worried. "What you really need is the authority to guarantee their liabilities," he advised Paulson shortly after the initial TARP bill was voted down. The two needed to work hand in hand.

At Treasury, we put in place a temporary guarantee against any losses on more than $3.4 trillion of money market mutual funds, after investors panicked in the days following the collapse of Lehman Brothers. Shortly thereafter, several of our European counterparts had guaranteed their bank debt, hoping to prevent runs from spreading across the European financial system. Once a government chooses to guarantee some assets or institutions, it can spark a run on those that are not protected, as investors flee to safety.

The Treasury did not have the debt guarantee authority; those powers belonged to the FDIC (under certain circumstances), which had traditionally used them in resolving failed financial institutions. To guarantee all U.S. bank debts, we would need to ask the FDIC to extend its mandate to banks that had not yet failed—and even to bank holding companies and consumer credit companies, which the FDIC did not formally oversee.

Leadership of both the Treasury and the Fed strongly advocated for the FDIC to establish what became known as the Debt Guarantee Program of the Temporary Liquidity Guarantee Program (TLGP). Paulson argued that the more risk the Treasury and the FDIC took on today, the fewer losses we would see in the future. Sheila Bair, chairman of the FDIC, was understandably reluctant to take on such significant additional exposure. But after consulting with her colleagues, she returned saying that the FDIC could invoke the systemic risk exception to establish a program. However, she wanted to be certain the banks would pay a fair price.

When paired with the CPP bank investments, the TLGP made the broader recapitalization effort far more powerful. The CPP investments strengthened the banks' capital levels, while the TLGP made them less susceptible to a run. Together the programs strengthened equity capital materially and sharply curtailed the run risk, thereby ensuring the ability of the banks to finance themselves in the private market with debt securities. The FDIC ultimately agreed to guarantee new U.S. bank debt as of October 14, 2008.

One question about the program was just how many banks would participate. Even though we anticipated opening CPP to all healthy institutions, we didn't have the infrastructure in place to support a broad rollout. Instead, we decided to begin with the largest banks and the most systemically important banks. The thought was that these sophisticated institutions had the resources to retain counsel to identify any and all unintended concepts or problems with the program. Every other institution would be treated identically. We allocated $125 billion, roughly half of the TARP funds that we had designated for the bank investment program. To minimize political interference, we deferred to the Federal Reserve Bank of New York to designate the first banks and corresponding capital amounts. FRBNY settled on nine systemically important institutions—a group consisting of the four largest banks: Citigroup, Bank of America, JPMorgan Chase, and Wells Fargo; such traditional Wall Street banks as Goldman Sachs, Merrill Lynch, and Morgan Stanley; and the custodial banks Bank of New York Mellon and State Street. At the time, these banks accounted for 55 percent of U.S. banking assets.[7] The financial health of those institutions varied. That, however, drove home the point: We were giving all banks government capital so they could more easily absorb losses and continue lending through the downturn—and not distinguishing the weak from the strong. (See Figure 8.2.)

Meanwhile, we wanted immediate participation. We invited the chief executives of the nine banks with their financial regulators to the Treasury Department for a confidential meeting on Columbus Day to reveal how CPP and TLGP would work. This rather dramatic meeting was driven by pragmatism. It allowed us to explain the deal to all nine banks at once and then ask for an immediate decision. In fact, we used the offices of nine senior Treasury officials so that every bank's chief executive would have his own breakout room to have private discussions with the general counsels and boards. Although quite a bit has been written about the theatrics of the meeting itself, the fact is that our plan worked and every bank participated.

7. Government Accountability Office, Report, *Capital Purchase Program: Revenues Have Exceeded Investments, but Concerns about Outstanding Investments Remain,* March 2012, 7, https://www.gao.gov/assets/590/589127.pdf.

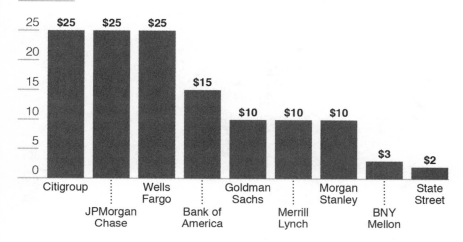

$30 billion

	Citigroup	JPMorgan Chase	Wells Fargo	Bank of America	Goldman Sachs	Merrill Lynch	Morgan Stanley	BNY Mellon	State Street
	$25	$25	$25	$15	$10	$10	$10	$3	$2

Figure 8.2 **Initial CPP Investments in Large U.S. Financial Institutions**

Notes: (1) Treasury announced the Capital Purchase Program (CPP) on Oct. 14, 2008, and distributed $125 billion to nine banks as shown here. The program ultimately disbursed a total of $205 billion to 707 banks in 48 states, Puerto Rico, and the District of Columbia. (2) Bank of America received the initial investment in Merrill Lynch after it acquired the firm.

Source: U.S. Treasury

This marked just the start of the CPP's bank investments. With the nine lead banks in the fold, we moved quickly to broaden the program to 707 financial institutions—large and small, publicly traded and privately held, and from 48 states. (See Figure 8.3.) It would require us to build out a dedicated office, led by a "chief investment officer" who would work closely with the independent banking regulators to award investments to viable institutions. (For more details on the management of the CPP, see Chapter 14.) After investing the first $125 billion in the nine largest banks, we invested an additional $69 billion by January 16, 2009— or roughly 78 percent of the total amount before the end of the Bush administration. Investing the money quickly was crucial to the success of the program.

In addition to CPP, some firms required additional capital injections. For example, Citigroup required a second capital injection (and later, a third injection of common equity through a conversion of preferred stock into common stock). In November 2008, as Citigroup's losses worsened and the market's confidence in the company declined further, Citigroup faced the prospect of

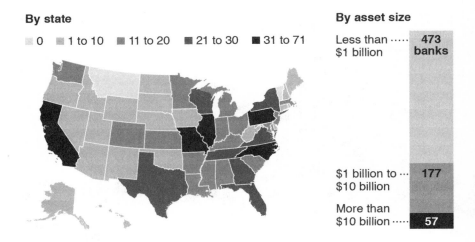

By state

0 ■ 1 to 10 ■ 11 to 20 ■ 21 to 30 ■ 31 to 71

By asset size

Less than ····· **473**
$1 billion   **banks**

$1 billion to ··· **177**
$10 billion

More than
$10 billion ····· **57**

Figure 8.3 **Distribution of Banks Participating in the CPP, by State and by Size**

Sources: By location: authors' calculations, based on U.S. Treasury TARP Investment Programs transaction reports; by size: U.S. Treasury, "Troubled Asset Relief Program: Two Year Retrospective," SNL Financial

becoming illiquid within a matter of days. To prevent the failure of a systemically important international bank—and the potential for a disorderly receivership in the midst of a market crisis—we agreed to provide another $20 billion of government capital on top of the $25 billion Citigroup had received at the Columbus Day meeting. We also put together a program that would insure against losses on up to $306 billion of Citi's most illiquid assets—an innovative crisis response tool known as a ring-fence guarantee, or, more formally, as the Asset Guarantee Program (AGP).[8]

Under the AGP, Citigroup would agree to take the first losses. But after that, Treasury would put up a modest amount of TARP capital as a second loss position, the FDIC would take the next set of losses, and the FRBNY would take on the rest of the downside risk.

8. We would take similar actions to stabilize Bank of America in January 2009. Shortly before our administration ended, we agreed to provide an additional $20 billion of government capital on top of the $25 billion investment that was announced on Columbus Day. We agreed to provide an AGP ring-fence guarantee on a pool of troubled assets, although Bank of America exited the program before it was deployed.

Although the asset ring-fence was initially greeted favorably by the market, it ultimately failed to stabilize Citigroup. One reason is that the $306 billion of insured assets paled in comparison to Citigroup's $2 trillion balance sheet. Another is that it was complicated and time-consuming to determine which assets would be included in the ring-fence.

ASSESSMENT AND LESSONS LEARNED

Lesson 1:
Bank capital standards and supervision were not adequate.

Before the crisis, the regulatory capital regime and supervision were inadequate. Although most banks were in compliance with regulatory capital standards, the markets did not have confidence in capitalization levels or the supervision provided by regulators. As a consequence of this lack of confidence, a number of well-capitalized banks failed or nearly failed during the crisis. Strong capital requirements and more forward-looking supervision (such as capital and liquidity buffers / stress supervision) must be the first line of defense.

Lesson 2:
The Capital Purchase Program was a critical component of our crisis response.

From a policy perspective, this program was unique in its scale, speed, and broad-based approach. It marked the first time that a recapitalization program centered on assisting healthy financial institutions in the United States rather than nationalizing failed banks. The capital injections were fast, efficient, and effective, helping to avoid the potential failure of scores of firms.

Lesson 3:
The government received proceeds in excess of its investments.

Although profit was not the motive for the CPP investments and should not be the sole or primary basis for evaluating the program, the government received proceeds in excess of the funds it invested. Many observers predicted steep losses, which did not materialize. Through the CPP and other direct bank programs, the government committed $250 billion and has received total proceeds of $275 billion from the repayment of preferred stock, dividends, and warrant proceeds.[9] In addition, the banks repaid us far more quickly than we initially anticipated. By December 2009, eight of the nine initial TARP recipients had redeemed their preferred stock. As of December 2018, all but three of the more than 700 banks have redeemed their preferreds. We also put in place strong controls and oversight mechanisms that ensured that every dollar was accounted for and no fraudulent investments were made. The CPP received a clean audit every year. This is important for building public confidence in government's ability to be a good steward of taxpayer funds.

Lesson 4:
The Capital Purchase Program provided the foundation for future actions.

The CPP by itself did not fully stabilize or recapitalize the financial system. A number of banks were so severely undercapitalized that they would need to raise billions of additional capital from private investors; and, in two cases, the banks had to return to the government for additional TARP capital from the Targeted Investment Program (TIP) and the AGP. The CPP, together with the FDIC guarantee, calmed markets and bought some much-needed time during a presidential transition, allowing a broader recovery strategy including fiscal stimulus. In addition, the CPP provided a key and necessary cornerstone to restore the banking system—and the broader economy—to normal functioning. The important stress tests carried out by the Federal Reserve in 2009, and the subsequent private recapitalizations, would not have been successful without the base of equity provided by the CPP.

Lesson 5:
Political and public support were low.

Putting government funds into private institutions is rightfully unpopular in America. The government's investments, while stabilizing the financial system, did help the banks that the public blamed for causing the crisis. Understand-

---

9. U.S. Department of the Treasury, Monthly TARP Update for 09/01/2018, Sept. 1, 2018, https://www.treasury.gov/initiatives/financial-stability/reports/Documents /Monthly_TARP_Update - 09.01.2018.pdf.

ably, this violated many people's fundamental sense of fairness. This unintended consequence is something that future policymakers must take into account.

Lesson 6:
Policymakers should carefully consider the requirements to use emergency authorities.

Financial institutions are unique in that their business models and viability are tied to the confidence of their customers. No other business enterprise's viability is tied as closely to this perception, and thus financial institutions are susceptible to banking runs. These runs, in turn, can turn into systemic threats to the entire economy. This concern is the foundation for FDIC deposit insurance and the Federal Reserve's lender-of-last-resort authority.

Congress must take this into account when crafting policy for bank stability. As discussed in this chapter, capital injections and guarantees were effective in stabilizing a teetering banking system. However, government investments into private enterprises create significant policy issues. Any decision-making must be transparent and subject to scrutiny.

Lesson 7:
Clarity and communication are critical.

To stop a panic, interventions need to be easily understood by market participants and must be capable of being implemented quickly. You can have great ideas, but you need to be able to operationalize them. The best chance for building political and public support is straightforward communication.

Lesson 8:
Plan for a crisis.

The best time to plan for a crisis and evaluate alternatives is before a crisis begins. Once a crisis begins, policy options can be constrained by political or market considerations. Since banking and financial crises have occurred throughout the history of the United States and other countries, advance planning before the next crisis is warranted.

CHAPTER NINE

The Temporary Liquidity Guarantee Program

MICHAEL H. KRIMMINGER

SETTING THE STAGE

The Federal Deposit Insurance Corporation (FDIC) was created during the Great Depression to restore public confidence in the banking system and to stem the bank runs then undermining financial stability by assuring depositors their money was safe and quickly resolving failing banks. During much of the 2008 financial crisis, the FDIC continued to focus on the roles it was known for: the protection of insured depositors and resolving failing banks.

However, the severity of the 2008 financial crisis required more of the FDIC. In an effort to address the risks to insured banks and thrifts, the FDIC sought new solutions, including by seeking solutions to mortgage distress, pursuing additional flexibility for investment in banks, and introducing or expanding a number of techniques for resolving failing banks.

This chapter examines one of the most significant, and unprecedented, uses of the FDIC's authority in the government-wide effort to restore public confidence: the Temporary Liquidity Guarantee Program (TLGP). The TLGP con-

I wish to thank my colleague at Cleary Gottlieb, Luca Amorello, for his invaluable assistance during the development of this chapter. In addition, I wish to thank Art Murton, Diane Ellis, and Matthew Green of the FDIC for their assistance. However, any errors of fact or analysis are solely my responsibility. The analyses and decisions by the FDIC described in this chapter were the product of work by Art, Diane, Matthew, and many others, and I benefited enormously from their work then and subsequently. However, I would be remiss if I did not express particular appreciation to Chairman Sheila Bair for her leadership, creativity in devising new solutions, and tireless dedication to the public interest.

sisted of two guarantees—a limited-term guarantee for certain new debt issued by banks and certain other financial companies, and a full guarantee of all funds in non-interest-bearing transaction deposit accounts in banks. These guarantees were an integral part of the set of government actions taken in October 2008 at a critical time in the crisis, when investors and creditors had lost confidence that the banking system was solvent, and helped avert a more costly financial crisis. We review the key policy issues and the choices made by the FDIC and offer some lessons for the future.

After Lehman Brothers defaulted on September 15, 2008, the Reserve Primary Fund, one of the largest U.S. money market funds, stunned nearly everyone with the disclosure that, because it was holding at least $785 million of Lehman's commercial paper, it would no longer be able to redeem shares at $1 a share—it "broke the buck." This triggered a run on the fund, which quickly spread across the money market industry. Although the Treasury was able to stem the contagion effects by announcing a guarantee for all losses on money market funds, investors concluded that commercial paper was no longer safe. As a result, it became clear that any financial institution relying on market-based funding would face increasing difficulty.

By late September 2008, interbank markets in many financial assets were illiquid and financial institutions were virtually unable to issue new debt or roll over existing debt.[1] The financial system stood poised on the precipice of illiquidity, and if the markets froze, mass insolvency.[2] The growing loss of market liquidity was triggered by uncertainty over the extent of the impairment of mortgage-related assets and the consequences for the balance sheets of banks, broker-dealers, and other financial institutions. This uncertainty was heightened by the shocks from the collapse of Lehman Brothers, the failure of Washington Mutual (WaMu) on September 25, and the threats to the stability of other, bigger financial institutions. Suspicion that the scope and severity of the losses from mortgage-related assets, including mortgage-backed securities and synthetic derivatives, were understated was rampant. This led market

1. Federal Deposit Insurance Corporation (FDIC), *Crisis and Response: An FDIC History, 2008–2013* (Washington, D.C.: FDIC, 2017), chapter 2, 40. I am particularly grateful for the descriptions and analyses provided by the FDIC in this volume.
2. For a comparable judgment, see Sheila Bair, *Bull by the Horns: Fighting to Save Main Street from Wall Street and Wall Street from Itself* (New York: Free Press, 2012), 107; Ben S. Bernanke, *The Courage to Act: A Memoir of a Crisis and Its Aftermath* (New York: W. W. Norton, 2015), 153–66, 336–37.

participants to deeply discount mortgage-related assets and financial institutions' balance sheets.

This market uncertainty over the severity of the impact of the mortgage-related problems buffeting the financial system was, in part, a product of significant changes in mortgage finance prior to the crisis. Leading up to the crisis, banks had often found themselves chasing, rather than setting, pricing and risk tolerance trends. With many financing activities occurring formally off the balance sheets of banks and other financial firms, banking regulators also found themselves less able to monitor market developments and assess the true risks in the system. For the FDIC, this meant that some standard sources of information available about banks were insufficient to permit accurate assessment of the timing or severity of the challenges. Banks were buffeted by broad market issues, the opacity of funding vehicles, and a growing and broad investor aversion to real estate–related assets. While the FDIC was accustomed to assessing bank-specific challenges, the assessment of the impact of broader market factors was necessarily directional rather than predictive.

As the crisis deepened, the decline in market-based funding was paralleled to a much lesser degree by accelerated withdrawals of uninsured deposits from banks viewed as troubled. Significant withdrawals occurred even from generally healthy banks.[3] Bankers were particularly concerned about stability in deposit funding and the ability to retain small-business accounts exceeding the deposit insurance limits. While this issue had been addressed to some degree by an increase in insurance coverage to $250,000, the overall level of consumer and business uncertainty created concern that deposit volatility could engender additional stress on banks.

THE TEMPORARY LIQUIDITY GUARANTEE PROGRAM

On October 14, 2008, FDIC chairman Sheila Bair, secretary of the Treasury Henry M. Paulson, Jr., and Federal Reserve chairman Ben S. Bernanke announced the TLGP along with the Capital Purchase Program (CPP) and details about the Commercial Paper Funding Facility (CPFF), signaling a coordinated government response to stem the deterioration of the financial system and laying a foundation for further efforts. As part of this package of initiatives, the FDIC's TLGP played a critical role in returning liquidity to

---

3. FDIC, *Crisis and Response,* 40.

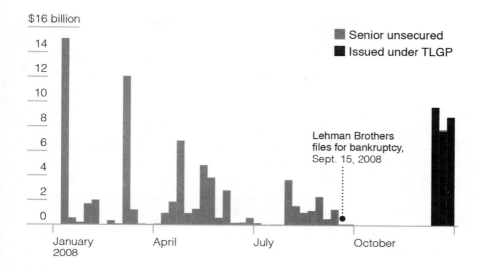

$16 billion

- ■ Senior unsecured
- ■ Issued under TLGP

Lehman Brothers
files for bankruptcy,
Sept. 15, 2008

January 2008   April   July   October

Figure 9.1 Senior Unsecured U.S. Bank Debt Issuance before and after September 2008

Notes: (1) Issuance data are weekly. (2) TLGP is the Temporary Liquidity Guarantee Program.

Source: Bloomberg Finance L.P., based on Figure 2.2 from FDIC, *Crisis and Response: An FDIC History, 2008–2013* (2017)

banks and their affiliates. By combining both a debt guarantee and a transaction account guarantee, the TLGP provided targeted support to address the challenges banks were facing in the debt markets and for deposit funding. (See Figure 9.1.)

The initiatives announced included elements to address the immediate liquidity challenges as well as the underlying capital shortfall that had shaken the market. Both were important to policymakers. While a guarantee of liquidity was essential to stem the risk of spreading financial system illiquidity and insolvency, pairing it with capital from the Troubled Assets Relief Program (TARP) signaled the government's determination to address underlying systemic solvency. While a complete package of guarantees and capital was needed, rolling out this package of initiatives was complicated by the fact that no one agency had plenary authority to create all of the needed initiatives, and each participating agency had to work within its own mandates and legal authorities.

The TLGP and CPP also were interconnected in other ways. While the TLGP generally was a voluntary program, the greatest risk of loss to the FDIC was from the largest banks—which also were most reliant on the debt markets. As a result, it was important for the FDIC debt guarantees to be paired with TARP capital to provide a cushion against loss. When the programs were presented to the nine largest U.S. banks on October 13, these banks were informed that they were required to accept both TARP capital and the TLGP guarantees. For these banks, TARP and the FDIC debt guarantees were inextricably tied—participation in TARP was a condition of participation in the debt guarantees.[4] The presence of TARP capital—along with the other programs that assisted the largest financial companies—provided a cushion against loss precisely from those banks whose default could have devastated the FDIC's Deposit Insurance Fund (DIF) and impaired public confidence in the deposit guarantee.

The TLGP was composed of two distinct but related components. The Debt Guarantee Program (DGP) provided a limited-term guarantee for certain new debt issued by banks, thrifts, and financial holding companies and eligible subsidiaries. The Transaction Account Guarantee Program (TAGP) fully guaranteed specified non-interest-bearing transaction deposit accounts held by insured depository institutions.

When the TLGP was announced, all institutions that met the eligibility criteria were automatically enrolled at no cost for 30 days. After this initial period, eligible entities could opt out of either the DGP or the TAGP or both. Once the TLGP became optional, more than half of the eligible entities elected to remain in the DGP before its 2009 extension, and more than 86 percent of FDIC-insured banks and thrifts remained in the TAGP. The first FDIC-guaranteed debt was issued by eligible institutions on October 14.[5] Ultimately, outstanding DGP-guaranteed debt exceeded $340 billion, while TAGP-covered deposits exceeded $800 billion.[6]

THE DEBT GUARANTEE PROGRAM

The DGP guaranteed newly issued, senior unsecured debt by FDIC-insured depository institutions, their holding companies, and other eligible financial

---

4. Henry M. Paulson, Jr., *On the Brink: Inside the Race to Stop the Collapse of the Global Financial System* (New York: Business Plus, Hachette Book Group, 2010), 364.
5. See FDIC, "TLGP Debt Guarantee Program: Issuer Reported Debt Details," accessed June 2, 2019, https://www.fdic.gov/regulations/resources/tlgp/totaldebt.pdf.
6. FDIC, *Crisis and Response,* 33, 43.

institutions.[7] Bank and savings and loan holding companies were required to have at least one insured and operating depository institution, but the FDIC could make other affiliates eligible on a case-by-case basis after written request and with the agreement of the appropriate federal banking agency.

The DGP capped the debt guarantee at 125 percent of the par value of the issuer's senior unsecured debt to allow participants to roll over existing debt and provide for a modest growth of debt issuance. The interim final rule of October 14, 2008 (Interim Rule) provided that the payment of claims was to be triggered by receivership for banks and bankruptcy for bank holding companies.[8] Pricing under the Interim Rule was on an annualized flat rate of 75 basis points. The Final Rule of November 21, 2008, changed the trigger for the payment to an issuer's payment default. The FDIC also altered the flat-rate pricing approach to a sliding-fee schedule ranging from 50 to 100 basis points.[9]

THE TRANSACTION ACCOUNT GUARANTEE PROGRAM

The TAGP extended deposit insurance coverage to all deposits in non-interest-bearing transaction accounts, as well as accounts that pay minimal interest. The goal of the TAGP was simply to stabilize deposit funding for banks by mitigating the risk that larger deposits would run and lead to further bank failures.

As was the case with the DGP, the TAGP received direct user fees. A surcharge of 10 basis points was applied to deposits in non-interest-bearing transaction accounts not otherwise covered by the existing deposit insurance limit of $250,000. The surcharge was added to the participating bank's risk-based

---

7. The DGP guarantee applied to (1) FDIC-insured depository institutions, (2) U.S. bank holding companies, and (3) U.S. savings and loan holding companies that either engaged only in activities permissible for financial holding companies under Section 4(k) of the Bank Holding Company Act (BHCA) or had an insured depository institution subsidiary that was the subject of an application under Section 4(c)(8) of the BHCA regarding activities closely related to banking. 12 C.F.R. 370.2(a) (2008) (note that following the expiration of the TLGP, Part 370 was repurposed); see Temporary Liquidity Guarantee Program: Final Rule, 73 Fed. Reg. 72244 (Nov. 26, 2008) (Federal Register publication of Final Rule adopted by FDIC board on Nov. 21, 2008).
8. See FDIC, *Crisis and Response*, 15: "As a result, the initial interim rule the FDIC put forward for the payment of claims relied for triggers on the receivership process for banks and on bankruptcy filings for BHCs."
9. FDIC, *Crisis and Response*, 45.

deposit premium. The FDIC determined the continued eligibility requirements and parameters for use. With the extension of the program, fees were increased.

DEVELOPING THE FRAMEWORK: SORTING OUT THE POLICY ISSUES

On October 14, 2008, the FDIC board of directors approved the Interim Rule and on November 21 adopted the Final Rule establishing the TLGP.[10]

The two weeks preceding the October 14 announcement were filled with dire news about the financial system and intense interagency debates over the government response. Even as financial institutions began to issue FDIC-guaranteed debt after October 14, many of the operational details continued to be debated and refined. In retrospect, it is remarkable how quickly the TLGP was developed and options tested and revised during a period of a few weeks in October and early November 2008.

The FDIC developed the program's final form in consultation with other agencies and through discussions with bankers, market contacts, credit rating agencies, advisory firms, and law firms. Within the FDIC, the development of the TLGP was fueled by an interdisciplinary approach across the agency's supervisory, resolution, research, deposit insurance, consumer outreach, and legal teams. We also consulted constantly with members of the FDIC's board.

Outside the FDIC, Chairman Bair sought feedback from other regulators both to gather additional information and to benefit from their expertise. The FDIC has a different role and different responsibilities from those of the Office of the Comptroller of the Currency (OCC), the Federal Reserve, or the Treasury. While the FDIC has statutory power to respond to systemic risks, its statutory powers focus on protecting insured deposits and preserving the strength of the Deposit Insurance Fund that stands behind deposit insurance.[11] The OCC and the former Office of Thrift Supervision have the power to charter new federal depository and trust institutions and principally supervise those institutions. The Federal Reserve, while exercising broad supervisory power over bank holding companies and a subset of banks, must consider the stabil-

10. 73 Fed. Reg. 72244 (Nov. 26, 2008). Before issuing the Final Rule, the FDIC issued the Interim Rule with a request for comments, which was published at 73 Fed. Reg. 64179 (Oct. 29, 2008), and an Amendment to the Interim Rule, which was published at 73 Fed. Reg. 66160 (Nov. 7, 2008).
11. See Bair, *Bull by the Horns*, 12–13; 12 U.S.C. §§ 1821–23.

ity of the financial system as well as monetary policy.[12] Treasury likewise has broad responsibilities but does not act as a supervisor or chartering authority, and, as was evident during the crisis, has very limited, unappropriated financial resources.[13]

These different experiences, responsibilities, and powers meant that each agency and the Federal Reserve came to the crisis and the questions about the TLGP with different perspectives and preconceptions. While this led to intense debates and disagreements, the differences helped prevent groupthink and ensured that diverse options and consequences were fully vetted.[14] While this multiplicity of actors may be inefficient at times, my experience is that this competition of ideas usually achieves better and more thoroughly considered decisions than those made by a single authority. It is important not to overlook the value added by analysis and advocacy from the unique perspectives of different statutory and regulatory authorities. In the crisis, we were successful in combining consultation with quick decision-making and decisive action.

Also important in framing the policy issues is to remember that the U.S. actions did not occur in a vacuum. In Europe, the United Kingdom and other countries had already put in place certain guarantees and continued to explore additional options.[15] U.S. regulators were conscious of the potential for U.S. banks to be placed at a competitive disadvantage if these varying government support actions appeared to provide foreign banks with clearer and more reliable support.

The DGP and the TAGP presented different policy questions. Fundamentally, the policy issues surrounding the TAGP were much simpler. It was an expansion of the deposit guarantees embodied in the FDIC's historical mission. However, development of the TAGP required careful consideration of how this expansion could be implemented in the most effective manner. While the FDIC had provided deposit guarantees for 75 years by 2008, it was vital to calibrate the expansion to avoid unanticipated and unintended consequences. The TAGP was especially important for smaller banks, which sometimes

---

12. See Bernanke, *Memoir of a Crisis*, 48–49; 12 U.S.C. § 248.
13. See Paulson, *On the Brink*, 49–50.
14. Somewhat indirect confirmation is provided in Bair, *Bull by the Horns*, 111–15; Timothy F. Geithner, *Stress Test: Reflections on Financial Crises* (New York: Crown Publishers, 2014), 230–34.
15. FDIC, *Crisis and Response*, 34.

viewed the DGP as designed principally to support the largest banks with their much greater reliance on market-based funding.[16] If government support appeared focused on larger banks, smaller banks feared the loss of deposits to the "too big to fail" banks. In fact, by October 2008, the FDIC had some evidence that deposits had been moving to larger banks.[17]

The policy issues involved in development of the DGP were considerably more complex and ones with which the FDIC had comparatively little experience. However, in comparison with equity investments, the FDIC had long considered guarantees to be simpler to adopt and exit. This was one reason for the preference for loss sharing, which is simply a guarantee against tail risk, over equity or other forms of support to purchasing banks. Guarantees were viewed as simpler to implement, since there are no securities to purchase or sell, and as providing more leverage for the funds committed since actual payment was required only on default rather than at investment. Nonetheless, the guarantees planned under the DGP were quite different from guarantees for individual banks, such as in the open bank assistance transactions principally in the 1980s or closed bank resolutions involving bridge banks.[18] No prior assistance transactions had involved guarantees of the magnitude contemplated by the DGP. Given the virtual collapse of the bank-related debt markets by early October 2008 and the interagency consensus that capital alone was insufficient, it was imperative to address the moribund debt markets. In effect, the conclusion was that the only prospect for doing this was to use the systemic risk exception to allow for a greatly expanded use of open bank assistance by the FDIC.

16. See Final Rule Regarding Amendment of the Temporary Liquidity Guarantee Program to Extend the Transaction Account Guarantee Program (Federal Register, vol. 75, no. 123, 36506, June 28, 2010), stating that "the TAG component of the TLGP was developed, in part, to address concerns that a large number of account holders might withdraw their uninsured deposits from IDIs due to then prevailing economic uncertainties. Such withdrawals could have further destabilized financial markets and impaired the funding structure of smaller banks that rely on deposits as a primary source of funding."

17. For example, see Sheila Bair, Statement at the U.S. Treasury, Federal Reserve, FDIC Joint Press Conference, Oct. 14, 2008, arguing that "many smaller, healthy banks have been losing these accounts to their much larger competitors because of uncertainties in the financial system."

18. See, for example, FDIC, *Managing the Crisis: The FDIC and RTC Experience 1980–1994* (Washington, D.C.: FDIC, 1998), vol. 1, chaps. 5 and 6.

The key issues considered and addressed in the development of the DGP were the following:

1. Did the FDIC have the necessary legal authority to create the program?
2. Who should be eligible to participate?
3. What types of debt should be guaranteed?
4. What should the terms and conditions be for payment, reporting, and documentation?
5. How much should participants pay for the guarantee?

THE FINE PRINT: THE SYSTEMIC RISK EXCEPTION AND ELIGIBILITY

THE KEY POLICY ISSUES IMPLICATED BY TLGP

Legal Issues—Applicability of the "Systemic Risk Exception"

Since Congress passed the Federal Deposit Insurance Corporation Improvement Act of 1991 (FDICIA) in the wake of the thrift crisis, the FDIC has been required to use the resolution strategy that is the "least costly" to the DIF when resolving failing insured banks or thrifts. One exception to this requirement is allowed. If the "least costly" resolution "would have serious adverse effects on economic conditions or financial stability," the FDIC can take an alternative "action or assistance" if doing so "would avoid or mitigate such adverse effects." This is commonly referred to as a systemic risk exception. This decision cannot be made by the FDIC alone. The secretary of the Treasury, in consultation with the president, must decide to use the exception following the recommendation of two-thirds votes of the FDIC board of directors and the Federal Reserve Board of Governors.[19] Before 2008, the exception had never been invoked.

The initial legal question was whether a provision expressly permitting an exception "with respect to an insured depository institution" could be applied to a program of assistance for many financial institutions at one time.[20] The FDIC ultimately concluded that the statutory language, and the context in which it was used, demonstrated sufficiently that the systemic risk exception could be applied to multiple financial institutions at once because the remedy

---

19. See 12 U.S.C. § 1823(c)(4)(G).
20. There is little legislative history on the systemic risk provision and nothing addressing the precise scope of this language.

had to be broad enough to mitigate the "serious adverse effects on economic conditions or financial stability" that the provision was designed to address. In particular, the statute did not specifically require an institution-by-institution determination of systemic risks. Moreover, the application of a "systemic risk exception" would necessarily entail situations of "systemic relevance"—that is, situations involving multiple institutions. Examined in context, the FDIC concluded, Congress inherently required an evaluation of the consequences on multiple financial institutions.

As a result, the FDIC concluded that the statutory language permitted the FDIC to fashion a remedy commensurate with the "serious adverse effects."[21] While this was a reasonable interpretation that provided flexibility in designing a solution to meet the problem, it did not go unchallenged. In its later analysis, the Government Accountability Office concluded that "there are questions about these interpretations" and therefore "the statutory requirements may require clarification." Congress later imposed limitations on the FDIC's authority to create a future TLGP-style program in the Dodd-Frank Wall Street Reform and Consumer Protection Act of 2010.[22]

Did the conditions in the fall of 2008 meet the statutory standard? Certainly, market conditions were dire. The short-term lending markets and credit markets were essentially frozen, and there was almost no interbank or federal funds lending. The shocks from the failures of Lehman and WaMu, and increasing stress on other large financial institutions, had led to further tightening in funding and withdrawals of deposits from some banks. The conditions amply demonstrated "serious adverse effects on economic conditions or financial stability."[23] In this context, it is difficult to question a conclusion that applying

21. The language of U.S.C. § 1823(c)(4)(G) clearly connected the use of the "least costly resolution method" for an insured depository institution to the risk of "serious adverse effects on economic conditions or financial stability" and provided broad flexibility in choosing steps that could be taken to address those "serious adverse effects" so long as those steps reasonably would help mitigate those effects. Nothing in the statute specifically limited the *remedy* to action to assist a single insured depository institution.

22. See FDIC, *Crisis and Response*, 41; Government Accountability Office (GAO), *Regulators' Use of Systemic Risk Exception Raises Moral Hazard Concerns and Opportunities Exist to Clarify the Provision* (Washington, D.C.: GAO, 2010), appendix II.

23. FDIC, *Crisis and Response*, 38–40; see also John F. Bovenzi, *Inside the FDIC: Thirty Years of Bank Failures, Bailouts, and Regulatory Battles* (Hoboken, NJ: John Wiley & Sons, 2015), 173–78.

the "least costly" resolution process on a bank-by-bank basis "would have serious adverse effects on economic conditions or financial stability" and would not mitigate the crisis. Although it was impossible to know whether the TLGP "would avoid or mitigate such adverse effects," it certainly appeared much more likely to address the underlying market illiquidity. The prospects of success were greatly improved by combining the DGP with capital intervention by Treasury and additional liquidity intervention by the Federal Reserve.

Eligibility

The policy debates over eligibility also posed significant legal questions of FDIC authority and appropriate policy. Providing a broader guarantee of deposits was relatively simple and clearly within the FDIC's mandate. In addition, doing so would respond to concerns at smaller banks that only the largest money-center banks had received assistance to date. To partially address the potential for deposit runs by depositors with balances of more than $100,000, the TARP legislation included an increase in the deposit insurance coverage to $250,000. However, given the increasing liquidity stress at banks, a broader guarantee focused on business transaction accounts, which became TAGP, seemed in order.

Broad debt guarantees were different. Initially, Treasury and the Federal Reserve asked the FDIC to guarantee all bank liabilities, as well as those of bank and thrift holding companies. The FDIC instead proposed to apply the DGP only to new, senior unsecured debt issued by FDIC-insured depository institutions. But given the limitations of the TARP and the just-announced Federal Reserve programs, Treasury and the Federal Reserve were concerned that this would be insufficient.[24]

To the FDIC, extension of the proposed guarantees beyond banks posed legal and policy questions given the focus of the FDIC's powers on the protection of depositors in insured banks and thrifts. The FDIC's past experience had been in addressing issues at insured depository institutions, not at their holding companies. The statutory language creating the systemic risk exception potentially implies authority considerably broader than redressing issues at insured depository institutions. That language authorizes the FDIC to use the exception to provide "assistance" if doing so would mitigate "serious adverse effects on

---

24. See Bair, *Bull by the Horns*, 113; Geithner, *Stress Test*, 230–34; Paulson, *On the Brink*, 340–41.

economic conditions or financial stability." While this language reasonably may be viewed as tied to resolving an insured depository institution, it potentially could cover U.S. bank holding companies, U.S. savings and loan holding companies, and certain types of thrift holding companies if necessary to address the underlying "serious adverse effects" on the economy or financial stability. But could it extend beyond that?

The FDIC was concerned that providing debt guarantees to financial companies other than insured depository institutions and their holding companies also could potentially undercut the credibility of the guarantee of insured deposits as well as of the new guarantees under the TLGP. Given the available resources, would the markets question the credibility of broader guarantees? The DIF had a finite balance, which had already been questioned earlier in 2008. On a financial basis, backing by the "full faith and credit of the United States" and the ability to borrow from Treasury may be sufficient. However, a financial analysis ignores the fragile nature of public confidence during a crisis—and the importance of a "fund" available to meet depositors' claims.

Treasury and the Federal Reserve expressed concern that limiting TLGP—particularly given the limitations of TARP—could place nonbank financial companies at a severe disadvantage.[25] For the FDIC, providing guarantees to financial companies other than insured depository institutions and their holding companies posed a broader challenge because the agency did not have information to assess the risk posed by broader guarantees.[26] To address this concern, the FDIC, Treasury, and the Federal Reserve ultimately agreed to broaden the eligible entities to include both financial companies that were not bank holding companies and nonbank affiliates of bank holding companies. To give the FDIC authority to manage the potential risks, guarantees to those companies would be subject to FDIC approval, in its sole discretion, on a case-by-case basis on written request and positive recommendation by the appro-

---

25. General Electric Capital Corporation (GECC) was a savings and loan holding company, but it was not solely engaged in activities permissible for a financial holding company under section 4(k) of the Bank Holding Company Act. For additional details, see Mark Barber, "Written Submission of GE Capital to the Financial Crisis Inquiry Commission," May 6, 2010, https://fcic-static.law.stanford.edu/cdn_media/fcic-testimony/2010-0506-Barber.pdf.
26. See Bair, *Bull by the Horns*, 118.

priate federal banking agency. The FDIC also would have an opportunity to consider additional information to assess the risks. In making this determination, the FDIC would consider the following factors: (1) the extent of the financial activity of the entities within the holding company structure; (2) the strength, from a ratings perspective, of the issuer of the obligations that would be guaranteed; and (3) the size and extent of the activities of the organization.

One example of the use of this discretion was GE Capital Corporation (GECC). Jeffrey Immelt, the CEO of GECC parent General Electric (GE), approached several policymakers to seek guarantees under the DGP to ease GECC's access to market funding. After discussions between FDIC's Bair and Immelt and a review of GECC's capital, risk management, and information controls, the FDIC approved that firm's participation. The FDIC considered GECC's capital and risk management to be solid, and since GE was then triple-A rated and had agreed to guarantee the FDIC against loss, direct risk appeared to be limited.

As noted above, given the risk posed to the FDIC by any default by the nine largest U.S. banks, one condition for extending the DGP to those banks was that each also had to accept TARP capital.[27] TARP capital and the CPFF, which was designed to provide a liquidity backstop to issuers of commercial paper, provided a cushion against substantial losses in the event of a default by one of these institutions. Another consideration for requiring all nine banks to participate was the significant concern at that stage of the crisis that if one or more of the stronger institutions elected not to participate, that decision could be taken as a "signal" that those participating in the programs were weaker, and this in turn could create additional dangerous downward market pressure on program participants.

Similarly, there was the risk of adverse selection if only the weakest institutions elected to receive guarantees under the DGP. Given the great disparity in the use of the DGP by different financial companies, with Citigroup, GECC, and Bank of America by far the greatest issuers of guaranteed debt, perhaps fears over the signaling effect were overblown.[28] Nonetheless, in October 2008, it was imperative not to take such risks. Interestingly, many of the largest banks continued to use the DGP for an extended period as it provided useful support

27. Paulson, *On the Brink,* 364.
28. See FDIC, *Crisis and Response,* 50–51.

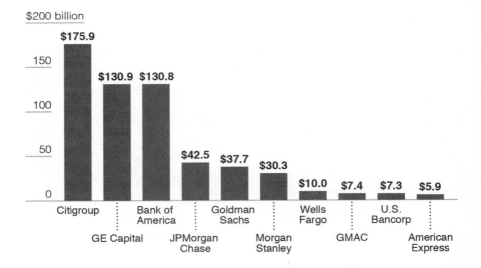

$200 billion

150 — $175.9 (Citigroup)

$130.9 (Bank of America) $130.8 (GE Capital)

100

50 — $42.5 (Goldman Sachs) $37.7 (JPMorgan Chase) $30.3 (Morgan Stanley)

0 — $10.0 (Wells Fargo) $7.4 (GMAC) $7.3 (U.S. Bancorp) $5.9 (American Express)

| Citigroup | Bank of America | Goldman Sachs | Wells Fargo | U.S. Bancorp |
| GE Capital | JPMorgan Chase | Morgan Stanley | GMAC | American Express |

Figure 9.2 Top Ten Debt Guarantee Program Issuers, by Dollar Amount

Source: FDIC, *Crisis and Response: An FDIC History, 2008–2013* (2017)

for debt issuances. Smaller banks were not required to participate in TARP to access the DGP. (See Figure 9.2.)

After the opt-out date, only those institutions still participating in the program were subject to fee assessments. However, participation rates remained high even though continued participation was voluntary. For example, at the end of March 2009, more than 90 percent of insured deposit institutions with assets greater than $10 billion remained in the DGP. The explanation for this high rate of participation is straightforward: Banks were concerned about their ability to access market funding.

MANAGING THE RISK: PRICING AND OPERATIONALIZING THE GUARANTEES

In addition to the questions about authority and eligibility, implementation of the DGP required weighing the issues presented by several key features. First, the FDIC had to define the types of debt that would be guaranteed. Second, it had to define the contractual terms and conditions under which the guarantee would be provided. Third, it had to price the guarantees. Each of these questions required striking a balance between the imperative of strong and quick action to stem growing banking system illiquidity and managing the risk to the FDIC. This was all the more challenging given the limited available information and the novelty of the proposed solution.

There was a strong recognition within the FDIC that making the terms too strict could impair the fundamental goal of reducing funding costs and loosening credit flows to the economy. In addition, if the terms were too strict, the risk of adverse selection was much greater, which could have the noted signaling effect and, in fact, increase risks to the FDIC. Conversely, terms that were too lax could yield heightened risk to the FDIC by spurring overuse and eliminating encouragement to turn to unguaranteed private debt markets as soon as feasible.

TYPES OF DEBT

An initial definitional issue was to specify what types of debt would be guaranteed and with what maturities. While the debates over eligibility resolved the question of whose debt could be included in the DGP, the question of whether preexisting debt should be guaranteed remained. Treasury and the Federal Reserve argued that preexisting as well as new debt should be guaranteed. In response, the FDIC noted that while it would be important to ensure that eligible institutions could roll over existing debt if necessary, preexisting debtholders had already made their bargain. Issuing new debt would, in contrast, allow refinancing of prior debt and continue access to the markets.[29]

The FDIC made clear its focus on enhancing liquidity and not creating opportunities for arbitrage in more exotic debt. Many comments on the October 14 proposal were in favor of FDIC guarantees for letters of credit, structured notes, and derivatives more broadly. Those arguments were quickly rejected as outside the goal of improved debt liquidity. Other commenters sought longer-term guarantees to support long-term debt issuance. While the FDIC was conscious that short-term markets (30 days or under) had begun to stabilize by the November approval of the Final Rule, the risk of longer-term guarantees would have extended the FDIC's guarantee exposure far beyond the horizon of expected need and impaired the transition to unguaranteed debt.

29. See Bair, *Bull by the Horns*, 112–13; Geithner, *Stress Test*, 234.

This is an important lesson—a balance must be struck between immediate government support and avoiding a longer-term dependence on a government-guaranteed market. The potential for private market distortion was a constant consideration. As a result, the FDIC agreed to guarantee all senior unsecured debt, as defined in the Final Rule, issued by a participating institution until the maturity date or June 30, 2012, whichever came first.[30]

GENERAL TERMS AND CONDITIONS

A further important operational element was to settle on the terms of the Master Agreement with the FDIC required for eligible entities to participate in the TLGP.

An important initial "term" was confirmation that the FDIC's guarantee was backed by the full faith and credit of the United States. As a legal question, this was relatively straightforward since the guarantees clearly met the statutory criteria, but clarity was crucial to achieving confidence in the program. Clarity that the guarantees were backed by the United States also was essential to ensure that TLGP-guaranteed debt had a preferential risk-weighted treatment for regulatory capital purposes. The Final Rule resolved any questions by confirming that the FDIC's guarantee of qualifying debt under the DGP was subject to the full faith and credit of the United States pursuant to section 15(d) of the Federal Deposit Insurance Act (FDIA), 12 U.S.C. § 1825(d).

Equally essential to achieving market confidence was to ensure that any guarantee payments met market expectations for timing and full satisfaction of the obligation. In the Interim Rule, the FDIC planned for payments to be made consistent with its experience with deposit insurance—upon insolvency

---

30. "Senior unsecured debt" was defined to include noncontingent, unsubordinated debt with a fixed principal amount without embedded derivatives. Accordingly, permissible debt could include federal funds purchased; promissory notes; commercial paper; unsubordinated unsecured notes, including zero-coupon bonds; U.S. dollar–denominated certificates of deposit owed to an insured depository institution, an insured credit union as defined in the Federal Credit Union Act, or a foreign bank; U.S. dollar–denominated deposits in an international banking facility (IBF) of an insured depository institution owed to an insured depository institution or a foreign bank; and U.S. dollar–denominated deposits on the books and records of foreign branches of U.S. insured depository institutions that are owed to an insured depository institution or a foreign bank. 12 C.F.R. 370.2(e).

of the issuing institution. However, through feedback from bankers, advisers, and credit rating agencies, it became obvious that anything less than an obligation to pay all amounts due upon the issuer's nonpayment likely would severely curtail demand for guaranteed debt and undermine the entire goal of the DGP. Similar guarantees upon nonpayment had been introduced in the United Kingdom, and this further signified the market expectation.

The original repayment terms in the Interim Rule led Standard & Poor's to question whether FDIC-guaranteed debt should be rated consistently with U.S. government debt.[31] If the payment on the guarantee was not "unconditional, irrevocable, and timely" and there was a risk of significant delay in payment, the FDIC-guaranteed debt would not receive a triple-A rating. This created a real concern at the FDIC that a less than triple-A rating could be viewed as a vote of no confidence in the FDIC's ability to perform—including in protecting insured deposits. Once the market and credit rating agency reaction was clear, there was limited debate. Payment on the debt guarantee would be triggered by payment default rather than bankruptcy or receivership.[32] With these revisions in the Final Rule, Standard & Poor's agreed that payment could reliably be expected upon payment default and provided the triple-A rating.[33]

The Master Agreement also included provisions facilitating repayment. For example, the Master Agreement included a clause permitting the FDIC to recover guarantee payments made to debtholders through subrogation or assignment. In addition, the defaulting bank was required to reimburse the FDIC for any payments made on the guarantee and pay interest on any unpaid reimbursement payments at an interest rate equal to 1 percent of the guaranteed debt instrument.

The FDIC also used other tools under the Final Rule to control its risk in the DGP. The Final Rule permitted the FDIC, working with an institution's primary federal regulator, to increase, reduce, or restrict the institution's ability to issue debt. This tool was used extensively by the FDIC. For example, in some cases the FDIC, in consultation with other agencies, reduced to zero the amount of guaranteed debt the company could issue.[34]

---

31. See FDIC, *Crisis and Response*, 48.
32. See Final Rule, 73 Fed. Reg. 72248; Bovenzi, *Inside the FDIC*, 192.
33. Bovenzi, *Inside the FDIC*, 192.
34. FDIC, *Crisis and Response*, 46–47; 73 Fed. Reg. 72268 (Nov. 26, 2008).

PRICING

The tension between achieving widespread adoption and managing risk and incentives was most acute in pricing. Both components of the TLGP had to generate fees to compensate the FDIC for the costs and risks of the protection. It was equally important to balance the necessity for supporting liquidity during the crisis with ensuring that pricing provided an incentive to move to unsupported debt markets in the future. In other words, if the price were too high, it could discourage companies from using the liquidity guarantees while they needed them; but if the price were too low, it could encourage overreliance on government support over the longer term and displace private markets.

Pricing for the TAGP was simpler since that component was an extension of the preexisting depositor protection. The FDIC assessed eligible insured institutions as of November 13, 2008, an annualized 10 basis points on balances in non-interest-bearing transaction accounts that exceeded the existing deposit insurance limit of $250,000.

Pricing for the DGP was more complex. If the price were too high, only the riskiest institutions would participate. This could have two negative consequences: signaling which institutions were weakest (though that was generally known at the time) and leaving the FDIC to guarantee debt issued only by those more desperate institutions. There was also a risk if the guarantees were underpriced. Underpricing would increase the risk of substantial losses to the FDIC, but it also could lead banks and affiliated companies (given the expanded eligibility) to become overreliant on guaranteed debt, thereby distorting funding markets and reducing incentives for a return to normal, unsupported debt markets. The FDIC considered a variety of flat-fee and calibrated-fee structures adjusted using risk-based factors.

In the end, the FDIC sought to balance these considerations by trying to replicate pricing for banks' funding costs in a normal market. Preliminary conclusions on pricing were included in the Interim Rule, which proposed to charge an annualized fee of 75 basis points on the amount of guaranteed debt. This was based on analyses suggesting that this flat fee was substantially above normal funding costs but far lower than the funding costs in October 2008.[35] Participating entities were limited to a maximum amount of guaranteed debt

---

35. FDIC, *Crisis and Response*, 45.

Table 9.1 **TLGP Guarantee Fees**

For debt with a maturity of:	The annualized assessment rate in basis points is:
180 days or less (excluding overnight debt)	50
181–364 days	75
365 days or longer	100

Source: Final Rule Regarding the Temporary Liquidity Guarantee Program, *Federal Register* (Nov. 26, 2008), Vol. 73, No. 229

and were prohibited from issuing nonguaranteed debt until the maximum allowable amount of guaranteed debt had been issued.

Many commenters on the Interim Rule criticized this fee structure. Some participants criticized this pricing structure as setting fees that were too high for short-term instruments.[36] Although the initial proposed flat fee would have benefited many issuers, the FDIC was asked to take into account a variety of factors to determine the appropriate fee structure, including the riskiness of the eligible entity, the term of the borrowings, the size of the financial institutions, and the maturity of the guarantee debts.

The FDIC examined the consistency and implications of the proposals suggested by the industry. The FDIC considered, but rejected, a risk-based pricing model for the DGP with guarantee fees based on a bank's CAMELS rating and the term of the borrowings.[37] Conversely, the FDIC concluded that a flat 75-basis-point rate could make the guarantee uneconomical for shorter-term debt and significantly understate its value for longer-term debt. For this reason, the Final Rule incorporated a sliding-scale structure for fees based on the maturity of the instruments with the rates shown in Table 9.1.

However, an extended program of debt guarantee with this pricing could have negative effects in the long run. In fact, the FDIC was aware of the potential

36. See Final Rule, 73 Fed. Reg. 72251.
37. Banks are rated by supervisors on a scale from 1 to 5, from strongest to weakest. The ratings criteria cover six components—capital adequacy, asset quality, management, earnings, liquidity, and sensitivity to market risk—and are referred to as the CAMELS ratings. Each bank is assigned a rating from 1 to 5 as well as a composite rating on the same scale. See FDIC, *Crisis and Response,* 70, footnote 3.

cliff effect that a sudden exit from the debt guarantee scheme could have for eligible institutions. So when the FDIC in March 2009 extended the program until October 31, 2009, it imposed certain fee surcharges (beginning on April 1, 2009) for those institutions willing to continue their participation in the program.[38] The additional fees consisted of a surcharge on assessments: 25 basis points for insured depository institutions and 50 basis points for other participating entities for FDIC-guaranteed debt that was either issued on or after April 1, 2009, with a maturity date after June 30, 2012, or issued after June 30, 2009.

Under the FDIA, the net cost of any use of the systemic risk exception must be recovered through a special assessment on the industry.[39] As a result, the FDIC created a separate account, through which it recorded fees collected and expenditures for payments on guarantees. Ultimately, the TLGP was fully financed by the fees participating institutions paid.

TEN YEARS LATER: A CRITICAL ASSESSMENT OF THE TLGP

WHY THE TLGP PROVED SUCCESSFUL

The TLGP was a key part of a multifaceted government response to the solvency and liquidity challenges the U.S. financial system faced in the fall of 2008.[40] More than half of the approximately 14,000 eligible entities participated in the DGP. While unguaranteed debt continued to be issued, between October 2008 and October 2009—the height of the disruption in the debt markets— almost two-thirds of the debt issued by eligible entities was DGP guaranteed. Further, the FDIC's analysis shows that over time, DGP-guaranteed debt moved from shorter-term notes to longer maturities.[41]

DGP-guaranteed debt was highly concentrated in a few U.S.-based institutions. The top 29 issuers of DGP-guaranteed debt accounted for about 99.7 percent of the cumulative total of guaranteed debt issued during the program, or more than $616.56 billion. Of that total, more than $578.6 billion was issued by the top ten issuers. Citigroup, GECC, and Bank of America, in that

---

38. 74 Fed. Reg. 26521 (June 3, 2009).
39. See 12 U.S.C. § 1823(c)(4)(G).
40. The FDIC provides an excellent overview of the data on the TLGP in chapter 2 of *Crisis and Response*. The following data are extracted from its analysis.
41. FDIC, *Crisis and Response*, 54–56, figure 2.8.

order, were by far the largest issuers While a number of U.S. bank subsidiaries of foreign banks issued guaranteed debt, only four were among the top 29 issuers and collectively accounted for only $8.63 billion total in guaranteed debt.[42]

In contrast, the TAGP was spread much more broadly across all insured depository institutions. In fact, during the extended period for the TAGP through 2010, the proportional participation by banks with more than $10 billion in total assets dropped far more than did the proportional participation of smaller banks. With other support programs—including the DGP—viewed as predominantly assisting larger institutions, the TAGP was viewed as essential to avoid smaller banks losing deposits to larger banks.

Ten years after the TLGP was created, it is appropriate to review a few of the successes and criticisms.

Public Acceptance: Building on Existing Programs

The TLGP generally received less criticism than other government interventions.[43] The FDIC benefited from a decades-long reputation as a federal agency that protected Main Street and consumers directly through deposit insurance. This is not a complex exchange: a bank fails and depositors are protected. The components of the TLGP drew directly on this relationship. In effect, the TAGP simply expanded depositor protections, while the DGP—though an enormous expansion of the FDIC's role—functioned much like insurance for debt. Both the public and the market understood guarantees, and both the TAGP and the DGP benefited Main Street as well as Wall Street. This combination spread the benefits and muted the outcry. A long-standing key to acceptance of any federal program is to have a constituent that benefits in every congressional district.

The FDIC is popularly viewed, rightly or wrongly, as independent from the political branches of the government. In addition, by the fall of 2008, Chairman Bair was seen as an advocate for homeowners and depositors. As a result, the TLGP was understood as being shielded from most political pressures, thereby enhancing its popular credibility. Finally, the FDIC also actively broadcast that the TLGP was paid for by the industry, like deposit insurance. As a result, while institutions paid for other programs as well, the TLGP appeared to be viewed, like deposit insurance, as industry funded.

---

42. FDIC, *Crisis and Response,* 61–62, appendix table 2-A.
43. See Bair, *Bull by the Horns,* 118.

Bair best summarized the key reasons for TLGP's acceptability: It relied on industry payments up front, and the amounts guaranteed, while substantial, were simply smaller compared with some other crisis programs.[44]

Guarantees Provide Efficient Use of Resources

Guarantees are financially efficient both in providing benefits where they are needed and in using available resources. The estimates of the cost of any guarantee program are generally based on the expected losses, not on the total amount guaranteed. In my view, this analysis more accurately reflects the fact that only a subset of total guaranteed debt will require payment by the guarantor. As a result, guarantees allow available resources to be efficiently leveraged where expected losses are limited; and, in comparison with equity injections or asset purchases, guarantees can potentially have a much greater economic effect given the same resources. This is a principle that the FDIC has long used in its loss-share and related programs for the resolution of banks and thrifts and that was applied in the ring-fence programs created for Citigroup and Bank of America.[45] While equity injections and asset purchases were necessary components of a broad-based program in a crisis as severe as the one we experienced in 2008, they do not provide the same targeting of benefits or leveraging of resources.

The TLGP targeted the guarantee benefits to discrete operations—deposit and debt funding. This ensured that the program could, and likely would, be used by a large number of banks and, with the eligibility expansion to affiliated entities, by a very large number of entities. This potential widespread targeted application was one of the reasons for the FDIC's focus on controlling risks, defining terms and conditions, and calibrating pricing. As noted above, the main purpose of the TLGP was to permit eligible institutions to meet their liquidity needs during a period of severe funding distress, helping the credit market to restore its transmission channels in times of economic recession and financial downswings. By design, the TLGP focused most directly on allowing eligible financial institutions to roll over and issue debt by providing a critical backstop guarantee. This focus was possible because the TLGP was only one part in a multipronged U.S. governmental effort to stabilize the financial

---

44. Bair, *Bull by the Horns,* 118.
45. See FDIC, *Crisis and Response,* 83.

markets. As funding became more stable, the liquidity positions of banks that opted into the TLGP improved substantially.

The TLGP Improved Liquidity

Although there is no precise way to assess the comparative contribution of the various elements of the October 14 package, it is generally recognized that banks' liquidity positions would not have been restored without the DGP. This is not surprising. The DGP was focused on a specific problem—the inability of financial institutions to issue debt—and the improvement in funding costs after initiation of the program was dramatic.

Studies that the FDIC noted in its retrospective analysis *Crisis and Response: An FDIC History, 2008–2013* showed significant improvements in liquidity, much lower funding costs, and decreasing yield spreads shortly after the start of the DGP. For example, immediately after the announcement of the combined U.S. governmental effort on October 14, institutions were able to access liquidity at much lower funding costs compared with those available in the markets. From October 13, 2008, to September 30, 2009, the cost of Libor credit declined by 446 basis points and the TED spread (three-month U.S. Libor / three-month Treasury bill) declined by 443 basis points.[46] Additional contributions to liquidity improvements could be observed in the easing of short-term and intermediate-term funding markets.[47] These developments once again allowed financial institutions access to market funding, while the TAGP allowed insured depository institutions to stem deposit withdrawals. (See Figure 9.3.)

The TLGP Did Not Impose a Net Loss on the DIF

A common measure of success is whether a program suffered a net loss. For the DGP, the FDIC collected more than $10 billion in fees and surcharges while paying out only $153 million for losses. For the TAGP, the FDIC collected $1.2 billion in fees while the cumulative losses at the end of 2016 amounted to $1.5 billion.[48] As a result, the gains derived from the TLGP substantially

---

46. FDIC, *Crisis and Response*, 56, figure 2.7.
47. FDIC, *Crisis and Response*, 56.
48. See FDIC, *Crisis and Response*, 58. More than half of the losses incurred by the TAGP were incurred in five bank failures: Silverton, Irwin Union Bank and Trust, Colonial Bank, Georgian Bank, and ShoreBank.

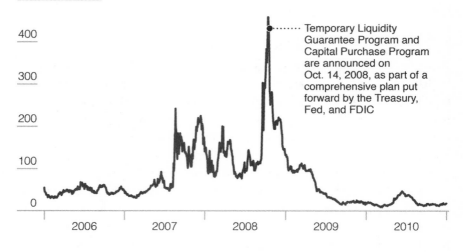

500 basis points

400

300

200

100

0

2006   2007   2008   2009   2010

Temporary Liquidity
Guarantee Program and
Capital Purchase Program
are announced on
Oct. 14, 2008, as part of a
comprehensive plan put
forward by the Treasury,
Fed, and FDIC

Figure 9.3 **TED Spread**

Note: The TED spread is the spread between three-month U.S. Libor and the three-month Treasury bill.

Source: Federal Reserve Bank of St. Louis

outweighed the FDIC's disbursements, with a net total of about $9.3 billion in fees deposited into the DIF.

The pricing structure of the TLGP was risk based. There has been considerable debate since the program ended about whether the FDIC properly priced the DGP and TAGP. Some have criticized the FDIC's pricing mechanism as insufficiently targeted to riskier institutions or as not incorporating market-based measures, such as an institution's credit default swap spread over government securities.[49] While these are reasonable considerations, these criticisms must be considered within the overall context of the goals of the program as well as other controls for risk used by the FDIC. As noted above, the TLGP was simply one part of a governmental response to the extraordinary loss of liquidity and the risks to solvency during the fall of 2008. TARP, the CPFF, and the TLGP together were intended to provide a cohesive response that would help

49. See discussion in FDIC, *Crisis and Response,* 46.

stabilize the financial system. The FDIC was conscious of the need to balance risk-based pricing against the imperative to reverse the growing slide to market illiquidity. And, the FDIC had other tools to control its risks. While the FDIC priced the debt guarantee at levels slightly above normal market conditions, it consciously priced the DGP guarantee well below the then-current costs of credit default spreads, which helped reopen the debt markets to eligible entities. The FDIC also sought to control its risks by a number of other mechanisms. As noted above, the FDIC used the discretion provided by the Final Rule to place limitations on the terms and debt it would guarantee for weaker institutions.

CRITICISMS

Congress did not focus on the TLGP at the time of its implementation. However, the Dodd-Frank legislation ultimately limited the FDIC's authority to extend guarantees in the future without congressional approval. It is reasonable to surmise that the proponents of this legislative change were reacting to the overall pushback against the "bailouts" of the financial crisis and to questions about the FDIC's expansionary reading of its systemic risk exception authority.

The Dodd-Frank Act significantly restricted the FDIC's ability to create a future TLGP. The new provision allows the Treasury secretary to request the FDIC and the Federal Reserve to determine that a "liquidity event exists." This determination requires the affirmative vote of two-thirds of the FDIC board and the Fed Board of Governors. With the written consent of the secretary, the FDIC can then create a "widely available" program of guarantees. The implementation of this program requires approval by a joint resolution of Congress. The guarantee program would be funded by fees and assessments paid by all participants in the program. Moreover, any excess funds would be deposited in the general fund of the Treasury. As a result, Congress controls whether the FDIC can create a TLGP-style guarantee program in the future.[50]

The Dodd-Frank Act amendments limit the FDIC's flexibility in dealing with liquidity shocks during future financial crises. Given these constraints, it will be more difficult in the future for the FDIC to implement a similar program in a timely fashion.

50. 12 U.S.C. §§ 5511–12.

LESSONS FOR THE FUTURE

Lesson 1:
Guarantees provide targeted support.

The TLGP was only one part of the coordinated government response to the capital and liquidity threats in the fall of 2008. Liquidity alone could not address that crisis. However, as part of a multipronged effort, the TLGP did effectively deploy guarantees to support a restart in the debt markets and stem the risks of deposit runs. Along with other tools, guarantees can provide an efficient mechanism to support existing market practices, rather than replacing them, and may be particularly suited to ease the return to an unsupported market. The FDIC had to address the potential cliff effect from the termination deadline but appeared to achieve a gradual weaning of the market from the guarantees through stepped-up surcharges.

Lesson 2:
Market and public support are important.

Public policy in the United States has been marked for the past ten years by reactions to the government interventions in 2008. The TLGP appeared to garner relatively positive public acceptance perhaps because it was an extension of a long-supported program, deposit insurance, and because it provided a direct benefit to depositors through the TAGP. In addition, the TLGP was funded by user fees, and not repaid over time, and as a result generally was not viewed as a bailout. Other programs, such as TARP and the Federal Reserve liquidity programs that were repaid over time, received much greater criticism. The apparent simplicity of guarantees and their similarity to deposit insurance and other popular programs, such as guaranteed loans for small businesses, also likely contributed to public acceptance. In effect, the perceived social cost of the TLGP guarantees was relatively low while the benefits for the markets, and the economy as a whole, were viewed as substantial and similar to the FDIC's existing programs.

Lesson 3:
Seek to understand market needs in tailoring programs.

The development of the TLGP was marked by discussions with governmental and private-sector stakeholders in an effort to ensure that the program would be targeted and elaborated in a way that accomplished the desired goals. For example, in tailoring the TLGP, the FDIC was fortunate in being able to respond to feedback after the Interim Rule by incorporating changes to address market requirements to include certain specific mechanics, such as a procedure for timely payments of debt guarantees. Future policymakers should ensure that they are open to outside input and analysis and incorporate this feedback in developing any programs like the TLGP.

Lesson 4:
Collaboration across agencies is critical.

The TLGP would not have been successful on its own. Only a combined governmental effort with TLGP, TARP, and CPFF could have achieved the relative success of the governmental effort launched in the fall of 2008. The severity of the crisis clearly demanded a unified approach. In any crisis, it is critical to assess how different authorities can deploy different initiatives to achieve a coordinated response. Equally critical is collaboration across agencies in the design of the efforts. More could have been done to collaborate during the fall of 2008, but the interagency discussions allowed faster innovation and helped avoid damaging false starts. This approach is essential to improving consumer, market, and institutional confidence, which itself is a key element in any successful intervention.

Lesson 5:
Be flexible.

This is paramount. All government agencies are bound by their statutory authorities and missions. But, in a crisis, solutions may depend on the creative application of preexisting tools and a clear understanding of when additional authority may be needed. The development of the TLGP exemplified flexibility in interpreting statutory authority and considering new options permitted under the FDIC's authority and mission. Other authorities, clearly including Treasury and the Federal Reserve, exercised creativity and flexibility in tailoring their tools and resources to meet the crisis. Without openness to considering such steps, the U.S. response to the crisis would have been hamstrung from the start.

CHAPTER TEN

Bank Capital

Reviving the System

TIM CLARK, MATTHEW KABAKER, AND LEE SACHS

THE STATE OF THE ECONOMY AND THE FINANCIAL SYSTEM DURING THE PRESIDENTIAL TRANSITION

By the time President Barack Obama was sworn into office, the economic fallout of the crisis had proved to be much more damaging than had been feared. The real economy was deteriorating and the financial sector remained under severe stress. The Treasury Department, the Federal Reserve, and the Federal Deposit Insurance Corporation (FDIC) had responded aggressively with a series of innovative programs during the fall of 2008. Treasury secretary Henry M. Paulson, Jr., successfully lobbied Congress for an early fiscal stimulus package and, despite an initial setback, $700 billion to fund the Troubled Assets Relief Program (TARP).[1] That allowed Treasury to inject capital into nearly 700 lenders. To avoid further damage from the fallout of the Lehman Brothers bankruptcy and the collapse of AIG, the Fed slashed interest rates and pumped

The authors acknowledge and thank the many staff members of the Federal Reserve System, U.S. Department of the Treasury, and the banking agencies that contributed to the efforts discussed in this chapter and throughout this book. Their dedication, creativity, and outstanding work on behalf of the American people under tremendous pressure and extremely tight time constraints were critical to the success of the many U.S. government programs undertaken to address the financial crisis.

1. Though the legislation provided for a total of $700 billion, it allowed the administration to draw only $350 billion initially. The incoming team would have to secure the second $350 billion before taking office in January.

trillions of dollars of liquidity into U.S. and global markets. The FDIC took the unprecedented step of guaranteeing all new bank debt for the financial system, a program that more than 100 banks participated in directly. Treasury designed and implemented a program to guarantee investments in money market mutual funds. And Treasury and the Fed orchestrated several programs aimed at restarting the mortgage and consumer lending markets, which had become all but frozen.

These actions were essential in breaking the panic of the autumn and preventing the collapse of the financial system. They helped forestall another Great Depression and bought valuable time for a new administration to decide what should come next.

The leadership and staff at the financial regulatory agencies and Treasury worked diligently throughout the transition to ensure the incoming administration completely understood the actions they were taking, why they had made these choices, and the trade-offs that had to be made. Their efforts provided the essential foundation to our response, which ultimately required only a modest additional use of taxpayer resources.

But these and other actions were not enough to stem the crisis. Even with all the powerful financial interventions during the autumn, the markets and the economy were in a downward spiral, with GDP falling at a real annual rate of 8 percent in the fourth quarter of 2008. Jobs declined by more than 700,000 in the month of January alone. A deepening economic slowdown raised fears about further home price declines and consumer defaults, which could lead to additional losses on mortgages and other loans as well as on the asset-backed securities (ABS) to which their performance was tied. In response, asset values declined, raising concerns about the solvency of the biggest holders of those assets: banks and other financial institutions. Fears of another solvency crisis and a pullback in lending only exacerbated concerns that the economy would continue to fall, causing the cycle of worry to begin again.

Making matters worse was the uncertainty over what steps the U.S. government would take. In part because of the sheer amount of government action in so many areas, it appeared to investors that Washington kept changing the rules of the game, and they were concerned about the actions that a new Democratic administration might take. Some on the Obama team talked during the transition about the idea of nationalizing some banks and imposing broader losses on creditors, leading to a chain reaction of rumors and unfounded speculation and contributing to further downward pressure on financial institutions (see Figure 10.1).

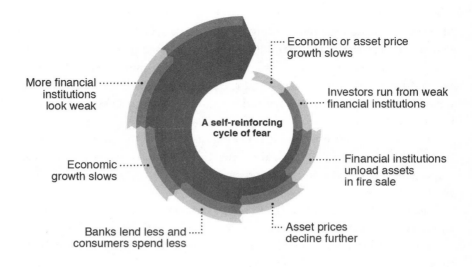

Figure 10.1 **Fear Cycle**

Just as worrisome, we were acutely aware that the financial resources available to us were limited and potentially inadequate. The International Monetary Fund (IMF) estimated, along with some private analysts, that U.S. financial institutions might have up to $2 trillion in losses. Yet we had only $250 billion to $300 billion of TARP government capital left to spend after commitments to other programs. We were concerned we would not have enough financial firepower to address the growing list of challenges we faced—and perhaps more important, we were fearful the markets would start to believe that we were out of ammunition.

We also knew these loss estimates were not static; the total would ultimately depend, in part, on what we did. An undersized fiscal response, a financial system left to resolve itself, and a continued confidence deficit would make it more likely that losses would be higher and the system would require more capital. By contrast, a credible fiscal program that reduced the risk of further economic contraction, paired with sensible policies to recapitalize the financial system and push against some of the fire-sale dynamics in credit markets, could create an environment where assessments of worst-case loss estimates might contract and the ultimate capital need might be more modest. Although this chapter focuses on the aspects of the strategy that directly addressed financial institutions and markets, the active fiscal and monetary measures would also prove critical in helping to reduce the risk of a major economic depression and allow our programs to succeed with much more modest outlays by both the public sector and the private sector than initially forecast.

We needed to come up with a convincing strategy, one that would reduce uncertainty and have credibility with the markets. The strategy also needed to make clear what we would not do: allow another wave of damaging financial failures, for example. We knew we needed to build on the government-sponsored enterprise (GSE) conservatorship, the initial deployment of TARP capital, the FDIC's guarantees, the Fed's introduction of innovative liquidity programs, Treasury's money market fund guarantee program, and other actions to create a clear plan to get the financial system working again so that the economy could start growing again.

We had two main objectives. First, we needed to recapitalize our financial system to mitigate the fear of a solvency crisis. Second, we needed to focus on ensuring that the credit markets were functioning and that prices in these markets better reflected fundamentals and did not continue to reinforce the downward spiral.

Most important, we were determined to adopt policies that attracted private capital back into the financial system. This was the linchpin of our strategy: We wanted private investors to do most of the work for us—to recapitalize banks, to invest in credit assets, to see opportunity instead of risk. Designing policies that made financial institutions and financial assets investable again was necessary in part because of the limitations on our resources but also because of the risk and costs of a prolonged period of direct government management of the financial system. Each policy was tested through these lenses. Would it help restore confidence? Would it increase the probability that private capital would mobilize?

Over the next six months, we rolled out an ambitious response plan that would ultimately achieve these goals. Admittedly, it was far from flawless. Nor did it always seem just. We struggled to communicate what we were doing and why we were doing it. But our core policy decision was to focus on stabilizing the financial system to help it support revitalization of the real economy. To engineer a sustainable economic recovery, it was necessary to fix the machines that provided credit to families and businesses. That meant resuscitating the very markets and institutions that had led us into the financial disaster: the credit markets and banks. For the general public, that was hard to understand, but we believed there was no plausible alternative.

THE NEXT STAGE OF THE FINANCIAL CRISIS RESPONSE

Our initial policy debates during the transition echoed those of the previous administration and those of governments in earlier financial crises. Should the policy response target the financial system and its major institutions or the households and businesses that depend on that system? To fix a broken financial system, was it better to buy assets, forgive debt, and provide assistance to affected borrowers or to inject capital into the system itself?[2]

Those of us who were members of the Obama economic policy team revisited this fundamental debate. At the beginning, each alternative seemed like a better choice than taking on the politically difficult task of recapitalizing financial institutions. Despite trying to design the best version of each idea, we encountered the same challenges that had left our predecessors in the Bush administration perplexed:

- *How should we value assets that are transferred to the government?* If the assets are priced too high (so that the government overpays), a hidden subsidy would go to the existing owner or financial institution. If the assets are priced too low, no institution would voluntarily sell—and the problem we are trying to solve would metastasize, as these legacy assets continue to reside on the banks' balance sheets.
- *How should the government dispose of the assets?* We feared creating a shadow overhang of troubled assets; likewise, we were sensitive to the fact that reselling the assets to new buyers at such attractive prices would create a political backlash, suggesting taxpayers were getting ripped off.
- *How should we treat the borrowers?* Should we be willing to make accommodations—including principal reduction—and who should decide? How would this be fair to borrowers with mortgages that were not purchased by the government? How would it be fair to those who continue to pay their mortgages—the "good" assets?

---

2. This was as much a political problem as an economic one. That is because the institutions most in need of assistance are usually the ones that through incompetence, ignorance, or guile acquired the largest quantity of the "root cause" loans or securities that caused the financial crisis in the first order. It is the most culpable that become the most vulnerable. And it is relatively simple for commentators to make an argument that concentrating one's efforts on restoring basic function to the financial system rewards the most offensive contributors to the crisis itself.

We also revisited another core debate in financial crises: Was this a liquidity crisis or a solvency crisis? Despite the earlier capital injections into Fannie Mae, Freddie Mac, and the banking system, both private-sector and government economists were still raising concerns about the solvency of the broader financial system. Wall Street analysts were projecting that the financial system would be severely undercapitalized once the banks began realizing the losses in their portfolios produced by the deepening recession. Analysts at the Fed also warned of a substantial shortfall of remaining capital. In late 2008, the New York Fed was privately projecting that the banks could still face as much as a $290 billion capital deficit if the economy worsened under a "stress scenario," and up to $684 billion in an extreme case, with about 80 percent of those losses concentrated in the 15 largest banks.[3]

The market was also sending clear signals. Many of the critical measures of system solvency—equity values of banks, the price banks paid for short-term borrowing, the price of insurance against the risk of bank failure—still signaled acute distress. The initial power of the bank preferred stock investments and the effective nationalization of Fannie and Freddie under the Bush administration appeared to be waning. One inference was that the earlier capital injections were undersized, particularly in light of the deteriorating economy. We thought this might be only part of the answer.

The combination of the market signals, the preliminary Fed assessment of potential capital shortfall, and numerous private forecasts led us to conclude that in addition to a liquidity crisis, the system was very likely undercapitalized. Whether individual institutions were also insolvent was an open question. What was clear was that enough market participants and counterparties *believed* they were insolvent. One reason was that investors started paying close attention not only to the *amount* of capital held by the banks but also to the *type* of capital on hand.

In its effort to recapitalize the banks while avoiding government control or nationalization, the Treasury Department under Paulson elected to make

---

3. Timothy F. Geithner, *Stress Test: Reflections on Financial Crises* (New York: Crown Publishers, 2014), 283. These projections were rough estimates and constantly in flux. They were also unsophisticated in that they were not capital need models (with full accounting for taxes, earnings, etc.) but rather gross loss estimates. The development of stress tests, as mentioned in the appendix to this chapter, would allow Fed economists to make far more accurate projections of capital deficits for each bank in different gross loss scenarios.

nonvoting preferred stock investments in the banks. That, along with an escalating dividend rate (which stepped up after five years) and additional compensation restrictions (required by the TARP legislation), led the market to believe that this capital was not permanent. It would need to be repaid, with interest, to avoid further opprobrium or penalties. What started as government equity capital, in other words, began to look like a government loan.

As we prepared to move into the Treasury Department amid a deteriorating economy, we became convinced that we needed to address more definitively the remaining concerns about solvency. Not only did we need to add or attract more capital to the system, but we also needed to inject higher-quality capital that could more easily absorb losses, or so-called tangible common equity. Taken together, this approach might create its own virtuous cycle: If the financial system were healthier, lending would pick up, the real economy would be healthier, and—though we knew we were in for a harsh downturn and a protracted recovery—the most adverse outcomes would be avoided. The question then became: how?

RECAPITALIZING THE FINANCIAL SYSTEM: EVALUATING THE ALTERNATIVES

Undercapitalized financial institutions exacerbate a crisis. They constrain lending activities as they seek to deleverage their balance sheets. The debt overhang can create heightened volatility in their equity, which can attract short-sellers. Their debt can trade at a discount or at a wide spread, which increases borrowing costs. They may face incentives to gamble for redemption and make high-risk investments at inopportune times.

Recapitalization, or the process of changing the mix of debt and equity, alleviates many of these concerns and puts the financial system on a substantially more stable footing. Here, we had four main alternatives:

1. *Forbearance.* Policymakers attempt to buy time to give financial institutions the room to recapitalize from operating earnings. They waive capital requirements, provide liquidity, and commit to avoiding catastrophic failure for the institutions. This can often take quite a long time, and during that period, banks are likely to exhibit many of the counterproductive behaviors described above.

2. *Resolution.* Policymakers force debtholders of financial institutions to cancel their debts and replace them with equity. In the United States,

this is traditionally how the FDIC recapitalizes insolvent financial institutions and how corporate entities recapitalize under U.S. bankruptcy laws.

3. *Loss Absorption*. Policymakers choose to assume losses that would otherwise be borne by the banking system. By absolving the banks of the need to pay these losses, equity capital is created and recapitalization achieved. This is often done through the use of asset purchases or guarantee programs.

4. *Equity Injections*. Policymakers attempt to create incentives for private investors to inject capital into banks or inject it themselves using taxpayer resources. This was the primary approach of our predecessors in the Paulson administration.

FORBEARANCE

We ruled out forbearance. President Obama made that call. He would admiringly cite examples of countries that he felt had pursued aggressive responses to financial crises. "Do Sweden, not Japan," was his common refrain. In other words, we were to take decisive action and differentiate ourselves from countries that had pursued a more gradual strategy of incremental, temporizing measures. The president embraced the foreign policy analogy used by Larry Summers, the director of the National Economic Council, who suggested we apply the so-called Powell Doctrine—the belief that a nation engaging in war should act with every resource and tool at its disposal to achieve a quick and decisive victory. We needed to act with overwhelming force.

RESOLUTION

Resolution was our preferred tool for smaller, less complex institutions. The FDIC had legal authority, expertise, and a long track record of resolving small and midsize banks in an efficient and effective manner. Unfortunately, we did not have the same tools to resolve much larger, more complex, and more interconnected institutions[4] without potentially devastating consequences to

---

4. Ultimately defined roughly as those with greater than $100 billion in assets, the institutions that formed the initial 19 banks in the Supervisory Capital Assessment Program.

other financial firms and the broader economy. Equity injections seemed empirically less messy.

Proponents of resolution argued that this method was more just—that it would punish institutions for their wrongdoing. As we saw it, the punishment was not being delivered to the institution itself and its executives but rather to the debtholders, who would be forced to exchange their debt for equity.

More important, resolution presented risks of a substantial contagion effect associated with imposing uncertain losses on a wide variety of creditor classes in the midst of the crisis. If these creditors saw losses being imposed on senior creditors of the bank, those that provided credit to other banks on a pari passu basis (equal ranking), but with shorter or demand maturities, might pull back from funding. These financial holding companies were organized in such a way that those in trading relationships or holding derivative contract counterparties with credit balances or providing wholesale funding were often pari passu creditors in the same legal entities as the long-term debt that would be subject to a haircut in a resolution. The risk of these creditors running from resolved institutions or others was potentially catastrophic.[5]

The use of resolution also risked spooking these same private investors, whom we were trying to attract to invest fresh equity capital into the banks. They were seeking clarity and certainty; forcing haircuts would muddy the rules and potentially cause anxious investors to flee.

Finally, there were serious governance concerns with a resolution-centric policy, especially if the government controlled a bank for any period of time. Governments are historically poor owners of operating businesses, and the exit path from crisis management would become much more challenging.

Nevertheless, we agreed with the spirit of these arguments: Resolution can work, and ideally, if you have enough time and a stable legal process where creditors and shareholders who knowingly assumed additional risk would ultimately reap the consequences of that bargain to help recapitalize an institu-

---

5. The financial system at the time was funded to a great degree by short-term creditors. If those creditors believed that the government was going to force haircuts on senior creditors, they would run from other institutions, forcing those institutions to quickly sell assets that they could no longer afford to finance. In our view, this would have put further downward pressure on the assets, causing more fire sales and exacerbating the fallout in the housing and other markets as borrowing rates rose even further. It had the risk of unraveling all the work that had gone into stabilizing the system.

tion, it can be a powerful and effective tool. We used it sparingly: The GSEs were formally resolved, and the FDIC managed nearly 500 smaller bank failures during the crisis using its time-tested resolution tool kit. These situations were distinguished mostly by the fact that we had a legal framework for resolution in both cases that did not exist for bank holding companies or for any nonbank financial institution, like AIG, GE Capital, and the major investment banks.

LOSS ABSORPTION (ASSET PURCHASES AND GUARANTEES)

The use of asset purchases or guarantees has significant conceptual appeal. As a policy choice, it can seem almost perfect in design: The government can buy assets or apply a guarantee to a basket of affected assets and agree to assume losses on those assets if they reach an agreed-upon "out of the money" level. This is a form of synthetic capital to a bank. At its simplest level, if you are willing to buy (or guarantee) assets at the banks' elevated marks, you can use this to create capital. Calibration of the level of the guarantee and the basket of assets can be used to adjust the level of capital support provided. Loss absorption on a more aggressive basis has also been used (during the Mexican peso crisis in 1994, for example), where the government explicitly assumed realized losses for no compensation or for equity.

We spent considerable time exploring asset purchase schemes. With respect to asset guarantees, our predecessors announced this approach for Citigroup and Bank of America during the transition, promising that the Asset Guarantee Program (AGP) would absorb losses on approximately $300 billion and $120 billion of assets, respectively. But the program proved to be exceptionally difficult to implement. For example, we struggled to identify a way of setting a fair price on literally thousands of securities. Other challenges included determining the appropriate loss mechanism—mark-to-market, realized loss, or another calculation—and then deciding how we would adjudicate, and who had control over, the settlement of the losses.[6] Finally, loss absorption did not have the scalability of other policy designs. Despite a significant effort to make it work for Citigroup and Bank of America and consideration of their broader

---

6. The Asset Guarantee Program was one of the few instances of an action that was announced—in this case a ring-fence of assets at Bank of America—but was never actually implemented.

applicability, it did not play a large role in the policy response. Loss absorption ultimately was a component of some contingency planning, as discussed later with regard to the Legacy Loan Program (LLP).

A HYBRID APPROACH: "OPEN BANK RESOLUTION" AND EQUITY INJECTIONS

We ultimately tried to reconcile the attractive features of resolutions and equity injections in our policy formulation. Internally, we referred to the series of policies we adopted as "open bank resolution." Our idea was that we could potentially realize some of the attractive attributes of resolution—chiefly the ability to have some of the need for new capital met by existing holders of subordinated debt and preferred equity—while avoiding the contagion effects of imposing losses on senior creditors or having institutions undergo a process of bankruptcy that was ill-suited for financial institutions.

The simplest path would have been to have Treasury inject common equity into the banks. Other countries, notably the United Kingdom, pursued this path. But like our colleagues in the Paulson Treasury, we feared that once the government owned an enterprise, it would be difficult to get out. That fear was borne out by the experiences of other countries that nationalized banks and of Fannie Mae and Freddie Mac in the United States, which have been owned by the U.S. government for more than a decade as of this writing. At the other extreme, we could have compelled private-sector involvement through resolution by forcing losses on existing creditors. For the reasons stated above, this was also suboptimal.

Instead, we challenged ourselves to attempt something more novel: to pursue a series of policies that might create an environment where the private sector would mostly complete the recapitalization itself. Further, we wanted to differentiate among institutions. We felt that we had to allow strong institutions to get credit for their relative solvency and make sure that the weak institutions did not get just a measured dose of capital but got all the capital they needed to survive even pessimistic assumptions on loss development.

The use of private instead of public capital was beneficial from both a policy and a political economy perspective. From a policy perspective, the potential pool of private capital was much deeper than the TARP funds that we had available. It would also minimize the expansion of the federal balance sheet.

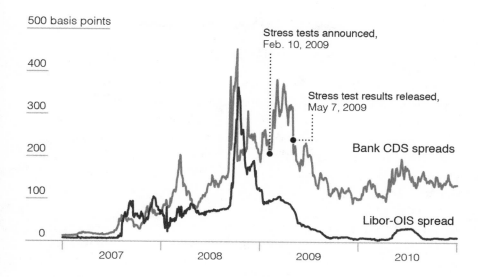

Figure 10.2 Bank CDS Spreads and Three-Month Libor-OIS Spread

Note: Credit default swap spreads shown are an equal-weighted average of Bank of America, Citigroup, Goldman Sachs, JPMorgan Chase, and Wells Fargo. Libor-OIS is the difference between the London Interbank Offered Rate (Libor) and the overnight indexed swap (OIS) rate.

Sources: Bloomberg Finance L.P.; IHS Markit

Still, it involved significant risk. We had to imagine the set of conditions under which private capital might invest substantial resources, and we had to plan for the case where we tried to encourage this investment and failed. Indeed, some of our colleagues believed it was unrealistic to expect private investors to provide the large amount of capital that would be required. But we did several analyses that suggested it was conceptually possible under the right set of public policies for the private sector to meet meaningful amounts of the new capital need. We believed there would be significant pent-up demand for bank equities if we could generate the conditions to cause this capital to become unlocked.[7] Our task was to figure out how to mobilize it.

7. We concluded this by looking at the short interest in banks, which was quite high, and the investment of the major mutual fund managers in the financial sector relative to the weighting of the financial sector in important indexes. Rough calculations of demand from short covering (back to even modestly elevated levels

STRESS TESTS AND BACKSTOP

SUPERVISORY CAPITAL ASSESSMENT PROGRAM

Restoring the banking system to health required that we determine where equity might be needed in the event of further economic pressure and that we be prepared to provide some of it to the extent that institutions could not raise the money from private investors. To accomplish that goal, we needed to put some bounds around the potential for further losses and provide clarity on how much capital banks needed and would be required to get. The Supervisory Capital Assessment Program (SCAP), better known as the bank stress tests, would be the critical tool (see Figure 10.3).

The stress tests marked the first time that regulators conducted an apples-to-apples analysis of potential losses across the banking system. It was a mammoth undertaking, led by the Fed and involving more than 150 bank supervisors, economists, and financial analysts from the three major banking regulatory agencies, supported by advisory teams of lawyers, accountants, and regulatory capital specialists. The assignment was to offer forward-looking projections of how much capital would be depleted by a severe economic downturn—including a scenario that was worse than the current dire forecasts coming from private-sector economists. As it turned out, the exercise ended up examining the ability of institutions to survive potential loan losses worse than those that banks suffered during the Great Depression. Any bank deemed to have a capital buffer that was not adequate to withstand severe further stress would be required to raise additional funds. And unlike most other bank exams, the results would be made *public*.

By providing clarity about potential losses and capital shortfalls (or the lack thereof) at each of the 19 largest banks—those with more than $100 billion in assets—that were required to participate, the stress tests would differentiate the weakest banks from those in a stronger position. The exercise would also help reduce the widespread uncertainty about the solvency of banks, one way or another.

Once completed, the test would then allow us to require those banks deemed to have fallen short to hold a significant buffer against worse-than-expected

---

instead of the peaks of early 2009) and a return of institutional investors from an "underweight" to an "equal weight" position suggested there could be meaningful demand for bank common equity.

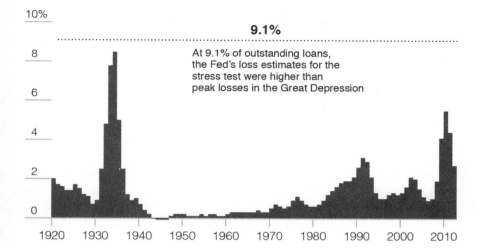

10%

9.1%

At 9.1% of outstanding loans,
the Fed's loss estimates for the
stress test were higher than
peak losses in the Great Depression

Figure 10.3 Historical Loan-Loss Rates and Bank Stress Tests

Note: Percentages reflect two-year bank loan-loss rates.

Sources: Federal Deposit Insurance Corp.; Federal Reserve Board; International Monetary Fund

losses, promoting confidence and reducing the likelihood that the worst-case scenario would occur. Importantly, it would also allow private investors to more precisely model the value of a specific bank. They could be reasonably assured that so long as the bank raised the required capital, the government would not intervene. This addressed one of the investment community's biggest fears—that it might commit capital to the banking system only to find the government had changed course and its investment was going to be wiped out.

But for this to work, the market had to believe the results were credible. Indeed, it was critically important that the exercise not be seen as a whitewash meant simply to provide false confidence, which many observers were already claiming was likely to be the case. Our economic scenarios, loss projections, and net revenue estimates needed to be transparent to investors—and seen as sufficiently tough. (For details on key design decisions, see the appendix to this chapter.) To remove any appearance of political interference, the stress test had to be administered by the Fed and the other banking agencies—independent of the U.S. Treasury. We had to run the test without preconceived notions of the outcome, and we all had to be prepared to accept and address the results.

None of this was without concern or controversy. Given the widespread use of stress tests today, it is easy to forget how unusual it was at the time for U.S. supervisors to require banks to capitalize against a hypothetical outcome. U.S. bank supervisors had never used a scenario-based stress test to assess the capital adequacy of banks and then required capital increases based on what those results showed was needed. Many thought it might not be possible under then existing legal authorities to require a bank that was currently meeting all regulatory capital requirements to raise additional capital based on a hypothetical scenario. There were concerns that if we suggested a bank was "insolvent" by identifying a need for additional capital but did not resolve the bank immediately, we risked exacerbating the situation. But the extreme market pressures that banks were under indicated to supervisors that there were clear safety and soundness concerns. On those grounds, the Fed determined it had the authority to require additional capital.

We also had to grapple with how transparent we should be about the specifics of the stress test and the bank-by-bank results. On the one hand, if we were going to reduce the prevailing uncertainty and provide useful information about the state of the banking system, investors and others would need to be able to parse the analysis with adequate granularity. They would essentially need to be able to use the data for their own analyses to determine their credibility. Otherwise there would be continuing suspicion that we had finessed the results to make the banks look stronger than they were. On the other hand, this level of transparency ran counter to decades of a banking supervision philosophy that extolled the virtues of confidentiality. The disclosure proposals led to contentious internal debates. There were concerns about setting what some deemed a bad precedent for supervision by increasing expectations for greater transparency in all future efforts. Worse still, we might risk calling attention to weaker banks—or possibly show they were all weaker than assumed—and prompt the very types of bank runs we were trying to avoid. The banks and some supervisors were concerned too much transparency would be destabilizing.

Ultimately, most of the skeptics came around to the need for greater transparency. Chairman Ben S. Bernanke and the Board of Governors decided we would let the public see the results in great detail and decide for themselves whether our stress test was sufficiently rigorous and credible.

The stress tests offered substantial practical advantages. First, they provided the information Treasury officials needed to size a government capital injection backstop. Second, they allowed for differentiation between stronger and weaker institutions because like assets were treated similarly across the financial system and each bank received a unique assessment according to its circumstances.

Third, by its design, it pushed back on the narrative that banks should be held to a mark-to-market standard. By measuring impairment in a stress scenario (but not necessarily assuming distressed-market discount rates) and including a bank's pre-provision net revenue in the calculation, we reinforced what some Treasury staff called the theory of special bank relativity—that banks exist through time and shouldn't be judged simply by how they stand at a certain point in time. Banks are designed to be "unstable" in this way, with demand deposits and short-term liabilities funding illiquid and long-term assets. If you force the banks to value their assets using a mark-to-market standard at the low point of the cycle, you undermine a key reason they are so important for supporting economic activity in the first place.

Fourth, the stress tests allowed the supervisors to define capital adequacy in a period of great uncertainty and compelled the banks to raise additional capital they needed to reduce concerns about potential insolvency. The SCAP created essentially a new capital benchmark, known as post-stress capital, which required banks to hold at least 4 percent of their risk-weighted assets after the impact of the stress in a newly created and stronger capital form, "Tier 1 Common." Through this mechanism, we were able to substantially increase both the quantity and the quality of capital that banks were required to hold and to support credit availability.

The intent was to capitalize the banks so they could continue lending at least at current levels even if conditions worsened. Normally, the easiest way to maintain a required capital ratio in a downturn is to pull back from lending or shed assets—activities that only make a downturn worse. To address this concern, we measured capital needs using a post-stress ratio—the "bogey," as we came to call it—based on an assumption that banks' balance sheets at the end of the scenario were essentially the same size and composition as they were at the start. We then translated that into an absolute dollar amount of capital we would require firms to raise rather than allowing them to shrink their balance sheets to meet the ratio.

CAPITAL ASSISTANCE PROGRAM

We were concerned that instead of helping attract capital back into the banking system, the stress tests could potentially make things worse—especially if a bank deemed undercapitalized or insolvent by the exam was unable to raise private capital and was left to sink or swim. We also knew that any credible stress test would take months to complete and that investors would likely assume the worst during that time. The stress tests could have even sparked the very types of bank runs we were trying to avoid. Some form of backstop was necessary. Shortly before the banks underwent the stress tests, we made clear that any bank unable to raise the necessary capital to meet the post-stress requirement under the SCAP would have access to additional government capital.

Enter the Capital Assistance Program (CAP). Treasury agreed to subscribe to a form of contingent equity security in an *unlimited* quantity as necessary.[8] Further, we noted that the security would be convertible as necessary into tangible common equity of a bank, and we defined the price at which it would convert based on the price of the bank's common equity as of the close of trading on the day before the announcement of the plan. The banks could convert their preferred stock provided by the previous administration under the Capital Purchase Program, or CPP (the preferred that had come to be viewed as most debt-like by market participants), into the new security that was convertible into tangible common equity. This helped us partly address the math problem of having only approximately $100 billion left of uncommitted appropriation in the TARP: By allowing the conversion of the previously issued preferred, we added approximately $200 billion of capacity to the program.

In a joint statement on February 10, 2009, Secretary Timothy F. Geithner, Chairman Bernanke, Chairman Sheila Bair, Comptroller John Dugan, and Director John Reich noted: "Our expectation is that the capital provided under the [Capital Assistance Program] will be in the form of a preferred security that is convertible into common equity, with a dividend rate to be specified and a conversion price *set at a modest discount from the prevailing level of the institution's stock price up to February 9, 2009*" (emphasis added). That final phrase was in brackets until moments before the release was finalized. The scope of the announcement we were making was sobering—we were committing the government to buy an indeterminate amount of common stock in the

8. Treasury offered the CAP to all banks and qualifying institutions, unlike the SCAP, which was limited to the 19 largest bank holding companies. Bank holding companies had six months to raise additional capital after publication of the SCAP results. A firm could, however, apply to the CAP immediately after the release of the SCAP results but delay the actual funding for six months while it raised as much private capital as possible.

banking system at a fixed price. It would be up to the regulators to determine how much capital the system needed and up to the banks to see whether they could raise this capital at better terms. The government was standing behind the system and the stress tests, and this fact alone provided some certainty and alleviated many of the widespread concerns about what the government might do with the banks.

On the positive side, this program allowed market participants to invest in any individual bank knowing that there would not be a catastrophic failure at any other major institution that might threaten to cause a cascading downward spiral. On the negative side, existing owners of bank equities knew that if they could not raise capital at better terms than those of the CAP backstop, they would have to accept government capital and significant dilution.

Shortly before the stress test results were released on May 7, a joint statement from the independent banking regulators made it clear that bank holding companies should "design capital plans that, wherever possible, actively seek to raise new capital from private sources," including specifically "restructuring current capital instruments."[9]

Indeed, we had called our program "open bank resolution" because we saw several sources of capital to meet the banks' needs under the SCAP other than raising "fresh" equity from market participants or from Treasury. We wanted the banks to undertake "self-resolution" by seeking to convert their junior creditors to equity and wanted them to know that if they couldn't find new private capital, targeting debt-for-equity exchanges of their junior creditors was the preferred path before they sought government capital. Although we had always been clear that from a policy perspective we did not seek impairment of senior bank creditors, we also significantly hardened our language in stating that junior creditors—holders of subordinated debt or other preferred securities—should expect to bear losses.[10]

9. Federal Reserve Board of Governors press release, May 6, 2009. Joint statement by the Federal Reserve, the Treasury, the FDIC, and the Office of the Comptroller of the Currency on the Treasury Capital Assistance Program and the SCAP.
10. The top 19 banks at the time had approximately $300 billion of these securities outstanding, which again helped us manage our budget constraints. Among the $100 billion of remaining availability in TARP, the $200 billion of CPP preferred stock, and the existing stock of subordinated debt and preferred stock, there was $600 billion of capacity to help meet the stress test requirements without needing to raise any new equity.

We also wanted to give the market a road map that demonstrated how firms could execute "open bank resolution." Citigroup approached us in early 2009, and we saw an opportunity to announce—nearly concurrently with the Financial Stability Plan (FSP)—a restructuring proposal that was consistent with our principles. In this transaction, announced on February 27, we agreed to convert a portion of the preferred stock held by Treasury ($25 billion) into common stock at $3.25 per share if Citigroup could convert an equal amount of subordinated debt and private preferred securities at the same price. We viewed this individual action as an important part of the plan because it demonstrated to market participants how the broader program could be executed.

It was only after the Citigroup transaction that we began to see evidence that the market understood what we were trying to do. A report from the Oppenheimer Group on March 2, titled *Geithner's Evil Genius,* provided the following evaluation: "Treasury is telling the marketplace, by its actions if not its words, that it wants to ensure that the company has access to common equity at roughly [the CAP price]. Treasury will either supply the capital itself or it will drill into the more senior layers of the parent company capital structure to do it. Treasury is, of course, not just sending this message with regard to Citi. The clear implication is, of course, that this two-piece tool kit can be used in all the other BHCs."

The SCAP results were published in May. Ten of the 19 banks were found to have had a combined capital shortfall of $185 billion based on the December 31 as-of date used in SCAP, with $75 billion of that shortfall still needing to be raised in May when the results were released. The incremental capital need was sized at approximately 2.3 percent of risk-weighted assets. This was on top of the 3.0 percent of assets they had received in the Columbus Day injections, with a major distinction being that the SCAP required the banks to raise common equity (TARP/CPP was preferred stock). By restructuring existing capital instruments after the SCAP as-of date, as in the Citigroup example, taking account of their pre-provision earnings in the first quarter, which had not been captured in the stress test, and new common equity raises from private investors, nine banks were able to satisfy the entire incremental requirement stemming from the stress test without turning to the government for capital through the CAP. The capital need of the tenth bank, GMAC, was resolved separately as part of the auto rescue.

Following the SCAP, a number of those banks wanted to quickly pay back the government investments they had received through TARP. To boost the quality of capital further in advance of additional planned supervisory work

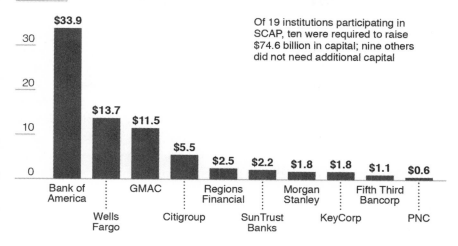

$40 billion

$33.9

Of 19 institutions participating in SCAP, ten were required to raise $74.6 billion in capital; nine others did not need additional capital

$13.7
$11.5
$5.5
$2.5 $2.2 $1.8 $1.8 $1.1 $0.6

Bank of America   GMAC   Regions Financial   Morgan Stanley   Fifth Third Bancorp
Wells Fargo   Citigroup   SunTrust Banks   KeyCorp   PNC

Figure 10.4 Stress Test Results: Capital Raises Needed

Notes: (1) $74.6 billion in required capital is after earnings and capital measures in the first quarter of 2009. Citigroup's requirement, for example, fell from $92.6 billion to $5.5 billion after adjusting for capital actions and earnings in the first quarter of 2009 and its plan to convert approximately $58 billion of preferred stock into common equity. (2) SCAP is the Supervisory Capital Assessment Program.

Source: Federal Reserve Board

on capital adequacy, the Fed required firms that wanted to repay the investments to raise roughly $1 of additional common equity for every $2 of TARP funds redeemed. By late January 2010, these firms had raised enough additional capital to repay the government's investment.

Meanwhile, the CAP was terminated—having never made a single investment. We saw this as a strong indication of its success, as our objective in the first place was to recapitalize the system with private capital.

THE LEGACY LOAN PROGRAM CONTINGENCY

Ultimately, we were relieved that the private sector mobilized for all institutions—strong and weak. This was by no means preordained. In fact, while the major banking regulators were conducting the stress tests, we spent a good part of March, April, and early May preparing for a worst-case scenario:

What if the institutions were unable to raise any of the additional capital need in private markets? What if the additional capital that the banks raised after the stress tests was still inadequate? How would we escalate our response to contend with a deepening crisis?[11]

For this, we knew we needed to partner with the FDIC. After all, it not only had the wherewithal and the authority (nearly unlimited) but also was the expert on resolution. Working closely with the FDIC's Department of Resolution, we designed a mechanism that would essentially replicate resolution for an open institution. If the government had to use the CAP to inject equity into a financial institution, resulting in implied ownership (upon conversion of the equity instrument) of more than 50 percent, we were prepared to implement these more radical approaches.

One of our policy tools was called the Legacy Loan Program, which offered a way to separate troubled assets from regulated banks. The FDIC agreed to finance the "purchase" of these assets from the banks by private-sector investors and Treasury. And unlike with TARP, there was no limit on the size of the program. In early 2009, for example, Citigroup, a bank holding company with approximately $2 trillion of assets, announced that it was moving $850 billion of troubled assets to an entity it called Citi Holdings.

One could imagine that the Legacy Loan Program might have been used to fully segregate these assets into a new entity, with financing by the FDIC. The "old" bank, now with $1.15 trillion of supposedly healthier assets and all the operating businesses, could continue as a listed company (although in this scenario most likely owned almost entirely by Treasury), but without going through a disruptive bankruptcy proceeding.

This was not nearly as simple as this example implies. There were questions of authority, legal structure, burden sharing for the various debt and equity holders of an impacted institution, and raising the funding itself. But we viewed the Legacy Loan Program as an important tool in Plan B. So as not to raise alarm, we didn't talk about this program very much or how we intended to use it. It required a systemic risk determination that we quietly pursued— the Board of Governors of the Fed and the FDIC Board approved the pro-

---

11. The same restrictions on authority still applied: How could we accomplish an intensive open bank resolution without having to use the bankruptcy process and without further increasing uncertainty and fears of nationalization and capricious government action?

gram. All that was needed was the signature of the Treasury secretary to launch the program.

The necessary document was never signed. In June 2009, FDIC chairman Bair released a formal announcement that the program was being postponed. In that release, she noted, "Banks have been able to raise capital without having to sell bad assets through the LLP, which reflects renewed investor confidence in our banking system."

REVIVING THE ASSET-BACKED SECURITIES MARKET

It was not enough to simply recapitalize the banks. We also needed to revitalize the asset-backed securities markets, which provided a critical source of funding to consumers and businesses. Over the previous three decades, that market had grown to more than $2 trillion, and by early 2009 it was showing signs of real stress. The sharp drop in prices of these securities was deeply problematic, and its impact extended beyond the realized losses to holders of the securities themselves. These distressed prices were being used to infer what the market thought the ultimate losses might represent for the entire financial system. The market could then apply this information to the owners of these securities and determine what losses their owners might face. The fear of increased losses often rippled first through these markets and then ultimately to perceived fears of insolvency for the institutions that owned these assets or faced similar credit risk.

What's more, the conditions in these markets posed a drag on lending. The prices of these securities reflected the yield or return that investors were seeking to own these assets. And these yields raised the benchmark for new loans. If an investor could buy a liquid security secured by car loans and make a 15 to 20 percent return, why would that same investor buy a new security backed by similar car loans or lend to a consumer looking to buy a new SUV at 4 percent?

Restoring confidence would require some intervention in these markets. We needed security prices to more accurately reflect underlying perceptions of default risk instead of the fire sale prices seen every day in the credit markets. We needed to bring down the yield of these *legacy* securities to promote the formation of new securities, which would support lending. Our policy challenge was how, with limited resources, to sway such a large market. Like our predecessors in the Paulson Treasury, we rejected plans to use TARP funds to purchase these assets. Meanwhile, our colleagues at the Fed made it clear that the law limited large-scale asset purchases under their quantitative easing initiatives to Treasuries and GSE securities.

Our assessment was that one of the biggest factors leading to a divergence between actual security prices and fundamentals of ABS was the so-called falling-knife problem. Without a sense of how bad things could get, no prudent investor would invest. But there was another problem. Before the crisis, most of these securities—the triple-A-labeled and super-senior-rated tranches of mortgage-backed securities (MBS)—had been purchased with significant amounts of leverage and little equity. An investor might have put down $1 million to finance a $100 million purchase of these securities. By early 2009, that same investor would have to put down $50 million or $60 million to execute the same transaction.

Just as we were constrained by limited TARP funds, the private sector was potentially capital-constrained. But if we could provide financing to support the purchase of these securities, we could lower the effective discount rate to own the securities and lower the amount of capital required (through leverage) to purchase the securities. This is similar to the lender-of-last-resort policies pursued by the Fed to expand the use of the discount window. But those policies were institution-centric: The Fed lent to primary dealers and regulated financial institutions. Our belief was that it could be even more effective and equally conservative to focus on the collateral itself without regard to the institution that owned it. We were trying to create a form of discount window lending to provide leverage directly to the nonbank market.

Some thought it paradoxical that our solution to a crisis of overleverage was to apply more leverage. But we thought the market had overcorrected in the other direction. So the medicine was much like a vaccine. We had to apply a bit more leverage, judiciously, to try to break the fire sale fever.

THE TERM ASSET-BACKED SECURITIES LOAN FACILITY

The Term Asset-Backed Securities Loan Facility (TALF) was announced on November 25, 2008, but by Inauguration Day it still had not been implemented, as the Fed wrestled with how to fit the program within its own legal constraints. The TALF had initially been designed by the Fed and the Paulson Treasury. Even among some highly innovative programs, we felt it was one of the most promising. It provided a chassis to accomplish the policy objectives we describe above. The program was set up with an initial $200 billion and was intended to provide asset-level, nonrecourse leverage to any purchaser of certain triple-A-rated ABS regardless of that purchaser's discount window eligibility. The terms of the loans—how much the Fed would be willing to lend against the collateral—would be determined by the Fed itself and set at a level to ensure that the central bank was protected in all but the most catastrophic scenarios. Importantly, it was targeted directly at capital formation: The Fed made the TALF available only to certain kinds of newly issued securities (auto, student, credit card, and Small Business Administration), all with the intention of reviving basic consumer and small business lending and borrowing at reasonable rates to foster an economic revival.

The architecture of the program also tied the Fed and Treasury together. To support the $200 billion of lending, the Fed required Treasury, through the TARP, to provide a first-loss layer of $20 billion to further protect the Fed from any losses under the program. This allowed a limited amount of TARP resources to have an outsize impact, 10 times as large as devoting TARP resources directly to lending or purchasing securities.

Our plan was to create a greatly expanded version of this excellent idea to demonstrate to the markets that there was a capable mechanism to restore function to asset-backed lending markets for all types of collateral. The Fed agreed to expand the program to other kinds of collateral for new security issuances and to increase its size. We felt this would send an important message, and, as part of the consolidated set of announcements in early February, the Fed announced a massive TALF expansion, to $1 trillion; extended the maturity of the eligible loans; and added most other asset classes, including commercial and residential mortgage securities. Markets quickly took note of the scope of the program. The TALF was officially launched in early March 2009.

We continued discussions with the Fed on our final frontier—expanding the TALF to finance so-called legacy securities as opposed to only new securitizations. The high yields available on legacy securities continued to have allure and forced pricing for new credit origination higher, drawing capital away from fresh lending.

This proved to be a real challenge for the Fed. It was concerned about how to define the eligible group of securities, how to create a methodology to determine the advance rate, and the political economy of lending to investment funds with a difficult-to-explain connection to new credit formation. We understood its concerns but believed the benefits outweighed the potential costs. As these discussions continued, we feared we would not reach agreement and began to consider other ways we could potentially achieve our objectives.

We faced the same set of consistent challenges in designing another program to restart lending. The germ of the idea came from Warren Buffett, who outlined a concept to Secretary Geithner wherein the government and private investors would coinvest in legacy assets. The government would be a silent partner—outsourcing decision-making on the assets purchased and their price to their private-sector partners. Similar models had been deployed by the Resolution Trust Corporation in the cleanup of the savings-and-loan disaster, relying on so-called partnership transactions that sold partial interests in acquired assets to private investors, who then pursued recovery and workouts of the underlying loans. The government participated in the ultimate value recovery through a retained stake.

THE PUBLIC-PRIVATE INVESTMENT PROGRAM

The Public-Private Investment Program (PPIP) was announced in late March, concurrently with the announcement that the Fed had ultimately agreed to consider expanding the TALF to include legacy residential and commercial mortgage-backed securities. Between the two programs, we were able to announce the potential to generate up to $1 trillion in purchasing power in the market for these legacy assets. It was not necessarily important to us how much was ultimately purchased. In hindsight, the announcement itself marked the beginning of the turnaround in the markets for residential and commercial MBS. In fact, as President Obama remarked in a meeting shortly after, why hadn't we announced this program earlier?

The PPIP solicited private-sector fund managers to raise funds explicitly for the purpose of purchasing eligible legacy securities as determined under the program. Any private funds raised by these managers would be matched dollar for dollar with TARP funds, and Treasury agreed to provide a credit facility for these funds in a 1:1 ratio with the total capital raised. This credit facility was a further inducement for investors—retail and institutional—to commit capital to these new funds.

In this way, $1 of private capital raised could be matched with $3 of government capital ($1 of equity and $2 of debt). We also conceived that these private-public investment funds would be heavy users of the TALF. So the capital in the PPIP, when combined with the financing provided by the Fed through the TALF program, could theoretically support purchasing power of up to $1 trillion, which was the figure we cited in public announcements.

The asset managers would make all the purchase decisions, and because of their fiduciary obligation to their investors, they would have to apply the same rigor to the performance of these funds as to that of their other investment vehicles. They would also control the disposition of the assets and any restructuring decisions that needed to be made to optimize value. Originally, we had the idea that we would select five fund managers through a comprehensive bidding process administered by Treasury.

We received more than 100 applications and ultimately were so impressed with the quality of the applicants that we approved nine managers to seek capital for their public-private investment funds, who subsequently raised $6 billion. With the match from Treasury and the credit facility, these funds ultimately deployed $25 billion of purchasing power.

IMPACT OF THE TALF EXPANSION AND THE PPIP

The Legacy TALF continued to be difficult to implement. It was officially launched for commercial mortgages in May 2009 but was never ultimately expanded to include residential mortgage-backed securities. Usage of the TALF program in aggregate peaked in 2010 at about $50 billion. These numbers, even combined, were quite a bit less than the $1 trillion of purchasing power we had announced. As with the CAP, the mark of success of these programs was perhaps their modest usage. In fact, we succeeded in bringing down spreads in the asset classes we were targeting; by this yardstick, we accomplished our objective. Simply announcing the program had a meaningful impact—by demonstrating that we had the mechanism, capacity, and intent to support the market if necessary, the market began to do our work for us.

Treasury published its last quarterly report on the PPIP in 2013, when the last fund had liquidated its remaining holdings. All the managers performed extremely well: The worst-performing manager generated an 18.7 percent return, and the best had a 26.3 percent return. In the end, Treasury invested $18.6 billion, on which it made a profit of $3.8 billion.

RESULTS AND LESSONS LEARNED

We were optimistic about our financial stability plan when we announced it in February 2009, but even we were surprised by the speed and capacity of the private sector to mobilize and reverse the negative trends. Building on the critically important capital injections and guarantees of October 2008, the overall mix of policies from the new administration and the Fed created a credible sense of our intent and capacity to keep the nation out of a second Great Depression. As a result, the market's views of the amount of capital required to manage through the downturn improved with time rather than deteriorating. The broader integrated strategy—including a credible backstop for senior creditors, complementary policies (like the PPIP and the TALF) to help restore the functioning of other credit markets and limit fire sale pressures, and supportive macroeconomic policies—was key to making the financial sector recapitalization strategy successful.

Within that recapitalization strategy, a credible stress test regime combined with a well-structured capital backstop and an effort to foster restructuring of junior debt and capital securities proved powerful. The credibility was driven by loss estimates judged to be severe and defined independently of fiscal authorities, with full transparency into individual banks. The capital requirement was set as a numerator (a minimum level of common equity post net losses) to avoid reinforcing deleveraging pressure. The backstop was appropriately sized and designed with a fixed price floor on public injections defined ex ante. This limited the amount of dilution possible in extreme cases, and therefore supported equity prices and the ability of the private sector to act in place of the government.

Charles Eames, the famous modernist furniture designer, asserted that "design depends largely on constraints" and that one's "willingness and enthusiasm" to work within and around unchangeable elements determines success or failure. The response to the financial crisis clearly follows this rule. The policy objective was relatively simple: Recapitalize the financial system and support credit formation. The challenge and the creativity required were in the design. Our success came from putting people of many different backgrounds— regulators, bank liquidators, supervisors, monetary policy experts, economists, and financial market experts—into dialogue and forcing ourselves to challenge orthodoxy and come up with novel solutions.

Lesson 1:
Collaboration is key.

Importantly, we worked together, across administrations and across agencies, with broad continuity in strategy and approach. Part of the political economy of crisis management was designing a set of programs that created the political space to allow the independent agencies with substantial crisis-fighting statutory authority to use these tools in the most effective manner. The various joint statements, joint releases, and board resolutions, along with a series of bilateral letters written between Treasury and the Fed, were all part of an architecture that made sure no agency was left on its own to defend politically the consolidated set of actions required to stabilize the system.

Lesson 2:
A weak capital regime can be difficult to recognize until it's too late.

There are significant benefits to having higher capital requirements at all points in the economic cycle. It can be hard to force undercapitalized banks to raise or conserve enough capital before it becomes too hard and expensive to do so in the early stages of a crisis. The precrisis capital regime was poorly designed. It permitted low-quality capital, relied on relatively benign point-in-time measures of risk, was backward looking, and did not incorporate contingent claims on capital or liquidity. Improvements have been made. To reduce the likelihood that the banking system will exacerbate an economic downturn and/ or market turmoil, the current capital regime requires systemically important banks to be capitalized in good times to withstand severe distress and continue to function. Appropriately, these banks now pay the cost ex ante of holding capital against potential severe distress.

Our successful experience with conversion of junior capital securities into high-quality tangible common equity also suggests that recent changes to encourage institutions to manage to a constant and substantial layer of total loss-absorbing capacity (TLAC) at their holding companies *might* also be a useful development in a future crisis if institutions attempt such exchanges earlier and avoid more distressed equity raises or deleveraging.

Lesson 3:
Uncertainty is the hardest variable to change.

The fear of a severe recession and a collapse of the financial system through destabilizing runs creates upward pressure on loss estimates and can be paralyzing to stabilization efforts. Recapitalization is essential but insufficient to change the curve of expectations. A broader set of policies—including guarantees of bank and other financial system liabilities and a forceful Keynesian response—is required. The public and market participants need to believe that the government understands the scale of the problem, has the desire to resolve the crisis even at a political cost, and has the wherewithal and a credible mechanism to do so. It is important to ultimately have an anchor for expectations—

with assurances that the system will be forced to raise (or be provided with) the capital to withstand losses in reasonably negative scenarios, and also that the most adverse scenarios (economic depression) can be avoided.

Lesson 4:
Prioritize private capital solutions.

Our overarching theme of bringing the private sector back to the table—making the financial system investable—was a highly useful framework. But it was much harder to design these policies than to rely on government intervention like simple equity injections or asset purchases. They required a broad set of independent investors taking actions that were in their own self-interest, all at about the same time. On the other side of the ledger, the benefit for the public is that the response can be self-perpetuating, the exit from the policy response can be much easier, and the recovery can be self-generating and faster.

Lesson 5:
The breadth of the response is important.

In a crisis, it is useful to think about the system as a whole, not just to triage the weakest institutions. The strength of our approach was the speed, level, and breadth of the recapitalization (GSEs, investment banks, AIG, auto finance companies, the largest bank holding companies, hundreds of smaller banks). A piecemeal approach can succeed and may be necessary in the early stages, when policymakers are testing whether there is a solvency crisis or when events intervene and there is simply no time. But a comprehensive response is necessary to ultimately carry the day.

Lesson 6:
Provide insurance against adverse outcomes.

Sometimes the best programs are the ones that sit on the shelf. Ideally, in a crisis response, the government demonstrates a willingness to assume the risk in the tail—the risk of catastrophe—but leaves the private sector to manage the more attritional risk. Heavy program usage outside of the tail may suggest miscalibration of the program. The existence of the program, or insurance, in the event circumstances deteriorate often provides the confidence necessary to avoid more catastrophic outcomes in the first order.

Final thought:
We made mistakes.

The initial outlines of our strategy, without the necessary details, caused another wave of uncertainty and concerns in the market about our intentions. The programs took longer to execute than we had hoped. We were less than successful in managing the political economy of the crisis response, in explaining what we were doing and why the focus on repairing the financial sector was so important to restoring growth in employment and incomes.

All that said, if you compare our response with those of other advanced countries in similar circumstances, we were able to achieve recapitalization and ultimately unwind government support over a relatively short period of time. The real economy was therefore able to recover more rapidly than elsewhere.

APPENDIX: DESIGNING THE STRESS TESTS

Although the idea of a stress test was conceptually fairly simple, running the exercise was analytically and operationally complex. We (the Fed and banking regulators) had to develop a set of practices in real time to carry out an exercise that supervisors had never done before—and do it under substantial pressure from outside and inside the government. For it to work, the market had to believe the results were credible, and we took great care at every step along the way to make sure that its design was rigorous and robust. Here is a look at a number of the policy choices that we made.

DEFINING THE UNIVERSE OF FINANCIAL INSTITUTIONS

There was significant discussion about how many institutions would undertake the stress tests. On the one hand, some of us at the Fed were concerned about our capacity to carry out the exercise with a large number of firms simultaneously. On the other, we wanted to make sure that we covered a suitably large swath of the banking system and the troubled mortgage assets. After exploring the merits of looking at just the ten largest firms, we drew the line at banks with more than $100 billion in assets on a consolidated basis. That group was made up of the 19 largest domestic bank holding companies,[12] which together held more than two-thirds of the assets and nearly half of the loans in the U.S. banking system.[13] The group covered banks that were engaged in a wide range of complex activities, such as JPMorgan Chase and Goldman Sachs, as well as more traditional large regional banks with balance sheets consisting largely of loans and securities.

DEVELOPING THE ECONOMIC SCENARIOS

The steady stream of bad economic news and deteriorating conditions in early 2009 made coming up with the more adverse economic scenario complicated. For our exercise to be credible, we needed to stay at least one step ahead of the ongoing deterioration in the outlook and develop a test that was more severe than what was actually expected to occur.[14]

The Fed developed two scenarios. A "baseline" scenario was used to provide a rough benchmark of a weak economy. The Fed was especially attuned to the risk that the markets could perceive that the baseline scenario it released for the stress tests was the same one being used by the Federal Open Market Committee (FOMC) for the setting of monetary policy. Thus it used an average of three major publicly available macro forecasts as of February 2009.[15] The "more adverse" scenario was meant to be significantly more severe than what was expected and was the main focus for most observers of the stress tests. We were careful to point out that it was meant to be neither a "worst case" scenario nor the Fed's forecast of expectations. Instead, it represented a scenario that, though very severe, was plausible given the current environment. It was

---

12. As measured according to the assets reported for fourth-quarter 2008 in the Federal Reserve's Consolidated Financial Statements for Bank Holding Companies (FR Y-9C).
13. Federal Reserve Board, "The Supervisory Capital Assessment Program: Design and Implementation," April 2009, https://www.federalreserve.gov/bankinforeg /bcreg20090424a1.pdf.
14. The more adverse case assumed a very severe recession with a sharp drop in housing prices. In particular, it assumed a 3.3 percent drop in GDP in 2009 and a 0.5 percent increase in 2010; an unemployment rate of 8.9 percent in 2009 that would rise to 10.3 percent in 2010; and a 22 percent drop in housing prices in 2009 as measured by the Case-Schiller Index, followed by a 7 percent decline in 2010.
15. Federal Reserve Board, "The Supervisory Capital Assessment Program."

based in part on an analysis of the historical record of previous U.S. recessions and national housing price declines (going back to before World War II), but was adjusted for the unprecedented decline in national housing prices that was currently occurring. As it turned out, the rapidly deteriorating economy led to an increase in the unemployment rate in early 2009 that ended up tracking very closely to the rise in the more adverse scenario. Housing prices continued to fall substantially, increasing the risk that any stress test results to be announced later that spring might not be viewed as credible.

GAUGING "POST-STRESS" CAPITAL ADEQUACY

To determine whether a bank had enough capital to withstand a hypothetical severe economic downturn involved three moving pieces: projecting the potential losses an institution would face, evaluating how much revenue that institution would earn, and deciding where to set the bar for "post-stress" capital adequacy.

Projecting Potential Losses

A key decision was made early on that we would run the stress test largely in keeping with traditional bank accounting standards, with the important distinction that we were assessing potential performance under hypothetical scenarios. Loss estimates for loans and securities in investment portfolios would not result from trying to mark the positions to market, as many analysts were trying to do on the backs of envelopes, but rather by assessing their potential performance under the hypothetical scenarios, consistent with accepted accounting practices. The resulting loss and revenue estimates would then be run through banks' income statements.

The preferred option for generating the stress loss estimates would have been to require all the banks to provide data that could be independently analyzed by regulators. But the Fed had yet to develop the robust stress testing infrastructure that exists today, nor did it have the time to create that capacity. We decided we would give the banks the scenarios, have them run the stress tests themselves, and then analyze and adjust the results they provided. Given how bad many of the banks had proven at measuring their risks, our confidence in their practices was far from high. Moreover, we were well aware of their strong incentive to be overly optimistic. But there was no other feasible way to do this. Our focus would have to be on assessing their submissions and making whatever adjustments were necessary based on all available information, including a deep understanding of their operations informed by years of supervising the banks.

To support these efforts, economists at the Fed, the FDIC, and the Office of the Comptroller of the Currency worked together to develop a set of loss estimates—known as "indicative loss ranges"—for each major loan class based on industry-wide asset characteristics. If a firm's analysis resulted in estimates that were significantly outside the ranges, the firm would have to explain why. This made it harder for the banks to game the tests. It also put the onus on them to show us the data they had to support the contention that their portfolios would perform better than average. One thing we had not counted on was the extent to which many banks did not have the risk measurement information needed to estimate potential losses under stress. If not a complete shock, this fact certainly complicated our work.

During those few months, there was substantial back-and-forth between the supervisors and the banks to get additional information about the risk characteristics of loans held by each of the banks. We benefited greatly from being able to look across all the firms simultaneously. From this "horizontal" perspective we were able to see details on huge swaths of the system's loans and then drill down into each firm's specific portfolios. This allowed us to come up with adjusted estimates that were both consistent across loan categories (for example, if two banks had the exact same loan, the result would be the same for both) and specific to the riskiness of each bank's particular portfolios. In other words, loss estimates were informed by a system-wide view of the major loan categories (residential mortgages, commercial loans, and so forth), and banks that held loans with riskier characteristics would appropriately generate bigger losses in the stress tests.

A challenge arose with respect to firms with substantial trading activities, of which there were five, including two (Goldman Sachs and Morgan Stanley) that had only recently become regulated bank holding companies and whose assets were held mostly in the trading book. Trading had generated huge losses already, largely in the structured credit positions that were the source of so much uncertainty.

Trading positions are marked to market regularly by banks and can change in composition more rapidly than the assets held in loan and investment portfolios. How could we estimate potential losses in trading-related exposures over the nine-quarter scenario time frame? The only practical alternative was to have the banks test their trading positions by applying a technique they had long used in a much more limited way: They would assume a sudden shift in global market values (and the risk factors that drive them). Extreme market volatility had already led to significant swings in valuation over the second half of 2008. There was no reason to think this could not continue. Trading firms would be required to hold enough capital to withstand both a severe macroeconomic downturn *and* an extreme market meltdown. Of the $600 billion of total losses estimated across all 19 firms in the stress tests, $100 billion was from trading-related exposures, including credit exposures to trading counterparties, at these five banks.

Estimating Potential Revenue

Even while taking huge losses from deteriorating asset values and loans that will not be repaid, banks would continue to generate revenue from interest earned on loans and securities, trading activities, and other fee-based services over the scenario horizon. This "preprovision net revenue," or PPNR, was a critical consideration and one that was largely being ignored by private-sector analysts and others focused on marking to market the banks' balance sheets. But how would we calculate those net revenues and the impact they would have in offsetting the erosion of banks' capital under the prescribed scenario?

Again, the starting point was estimates submitted by the banks, which had extremely rosy views of their revenue prospects under severe stress. Indeed, it was with some alarm (and a few chuckles) that we noted the banks had estimated that their aggregate PPNR under the more adverse scenario stress would be greater than what they had actually generated over *any* historical period of the same length. Internally, we used statistical analysis of industry earnings to derive revenue estimates for the firms' various revenue streams, and these informed the final estimates.

Determining the Capital Buffer

Importantly, the post-stress capital requirement needed to be seen not only as a qualitative improvement over existing requirements but also as sufficiently high to allow firms to continue to operate and lend during a deep downturn. Traditional, point-in-time capital measures had missed important risks and had little to no value for assessing banks in a rapidly deteriorating environment. Moreover, they included a significant amount of "hybrid" debt and debt securities that the markets discounted as a source of loss absorption. In essence, nobody trusted the reported capital numbers based on the current standards.

The SCAP required banks to hold so-called post-stress capital, or a capital cushion after the impact of the stress test, equivalent to at least 4 percent of their risk-weighted assets in Tier 1 Common Equity. This new measure was developed specifically for the stress test and ruled out most non–common equity elements. This was a significant strengthening of the quality and quantity of required capital.

The final results from the more adverse scenario represented extreme levels of losses—losses on loans of roughly $450 billion accounted for approximately three-quarters of the $600 billion of estimated losses in the stress test. That equaled more than 9 percent of total loans outstanding, higher even than the loan loss rate in the Great Depression. In addition, estimates of PPNR showed a significant hit to revenues. Illustrating that the stress test had closely looked into all the portfolios at each of the firms, loan losses appropriately differed by loan type and across the banks. For example, aggregate commercial loans to businesses averaged a 6.1 percent loss rate, ranging from a low of less than 2 percent at two firms to more than 20 percent at a third. Credit card losses averaged 23 percent, ranging from 18 percent to a high of almost 40 percent. After a long wait, anxious observers could see that the stress test results indeed represented a severely stressful outcome. In the end, most experts agreed that the test had been credible.

CHAPTER ELEVEN

Lessening the Impact of Bank Failures

JAMES R. WIGAND

INTRODUCTION: SUDDENLY, A CASCADE OF FAILURES

In the fall of 2007, the failure of NetBank, a $2.2 billion institution based in Alpharetta, Georgia, was ominous for two reasons. It was the largest U.S. bank failure in 14 years,[1] and it was the first bank to collapse in what became a wave of failures from mortgage defaults. Its story is now painfully familiar.

NetBank had experienced rapid growth through its internet-based deposit platform since its founding in 1996. In search of a profitable business line, it purchased Market Street Mortgage, a Florida-based retail mortgage lender, in 2001 and Resource Bancshares Mortgage Group, a wholesale mortgage banking company with a nationwide network of correspondents and brokers, in

I want to acknowledge and thank my colleagues at the FDIC for their tireless dedication, creative spirit, and hard work in making the programs discussed in this chapter possible. Diane Ellis, Matthew S. Kabaker, Michael H. Krimminger, and Margaret M. McConnell advised on this chapter. Ellis is director of the FDIC's Division of Insurance and Research. Kabaker was a senior adviser to secretary of the Treasury Timothy F. Geithner. Krimminger served as special adviser for policy to FDIC chairman Sheila Bair. McConnell served from 2007 to 2011 as the deputy chief of staff for policy at the Federal Reserve Bank of New York.

1. "Bank Failures and Assistance Data," Federal Deposit Insurance Corporation (FDIC) Research Statistics, accessed June 10, 2019, https://banks.data.fdic.gov /explore/failures/?aggReport=detail&displayFields=NAME%2CCERT%2CFIN%2C CITYST%2CFAILDATE%2CSAVR%2CRESTYPE%2CCOST%2CRESTYPE1%2CC HCLASS1%2CQBFDEP%2CQBFASSET&endFailYear=2007&sortField =QBFASSET&sortOrder=desc&startFailYear=1993#panel-filters.

2002.[2] Through these acquisitions, NetBank became dependent on mortgage banking to generate earnings. When the secondary mortgage market began to contract in 2005, NetBank responded by lowering its underwriting standards to maintain volume, originating "low or no doc" mortgages, interest-only payments, and high loan-to-value/low-down-payment features.

These products resulted in increased early defaults.[3] NetBank had sold many of the loans to investors and was forced to repurchase the defaulted loans under recourse provisions. Ultimately, the losses arising from the repurchases, coupled with declining loan production and other poor business strategies, caused NetBank to fail.[4] The Federal Deposit Insurance Corporation (FDIC) insurance fund lost $124 million from the failure.[5]

NetBank was one of only three banks to fail in 2007, out of about 8,550 insured institutions. Industry equity capital at the end of the year totaled $1.35 trillion.[6] The FDIC's Deposit Insurance Fund (DIF) balance stood at $52.4 billion.[7] Quarterly net income for commercial banks for the second quarter of 2007 was the fourth highest ever, although short of the highest quarterly earnings records broken in 2006.[8]

However, the good times were already over. Industry net income nose-dived in the fourth quarter of 2007, falling from $28.8 billion to $646 million—the lowest quarterly amount since the banking/thrift crisis of the late 1980s and early 1990s.[9] Loan-loss provisions hit a record $31.3 billion in the fourth quarter, and for the first time, the industry reported a net trading loss, totaling $10.6 billion. By the end of the second quarter of 2008, quarterly loan-loss provisions exceeded $50 billion.

2. See U.S. Department of the Treasury, Office of Inspector General (OIG), *Safety and Soundness: Material Loss Review of NetBank, FSB*, OIG-08-032, April 23, 2008.
3. Early defaults meant that the borrower defaulted or was delinquent within the first 90–180 days of the loan, or defaulted or was delinquent on the loan's first payment.
4. U.S. Department of the Treasury, Office of Inspector General (OIG), *Safety and Soundness*.
5. See FDIC Research Statistics, "Bank Failures and Assistance Data."
6. FDIC, Quarterly Banking Profile: Fourth Quarter 2007, table II-A, 5, https://www5 .fdic.gov/qbp/2007dec/qbp.pdf.
7. FDIC, Quarterly Banking Profile: Fourth Quarter 2007.
8. FDIC, Quarterly Banking Profile: Second Quarter 2007, 1, https://www5.fdic.gov/qbp /2007jun/qbp.pdf; and FDIC Quarterly Banking Profile: Fourth Quarter 2006, 1, https://www5.fdic.gov/qbp/2006dec/qbp.pdf.
9. See FDIC, Quarterly Banking Profile: First Quarter 2008, https://www5.fdic.gov/qbp /2008mar/qbp.pdf.

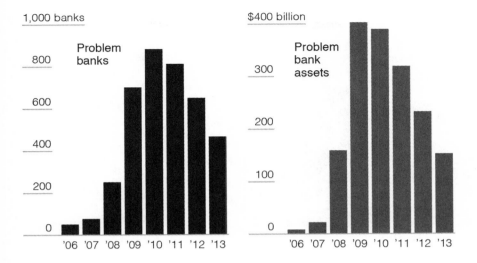

Figure 11.1 **Problem Banks and Problem Bank Assets**

Source: FDIC, *Annual Reports,* 2006–2013

Although signs of weakness in residential real estate prices, subprime loan products, and mortgage banking were emerging in 2005 and 2006, the Problem Bank List, which factors into the FDIC's contingent-loss reserve for the DIF, did not reflect an increase until 2007.[10] Then the number of troubled institutions soared, with a net increase of more than 600 in 2008 and 2009. Assets of problem banks peaked in 2009, although the number of troubled institutions peaked in 2010, suggesting, consistent with performance metrics from reported data of large versus small banks, that stresses became apparent in larger institutions earlier than in smaller ones.[11] (See Figure 11.1.)

10. The Problem Bank List is a confidential list composed of all banks having a composite CAMELS rating of 4 or 5. CAMELS is a widely used system to rate a bank's overall financial condition, assessing capital, assets, management, earnings, liquidity, and sensitivity to risk, with 1 being the strongest and 5 being the weakest.
11. Whether the difference in timing of the appearance of stress in large versus small banks was due to differences in the underlying asset portfolios, accounting recognition, or exam cycle timing (for example, dedicated examiners present at large banks versus periodic examinations of small banks) would be an interesting area of further research. For a comparison of performance metrics for large versus small banks, see FDIC, Quarterly Banking Profile: Second Quarter 2008, https://www5.fdic.gov/qbp /2008jun/qbp.pdf.

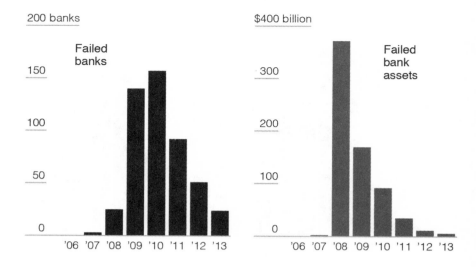

Figure 11.2 Failed Banks and Failed Bank Assets

Source: FDIC, *Annual Reports*, 2006–2013

Bank failures jumped from 25 in 2008 to 140 in 2009 and 157 in 2010. Assets in failed banks peaked in 2008, when IndyMac and Washington Mutual (WaMu) became the two largest insured institutions to collapse in the crisis. (See Figure 11.2.) These banks' lack of liquidity to fund deposit withdrawals drove the timing of their closure, although both also had significant underlying problems with asset quality. The Government Accountability Office (GAO) found that high concentrations of commercial real estate loans, especially acquisition, development, and construction loans; aggressive use of brokered deposits and other high-risk funding sources; and weak underwriting and credit administration practices were significant contributing factors in the failures of small and medium-size banks (less than $10 billion).[12]

In the end, the 489 banks that failed between 2008 and 2013 cost the FDIC's insurance fund $72.5 billion, an amount greater than the fund's balance when the crisis started. That placed the FDIC in the difficult position of having to find ways to replenish the DIF in the midst of the crisis.

12. See U.S. Government Accountability Office (GAO), *Financial Institutions: Causes and Consequences of Recent Bank Failures,* GAO-13-71, Jan. 3, 2013.

At the same time, the collapse of so many banks created a mountain of failed-bank assets, ultimately totaling more than $680 billion, which the FDIC was charged with managing and liquidating. That put the agency in a second difficult position: getting around the specter of fire sales in depressed markets that would yield low recovery values and potentially further depress asset values, impairing the capital of open banks.

How did the FDIC keep the insurance fund solvent, and why was it important to do so? How did it handle the asset sales without making the crisis worse?

This chapter describes the key policy decisions and programs that the FDIC used to solve those challenges. The agency's decisions and actions didn't come without debate, however, and several remain the subject of controversy, which the chapter also addresses.

Several new statutory provisions that could have helped during the crisis are now available. These include changes to the FDIC's deposit insurance assessment structure, the authority for orderly liquidation of systemically important financial companies, and the establishment of "living will" resolution-planning requirements. But it is also the case that several of the authorities that the FDIC used to address systemic risk situations have been curtailed by Congress. Most notably, the legislature has eliminated the agency's ability to provide open-bank assistance to failing institutions, even those that pose systemic risk—Congress must now authorize the agency to offer such assistance.

MANAGING THE DEPOSIT INSURANCE FUND

The DIF has two key purposes. First, it serves as the source of funds to satisfy FDIC's deposit insurance obligations.[13] When a bank fails, the FDIC will pay the full amount of a depositor's insured funds and in return become a claimant for that amount in the failed bank's receivership estate. Second, the DIF serves as a source of working capital to facilitate an orderly resolution process. The DIF advances the funds necessary to administer the receivership, preserve assets, and ensure an orderly resolution from the time a receivership estate is established to when asset collection and sales proceeds are sufficient to fund the estate's operations.

The funding requirements associated with a bank's prospective resolution are determined by (1) the initial outlay to honor deposit insurance obligations,

---

13. See 12 U.S.C. § 1823(c)(4)(A)(i).

(2) the initial period and amount of the receivership's operating expenses, (3) the losses arising from the FDIC's claim (as subrogee) on the assets, (4) the amount of liquid assets at the failed bank, and (5) the timing of the receivership estate's distribution of funds to its creditors. These factors impact the DIF's liquidity and its "capital" balance, which is more commonly known as the "DIF balance."[14]

That balance plummeted after the first quarter of 2008, falling from $52.8 billion to $17.3 billion at the end of the year. An increase in contingent-loss reserves for future bank failures (from $0.6 billion to $24.0 billion) accounted for most of the decline, and an additional $10.7 billion of the DIF's fall was for the resolution of IndyMac, which caused the largest loss arising from a single bank failure in FDIC's history.[15] The decline of the fund's liquidity, which is directly linked to resolution activity, was not as marked, falling from $55.1 billion at the end of the first quarter to $33.7 billion at the end of the year. (The "capital" balance is the amount in the fund, including cash and Treasury securities, plus the estimated value of the FDIC's claims in receivership estates [a receivable] less the amount set aside [reserved] for estimated losses arising from future bank failures [that is, contingent-loss reserves] and any liabilities due to resolutions. The liquidity balance is composed of essentially cash and Treasury securities.)[16]

14. By the time a bank fails, losses on its assets and the amount of its liabilities are to a large extent fixed. Although resolution strategy does have an impact on creditor and FDIC losses/recoveries, the FDIC's liquidity needs are significantly more affected by the range of resolution alternatives for paying the bank's deposit insurance obligations and managing the receivership estate than are its losses/recoveries.

15. See FDIC, *Annual Report,* 2008; and FDIC, *Crisis and Response: An FDIC History, 2008–2013* (Washington, D.C.: FDIC, 2017).

16. To illustrate how resolution activity affects the DIF liquidity and capital balances, suppose the liquidity balance on June 1 is $100 and, due to a contingent-loss reserve for future bank failures of $10, the capital balance is $90. Now, assume on June 30 that hypothetical Bank Zed fails, having $40 in insured deposits. Let's also assume that the FDIC had to pay out the $40 in insured deposits (i.e., pay the insured depositors directly) and estimate that it will lose $6 from Bank Zed's failure, projecting that it will collect $34 (over a period of years) from the bank's receivership estate. The capital balance would remain at $90, with the contingent-loss reserve absorbing the $6 loss and declining from $10 to $4. However, the liquidity balance would decrease by $40. As distributions from Bank Zed's receivership estate are made over time, the liquidity balance would be expected to increase by $34.

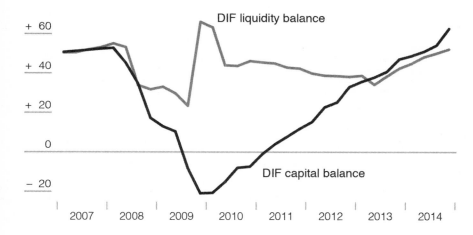

+$80 billion

+ 60

+ 40

+ 20

0

− 20

DIF liquidity balance

DIF capital balance

2007   2008   2009   2010   2011   2012   2013   2014

Figure 11.3 **Deposit Insurance Fund Liquidity and Capital Balances**

Source: FDIC Division of Insurance and Research

The big increase in 2008 of contingent-loss reserves, however, indicated that the fund's liquidity would become depleted if the provisioned-for failures occurred—especially if the FDIC had to honor its deposit insurance coverage through payouts. Moreover, adding to the possible shortfall, FDIC's insurance obligations increased after deposit insurance coverage was raised to $250,000, from $100,000, as part of a broader effort to stabilize the financial system; this increase later became permanent.[17] (See Figure 11.3.)

17. See FDIC, "Emergency Economic Stabilization Act of 2008 Temporarily Increases Basic FDIC Insurance Coverage from $100,000 to $250,000 per Depositor," press release PR-93-2008, Oct. 7, 2008. On October 14, 2008, the FDIC approved the Transaction Account Guarantee Program, which provided unlimited deposit insurance coverage for non-interest-bearing transaction accounts. See FDIC, "FDIC Announces Plan to Free Up Bank Liquidity," press release PR-100-2008, Oct. 14, 2008. The unlimited coverage expired in December 2012. See 12 C.F.R. Part 330; and 12 C.F.R. Part 370. However, the Dodd-Frank Wall Street Reform and Consumer and Protection Act of 2010 (Dodd-Frank) permanently raised coverage to $250,000 for all types of deposit accounts.

INDUSTRY PAYMENTS FOR DEPOSIT INSURANCE

The Federal Deposit Insurance Reform Act of 2005 (FDIRA), which took effect in 2006, ended a ten-year statutory restriction on the FDIC's ability to charge most banks for deposit insurance.[18] During that period, due to deposit growth and little premium inflow, the ratio of the DIF balance to estimated insured deposits (the reserve ratio) fell from 1.33 percent to 1.21 percent. FDIRA permitted the FDIC to charge all banks, not just less-healthy ones, regardless of the level of the authorized reserve ratio, thus restoring the FDIC's ability to price deposit insurance according to the risk a bank posed to the DIF. The new law also allowed the FDIC to increase the DIF balance to 1.5 percent of insured deposits.

One of the objectives of FDIRA was to mitigate the procyclical nature of deposit insurance assessments by collecting premiums and building up the DIF when times are good, so that the FDIC doesn't have to increase premiums or make special assessments when times are bad. However, the Great Recession followed too closely to the enactment of FDIRA to avoid a repeat of the historical pattern. As was the case in previous periods when the DIF balance began to decline, the FDIC responded by increasing premiums, this time by 7 basis points in October 2008.

The collection of insurance premiums and special assessments benefits the DIF in two ways. First, the cash inflow improves the DIF's liquidity—making funds available to pay deposit insurance obligations and to provide working capital for bank resolution. Second, the DIF's capital position also increases—offsetting losses arising from actual resolution activity or from provisioning for future losses. Earnings on the DIF's investment account and insurance premiums/assessments are the only sources of DIF capital.

As bank failures increased during 2009, cash inflows from premiums proved not to be sufficient to avoid the prospect of the fund becoming "capital" insol-

---

18. Under the ten-year restriction, if the DIF's Designated Reserve Ratio (i.e., the target ratio of the DIF balance to estimated insured deposits) was 1.25 percent or greater, the FDIC could not charge banks that were well capitalized and had composite CAMELS ratings of 1 or 2. More than 90 percent of insured banks avoided premiums for any given assessment period between 1996 and 2006. FDIRA required the FDIC to return one-half of excess premium collections to the industry when the reserve ratio reached 1.35 percent and all excess collections at 1.5 percent.

vent or to meet forecasted liquidity needs. In reaction, the FDIC approved a special assessment of $5.5 billion in June 2009 and collected the funds at the end of September. This, too, proved insufficient, and the fund went negative at the end of the third quarter. Increasingly, the FDIC's focus shifted from the "capital" balance of the fund to projected liquidity needs as provisioned-for failures were realized.

Whether the FDIC should have imposed the premium increase and special assessment during the crisis was, and continues to be, a topic of debate. The agency was concerned about the loss of public confidence in its ability to honor its deposit insurance guarantee during the financial panic.[19] It also was concerned about the perception that the government would need to "bail out" the FDIC—reminiscent of what occurred with the Federal Savings and Loan Insurance Corporation (FSLIC) in 1989. Several banking industry officials were advocating the need for an "RTC-like solution."[20] But agency leadership viewed the continuation of banking-industry funding as a signal of confidence that the industry had the wherewithal to support the DIF, that it would be held accountable for doing so, and that the FDIC did not need to turn to Treasury for support.[21] (See Appendix A: A Different Problem, a Different Approach: Lessons Learned from the S&L Crisis.)

The other side of the debate was that increased premiums and special assessments would result in more stress to an industry that was already highly stressed. Imposing additional costs on the industry when losses were increasing, earnings were under pressure, and equity capital was either too expensive

---

19. When IndyMac failed in July 2008, long queues formed outside several branches even though the FDIC was appointed conservator of the bank and depositors had full access to their insured funds the following day. The withdrawal of deposits continued for two weeks. See John F. Bovenzi, *Inside the FDIC: Thirty Years of Bank Failures, Bailouts, and Regulatory Battles* (Hoboken, NJ: John Wiley & Sons, 2015), 14–16.

20. The Resolution Trust Corporation (RTC) was established in 1989 to resolve failing savings and loans after the FSLIC became insolvent. RTC's funding came from appropriations by the federal government, assessments on the savings and loan industry (including Federal Home Loan Banks), and borrowings from the Federal Financing Bank. The GAO estimated taxpayers bore 83 percent of the $160 billion direct and indirect costs of the S&L cleanup. See GAO, *Financial Audit: Resolution Trust Corporation's 1995 and 1994 Financial Statements*, AIMD-96-123, July 2, 1996.

21. See Sheila Bair, *Bull by the Horns: Fighting to Save Main Street from Wall Street and Wall Street from Itself* (New York: Free Press, 2012), 292–93.

or difficult to raise could, at the margin, increase the number of failing banks, thereby imposing additional losses on the DIF.[22] The agency was also concerned that the additional costs could impede lending, affecting economic recovery. The FDIC had borrowing authorities to ensure adequate liquidity. And it could restore the fund's "capital" position over time through special assessments after the crisis passed. Would the public even care about the DIF balance, knowing that the fund is backed by the full faith and credit of the United States?

The FDIC was experiencing the same dilemma it faced in the crisis of the late 1980s and early 1990s: one alternative reinforced procyclicality, while the other would stoke the perception of the severity of the crisis and that the deposit insurer needed a lifeline.

A NEW APPROACH

Weighing the pros and cons of the two sides of the debate, the FDIC decided in November 2009 to strike a balance by adopting a third approach: have insured institutions prepay their quarterly assessments due over the next 12 quarters—effectively, borrowing from the industry.[23]

The advantages over the two earlier alternatives were significant. First, the FDIC was able to quickly improve the DIF's liquidity and increase the funds available to resolve banks. However, unlike a special assessment, the prepayment alternative did not require banks to recognize the full amount paid as an immediate expense. Rather, only the quarterly amount due would need to be expensed, with an asset account reflecting the remaining balance of the prepayment on a bank's balance sheet.[24] At the bank level, the expensing of premiums occurred as it would in the normal course.

Second, given the alternative of the FDIC's tapping its borrowing lines with the Treasury or the Federal Financing Bank, the ultimate cost to the industry was less—allowing for future assessments to be allocated to restoring the fund. Assuming the DIF remained industry funded, insured banks would have to

---

22. The 2009 special assessment almost wiped out bank earnings for the year.
23. See 74 Fed. Reg. 59056 (Nov. 17, 2009).
24. The asset account for the prepaid expense had a zero percent risk weight. Accordingly, banks did not incur a capital charge for carrying the prepaid expense balance.

pay for the interest expense associated with FDIC borrowings through future assessments. The spread between a bank's opportunity cost for using the cash over the 12 quarters and the interest charges incurred on FDIC borrowings was the theoretical cost differential.[25] By the end of 2009, banks were holding substantial amounts of cash and excess reserves in the Federal Reserve.[26] The average bank's ratio of cash and balances due from other depository institutions, which includes reserves at the Federal Reserve, to total assets was 8.0 percent—a full 3 percentage points higher than the 2003–2007 average.[27] Banks had sufficient liquidity to make the prepayments and avoid paying the cost of FDIC borrowing.

Third, the DIF remained industry funded. By having the industry prepay assessments, the fund received the liquidity inflows that would have occurred over a three-year period—just accelerated to meet current needs. These were sufficient to meet FDIC's needs and avoided the perception that the DIF required a lifeline from the federal government.

Last, and important from a macroeconomic perspective, the relatively high cash/excess reserve balances of insured institutions suggested that the prepayments would not affect a bank's ability to provide credit. This was a significant concern, especially given the decline in bank lending in 2009.

The prepayment of premiums resulted in the DIF's receiving $45.7 billion on December 30, 2009, significantly improving the fund's liquidity.[28] As a result of

25. For example, in the fourth quarter of 2009, banks' excess reserves at the Federal Reserve earned 25 basis points. The FDIC's line of credit with a Treasury borrowing rate, assuming a three-year maturity, would have been about 1.5 percent—resulting in a spread of 125 basis points. The difference of 100 basis points represents the theoretical cost savings. Rate data from Board of Governors of the Federal Reserve System (U.S.), "Interest Rate on Excess Reserves (IOER)," FRED, Federal Reserve Bank of St. Louis, June 12, 2018, fred.stlouisfed.org/series/IOER; and Board of Governors of the Federal Reserve System (U.S.), "Three-Year Treasury Constant Maturity Rate (DGS3)," FRED, Federal Reserve Bank of St. Louis, June 13, 2018, fred .stlouisfed.org/series/DGS3.

26. There are multiple causes for the increase in the banks' cash holdings and excess reserves. However, by the end of 2009, the government's liquidity support programs, especially the Fed's asset-purchase program, materially affected excess reserve balances.

27. See FDIC, *Crisis and Response.*

28. See FDIC, *Annual Report, 2009.*

the infusion, FDIC's liquid assets never fell below $34 billion during the remaining crisis period.

MINIMIZING PAYOUTS

Although the FDIC can always honor its insurance obligations by issuing checks to a failed bank's depositors, this option results in undesirable outcomes for the FDIC and the customers.[29]

Significantly for the FDIC, a payout drains DIF liquidity dollar-for-insured-deposit-dollar immediately upon a bank's failure. The FDIC may eventually recover the lost liquidity once the failed bank's assets are sold and receivership claims are paid. But that process typically takes several years, requiring working capital to bridge the disbursement-collections gap. Finally, payouts may result in a large inventory of certain asset types or market concentrations that can depress pricing—whether through the "overhang" effect, as markets anticipate the FDIC liquidating the assets, or by large-volume selling that exceeds demand. This result negatively affects markets and open institutions in addition to FDIC's losses.

Given the undesirable attributes of payouts, the FDIC looked at how to minimize the likelihood of resolving failed banks with this method. Two major challenges had to be overcome. One was ensuring that the FDIC had sufficient information to market a failing bank's deposit franchise to a qualified prospective acquirer. The other was following the least-costly resolution requirement: any use of the DIF, other than a payout, must be the least expensive means to resolution. The option of avoiding a resolution altogether by providing assistance to an open institution could occur only with a systemic risk determination. (See Appendix B: The WaMu Resolution: Balancing Competing Policy Objectives.)

During the crisis, only 26 of the 489 failed banks—about 5 percent—were resolved through payouts. Excluding WaMu, purchase and assumption (P&A) transactions constituted 96 percent of failed-bank resolutions by assets.[30]

---

29. A payout (liquidation) is exempt from the statutory requirement that the resolution option be the least costly to the DIF of all possible methods for meeting the agency's insurance obligation. See 12 U.S.C. § 1823(c)(4)(A).

30. Inclusive of WaMu, 98 percent of failed banks were resolved through P&A transactions by assets. FDIC, Division of Resolutions and Receiverships, "Crisis Asset Reductions," https://www.fdic.gov/about/freedom/crisis-asset-reduction.pdf.

WHEN AND HOW TO SELL

In the years before the crisis, the FDIC answered the questions of when and how to sell a failed bank's assets by evaluating the characteristics of the institution and its asset portfolio within the context of the agency's statutory and policy mandates. Bank failures were relatively infrequent, and failed banks varied by geography, cause of failure, franchise/business lines, and portfolio characteristics. Each resolution and receivership estate generally would be handled independently. There were few opportunities to bundle similar asset types, including deposit franchises, across receiverships for a sale. Assets either would be liquidated through collections or sold as soon as they could be offered in transactions consistent with the FDIC's roles as deposit insurer and receiver.

The prospect of a large number of failures and large amounts of failed-bank assets over a relatively short time horizon called into question whether the FDIC's customary resolution approaches during times of financial stability would work. This crisis was even broader, deeper, and more severe than the banking and S&L crisis of 20 years earlier. It was national, even international, in scope rather than a rolling series of regionally concentrated recessions.[31]

The challenge for the FDIC was to find a way of conveying assets from failed banks quickly but avoid the discounts for liquidity and credit risks that were occurring as the crisis deepened, and importantly, avoid creating new risks for the DIF, the industry, and the economy.

Key additional considerations were that private-sector capital and liquidity would be more constrained, public confidence in the banking system more tentative, and counterparty viability and asset values less certain than at any time since the Great Depression.

Many banks would be ineligible to make acquisitions due to a lack of capital or be challenged managing their own problem asset portfolios, thereby reducing the pool of qualified deposit franchise and asset acquirers. Markets for certain asset types were depressed and would become more so if additional failed-bank assets were sold quickly.[32] What's more, liquidity failures, which

---

31. See FDIC, *History of the Eighties–Lessons for the Future: An Examination of the Banking Crisis of the 1980s and Early 1990s* (Washington, D.C.: FDIC, 1997).
32. Selling assets in distressed markets was also a concern during the thrift crisis. The Financial Institutions Reform, Recovery, and Enforcement Act of 1989 (FIRREA)

were very infrequent in the prior crisis, were occurring, forcing accelerated resolution timeframes.[33]

The FDIC needed to develop programs that addressed the speed with which banks failed, ensured a competitive pool of banks for acquisitions, and mitigated the high degree of risk aversion and asset value uncertainty. It did so through supervisory coordination, attracting private capital for failed banks and risk sharing.

SUPERVISORY COORDINATION: RAISE CAPITAL, SELL/MERGE, OR BE RESOLVED BY THE FDIC

The occurrence of liquidity failures made it imperative to solve the FDIC's long-running due-diligence problem in this area—that is, knowing, as deposit insurer, what its potential liability and funding obligations would be, and as receiver, what information it could make available to bidders when selling the franchise and assets.

The FDIC historically coordinated with a troubled bank's chartering authority and would send staff, as examiners, into an open institution to collect information necessary to conduct an orderly resolution process. That effort would include the development of an investor package and "war room" for franchise bidders.[34] After the crisis of the late 1980s and early 1990s, technology improvements facilitated the collection of more data through computer downloads than through on-site file reviews. The FDIC started using virtual data rooms to offer failing bank franchises and asset pools to prospective buyers.[35]

---

contained provisions requiring the RTC to evaluate whether its sales programs for real estate affected certain distressed markets. See P.L. 101–73 § 501(b)(12)(D)(ii).

33. The term "liquidity failure" means that the institution is unable to pay its obligations or meet its depositors' demands either presently or within the immediate future. Significant capital impairment typically precedes a liquidity failure.

34. Academic research and FDIC/RTC experience indicate that better pricing is achieved when bidders have sufficient information to make an informed bid. See Sudhir Nanda, James E. Owens, and Ronald C. Rogers, "An Analysis of Resolution Trust Corporation Transactions: Auction Market Process and Pricing," *Real Estate Economics* 25, no. 2 (1997): 271–94; and James A. Berkovec, John J. Mingo, and Xeuchun Zhang, "Premiums in Private versus Public Bank Branch Sales" (Federal Reserve Board's Finance and Economic Discussion Series Working Paper, 1997).

35. Contingency planning for Y2K initiated the FDIC's use of virtual data rooms for offering failing bank franchises to prospective buyers. Virtual data rooms were a

Although payouts and so-called clean-bank P&As require minimal due diligence, planning is necessary to ensure depositors quick access to their insured funds and to determine the likely holders and amounts of uninsured funds. The latter is important to assess economic and public confidence risks.

To help solve the failing bank due-diligence problem, the FDIC asked federal bank supervisors to order banks that fell below minimum requirements (and thus were subject to prompt corrective action) to attempt to raise capital or arrange for a sale and to do so with the assistance of a financial adviser.[36] Within the scope of its services, the adviser would create a virtual data room containing the information an investor/prospective buyer would need to perform due diligence, essentially the same information the FDIC would need to offer the bank in a resolution transaction.

The program achieved several objectives. Importantly, it forced recalcitrant banks to seek additional capital or to sell themselves without direct FDIC intervention and federal assistance. Often, bank owners/management resist equity dilution or a sale until it's too late to achieve one. Having supervisors require undercapitalized banks to do so increased the probability that an open-bank solution could be found. The added incentive for the bank was to control its own destiny rather than cede that to the FDIC. A number of banks successfully raised capital or were sold that otherwise might have required FDIC action to resolve.

Second, the program resulted in the creation of virtual data rooms in which prospective bidders, solicited in any future FDIC offering, would find the due-diligence information they needed to make an informed bid. Of note, the information was collected without sending FDIC staff into the bank, which might have signaled to internal bank staff that the institution was about to fail.

Finally, if the bank progressed sufficiently through the capital raise or sale and then was not able to close on the transaction or failed for liquidity reasons,

---

quick and efficient channel for providing due-diligence information. However, many community banks at the time did not have the internet connectivity required for using a virtual data room. Accordingly, the FDIC had to run a parallel system of paper-file due-diligence war rooms in the early 2000s.

36. Prompt corrective action is a set of progressive supervisory measures imposed as a bank's capital ratio declines through thresholds set by statute. Undercapitalized banks are required to submit a capital restoration plan. However, the plan does not require either a capital raise or sale, unless the bank's supervisor conditions approval of the plan by doing so. A bank's supervisor may require a significantly undercapitalized bank to raise capital or to be acquired. See 12 U.S.C. § 1831o.

the prospective investors/buyers who already had conducted due diligence could serve as a solicitation list for an accelerated FDIC resolution process.

ATTRACTING PRIVATE CAPITAL: EXPANDING THE POOL OF POTENTIAL ACQUIRERS

Another concern was whether a sufficient pool of potential bidders would be available to allow for competitive sales of deposit franchises.[37] As discussed earlier, payouts were a transaction of last resort. Furthermore, a competitive auction process supports achieving a fair market price for the franchise and substantiates the FDIC's least-costly resolution requirement.[38]

Although a potential acquirer is qualified based on multiple factors, capital adequacy was of greatest concern. The capital depletion arising from operating losses and asset repricing narrowed the field of eligible or interested buyers. Capital needed to flow into the industry, not just to support capital-deficient banks in distress but to facilitate the acquisition of failing and failed institutions.[39]

Capital for acquisitions could flow into either new bank charters or existing charters. However, the FDIC neither issues new charters nor conveys existing ones in resolution transactions. When private equity investors sought to invest in failing banks, FDIC staff welcomed the interest but directed the investors to the Office of the Comptroller of the Currency (OCC), Office of Thrift Supervision (OTS), or state chartering authorities to apply for a charter or suggested investing in an existing bank to position it for acquiring a failing institution.

In November 2008, the OCC announced the availability of a shelf-charter application for investors seeking to acquire failing banks.[40] Shortly after, the

---

37. The FDIC sells a deposit franchise through a sealed-bid auction process.
38. The FDIC sought to have at least five or six potential acquirers conduct due diligence and have at least three of those parties submit bids. To ensure it executed the least-costly transaction, the FDIC always compared the resulting recoveries it would achieve from the submitted bids with a recovery following a deposit insurance payout, which assumed the collection and sale of assets over time from the receivership estate.
39. See Chapters 8 and 10 for discussion about capital support for distressed banks.
40. See U.S. Department of the Treasury, Office of the Comptroller of the Currency (OCC), "OCC Conditionally Approves First National Bank Shelf Charter to Expand

FDIC announced it would allow prospective investors to bid for failing banks while a charter application was pending.[41] By the first half of 2009, the OTS had approved applications to facilitate the acquisition of two failed thrifts, IndyMac and BankUnited, which brought $2.2 billion of new capital into the industry.[42] Besides bringing in new capital, these transactions were the least-costly resolutions for the DIF, saving almost $1 billion over the cover bid for IndyMac alone.[43]

As private equity investor interest in failed-bank acquisitions grew, the FDIC became concerned about the management, skills, and incentives of the prospective owners. Institutions with de novo charters fail at significantly higher rates than established banks.[44] Importantly, private equity investors have a relatively short time horizon for achieving a return on their investments, typically three to seven years, and frequently set up their investment vehicles through offshore entities, obscuring ownership. An underappreciation of the complexity of establishing a new bank from the ashes of a failed one and a slow economic recovery could result in the FDIC's having to resolve essentially the same bank twice. To respond to these concerns, the agency issued a policy statement that addressed capital and source-of-strength requirements, ownership structure, disclosure requirements, and continuity of ownership interests.[45]

During the course of the crisis, 18 private equity investor groups acquired $75 billion in failed-bank assets and 60 failed-bank deposit franchises, or 22 percent of all failed-bank assets, excluding WaMu. These investments added

Pool of Qualified Bidders for Troubled Institutions," OCC news release NR 2008-137, Nov. 21, 2008. A shelf charter provides conditional approval for a bank charter, which is granted once certain conditions are met.

41. See FDIC, "FDIC Expands Bidder List for Troubled Institutions," press release PR-127-2008, Nov. 26, 2008.

42. See FDIC, "Board Approves Letter of Intent to Sell IndyMac Federal," press release PR-1-2009, Jan. 2, 2009; and FDIC, "BankUnited Acquires the Banking Operations of BankUnited, FSB, Coral Gables, Florida," press release PR-72-2009, May 21, 2009.

43. See FDIC, "Bid Summary, IndyMac Federal Bank FSB," March 19, 2009, https://www.fdic.gov/bank/individual/failed/indymac-bid-summary.html.

44. Robert DeYoung, "De Novo Bank Exit," *Journal of Money, Banking and Credit* 35, no. 5 (2003): 711–28.

45. Key among the requirements was a tier-1 common equity capital ratio of at least 10 percent and prohibiting the sale of interests for three years without the FDIC's consent. See FDIC, "Final Statement of Policy on Qualifications of Failed Bank Acquisitions," 74 Fed. Reg. 45440-9 (Sept. 2, 2009).

$5.6 billion in capital to the industry.[46] All were the least-costly resolutions available, reducing the cost of the crisis to the DIF.

RISK SHARING: THE LOSS-SHARE PROPOSITION

A lesson learned from the crisis of the late 1980s and early 1990s was that the longer the FDIC or the Resolution Trust Corporation (RTC) had assets under its custodianship, the lower the overall net recoveries were, unless market conditions for that asset improved significantly.[47] Multiple factors—including not having the operational efficiencies of firms in the business and being in the public sector, where business decisions intersect with public policy considerations and objectives—contribute to this result.

Holding and liquidating assets through collections and targeted asset sales, similar to what the FDIC did before the crisis of the late 1980s and early 1990s, would require a large infrastructure and fully expose the FDIC to financial, operational, market, and public relations / political risks. But other considerations during the financial crisis—including recovery value, the liquidity implications for the DIF, and such public policy objectives as avoiding fire sales and home foreclosures that could further depress markets—were even more significant. The agency faced the additional challenge of ensuring that bidders had sufficient time and information to make an informed offer, especially when deposits and assets were to be conveyed at the time of resolution.

Like any insurance company, the FDIC mutualizes covered-event losses among its base of premium payers. The federal government serves as the FDIC's reinsurer, ultimately having the ability to mutualize FDIC's losses among taxpayers if needed.[48] This arrangement makes the FDIC uniquely positioned to efficiently bear the risk of high or catastrophic losses arising from bank failures.

Additionally, by the time a bank fails, the FDIC has already assumed most of the intrinsic loss associated with the bank's assets through its deposit insurance obligations.[49] A subsequent asset buyer, on the other hand, will be assuming

---

46. See FDIC, *Crisis and Response,* 199.
47. See FDIC, *Managing the Crisis: The FDIC and RTC Experience* (Washington, D.C.: FDIC, 1998), 47–48; and FDIC, *Crisis and Response,* 179–80.
48. This reinsurance role was triggered when the original deposit insurer for savings and loan associations, the FSLIC, became insolvent.
49. As subrogee for the failed bank's insured depositors, the FDIC bears a loss that is determined by the amount of loss associated with the failed bank's assets, the

any loss that the buyer hasn't factored into the price at the time of purchase. A risk-averse buyer will discount the purchase price for risks that cannot be determined, whether due to lack of information or the uncertainty of future events, resulting in lower receivership creditor recoveries and a higher loss to the FDIC.

These two concepts—that the FDIC is more efficiently positioned to bear the risk of high or catastrophic loss than the buyers of failed banks and their assets and that the buyers will be assuming any loss not factored into the failed banks' price—form the conceptual basis for the FDIC's loss-share program. The program is essentially an insurance wrap for credit loss on specified asset pools.[50] In the event credit losses on a covered pool exceeded a certain threshold, the insurance coverage kicked in and the receivership estate would share a percentage of the loss with the acquirer.[51] The loss-share covered was of sufficient duration to allow for the realization of intrinsic losses as well as to avoid losses, and the systemic consequences, arising from selling a large volume of assets in distressed markets.

The insurance wrap provided by loss-share made assets that banks otherwise would not acquire with a deposit franchise attractive for them to purchase.[52] Of key importance to the FDIC, it facilitated the agency's ability to execute whole-bank P&A transactions, in which almost all of a failed bank's assets and liabilities are conveyed to an acquirer at the time of resolution.[53]

---

amount of secured claims, and the amount of claims subordinate or pari passu to the depositors' subrogated claims.

50. See FDIC, *Managing the Crisis*, 194–209, for more detail about the earlier loss-sharing transactions.

51. For example, assume a failed bank had a commercial real estate loan on its books for $1,000 and $1,000 in insured deposits. The acquirer's bid terms set an 80 percent coverage threshold level at $100 of loss and a 95 percent threshold level at $200 of loss and included a $50 discount. At closing, the FDIC pays the acquirer $50. The first $100 of loan loss is covered by the acquirer (although the $50 payment offsets a portion). The next $100 of loan loss is shared 80 percent by the receiver and 20 percent by the acquirer, resulting in an $80 payment to the acquirer. The receiver covers 95 percent of the loss exceeding $200.

52. The loss-share indemnity is booked as an asset on the acquirer's balance sheet. If an acquirer's bid resulted in a "bargain purchase," the difference between the purchase price and the restated asset book values could be realized immediately as capital or accrete over time as earnings. Regardless, the effect of a bargain purchase was to add capital to the banking system. If the assets were sold to nonbanks, this would not be the case.

53. In a whole-bank P&A transaction, almost all of the assets and liabilities of the failed bank are conveyed from the receivership estate to an acquirer, except, for example, certain tax assets and director/officer liability claims.

Of the $312 billion in failed-bank assets conveyed in whole-bank P&As with loss-share provisions, $217 billion was placed into loss-share covered pools.[54] Commercial real estate loans—including those for acquisition, development, and construction—constituted the largest asset type in the pools, making up $98 billion (45 percent), followed by single-family residential loans, at $74.2 billion (35 percent). Many of these loans were in default at the time of resolution.[55]

As the crisis stabilized and market conditions improved, and as the FDIC acquired more experience with the program, the threshold levels and structure for coverage changed. For example, in the 2008 transactions, once losses reached a transaction-specified amount, the receivership estate would cover 80 percent of the credit loss. If a higher transaction-specified loss amount was breached later, then 95 percent of any additional loss was covered—catastrophic loss protection. But by the third quarter of 2010, 95 percent loss protection was no longer offered; the FDIC included "true-up" provisions to essentially share gains from overly discounted bids; and the program had a multitiered structure for coverage to more strongly incentivize an acquirer's asset-loss mitigation efforts.[56]

The loss-share program benefits the FDIC in its roles as deposit insurer and as receiver. As insurer, the FDIC has to either pay depositors directly for their insured amounts or pay an acquiring bank to assume the failed bank's insured deposits. As noted earlier, using cash to pay for this obligation drains the liquidity of the DIF very quickly. As receiver, the FDIC has to liquidate the assets of the failed bank in a manner that maximizes their net present value and minimizes losses and then distribute the proceeds to its creditors.[57] Paying an acquirer for the assumption of deposit liabilities with noncash assets helps the FDIC as insurer. Financing the sale of assets with low-cost deposits and only 10 percent equity, terms highly unlikely to be available to buyers of

---

54. See FDIC, *Annual Report,* 2013, 76.
55. See FDIC, *Crisis and Response,* 221.
56. The multitiered structure featured a "doughnut hole" in coverage, with, for example, a first-loss tranche having 80 percent of losses covered by the receiver, a second-loss tranche having 0 percent of losses covered, and a third-loss tranche again having 80 percent covered. The underpinning theory was that the markets would stabilize, asset pricing would become more certain, and losses would be contained, with proper servicing/management, within the first two tranches. The third tranche provided tail-risk protection.
57. See 12 U.S.C. § 1821(d)(13)(E); and 12 U.S.C. § 1823(d)(3)(D).

distressed assets, results in higher pricing and better recoveries for the receivership.[58]

During the crisis, the FDIC resolved 304 banks ($312.1 billion in assets) through whole-bank P&As with loss-share. These transactions made up 62 percent of the number of resolutions and 82 percent of failed-bank assets (excluding WaMu). Total estimated cost to the FDIC is $56.8 billion, an estimated savings of $42 billion compared with the cost of resolution through payouts.[59]

OTHER RISK-SHARING PROGRAMS

Of the remaining 18 percent of failed-bank assets not resolved through loss-share transactions, $12.9 billion, or only 3.4 percent, was resolved through whole-bank transactions. Payouts totaled $15.9 billion, and other types of P&A transactions accounted for $38.4 billion.[60] The FDIC used two other risk-sharing programs to liquidate most of the retained assets from these resolutions: equity partnerships and securitizations. Collectively, more than 90 percent of failed-bank assets either passed at resolution or were sold through risk-sharing sales programs. (See Figure 11.4.)

Equity partnerships are structured sales in which the FDIC created limited liability companies (LLCs) to acquire certain assets from receiverships.[61] As consideration for the sale, the receivership estates typically acquired all the equity interests in the LLC and a note from the LLC, secured by the conveyed

---

58. At the outset of the crisis, buyers of distressed assets were looking for annualized rates of return of 25–30 percent. The purchase would be funded through a combination of equity, often a minimum of 20 percent, and borrowed funds. Banks, as asset buyers, could fund the purchase with the amount of capital regulators required to support the assets and the deposits assumed in the transaction. Leverage is higher and the cost of equity capital is lower for banks than for buyers of distressed assets.
59. See FDIC, *Crisis and Response,* 202. The estimated costs of payouts (liquidation) were made at the time of resolution to satisfy the least-cost test and were not revised for any differences between assumed and actual variables.
60. See FDIC, *Crisis and Response,* 200. WaMu, which was resolved in a whole-bank P&A without loss-share, was excluded from these figures because of its "outlier" size.
61. This program was a variant of the equity partnership programs the RTC used. See FDIC, *Managing the Crisis,* 433–70, for more background on those earlier programs.

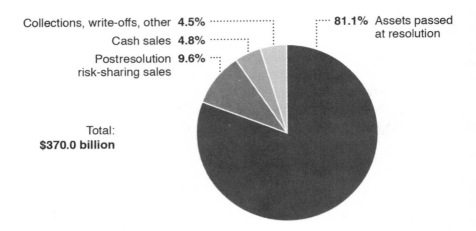

Collections, write-offs, other **4.5%**
Cash sales **4.8%**
Postresolution **9.6%**
risk-sharing sales

81.1% Assets passed
at resolution

Total:
$370.0 billion

Figure 11.4 **FDIC Asset Reductions, 2008–2013**

Note: Excludes Washington Mutual due to its size (all $298.8 billion of its assets were passed at resolution).

Source: FDIC Division of Resolutions and Receiverships

assets and equity interests.[62] The FDIC would then sell the managing member's interest—generally consisting of specified control rights and 40–50 percent of the equity—to a qualified, experienced investor team for cash. The managing member would then work out, collect, and sell the assets over a multiyear period. Distributions from the LLC were made to first pay off the note and then were split among the LLC's members based on their equity interests.

The program in many respects was the "other side of the coin" from loss-share: The partners shared in gains from the purchase price rather than sharing in loss from a failed bank's book value benchmark; the assets were sold to buyers of distressed assets rather than retained in the banking industry; and monitoring compliance with the partnering agreements was fully in FDIC's court rather than shared with a bank acquirer's supervisor. Of note, however, the program allowed the FDIC receiverships to share in value improvement as buyers applied their specialized expertise in managing and collecting on the assets and as markets stabilized and recovered. The program also avoided the consequences of selling highly distressed assets in very depressed markets.

62. About one-third of the structured sales did not include financing. The amount of leverage provided varied by underlying asset type.

The FDIC conveyed $26.2 billion of failed-bank assets to a total of 35 equity partnerships, of which 20 were established for working-out acquisition, development, and construction loans, eight for other commercial real estate loans, and seven for single-family residential loans. These sales represented about 30 percent of the assets not sold to bank acquirers at resolution. Recent estimates suggest the program will realize additional recoveries of $4.6 billion compared with the estimated bulk sales recoveries.[63]

LESSONS LEARNED

As noted earlier, during the financial crisis, the FDIC resolved 489 banks holding more than $680 billion in failed-bank assets, at an estimated cost to the DIF of $72.5 billion.[64] The idiosyncratic asset quality, capital structure, and degree of capital insolvency of failed banks make cost-effectiveness comparisons among resolution programs problematic, especially when one considers that both resolution authorities and acquirers select a resolution method based on those characteristics.

The programs the FDIC implemented during the crisis to manage the DIF and resolve failing banks, all of which facilitated the prompt payment of covered deposits, are generally viewed as having achieved their objectives: the public remained confident in the safety of their insured deposits, promoting financial stability; the industry continued to fund the DIF without the need for the FDIC to borrow from the Treasury; capital was brought into the industry through the resolution process; the overall financial and customer costs of resolutions were substantially less than if all resolutions were payouts; and when a bank failed, the resolution process was typically seamless, minimizing disruption to the bank's customers and the communities it served.

However, the programs were in response to the environment, circumstances, and events of this crisis and may not be as successful or applicable in the future. For example, the industry's ability to prepay deposit insurance premiums depended on the amount of available liquidity. If the DIF needs to borrow funds in the next crisis and the industry is severely strapped for liquidity, the FDIC may have to tap its borrowing lines with the Treasury and the Federal Financing Bank, as it did during the crisis of the late 1980s and early 1990s.

---

63. See FDIC, *Crisis and Response,* 219.
64. FDIC, *Crisis and Response,* 182.

Having banks prepay future insurance premium assessments was a creative solution for addressing the FDIC's liquidity needs in late 2009. The DIF received a much-needed boost in liquidity, and banks did not have to expense all of the funds immediately. Nonetheless, it was a solution to a problem that could have been avoided if the DIF had been sufficiently funded before the crisis.

Lesson 1:
Ensure that the DIF is sufficiently large during times of financial stability to avoid special assessments during times of stress.

Dodd-Frank lifted the statutory restrictions that historically constrained the size of the DIF. The FDIC is no longer required to return all excess premiums when the Designated Reserve Ratio (DRR) reaches 1.5 percent, which FDIRA mandated, and now has the flexibility to set the DRR at any level, provided a minimum DRR at 1.35 percent. The law also provided the agency with a greater ability to price for risk and required the assessment base for the DIF to change from domestic deposits to average consolidated total assets minus average tangible equity.[65]

In response to its new authorities, the FDIC looked back over a 60-year period that included the two most recent banking crises to determine how large the DIF needed to have been to avoid going negative at any point during that period.[66] With that analysis, the FDIC adopted a target DRR of 2.0 percent.[67] The agency also revised the DIF's assessment base to conform to the new statutory requirements and revised its risk-based pricing methodologies for large and small banks.[68]

These actions will mitigate the need to impose special assessments or increase insurance premiums when bank failures rise and industry conditions are poor. However, given the wide range of possible liquidity needs for honoring its insurance obligations and executing its resolution authorities, the FDIC

---

65. See Dodd-Frank, § 331–34, https://www.govinfo.gov/content/pkg/PLAW-111publ203/html/PLAW-111publ203.htm.
66. See Lee K. Davison and Ashley M. Carreon, "Toward a Long-Term Strategy for Deposit Insurance Fund Management," *FDIC Quarterly* 4, no. 4 (2010).
67. See 75 Fed. Reg. 79286 (Dec. 20, 2010).
68. See 79 Fed. Reg. 70427 (Nov. 26, 2014).

will continue to need access to the Treasury line of credit, the Federal Financing Bank, and other sources of short-term borrowing.

Lesson 2:
Revise and develop resolution strategies based on the facts and circumstances of the crisis.

Although the challenges for resolving banks in an orderly manner have recurrent themes, the economic environment and characteristics of the failing banks need to be factored into the programmatic responses. Private equity investments in distressed banks and de novo bank charters, for example, were successful mechanisms for bringing capital into the industry when it was needed and should be considered as potential resources in future crises when the lack of industry capital could constrain acquisitions. But private equity capital is expensive and may not be cost-effective when industry capital is readily available.

Loss-share proved to be very effective in making failed-bank assets attractive to acquirers buying deposit franchises. However, the magnitude of the program's benefits is dependent on the uncertainty of the underlying asset values. Risk-sharing programs should be updated and considered for use whenever systemic asset repricing results in value uncertainty. Although the administrative burden for compliance makes these programs unattractive during periods of stability, the potential benefits to the DIF, receivership creditors, and the macroeconomic environment can be significant when markets become atypically risk averse.

Lesson 3:
Have a "wish list" of statutory changes prepared before a crisis hits.

One program that the FDIC used in previous crises but could not in the crisis of 2008 without policymakers invoking the systemic risk exception was open-bank assistance. (The exception was invoked in 2008 for the Temporary Liquidity Guarantee Program and for assistance provided to Citigroup—see Chapters 9 and 10.) A series of legislative changes since 1991 have restricted the ability of the FDIC to provide open-bank assistance, most recently in

Dodd-Frank, which eliminated the systemic risk exception.[69] Any use of the DIF for open-bank assistance now requires congressional authorization.

This limitation is one that policymakers may want to revise in order to be prepared for the next crisis. With properly tailored constraints that address moral hazard and accountability concerns, open-bank assistance can be an effective and efficient resolution approach.

A case in point was when mutual savings banks were failing in the early 1980s. The cause was a negative spread, or net interest margin, between the banks' assets and their deposit liabilities due to the lifting of interest rate restrictions—credit quality was not an issue. The FDIC primarily resolved the banks through assisted mergers, whereby the FDIC paid acquiring institutions the spread between the acquired earning assets and the average cost of funds for the savings banks.[70]

This result was accomplished with the FDIC's open-bank assistance authority at a lower cost to the fund and to the banks' served communities than liquidation.

APPENDIX A: A DIFFERENT PROBLEM, A DIFFERENT APPROACH: LESSONS LEARNED FROM THE S&L CRISIS

Different problems require different solutions. That truism helps explain the different approaches that Washington applied to the banking/S&L crisis of the late 1980s and early 1990s and the financial crisis of 2008. These disruptive events arose from different market and industry forces and ran their courses in different economic environments. Because of those contrasts in circumstance and the advantage of applying lessons learned from the earlier crisis, the Federal Deposit Insurance Corporation (FDIC) went in a different direction in 2008 in resolving failing banks and selling their assets.

Many savings and loans were insolvent in early 1989 owing to years of regulatory forbearance. Having no funds for resolution, the government began placing insolvent thrifts into government-controlled conservatorships. Ulti-

---

69. FIRREA, the Federal Deposit Insurance Corporation Improvement Act of 1991 (FDICIA), the RTC Completion Act of 1993, and most recently Dodd-Frank have each resulted in narrowing the FDIC's authority for providing open-bank assistance.
70. The FDIC resolved 14 mutual savings banks with open-bank assistance in 1981–1983. See FDIC, *Managing the Crisis*, 159.

mately, 262 savings and loans went into conservatorship from the time legislation was proposed to create and fund the Resolution Trust Corporation (RTC) until it passed. The RTC, a government-owned corporation, was charged with resolving all failed savings and loans and overseeing the disposition of the failed institutions' assets.

The value of these core deposit franchises deteriorated during conservatorship due to customer attrition and changing market conditions, resulting in a high percentage of payouts when the affected thrifts ultimately were resolved. However, leaving the S&Ls under the control of their owners presented risks of even greater loss.

For thrifts that were not placed into conservatorship, the typical resolution was a clean-bank purchase and assumption, known as a "clean-bank P&A," in which only "clean assets," essentially vault cash and cash-like equivalents, were offered and conveyed with the deposit franchise to a bank acquirer. These transactions were common because they did not require significant due diligence by either the RTC or prospective buyers. Such a review was difficult, if not impossible, to perform, due to the lack of pertinent information and/or the compressed resolution time frame prior to a thrift's closing.

The remaining assets—mostly loans, real estate, non-readily-marketable securities, and investments in subsidiaries—would be held in the RTC receiverships and wound down over time, through collections, workouts, and/or sales. The collections activity took the form of servicing the performing loans and other credits, until they matured within a few years and were paid off, and negotiating workouts and settlements on nonperforming credits. Generally, the other assets would be sold, typically through sealed-bid auctions.

These initial approaches resulted in failed-bank assets building up in inventory much more quickly than they were being liquidated. For the RTC, the problem was particularly severe. The FDIC was able to expand the volume of assets conveyed at the time a bank was resolved by offering options to deposit franchise buyers for high-quality loan pools. But the RTC's funding dynamic requiring congressional appropriations resulted in having to sell conservatorship assets before funds became available to resolve the conservatorship, thereby reducing the pool of assets available to convey to a bank acquirer with the deposit franchise.

A silver-lining outcome of this tension was the development of new portfolio sales programs, including some that securitized mortgages and others that created partnerships between the RTC and the private sector, which tapped into private capital and distressed-asset management expertise. (See Figure 11.5.)

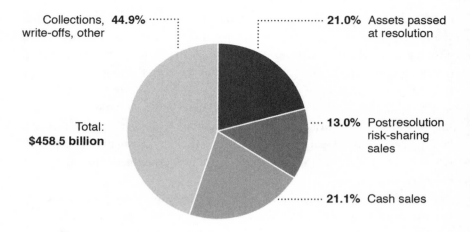

Collections, **44.9%** ⋯⋯⋯⋯
write-offs, other

⋯⋯⋯⋯⋯⋯ **21.0%** Assets passed
at resolution

Total:
$458.5 billion

⋯⋯ **13.0%** Postresolution
risk-sharing
sales

⋯⋯⋯⋯⋯⋯ **21.1%** Cash sales

Figure 11.5 **Resolution Trust Corporation Asset Reductions, 1989–1995**

Source: Thrift Depositor Protection Board, *Annual Report,* 1995

A downside of the RTC approach was that it required a massive operational infrastructure. At the beginning of 1992, the RTC had under its custodianship more than $130 billion in failed-thrift assets. To handle the workload, the RTC established 20 offices throughout the United States, assembled a staff of more than 8,600 direct employees, and had in excess of $3.5 billion in annual administrative expenses.[71] Managing this huge volume of assets exposed the RTC to financial, operational, and public relations risks. Its infrastructure took two years to set up, even with the jump-start provided from existing FDIC and former Federal Savings and Loan Insurance Corporation (FSLIC) operations, and took 14 years to wind down.

Arguably, the most significant effect of this approach was the value loss arising from splitting the sale of deposits from the sale of a failed bank's other assets. Deposit acquirers receiving a large cash transfer from the FDIC for the insured deposits have to quickly find a way to invest those proceeds at a posi-

71. See appendix table B of the "Report by the Chairperson of the Thrift Depositor Protection Oversight Board on Loss Funds Provided by the Congress for Use by the Resolution Trust Corporation" included in Thrift Depositor Protection Board, *Annual Report,* 1995, https://fraser.stlouisfed.org/files/docs/publications/rtc/ar_rtc _1995.pdf.

tive margin—or risk losing the customer relationships they just paid to acquire. To compensate for the reinvestment and deposit attrition risks, banks offer a lower premium for the deposit franchise.

Conversely, asset buyers have to find the equity and financing necessary to purchase a failed bank's assets. If the seller isn't providing financing, the purchase price is discounted to reflect the leverage structure and financing the buyer can obtain under existing market conditions, which can be restrictive in depressed credit cycles. Finally, the business franchise value of a customer's linked-product relationships is lost.

The lessons learned from the previous crisis greatly informed the FDIC's response to the crisis of 2008. This time around, by conveying most of a failed bank's assets at the time of resolution whenever possible, losses were minimized, customer relationships were preserved, community impact was lessened, and the FDIC's working-capital needs were reduced. Importantly, the seamless resolutions fostered confidence in deposit insurance and the commercial banking system.

Because the next crisis will also have its own unique circumstances and require its own special solutions, future policymakers would do well to study both of these earlier crises to see what other lessons might have value in shaping their decisions.

APPENDIX B: THE WAMU RESOLUTION: BALANCING COMPETING POLICY OBJECTIVES

The case of Washington Mutual (WaMu) is a notable illustration of the tension between competing government policy objectives in bank resolution.

Because of concerns about accountability, market discipline, and long-term financial stability, Congress prohibited the Deposit Insurance Fund (DIF) from benefiting shareholders of a distressed bank and mandated that it be used for the least-costly resolution option available. However, a systemic risk exception of these restrictions was allowed under the Federal Deposit Insurance Corporation Improvement Act of 1991 (FDICIA). Invocation of the exception required supermajorities of the FDIC and the Federal Reserve boards to recommend authorizing its use, and the subsequent authorization by the Treasury secretary after consultation with the president.

The first potential use of the exception was with WaMu. The issues for policy-makers were (1) under what circumstances should the exception be authorized, and (2) did WaMu qualify for the exception in September 2008.[72] These issues, in turn, led to the question of how to balance long-term financial stability objectives with the immediate risks of financial instability.

When the September 2008 deposit run on WaMu started to accelerate, the FDIC considered whether the bank warranted invoking the systemic risk exception, which would allow the agency to provide open-bank assistance and avoid the prospect of WaMu's creditors suffering losses if it failed. The authorizing agencies had already developed procedures for triggering the exception. And market indicators recognized the bank's distress: Its stock was trading at less than $2, its debt had been downgraded to junk or near-junk status and was trading at deep discounts, and credit default swap pricing suggested the market expected default. Wall Street analysts openly speculated that the bank would soon be capital insolvent.[73]

The FDIC reviewed the asset book of the bank, the services it provided, its deposit base and capital stack, and its interconnections with the financial system. It concluded that should WaMu fail, haircuts imposed on WaMu's depositors would be destabilizing, given the large amount of uninsured funds.

After a sales effort by the bank's parent was unsuccessful, the FDIC offered WaMu to bidders in an approach that indirectly solicited the potential acquirers' views of the effect of impairing various classes of WaMu's capital stack. Unlike standard FDIC resolution offerings—in which bidders are offered bid options to assume only liabilities secured by assets they seek to acquire in the transaction, insured deposits, or all of the bank's deposits—in the case of WaMu, the FDIC offered bid options that included the assumption of subordinated and senior unsecured debt. This gave potential acquirers the ability to make a bid in which the DIF supported the acquirer's assumption of layers in the capital stack that it considered important.

72. The systemic risk exception allowed the FDIC to provide assistance to open banks if compliance with the least-cost and no-shareholder-benefit restrictions would have serious adverse effects on economic conditions or financial stability and if bypassing the restrictions would avoid or mitigate such adverse effects.
73. See Eric Dash and Geraldine Fabrikant, "Washington Mutual Stock Falls on Investor Fears," *New York Times,* Sept. 10, 2008, http://www.nytimes.com/2008/09/11/business/11bank.html.

When bids came in, they indicated that all of WaMu's deposits needed to be assumed. Bond and equity holders would suffer losses. The DIF incurred no cost for WaMu's resolution. Equity market reaction suggested that WaMu's resolution met the market's expectations.

However, that's not the end of the story.

After the failure of Lehman Brothers, and now WaMu, the credit markets, unaccustomed to experiencing loss from financial institution exposure, immediately focused on which bank was likely to fail next. Given the similarity of Wachovia's asset book to WaMu's, its funding immediately came under more stress: It would need to be acquired or resolved in short order.

Although the systemic risk exception was not used for WaMu, its resolution, combined with Lehman's, signaled that financial institution creditors were at risk at a time when contagion was increasing. Could a systemic determination for WaMu have mitigated the spreading contagion in the credit markets?

We'll never know the answer. However, given the breadth of the asset repricing and uncertainty of values in the third week of September 2008, system-wide support clearly was needed.

CHAPTER TWELVE

Crisis-Era Housing Programs

MICHAEL BARR, NEEL T. KASHKARI, ANDREAS LEHNERT, AND PHILLIP SWAGEL

INTRODUCTION

Housing was at the center of the financial crisis. Losses from financial instruments based on defaulted mortgages were the initial spark that started the downturn, while the corresponding wave of foreclosures led to some of its most profound and long-lasting consequences for American families. Credit expansion, including through subprime and Alt-A mortgage products, gave rise to mutually reinforcing increases in home prices and household debt, creating an unsustainable situation that began to unwind after house prices peaked in 2006.[1] As prices flattened, then declined, and the economy entered a recession

The authors thank the following people for their comments and feedback: Ben S. Bernanke, Timothy F. Geithner, Henry M. Paulson, Jr., Richard Brown, Phyllis Caldwell, Eric Dash, Laurie Goodman, Nellie Liang, Tim Massad, Pascal Noel, Jim Parrott, Tom Redburn, Seth Wheeler, and John Worth. The authors would also like to thank Anthony Cozart, Annabel Jouard, and Jongeun You of the University of Michigan's Center on Finance, Law, and Policy; Benjamin Henken of the Yale Program on Financial Stability; and Alex Martin from the Federal Reserve Board for their invaluable research assistance. A huge number of people across both administrations contributed to the development and implementation of the mortgage-related programs described in this chapter. Their efforts and dedication made a difference to the nation and to millions of American families.

1. Subprime loans are made by creditors that specialize in lending to borrowers with FICO scores generally below 620. Alt-A loans do not meet standard underwriting guidelines; for example, many Alt-A loans lack full documentation of borrower income or have unusual features such as nonamortizing monthly mortgage payments.

that led to widespread job losses, it became more difficult for homeowners to refinance or service their mortgages. Defaults grew, first in the subprime sector and then more broadly.[2] With the expiration of teaser rates, many homeowners faced further challenges from increasing monthly mortgage payments. A vicious cycle of rising defaults, sinking home prices, and declining housing construction led to immense losses on housing-related assets, pushing the undercapitalized financial system to the brink of collapse.

A broad set of policies and initiatives stabilized and improved housing markets during the crisis. Under the July 2008 Housing and Economic Recovery Act (HERA), the Treasury provided backstops to the government-sponsored enterprises (GSEs)—Fannie Mae and Freddie Mac—that ensured mortgage financing remained available even as many financial markets experienced severe strains and as mortgage funding outside the government-guaranteed sector dried up. Capital injections through the Troubled Assets Relief Program (TARP) stabilized a wide range of financial institutions, including some of the largest that played key roles in the mortgage market. Monetary policy easing by the Fed, which included purchases of mortgage-backed securities (MBS) as part of quantitative easing (QE), aided millions of homeowners and housing markets more broadly by driving down interest rates and supporting the overall economy. Fiscal stimuli enacted in January 2008 and February 2009 (and thereafter) supported consumer and business spending. A common criticism of the Bush and Obama responses to the crisis is that too much attention was focused on financial institutions at the expense of individual homeowners, but helping homeowners required stabilizing the financial system and ensuring that the mortgage market continued to function.

The focus of this chapter is on policies aimed at helping homeowners avoid foreclosure. Some programs were put in place during the Bush administration: HERA and the Emergency Economic Stabilization Act (EESA), enacted in October 2008, provided authorities and funding that were eventually used to implement a wide range of housing-related programs. But the main use of taxpayer funds for foreclosure prevention started in 2009. Within its first few weeks, the Obama administration announced programs aimed at helping

2. "S&P/Case-Shiller U.S. National Home Price Index," S&P Dow Jones Indices, McGraw Hill Financial, accessed Jan. 18, 2019, http://us.spindices.com/indices/real -estate/sp-case-shiller-us-national-home-price-index.

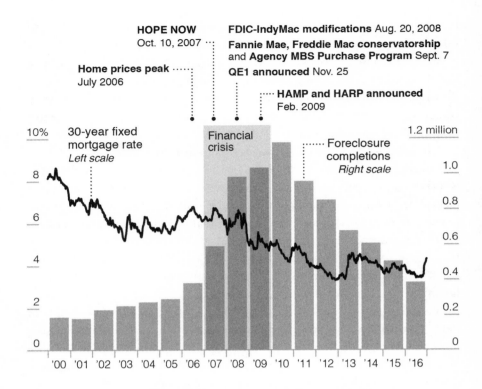

HOPE NOW Oct. 10, 2007

FDIC-IndyMac modifications Aug. 20, 2008

Fannie Mae, Freddie Mac conservatorship and **Agency MBS Purchase Program** Sept. 7

Home prices peak July 2006

QE1 announced Nov. 25

HAMP and HARP announced Feb. 2009

10% — 30-year fixed mortgage rate *Left scale*

Financial crisis

Foreclosure completions *Right scale*

1.2 million

Figure 12.1 Programs, Mortgage Rates, and Foreclosure Completions

Note: Acronyms used in this figure are defined in the list of abbreviations at the front of this book.

Sources: Mortgage rates: Freddie Mac via Federal Reserve Economic Data; foreclosure completions: CoreLogic

homeowners, notably the Home Affordable Refinance Program (HARP) and the Home Affordable Modification Program (HAMP). Efforts to improve these programs continued for years. The administration also sought to catalyze modifications of GSE-guaranteed mortgages outside of TARP, launched a new Federal Housing Administration (FHA) refinance program, and provided funds to state and local Housing Finance Agencies (HFAs) and Community Development Financial Institutions (CDFIs) to support their responses to the foreclosure crisis. Efforts in some of these dimensions, such as expanded use of FHA refinancing, were also undertaken during the Bush administration. Figure 12.1 illustrates a timeline of major programs as well as the level of mortgage rates and foreclosure completions.

Despite these programs and the broad-based effort to overcome the crisis, federal housing policy was widely seen as having been unsuccessful because the programs prevented fewer foreclosures than predicted and produced results at a slower pace than expected. Millions of foreclosures took place. Americans suffered greatly during the crisis, and this experience has had a long-standing effect on housing choices as well as the opportunities available to households to get access to mortgage credit.

We understand critics' frustration with mortgage modifications: The policy responses did not resolve the housing crisis and were not as effective as hoped or predicted. Even so, foreclosure prevention policies were more consequential than commonly thought, with positive impacts on millions of families, and the full suite of housing-related policies together contributed to the housing market and macroeconomic recovery. Although HAMP directly reached only a third of delinquent borrowers with government-subsidized loan modifications, private-sector modifications modeled on HAMP but not involving taxpayer money helped many others, as did other GSE, FHA, and other governmental modification programs.[3] The programs we implemented led to 8.2 million mortgage modifications, 9.5 million targeted refinancings, and 5.3 million other mortgage assistance actions.

Future policymakers can learn from these responses, specifically from how our thinking evolved as the crisis unfolded. With uncertain data and analytic frames, we proceeded with the options we thought would best serve the most people. In hindsight, pushing more quickly to bolder options would have been better. At the same time, legal and operational constraints affected the policy responses, and political constraints limited our ability to obtain new authority to overcome some of the obstacles we faced.

DIAGNOSING THE PROBLEM AND CONSTRAINTS

Figure 12.2 summarizes some of the key variables that affected our policy choices: house prices, consumer bankruptcy filings, the initial notices of default (NOD) that marked the start of the foreclosure process, and the delinquency rate on mortgages. During the peak years of the foreclosure crisis, from 2007 to

---

3. Sumit Agarwal, Gene Amromin, Itzhak Ben-David, Souphala Chomsisengphet, Tomasz Piskorski, and Amit Seru, "Policy Intervention in Debt Renegotiation: Evidence from the Home Affordable Modification Program," *Journal of Political Economy* 125, no. 3 (2017): 654–712.

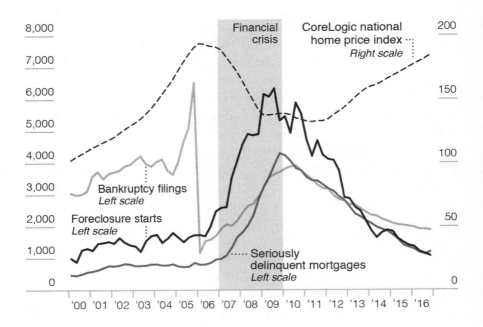

Figure 12.2 **Housing Market Trends during the Crisis**

Note: U.S. Courts Chapter 7 and Chapter 13 bankruptcy filings as well as foreclosure starts are charted in hundreds. Seriously delinquent mortgages are charted in thousands.

Sources: Bankruptcy filings: U.S. Courts; foreclosure starts and seriously delinquent mortgages: Mortgage Bankers Association National Delinquency Survey; CoreLogic House Price Index: CoreLogic via Financial Accounts of the United States, Federal Reserve Board (Z.1 Release)

2010, about 5.8 million households received their first NODs, compared with 2.5 million during the precrisis period, suggesting something like 3.3 million additional foreclosure starts attributable to the crisis itself (Table 12.1). Many, but not all, of these initiated foreclosures ultimately forced households out of their homes, causing harm to the families affected and to their communities.

Several factors explain the high level of foreclosures during the crisis, including changes in mortgage origination practices, serious problems in mortgage securitization, the speculative nature of the housing boom, and then, as the boom turned to bust, rapidly falling house prices combined with widespread job losses. Most obviously, large volumes of mortgages were originated requiring little equity on properties where values were stretched, and with not enough attention to borrowers' ability to pay. Although such origination prac-

Table 12.1 **Foreclosures before and during the Crisis**

Years	Foreclosures started (in millions)	Households receiving first notice of delinquency (in millions)	Difference: Proxy for investor-owned (in millions)
Precrisis (2003–2006)	2.7	2.5	0.2
Crisis (2007–2010)	7.8	5.8	2.0
Difference: "Excess" foreclosures	5.1	3.3	1.8

Sources: Foreclosures started: Mortgage Bankers Association National Delinquency Survey; households receiving first notice of delinquency: Equifax, Federal Reserve Bank of New York

tices became widespread throughout the industry, they were particularly prevalent in loans destined for securities packaged through so-called private mortgage conduits, meaning by companies other than the GSEs or the government-backed loans of the FHA and the Department of Veterans Affairs. As shown in Figure 12.3, these private-label mortgages formed a growing share of total mortgages outstanding from the late 1990s through 2006. But by the time the GSEs were put into conservatorship in September 2008, the private-label market driven by securitization had collapsed.

Some of the worst underwriting practices were evident among the subprime sector, but the misconduct was especially notable in Alt-A lending and beyond. Although subprime losses were large, they alone do not account for the magnitude of the Great Recession.[4] The recession's depth and severity were the result of losses from poorly underwritten mortgages hitting an economy that featured overextended households, highly leveraged financial institutions, and large volumes of assets held in unstable funding structures vulnerable to runs. Moreover, basic information was lacking on the extent of poorly underwritten mortgages and their distribution through the system, feeding contagion across institutions and sectors. The system was highly interconnected because

4. Statement by Ben S. Bernanke, chairman of the Board of Governors of the Federal Reserve System, before the Financial Crisis Inquiry Commission, Sept. 2, 2010, https://www.federalreserve.gov/newsevents/testimony/bernanke20100902a.pdf.

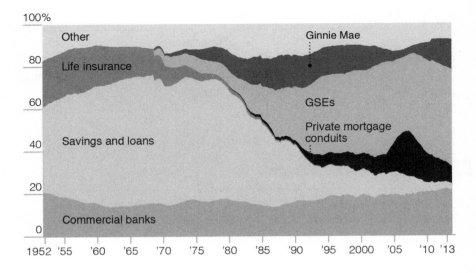

Figure 12.3 **Distribution of Outstanding Single-Family Mortgages**

Note: GSEs are government-sponsored enterprises.

Source: Michael S. Barr, Howell E. Jackson, and Margaret E. Tahyar, *Financial Regulation: Law and Policy, Second Edition* (St. Paul, MN: Foundation Press, 2018), relying on original chart from Laurie Goodman, "A Realistic Assessment of Housing Finance Reform" (Washington, D.C.: Urban Institute, 2014)

risk was spread throughout the financial sector in asset-backed securities, derivatives, and collateralized debt obligations.

Diagnosing the problem in real time was difficult. Basic data of the kind we now take for granted were not available. Thus, estimates of total losses, the distribution of those losses, the extent and distribution of negative equity, and other key statistics were subject to even greater uncertainty than normal. Further, there was no consensus at the time on the degree to which households defaulted strategically—responding to negative equity or program eligibility requirements—rather than when faced with cash flow problems that made it impossible for them to make their monthly payment. Contemporaneous evidence, including a host of anecdotes, supported both views. We fundamentally did not know whether the most important problem was household cash flow or negative equity.

The policy responses of both administrations were also seriously hampered by a series of practices within the industry that had grown during the credit boom.

First, commonly used securitization structures frustrated attempts to modify loans. Private-label securities, at their peak, had bundled loans worth a quarter of mortgage debt outstanding (Figure 12.3); an even larger share of the most troubled mortgages, notably subprime and Alt-A, were securitized in the private-label system. In such securitizations, the underlying mortgages were transferred to a special purpose vehicle (SPV) that issued securities backed by the cash flows from these mortgages, including regular monthly payments, the proceeds of refinancings, and any prepayment penalties or other fees. Ownership of these securities was highly dispersed, and the timing and priority of payments to various securities often resulted in sharply differing incentives to modify the underlying loans. Further, the legal structure of the SPVs did not allow for large-scale changes in the underlying loans, and in many structures, modifications were prohibited or severely restricted. The SPVs were designed to operate entirely on automatic pilot, with no active management by the securitizing institution, the trustee, or in many cases the servicers of the underlying loans. Each SPV was overseen by a trustee, typically a large bank. Trustees acted as custodians and undertook additional administrative functions but were not expected to broker deals among owners of the SPV or between the SPV and the government.

Second, the holders of junior liens had to agree to foreclosure alternatives such as loan modifications, presenting both operational hurdles and a classic "hold up" problem, meaning that junior lien holders could try to block modifications. Gerardi et al. show that the use of junior liens was instrumental in permitting the increase in leverage among subprime borrowers; nearly 30 percent of subprime loans at their peak originated simultaneously with a second lien.[5] Because of underreporting, the true prevalence of such loans was higher. In principle, once house prices had fallen sufficiently to wipe out their equity, junior liens should have been worth very little; nonetheless, the lien holder's consent was required for modification programs, effectively giving them a veto. Moreover, distressed homeowners were surprisingly likely to make payments on a junior lien even after having gone delinquent on the senior lien, presumably because the payment was smaller and thus easier to meet. In cases where junior lien holders were getting paid, they had little incentive

5. Kristopher Gerardi, Andreas Lehnert, Shane M. Sherlund, and Paul Willen, "Making Sense of the Subprime Crisis," Brookings Papers on Economic Activity, 2008 (2), 69–159.

to cooperate. Addressing this problem required time and resources during the design and implementation phases of the mortgage rescue programs.

A third hurdle was the lack of capacity or willingness among many mortgage servicers to modify loans. Indeed, had the lower end of the servicer spectrum been as effective as the top tier, the number of permanent modifications would have been 70 percent higher. Yet the performance of even the best servicers fell well short of what we expected.[6] Servicers had not anticipated the need to undertake large-scale actions to modify loans to avoid foreclosures, so they did not have the resources or systems needed for the efforts they were called on to make (and which, indeed, they were contractually obligated to make). Problems in servicing were widespread and a tremendous obstacle to the implementation of policies aimed at avoiding foreclosures. We knew servicers were ill-equipped to handle the foreclosure crisis, but we underestimated how badly they would perform, effectively preventing hundreds of thousands of borrowers from obtaining relief to avoid foreclosure. This was later revealed in spades, as the robo-signing scandals and subsequent lawsuits showed just how badly the mortgage servicers performed.

Fourth, policy coordination within the administration, across states, and with independent agencies, including the Federal Housing Finance Agency (the newly created regulator of the GSEs, known as FHFA, which effectively controlled Fannie and Freddie in conservatorship), was difficult. No one entity had full authority to act, and several key agencies were independent.

Fifth, compliance and administration costs were large, creating frictions that reduced the effectiveness of our programs. Congress; the Special Inspector General for the TARP (SIGTARP), the internal auditor responsible for monitoring the program; Treasury; FHFA; and others were focused on preventing fraud and ensuring appropriate use of taxpayer dollars—laudable goals—but this instilled a caution and paperwork burden that made it much harder to scale up a program in the midst of the crisis.

Last, there were trade-offs between using the limited funds available for homeowner assistance or for broader financial stability initiatives.

As policymakers we understood the interplay between macrolevel and microlevel policy. The impacts ran in both directions. Mortgage modification and refinancing programs could help stabilize financial markets and improve the broader economy, while policies that brought an improved economy and fi-

---

6. Agarwal et al., "Policy Intervention in Debt Renegotiation."

nancial sector would help stabilize housing markets and assist individual families. While recognizing the intensity of the political opposition to mortgage modifications (many saw them as unfair to responsible homeowners who paid their mortgages and had not overextended themselves), we viewed reducing the negative externalities from foreclosure as the right thing to do as a matter of economic policy. It was also morally fair to the many troubled borrowers who had been taken advantage of in the mortgage process. Even so, we took care to ensure that public subsidies were targeted to homeowners rather than to investors, and we focused on homeowners who had the financial wherewithal to stay in their homes with a reasonable amount of assistance. We recognized that not every foreclosure could (or should) be avoided, although families and communities affected would need further help.

Homeowners with securitized subprime and Alt-A loans suffered disproportionately from foreclosures early in the housing bust, although the problems spread throughout the housing sector as job losses spiked and the Great Recession set in. In principle, securitizations could replicate the incentive structure built into old-fashioned bank lending, but in practice, misaligned incentives, lack of transparency, misrepresentation, and fraud, as well as credit rating agency abuses, caused widespread harms. In addition, as one can see from Figure 12.2, consumer bankruptcy filings plummeted after the 2005 legislation that restricted access to bankruptcy court, perhaps providing consumers with less flexibility in coping with their consumer debts and contributing to pressures on mortgage payments and increasing delinquencies.[7] Moreover, even those homeowners who managed to file for protection could not modify their mortgages in bankruptcy. All of this limited the power of homeowners in negotiating mortgage restructuring. Political constraints in getting Congress to change the law were significant—and there is still a vigorous debate about whether a change is desirable.

Despite all these challenges, the policy responses helped millions of borrowers, lessened the severity of the financial crisis, and contributed to the stabilization of the housing sector and to the macroeconomic recovery. The choice to reduce monthly mortgage payments rather than to write down mortgage principal turned out to be much more cost-effective for a given amount of

7. Michelle White, Wenli Li, and Ning Zhu, "Did Bankruptcy Reform Cause Mortgage Defaults to Rise?," *American Economic Journal: Economic Policy* 3 (2011): 123–47, http://econweb.ucsd.edu/~miwhite/AEJ_Policy_Li_White.pdf.

taxpayer dollars.[8] At the time, we wanted to experiment more with principal reduction, but we were worried initially about blowing through available resources and were blocked later by FHFA objections to letting the GSEs engage in principal reduction. Even so, although the focus on payments was the right approach from the perspective of the efficiency of taxpayer resources, it is possible that the overhang of negative equity affected consumer spending and slowed the economic recovery.[9]

POLICY RESPONSE: DESIGN AND IMPLEMENTATION

During the Bush administration, we organized and led private-sector initiatives (that is, not involving taxpayer funds) that sought to make it easier for homeowners and servicers to modify private-sector mortgages, and acted to promote refinancing into FHA-backed mortgages. We introduced a national hotline in 2007 to make beginning a modification easier, as well as a private-sector-led program, HOPE NOW, which helped homeowners obtain modifications that, among other things, allowed some to delay or limit interest rate resets. In the fall of 2007, we worked with Congress to enact bipartisan tax legislation that allowed homeowners who benefited from the reduction of principal on their mortgage debt as part of a restructuring to avoid paying the capital gains tax on the debt extinguishment. This legislation helped all later programs that addressed negative equity.

Housing-related policies ramped up significantly starting in the summer of 2008, as the number of foreclosures continued to increase.[10] The most visible

8. Among those supporting this view are Therese C. Sharlemann and Stephen H. Shore, "The Effect of Negative Equity on Mortgage Default: Evidence from HAMP's Principal Reduction Alternative," *Review of Financial Studies* 29, no. 10 (2016): 2850–83, https://academic.oup.com/rfs/article/29/10/2850/2223370; Janice Eberly and Arvind Krishnamurthy, "Efficient Credit Policies in a Housing Debt Crisis," Brookings Papers on Economic Activity, Fall 2014, https://www.brookings.edu/wp-content/uploads/2016/07/Fall2014BPEA_Eberly_Krishnamurthy.pdf; and Peter Ganong and Pascal Noel, "Liquidity vs. Wealth in Household Debt Obligations: Evidence from Housing Policy in the Great Recession" (NBER Working Paper, 2018), http://www.nber.org/papers/w24964.
9. Atif Mian and Amir Sufi, *House of Debt: How They (and You) Caused the Great Recession, and How We Can Prevent It from Happening Again* (Chicago: University of Chicago Press, 2014).
10. Ben S. Bernanke, "The Crisis and the Policy Response" (speech at the Stamp Lecture, London School of Economics, London, England, Jan. 13, 2009), https://www.federalreserve.gov/newsevents/speech/bernanke20090113a.htm.

policy response was the enactment of HERA, which established the FHFA (taking over for the GSEs' previous regulator), increased supervisory authority over Fannie and Freddie, and gave the agency the power to put each GSE into conservatorship or receivership. HERA also authorized Treasury to provide support for Fannie and Freddie.[11] Backing the GSEs was essential to stabilize these institutions, which had $5.4 trillion in securities outstanding, and was critical to maintaining a vital source of mortgage financing during the crisis. The administration's view at the time, later summarized by Treasury secretary Henry M. Paulson, Jr., was that the GSEs "more than anyone else were the engine we needed to get through the [housing markets] problem."[12]

In early September, both Fannie and Freddie were taken into conservatorship by their independent regulator, and the Treasury committed $200 billion to ensure the continued operation of the GSEs as their capital positions deteriorated.[13] (The Obama administration later doubled that amount, to a total of $400 billion in February 2009, and let it float up further at the end of that year; by the end of 2012, Treasury's backstop of Fannie and Freddie totaled $445.5 billion.)[14] Fannie and Freddie were essential to housing markets and the economy; it was crucial to have these firms operating both to ensure the continued flow of mortgage credit and to serve as vital participants in mortgage modification programs.

HERA also authorized a new program called Hope for Homeowners, which sought to help up to 400,000 homeowners through FHA refinancings and lender write-downs of mortgage principal. The actual impact, however, was minuscule, largely because the program was hobbled by design flaws in the legislation that overly restricted borrower eligibility and made it more expensive for lenders to participate than to take other modification actions or to foreclose.

11. Housing and Economic Recovery Act, 12 U.S.C. § 4501.
12. Interview with former Treasury secretary Henry M. Paulson, Jr., Financial Crisis Inquiry Commission, April 2, 2010, http://fcic-static.law.stanford.edu/cdn_media /fcic-docs/2010-04-02%20FCIC%20memo%20of%20staff%20interview%20with%20 Henry%20Paulson,%20U.S.%20Treasury.pdf.
13. Statement by Secretary Henry M. Paulson, Jr., on Treasury and Federal Housing Finance Agency Action to Protect Financial Markets and Taxpayers, Sept. 7, 2008, https://www.treasury.gov/press-center/press-releases/Pages/hp1129 .aspx.
14. Michael S. Barr, Howell E. Jackson, and Margaret E. Tahyar, *Financial Regulation: Law and Policy,* 2nd ed. (St. Paul, MN: Foundation Press, 2018), 1289.

In October 2008, after the failure of Lehman Brothers and the rescue of American International Group, Congress passed the Emergency Economic Stabilization Act, authorizing the deployment of up to $700 billion in several tranches and giving "the Treasury Secretary broad and flexible authority to purchase and insure mortgages and other troubled assets."[15] EESA authorized TARP, which, in addition to being used for financial stability initiatives, eventually was used to implement a range of mortgage- and housing-related programs. The priority of TARP under the Bush administration was to prevent the collapse of the financial system, which is why the first $350 billion made available to the Treasury was used to inject capital into banks and other financial institutions (and then later to provide bridge financing to General Motors and Chrysler to prevent the collapse of the two automakers). Democrats in Congress made clear that they expected TARP funding to support a program for homeowner relief. Incoming Obama administration officials started to study the issue, conferring with Bush Treasury staff, consumer and community groups, think tanks, and academic experts, and many others during the transition about various options.

There was no existing infrastructure in place for the Treasury to price and purchase individual mortgages or subprime MBS. Efforts to build out the programs were put on the shelf by the Bush administration as it became clear that capital injections into financial institutions could be implemented more quickly. Among the options analyzed by Treasury staff in the Bush administration to support the housing market and prevent foreclosures was for Treasury to buy MBS at a price that would result in a low interest rate (say, 4 percent) for borrowers. The combination of the GSE conservatorship and the Fed's QE actions to purchase Treasuries and agency MBS ultimately reached that goal, helping millions of homeowners, but it was too late for many homeowners early in the crisis.

President Obama took office in January 2009 determined to address the worsening housing crisis and deep recession. Fannie and Freddie were quickly using up their initial capital backstops, and in February 2009 the Treasury doubled its commitment to each GSE to $200 billion (and even then we did not know whether that would be sufficient to stave off collapse). That month the

15. Neel Kashkari, "Remarks before the Institute of International Bankers," Oct. 13, 2008, https://www.treasury.gov/press-center/press-releases/Pages/hp1199.aspx.

administration also announced two new initiatives, together referred to as the Making Home Affordable Program.

The first, HARP, encouraged refinancing of underwater and high loan-to-value (LTV) mortgages owned by the GSEs, those with LTVs between 80 and 125 percent. Broad refinancing would reinforce the effects of the Fed's policies to lower mortgage interest rates. Lower payments would also support consumer spending and thereby the overall economy—in this way expansionary monetary policy combined with housing-related efforts. It was clear, however, that many homeowners were not initially able to refinance their mortgages, because they were underwater, had high LTVs, or had impaired credit, and thus could not qualify for a GSE refinance to benefit from the lower interest rates. Addressing this challenge through HARP and other means was the focus of ongoing efforts that were ultimately fruitful.

The second program, HAMP, involved government subsidies to induce mortgage servicers to carry out more modifications for loans originated before 2009 that were either more than 60 days delinquent or at risk of imminent default. HAMP modifications began with a trial period (typically three months) that allowed homeowners to demonstrate the ability to make timely mortgage payments and document their eligibility, after which the mortgage servicer could execute a permanent modification. We offered up-front and continuing payments to servicers, mortgage holders, and borrowers on successfully restructured loans. These continuing "pay for success" payments were designed to provide ongoing incentives to avoid default and foreclosure. We required modifications to reduce monthly payments enough so that they accounted for at most 31 percent of a borrower's income (a debt-to-income ratio, or DTI, of 31 percent). We also initially limited the availability of HAMP modifications to owner-occupied property, not allowing investor-owned properties to receive government subsidies. We began a process to coordinate modifications across first and second liens, although this proved difficult and time-consuming, delaying implementation of second lien modifications. To assist unemployed borrowers, unemployment insurance would count as available income to make modified mortgage payments under a forbearance plan, prior to consideration for a permanent HAMP modification.[16]

16. Supplemental Directive 10-04, Home Affordable Unemployment Program, May 11, 2010.

HARP and HAMP were designed to limit foreclosures. Both also provided broader macroeconomic benefits since the prevention of foreclosures would raise home values above the levels that otherwise would have prevailed, and a reduction in mortgage expenses would increase the amount of household income for other spending. The payments to borrowers under the "pay for success" program were also structured to reduce, albeit modestly, the mortgage principal owed, helping borrowers make progress on reducing the extent of being underwater.

The idea to offer mortgage servicers financial incentives to modify mortgages had been discussed but not undertaken at the Treasury in 2007 and 2008.[17] FDIC chairman Sheila Bair was an early advocate of such efforts (even while criticizing the precise program eventually undertaken). She argued that a modification program would have important positive spillover effects for the economy. The FDIC had introduced a loan modification program for distressed IndyMac mortgages after taking over that institution in August 2008.[18] We expected lenders, investors, and servicers largely to support these efforts, as they were structured to make financial sense to modify a mortgage rather than foreclose. The government would not require servicers to modify loans, but instead would use taxpayer money to change the economics in favor of modifications. That proved much more challenging than we had anticipated.

Uncertain about what would work best, we introduced a range of other policies beyond HAMP and HARP in the spirit of trying many ideas to stem foreclosures and to support and rebuild communities (see Table 12.2). For example, we expanded modifications and other foreclosure mitigation alternatives available through the FHA. We developed a new initiative under HERA that provided $23.5 billion in financing through the GSEs to state and local Housing Finance Agencies to help them restructure their balance sheets and to continue lending during the crisis; this proved effective in continuing housing support for low-income households. We disbursed TARP funds in three new initiatives: one to state and local HFAs for homeowners in the

---

17. The various options to reduce foreclosures are discussed in Phillip Swagel, "The Financial Crisis: An Inside View," Brookings Papers on Economic Activity, April 2009.
18. "FDIC Implements Loan Modification Program for Distressed IndyMac Mortgage Loans," press release, FDIC, Aug. 20, 2008, https://www.fdic.gov/news/news/press /2008/pr08067.html. See also Sheila C. Bair, "Fix Rates to Save Loans," *New York Times,* Oct. 19, 2007, https://www.nytimes.com/2007/10/19/opinion/19bair.html.

Table 12.2 Housing Program Evolution

October 2007: HOPE NOW established to help distressed homeowners

December 2007: Mortgage Forgiveness Debt Relief Act passed, exempting homeowners from a capital gains tax on forgiven principal balances

July 2008: HERA passed, establishing FHFA and homeowner assistance programs (refinances, principal write-downs) through FHA

February 2009: HARP and HAMP announced; implementation begins in March

July 2009: Loan-to-value ceiling raised, allowing borrowers more deeply underwater to refinance through HARP

August 2009: Second Lien Modification Program (2MP) launched, expanding HAMP to second lien mortgages for those who qualified for a first lien modification

February 2010: Hardest Hit Fund launched, providing aid to Housing Finance Agencies in states with the highest rates of unemployment and foreclosure

March 2010: HAMP revised to encourage some principal write-downs to address negative equity, allowing unemployed homeowners to take up to six-month deferments of mortgage payments; made FHA-issued mortgages eligible for servicer modification incentives

April 2010: Home Affordable Foreclosure Alternatives launched, providing alternatives such as short sales or deeds-in-lieu of foreclosure

September 2010: State and Local Housing Finance Agency initiative launched

July 2011: Aid provided to unemployed borrowers by extending mortgage payment deferments to 12 months for HAMP and FHA programs

January 2012: HARP 2.0 introduced, easing representation and warranty requirements to increase pool of eligible borrowers and increase servicer participation; HAMP Tier 2 established, facilitating modifications for non-GSE borrowers

July 2015: Streamline HAMP launched, allowing modifications for seriously delinquent borrowers with limited hardship documentation and limited or no income documentation

April 2016: Principal Reduction Modification program launched for seriously delinquent and underwater borrowers

Incremental changes during the lifetime of HARP and HAMP: Streamlined administrative processes; increased incentives payable to servicers; provided more flexibility on debt-to-income determinations; included some investor-owned properties

Sources: Financial Stability Report, 4Q2017, https://www.treasury.gov/initiatives/financial-stability/reports/Documents/4Q17%20MHA%20Report%20Final.pdf; HUD press release, "Obama Administration Announces $1 Billion in Additional Help for Struggling Homeowners in 32 States and Puerto Rico," Oct. 2010, https://archives.hud.gov/news/2010/pr10-225.cfm; "Written Testimony of Chief of Homeownership Preservation Office Phyllis Caldwell Before the House Financial Services Subcommittee on Housing and Community Opportunity," Nov. 2010, https://www.treasury.gov/press-center/press-releases/Pages/tg960.aspx; HUD press release, "Obama Administration Offers Additional Mortgage Relief to Unemployed Borrowers," July 2011, https://archives.hud.gov/news/2011/pr11-139.cfm

"hardest hit" areas, another to combat blight from abandoned homes, and a third to support CDFIs serving low-income households.

Over the next several years, we continually modified HAMP and HARP in response to operational problems, a lack of servicer capacity, and our experience overcoming borrower mistrust. As we were designing and implementing this mix of mortgage and housing programs, fiscal stimulus and the Fed's monetary policy programs were also supporting housing markets. On paper, QE could have been the biggest crisis-era mortgage refinancing program, but newly stringent underwriting standards by mortgage lenders meant that many families, especially those with negative equity, could not refinance and paid higher rates than those for new loans.[19] We sought to counteract this barrier by encouraging mortgage refinancing through programs with broader eligibility criteria, including an expanded HARP to refinance more underwater loans insured by the GSEs, and through a new FHA "Short Refi" program that permitted FHA refinancing of a privately issued or held mortgage after lender write-downs for underwater and high LTV loans. Still, those who most needed help often had the hardest time refinancing or getting modifications, given the difficulties of navigating servicers and program participation.

HARP and HAMP were our most well-known policy responses, and both programs highlight a trade-off we faced. We sought to design both programs to be broad enough to improve housing markets, but at the same time to target assistance to avoid wasting taxpayer funds. We did not know what level of incentive to borrowers, creditors, and servicers would be effective, and we were worried we would quickly exhaust available funds while helping fewer homeowners than we could. (The latter concern turned out to have been misplaced, since the funds set aside for housing were not fully utilized, but this was hard to know at the time.) As a result, we initially designed HARP and HAMP with a relatively narrow aperture to define eligibility, although the extent of the narrowness of the program only became clear with time as we encountered problems with documentation, trials, and servicer friction. We sought to prevent foreclosures for homeowners who could remain current if their monthly mortgage payments were reduced to a sustainable level—the 31 percent debt-to-income ratio—and borrowers who could not document their income were

19. Karen Dynan, "Want a Stronger Economic Recovery? Encourage More Home Refinancing," Brookings, Feb. 20, 2013, https://www.brookings.edu/opinions/want-a-stronger-economic-recovery-encourage-more-home-refinancing/.

excluded from permanent modifications. We did not want to overpay creditors or servicers, so we initially set payments at levels that may have been too low to induce full participation. And we did not want to help investors, speculators, home flippers, or others whom Congress, SIGTARP, or taxpayers would view as undeserving, even though the spillover effects from foreclosures in those circumstances could harm communities. Individually, these choices each may have made sense, but together they limited the initial impact of the programs.

Throughout 2009 and 2010, we made dozens of adjustments to both programs to encourage more modifications and refinancings, even while largely maintaining the initial narrow aperture in terms of the borrowers who could qualify. (Although our ability to modify HAMP was legally constrained after September 2010, we were able to make a few additional adjustments thereafter.) In July 2009, we raised the HARP loan-to-value ceiling to allow borrowers who were more deeply underwater (beyond 125 percent LTV) to refinance. In August and again in October, we sought to streamline administrative processes in HAMP. In March 2010, we revised HAMP to encourage some principal write-downs to address negative equity, as well as to offer additional incentives to both servicers and borrowers.[20] We also made FHA-insured mortgages eligible for servicer modification incentives. We allowed homeowners to take six-month (and later 12-month) deferments of their mortgage payments to help families with unemployed breadwinners stay in their homes. We also provided for modifications of second liens consistent with the first lien modification, provided more flexibility on debt-to-income determinations, and included some investor-owned rental properties as well. These were largely incremental steps, taken while servicers slowly built capacity from 2008 onward. Figure 12.4 maps these iterations, along with foreclosure completions, which begin to decline in 2010.

Mortgage servicers were the key institutions that borrowers had to deal with; unfortunately, servicers struggled to implement even simple and (from their perspective) profitable programs in which they were effectively paid to modify loans. The modifications called for in the crisis were far more comprehensive

---

20. Department of the Treasury, "Written Testimony of Chief of Homeownership Preservation Office Phyllis Caldwell Before the House Financial Services Subcommittee on Housing and Community Opportunity," Nov. 2010, https://www.treasury.gov/press-center/press-releases/Pages/tg960.aspx.

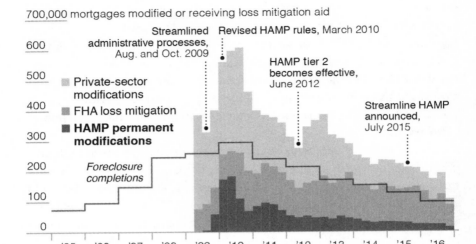

700,000 mortgages modified or receiving loss mitigation aid

Figure 12.4 **Housing Programs and Foreclosure Completions**

Notes: (1) Private-sector modifications through November 2016; other program results through 2016. Foreclosure completions are annual figures distributed evenly across four quarters. (2) Acronyms used in this figure are defined in the list of abbreviations at the front of this book.

Sources: FHA loss mitigation: U.S. Dept. of Housing and Urban Development; HAMP modifications: U.S. Treasury; private-sector modifications: HOPE NOW; foreclosure completions: CoreLogic

than typical precrisis modifications, which usually had been limited to forbearance on a few missed payments. Servicers needed to make fundamental changes to each mortgage, such as adjusting the expected monthly payment, the fixed versus floating nature of the rate, amortization schedules, or, in some cases, the principal owed. Years of low delinquency rates before the crisis had allowed servicers to cut operational costs and capacity, meaning that they lacked data and even basic calculation tools needed to evaluate potential modifications. Economics also played a role: The cost of servicing mortgages increased greatly during the crisis, while the revenue model was largely unchanged. Servicers were inexperienced in connecting with delinquent borrowers to offer a modification, and they had limited capacity to engage repeatedly with delinquent borrowers. By contrast, they had a great deal of experience in foreclosing on delinquent loans, so that simple inertia, along with legal, financial, and regulatory incentives, servicer culture, and other factors tilted their decisions in that direction, limiting the initial impact of HARP and HAMP.

In October 2011, the Treasury announced HARP 2.0, aimed at helping more homeowners refinance into lower-rate mortgages.[21] These adjustments sought to broaden the pool of eligible borrowers and to increase servicer participation. In retrospect, it would have been better if the broader parameters of HARP 2.0 had been in place from the start, but this was difficult to know in real time. A major change that made HARP 2.0 more effective was easing representation and warranty requirements on refinanced loans. We did not realize until several years into HARP the extent to which lenders hesitated to refinance loans out of concern over their legal exposure, or "putback risk," from the GSEs if a refinanced mortgage were to default early. This especially was preventing banks from refinancing mortgages that had been originated by another firm, driven by a concern that they might face liability if there had been defects in the original mortgage decision. After extensive discussions with Treasury, the FHFA worked with the GSEs to provide lenders with greater certainty about putbacks. Participation in the refinancing program increased significantly. Yet even if we had implemented HARP 2.0 in early 2009 instead of nearly three years later, deficiencies among the servicers and still-declining home prices most likely would have still significantly reduced the benefits of a broader program. Figure 12.5 illustrates the positive impact of HARP 2.0 on the number of loans refinanced.

We created our programs in a political context that reflected conflicting sentiments, with substantial support for government efforts to help reduce the risk of foreclosures existing alongside substantial aversion to bailing out "irresponsible" homeowners. We wanted to help soften the blow of the recession by mitigating the number of foreclosures without spending large amounts of money on "undeserving" borrowers, servicers, or investors.[22] Just months into President Barack Obama's first term, even Democratic senators were questioning whether the government should be bailing out irresponsible homeowners. When Senator Evan Bayh (D-IN) asked this question of Fed chairman Ben S.

21. "FHFA, Fannie Mae and Freddie Mac Announce HARP Changes to Reach More Borrowers," Federal Housing Finance Agency, Oct. 24, 2011, https://www.fhfa.gov/Media/PublicAffairs/Pages/FHFA-Fannie-Mae-and-Freddie-Mac-Announce-HARP-Changesto-Reach-More-Borrowers.aspx.
22. "Mortgage Tightrope," *Los Angeles Times,* Sept. 6, 2007, http://www.latimes.com/opinion/la-ed-mortgage6sep06-story.html.

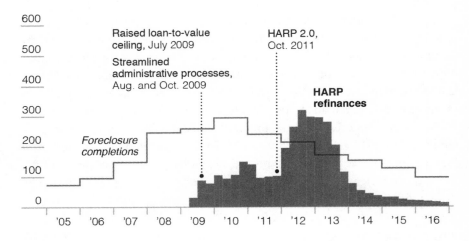

700,000 loans refinanced through HARP

Figure 12.5 **HARP Refinances and Foreclosure Completions**

Notes: (1) Foreclosure completions are annual figures distributed evenly across four quarters. (2) HARP is the Home Affordable Refinance Program.

Sources: Federal Housing Finance Agency; CoreLogic

Bernanke in a 2009 hearing, Bernanke responded with an analogy to a person who sees his neighbor's house on fire and knows that the neighbor tends to act irresponsibly by smoking in bed. Bernanke explained that while it might be tempting to let the irresponsible neighbor suffer to teach him a lesson, it was better to call the local fire department, since among the potential consequences is that "your entire neighborhood would have burned down."[23] Many Americans, however, disagreed with this logic.

ALTERNATIVE PATHS

During the crisis we considered four primary alternatives to the path we chose. The first alternative was to provide for wide eligibility for HAMP and HARP

23. Catherine Rampell and Jack Healy, "Fed Chairman Says Recession Will Extend through the Year," *New York Times*, Feb. 24, 2009, https://www.nytimes.com/2009/02/25/business/economy/25econ.html.

right away and to devote more taxpayer resources to borrowers with negative equity. This would have increased the support to homeowners and provided faster relief to hard-hit communities; however, one risk of a big negative equity program is that it might have blown through available resources and helped fewer homeowners than would otherwise have been helped with payment reductions (since principal reduction is a more expensive way to prevent foreclosures than reducing monthly payments through interest rate reductions). Such a program might have also increased moral hazard, probably adding to the number of defaults, and it would have funneled more taxpayer resources to investors and speculators.

An aspect of broader eligibility could have included "no doc" or "low doc" modifications. We had insisted on exacting loan documentation for permanent modifications, both to protect taxpayer resources (amplified by concerns about SIGTARP and congressional criticism of the program) and to avoid lawsuits from mortgage holders if we did not document borrower qualification for modifications. This was a consequential choice: Many hundreds of thousands of borrowers were denied permanent modifications because of a lack of documentation, the result of both servicer dysfunction (for example, repeatedly losing documents submitted by borrowers) and borrower inability to take advantage of the programs (because of fear of servicers, lack of knowledge and resources, or unwillingness to confront a difficult fact). Treasury later instituted a streamlined HAMP without up-front documentation requirements.

The second alternative considered was bulk refinancing, in which the government would have purchased pools of mortgages from banks and securitization trusts, modified the problematic mortgages, and then created new securitizations to be resold to banks and investors. The idea was widely discussed, including at the Treasury in 2007 and 2008. Some described this as bailing out the financial system "from the bottom up."[24] At the time, the idea was often compared to our government's response during the Great Depression, when the Home Owners' Loan Corporation (HOLC) bought and modified defaulted

---

24. See generally Swagel, "The Financial Crisis"; and Michael S. Barr, "Strengthening Our Economy: Foreclosure Prevention and Neighborhood Preservation," Testimony before the United States Senate Committee on Banking, Housing, and Urban Affairs, Jan. 31, 2008, https://www.americanprogress.org/issues/economy/news/2008/01/31/3858/strengthening-our-economy-foreclosure-prevention-and-neighborhood-preservation/.

mortgages from banks.[25] By 2008, many housing experts felt that bulk refinancing, at least in theory, would be an effective policy option.

Many in both administrations pursued this option, in fact, but bulk refinancing faced numerous practical, legal, and political challenges. To begin with, it would be difficult to devise a practical pricing mechanism (an effective auction in a dysfunctional market) to minimize the risk that the government would overpay for mortgages. This was especially a concern given the heterogeneity in mortgages, the problem of adverse selection (willing sellers would sell the worst loans), and asymmetric information (sellers would know more about the loans than the government buyer). The second barrier was legal. Securitization trusts owned many of the country's mortgages, and in many instances they lacked the legal authority to sell the bad mortgages from their securitized loan pools to the government.[26] We made some progress in 2009 in changing the rules under the Real Estate Mortgage Investment Conduit (REMIC) statute to permit sales, but the underlying problems with many trust and pooling and servicing agreements remained. The third barrier was operational. There was no existing capacity to run such a program, and the government would have had to launch it from scratch. Fannie and Freddie could have been enlisted—as they were for HAMP and HARP—but it would have taken a great deal of time to build such a program, even with the GSEs as the platform. And it would have exposed taxpayers to additional losses by transferring the risk of further defaults from the private owners of non-GSE loans, including subprime and Alt-A mortgages, to the government.

That said, bulk refinancing may have been a missed opportunity. This is especially the case since the idea may have been more politically viable than other alternatives. In the fall of 2008, for example, Senator John McCain, the Republican presidential candidate, proposed buying and refinancing $300 billion worth of subprime mortgages.[27] The public mood in 2008 and 2009 may

25. Alex J. Pollack, "A 1930s Loan Rescue Lesson," *Washington Post*, March 14, 2008, http://www.washingtonpost.com/wp-dyn/content/article/2008/03/13/AR2008031303174.html.
26. Michael S. Barr and James A. Feldman, "Issue Brief: Overcoming Legal Barriers to the Bulk Sale of At-Risk Mortgages," Center for American Progress, April 2008, https://repository.law.umich.edu/cgi/viewcontent.cgi?referer=https://scholar.google.es/&httpsredir=1&article=1018&context=other.
27. Edmund L. Andrews, Shan Carter, Jonathan Ellis, Farhana Hossain, and Alan McLean, "On the Issues: Housing," *New York Times*, accessed Jan. 18, 2019, https://www.nytimes.com/elections/2008/president/issues/housing.html.

have been opposed to homeowner assistance, but McCain's stance suggests that it might have been possible to generate bipartisan support for moving beyond the complaint that it was unfair for undeserving borrowers to get assistance while responsible people paid their mortgages.

The third policy alternative was to change bankruptcy laws to permit judges to discharge the unsecured portions of mortgages as home prices fell during the crisis. This option, typically referred to as "cramdown," could have been another policy tool to encourage servicers to modify mortgages because borrowers could have sought bankruptcy relief to reduce mortgage payments, and to provide borrowers with an additional avenue of relief through the bankruptcy courts, at a time when other mechanisms had problems. Cramdown would have required an act of Congress, and several attempts failed, although critics charged that the Obama administration did not push hard enough. In April 2009, the Obama administration supported cramdown legislation but prioritized the stimulus focused on job creation, and support for including cramdown lacked even a simple majority in the Senate—let alone the 60 votes needed to overcome a filibuster and proceed to a vote for enactment.[28]

Some economists have since argued that we should have done more to reduce household debt,[29] but experts remain divided on the merits of cramdown (as do the authors of this chapter).[30] Cramdown would have retroactively changed the rules for mortgages, and opponents feared that change would have further depressed the collateral value of homes, driving down home sale prices and increasing mortgage rates, as creditors responded to higher loss risk by raising borrowing costs. Moreover, by raising questions about the value of collateral, cramdown might have affected credit conditions in collateralized lending outside of housing. Still, policymakers may wish to consider prospectively changing home mortgage bankruptcy rules in normal economic times to avoid crisis-induced legal changes and to provide further channels for mortgage relief at a time of crisis.

A fourth alternative was to use eminent domain to purchase mortgages directly from securitization pools. This approach would have been similar to

28. S.896 - Helping Families Save Their Homes Act of 2009, 111th Congress (2009–2010), https://www.congress.gov/bill/111th-congress/senate-bill/896.
29. Notably, Mian and Sufi, *House of Debt*.
30. See generally Lawrence Summers, "House of Debt," *Financial Times*, June 6, 2014.

cramdown in that it would help borrowers reduce their outstanding principal while forcing losses on investors. It would also have shared its drawbacks. Opponents from the banking and real estate sector argued that using eminent domain would increase borrowing costs overall. Some cities used eminent domain to purchase underwater mortgages and then wrote down the debt and allowed those homeowners to refinance; these efforts faced litigation as well as regulatory barriers and were not implemented on any large scale.[31]

In addition to these four main alternatives, many other policy options were proposed or considered, but most would have required difficult-to-pass new legislation. For example, some called for legislation to "require a call option on potentially risky mortgages that would allow for easy government restructuring in the event of another major downturn in real estate prices in the future."[32] Others suggested a foreclosure moratorium, government guarantees, and policies to prevent interest rate resets.[33]

PROGRAMMATIC RESULTS AND POLICY ASSESSMENT

For all the flaws in the policy responses we adopted, key metrics and several academic studies make clear that these efforts helped millions of homeowners and eased housing market conditions. We evaluate these policies in terms of the numbers of households assisted, the quality of mortgage modifications, and the effects on communities. There are a number of ways of assessing effectiveness. We discuss several measures and then summarize our findings in Table 12.3.

It may help to get a sense of the scale and scope of the programs by first looking at individual results and then rolling those up together, as we do in

---

31. Barr, Jackson, and Tahyar, *Financial Regulation*, 1253.
32. Barr, Jackson, and Tahyar, *Financial Regulation*, 1254. See also John Campbell, Andreas Fuster, David Lucca, Stijn Van Nieuwerburgh, and James Vickery, "Rethinking Mortgage Design," Liberty Street Economics, Federal Reserve Bank of New York, Aug. 24, 2015, https://libertystreeteconomics.newyorkfed.org/2015/08/rethinking-mortgage-design.html.
33. See generally Swagel, "The Financial Crisis." See also John Geanakoplos and Susan Koniak, "Mortgage Justice Is Blind," *New York Times*, Oct. 29, 2008, for a proposal for a form of eminent domain in which government-appointed trustees would take over administration of securitization trusts to determine mortgage modifications.

Table 12.3. For example, according to one measure (narrower than that used in Table 12.3), in the Department of Housing and Urban Development's Housing Scorecard, "nearly 11.1 million mortgage modifications and other forms of mortgage assistance arrangements were completed between April 2009 and the end of November 2016."[34] Looking at the individual measures and using these to derive totals in Table 12.3, HAMP provided more than 2.5 million temporary modifications and 1.7 million permanent modifications (although approximately 650,000 of these later re-defaulted or were otherwise disqualified), reduced principal by approximately $24.5 billion, and saved borrowers approximately $55 billion in mortgage payments.[35] A further 3.4 million households were helped through the FHA's loss mitigation programs, including 450,000 modifications by 2012.[36] Fannie and Freddie made 1.5 million modifications in addition to HAMP and refinanced 26 million loans from April 2009 to 2017, including 3.4 million refinancings of high loan-to-value mortgages under HARP and 4 million streamlined refinancings outside of HARP.[37] The GSEs engaged in other initiatives to avoid foreclosures, including nearly 700,000 charge-offs-in-lieu, short sales, and deeds-in-lieu.[38] Treasury also supported state and local Housing Finance Agencies with $15.3 billion in a New Issue Bond Program and an $8.2 billion Temporary

34. U.S. Department of Housing and Urban Development (HUD), "The Obama Administration's Efforts to Stabilize the Housing Market and Help American Homeowners," Dec. 2016 Scorecard.

35. U.S. Department of the Treasury, *Making Home Affordable Program Performance Report,* through the Fourth Quarter of 2017, https://www.treasury.gov/initiatives /financial-stability/reports/Documents/4Q17%20MHA%20Report%20Final.pdf. See generally Barr, Jackson, and Tahyar, *Financial Regulation,* 1251; Office of the Comptroller of the Currency, *OCC Mortgage Metrics Report,* Fourth Quarter 2017, https://www.occ.gov/publications/publications-by-type/other-publications-reports /mortgage-metrics/mortgage-metrics-q4-2017.pdf.

36. Data available disaggregated through 2012 only; included in the "FHA Loss Mitigation Interventions" total through 2017. Source (used April 1, 2009, forward to match HUD Housing Scorecard data): "Monthly Report to the FHA Commissioner," Department of Housing and Urban Development, April 2009 through Dec. 2012, accessed Jan. 18, 2019, https://www.hud.gov/program_offices/housing/rmra/oe/rpts /com/commenu.

37. FHFA, *Refinance Report,* Oct. 2017, 3, https://www.fhfa.gov/AboutUs/Reports /ReportDocuments/Refi_Oct2017.pdf.

38. FHFA, *Foreclosure Prevention Report,* Oct. 2017, 4, accessed Jan. 18, 2019, https:// www.fhfa.gov/AboutUs/Reports/ReportDocuments/FPR_OCT2017.pdf.

Credit and Liquidity Program, financed under HERA authorities.[39] The programs prevented the collapse of state and local HFAs, and the New Issue Bond Program alone enabled HFAs to finance more than 100,000 single-family homes in just two years.[40]

Outside of HAMP, GSEs and the private sector made 6.6 million mortgage modifications from 2007 to 2017, most of which conformed to HAMP's debt-to-income and other modification requirements (see Table 12.3). Our policy response changed many mortgage industry practices (for example, establishing a standard approach to providing mortgage assistance) and improved the quality of modifications.[41] These changes remain and will be a long-lasting achievement of the policy response.

Numerous studies have used the various policy responses as natural experiments. Agarwal et al. estimate that through 2012, HAMP induced an additional 1 million permanent modifications that would not have otherwise taken place and reduced the number of completed foreclosures by 600,000. They find that HAMP had the largest effect in the first two years and among already delinquent loans, and that it did not have a meaningful "crowd-out" effect on private behavior in the sense of leading to fewer modifications without government assistance.[42] Several other studies estimate that refinancing under HARP roughly halved the probability of default.[43]

39. "Administration Completes Implementation of Initiative to Support State and Local Housing Finance Agencies," U.S. Treasury, Jan. 13, 2010, https://www.treasury.gov /press-center/press-releases/Pages/20101131429486865.aspx. See also National Association of Local Housing Finance Agencies, in collaboration with Freddie Mac, *Local Housing Finance Agency Participation in the Treasury/Government Sponsored Enterprises New Issue Bond Purchase Program (NIBP): A Tremendous Story of Success,* Nov. 2011, http://www.munibondsforamerica.org/cms/wp-content/uploads /2012/11/Final-Report-on-NIBP-12-1-11.pdf.
40. Jordan Eizenga, "A House America Bond for State Housing Finance Agencies," Center for American Progress, March 1, 2012, https://www.americanprogress.org /issues/economy/reports/2012/03/01/11176/a-house-america-bond-for-state-housing -finance-agencies/.
41. Sumit Agarwal, Gene Amromin, Souphala Chomsisengphet, Tomasz Piskorski, Amit Seru, and Vincent Yao, "Mortgage Refinancing, Consumer Spending, and Competition: Evidence from the Home Affordable Refinancing Program" (Kreisman Working Papers Series in Housing Law and Policy, no. 27, 2015), https://chicagounbound.uchicago.edu /cgi/viewcontent.cgi?article=1044&context=housing_law_and_policy.
42. Agarwal et al., "Policy Intervention in Debt Renegotiation," 658.
43. Kadiri Karamon, Douglas A. McManus, and Jun Zhu, "Refinance and Mortgage Default: A Regression Discontinuity Analysis of HARP's Impact on Default Rates,"

Table 12.3 shows that the cumulative impact of these programs was large: More than 8.2 million mortgage modifications, 9.5 million refinancings, and 5.3 million other foreclosure prevention actions were completed as a direct result of these programs.

These results can be compared to those of the Home Owners' Loan Corporation during the Great Depression. At the time, mortgages commonly had short maturities and large balloon payments. HOLC, created in 1933, had by 1936 modified and refinanced about 1 million loans, or 20 percent of homes with mortgages, worth a total of $3.1 billion (or $49 billion in 2008 dollars).[44] HOLC, however, had serious problems; it was wasteful, as a result of systematic overappraisal and asset sales.[45] Moreover, implementation was easier in the 1930s: With a bank-based financial system, modifications were easier to execute because banks held whole loans on their balance sheets. And paradoxically, Depression-era programs—designed in part to move risk off the balance sheets of banks to reduce systemic risk—ultimately grew into Fannie, Freddie, FHA, and the private-label securitization markets that contributed to the dispersed ownership of loans that was such a challenge during the Great Recession.[46]

Journal of Real Estate Finance and Economics 55, no. 4 (2017): 457–75, https://papers .ssrn.com/sol3/papers.cfm?abstract_id=2793661. See also Gabriel Ehrlich and Jeffrey Perry, "Do Large-Scale Refinancing Programs Reduce Mortgage Defaults? Evidence from a Regression Discontinuity Design," *Journal of Real Estate Finance and Economics* 55, no. 2 (2015), https://papers.ssrn.com/sol3/papers.cfm?abstract_id =2678425; and Joshua Abel and Andreas Fuster, "How Do Mortgage Refinances Affect Debt, Default, and Spending? Evidence from HARP," Federal Reserve Bank of New York Staff Reports #841, 2018, https://www.newyorkfed.org/research/staff _reports/sr841.html.

44. Daniel Immergluck, "Private Risk, Public Risk: Public Policy, Market Development, and the Mortgage Crisis," *Fordham Urban Law Journal* 36, no. 3 (2009): 447–88. For 2008 dollar terms of HOLC loan book, see Price V. Fishback et al., "The Influence of the Home Owner's Loan Corporation on Housing Markets during the 1930s" (NBER Working Paper, no. 15824, 2010), 7. See generally Barr, Jackson, Tahyar, *Financial Regulation*.

45. C. Lowell Harriss, "History and Policies of the Home Owners' Loan Corporation," National Bureau of Economic Research 1–2, 1951, http://www.nber.org/chapters /c3205.pdf; and Fishback et al., "The Influence of the Home Owner's Loan Corporation," 7.

46. See David C. Wheelock, "The Federal Response to Home Mortgage Distress: Lessons from the Great Depression," Federal Reserve Bank of St. Louis, May/ June 2008.

Table 12.3 **Cumulative Impact of Crisis-Era Housing Policies**

Program	Through 2012	Through 2017
HAMP permanent modifications (less disqualified)[A]	851,135	1,087,104
HAMP trial modifications (all)[B]	1,975,649	2,537,629
HAMP permanent modifications (all)[C]	1,136,482	1,735,141
HOPE NOW "Proprietary Modifications"[D]	4,079,023	5,176,329
GSE standard and streamlined modifications[E]	859,184	1,490,580
FHA modifications[F]	450,194	450,194
HARP completed refinances[G]	2,165,021	3,484,025
FHFA streamline refinances[H]	2,517,960	4,010,098
FHA streamline refinances[I]	N/A	2,013,000
FHFA HomeSaver Advance[J]	70,178	70,178
FHFA repayment plans	665,796	904,843
FHFA forbearance plans	147,602	216,828
FHFA foreclosure alternatives[K]	455,313	697,463
FHA loss mitigation interventions[L]	1,145,806	2,979,806
Hardest Hit Funds—borrowers assisted[M]	94,056	347,417
State and Local Housing Finance Agency Initiative—mortgages and units financed[N]	100,000 single-family mortgages; 24,000 multifamily units	
Total modifications[O]	**6,239,536**	**8,204,207**
Total special refinancing[P]	**4,682,981**	**9,507,123**
Total other borrower assistance[Q]	**2,702,752**	**5,340,535**

[A] Sources: Making Home Affordable, Program Performance Report through Fourth Quarter 2017, published March 16, 2018, https://www.treasury.gov/initiatives/financial -stability/reports/Documents/4Q17%20MHA%20Report%20Final.pdf; Making Home Affordable, Program Performance Report through Dec. 2012, published Feb. 8, 2013, https://www.treasury.gov/initiatives/financial-stability/reports/Documents /December%202012%20MHA%20Report%20Final.pdf.

[B] This shows HAMP's reach, or intent to treat; disqualified trial modifications are not removed. Sources: Making Home Affordable, Program performance reports.

[C] All permanent modifications less disqualified permanent modifications is one measure of HAMP's success; it does not account for crowd-out (discussed in depth by Agarwal et al., "Policy Intervention in Debt Renegotiation"). Sources: Making Home Affordable, Program performance reports.

[D] "Proprietary Modifications" reported by HOPE NOW exclude HAMP modifications and non-HAMP GSE modifications. Source: HOPE NOW, December 2017 Full Report, accessed Jan. 18, 2019, http://www.hopenow.com/industry-data/HopeNow.FullReport .Updated(December).pdf.

[E] Using permanent modifications started; total FHFA loan modifications less HAMP permanent modifications through GSEs. FHFA loan modifications sourced from FHFA, Foreclosure Prevention Report of Fourth Quarter 2017, published March 22, 2018, https://www.fhfa.gov/AboutUs/Reports/ReportDocuments/4Q2017_FPR.pdf; and FHFA,

Foreclosure Prevention Report of Fourth Quarter 2012, published March 19, 2013, https://www.fhfa.gov/AboutUs/Reports/ReportDocuments/20124Q_FPR_N508.pdf. HAMP permanent modifications through GSEs sourced through the Making Home Affordable Program performance reports.

[F] Data available disaggregated through 2012 only; included in the "FHA Loss Mitigation Interventions" total through 2017. Sourced from the Monthly Reports to the FHA Commissioner, Department of Housing and Urban Development, April 2009 through Dec. 2012, accessed Jan. 18, 2018 (used April 1, 2009, forward to match HUD Housing Scorecard data), https://www.hud.gov/program_offices/housing/rmra/oe/rpts/com/commenu.

[G] The FHFA does not report the number of attempted refinances (instances where a borrower starts the process of HARP refinancing). Consequently, we don't have a measure of HARP's reach, just an estimate of success. Sources: FHFA, Refinance Report of Fourth Quarter 2017, published Feb. 14, 2018, https://www.fhfa.gov/AboutUs/Reports/ReportDocuments/4Q17-Refi-Report.pdf; FHFA, Refinance Report of December 2012, published March 13, 2013, https://www.fhfa.gov/AboutUs/Reports/ReportDocuments/201212_RefiReport_508.pdf.

[H] Sources: FHFA refinance reports.

[I] 2012 and 2017 data not available; September 2015 and December 2016 used, respectively. Data sourced from HUD, Housing Scorecard of September 2015, accessed Jan. 18, 2019, https://archives.hud.gov/initiatives/housing_scorecard/scorecard2015_09_508c.pdf; and HUD Housing Scorecard of December 2012, accessed Jan. 18, 2019, https://www.hud.gov/sites/documents/SCORECARD_2016_12_508C.PDF.

[J] HomeSaver Advance program ended in 2010. For this and following FHFA actions, data sourced from the FHFA, Foreclosure Prevention Reports.

[K] Includes charge-offs-in-lieu, short sales, and deeds-in-lieu.

[L] 2017 data not available; December 2016 used. Loss mitigation interventions include forbearance, modifications, partial claims, preforeclosure sales, and short sales. Modifications through 2012 subtracted from totals; remaining data included in total other borrower assistance totals, as modification data were not available disaggregated. Data sourced from the HUD Housing Scorecards.

[M] Data sourced from the Housing Finance Agency, Quarterly Report of Fourth Quarter 2012, accessed Jan. 18, 2019, https://www.treasury.gov/initiatives/financial-stability/reports/Documents/HFA%20Quarterly%20Report.Q42012.pdf; and HFA, Final Report of Fourth Quarter 2017, accessed Jan. 18, 2019, https://www.treasury.gov/initiatives/financial-stability/reports/Documents/HFA%20Aggregate%20Q42017%20Report%20Final.pdf.

[N] Program ended in 2012; no 2017 data available. Source: Jordan Eizenga, "A House America Bond for State Housing Finance Agencies," Center for American Progress, 2012, https://cdn.americanprogress.org/wp-content/uploads/issues/2012/02/pdf/house_america_bonds.pdf.

[O] Totals HAMP permanent modifications (less disqualified), HOPE NOW "Proprietary Modifications," and GSE standard and streamlined modifications.

[P] Totals HARP completed refinances, FHFA streamline refinances, and FHA streamline refinances.

[Q] Totals FHFA Home Saver Advance; FHFA repayment plans, forbearance plans, and foreclosure alternatives; FHA loss mitigation interventions; Hardest Hit Funds; and state and local HFA initiative mortgages and units financed.

Successful HAMP modifications totaled just over 1 million through the end of 2017, representing just under 4 percent of homes with mortgages.[47] More broadly, however, the breadth of our programs beyond HAMP were large, producing 8.2 million mortgage modifications, representing 29 percent of all mortgages. Our efforts also led to 9.5 million refinances, representing 33 percent of mortgages, and 5.2 million other borrower assistance and loss mitigation actions, representing 19 percent of total mortgages. These results compare favorably with HOLC's 20 percent.

The quality of modifications also improved considerably over the course of the policy response, providing borrowers with more payment relief. As shown in Table 12.4, before HAMP, 54 percent of GSE and 32 percent of industry loan modifications in 2008 actually resulted in an increased monthly payment, which could happen, for example, if past missed payments were added back into future mortgage payments. By contrast, the share of loan modifications that decreased monthly payments climbed as the programs went into effect. The effects lasted well after the crisis was over: By 2017, the vast majority of mortgage modifications resulted in lower payments.

A further important indicator of improved quality of loan modifications was the decline over time in borrowers who received modifications but then subsequently defaulted on their mortgage, a phenomenon known as a re-default. Re-default rates of borrowers with loans modified under HAMP were considerably lower by 2012 than was the case in 2009.[48]

Re-default rates similarly declined for both GSE and private loans within and outside HAMP as modification quality improved. As shown in Table 12.5, loans modified in 2008 exceeded 60 percent re-default rates in the months and

47. Immergluck, "Private Risk, Public Risk." See also Charles Courtemanche and Kenneth Snowden, "Repairing a Mortgage Crisis: HOLC Lending and Its Impact on Local Housing Markets," *Journal of Economic History* 71, no. 2 (2011), https://www .cambridge.org/core/journals/journal-of-economic-history/article/div -classtitlerepairing-a-mortgage-crisis-holc-lending-and-its-impact-on-local-housing -marketsdiv/AAAEDA3641C19BB9090522C7461D087C. HAMP targeted roughly 3 million–4 million heavily indebted households (see Agarwal et al., "Policy Intervention in Debt Renegotiation"; HAMP helped a smaller fraction of all borrowers than HOLC. Data on total mortgages provided by the Federal Reserve Board, using estimates from the Consumer Expenditure Survey).

48. U.S. Department of the Treasury, *Making Home Affordable Program Performance Report,* through the Third Quarter of 2017, 6, https://www.treasury.gov/initiatives /financial-stability/reports/Documents/3Q17%20MHA%20Report%20Final.pdf.

Table 12.4 Loan Modification Quality Measures

Quality measures—loan modifications	2008 average	2012 average	2017 average
Percentage of GSE modifications that decreased monthly mortgage payments[A]	45	96	82
Percentage of GSE modifications that decreased monthly mortgage payments *by 20 percent or more*	*20*	*69*	*44*
Percentage of industry modifications that decreased monthly mortgage payments[B]	42	90	83
Percentage of industry modifications that decreased monthly mortgage payments *by 10 percent or more*[C]	*29*	*77*	*65*
Percentage of GSE modifications that increased monthly mortgage payments	54	4	6
Percentage of industry modifications that increased monthly mortgage payments	32	6	15
Percentage of HOPE NOW "Proprietary Modifications" that reduced principal and interest by 10 percent or more[D]	—	75	53

[A] Source for all GSE modification data is the FHFA Foreclosure Prevention Report of First Quarter 2018, published June 21, 2018, https://www.fhfa.gov/AboutUs/Reports /ReportDocuments/FPR_1Q2018.pdf.

[B] Source for all industry modification data is the Office of the Comptroller of the Currency's Monthly Metrics Report, which tracks first-lien residential mortgages serviced by the seven largest banks, covering a majority of all mortgages outstanding: Fourth Quarter 2008, published April 2009, https://www.occ.gov/publications /publications-by-type/other-publications-reports/mortgage-metrics/mortgage-metrics -q4-2008-pdf; Fourth Quarter 2012, published March 2013, https://www.occ.gov /publications/publications-by-type/other-publications-reports/mortgage-metrics /mortgage-metrics-q4-2012.pdf; First Quarter 2017, published July 2017, https://www.occ .gov/publications/publications-by-type/other-publications-reports/mortgage-metrics /mortgage-metrics-q1-2017.pdf; Second Quarter 2017, published Sept. 2018, https://www .occ.gov/publications/publications-by-type/other-publications-reports/mortgage -metrics/mortgage-metrics-q2-2017.pdf; Third Quarter 2017, published Dec. 2017, https://www.occ.gov/publications/publications-by-type/other-publications-reports /mortgage-metrics/mortgage-metrics-q3-2017.pdf; and Fourth Quarter 2017, published March 2018, https://www.occ.gov/publications/publications-by-type/other-publications -reports/mortgage-metrics/mortgage-metrics-q4-2017.pdf.

[C] Data not available for payment reductions of 20 percent or more in 2008; 10 percent used for continuity across years.

[D] Data not available for 2008. Sourced from the HOPE NOW Dec. 2017 Full Report, accessed Jan. 18, 2019, http://www.hopenow.com/industry-data/HopeNow.FullReport .Updated(December).pdf; and the HOPE NOW Dec. 2012 Full Report, published Feb. 7, 2013, http://www.hopenow.com/press_release/files/HN-2012-Full-Data-FINAL.pdf.

Table 12.5 Modified Loan Re-default Rates, by Vintage of Modification and Investor

Months after modification	2008		2010		2013	
	GSE	Private	GSE	Private	GSE	Private
	(percent)					
6	45	49	13	20	11	11
12	59	61	19	28	16	14
18	64	67	22	33	18	15
24	63	68	23	34	16	14
36	57	68	22	29	—	—

Source: Data unavailable after Third Quarter 2015; data for all metrics in table sourced from the Office of the Comptroller of the Currency, Mortgage Metrics Report, published Dec. 2015, https://www.occ.gov/publications/publications-by-type/other-publications-reports/mortgage -metrics/mortgage-metrics-q3-2015.pdf.

years following a modification; by 2013, re-default rates remained less than 20 percent in the same time frame.

Apart from loan modification programs, interest rate declines beginning in 2009 helped millions of borrowers, with especially steep declines for nonprime borrowers with adjustable mortgages. Figure 12.6 shows the average interest rate paid for different groups of borrowers (excluding junior liens). The mean interest rate paid by all borrowers fell steeply beginning in 2009. Many of the loans at the center of the foreclosure crisis had adjustable rates— for example, pay-option adjustable-rate mortgages and 2/28s.[49] The dark gray line shows the average rate paid on adjustable-rate loans to nonprime borrowers. As shown, rates on these loans rose in the lead-up to the crisis as teaser rates expired; however, by 2009, as risk-free rates fell, so did rates on these loans. This was a powerful source of support for struggling borrowers. But the benefits from lower rates were not distributed equally. The black line shows that rates paid by mortgage holders facing the highest borrowing costs before 2009 fell less steeply. Because negative equity was widespread and many mortgage

49. A 2/28 is a type of 30-year mortgage with a fixed rate for 2 years and a variable rate for the 28 years thereafter.

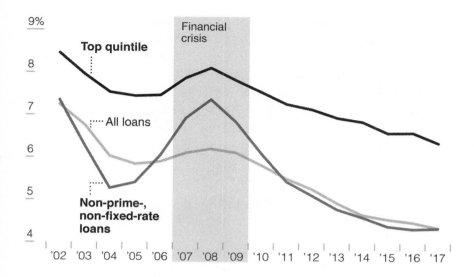

Figure 12.6 **Average Mortgage Interest Rates, 2002–2017, by Selected Loan Categories**

Source: Black Knight McDash data

originators were imposing tougher underwriting standards, many borrowers found it difficult to take advantage of lower mortgage rates. Many of the borrowers who most needed help tended to get less of it, in many cases because of missing or incorrect documentation (made worse by the lack of digitization) and inadequacies on the part of servicers. Nonetheless, lower rates provided powerful help to many borrowers.

Beyond modifications and re-default rates, the housing boom and bust left a long-standing imprint on Americans' choices and opportunities. During the 1990s and early 2000s, the homeownership rate climbed steadily, to a record high in 2005 of 69 percent, but it fell during the crisis to levels last seen in the late 1960s. Homeownership has since risen from those lows but remains at levels from the early 1990s at 64 percent. The greatest impact was on families in the lower half of the income distribution, who have clearly fallen behind what seemed the typical lifecycle trajectory for homeownership. Minority households fared far worse in the financial crisis than white households and have recovered from the crisis much more slowly. Leading up to the crisis, minority borrowers were more likely to have subprime loans than white borrowers with similar risk profiles.[50] Minority households held a larger share of their household wealth in home equity and experienced larger and longer declines in wealth.[51] In low- and moderate-income communities already in difficult economic circumstances, the crisis was devastating. In Detroit, for example, mean home values in low- and moderate-income neighborhoods fell by $44,006, and the number of underwater homes increased by 62 percentage points.[52] For all the positive results cited in this chapter, we see these outcomes as an especially troubling legacy of the crisis that illustrates the degree to which the policy response fell short.

LESSONS LEARNED

While the design of our policy response was affected by uncertainty in the midst of the crisis, limited resources, politics, and legal authority, at a higher level it was directed by our answers to more philosophical questions: What is the proper role of government to stabilize housing markets and to help individual homeowners? And when should the government intervene?

In evaluating the housing policy response put in place during the Bush administration, it is fair to say that we were always "late" (or "later") to respond, in part because of the belief that intervening in housing markets had efficiency costs and that it was better to support the overall economy while an inevitable adjustment in the housing sector proceeded. One might reasonably take the view that helping overstretched homeowners will always be politically difficult and that supporting the broader economy is fairer and more transparent.

50. Henock Louis, "Minority Borrowers and the Subprime Foreclosure Crisis: Unintended Consequences of Regulations vs. Unfair Lending," Sept. 12, 2013, https://ssrn .com/abstract=2128313.
51. Sarah Burd-Sharps and Rebecca Rasch, *Impact of the U.S. Housing Crisis on the Racial Wealth Gap across Generations,* Social Science Research Council, June 2015, https://www.aclu.org/files/field_document/discrimlend_final.pdf. See also Rakesh Kochhar and Anthony Cilluffo, "How Wealth Inequality Has Changed in the U.S. Since the Great Recession, by Race, Ethnicity and Income," Pew Research Center FacTank, Nov. 1, 2017, http://www.pewresearch.org/fact-tank/2017/11/01/how -wealth-inequality-has-changed-in-the-u-s-since-the-great-recession-by-race -ethnicity-and-income/.
52. Michael S. Barr and Daniel Schaffa, "Nothing Left to Lose? Changes Experienced by Detroit Low- and Moderate-Income Households during the Great Recession" (Washington Center for Equitable Growth Working Paper, 2016), https://papers.ssrn .com/sol3/papers.cfm?abstract_id=2836589.

As a practical matter, Congress did not make sizable funds available for subsidizing foreclosure reduction until the enactment of the TARP in October 2008; the earlier Hope for Homeowners program in July 2008 had legislative restrictions that made it ineffective because lenders were better off using other FHA programs that provided less relief for borrowers. The initial housing-related policy efforts largely focused on improving the private-sector response, complemented by some increased refinancing through the FHA. During the Bush administration, the most powerful housing program was the government conservatorship and capital backstop for the GSEs, which ensured that Fannie and Freddie remained the primary source of mortgage finance during the crisis. Without the conservatorship, the mortgage market would have collapsed, housing prices would likely have been far lower, and foreclosure rates would have been much higher.

The Obama administration came in committed to using government resources to reduce foreclosures. We acted quickly and aggressively to launch mortgage modification and refinancing programs. We bolstered the government backstops of the GSEs, launched innovative programs with state and local Housing Finance Agencies, and repeatedly experimented with new initiatives to improve and expand our programs. Yet our policy response in early 2009 was inadequate. Households would have been better off had we acted earlier and more aggressively during both administrations, such as by implementing the broader parameters of HARP 2.0 from the start to allow more people to refinance.

Our experience offers several lessons for future policymakers.

Lesson 1:
Do not overweight the potential for waste and moral hazard in helping "undeserving" borrowers.

Continuing with Chairman Bernanke's analogy, firefighters routinely waste a tremendous amount of water in putting out a five-alarm fire, and that is okay. Prudence and the desire to minimize waste may lead to underwhelming results—or even allow the problem to get worse. Our approach was judged ex post more cost-effective than calls for broad principal write-downs, but ex ante we could have engaged in more aggressive additional experimentation with principal write-downs given the uncertainty about relevant policy trade-offs in helping more households. Research since the crisis also suggests that policymakers might want to focus more on the extent of payment reduction rather than the goal of a debt-to-income level.[53]

Uncertainty about the course of the housing crisis and about the correct policy responses, substantive concerns about the fragility of financial markets, and judgments about the political acceptability of directly helping homeowners led both administrations to take more moderate approaches than in retrospect we believe were warranted.

Lesson 2:
Be ready to act forcefully in the face of uncertainty.

It is difficult, early on in a crisis, to distinguish a five-alarm fire from a more isolated one. Initially, there was no consensus on the nature of the problem, with many arguing that modifications would merely prolong the necessary adjustment in the housing market. Foreclosure prevention events in 2007 and 2008 attracted thousands of distressed borrowers, and by the spring of 2008 we knew mortgage segments and geographic regions had real problems. But it was not clear whether these problems were simply bad for the subprime market or for overstretched places like Florida, or instead foreshadowed a cataclysm for the broader economy. Another reason we were too cautious was that we focused too much on the modal path and outcome. We were surprised by the extreme dysfunction of markets, servicers, and originators when confronted by an unprecedented foreclosure wave. Given the enormous uncertainty involved, policymakers should consider forceful policies to hedge against the bad tail outcomes. Policymakers need to act quickly to get interest rates down, reduce barriers to refinancing, and pursue payment reduction modifications. A challenge for future policymakers will be that forceful actions could be politically difficult when they appear to be helping undeserving borrowers.

Lesson 3:
Put the proper regulatory and supervisory framework in place
before a crisis unfolds.

Before the crisis, regulators did not use their supervisory authorities to crack down on risky practices. Federal banking regulators (which at the time in-

---

53. Ganong and Noel, "Liquidity vs. Wealth in Household Debt Obligations."

cluded the now-defunct Office of Thrift Supervision) had ample authority to limit underwriting practices that allowed for no-doc loans and practically non-existent down payments made by regulated depository institutions. Regulators, including those at the Federal Reserve, failed to use their authority in a timely and sufficiently strong manner. One can debate the trade-offs between the added safety in the financial system and economic costs in terms of lost activity and less innovation, but regulators need to ensure that rules on consumer protection, and on banking safety and soundness, are effective and enforced. Although legislation since the crisis has addressed many of these issues, there is a serious risk of backsliding. Regulators should also take further steps as well to ensure clear accountability across all the relevant agencies for crisis fighting.

Lesson 4:
Implementing responses to housing market turmoil will be more difficult than future policymakers expect.

We knew that the operational and other frictions would be severe, but they were much worse than we thought. Policy experimentation around the margins of HAMP and HARP resolved some of these constraints, but we should have pursued bolder responses. The active involvement of the GSEs was crucial because of their operational experience, scale, and relationships with servicers. Indeed, because the mortgage servicing industry was, at best, simply paralyzed or, at worst, actively resisting the implementation of modifications, we should have considered more seriously policy options that we perceived as infeasible.

Future policymakers should seek to understand the sources of, and reasons for, friction when designing policy. Normal competitive dynamics could easily leave the private sector lacking the organizational capacity or will to enact far-reaching and dramatic policies; our experience suggests this is especially true in housing markets, and that to overcome this, the government may have to overpay servicers to implement policy. One road not taken—a policy we have since given much thought to—would have been to address the lack of capacity and deep inertia in the mortgage servicing industry by creating a twenty-first-century Home Owners' Loan Corporation—that is, a new agency to collect and distribute mortgage payments, contact and negotiate with borrowers, and, when necessary, foreclose on properties. This is something policymakers should consider in deciding what role the GSE, the FHA, and the broader government should play in the housing finance system.

Lesson 5:
Have a more powerful mix of carrots and sticks to induce servicers and investors to resolve problems.

Even though we offered incentives to servicers, many failed to modify or refinance mortgages (even when it made financial sense to do so). We should have used stronger sticks—looking for ways to force servicers to act—together with larger carrots (say, financial incentives). Bank capital injections were based on the idea of using overwhelming force to stabilize the financial sector, but our housing programs were much more modest in scale. One such stick, if it had been in place in advance, could have been bankruptcy reform permitting judicial restructuring of mortgages. More research would be useful to quantify the balance of pros and cons to this change.

CONCLUSION

Ultimately, our policy response helped millions of families at a modest cost to taxpayers and contributed to the recovery in the broader economy. But the policy response was not adequate to the challenge, and millions of families lost their homes—many of them needlessly. In retrospect, we acted too "prudently" and should have instead acted more forcefully from the start.

| CHAPTER THIRTEEN |

The Rescue and Restructuring of General Motors and Chrysler

BRIAN DEESE, STEVEN M. SHAFRAN, AND DAN JESTER

The rescue and restructuring of General Motors and Chrysler, and their financing arms, required us to confront a series of economic, policy, and political challenges that bridged the Bush and Obama administrations.

Never before had major industrial companies approached the federal government for such a large infusion of cash. Never before had the federal government become a majority owner in an industrial powerhouse like General Motors.

In the end, both administrations shared the same overarching goal—to blunt the impact of the worst economic downturn since the Great Depression and to save hundreds of thousands of jobs at a perilous time for the American economy. But to get there, each administration took different paths and had different objectives.

For those of us in the Bush administration, our goal was to keep GM and Chrysler alive so that officials in the Obama administration could craft their own plan. In the waning months of the Bush presidency, we did not have the time to decide the long-term fate of two industrial behemoths like GM and Chrysler, which had not done any contingency planning for bankruptcy. We wanted only to devise terms of bridge loans that would allow for our successors

The authors would like to recognize the many contributions from their colleagues throughout both administrations, without whom none of these programs would have been possible. We wish to thank Michael Tae, who worked with the Treasury Department's Office of Financial Stability as director of investments and senior policy adviser, for his contribution to the discussion of the auto financing companies.

to find a more permanent solution, whatever it ended up being. We wrestled with how restrictive to make those terms—to find the balance between driving to a prompt resolution within an established framework while giving leverage to our successors and not deepening the crisis.

For those of us in the Obama administration, we were tasked with devising a framework that would put the automakers on stable footing. This was different from the rescues of financial institutions such as American International Group (AIG), which posed an immediate systemic risk to markets and the economy. Instead, this rescue was, in effect, an extension of our broader effort to blunt the worst effects of an economy in freefall and provide stimulus to accelerate an economic recovery.

And perhaps because of that, it was one of the most politically charged of the financial restructurings during the crisis. We worked to fend off attempts by stakeholders on all sides of the issue to meddle in granular decision-making over which dealerships to close or which plants to shut down. We were the subject of intense criticism from both free-market advocates and progressive activists.

But we believed that the risk of inaction outweighed the risk of action. Although there were limits to how far we would go in rescuing a troubled industry, the prospect of uncontrolled bankruptcies of GM and Chrysler posed a great enough threat to the economy that we were prepared to consider extraordinary interventions. If left alone, these companies were facing a liquidation under Chapter 7 of the U.S. bankruptcy code, in which a trustee sells whatever assets are left, pays back creditors, and closes the business. There was no real chance for a reorganization outside of court or even a fresh start via a normal Chapter 11 bankruptcy. Financing in the private markets was not available, and there was not enough time for a normal Chapter 11 process.

Even without the collapse of GM and Chrysler, the economic news was alarming, with reported job losses of 533,000 in November[1] and estimated gross domestic product falling by 6.2 percent—later revised to 6.3 percent—in the fourth quarter of the year.[2]

We considered the alternatives. As noted, the do-nothing approach was to step back and let GM and Chrysler go into liquidation. Let the process work

---

1. Bureau of Labor Statistics monthly report, Nov. 2008.
2. U.S. Department of Commerce, Bureau of Economic Analysis (BEA) final report for fourth quarter 2008, March 26, 2009.

itself out. But the auto companies are connected to a network of suppliers—and to one another—and in late 2008, the entire system was under historic stress. An uncontrolled Chapter 7 liquidation of GM would have brought down major companies in the auto supply chain, dragging Ford and other, healthier automakers like Toyota and Honda in the downdraft. (This is why Ford and other automakers supported our intervention with GM and Chrysler.) At the other end of the spectrum, the companies themselves were asking for federal funds with few strings attached.

The Bush administration was blunt in its warning when it announced the lifeline on December 19, 2008: "The direct costs of American automakers failing and laying off their workers in the near term would result in a more than one-percent reduction in real GDP growth and about 1.1 million workers losing their jobs, including workers from auto suppliers and dealers."[3]

Beyond crippling the auto industry and its workers, uncontrolled bankruptcies would also have had a destabilizing effect on the cities and towns dependent on the tax revenues of the plants and their workers. A large portion of the pension obligations for tens of thousands of workers and retirees would be kicked over to the federal government.

The rescue and restructuring can be broken down into two phases—actions taken by the Bush administration and those taken by the Obama administration.

SETTING THE STAGE

In the fall of 2008, two of the three major domestic automakers, General Motors and Chrysler, were tumbling toward bankruptcy.

With credit markets frozen, consumers could not get loans to buy new cars at affordable rates. Dealers, likewise, did not have access to competitive financing that would allow them to put the latest vehicles on their lots, hurting cash flow to automakers. Adding to the pressure was the soaring price of oil, which had surpassed $140 a barrel that summer, leaving fleets of low-mileage sport utility vehicles and trucks—the engine of profits for automakers—languishing on dealers' lots.

---

3. "Fact Sheet: Financing Assistance to Facilitate the Restructuring of Auto Manufacturers to Attain Financial Viability," White House archives, Dec. 19, 2008.

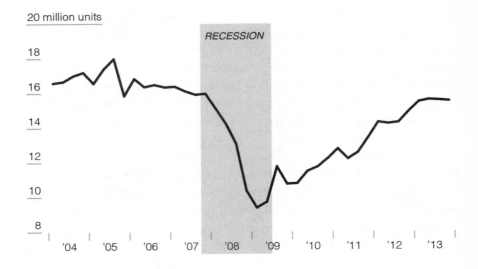

Figure 13.1 Light Weight Vehicle Sales

Note: Series is quarterly, seasonally adjusted annual rate.

Source: U.S. Bureau of Economic Analysis via Federal Reserve Economic Data (FRED)

The result was a plunge in sales. Monthly auto sales (the seasonally adjusted annual rate, or SAAR) would fall from more than 17 million a year in July 2006 to just over 9 million in February 2009.[4] With cash reserves dwindling, General Motors and Chrysler were in a desperate race to maintain liquidity. (Ford had presciently locked in billions in long-term debt with low rates in 2006, when financing was inexpensive, and had more breathing room.)

The downturn had exposed the long-term, structural problems of the domestic automakers, which for years had been losing market share to more-nimble foreign competitors that had lower costs and fewer long-term liabilities, and, in the eyes of many consumers, produced higher-quality cars.

There was no better illustration of this dichotomy than a joint venture started in 1984 by General Motors and Toyota in Fremont, California. Called New United Motor Manufacturing Inc., or NUMMI, the plant produced essentially the same car under two different makes and models—the Pontiac Vibe

---

4. BEA, "Light Weight Vehicle Sales: Autos and Light Trucks," Federal Reserve Bank of St. Louis, accessed May 31, 2019, https://fred.stlouisfed.org/series/ALTSALES.

and the Toyota Matrix. The notable difference was that Toyota made significantly more profit per car.

General Motors was shedding capacity, laying off workers, suspending its dividend, and selling off assets. Chrysler, owned by the private equity firm Cerberus Capital Management, approached many auto companies, including GM, about a merger. But the financial crisis overwhelmed any measures they took. The earnings reports alone told the story of an industry in distress. General Motors reported a loss of $15.5 billion in the second quarter of 2008, burning through $3.6 billion in cash.[5] Ford reported a loss of $8.7 billion that quarter, though it had enough liquidity to ride out the downturn.[6] And Chrysler was struggling to manage the debt from its $7.4 billion takeover by Cerberus.

The decline was spreading to the supply chain as well. As assembly lines went idle, the vast network of companies that provided parts began to feel the pinch. GM at the time spent $31 billion a year on parts from 2,100 suppliers, just in the United States.[7] In all, auto suppliers accounted for 607,700 jobs in 2007, according to the Bureau of Labor Statistics.[8]

GM, which had already been sounding out members of Congress and the Commerce Department for relief, turned to the Bush administration for help. On October 13, 2008, Rick Wagoner, GM's chief executive, arrived with a delegation at the office of Treasury secretary Henry M. Paulson, Jr. He wanted a $10 billion lifeline for GM—$5 billion as a loan and $5 billion in a revolving line of credit—and soon. He didn't get very far. Paulson told Wagoner that he did not have the authority to grant any government assistance, particularly from the $350 billion Troubled Assets Relief Program (TARP) that Congress had recently approved. He was also skeptical of Wagoner's timeline, coming so close to a presidential election. While financial institutions can collapse in a matter of days once the market loses confidence, industrial companies like GM take more time to unravel, Paulson believed. He directed Wagoner to Congress.

5. Kevin Krolicki and David Bailey, "GM Posts $15.5 Billion Loss as Sales Sputter," Reuters, July 31, 2008.
6. David Bailey and Kevin Krolicki, "Ford Posts $8.7 Billion Second-Quarter Loss on Truck Slump," Reuters, July 24, 2008.
7. Peter Valdes-Dapena, "GM Failure: The Shockwave," CNN Money, Nov. 25, 2008.
8. Thomas H. Klier and James Rubenstein, "Detroit back from the Brink? Auto Industry Crisis and Restructuring, 2008–2011," Federal Reserve Bank of Chicago, 2012.

At the same meeting, Commerce secretary Carlos Gutierrez brought up the possibility that GM go through an orderly transition using the established bankruptcy process. But Wagoner refused to consider any such thing. In fact, GM had not done any contingency planning for bankruptcy—a decision that Steven Rattner, the investment banker hired by President Barack Obama to help lead his effort on autos, later said "would add materially to the cost of the eventual rescue."[9] Wagoner maintained that the mere talk of bankruptcy would scare off consumers, who would fear that warranties would not be honored. Wagoner and his delegation left Paulson's office empty-handed. Following Paulson's advice, they took their message to Congress.

By December, both the House and the Senate had considered proposals to offer a bridge loan to the automakers, using funds from a $25 billion program meant to encourage the development of energy-efficient vehicles. On December 10, 2008, the House passed such a bill, 237–170, that would provide $14 billion in emergency loans.[10] But talks in the Senate stumbled over the issue of concessions by labor unions. While the supporters of the plan gained a majority in support, 52–35, they could never gain the 60 votes needed to close off debate and bring the rescue plan for consideration.[11] The measure died the next day.[12]

Around that time, a group of senior Democratic congressional leaders had approached Federal Reserve chairman Ben S. Bernanke about lending to the auto companies. But Bernanke was highly reluctant, feeling that the Fed's energies were best spent on the financial panic. "We were hardly the right agency to oversee the restructuring of a sprawling manufacturing industry, an area where we had little or no expertise," he later wrote.[13] He also echoed Paulson's view that threats to the auto industry would be slower to be realized than dis-

9. Steven Rattner, *Overhaul: An Insider's Account of the Obama Administration's Emergency Rescue of the Auto Industry* (New York: Mariner Books, 2010), 27.
10. David M. Herszenhorn and David E. Sanger, "House Passes Auto Rescue Plan," *New York Times,* Dec. 10, 2018.
11. The vote had a measure of bipartisan support, with ten Republicans, 40 Democrats, and two Independents voting in favor. To those of us in the Bush administration, that support was a significant factor when we considered the desirability of a rescue and the decision to incorporate certain terms of the legislation into the framework.
12. David M. Herszenhorn and David E. Sanger, "Senate Abandons Automaker Bailout Bid," *New York Times,* Dec. 11, 2018.
13. Ben S. Bernanke, *The Courage to Act: A Memoir of a Crisis and Its Aftermath* (New York: W. W. Norton, 2015), 377.

tressed financial institutions, which needed a quick response. He believed that Congress and the administration would have more time to consider options.[14]

By mid-December, the issue was back in the Bush administration's hands. The president was faced with a choice between bad and worse—either extend a lifeline to two companies, and their financing arms, that had been mismanaged for years or let them fail.

THE RESCUE, PART I—BUSH ADMINISTRATION

On December 19, 2008, with only 31 days left in his presidency, President George W. Bush, who at first opposed helping the automakers, announced that the federal government would provide a lifeline to GM and Chrysler. As Paulson later recalled, "For President Bush an auto bailout was a bitter pill to swallow, especially in the last major economic decision of his administration. He disliked bailouts, and he disdained Detroit for not making cars people wanted to buy." But President Bush could see the downsides of not acting. "The consequences for the economy would be devastating," Paulson wrote.[15]

President Bush had decided that he did not want an unplanned bankruptcy to occur on his watch. The financial system was so weak that there was simply not enough money in the private sector for the normal bankruptcy process— debtor-in-possession financing—to work for a company like General Motors. Without that option, and without federal money, the only bankruptcy option at the time was a disorderly forced liquidation under Chapter 7 of the bankruptcy code. That would be a disaster, taking down big parts of the auto industry, and it would be too consequential of an outcome, Bush decided, to allow in the last days of an administration.

To support this policy shift, we needed to revisit the idea of using TARP funds. This determination relied on a central question: Could the auto companies qualify for financial assistance under the statutory definition of the Troubled Assets Relief Program? Asking this question marked a significant shift from the Bush administration's position in its first meeting with GM and generated considerable opposition from the political right. After talks for a

---

14. Bernanke, *Courage to Act*, 377.
15. Henry M. Paulson, Jr., *On the Brink: Inside the Race to Stop the Collapse of the Global Financial System* (New York: Business Plus, Hachette Book Group, 2010), 424.

legislative solution broke down in the Senate, the Bush administration obtained an opinion from the Treasury Department's general counsel that allowed us to use TARP funds to make bridge loans to General Motors and Chrysler.

The Obama administration subsequently agreed with that judgment, using the Bush administration's legal interpretation as a basis. That decision would stand up to further challenges during the Obama administration.

The Bush Treasury team designed three programs in the final two months of the administration:

- We used TARP funds to make short-term loans to each of GM and Chrysler, ensuring that they would not run out of money for several months. We wanted to establish a framework for prompt resolution while giving leverage to our successors and not deepening the crisis. We tried to give enough time for the Obama administration to develop a solution it deemed appropriate.
- We used TARP funds to provide support for the finance subsidiaries of GM and Chrysler. This was similar to the support we had provided to large and small banks around the country.
- We designed and announced the Term Asset-Backed Securities Loan Facility, or TALF, a program developed in coordination with the Fed that would address the problems in the securitization marketplace. Precrisis, the securitization market had been very important to the financial structure of the auto industry, and it would need to restart if the industry was going to get back on its feet.

LENDING TO GM AND CHRYSLER

In Washington, during a presidential transition, there is a saying that you have only one president at a time. The idea is that the new president shouldn't make policy on issues that are the responsibility of the outgoing administration. While there is a lot of logic to this unwritten policy, the reality was that the Bush administration was not going to design a long-term fix for the auto industry in the waning days of its tenure. And the Obama administration, by extension, was not in position to take a significant role in the nine weeks between the election and taking office.

Hank Paulson appealed, unsuccessfully, to Lawrence Summers and other Obama officials for greater cooperation. He proposed that the Bush administration would support an auto rescue, which it had previously opposed, in exchange for Obama's support for another round of TARP funding from Congress. The conversation culminated in a meeting on November 30, the Sunday of Thanksgiving weekend, in Paulson's office. A skeptical Summers heard Paulson out but ultimately declined to go along. Paulson was disappointed but later acknowledged that it was the right decision.

We needed to hand the companies over to the next team and let it determine the government's response to this piece of the crisis. We did not want to set anything in stone, and we did not want to do anything that would hamper the next team's flexibility. We wanted to consult with the new administration on the specific trade-offs we were weighing, but that would violate the doctrine of one president at a time. Thus, it was left to us in the Bush administration to set up the terms of the loans and trust that we did no harm to our successors.

In designing the loans to GM and Chrysler, there were several moving pieces in the structure that were debated internally and negotiated with the borrowers:

- *How much should we lend?* Too much, and we could be accused of wasting taxpayer dollars. Too little, and the Obama administration would be consumed on day one with an out-of-control crisis.
- *When should the loans be due?* The maturity date on a loan is the "gun to the head" of a borrower who can't pay you back. Everyone knew that these short-term loans were never going to be repaid by any third-party financing, so the maturity date was really the same as the drop-dead date for the Obama administration and the car companies to come to a solution. Too soon had obvious risks. Too long, and it might give the car companies more latitude and time than would be helpful.
- *What covenants should we ask for?* No covenants was a strong choice, given that the loans were intended as a bridge and not to constrain the next administration's decision space. Yet this option seemed to be a gift to these borrowers that had not done a thing to prepare for the inevitable pain of restructuring.

The bridge loan deal was announced on December 19, a week after the Senate negotiations collapsed. The automakers were given $17.4 billion in loans—$13.4 billion for GM and $4 billion for Chrysler.[16] The key covenant we

16. "Fact Sheet: Financing Assistance to Facilitate the Restructuring of Auto Manufacturers to Attain Financial Viability," White House Archives, Dec. 19, 2008.

inserted required GM and Chrysler to submit restructuring plans to the new administration by February 17, 2009, that would show how they would repay the loans and become viable companies again.

The plans we demanded required each company to show how it would "achieve and sustain long-term viability, international competitiveness and energy efficiency." The idea was that all stakeholders—labor, management, debtholders, stockholders—would have to make concessions to receive financial assistance and put the automakers on a path to viability.

We wanted to provide adequate time, approximately two months, for the companies to develop plans, and we envisioned that during this process they would engage in meaningful discussions with key stakeholders. We didn't want to make the timeline any shorter, because we did not want to place the problem on the doorstep of the incoming administration. We wanted to provide President Obama with the time to assemble a team and begin work on formulating the next steps. At the same time, since the companies were losing money, it was important to establish a tight timeline.

To increase the chances that the proposed plan would be effective, we required the president's designee to certify by March 31 that the plans had met the specified requirements. If the plans did not meet the requirements, the loans would become due, effectively forcing bankruptcy. We included restructuring targets and various term sheet requirements.

The goal of our plan was to put the automakers on a path of reorganization through bankruptcy proceedings. As Paulson wrote in *On the Brink*, "We knew it would be almost impossible to win major concessions from all parties without this pressure."[17]

SUPPORTING GMAC AND CHRYSLER FINANCIAL

We recognized early on that if we were going to prevent a collapse of the auto industry in the short run, and support a recovery in the long run, it would require stabilizing the auto finance industry. Purchases of automobiles in the United States rely heavily on financing. About three-quarters of all consumer automobile purchases in early 2008 were financed,[18] as were substantially all

17. Paulson, *On the Brink,* 428.
18. Ralf R. Meisenzahl, "Auto Financing during and after the Great Recession," FEDS Notes, the Federal Reserve, June 22, 2017, https://www.federalreserve.gov/econres

dealer loans (known as "floor plan" loans). Leading up to the financial crisis, the auto industry largely relied on dedicated financing arms to support sales, given their specialized resources, embedded infrastructure, and long-term experience in underwriting automotive credit.

These dedicated finance companies faced severe funding and liquidity challenges in the fall of 2008. Securitization markets were a primary source of funding for these entities, and distress in the markets affected GMAC's and Chrysler Financial's ability to finance operations. Investors' fears were magnified by the distress among their parent automakers, including the threat of both GM and Chrysler bankruptcies. On top of this, GMAC had made ill-fated ventures into markets beyond auto loans. Its residential real estate division, ResCap, was caught in the housing downturn and was bleeding billions of dollars.

Alternative sources of funding, such as the unsecured bond market, were not available. Ultimately, without government assistance to the automotive finance companies, limited financing for auto consumers and dealerships would translate into a slowdown of automobile production, which would have added significant stress to the parent automobile companies.

To demonstrate this point, at the time we provided assistance to GMAC, it managed approximately $26.5 billion of wholesale auto loans, $23.3 billion of which supported GM dealers. Had Treasury allowed GMAC to fail, no single competitor or group of competitors could have stepped in to absorb GMAC's entire loan portfolio, partially because of the size and capital requirements of the portfolio, and partially because most of the large national banks faced significant threats to their own financial health.

In December 2008, GMAC received $5 billion, and in January 2009, Chrysler Financial received $1.5 billion in loans from TARP funds. This financial intervention avoided liquidations that would have been devastating to the auto market. GMAC also applied for and received approval from the Federal Reserve to become a bank holding company during this time. This gave GMAC the ability to use its bank deposits to fund its automotive finance originations.

The loans we made during that time gave GM and Chrysler the desired lifeline to the Obama administration.

/notes/feds-notes/auto-financing-during-and-after-the-great-recession-20170622
.htm.

CONCEIVING THE TERM ASSET-BACKED SECURITIES LOAN FACILITY

In addition to the actions to bolster the auto financing arms, we also intervened to ease the gridlock in the auto lending securitization market. With the collapse of Lehman Brothers in September, demand for asset-backed securities backed by car loans to consumers and floor plan loans had all but evaporated. Mike Jackson, chief executive of AutoNation, highlighted just how dramatic the decline in loans to consumers had been: From December 2007 to December 2008, GMAC's acceptance of new loans to consumers had plunged from 1,527 to 9. Chrysler Financial's had dropped from 823 to 22.[19]

We had to bring this vital market back to life, and we needed to send a signal to the market. So, while we addressed the immediate funding problems at the manufacturers and their finance subsidiaries, we also worked to address this market-wide challenge.

The Bush Treasury team began working with the Federal Reserve Bank of New York to create a lending program called the Term Asset-Backed Securities Loan Facility, or TALF. This program was jointly created and funded by the Fed and Treasury, and it would play a prominent role in reviving the asset-backed securities market.

The idea was to use the Fed's lending authority to bring more firepower to the TARP funds. The Fed initially authorized up to $200 billion in loans under TALF, backed by $20 billion in TARP funds from Treasury.

A key distinction in TALF was that its loans were nonrecourse, meaning that the borrower need give back only the collateral, and nothing extra, if its collateral did not cover the full cost of the loan.

When the program went live in March 2009, TALF provided liquidity in the least risky part of the asset-backed securities market, covering assets from student loans to credit cards to small businesses. But a key driver of the program was to revive lending for car buyers and car dealers.

By the time it was closed in June 2010, TALF had had a significant impact in reviving the auto lending market. It ultimately was responsible for $71 billion for all types of loans.[20] All of it would be paid back in full.[21]

---

19. Presentation to Automotive Outlook Symposium, Federal Reserve Bank of Chicago–Detroit branch, June 5, 2009.
20. The Federal Reserve, press release, Jan. 15, 2013.
21. Federal Reserve Bank of New York, programs archive.

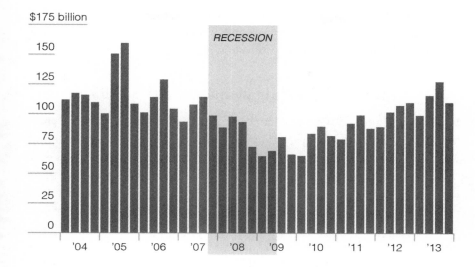

$175 billion

RECESSION

'04   '05   '06   '07   '08   '09   '10   '11   '12   '13

Figure 13.2 Auto Loan Origination Volume

Source: Chart based on data from New York Fed Consumer Credit Panel/Equifax, accessed Nov. 16, 2018, www.newyorkfed.org

There was little mystery why it worked: The program lowered interest rates for the auto loans at a time when lenders had significantly tightened standards. As Brian Sack, executive vice president of the New York Fed, said in a speech in June 2010, "Nearly all of the auto lenders supported by the TALF reported that the facility enabled them to offer more credit to consumers at lower rates."[22]

SUMMARY

In the end, it was the TARP funds that allowed us to build a bridge to the Obama administration. Those funds would prove important politically as well. The fact that the Bush administration had made the legal determination that TARP funds could be used for auto companies inoculated the Obama administration, to some degree, from the criticism that the executive branch was acting without legal authority, and it provided a degree of consistency across administrations.

22. Brian P. Sack, remarks at the New York Association for Business Economics, June 9, 2010, Federal Reserve Bank of New York, speeches archive.

The Obama administration now had some breathing room—measured in weeks rather than days. Not a lot of time, but enough to craft the plan that would put the automakers on a path to solvency.

THE RESCUE, PART II—OBAMA ADMINISTRATION

We on the Obama team reported to work in late January faced with the challenge of crafting a long-term solution to the ailing auto industry in a matter of weeks. We had been intensively studying and devising potential options over the course of the transition. Upon taking office, we had to begin to put these ideas into practice. The experience and decisions of the prior administration provided important context. We considered and immediately rejected the idea of going back to Congress for authority, based on the failed congressional votes only six weeks earlier. We reviewed and agreed with the prior administration's legal judgment that TARP funds could be used to support auto companies—so we had limited but powerful policy tools at our disposal. With that, we focused on a core set of questions that would define the structure of our policy interventions:

- *The bankruptcy question:* Was there a viable path for these companies to restructure under the bankruptcy code?
- *The Chrysler question:* Was there a sufficient case to use precious taxpayer resources to backstop GM and—the more difficult question—Chrysler?
- *The government ownership question:* How should the government manage its stake as a majority owner of a major industrial company?

THE BANKRUPTCY QUESTION

It was a central issue of the autos rescue: Was there a way for these companies to restructure using the bankruptcy code?

Early on, we made the determination that for these companies to have any real chance of reaching financial viability, they would need to shed substantial liabilities. The debt burden of both GM and Chrysler was so great that a restructuring that did not involve forcing creditors to take real losses would have required an enormous amount of money—an amount that we didn't necessarily have within TARP, nor that we could justify as a prudent use of taxpayer resources.

For these reasons, we focused our analysis on bankruptcy restructurings that would enable the companies to use the protections of the bankruptcy code to shed liabilities and fundamentally restructure. But the question of whether and how bankruptcy would work in this context was difficult—there were real risks and unknowns.

One of those risks was the "melting ice cube" problem. Whenever a company goes into bankruptcy, there is a risk that people will stop buying its products because they lose trust in the brand. The longer a bankruptcy restructuring goes on, the more consumer trust erodes, and the more the ice cube melts. Automakers felt particularly vulnerable to this since warranties are a central part of consumer decision-making. This risk was felt not only by the auto companies—we faced pressure from other stakeholders from lawmakers to labor leaders to avoid discussing the restructurings as bankruptcy, for fear that it would be interpreted as the death knell for the industry. Some stakeholders implored us during the winter of 2009 to not even use the "B" word publicly for fear that doing so would cause communities and consumers to panic, run away from the companies' products, and make the problem worse.

A second, related risk of bankruptcy is that it could drag on indefinitely as creditors fought it out in court. The average period for a company in Chapter 11 proceedings was measured in months, not weeks—time we did not have.

We continued to believe that, if feasible, a managed bankruptcy was the best course. The cost to taxpayers of financing a restructuring without major concessions was simply too high; and given these companies' track records of avoiding difficult decisions, the risk of simply kicking the can once again was too high as well.

The challenge was to determine what form the bankruptcy would take. We needed a way to mitigate the risks—to reduce uncertainty and move through the process quickly.

There are two basic ways to accelerate the bankruptcy process. First, there is a prepackaged bankruptcy, or a "prepack," in which all the major creditor groups agree in advance and a plan is presented to the bankruptcy judge.

Then there's the approach called a 363 sale, named for a section of the U.S. bankruptcy code. In that scenario, a single entity makes a stalking-horse bid to buy the company out of bankruptcy. Any other player can come in and bid on that sale, but once the highest price is determined and the sale is approved, the debate and deliberation around the terms of the restructuring are curtailed.

We settled on the 363 sale. We were under intense time pressure—it was costing taxpayers dearly to keep the companies afloat as administrations changed. Rattner wrote that it cost from $500 million to $1 billion a month to keep Chrysler afloat and as much as $2 billion a month to keep GM going.[23] The longer the bankruptcy process dragged out, the greater the chance that the ice cube would melt and the companies would need to be liquidated. In that case, more taxpayer dollars would be wasted, creditors would end up with virtually nothing, and the country would suffer the damage to the economy that we feared from the outset.

While a prepack bankruptcy could have afforded similar speed, in the case of GM the number of creditors and shareholders was too large to realistically drive agreement. With Chrysler, we would leave open that prospect, but the tool of the 363 sale allowed us to drive forward if unanimity among the creditors could not be reached.

For GM, the direct buyer was a "new" GM, underwritten by taxpayer dollars. For Chrysler, Fiat was that controlling buyer in the 363 sale, using proceeds from the U.S. Treasury to underwrite the deal. Not surprisingly, these arrangements were controversial. We faced heated criticism from creditors, who felt that we were subverting the normal hierarchy of the bankruptcy code and that the 363 sales in this context were "sham" transactions. They litigated every step of the way—to the Supreme Court in the case of Chrysler—only to lose.

The multiple courts that looked at the issue found that while the circumstances surrounding these restructurings were as unique as you can get, in bankruptcy terms, the transactions were actually quite ordinary.

In an opinion that cleared the way for the sale of Chrysler's assets to Fiat, Judge Arthur J. Gonzalez of the U.S. Bankruptcy Court for the Southern District of New York granted our motion in its entirety.

"Notwithstanding the highly publicized and extensive efforts that have been expended in the last two years to seek various alliances for Chrysler, the Fiat Transaction is the only option that is currently viable," he wrote in his 47-page opinion. "The only other alternative is the immediate liquidation of the company."[24]

23. Rattner, *Overhaul*, 127.
24. Judge Arthur J. Gonzalez, U.S. Bankruptcy Court Southern District of New York, in Re Chrysler LLC et al., "Opinion Granting Debtors Motion," Case No. 09 B 50002 (AJG), 16–17.

The fact remained that there was an open sale process. Every creditor and indeed any external party had the opportunity to outbid Fiat or "new GM" in the process. With Chrysler, the sale price was $2 billion—far from the $7.4 billion Cerberus paid for it in 2007 but nearly twice the $1.1 billion that Chrysler had estimated was its liquidation value. Had any creditor come in and bid $2 billion and a dollar, that creditor would have become the buyer and dictated the terms of the restructuring. Likewise, had we decided not to fund the stalking-horse bid, Chrysler would have entered liquidation and creditors would have received far less.

There's an old saying in finance called the golden rule of bankruptcy: He who has the gold makes the rules. That was the dynamic in a 363 bankruptcy.

This dynamic also meant that Fiat and the new GM management team were positioned to determine which liabilities to bring through the process and which to shed, in consultation with our team. The approach we employed was based on the commercial logic of what was essential for the company to operate on the other side. As a result, liabilities like warranties and key supplier commitments were honored in full. It is hard to sell cars without warranties or steering wheels. Other liabilities were shed or significantly restructured. The most contentious were union contracts, health care and pension obligations, product liability claims, and dealer contracts.

The final concessions agreed to under the 363 sales tracked a blueprint developed by Senator Bob Corker (R-TN) during the failed congressional negotiations in December. Under that blueprint, Corker laid out representative concessions on wage and hour provisions for union workers and haircuts on health and pension obligations. While the blueprint was rejected by Democrats at the time for going too far in penalizing workers, and was not controlling, it nonetheless provided a guidepost for the Obama team in assessing the required concessions among all stakeholders. In the end, the final agreements included deeper cuts than envisioned under the Corker blueprint—both to workers' obligations (wage, health care, and pensions) and to other key creditors' claims, including auto dealers' claims. This reflected our assessment of the dire financial position of these companies and the deeper restructuring necessary to put them on a viable path.

We aimed to work with but ultimately empower the new management teams at GM and Fiat to make the decisions that would drive these newly restructured companies forward. Although the unprecedented nature of the federal government underwriting the process with taxpayer dollars led to cries of unfairness and political favoritism, in the end, the creditors got significantly more than they would have received in a liquidation. By deciding not to step up and bid for the companies in the 363 sale, they gave up their right to dictate the terms of the restructuring. In the end, unions received *deeper* wage, health care, and pension haircuts than what Republicans in Congress had proposed and failed to pass just a few months earlier. But the process would become the story, and the cries of unfairness would persist.

In his Chrysler decision, Gonzalez saw no basis for the complaints about fairness: "The Debtors are receiving fair value for the assets being sold. Not one penny of value of the Debtors' assets is going to anyone other than the First-Lien Lenders."[25]

When we were making our estimates of just how quickly this could happen, we thought it was possible for the bankruptcy process to move within a month. We thought that was possible but by no means guaranteed. We had scenarios where the process was two or three or four months.

In fact, Chrysler spent 31 days in bankruptcy and GM spent 40, making them not only two of the largest industrial bankruptcies in history but also two of the fastest. That speed saved taxpayer resources and helped keep the ice cube cold.

SAVING CHRYSLER

While there was a consensus within the Obama team on the economic argument for saving GM, there was no such broad agreement when it came to Chrysler.

Rescuing GM was an easier decision for two reasons. First, it was a larger company with a larger employment base and a larger impact across the auto supply chain. The economic implications of letting it go into a disorderly bankruptcy were more clearly negative.

Second, despite its many troubles and management shortcomings, GM had valuable assets that we felt could form the core of a newly restructured company. GM, to its credit, had made a set of decisions over the previous couple of years to at least start putting in place the building blocks of a new, repositioned company.

We laid out a scenario in which GM would keep the strong assets while shedding the weak ones. We internally referred to the new company as "Shiny

25. Gonzalez, "Opinion Granting Debtors Motion," 18.

New GM," with Chevrolet, Cadillac, GMC, and Buick forming the core. The rest—including Saturn, Pontiac, Saab, and Hummer—would be put into "Old GM" and wound down. We believed that Shiny New GM could be a viable company—if we could get enough cash into the company, get enough of its liabilities removed, and get a competent management team and board in place.

At Chrysler, the picture wasn't as clear.

The perennial odd man out of the domestic automakers, Chrysler had been hollowed out. Although it had a strong brand in Jeep, new product development had suffered under a series of owners. When the downturn hit, Chrysler was struggling to service the debt it had acquired with its buyout by Cerberus. Add to that the trouble Chrysler had selling its existing vehicle lineup, and we saw an automaker with little ability to compete on its own. It needed a partner.

This judgment was reinforced by the fact that Chrysler had essentially been up for sale for the previous two years. GM had looked at it. And we, internally, looked for a bit at whether it would make sense for GM to buy Chrysler as part of this restructuring. It would have been an arranged marriage by the U.S. government. It sounded like a crazy idea, but when the annual sales rate is in a free fall, all ideas are on the table.

We also had to ask the question, what if Chrysler could not find a partner? What if Chrysler had to liquidate? It had a smaller economic, geographic, and employment footprint than GM, so the impact of Chrysler alone liquidating would be less significant than if GM were to do so, or if both GM and Chrysler together did so. But there was more to it than that, and the question became the subject of intense internal debate.

Economists, it is said, never agree, even with the same facts. We had people on both sides of that argument who brought facts to bear and, while never reaching agreement, focused on giving President Obama the most robust arguments on both sides in order to make a decision.

That day came on March 27, 2009, in the White House. In three days, President Obama was to announce his plan to rescue and restructure the auto industry. He called for a meeting of his autos team and senior members of his administration. It would begin in the Oval Office and continue that evening in the Roosevelt Room.

Those of us in favor of saving Chrysler laid out our assessment that Chrysler was not viable as an ongoing entity and that Fiat was the right, and willing, partner. The impact of a liquidation would go beyond Chrysler workers losing their jobs and suppliers being hurt, we said. It involved the knock-on impact of municipal bankruptcies in the jurisdictions where Chrysler was the dominant employer. It involved the costs to the federal government of the legacy health care obligations that, if Chrysler liquidated, would be borne by the federal government through Medicaid and Medicare. And it involved the transfer of pension obligations to the Pension Benefit Guaranty Corporation.

If the Fiat merger goes through and goes well, we argued, the chances of Chrysler continuing to survive as a thriving, ongoing entity over the next two to four years were probably 80 percent and beyond five years were probably 60 percent.

It was hardly a slam dunk. Adding to the uncertainty was that we were not asking for the president's approval on a fully negotiated deal. Instead, we were asking the president for his commitment allowing us to spend a month with Fiat and see if we could actually reach terms that would work.

Our team's bottom-line assessment to the president was that this was a 51–49 issue—barely in favor. With that as guidance, we asked for his approval on one of the most significant decisions in his young administration.

The case against saving Chrysler was made most forcefully by the Council of Economic Advisers, which was headed by Christina Romer. Austan Goolsbee, a University of Chicago economist who served on the council, was summoned to make the case against saving Chrysler.

In 2015, Goolsbee spelled out his arguments in the *Journal of Economic Perspectives*—a paper in which he acknowledged to being "pleased and a bit surprised" at the recovery in the domestic automakers.[26] First, he contended that there was not a big enough market for GM, Ford, and Chrysler all to survive, and therefore, saving two of the three would make all three less profitable and risk a lower return on the taxpayers' investment. Second, he said there was evidence to suggest that Chrysler customers would switch over and buy domestically produced vehicles, made by Ford, GM, or foreign transplants, since they had similar product lines. Third was the been-there-done-that argument. Chrysler had been owned by Daimler and then Cerberus—in flush times—and neither arrangement worked.[27]

26. Austan D. Goolsbee and Alan B. Krueger, "A Retrospective Look at Rescuing and Restructuring General Motors and Chrysler," *Journal of Economic Perspectives* 29, no. 2 (Spring 2015): 3–24.
27. Goolsbee and Krueger, "Retrospective Look," 9–11.

After hearing all arguments, President Obama gave his decision: "I think that we should give this a shot," he told us. "It's worth it."

He then made it clear that his only interest was in making Chrysler a viable company again. The deal, he stressed, needed to be free of social or economic policy objectives. "I want you to be tough, and I want you to be commercial," he said.

SHAREHOLDER IN CHIEF

The decision to back GM was easier. But the mechanics were harder. Because GM was carrying so much debt, the only way we could provide capital to the company and create a runway for it to succeed was to take equity in return for the government's stake. That created a stark reality—the U.S. government would be the majority shareholder in an iconic American institution. It presented a particularly thorny question for us in the Obama administration—how would we approach our new position? We called it U.S. Government as Shareholder. Critics called it Government Motors.

The challenge was to set up a framework that kept us at arm's length and out of the business of running a car company, yet held senior management accountable for its decisions and allowed us to protect the precious taxpayer dollars we had invested.

To begin, we decided that we had to change management and change the board. GM was receiving an infusion of $51 billion in taxpayer money, including the bridge loan. In our view, it was impossible to justify that magnitude of taxpayer investment while keeping Rick Wagoner and the management that had presided over the company's unwinding.

Timothy Geithner, the Treasury secretary under President Obama, said that replacing Wagoner as chief executive and overhauling the board of directors was consistent with the broader approach that both administrations took throughout the financial crisis. That is, the bigger the stake the government took in a troubled company, the more the government leaned toward replacing management. In the case of AIG, Fannie Mae, Freddie Mac, and GM—all of which were saved by substantial government investment—the senior management was replaced.

But along with this went an important corollary. Once we found a new chief executive, we were careful not to use our majority shareholder status to weigh in on commercial business decisions. Nor were we going to use our influence as a means of achieving broader policy outcomes.

We knew we were in a position of extraordinary authority and power. We faced pressure from all corners. There were calls for domestic content or domestic production floors, for commitments from GM and Chrysler to keep open certain plants, to help certain distressed communities, to make certain types of vehicles, or to hit certain fuel efficiency targets. At the same time, we faced criticism from others that the federal government's controlling stake in GM, and the overhauling of its senior management, amounted to creeping socialism.

We did our best to keep the outside pressure at bay. That's an easy thing to say ten years later, but we believe we were able to fend it off for the most part. We operated from the belief that if we let our focus drift from financial viability, we would end up further costing taxpayers. If we used our position to force the automakers to increase domestic production, for example, we risked making them less competitive, which would end up costing taxpayers more.

We spent a lot of time trying to create some arm's-length distance between our position representing the majority shareholder and the decisions that the management was making, both through the restructuring and then afterward in terms of managing the company and exiting our ownership stake. This was not easy, particularly given how directly involved our team had to be in positioning the initial restructuring as management was changing and as Fiat was coming on board.

We did consider alternatives to push our ownership stake even further away and inoculate ourselves from political intervention. We even explored handing over our equity stake to a third-party entity to manage. This was an alternative path that we didn't take; we ultimately decided it wasn't feasible or consistent with our obligation to manage taxpayer resources.

LESSONS LEARNED

The rescue and restructuring of General Motors and Chrysler, and their financing arms, required two administrations during a time of crisis to make independent but connected policy decisions, animated by a common goal—to blunt the impact of the worst economic downturn since the Great Depression.

In the period following the restructurings, the automakers returned to profitability and were in a far stronger position than they were in the years before the financial crisis. This happened more quickly than we anticipated. Indeed, during the period following the restructuring, the Detroit 3 collectively gained market share in the United States for the first time in more than two decades.

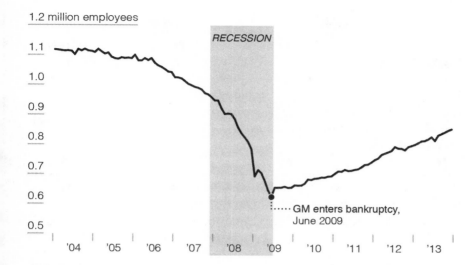

1.2 million employees

1.1

1.0

0.9

0.8

0.7

0.6

0.5

RECESSION

···· GM enters bankruptcy,
     June 2009

'04 '05 '06 '07 '08 '09 '10 '11 '12 '13

Figure 13.3 **Employment in Motor Vehicles and Parts Manufacturing**

Source: U.S. Bureau of Labor Statistics

The rebound in the auto industry as a whole—including the interconnected web of auto suppliers that we aimed to backstop with our actions—also revived more quickly than we expected. Employment among manufacturers of autos and parts grew from 623,000 in June 2009, when GM went into bankruptcy, to 825,000 four years later.[28] SAAR, which bottomed out at 9.023 million in February 2009, had rebounded to 14.6 million by February 2012, on its way to routinely topping 17 million.[29] The economic benefits of this resurgence should be measured not only in absolute terms but also relative to the counterfactual risk of precipitous job losses that would have come from uncontrolled liquidations.

From a financial perspective, the government exited the auto business more quickly than we anticipated. In May 2011, Chrysler had repaid what remained of the money it received under TARP. By the end of 2013, the government had unwound its equity stake in GM.

28. Motor vehicles and parts manufacturing employment, Bureau of Labor Statistics, U.S. Department of Labor.
29. BEA, "Light Weight Vehicle Sales."

Table 13.1 TARP Assistance to the U.S. Auto Industry

Recipient/Program	Amount disbursed ($ in billions)	Net gain/loss ($ in billions)
General Motors	49.5	−10.5
GMAC/Ally Financial	17.2	2.4
Chrysler (including Chrysler Financial)	12.0	−1.2
Suppliers and warranties	1.1	0.1
Total	**79.7**	**−9.1**

Notes: All amounts are as of Dec. 1, 2018. Net gain/loss equals total disbursements minus total cash back. Totals may not sum due to rounding.

Source: Monthly TARP Update for Dec. 1, 2018

Unlike the interventions in the financial sector, this rescue cost taxpayers money. After an investment of about $80 billion—a total that included GM, Chrysler, and Ally Financial (formerly called GMAC)—the government recouped about $70 billion. This included recouping $39 billion of its $51 billion investment in GM and $11.2 billion of its $12.5 billion investment in Chrysler. These were offset by the government's rescue of Ally Financial, which evolved out of GM's financing arm. That resulted in a gain of $2.4 billion on an investment of $17.2 billion.[30]

In the end, we feel that the actions we took fulfilled our mission—to stabilize an important driver of the American economy, save hundreds of thousands of jobs, and avoid economic dislocation at a particularly vulnerable time. Viewed from this perspective, we believe the cost to taxpayers was well justified. Across the landscape of crisis-era interventions to support the economy and jobs, this was one of the highest-returning investments the government made during the Great Recession.

Whether this revival was because of our foresight or luck or both will be debated for years. Ultimately, others will be the best judge of the lessons to take from our actions. But we offer a few reflections on this experience from our perspective:

30. U.S. Department of the Treasury, Office of Financial Stability, TARP programs, https://www.treasury.gov/initiatives/financial-stability/reports/Pages/TARP-Tracker .aspx#Auto.

Lesson 1:
Plan for downside scenarios.

The auto companies and the auto sector as a whole benefited from a stronger cyclical rebound than we anticipated at the time. It is tempting, for example, to look at Chrysler's strong performance and look back at the 51–49 decision as clearly the right one. However, the more difficult question is how the restructuring would have evolved had we not seen the same rebound. While we can never answer that question definitively, it is important to assess the intervention based on the fact that we planned for, and made decisions against, a significantly worse postcrisis economic trajectory. The goal of the restructurings—and the depth of the concessions required from stakeholders—was to position the companies to be competitive in a 10 million–11 million SAAR environment. Having planned for this more bearish outcome, the companies were positioned to take advantage of the upside surprise.

Lesson 2:
Crisis firefighting requires nonpartisan participation.

While the Bush and Obama administrations had different objectives, our teams were able to pass the baton on this issue in a way that allowed for considered policy judgments even in a period of intense crisis. Our actions were predicated both on the Bush team's willingness to create space for a subsequent administration to make decisions and on the Obama team's willingness to build from, rather than scrap, the prior administration's template and tools. That the two administrations were political rivals underscores the challenge and the accomplishment.

Lesson 3:
"One president at a time" is a valuable principle, but it comes at a cost.

The timing of the restructuring overlapping directly with the presidential transition meant that to maintain decision-making space for the incoming administration, the companies had to stay afloat. The period from mid-December until mid-March added to the total cost of the intervention and explains most of the net loss to taxpayers. We hope future policymakers will not face the bad timing of crises overlapping with presidential transitions. But if they do, this tension of speed and cost against the legitimacy of decisions made by one president at a time will be an important consideration.

Lesson 4:
Crisis-era tools are imperfect.

Congress's failure to act on the auto industry's need for help forced the Bush administration to consider the use of TARP to prevent the uncontrolled bankruptcies of GM and Chrysler, a decision we initially rejected and would have preferred to avoid. Once decided and justified, the Obama team spent little time considering other policy tools given the intense time pressure we were under. TARP was an imperfect mechanism to rescue GM and Chrysler, and it raised questions about the political legitimacy of the restructurings. On reflection, we believe it was the right decision—legally justified, as reinforced by the courts, and practically necessary, as the alternative was liquidation. Given the trajectory of legislation and political discourse since the crisis, the greater challenge facing future policymakers may well be even fewer and less well-suited policy tools. Skill and luck come into play, but ultimately policymakers are constrained by the tools they have to work with.

Lesson 5:
Being a reluctant shareholder is difficult, but it is an important goal.

We on the Obama team tried hard to live up to Obama's admonition to us to be tough and commercial—to focus on financial viability to protect taxpayers. In hindsight, it is tempting to think that, particularly given the stronger rebound in the auto industry, perhaps we could have achieved a greater set of objectives on behalf of the U.S. economy or U.S. workers for the investment we made. The issue of requiring U.S. companies to keep production in the United States rather than moving to lower-cost jurisdictions is a particularly pointed example of an issue that is resonant even absent a crisis environment. We believe on reflection that ultimately the principle of financial viability absent other policy goals was vital to executing these restructurings effectively and at the lowest direct cost to taxpayers.

| CHAPTER FOURTEEN |

Implementing TARP

The Administrative Architecture of the Troubled Assets Relief Program

TIMOTHY G. MASSAD AND NEEL T. KASHKARI

INTRODUCTION: RACING INTO THE UNKNOWN

There was no time to waste once Congress passed the law that created the Troubled Assets Relief Program (TARP)[1] in early October 2008. Although we were not certain how the funds would be used, we knew we needed to quickly cre-

The authors are grateful to several former colleagues for assistance in the preparation of this chapter, in particular Lorenzo Rasetti, as well as Steve Adamske, Lori Bettinger, Phyllis Caldwell, Tom Coleman, Don Hammond, Darius Kingsley, James Lambright, Jenni Main, Don McLellan, Duane Morse, Matthew Pendo, Anthony Salvatore, Howard Schweitzer, Michael Speaker, Phillip Swagel, and Paul Wolfteich. The authors also thank Ben S. Bernanke, Timothy F. Geithner, and Henry M. Paulson, Jr., for their comments and feedback, as well as Barry Adler and Benjamin Henken for their editorial and research assistance. The authors also wish to acknowledge the many other people who worked at the Office of Financial Stability from the first days in the fall of 2008 to the wind down of the program. We wish we could recognize all of them here. We are grateful for their hard work and willingness to serve our country. We also wish to thank, and to note our deep respect and admiration for, Herbert Allison, who served as assistant secretary for financial stability from June 2009 until September 2010. Mr. Allison passed away in 2013.

1. TARP, the Troubled Assets—plural—Relief Program, got its name from the Emergency Economic Stabilization Act of 2008 (EESA). The text of EESA is inconsistent in its references to TARP, sometimes calling it the Troubled Asset—singular—Relief Program, with the plural and the singular names even appearing on the same page. The Treasury Department has not been consistent in its references to TARP either. We have elected to use the plural.

ate an organization that could implement whatever those uses were, wisely and efficiently, and with the highest standards of transparency, fairness, and accountability—and one that could successfully straddle presidential administrations.

The Emergency Economic Stabilization Act of 2008 (EESA) authorized the Treasury secretary to establish TARP and provided $700 billion in funding, half of which was available initially. The law did not define exactly how the money should be used. Instead, it stated a broad purpose—to "provide authority and facilities that the Secretary of the Treasury can use to restore liquidity and stability to the financial system"—while setting parameters and limitations on the use of that authority. It also provided that an Office of Financial Stability (OFS) be created within Treasury to administer TARP. It was otherwise left to Treasury to determine TARP's substance and structure.

Treasury had no existing division that could handle the job. The department could provide some support functions but lacked the capability to implement programs involving the disbursement of hundreds of billions of dollars.

There was no good historical precedent either. The Resolution Trust Corporation was not a relevant model: It was established in 1989 to sell the assets of savings and loan associations that had already failed and been seized by the Federal Deposit Insurance Corporation (FDIC). In 2008, we were seeking to stop a crisis as it was intensifying—one that was already causing a panic, was far worse than the S&L crisis, and had the potential to be worse than the Great Depression.[2]

Over the next two years, we designed the administrative structure and processes for a variety of investment programs—as well as programs to help alleviate the housing crisis—and then managed and implemented them. The investments involved capital injections into financial institutions, support for the credit markets, and restructurings of the auto industry. We also planned for exiting investments as the need for them ended.

It is not surprising that we believe that TARP was a success. People may continue to debate the merits of the various policies and programs that addressed the consequences of the financial crisis, including whether the government

---

2. We did not feel that there was a good international precedent either. For example, Sweden had a banking crisis in the early 1990s, but its financial system was much smaller and less diverse than the U.S. system.

should have done more—or less. But the work of the staff that created, managed, and then wound down TARP is an example of outstanding execution:

- In the face of an accelerating crisis, we rapidly built an administrative structure that supported a wide range of untested programs while enabling a seamless transition from one administration to the next. Ultimately, TARP will have disbursed $445 billion—$412 billion on the investment side and $33 billion for housing.[3] More than $250 billion of the authorized $700 billion was never disbursed.
- We put together a small army of financial, legal, and other specialists that handled thousands of transactions in the investment programs in just two years—and by the end of 2013 had recovered $433 billion, $21 billion *more* than those programs disbursed. (The separate distribution of $33 billion for housing assistance was never meant to be repaid.) (See Table 14.1 for program descriptions, disbursements, and recovery amounts.)[4]
- We provided full transparency: Anyone can find out when and how each dollar was spent, as well as whether it was recovered, and review every investment contract. We produced audited financial statements for TARP as a whole and extensive reporting for all programs. Moreover, we were subject to oversight by four agencies in addition to Congress—which meant there were often more people overseeing TARP than were working for it. (We ramped up from no personnel in October 2008 to 220 by 2010 and then back down to just a handful today.)

TARP did not exist in a vacuum; it succeeded in part because of the cumulative impact of the overall response to the crisis. Some luck also was involved. And there were things we could have done better. At the top of that list would be communicating more effectively why we did what we did—a shortcoming that characterized the effort to combat the crisis generally. Many Americans thought of TARP as a bailout for Wall Street, not something that helped Main Street. We did not successfully communicate why stabilization of the financial

---

3. As of August 1, 2019, $441 billion was disbursed; an additional $4 billion is expected to be disbursed under existing mortgage modifications.
4. The amount recovered includes proceeds from "additional" shares Treasury held in American International Group (AIG) as discussed later.

Table 14.1 TARP Disbursements and Recoveries as of August 1, 2019

TARP investment programs	Disbursed	Recovered
	($ in billions)	
Bank investment programs		
Capital Purchase Program (CPP)[A]	$204.9	$226.8
Targeted Investment Program (TIP)[B]	40.0	44.4
Asset Guarantee Program (AGP)[C]	0.0	4.1
Community Development Capital Initiative (CDCI)[D]	0.2	0.2
Supervisory Capital Assessment Program (SCAP)[E]	0.0	0.0
Subtotal: Bank investment programs	245.1	275.5
Credit market programs		
Public-Private Investment Program (PPIP)	18.6	22.5
Term Asset-Backed Securities Lending Program (TALF)	0.1	0.8
SBA 7(a) Securities Purchase Program	0.4	0.4
Subtotal: Credit market programs	19.1	23.6
Other investment programs		
Automotive Industry Financing Program	79.7	70.6
American International Group (AIG)[F]	67.8	72.9
Subtotal: Other investment programs	147.5	143.4
TARP housing programs[G]		
Making Home Affordable (MHA)	20.5	N/A[H]
Hardest Hit Fund (HHF)	9.3	N/A
Support for FHA Refinance Program	0.0	N/A
Subtotal: TARP housing programs	28.1	N/A
TARP total[I]	441.6	442.6
TARP total without additional AIG shares	441.6	425.0

[A] Under CPP, Treasury made investments in 707 banks.

[B] Under TIP, Treasury purchased $20 billion in preferred stock from each of Bank of America and Citigroup, Inc., for a total of $40 billion.

[C] Under the AGP, TARP commitments were used to support two institutions, Bank of America and Citigroup. Treasury made no disbursements under the program. Amounts recovered represent premiums and fees.

[D] Under the CDCI, Treasury made investments in 84 Community Development Financial Institutions. Some banks that received CPP investments converted into CDCI. Those conversions, totaling $363 million, are not included in the CDCI disbursements in this presentation. In addition, the recovery of those investments is included in the CPP totals, not CDCI. Approximately $550 million was recovered under the CDCI, factoring in these exchanges.

[E] SCAP was created to provide capital to any bank that needed to raise capital to meet stress test minimums but was unable to do so privately. No disbursements were made.

[F] Amount recovered includes approximately $17.6 billion in proceeds received by Treasury from its additional shares in AIG; that is, those from the trust created for the benefit of Treasury by the Federal Reserve.

[G] Treasury housing programs under TARP are expected to disburse up to $33 billion.

[H] Amounts disbursed for all housing programs were not intended to be recovered.

[I] Totals may not sum due to rounding.

Source: Monthly TARP Update for 08/01/2019

sector was so important to the health of the American economy, and how TARP and the other interventions likely prevented another Great Depression.

TARP was unusual. Any future crisis will be different yet may require a similar rapid deployment of people and resources in an environment of extreme uncertainty.

TARP's implementation can be divided into three phases, marked not by dates but rather by changes in the nature of the challenges we faced. The initial phase was from the passage of the law until shortly after the Obama administration took office in late January 2009; the urgent need was to get the organization up and running. The second phase ran from the early days of the Obama administration until September 2010, when we expanded the range of programs and the portfolio of investments. The third phase was from October 2010 onward, when the authority to make new investments expired and we focused on exiting the investment portfolio and downsizing the administrative operation, while continuing to implement the housing programs.[5]

The authors' terms in office did not overlap, and we did not work together.[6] But we speak collectively in a unified voice because the story we tell was the work of a terrific team of people, many of whom served with us both, and because TARP's implementation was essentially nonpartisan. Where necessary, we have noted differences in our views. But the challenges each of us faced, and the choices each of us and our teams made, were more similar than dissimilar.

TARP'S LEGAL UNDERPINNING: UNDERSTANDING THE SCOPE, DEALING WITH THE CONSTRAINTS

TARP was a creature of a complex law, one that Congress initially voted down. It was only after the Dow Jones Industrial Average dropped more than 700 points, or 7 percent, that the law passed, on a second vote, just days later. TARP was often seen as a $700 billion fund that Treasury could use however it saw

---

5. While the authority to make new investments terminated pursuant to the original legislation as of September 30, 2010, Section 1302 of the Dodd-Frank Wall Street Reform and Consumer Protection Act of 2010, adopted in July 2010, prohibited the use of TARP funds for programs or initiatives that were not initiated before June 25, 2010.
6. Timothy Massad joined the OFS as its chief counsel in the spring of 2009, just as Neel Kashkari was leaving and Herbert Allison was succeeding him as assistant secretary for financial stability. Allison served until September 2010, when Massad became assistant secretary.

fit. That was not the case. We had broad authority but also specific constraints on what we could do and how we could do it. It is therefore important to understand key provisions of the law that shaped the administrative architecture.

Scope of Authority

EESA gave Treasury authority to "purchase . . . troubled assets from any financial institution,"[7] a mandate that gave rise to three key considerations.

First, the breadth of authority, coupled with uncertainty about how the crisis would evolve and what we would do to end it, meant that we had to build an organization that from the start had great expertise but also great flexibility.

Second, the term "troubled assets"[8] was broad enough to allow Treasury to make the critical decision shortly after EESA became effective to infuse capital in banks through the purchase of preferred stock (the Capital Purchase Program, or CPP). The decision was made to focus on capital infusions rather than purchases of mortgage-related assets for two reasons. One was that the markets were deteriorating too quickly; we were on the cusp of an all-out run on the financial system. Treasury would not be able to implement an asset-buying program fast enough. The other reason: A program of capital infusions would stretch the TARP dollars further than would purchases of mortgage-related assets, particularly because the objective was to support healthy institutions rather than rescue failing ones. We did not have sufficient funds to buy trillions of dollars of mortgage-related assets.

The decision to create CPP and allocate $250 billion of the $350 billion initially available[9] had profound effects on the administrative architecture. The country had more than 8,000 FDIC-insured banks at the time. We didn't

---

7. See EESA Section 101. Treasury was also given the authority to guarantee troubled assets in Section 102, but this tool was not used extensively.
8. The definition had two parts. One part pertained to mortgage-related securities and obligations issued before March 14, 2008. The second—added late in the legislative process—covered "any financial instrument that the Secretary [of the Treasury], in consultation with the Chairman of the Board of Governors of the Federal Reserve System, determines the purchase of which is necessary to promote financial market stability." This determination had to be transmitted to Congress.
9. Treasury had to request the second $350 billion, and Congress had the ability to block its use.

know how many would apply for capital, but we assumed and hoped that hundreds, if not thousands, would. We had to establish an organization that could quickly evaluate those applications, make decisions, and then disburse and track billions of dollars in investments while avoiding conflicts of interest that could undermine the program's integrity or interference that could delay its impact.

The decision to invest in the banks meant we had to develop the capability to exit the investments because not all banks would repay on their own, and we could not force them to do so. The preferred shares we received were not traded; we were the only holder. There was no market price, and it was not clear who the buyers would be. There would need to be ways to exit that not only maximized price but also were fair and transparent.

As for the third consideration regarding scope of authority, although "troubled assets" was broadly defined, the law required that the purchase be from a "financial institution." The Treasury secretary and the chairman of the Federal Reserve had to certify that element to Congress in the case of the purchase of "any financial instrument" (as opposed to a purchase of a mortgage-related asset described in the first paragraph of the definition of "troubled asset"). This meant that we had to create a process to determine the legal authority for each program idea or amendment.

Many ideas for programs or modifications might have been helpful but could not meet these requirements. The challenge was to create an operation that had the capability of using all the authority at our disposal, particularly as we could not predict all the actions we would take at the outset.

Warrants and Guarantee Provisions

EESA's requirements with respect to warrants and guarantees also had significant influence on program design and administrative architecture.

The law required that Treasury receive warrants for common or preferred stock (or in some cases "senior debt instruments") in connection with any purchase of a troubled asset. Every investment program had to incorporate a warrants provision in order to provide taxpayers with potential upside from the investments. While incorporating a warrant feature was straightforward for publicly traded banks in the CPP, it was more complex for the many non–publicly traded banks (including smaller, community institutions) and for many other programs, such as the Public-Private Investment Program (PPIP). We needed staff who could solve these issues. We also needed to create the appropriate process to sell the warrants, which, like the preferred stocks in the CPP, were not traded securities.[10]

The law also provided that Treasury could guarantee troubled assets in lieu of purchasing them. Initially, some thought this provision would be used widely in order to stretch TARP dollars, and one program was launched early on that relied on it.[11] However, the law required that TARP-available funds be reduced by the amount of the guaranteed liabilities. This rule, coupled with premium requirements and the difficulty in valuing guaranteed assets, restricted the provision's use.[12]

Executive Compensation

The compensation of executives at banks receiving capital was one of the most challenging administrative issues. The original TARP legislation contained very limited compensation restrictions, and the CPP contracts did not expand these. The Bush administration team believed that doing so might cause banks not to participate. If banks declined to use the program, the financial system could collapse, devastating Main Street and undermining the entire purpose of the legislation. We viewed our highest priority as preventing a financial collapse, even if that meant we would take substantial criticism for our actions.

By the time the Obama administration took office, there was widespread public outrage over executive compensation at financial institutions that had received taxpayer support. In February 2009, Congress substantially increased the executive compensation restrictions contained in the original law.[13] The anger grew further following the news in March 2009 that AIG had paid large bonuses to employees of AIG Financial Products.

The Obama administration had to devise the best way to implement the new restrictions imposed by Congress. In June 2009, Treasury issued regulations and appointed Kenneth Feinberg as a "special master" to implement them.

---

10. EESA, Section 113(d).
11. This authority was used for additional assistance for Citigroup and Bank of America, though the latter decided not to use the guarantee program after the terms were agreed upon and announced publicly.
12. EESA, Section 102.
13. The tougher compensation restrictions were contained in the American Recovery and Reinvestment Act (ARRA), Division B, Title VII.

Feinberg, well known for devising compensation schemes in mass tort incidents, created a process that we believe worked well. His participation also helped minimize the time and effort that Treasury leadership and the rest of the OFS staff had to spend on the issue.[14]

However, as feared, many financial institutions, especially smaller ones, refused to take TARP funds because of the expanded restrictions. Their top officers were not compensated nearly as generously as those at large banks, and for institutions that had few employees, the restrictions reached well down the organizational chart. The restrictions also contributed to the decisions of many banks to repay TARP funds as quickly as possible.

They also affected program design. For example, the Obama administration spent a lot of time exploring whether TARP funds could be used to support small business lending. We were unable to come up with a viable approach. One principal reason was that potential recipients did not wish to comply with the compensation restrictions.[15]

Provisions Affecting the Exit from Investments

The law gave us discretion in how and when we could dispose of or recover investments. General provisions relating to asset sales required, among other things, that Treasury maximize returns. The American Recovery and Reinvestment Act (ARRA) added a provision that effectively allowed banks to repay earlier than CPP contracts stipulated.

Provisions Otherwise Affecting Program Management

The law affected how we designed and implemented the administrative structure. For example, it gave the secretary "direct hiring authority," which allowed

---

14. For further information on administration of these regulations, see Office of the Special Master for Executive Compensation, *Final Report of Special Master Kenneth Feinberg,* Sept. 10, 2010, https://www.treasury.gov/initiatives/financial-stability/exec _comp/Documents/Final Report of Kenneth Feinberg - FINAL.PDF.
15. Congress later passed separate legislation—the Small Business Lending Fund (SBLF)—that provided capital to community banks and community development loan funds to encourage small business lending. It did not contain executive compensation restrictions, and it permitted small banks that had received CPP funds to refinance into the SBLF, subject to certain conditions. Many did. See Figures 14.3 and 14.4.

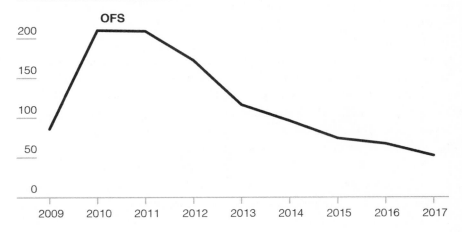

Figure 14.1 Staffing History (Full-Time Equivalents): Office of Financial Stability

Source: President's Budget appendixes

us to expedite hiring (because certain standard governmental procedures were not required), as well as authority to determine the administrative budget. It required production of stand-alone financial statements and cost accounting, as well as extensive and frequent reporting of transactions and other matters. In addition, as mentioned previously, it authorized four oversight agencies to review what we were doing.

These provisions made it essential from the start to establish strong financial accounting and control procedures, as well as overall mechanisms, to ensure accurate and timely record keeping and reporting.

STAFFING UP—AND DOWN

The task of staffing up the Office of Financial Stability in the fall of 2008 was daunting. Many of our staff would later refer to TARP as the world's largest start-up in the world's largest bureaucracy. Within a few months, we had to transition the operation to a new administration, and two years later, we began to wind it down. (See Figures 14.1 and 14.2 for OFS staffing levels and annual budgets, respectively.)

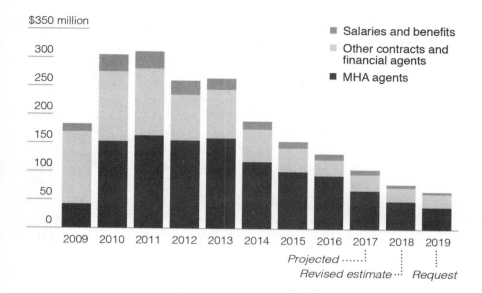

Figure 14.2 **TARP Administrative Budget History**

Notes: MHA refers to the Making Home Affordable program. Data are displayed on fiscal year terms.

Source: OFS Quarterly Administrative Activity Reports

THE INITIAL PHASE—STAFFING UP

On October 13, 2008, Treasury secretary Henry M. Paulson, Jr., Federal Reserve chairman Ben S. Bernanke, New York Federal Reserve president Timothy F. Geithner, FDIC chairman Sheila Bair, and comptroller of the Currency John Dugan met with the CEOs of the nation's nine largest banks. The next day, the Treasury announced the CPP. Treasury was providing a total of $125 billion in capital to these nine institutions and setting aside an additional $125 billion for any other bank that wished to apply and met the program criteria.

Now the challenge was implementation.

We needed to create a system for reviewing and approving bank applications, develop the governing contracts for the investments, and create the infrastructure for disbursing and monitoring investments as well as related financial and operational controls. And it all needed to be done "yesterday."

We also needed highly talented people, from both the private sector and government, with a wide range of special skills and experience—people with expertise in credit and investment analysis and investment management, as well as legal expertise in transactional and regulatory matters. And, oh yes, expertise in government accounting and financial control requirements. The fact that the program was under intense public scrutiny made it all the more critical to find top-notch staff.

The direct hiring authority meant we did not have to follow procedures otherwise required in the federal government, such as competitive rating and ranking. This expedited hiring.[16] Employees still had to meet strict conflict-of-interest and financial disclosure rules, which deterred a number of otherwise qualified candidates. Treasury hired almost 100 people within about three months. Staffing reached its highest level of 220 in March 2010.[17]

Many of the early employees were "detailed" (borrowed) from other agencies—the Federal Reserve, FDIC, Office of the Comptroller of the Currency (OCC), Office of Thrift Supervision (OTS), Internal Revenue Service (IRS), and the Securities and Exchange Commission (SEC). Interagency cooperation was strong and was critical to success, with agencies offering some of their best people for the initial effort. We could not have staffed up nearly as quickly without this cooperation.

We emphasized the following principles, among others, in hiring:

- Nonpartisanship—it did not matter whether candidates were Republicans or Democrats.
- Candidates needed to be self-starters capable of figuring things out on the fly, flexible because responsibilities would change, yet still humble—able to put aside their egos and work closely with others regardless of age, position, or experience.
- High personal integrity—there was simply no room for even the appearance of unethical or questionable behavior.
- Endurance and resilience—employees had to work hard in an extremely stressful environment and tolerate a high degree of public scrutiny and criticism.

---

16. EESA, Section 101(c).
17. This was the number on board for that month. The full-time equivalent basis for the year was 211.

We sought to build a culture that from the start emphasized these principles, particularly the themes of nonpartisanship, high integrity, and working for the common goal of stabilizing the financial system.

Responsibilities were divided among a number of "chiefs" who reported to the assistant secretary for financial stability. The Bush administration decided at the outset that the assistant secretary would be the only position filled by a political appointee. All other positions were career, to set a tone that emphasized performance and to ease the transition to a new administration. The Obama administration maintained this approach. The chief positions included, for example, chief investment, chief financial, and chief administrative officers.

In all phases of the operation, we relied on outside contractors to provide expertise. Initially, this enabled us to obtain the skills we needed more quickly; later, it made it easier to wind down operations. In particular, in the early days, it was critical to retain outside firms to set up the accounting systems and internal controls and prepare legal documentation for the initial investments. Some firms chose not to work with us because of our strict conflict-of-interest requirements.[18]

The first phase of operations under the Bush administration was marked by the need to maintain morale amid extremely long days, intense pressure, and uncertainty about whether our efforts would succeed. We needed to keep our staff operating at a high level of performance and collaboration without getting burned out. We held frequent meetings with all employees to keep everyone informed and did small things, like inviting staff to bring their children into the building on Halloween, to make the environment as "human" as possible.

It was also essential in those early days to give people a sense that their jobs would not end just because a new administration would be coming in soon, and to create an atmosphere where employees felt they might have opportunities to advance. These objectives reinforced the importance of keeping a nonpartisan culture.

---

18. EESA gave the secretary the authority to waive certain federal government requirements in order to expedite contracting if the circumstances were "urgent and compelling." We rarely, if ever, used this authority, because we felt it was important for transparency to abide by the standard contracting rules. Still, it was nice to know we had it. In a few cases, we were able to identify qualified advisers who already had contracts with the government. This helped accelerate the procurement process.

THE SECOND PHASE—TRANSITION AND EXPANSION

As the Obama administration took office, the second phase of operations was marked by more continuity than change in staffing. Neel Kashkari stayed on as interim assistant secretary until May 2009, when President Obama's nominee began work as a counselor to the secretary. There were few staffing changes—turnover throughout the program was driven by individual circumstances.

The second phase, particularly in 2009, was as frenetic and exhausting as the first. We were implementing new programs, including the restructurings (through bankruptcy) of General Motors and Chrysler, the credit market programs (TALF, PPIP, and SBA 7[a]), and HAMP.[19] Recruitment and maintaining morale were still huge challenges.

A significant difference in the second phase, particularly over time, was the intensifying criticism and scrutiny of TARP. The oversight agencies ramped up their staffing and activities and were constantly requesting information and conducting investigations. In addition, Congress continued to exercise vigorous oversight. The staff frequently repeated the story that a pollster had found "TARP" to be second only to "Guantanamo" as the most unpopular word in America.[20]

During this period, we made changes to the initial organizational structure—which had largely been built around the CPP—to accommodate the greater diversity of programs and complexity of operations.

THE THIRD PHASE—WINDING DOWN

As the Obama administration moved into the third phase, where we no longer had the authority to make new investments or disbursements (unless previously approved), we focused on winding down the operation as we reduced the portfolio of investments.

We were able to reduce staffing fairly quickly. Some employees left on their own, as they recognized that their work was largely completed. We did not extend employment for many of the workers who had been hired as term rather than permanent staff. Instead, we shifted their responsibilities to others. Many employees on detail were not extended either. We helped others find new jobs, including offering outplacement services.

---

19. Term Asset-Backed Securities Loan Facility, Public-Private Investment Program, the SBA 7(a) Securities Lending Program, and the Home Affordable Modification Program.
20. We have not been able to verify whether such a poll existed.

Because OFS was funded through a mandatory authorization, its employees were exempt from furloughs and could continue working during the government shutdown of October 2013. This was helpful to morale as well as program efficacy.

LESSONS LEARNED: STAFFING

Principal staffing and human resources lessons:

- Direct hiring authority is essential for a large program that must be implemented immediately and that requires diverse expertise from both the public and the private sectors.
- Employees detailed from other agencies greatly enable speed of implementation, interagency collaboration, and the gathering of expertise.
- Outside contractors are another immediate source of expertise, provided that strong standards are in place to avoid conflicts (and appearances of conflicts) and to ensure appropriate fees.
- Relying on term employees (rather than permanent ones) greatly facilitates the winding-down process.
- A nonpartisan, performance-oriented culture is key.

THE DEVIL IN THE DETAILS: PROGRAM IMPLEMENTATION

THE BANK PROGRAMS

Program implementation was a challenge across all the many TARP initiatives, and in particular with the bank and housing programs because of the many recipients involved. The Capital Purchase Program was the principal bank initiative and perhaps TARP's best-known effort. To launch it, we had to build systems for potentially hundreds or even thousands of applicants.

We incorporated peer review to make sure each regulator did not simply lobby for those applicants under its supervision. To obtain help, banks applied first to their primary regulator. If a bank had strong CAMELS ratings[21] and

---

21. CAMELS is a widely used system to rate a bank's overall financial condition, assessing capital adequacy, asset quality, management, earnings, liquidity, and sensitivity to risk.

its application was endorsed by the primary regulator, the application was given a "presumptive yes" and sent directly to the investment committee, which would decide whether to recommend approval by the assistant secretary.

Applications that did not receive a presumptive yes or had other factors warranting discussion were referred to the CPP Council, composed of representatives of all the bank regulators, with the CPP director facilitating. The council decided which applications to recommend to the investment committee. This process ensured consistent standards, regardless of the applicant's primary regulator.

An application that was likely to be denied was referred back to the relevant primary regulator, who would encourage the bank to withdraw its name. (We did not announce denials or withdrawals, as that might adversely affect a bank.)

Structural differences in small banks required minor adjustments in applications and procedures, producing still another challenge to get materials and processes up and running quickly.[22]

We used similar procedures for the Community Development Capital Initiative (CDCI), which provided capital to 84 Community Development Financial Institutions (CDFIs).

The Capital Assistance Program (CAP) was designed only for the 19 banks that went through stress testing, as a backstop in the event they needed to raise private capital to meet testing minimums but could not do so. Although ten banks were found to need more capital, all but one were able to raise it privately. The one that could not, Ally Financial (formerly GMAC, a division of General Motors), was assisted through TARP's Automotive Industry Financing Program (AIFP). Thus, CAP was never drawn on. Nonetheless, the fact that capital was available likely enhanced market support for the stress test process.

LESSONS LEARNED: PROGRAM IMPLEMENTATION

- The goal was to have a process for awarding TARP funds among competing applicants that was fair and fast and that could stand up to in-

---

22. For example, many of the nation's community banks are privately held "S corporations" for tax purposes, the shares of which must be held by a limited number of natural persons to qualify for certain tax benefits. As a result, we had to devise a substitute for the preferred equity with warrants structure that was used generally. We also modified the dividend rate in light of differences in tax treatment. Adjustments were needed as well for institutions owned by depositors rather than shareholders.

tense scrutiny. Not every applicant would receive funds. That meant it was important to design uniform application materials and consistent review procedures.

- We sought to make sure decision-making processes were free from political influence while remaining open and transparent with Congress. To that end, all congressional calls and input were directed to the assistant secretary and kept away from those reviewing applications.
- The rich diversity in types of banking institutions in our country created great complexity in implementing CPP. Having staff that could creatively adapt a program that was straightforward in concept so that it could be quickly available to different types of institutions was essential.
- The mere announcement of a new program was critical to stabilizing the system. It helped calm markets and boost confidence even before the program itself was implemented. We saw this with CPP, CAP, and other programs, such as the PPIP.

OTHER INVESTMENT PROGRAMS

Although the CPP was the largest vehicle for the use of TARP funds, all the other programs—which include the credit market programs such as PPIP and TALF, the programs supporting the auto industry and AIG—collectively invested slightly more. Because each had its own implementation issues, it is beyond the scope of this chapter to discuss them all. But the principles noted in the Lessons Learned section are equally applicable.

HOUSING

Because we did not have the resources to directly buy troubled mortgages on a scale that would have made an impact, the Obama administration developed the Home Affordable Modification Program, which used TARP funds to make mortgage modifications.[23] The first obstacle in HAMP's way was that EESA

---

23. Making Home Affordable (MHA) was the name of the collection of programs launched by the Obama administration to address the housing crisis. HAMP was the largest program within MHA and its largest conduit of TARP funds. Other MHA programs included the Home Affordable Refinancing Program (HARP), which was funded by government-sponsored enterprises (GSEs). See "Relief for Responsible Homeowners: Treasury Announces Requirements for the Making

referred to the importance of helping homeowners but did not provide specific authority to do so. A program had to be structured as the "purchase" of a "troubled asset" from a financial institution. Ultimately, we implemented the program by entering into contracts with mortgage servicers that incentivized those servicers to modify loans.[24]

The operational challenge was that the mortgage servicing industry was not equipped, at the beginning of the crisis and for quite some time thereafter, to implement the program effectively. The industry was structured for high-volume, technology-driven payment collections on performing loans, not to work with millions of homeowners to restructure their mortgages.

Mortgage modifications required a case-by-case understanding of a homeowner's situation. The servicers did not have the systems, staffing, or knowledge to engage directly with homeowners on a large scale. Moreover, they lacked basic information about their customers, because documentation was limited to begin with (as in the case of "low-doc" loans) or was missing or not transferred on the sale of the loan. Servicers in private securitizations were further constrained by contractual language that required them to maximize returns and did not address the possibility of widespread delinquencies.

We did not realize at the outset just how serious this problem was or how long it would take the servicers to restructure their operations. As a result, implementation of the program suffered. But it is not clear to us in hindsight that there was a good alternative as long as the program required extensive screening of borrowers, one at a time.

It would have taken even longer for Treasury to build such a massive infrastructure from scratch. And it is unlikely we could have crafted a solution involving third parties, because the servicers had legal responsibilities to the investors.

Looking back, a key question is whether we should have been less discriminating in choosing who to help, thereby increasing the number of modifications. That is, we could have eliminated up-front documentation and/or not screened applications for owner-occupied status or ability to sustain the modification. That might have intensified the already considerable public opposi-

---

Home Affordable Program," press release, U.S. Department of the Treasury, March 4, 2009, https://www.treasury.gov/press-center/press-releases/Pages /200934145912322.aspx.
24. Treasury counsel considered the entering into these contracts as a purchase of a financial instrument from a financial institution.

tion to the program growing out of the perception that people who had not acted "responsibly" or were not "deserving" were receiving assistance. It might have also led to higher re-default rates and possibly higher costs, but it might have still helped more people. (See also Chapter 12, on housing.)

We knew we needed agents to get the money to servicers and to oversee implementation and ensure consistency. Treasury did not have the resources nor did we believe we could build operations quickly. Therefore, we retained Fannie Mae as financial agent. Its responsibilities were to work with the servicers on implementation and administer the payments. We retained a division of Freddie Mac for compliance. Its job was to ensure that the servicers followed our standards and met their responsibilities to homeowners and to us.

We performed regular compliance reviews and met with the servicers frequently to pressure them to improve procedures and fix problems. In the spring of 2011, we began issuing public "servicer assessments"—simplified scorecards—based on our compliance examinations. This rating system got public attention and may have motivated the servicers to move faster to correct problems. We heard anecdotal evidence that the scorecards drew the attention of the servicers' boards of directors. In retrospect, we probably should have done this sooner.

We also required servicers to establish a single point of contact so that a knowledgeable case manager would guide a homeowner through the application process.

Over time, we relaxed certain program criteria, increasing eligibility and simplifying implementation slightly. For example, documentation standards were reduced, the debt-to-income ratio was relaxed, and we broadened eligibility criteria to include non-owner-occupied houses, subject to certain limits. (By contrast, some oversight agencies urged us to tighten the criteria.) However, we had only limited ability to make changes, regardless of what we learned on the ground, because of legislative restrictions. Under EESA, no new programs could be implemented after October 3, 2010. Therefore, any change after that date had to be evaluated to make sure it did not constitute a "new program." This restriction prohibited a variety of changes we considered.

Notwithstanding these problems, HAMP funded more than 2.5 million temporary and 1.7 million permanent modifications. Equally important, the program changed industry practices and set new standards, which contributed to millions more private modifications. (See Chapter 12, on housing.)

Among the other housing assistance programs, the largest was the Hardest Hit Fund, which was simpler to implement. We provided funds to state housing agencies, which helped hardest-hit neighborhoods in ways chosen by the agencies and approved by us.[25] Quality and speed of implementation varied. We performed compliance reviews on the states as well and worked to get underperforming states to improve.

MANAGING (AND EXITING) ONE OF THE WORLD'S LARGEST INVESTMENT PORTFOLIOS

Only a short time after ramping up the program, a new reality set in: Treasury was responsible for an investment portfolio that exceeded most sovereign wealth and private equity funds. The fact that Treasury held these investments only because of the need to stabilize the financial system shaped how we managed and exited them.

MANAGING INVESTMENTS

Use of Third-Party Advisers

Treasury retained third-party advisers to assist in managing almost all the investment programs. They provided industry expertise and experienced staff who could help value and monitor investments on an ongoing basis. They also helped plan and execute disposition strategies. The tasks of advisers varied by program. The CPP and CDCI together involved investments in close to 800 banks, so we needed help in tracking and exiting multiple similar investments. Investments in AIG and the auto industry, on the other hand, were much larger individually but involved businesses that needed to make complex restructurings, and our advisers helped evaluate restructuring strategies and progress. To avoid conflicts in incentives, we sought to retain as advisers firms that would not serve as underwriters or agents for sales of securities.

Transfer Investments to a Separate Entity?

We considered whether to transfer investments to a separate entity, such as a newly formed limited liability company that Treasury would own, for pur-

---

25. The state housing agencies were financial institutions, and these contracts were considered financial instruments.

poses of management and disposition. EESA permitted this, and some in Congress urged us to do it. Within Treasury, some felt TARP was adversely affecting the ability of the department to focus on other important priorities. We concluded, however, that the disadvantages of such a transfer outweighed any advantages. For one thing, such a transfer would not discharge Treasury from any responsibilities under the law for the management or sale of the investments, and we believed Treasury would retain the blame if poor decisions were made by a third party. Treasury would still be subject to oversight scrutiny. Moreover, a transfer would likely increase costs to the taxpayer because we would pay greater fees to third parties yet still need to retain a substantial staff to carry out our core responsibilities. Therefore, we decided it was preferable to hire third parties as advisers but to retain decision-making.

Exercising Voting Rights

We had to decide how to exercise voting rights that came with our equity ownership. Treasury's rights were limited because in most investments it purchased preferred stock rather than common, and the preferred had voting rights only in limited circumstances (such as failure to pay dividends). This was by design: Treasury generally did not seek voting rights, because our purpose was not to manage the firms. However, Treasury held common stock in some cases as a result of exchanges or restructurings or other events.

In the spring of 2009, the Obama administration developed a policy based on Treasury's status as a "reluctant shareholder," its holdings arising only as an unfortunate consequence of the financial crisis. It had no desire to retain ownership interests in private companies over the long term. Its overarching goal was to promote financial stability and foster economic growth. Therefore, Treasury should not interfere in the management of these companies.

Instead, the government would pursue up-front conditions at the time of investment to ensure that financial assistance promoted financial stability. These conditions might include changes to the board or management. Any voting rights would be exercised only in four areas: election and removal of directors, major corporate transactions, issuance of securities, and amendments to charter and by-laws. This policy was consistently followed. Even when Treasury had a large investment and the company required restructuring, Treasury observed this policy although it interacted more with management. Similarly, while some in Congress and in the public urged us to use our ownership informally to advance other policy goals (such as limits on offshoring or the production of more fuel-efficient cars), we declined.

Finding Directors

We had to find new board directors for some companies, such as AIG, GM, and Ally, where we owned voting stock. Because Treasury staff were prohibited by law from serving on outside boards, we chose unaffiliated persons as our nominees. While we were able to recruit highly qualified candidates, there were situations where it would have benefited the program and taxpayer return to nominate a Treasury employee. We did not direct how our nominees voted or acted, nor did we request information from them.

The CPP preferred stock gave Treasury the right to designate two directors in the event that a bank did not pay dividends for several quarters. In many cases where banks failed to pay, we worked out arrangements in which we sent Treasury employees as observers to board meetings. This was a way to have some oversight and input without recruiting a candidate for director, although we retained the right to designate directors.

Refusing to Interfere in Regulatory and Policy Matters

Many companies in which we had investments sought Treasury's help with matters pending before other agencies of the government, such as investigations by or requests for approvals from independent regulatory bodies. They assumed that maximizing Treasury's interest as a shareholder was more important to the government than the particular regulatory matter and therefore expected us to intervene on their behalf. We refused, explaining that each agency had to carry out its responsibilities.

Restructurings

Restructuring was planned from the start with the auto investments, and we also restructured some CPP investments as part of our overall strategy for winding down the portfolio. Banks would seek our assistance for a restructuring, or our own monitoring of the investment led us to raise the possibility. This issue posed some policy questions, particularly in the early cases. Do we decide our strategy based solely on the individual restructuring at hand (as a private investor would) and hold out for every dollar we could get? Or does our overall goal of restoring financial stability and getting out of private ownership by attracting private capital into the system generally require thinking about strategy differently? We decided the latter was the right principle but still sought to maximize returns within those parameters. In a few cases, restructurings involved third-party acquisitions in which we were able to exit the investment.

Minority Ownership Issues

We worked with the FDIC and representatives of minority groups to ensure that recipients of CPP funds that qualified as Minority Depository Institutions (MDIs) and that were not able to pay back the funds did not lose that qualification as a result of our disposition of the investment.[26] We are not aware of any cases where MDI status was lost.

Use of Funds

We did not direct or restrict how bank recipients used TARP funds, as the capital was fungible with all other capital. But we tracked lending levels. As the economy weakened further, lending continued to contract from the unsustainably high levels that caused the crisis. Starting in 2009, we published monthly reports on the lending levels of each CPP bank participant (by consumer, commercial, and other categories). But one oversight agency insisted that we should also know what each bank did with "these" particular funds. We therefore developed a "Uses of Capital" questionnaire requiring banks to check one or more broadly described uses.

Prohibited Trading

The risk existed that a Treasury employee might trade on the basis of inside information obtained from the management of investments, which would

---

26. The Financial Institutions Reform, Recovery, and Enforcement Act of 1989 "requires Treasury to consult with bank regulators to determine the best methods of preserving and encouraging minority ownership of depository institutions." See the letter dated April 22, 2002 (FIL-34-2002) from FDIC director Michael J. Zamorski on the adoption of its Policy Statement on Minority Depository Institutions, www.fdic.gov /news/news/financial/2002/fil0234.html.

have been very damaging to the perception of the program. Our employees were prohibited from holding investments in entities in which Treasury was invested. But how to ensure compliance, beyond just relying on an honor code and standard procedures, including periodic financial disclosures? Once we had a little breathing room from the crisis, we explored building a system to require more sophisticated monitoring and clearance of security trades. But this was too difficult to accomplish quickly. Our solution was to restrict access to nonpublic information as much as possible and to vigorously enforce existing policies (including regular financial disclosure requirements). We are not aware of any violations.

EXITING INVESTMENTS

One of the biggest challenges was exiting investments. While some recipients paid back TARP funds quickly, many did not. We had to decide whether to wait until an issuer could repay—which was difficult to predict—or sell to a third party. Moreover, if the form of the investment was common stock, the issuer had no obligation to repay; we had to sell to a third party (or to the issuer in a negotiated transaction). The form of the investment, as well as the condition of the issuer, thus could affect when and how we exited and whether we recovered 100 percent of TARP funds. (We recovered significantly more than our investment overall in the bank programs, and less in the auto industry program.)

Repayments, Restructurings, and Sales

CPP contracts originally forbade repayments for three years (unless a bank made a qualified equity offering). The Bush team felt it was important for the financial system to be fully recovered before the banks began repaying the loans. The ARRA legislation overruled this provision and required Treasury to accept repayments regardless of waiting period. Many banks, particularly larger ones, wanted to repay as quickly as possible to avoid the executive compensation restrictions. In addition, being a TARP recipient was seen as a negative, and banks did not want the government as an investor.

Banks needed regulatory approval to repay TARP, however, including, in the case of the largest banks, passing the stress tests. We coordinated with the appropriate regulator on whether a bank could repay.

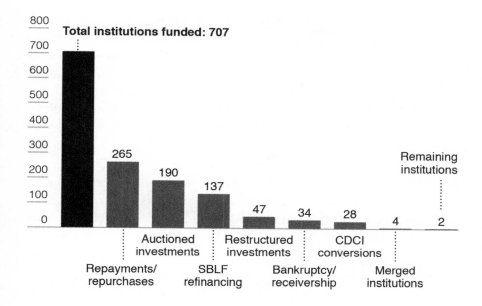

Figure 14.3 **Exit Method, by Number of Institutions: CPP**

Note: A total of 137 institutions refinanced from the Capital Purchase Program (CPP) to the Small Business Lending Fund (SBLF), representing $2.21 billion. In addition, 28 institutions exchanged their securities from CPP to the Community Development Capital Initiative (CDCI) program, totaling $363 million. Figures as of July 2019.

Source: Congressional monthly report

We sold or restructured almost as many CPP investments as there were repayments, when measured by number of banks. (See Figures 14.3 and 14.4, which show the method of exit in the case of CPP, measured both by number of banks and by dollars recovered.)

Determining the strategies to sell these and other investments, including the large stakes in the auto industry, AIG, and Citigroup, was the major focus in the third phase. The law required Treasury to maximize returns but otherwise did not specify price, process, or timing.

General Exit Principles

Treasury's publicly stated goal was to exit TARP investments as quickly as possible, subject to the following principles:

- Protect taxpayer investments and maximize overall investment returns within competing constraints;
- Promote financial stability and prevent disruption of financial markets and the economy;
- Bolster market confidence to increase private capital investments;
- Dispose of investments as soon as practicable, in a timely and orderly manner that minimizes the impact on the market and economy.[27]

Timing of Exit

With respect to each investment, we had to decide whether the advantages of a more rapid disposition outweighed the potential price discounts (or adverse consequences to financial stability) that might be realized from exiting too quickly. Our timing decisions were also based on our analysis of each company's health. We did not try to be market timers in the standard sense of that term.

With our advisers, we developed schedules for base case and accelerated exit strategies, and estimated returns on these trajectories on a program-by-program (and often investment-by-investment) basis. These estimates were frequently revised over time, in light of the results of our exit strategies as well as changes in financial markets and company conditions.

Public Offerings, Auctions, and Other Exit Strategies

We developed different strategies for sales depending on characteristics of the investments, including, in particular, liquidity. In each case, we sought market-driven and/or competitive pricing, so that the process was fair and defensible and to avoid forced selling. Our methods included public offerings, private offerings, at-the-market "dribble out" programs, negotiated repurchases, and auctions. As noted earlier, some restructurings also resulted in sales to an acquirer.

Where a public market for an investment existed, we typically chose to sell into that market. For example, we made six public offerings of AIG common stock, the first being a "re-IPO" in light of AIG's absence from the public markets. Two of these offerings included concurrent issuer re-

27. OFS, *Agency Financial Report,* 2009, 47, https://www.treasury.gov/initiatives /financial-stability/reports/Documents/OFS%20AFR%2009.pdf.

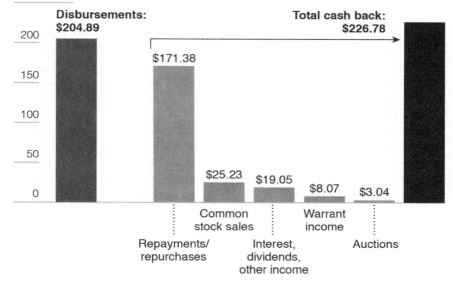

$250 billion

Disbursements:
$204.89

Total cash back:
$226.78

$171.38

$25.23　$19.05

$8.07　$3.04

Common
stock sales

Warrant
income

Repayments/
repurchases

Interest,
dividends,
other income

Auctions

Figure 14.4　Exit Method, by Dollar Volume: CPP

Note: A total of 137 institutions refinanced from the Capital Purchase Program (CPP) to the SBLF, representing $2.21 billion. In addition, 28 institutions exchanged their securities from CPP to the CDCI program, totaling $363 million. Figures as of July 2019.

Sources: Congressional monthly report and transaction report

purchases at the same price, which we believe were critical to the overall success. Our second-to-last AIG offering constituted the largest equity offering ever done as of that date ($21 billion). The AIG exit was complex because of the company's ongoing restructuring and because we assisted the Federal Reserve on the exit from its additional investments in AIG, the so-called Maiden Lane II and III investments. (See box, "A Time for Dynamite?")

The public trading of GM stock had ceased as a result of the company's bankruptcy. We conducted an initial public offering of GM stock, which was the largest IPO at the time. We also negotiated a repurchase by GM of some shares. Chrysler repaid debt and bought back our remaining position in a negotiated transaction. Ally involved private and public offerings. In the case of GM as well as Citigroup, we also established "dribble out" programs where

A Time for Dynamite?

We knew getting out of our investment in AIG would be difficult, but we did not anticipate what would happen on October 22, 2010, when AIG launched the offering to sell AIA, its Asian subsidiary. The Hong Kong underwriters contacted us to get the share certificates, which were pledged to Treasury. They wanted them flown to Hong Kong that Friday night so they could be delivered at the closing early the next week. But the certificates were in a vault at the Bank of New York Mellon (BNY), which had already closed for the weekend. The vault was on an automatic timer and would not open again until Monday morning.

"We have to blow the door off the vault," said a Treasury attorney. Others said that was crazy. But how else could we get the certificates to Hong Kong on time?

After much discussion and consultation with the vault manufacturer, BNY officials agreed to blow off the door, provided Treasury would reimburse the cost to repair or replace the vault, whatever it was. That made the Treasury lawyers pause. Even though $18 billion was at stake, no one wanted to sign off on an uncertain expense that was likely to be tens of thousands of dollars. They knew how frugal we were.

They tracked down Tony Salvatore, the OFS director of investment operations, figuring he would take responsibility. Tony was at a hospital in New Jersey because his father-in-law had just suffered a heart attack. His response was understandably terse and surprisingly negative: "It's too expensive. Tell the Hong Kong people they will have to close on the basis of a PDF copy, and we will deliver the share certificates later." He turned off his Blackberry and went back to his father-in-law.

The lawyers advising Treasury doubted this would work. But they dutifully followed their client's instructions, and after many phone calls, the Hong Kong underwriters agreed. "We just kept telling them, 'We are the U.S. Treasury; you have to trust us on this one.'"

In the end, the deal closed on time, $18 billion was transferred, and the certificates arrived a few days later.

---

incremental sales were made into the public market at the market price over time. We negotiated for very low underwriting fees by comparison with market standards in all of these transactions.

To dispose of the bank and other warrants, which were severable, we created a process under which a company had the option to repurchase them when it repaid TARP funds. We established criteria for determining price to ensure consistency across issuers.

If an issuer could not repay the CPP preferred stock, or if it repaid but chose not to repurchase the warrants, we established auction platforms in which third parties could bid to purchase the securities. Because the bank warrants were exercisable for common stock, we worked with the bank regulators to ensure that regulatory ownership restrictions were observed.

Avoiding Premature Disclosure of Exit

We did not announce any schedules or plans for the sale of specific investments to the market until we were ready to make a sale (beyond articulating the general exit principles noted earlier). In this way, we sought to minimize the risk that market participants might "front run," or trade against us. This allowed us to retain flexibility when there were different methods for exit. Nevertheless, some of the oversight agencies pressed us to announce our strategies and timetables in advance.

Coordination with Regulators

We notified bank regulators whenever we planned to sell a bank investment; however, they did not share confidential supervisory information with us, nor did they offer advice on exit strategies, such as when we should sell or how we should restructure a troubled investment. Although sharing information might have been useful to our decision-making, the principle of keeping supervisory information confidential was more important.

Unique Securities Law Challenges

We implemented special procedures to comply with securities laws in dispositions. The concern was not simply whether an offer and sale needed to be registered under the Securities Act but also whether it was compliant with the requirement that a selling shareholder not have material nonpublic information. Even though there were potential exceptions to the applicability of that standard in Treasury's case (including defenses based on sovereign immunity), we used our best efforts to make sure Treasury complied.

Before each sale, we implemented a process to confirm that no employee of OFS or officials up the chain, including the secretary, had any such knowledge.

We decided it was not appropriate or necessary, however, to go beyond that—so as to include the Office of the Comptroller of the Currency or the IRS, both of which are independent bureaus within Treasury. We faced a related concern as to whether one of the four agencies overseeing us—the Special Inspector General for TARP (SIGTARP), which was also part of Treasury and obviously closer to TARP—had such information. But SIGTARP was unwilling to share confidential information about its investigations, so we made the best decisions we could as to whether a serious probe of a company was pending.

TRANSPARENCY AND ACCOUNTABILITY: FINANCIAL CONTROLS AND REPORTING

The desire to maintain high standards of transparency and accountability affected all aspects of our operations. A critical part of achieving that goal was to build and maintain strong accounting and financial reporting systems. In addition, we made it a priority to provide timely and accurate reports about the program and post detailed information on our website.

Building an operation with strong controls was critical given the size of TARP, the discretion afforded Treasury in how to spend the money, and the public controversy over the program. Accurate financial statements and credible cost estimates, as well as processes to prevent misappropriation or abuse of funds, were essential to establishing and maintaining public confidence.

We retained an accounting firm to establish and document internal controls for each program as it was built. Accounting and reporting flowed directly from the program documentation. We retained a separate accounting firm to serve as internal auditor to review transactions as soon as they were booked. Although we used Treasury's general ledger system for top-line reporting, we also created internal systems (transaction processing and accounting sub-ledgers that held all the material terms of the transactions). This allowed us to transmit data directly to the cost models discussed in this chapter, which was key.

The law required the production of stand-alone financial statements for TARP that were audited by the Government Accountability Office (GAO). Our goal was to achieve unqualified audit opinions on those financial statements with no material weakness, including in the first year. We met that goal every year.

Estimates as to what the fiscal cost of TARP would be were a flash point in the public debate. For example, the Congressional Budget Office (CBO) estimated in January 2009 a subsidy cost of $64.9 billion, or about 26 percent of the initial $247 billion in investments. Many thought Treasury would lose even more.[28] EESA required that TARP's cost be calculated in accordance with the Federal Credit Reform Act of 1990 (FCRA) but using a discount rate adjusted to reflect market risk. This rate requirement was highly unusual for FCRA accounting. Moreover, there was no precedent nor any applicable government guidance on how to apply FCRA requirements to TARP's complex loan and equity investment transactions. There was also not enough time to seek a ruling from the Federal Accounting Standards Advisory Board. We had to build cost models in accordance with FCRA concepts and this rate requirement that could withstand substantial scrutiny from the GAO, the Office of Management and Budget (OMB), and others.

Given the lack of expertise or precedents in this area, we put together a team that combined people from the public sector (who understood FCRA) and the private sector who understood how to translate the complex transaction agreements into budget (cost) models and accounting records. We developed and revised these models over time.

REPORTING TO CONGRESS AND THE PUBLIC

In addition to our obligation to produce audited financial statements and cost accounting in accordance with FCRA, Treasury was required by EESA to provide several reports to Congress. These reports included notifications of asset purchases, sales and other transactions within two days, extensively detailed monthly reports on all programs as well as operating expenses, and periodic "tranche" reports providing, among other things, pricing information.

In addition, we produced a publicly available annual report that was more like that of a large corporation than of a typical government agency. Besides the audited financial statements, this report contained detailed accounting and cost reporting data as well as an extensive section on management's discussion

28. Congressional Budget Office, *The Troubled Assets Relief Program: Report on Transactions through December 31, 2008,* Jan.16, 2009, www.cbo.gov/sites/default/files/111th-congress-2009-2010/reports/01-16-tarp.pdf.

and analysis. The report won a government-wide award for clear presentation of complex information.[29]

We provided extensive additional reporting and information beyond what was required by law. Our website contained all program documentation forms, all executed program contracts and related documentation, and a list of all contracts entered into with third parties for services (such as law firms and accounting firms) and their material terms. The website also contained a daily TARP update, providing a snapshot of the amounts disbursed and recovered for each program. Anyone could see exactly what had been disbursed to whom for any investment, and the status of repayment or return of such funds. We created an interactive "TARP Tracker" that showed disbursements and collections for each program and contained descriptions and links to program details. We issued annual retrospective reports on the program that provided extensive detail. We produced additional reports on the disposition of warrants. The website lists more than 3,400 reports as of July 1, 2018.

For the housing program, we posted all program-related documentation on the website (including a lengthy MHA handbook setting forth all relevant requirements and guidance) as well as several periodic reports. These included the quarterly housing compliance scorecards described earlier, a monthly report on HAMP metrics, a monthly report on HAMP servicer activity by area, and reports on the Hardest Hit program. We also made available the HAMP loan-level data files on an anonymous basis.

Although we posted a lot of information about disbursements, collections, and cost estimates, there was a great deal of misunderstanding of basic facts among the public. Communicating the *fiscal cost* of TARP, as well as its *value* to the economy, was difficult, and it is probably fair to say we never succeeded.

Many people saw the program simply as a bailout for Wall Street; our explanations that stabilizing the financial system helped, even saved, Main Street did not resonate. And many assumed that the full amount authorized—$700 billion—was spent and was never coming back. (Numerous media stories began with a reference to "the $700 billion bailout.") The reality is that the

---

29. The Office of Financial Stability was awarded the Certificate of Excellence in Accountability Reporting by the Association of Government Accountants for four consecutive periods (2009, 2010, 2011, and 2012). See U.S. Department of the Treasury, *Agency Financial Report,* Office of Financial Stability—Troubled Asset Relief Program, Fiscal Year 2013, vii, https://www.treasury.gov/initiatives/financial-stability/reports/Documents/AFR_FY2013_TARP-12-11-13_Final.pdf.

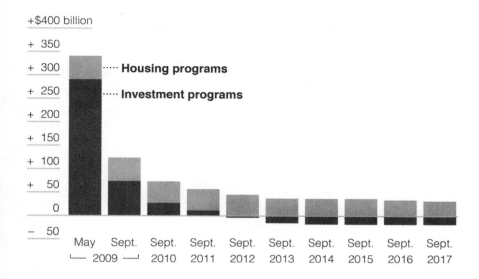

+$400 billion
+ 350
+ 300 ····· **Housing programs**
+ 250 ····· **Investment programs**
+ 200
+ 150
+ 100
+ 50
    0
− 50

May   Sept.   Sept.   Sept.   Sept.   Sept.   Sept.   Sept.   Sept.   Sept.
└─ 2009 ─┘   2010   2011   2012   2013   2014   2015   2016   2017

Figure 14.5 **Historical TARP Lifetime Cost Estimates**

Note: Includes proceeds from Treasury's additional AIG shares. Figures are on a net
present value basis. Negative costs reflect lifetime estimated income.

Source: OFS annual agency financial reports

net cost to taxpayers was just $12 billion after recovering $433 billion of the
expected total disbursements of about $445 billion, even including the $33 billion for housing assistance that was never intended to be repaid.[30] These fiscal
cost numbers, of course, do not take into account the incalculable value of stabilizing the financial system and the economy. (See Figure 14.5.)

30. While achieving a positive return is not necessarily a measure of success, we note
    the amount here because there was so much confusion about it. The total recovery of
    $433 billion includes amounts repaid, interest, dividends, gains on sales of warrants,
    and $17.55 billion in proceeds received by Treasury from its additional shares in
    AIG. Because those AIG shares originally came from the trust created by the Federal
    Reserve in connection with its initial loan to AIG rather than from a TARP
    disbursement, the proceeds are not included in official cost estimates for TARP. The
    most recent CBO estimate, which does not include the proceeds, is a net cost of
    $32 billion, or essentially the amount spent on the housing programs. Although the
    authority to obligate funds expired on October 3, 2010, Congress authorized an addi-
    tional $2 billion in unspent TARP money for the Hardest Hit Fund in Decem-
    ber 2015, which is included in these totals.

LESSON LEARNED: COMMUNICATION

We did not create a communications unit within OFS and instead relied on Treasury's public affairs department. The White House also had views about TARP communications. In retrospect, more resources devoted to communications might have been helpful, though we cannot say whether this would have changed the fundamental perceptions of TARP.

AN OVERDOSE OF OVERSIGHT?

TARP was the subject of excessive oversight.

As noted, EESA provided for oversight by four entities: the Congressional Oversight Panel (COP), SIGTARP, the GAO, and the Financial Stability Oversight Board (FinSOB).[31] In addition, numerous committees of Congress had extensive oversight roles, including the Senate Banking Committee, House Financial Services Committee, and House Committee on Oversight and Government Reform, as well as many subcommittees.

We believe strongly that oversight of TARP was essential. It contributed to accountability and transparency and certainly kept us on our toes. But the fact that we were monitored by four agencies that had largely overlapping responsibilities created layers of duplication and put enormous demands on our staff. At times, it made implementation of the program more difficult.

The FinSOB, created by EESA, consisted of five senior officials involved in the crisis response, including the Treasury secretary and the chairman of the Federal Reserve. It met monthly with OFS leadership to review the program's progress and to provide advice on design and implementation. It did not have its own staff.

COP and SIGTARP were created by EESA specifically for TARP. Both built up significant staffs and operations. COP was required by law to produce one report a month. SIGTARP produced a quarterly report as well as additional

---

31. Secretary Paulson recounted in his book *On the Brink: Inside the Race to Stop the Collapse of the Global Financial System* (New York: Business Plus, Hachette Book Group, 2010), 307–8, how the members of Congress with whom he negotiated the legislation all agreed there were too many oversight agencies, but no one wanted to give up a favorite. To get the legislation passed, he reluctantly accepted all of the agencies.

reports and audits. COP, SIGTARP, and GAO issued more than 170 reports (including audits) on TARP.

Each of these three entities operated independently and generally did not coordinate their work. They wrote reports on the same subjects and often proposed different and conflicting recommendations. We often disagreed with the merits of those recommendations.[32]

Our staff spent significant time responding to extensive and often duplicative document production and interview requests from the oversight agencies and Congress. And we also had moments of contention. At one point, SIGTARP sought to prevent OFS employees whom it wished to interview from bringing a lawyer, if they wanted one. We believe this led to intimidation of our employees that was not constructive.

At times, there were more overseers than employees implementing TARP. Indeed, SIGTARP alone had more full-time equivalent staff than OFS from fiscal year 2012 onward (see Figure 14.6). Even now, SIGTARP has more than 100 employees, whereas OFS has fewer than 30.

CONCLUSION

TARP worked. Its implementation was efficient and nonpartisan. Its fiscal cost was minimal. Its value—by helping to prevent another Great Depression—was enormous.

While the circumstances that led to the creation of TARP were deeply regrettable, we have no reservations about declaring its administration a success. There were mistakes and failings—we have noted some and undoubtedly there were others. But in the middle of the worst financial crisis since the Great Depression, a group of people came together to create a program of enormous scale and complexity from scratch. They designed it to operate seamlessly

---

32. For example, the housing programs were criticized for not reaching more people, yet one of the few specific recommendations made by one oversight agency was that we require notarized signatures and thumbprints of all applicants. That would have surely intimidated some applicants, slowed down administration, and resulted in fewer modifications. When it came to exiting investments, some of the oversight agencies called on us to commit to and disclose specific strategies before we struck a deal or made an arrangement to sell. We believed this would have only reduced our flexibility and leverage, thereby likely reducing returns to the taxpayer. We felt public transparency was properly served by disclosure of our general plans followed by specific disclosures once a transaction was agreed to or executed.

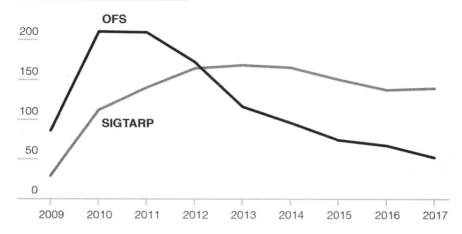

Figure 14.6 Staffing History (Full-Time Equivalents): Office of Financial Stability and Special Inspector General for TARP

Source: President's Budget appendixes

across two administrations, to be flexible enough to accommodate wide-ranging programs in a rapidly changing economic environment, to be temporary, and to protect taxpayers, first by stabilizing the financial system and then by getting their money back. And they succeeded—in the best tradition of public service.

We again thank the terrific group of people from the public and private sectors with whom we worked. They stepped forward and put in long and hard hours because they wanted to help the country. It was a privilege to work with them. We do not wish to repeat the experience, but we are grateful and proud to have been part of this effort to respond to a national crisis.

CHAPTER FIFTEEN

Monetary Policy during the Financial Crisis

DONALD KOHN AND BRIAN SACK

INTRODUCTION

The Federal Reserve's monetary policy was critical to the government's response to the financial crisis. Like other policymakers, Fed officials were required to come up with new, untested approaches when conventional policies were exhausted and more support for the economy was needed. Because there were no comparable precedents, policymakers operated under tremendous uncertainty—about the evolution of financial conditions, the impact of those conditions on the economy, and the efficacy of the tools at their disposal. The fog of war enveloped the Fed's monetary policy decision-making body, the Federal Open Market Committee (FOMC), just as it did other policymakers over that period.

Given the magnitude of the disruptions to the financial system, monetary policy easing was not, by itself, capable of preventing a recession or sparking a rapid rebound from the downturn once it occurred. The flight to liquidity and safety by investors led to sharp declines in asset prices, considerable pressure on many lenders, and a breakdown in the functioning of financial markets, causing credit to households, businesses, and state and local governments to become scarcer and more expensive before drying up entirely in the fall of 2008. A self-reinforcing dynamic of tightening credit conditions and worsening economic outcomes emerged.

Stemming this dynamic required action across a broad front, as detailed in other chapters in this volume. The Fed and other arms of the federal

The authors would like to thank Ben S. Bernanke, Timothy F. Geithner, David Wessel, J. Nellie Liang, David Wilcox, David Stockton, and Bob Tetlow for their comments, as well as Ankit Mital for his research support.

government guaranteed debt, served as a lender of last resort, rebuilt capital in the financial system, and provided fiscal stimulus when private demand collapsed. All those efforts were important for restoring confidence in financial firms, restarting markets, and getting credit flowing again. That said, monetary policy played an essential role, given that it is among the most visible policy actions with the widest effects on financial conditions. Financial markets, as well as businesses and households around the world, looked to the Fed to respond, and the central bank repeatedly pledged to employ all available tools to promote economic recovery and preserve price stability.

The FOMC reacted forcefully and creatively to the unfolding situation in ways that mitigated some of the detrimental consequences of the financial distress on household wealth and on the safety and soundness of banks and other intermediaries. In addition, the lower interest rates and higher asset prices that resulted from monetary policy actions were essential to encouraging a rebound in spending once the financial system had been stabilized.

None of the policymakers had ever experienced anything like the rolling crisis atmosphere that began in 2007, making it difficult to anticipate the severity of the disruptions that would take place and to project the extent of the damage to spending and employment that would result. Adding to the challenge, Fed officials at times were constrained by the perceived costs of the policy innovations they developed, even though, in hindsight, these costs turned out to be less serious than many feared at the time. Overall, the experience of setting monetary policy through this period provides some important lessons for future officials should they ever find themselves in a remotely similar situation.

A CRISIS-DRIVEN ENVIRONMENT FOR MONETARY POLICY DECISIONS

We begin with a narrative of monetary policy decisions over the financial crisis period, focusing on information that was available to policymakers in real time. It is helpful to break this history into two periods. The first ran from August 2007 through August 2008, when the primary challenge was calibrating the negative effects of the crisis on the economy and the appropriate degree to which the federal funds rate—the overnight interest rate that is the traditional policy instrument of the Fed—should respond. The second began in September 2008, when the trajectory of market disruption and recession steepened and the nominal federal funds rate fell to almost zero, so that policy was constrained by the so-called zero lower bound (ZLB), and the FOMC had to innovate to stimulate economic activity.

AUGUST 2007 THROUGH AUGUST 2008

Over the spring and early summer of 2007, financial markets began to feel the tremors of the oncoming financial crisis. House prices were declining, and the prices of securities tied to subprime loans were plummeting. Markets for those securities became illiquid, and they were hard to value, making it difficult to judge the creditworthiness of those holding them. Nonetheless, the broader economy was doing reasonably well. The unemployment rate was somewhat below the level the Fed staff and many others thought sustainable over the long run, and headline and core inflation were running just above 2 percent.

The financial tremors intensified in August 2007, when a French bank, BNP Paribas, suspended redemptions in three investment funds holding U.S. subprime mortgage securities. That news fed already rising doubts about the health of banks and nonbanks with similar exposures. Lenders of unsecured funding for banks began to demand larger risk premiums, especially for loans extending beyond a few days. Other funding sources for holders of subprime-related assets, such as commercial paper backed by these assets, began to dry up.

Through the late summer and the fall, credit conditions deteriorated further as lenders witnessed escalating risks and became far less willing to take those risks. The effects were particularly acute in mortgage markets, but banks were tightening terms and conditions across a broad swath of credit, and spreads on both investment-grade and below-investment-grade corporate bonds widened substantially.

Much of the Fed's focus over that period was on supplying liquidity to the financial sector to counter the effects of impaired funding markets. Open market operations (OMOs) to supply reserves to banks had to become more active and more generous to hold the federal funds rate at the FOMC's target given strong demand for short-term dollar liquidity, especially from foreign banks that had become quite dependent on borrowing dollars. To supplement market sources of funding, the Fed took steps to increase dollar liquidity directly to domestic and foreign banks through U.S. and foreign central bank discount windows, as detailed in other chapters in this volume.

Still, it was clear that those lending operations could not entirely counter the growing credit stringency, which at some point would begin to constrain spending. Both FOMC participants and Board staff wrestled with the extent to which their growth forecasts should be revised lower. Models provided limited guidance because they generally included only elementary financial sectors. Moreover, history pointed to examples in which financial headwinds had held back growth (the 1990–1991 credit crunch), but also to circumstances in which sharp financial market corrections had had little effect on spending in the United States (the 1998–1999 Asian financial crisis and the failure of hedge fund Long-Term Capital Management).

Incoming data on aggregate spending and employment showed little sign of weakening over the second half of 2007. The economy continued to operate near its potential, as upside inflation and inflation risks persisted because of increases in energy and food prices as well as high levels of employment. Nonetheless, the FOMC grew worried about the effects of increased credit stringency on the path of spending, leading to a cut in the federal funds rate target by a percentage point, to 4.25 percent, between August and the end of the year. We on the FOMC saw this response as adequate to keep the economy on track, with unemployment low and inflation expected to settle near 2 percent. Board staff concurred. By December, however, market participants had priced in considerably more easing of monetary policy than assumed in the staff forecast presented in the Greenbook, reflecting a darker assessment of the market turmoil and its effects.[1]

In early 2008, it became clear to Fed officials that the disruption in financial markets was becoming far more severe and was feeding through more decisively to the economy. Many banks and other intermediaries were facing greater resistance in funding markets, and they cut back on lending and market-making activity. The cost of credit for households and businesses rose, and it became increasingly difficult to tap. House prices continued to decline rapidly, equity prices fell, and credit spreads widened. The contraction in housing construction deepened, and the effects of tighter credit and lower wealth on spending became considerably more widespread, with production and employment starting to decline. By March, the Fed staff's forecast had switched to a "recession-like" scenario in which spending forecasts were weakened to reflect some of the negative dynamics typical of recessionary periods.

The FOMC's discussion focused increasingly on an adverse feedback loop between financial markets and the real economy, and the Board's staff presented estimates of losses on mortgages under a variety of house price sce-

---

1. The Greenbook is a document prepared for the FOMC by the Federal Reserve Board staff ahead of each policy meeting. It includes the staff forecast of the economy and analysis of various issues affecting the economic outlook.

narios and the feedback of those developments on the economy. But anticipating the evolution of the financial stress and its impact on the economy proved difficult; with no comparable experience to guide them, the projections failed to capture the severe, discontinuous disruptions to market functioning and credit flows that came to prevail during 2008. Financial difficulties intensified in mid-March, when the failure of Bear Stearns demonstrated the fragility of even collateralized sources of funds, intensifying the deleveraging pressures across a broad range of intermediaries. In securities markets, yield spreads jumped and equity prices fell substantially further.

The FOMC reacted to the deteriorating situation by easing policy aggressively, beginning with a 75-basis-point cut in its federal funds rate target in mid-January before its scheduled meeting, followed by an additional 50-basis-point reduction at the scheduled meeting at the end of the month. The funds rate was reduced a further 75 basis points in March after the Bear Stearns collapse, and an additional 25 basis points in April. Altogether, over the first four months of 2008, the target was cut by 225 basis points, to 2 percent. Those decreases were seen as enough to prevent a substantial deterioration in employment—though not enough to hold the economy at full employment. The staff forecast in April predicted an unemployment rate of 5.75 percent at the end of 2008 and 5.5 percent at the end of 2009, under an assumption that policy would ease a further 25 basis points in June and then hold at that lower rate through the end of 2009. FOMC participants' projections of the unemployment rate clustered around the same level as the staff projection.

The behavior of inflation and inflation expectations undoubtedly influenced policy decisions not to ease more aggressively to reduce unemployment. Oil and other commodity prices spiked over the second half of 2007 and the first half of 2008, boosting headline inflation to more than 4 percent in July 2008. Core inflation measures were not immune to spillovers from commodities and a weaker dollar, remaining above 2 percent through the first half of 2008. In response, some measures of inflation expectations moved higher, adding to the FOMC's concerns about achieving its price stability objective. Although commodity prices fell sharply beginning in July 2008, inflation and inflation expectations remained a focus for the FOMC through the summer.

Moreover, economic activity in the first half of 2008 turned out to be substantially stronger than it had seemed earlier in the year. Viewed with the data that were available at the time of the August FOMC Greenbook, not only had there been no recession, but growth was estimated to have been solidly positive in the first half of 2008, at 1.8 percent, with upside surprises in many spending categories. The economic expansion was expected to continue in the second half, albeit at an anemic pace of less than 1 percent. Indeed, at the Jackson Hole conference in August 2008, Stanley Fischer (then governor of the Bank of Israel) mused: "The disconnect between the seriousness of the financial crisis and the impact—so far—on the real economy is striking."

In this environment, the FOMC kept its policy rate at 2 percent at its June and August meetings and cited upside risks to inflation along with downside risks to growth in its announcements.

As the FOMC wrestled with the appropriate path of the federal funds rate, the Open Market Desk at the New York Fed (the Desk) faced challenges related to the implementation of policy decisions. Achieving the FOMC's federal funds rate target on a consistent basis was proving difficult given the considerable volume of reserves flowing into the system from borrowing under the various new liquidity facilities. Those facilities were intended to address problems in various funding markets, but they also created a degree of liquidity in the overnight funding market that threatened to undermine the Desk's control of the federal funds rate.

At the time, the Federal Reserve was not permitted to pay interest on those reserve balances, and banks' efforts to shed reserves and invest in interest-earning assets would have reduced the federal funds rate to well below the FOMC target.[2] To hold the funds rate to the target, the Desk attempted to absorb the extra reserves by selling assets; it redeemed and sold $275 billion of Treasury securities over the first eight and a half months of 2008. But the Federal Reserve System's supply of Treasuries was limited, potentially constraining the Desk's capacity to drain reserves.[3] Facing such constraints, Bill Dudley (then the head of the Desk) announced at the August meeting that an agreement had been reached with the Treasury for it to issue special bills and to deposit the proceeds in its Federal Reserve account to absorb reserves (the

2. Another challenge was the volatility of the demand for reserves, even on an intraday basis. The funds rate often traded firm to the target in the morning, amid strong demand from European banks, but then dropped precipitously in the afternoon, reflecting the Desk's provision of extra reserves to lean against the earlier tightness, leaving considerable uncertainty about the amount of reserves that needed to be injected on any given day.
3. In addition, some amount of Treasuries was required to operate the Treasury Securities Lending Facility, which was aimed at supporting market functioning by exchanging Treasury securities for less-liquid assets on the balance sheets of the broker-dealers.

Supplementary Financing Program, or SFP), and that the Federal Reserve was trying to gain congressional approval to accelerate its ability to pay interest on reserves to help set a floor for the federal funds rate. These steps would be activated after the collapse of Lehman Brothers in mid-September.

In financial markets, the actions around Bear Stearns—the resolution of the firm, the capital raised by the private sector, the liquidity provision to broker-dealers, and monetary policy easing—appeared to stabilize the situation and even to spark a bit of a recovery in the spring. But the underlying weaknesses at a number of intermediaries—including large commercial banks and thrifts, investment banks, and Fannie and Freddie—led once again to rising funding pressures and sharply falling equity prices by the summer, which in turn caused credit to households and businesses to become even more expensive and less available. And we now know, after many data revisions, that the economy was already in decline. The stage was set for the events of September 2008.

SEPTEMBER 2008 TO JUNE 2010

The failure of Lehman on September 15, 2008, occurred one day before a scheduled FOMC meeting. When the Committee gathered that Tuesday morning, the attention of Fed officials was fully focused on the spreading strains in financial markets in the aftermath of the Lehman failure and the potential failure of another important institution, AIG. These were immediate and severe threats to the financial system, and the implications for the economy and for monetary policy temporarily took a backseat. Indeed, with senior officials occupied with the emerging crisis, the meeting began late and was shortened. New York Fed president Timothy F. Geithner (vice chairman of the FOMC) stayed in New York. At the meeting, Chairman Ben S. Bernanke highlighted both the underlying weakness in the economic outlook and the huge uncertainty from the market disruptions. Yet the FOMC felt that it did not have enough information at that time to adjust policy, and it left the funds rate unchanged, at 2 percent.

Over the second half of September and into October, the severe stresses in a broad range of financial markets dominated the attention of the FOMC and the Fed staff. The resulting sharp reduction in business and household spending quickly became apparent. The financial panic was global, with the viability of major financial institutions everywhere called into question. All of those institutions strove to protect themselves by hoarding liquidity and curtailing lending, propelling the global economy into a deep recession. In the United

States, employment entered a free fall; the economy was shedding jobs at a pace of more than 600,000 per month by the end of the year, with no end in sight.

As with the earlier phases of the financial crisis, efforts to stem the panic and limit the damage to the economy involved a broad array of policy innovations. The FOMC cut its interest rate target by 50 basis points in early October in an action coordinated among the major central banks. That action, discussed in more detail in Chapter 17, was important in making the move toward monetary accommodation global in scope, and it was hoped that the sight of the key central banks working together would bolster confidence.

But that wasn't enough to counter the fear gripping the economic system and meaningfully limit the sharp declines in output and employment that were taking place. The FOMC took another 50 basis points off its federal funds target three weeks later, at the October meeting, lowering it to 1 percent. Nonetheless, many of us recognized that even more monetary policy action would be required to combat the deepening recession. Despite the easing, households and businesses were looking at sharp increases in the cost of credit and steep declines in wealth, and contacts in the business community in every Federal Reserve district expressed great concern. The projections of FOMC participants for the unemployment rate centered at just over 7 percent in the fourth quarter of 2009, with only modest improvement to just under 7 percent at the end of 2010. By any reasonable estimate, this fell far short of full employment.

An optimal-control exercise in the Bluebook[4]—a simulation designed to indicate the policy that had the best chances of minimizing deviations from the FOMC's employment and inflation objectives—indicated that if it were unconstrained by the lower bound, the federal funds rate should fall to negative 3 percent. Some FOMC participants wondered about the efficacy of additional policy easing when many transmission channels appeared clogged, but the chairman and others argued that reductions in actual and expected interest rates would help lower the cost of credit—even if it remained elevated—and stabilize asset prices.

At the end of the meeting, the chairman instructed the staff to update the analysis of monetary policy near the zero lower bound that it had conducted

---

4. The Bluebook is a document focused on policy issues and alternative policy choices for the FOMC that was written by Board staff and circulated to the FOMC in conjunction with the Greenbook. The Greenbook and the Bluebook were combined into a single document, called the Tealbook, beginning at the June 2010 FOMC meeting.

in 2003, when the policy rate last got to 1 percent. That work would review the costs and benefits of reducing the target rate even further—to near zero—and assess the other policy tools that might be available when the federal funds rate was at its minimum.

Meanwhile, the sharp increase in the use of Fed liquidity facilities after the Lehman failure—by banks, nonbanks, and foreign central banks—outran the Desk's capacity to drain reserves, and the federal funds rate began to trade notably soft to the Committee's target, even with the additional tool to sterilize reserves provided by the SFP. Congress had accelerated the Fed's ability to pay interest on reserves, and that authority was implemented in early October. But interest on reserves did not provide the floor to federal funds trading that had been anticipated. Interest on excess reserves (IOER) was initially set at 75 basis points under the FOMC's funds rate target, and that spread was narrowed in two steps until the rate was made equal to the target in early November. Still, the balance sheet pressure on banks made them unwilling to arbitrage between the low rate in the market and the higher rate offered by the Fed, and the daily effective funds rate was persistently 50 basis points or more below the Committee's target between mid-September and the December FOMC meeting.

The market dysfunction over this period also extended to government agency and agency-guaranteed mortgage-backed securities (MBS), despite explicit Treasury support for Fannie and Freddie. Higher rates for these agency securities fed through to mortgage rates, impeding efforts to stabilize the residential real estate market. To address these issues, on November 25 the Federal Reserve announced that it would purchase up to $100 billion of agency direct obligations and up to $500 billion of agency-guaranteed MBS for the system open market account (SOMA). The announcement led to a decline in 30-year mortgage rates of more than 50 basis points.

As the FOMC gathered for its December meeting, it found itself facing dire circumstances: an economy falling further into recession, with both employment and production in steep decline, and financial markets that remained under severe strain, despite an alphabet soup of Fed facilities and additional capital from the congressionally authorized TARP. In addition, the settings of the FOMC's policy instruments had been moving over the intermeeting period in ways not anticipated at the October meeting: The Fed's securities portfolio was expanding, and the federal funds rate was trading close to zero, well below the Committee's target of 1 percent.

The discussion at the meeting was wide-ranging and intense. The Committee was provided with 21 memos from the staff on various aspects of moving the policy rate close to the zero lower bound and additional steps that could be taken. A consensus developed to act across many fronts: The FOMC needed to be aggressive in lowering the funds rate; its communications should provide some guidance on the future path of the funds rate target; it should give serious consideration to setting an explicit inflation target; and it should consider additional purchases of MBS and agency debt and expanding such purchases into longer-term Treasury securities.

Asset purchases were a new policy instrument with uncertain effects, leading to considerable debate about their use. An important point of disagreement was the relative emphasis on the asset and liability sides of the Fed's balance sheet. Many, including the chairman, thought their stimulative effects derived primarily from securities purchases driving down mortgage and other longer-term rates (and of lending programs reducing the cost of funding). At the meeting he noted, "In this case, rather than being a target of policy, the quantity of excess reserves in the system is a byproduct of the decisions to make these various types of credit available."[5]

Several participants, however, focused on the liability side of the balance sheet—bank reserves or the monetary base (bank deposits at the Federal Reserve plus currency)—in judging policy. They stressed the importance of expanding these measures to protect against deflationary psychology gaining traction. For example, at the meeting Richmond Fed president Jeff Lacker argued, "At the end of the day, monetary policy is about controlling the monetary base or bank reserves. . . . What is important about the nonstandard tools and credit market programs is their effect on the monetary base." Although most of the Committee shared Chairman Bernanke's perspective, the other viewpoint was part of the policy debate. It also played a role in the public discussion of asset purchases, including use of the label "QE," for quantitative easing, rather than the term "LSAPs," for large-scale asset purchases (which was used internally), or the chairman's preferred "credit easing."

As for the policy stance, the FOMC reduced the target range for the federal funds rate to 0 to 25 basis points, effectively adopting the level that the market had already reached. We endorsed the purchases of MBS and agency debt that had already been announced. At the same time, we indicated that we were giv-

5. "Meeting of the Federal Open Market Committee on December 15–16, 2008," transcript, 26, https://www.federalreserve.gov/monetarypolicy/files/FOMC20081216meeting.pdf.

ing serious consideration to additional easing by announcing our readiness to expand such purchases "as conditions warrant" and that we were "evaluating the potential benefits of purchasing longer-term Treasury securities." Moreover, we announced that we saw near-zero interest rates persisting "for some time" to head off any market expectations that the sharp easing of policy would soon be followed by a tightening, as had often occurred after more garden-variety recessions.[6]

By the time of the March FOMC meeting, the Obama administration had come into office, and its plans for shoring up the banking system and providing fiscal stimulus were becoming clearer. It was also evident, however, that the economy was in an even steeper decline than the very serious recession that had been foreseen at recent FOMC meetings. In addition, there were still grave concerns globally about the viability of many large financial institutions, despite government capital injections and declarations that systemically important institutions would not be allowed to fail. Fighting for their lives, banks continued to tighten the availability of their loans to households and businesses. Securities and securitization markets remained badly impaired.

The adverse feedback loop between the real economy and financial markets was on vivid display. The Greenbook made major downward revisions to its forecast of GDP growth, upward revisions to expected unemployment, and downward revisions to projected inflation. The unemployment rate was expected to peak at 9.5 percent and core inflation to drop to 0.5 percent in 2010. Recovery would be painfully slow, with the unemployment rate expected to decline only slowly, to 5.6 percent by 2013, and inflation was expected to remain below 1 percent. Reflecting these revisions, another optimal-control exercise for the Committee now suggested that, if it were unconstrained, the federal funds rate should be reduced to negative 6.5 percent to promote timely recovery. More monetary accommodation was desperately needed. With short-term rates at zero, we were left with two instruments—asset purchases and forward guidance. We deployed both at the March meeting.

On asset purchases, the FOMC extended the horizon and increased the pace meaningfully, promising to buy up to an additional $1.15 trillion by year-end—$750 billion of MBS, $100 billion of agency debt, and $300 billion of Treasuries. The staff forecast, the discussion at the meeting, and the reports from the

6. See the Dec. 16, 2008, FOMC statement, available at https://www.federalreserve.gov /newsevents/pressreleases/monetary20081216b.htm.

Fed districts were so downbeat that we readily reached agreement to do even more than the most accommodative policy option (Alternative A) included in the set of options circulated before the meeting, a distinct break with FOMC tradition. At the same time, we firmed up our forward guidance by noting that the near-zero rates were likely to persist "for an extended period." In the ritualized communication between the FOMC and market participants, an "extended period" was intended to be, and was interpreted as, longer than "some time."

These were the last substantial monetary policy actions taken until the fall of 2010, when disappointing economic growth would lead the Committee toward another round of asset purchases. From the spring of 2009 through the spring of 2010, incoming data on the economy and financial markets indicated that the recovery broadly was following the path expected: GDP growth recovered and the unemployment rate leveled out and showed signs of turning lower; core inflation, though not falling as far as had been feared, remained quite low; and financial conditions stopped tightening and began to improve.

But that outcome was hardly satisfactory: In its projections made over that period, the FOMC expected to undershoot both its employment and price stability objectives for many years to come. The staff estimated that the economic effects of the negative 6.5 percent funds rate level from the March exercise could be roughly replicated by additional asset purchases of about $2 trillion—much more than the $1.15 trillion undertaken. Yet we took no further steps until the outlook deteriorated further.

The decision not to take even larger policy actions reflected the perception that the benefits and costs associated with additional asset purchases appeared to be roughly balanced, even with those unsatisfactory economic outcomes. The benefits were seen as highly uncertain, with some FOMC members expecting a limited effect on long rates once market liquidity had been restored. On the cost side, various Committee members continued to worry about exiting, about affecting the allocation of capital in the economy by purchasing mortgage-backed securities, and about risking unanchoring inflation expectations by being perceived as "monetizing the debt" in our purchases of Treasury securities.[7]

---

7. Concerns about the fuzzier borders between monetary and fiscal policy that had developed in the crisis response were widely enough held in the Committee that the chairman negotiated a published understanding with the Treasury Department on respective roles. It emphasized the importance of the independence of the Federal Reserve in the conduct of monetary policy. It noted that the Federal Reserve was to

The policy that was in place felt extreme, and while most saw it as clearly warranted by the dire circumstances, it also prompted a sense of unease among some participants and outside observers. Indeed, a substantial portion of each FOMC meeting over this period was devoted to discussing how to exit from the unusually accommodative policy. Term deposits and reverse repurchase agreements with an expanded group of counterparties were developed to absorb excess reserves, and the sequencing of exit steps was debated. This discussion was pursued not because we were thinking of a near-term policy tightening. Rather, it was intended to make the Committee and the public more comfortable with the steps we had already taken and more accepting should additional accommodation need to be considered.

POLICY CHALLENGES ENCOUNTERED DURING THE CRISIS

As noted earlier, the FOMC had difficulty anticipating the severity of the financial crisis and its consequences for the economy, and it wrestled over the appropriate response of the federal funds rate, the use of asset purchases as an alternative policy instrument, and the role of central bank communications in shaping expectations.

THE DIFFICULTY OF ANTICIPATING THE EFFECTS OF THE FINANCIAL CRISIS

The primary responsibility of the FOMC during normal periods is to adjust the federal funds rate to the level that is appropriate given the outlook for economic conditions in order to achieve the mandate of full employment and stable prices. Making effective policy requires an assessment of the likely evolution of economic conditions—an exercise in which the Board staff's forecast plays a key role. Unfortunately, through much of the crisis period, economic projections dramatically underestimated the intensity of the financial crisis and

---

avoid credit risk and credit allocation—government influence over credit allocation was "the province of the fiscal authorities." And it stressed that purchases of securities and other actions to establish financial stability must not interfere with the FOMC's ability to accomplish its legislative objectives for monetary stability—the Treasury would work with the Fed to ensure it had the tools to absorb reserves and roll back accommodation at the appropriate time. This issue is also discussed in Chapter 3.

the severity of its negative effects on the economy. The forecast errors on output and employment that were made by the Fed staff, by FOMC participants, and by nearly all economic forecasters in the profession were massive by historical standards.

This pattern is clear in Figure 15.1, which shows the actual path of the unemployment rate compared with the paths forecasted by the Fed staff at various points in time. In December 2007, despite the financial strains that had been witnessed for months and had prompted the launch of the Term Auction Facility (TAF) and the foreign swap lines, the Board staff was forecasting only a modest rise in the unemployment rate, to 4.9 percent. For the March 2008 Greenbook, which was published when financial stress had brought Bear Stearns to the brink of failure and the Fed had launched the Term Securities Lending Facility (TSLF), the Fed staff included only a mild and short-lived recession in the forecast. The unemployment rate expected for the end of 2009 was just over 5.5 percent—about 4.5 percentage points below the level that would be realized.

Forecast errors of this magnitude are rare. Indeed, the FOMC minutes now report a measure of the amount of uncertainty that has typically surrounded economic forecasts over the past several decades. Based on that metric, the standard deviation of forecast errors for the unemployment rate at this horizon is just over 1 percentage point, implying that the error that took place in March 2008 was roughly a 4-standard-deviation outcome.

Not only was the baseline forecast too optimistic, but the Fed staff was not able to conceive of how damaging the financial crisis could become even when it explicitly set out to do so. The August 2008 Greenbook presented an alternative simulation to capture "severe financial stress," which it described as a severe deterioration in financial conditions and the emergence of solvency concerns for many institutions. This Greenbook was published amid mounting concern about Fannie and Freddie and other large financial institutions, so the possibility of further stress was not an unrealistic scenario. Nonetheless, the staff estimated that the unemployment rate would reach only 6.7 percent, just 0.2 percentage points worse than the "typical recession" scenario.

Why were economic forecasts so far off? One reason is that forecasters were not able to imagine just how stressed financial markets would become, as no one making forecasts had lived through anything like the tsunami that was overtaking the financial system. Another reason was that it was very difficult to calibrate the economic consequences of those developments, even had we known them, in part because they went beyond the scope of what was captured in our models. Indeed, although our economic models included several key

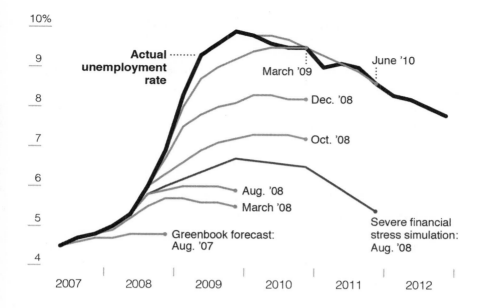

Figure 15.1 **Path of Unemployment Rate Compared with Greenbook Forecasts**

Sources: U.S. Bureau of Labor Statistics; Federal Reserve Board of Governors

variables that describe broad financial conditions, they did not contain enough detail about the financial sector to capture many critical aspects of the disruption to credit intermediation and market functioning that played out over this period. Moreover, those models were calibrated based on linear relationships estimated from moderate, more continuous adjustments in financial prices, whereas the economy was experiencing very abrupt changes and nonlinear adjustments arising from market dysfunction.

The difficulty of calibrating the effects of financial market developments is highlighted by the following exercise.[8] We took the forecast from the December 2006 vintage of the staff's primary macroeconomic model (FRB/US), adjusted to be consistent with the Greenbook forecast at the time, and we computed how the forecast would have changed in the FRB/US model if the financial sector shocks

8. We thank Bob Tetlow from the Federal Reserve Board staff for conducting this exercise for us. His expertise with the FRB/US model was critical for implementing this analysis.

that occurred over the subsequent several years had been known in advance.[9] Many of the financial variables in the model, such as credit spreads and equity prices, moved dramatically in a direction that would restrain economic growth. This exercise captures the extent to which the evolution of those financial variables explains the forecast misses described earlier. The portion that cannot be explained by these financial sector shocks is arguably a measure of how much of the financial crisis effects were "outside the model."[10]

The results, shown in Figure 15.2, indicate that the financial variables in the model would have produced a meaningful weakening of the economy, with the unemployment rate rising more than 2 percentage points. But this simulation still falls well short of capturing the magnitude and speed of the rise in the unemployment rate. That is, much of the weakening in the economy reflected the effects of financial sector developments not captured by the major financial variables included in FRB/US in 2006 and the measured sensitivities of economic conditions to those variables in that model.

This exercise, although focused specifically on FRB/US, is representative of the challenges FOMC members and Fed staff faced as they tried to assess the path of the economy over this period. The Fed staff was certainly aware of these shortcomings of economic models, and it made sizable adjustments to its models to account for the additional restraint coming from financial stress. In the September 2008 Greenbook, for example, the staff included a box on how it was incorporating judgmental effects of the financial turmoil by assuming deviations from the model's equations based on new financial stress indicators. These adjustments were enough to reduce GDP growth in 2008 by 1.5 percent-

9. More specifically, we take the realized residuals for seven financial variables relative to the values of those residuals that could be considered normal based on their history from 2003 to 2006. We then apply those shocks to the December 2006 extended Greenbook forecast to calculate how the forecast would have evolved with knowledge of those realized residuals. The variables included were the five-year Treasury term premium, the ten-year Treasury term premium, the spread of BAA-rated corporate bonds over Treasuries, the mortgage rate spread, the spread of the lending rate for consumer durable goods, the equity premium, and the nonequity wealth capital gain residual.

10. According to the FRB/US model, there were, of course, shocks other than financial market shocks that contributed to the Great Recession, including negative "demand" shocks and reductions in productivity. Whether these shocks are truly autonomous disturbances to the economy or were fundamentally induced by financial factors that are not incorporated within the model is a matter of debate.

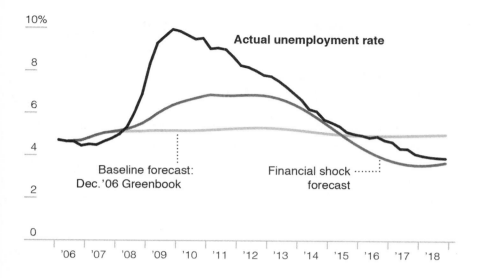

Figure 15.2 Path of Unemployment Rate Compared with FRB/US Simulation

Note: FRB/US is the Federal Reserve's large-scale estimated general equilibrium model of the U.S. economy.

Sources: U.S. Bureau of Labor Statistics; Federal Reserve Board of Governors

age points—a substantial effect. The effects on GDP growth were seen as transitory, as the adjustments lowered projected GDP growth in 2009 by only 0.2 percentage points.

With the information available at the time, policymakers faced a substantial challenge in assessing what was taking place in financial markets and the effects on the economy. Moreover, they had to formulate their decisions amid considerable uncertainty, relying on economic projections that chronically underestimated the extent of the financial disruptions and their consequences.

CALIBRATING THE APPROPRIATE RESPONSE FOR THE FEDERAL FUNDS RATE

Monetary policy eased aggressively in response to the deteriorating economic outlook, with the FOMC cutting the federal funds rate by 325 basis points by the middle of 2008. The willingness of the FOMC to act so forcefully, by historical standards, helped mitigate the negative effects of the financial crisis. The easing was not sufficient to prevent the sharp downturn in the economy, but the situation would have been even worse absent the aggressive easing.

The decline in the federal funds rate before September 2008 was about in line with what the Board staff assessed was needed to keep pace with the deterioration in the economic outlook. That pattern can be seen by looking at a policy benchmark computed by the Fed staff—the short-term equilibrium real federal funds rate (r*) consistent with the Greenbook. This measure represents the level of the real funds rate that, if maintained, would be expected to close the output gap within three years, taking into account all of the information incorporated into the staff forecast.

Figure 15.3 shows what this r* measure was reported to be in real time in the Bluebook, along with a range of similar measures computed under alternative models. The realized path for the real federal funds rate roughly kept pace with the r* measure through September 2008.

An important question is why the FOMC did not ease even more aggressively over this period. Indeed, some members of the FOMC and the Fed staff have argued that, in the presence of the zero lower bound on the policy rate, the Fed should ease more aggressively than normal in order to achieve a greater amount of accommodation and to limit the chances of getting stuck at the lower bound with a subpar outlook for economic growth.[11] In those circumstances, negative surprises could be more damaging than positive surprises, and policymakers may want to ease by more than normal to take out "insurance" against those outcomes. Thus, one might have expected the federal funds rate to be cut more quickly than was needed to keep up with the deterioration of the economic outlook. But, according to the r* measure, it appears that the FOMC did not take this approach.[12]

In retrospect, two factors prevented a more aggressive policy response. The first was that the outlook was deteriorating so quickly that the FOMC likely already felt that it was acting quite aggressively. Indeed, just keeping pace with the deterioration in the outlook required actions that were far more extreme than the more deliberate and inertial approach pursued during normal peri-

11. This argument has been made by Reifschneider and Williams (2000), among others.
12. This point was noted by some policymakers in real time. In January 2008, for example, Chairman Bernanke noted that the policy setting was "making little or no allowance for risk management considerations" and that insurance could be taken out by easing by more than seemed necessary based on the baseline economic outlook.

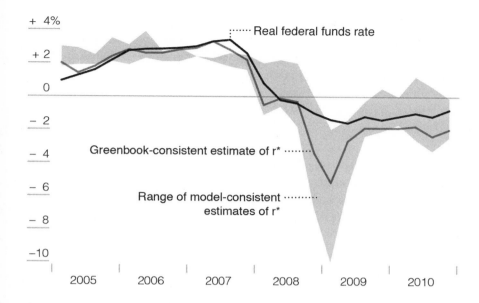

Figure 15.3 Real Federal Funds Rate Compared with Estimates of Its Equilibrium Level

Note: The equilibrium real federal funds rate (r*) is defined as the level that, if maintained, would be projected to return output to its potential over a period of 12 quarters under various economic models. The estimates shown are taken from the Bluebook/Tealbook published at that time.

Source: Federal Reserve Board of Governors

ods. The second was that the FOMC had ongoing concerns about higher inflation over much of the period before September 2008.

Another important consideration was just how low the FOMC could take the federal funds rate. The FOMC stopped at a target range of 0 to 25 basis points, but that decision was questioned by some FOMC members at the time, and the topic continued to be discussed into 2010. The arguments against moving overnight interest rates into negative territory, as presented in a staff memo in August 2010, were that doing so could impede the functioning of money markets (including strains on money market funds) and raise a variety of operational challenges. Yet several major central banks since then have taken rates into modestly negative territory, suggesting that the FOMC may wish to revisit this issue in the future.

Overall, it is clear that more-aggressive policy easing would not have prevented a deep recession, as the negative effects from financial stress were too rapid and powerful to be fully offset by a lower rate path. Nevertheless, we believe implementing additional policy easing earlier in 2008, in a manner consistent with guarding against downside risks, would have reduced the peak level of the unemployment rate to some degree.

ASSESSING THE BENEFITS AND COSTS OF ASSET PURCHASES

After the failure of Lehman, as financial conditions tightened dramatically and market functioning became impaired, the issue of calibrating the appropriate response of the federal funds rate became moot. Clearly the federal funds rate should move to the lowest level possible, which was reached in December 2008. At that point, the policy discussion turned to finding other instruments and measures that could be used to create more accommodative financial conditions and support the economy. Those included the launch of the Fed's first asset purchases, which ultimately led to a $1.75 trillion program that market participants now refer to as "QE1."[13]

The FOMC's use of large-scale asset purchases was nothing less than the creation of a new policy instrument. Although asset purchases had been previously used by the Bank of Japan, the channels through which the purchases initiated by the FOMC were expected to support the economy were novel.

Given this novelty, the FOMC entered into asset purchases after considerable debate. The key issues can be grouped into two categories—uncertainty about the effects and concerns about the associated costs. Both the benefits and the costs would have to be learned over time through experience.

As far as the benefits of asset purchases, it is important to recognize that they can serve two distinct functions. The first is to help restore market functioning, and the second is to affect interest rates and asset prices even in well-functioning markets. Both functions are aimed at making financial conditions more supportive of economic activity.

---

13. The actual amount of securities purchases in QE1 ended up being $1.725 trillion. The Fed's balance sheet expanded considerably over the next six years through a variety of additional asset purchase programs, including a second round of asset purchases launched in November 2010, the maturity extension program launched in September 2011, and a third round of asset purchases launched in September and December 2012 (for MBS and Treasury securities, respectively). When all of the programs were concluded, the Fed's securities holdings would stand more than $3.5 trillion above the levels in place before the financial crisis.

The first part of QE1 was largely aimed at restoring market functioning in the housing agency and agency-backed MBS markets, and it was successful in that regard. Spreads in those markets had become unusually wide, as many investors were shedding their holdings of those assets, even though the government had taken the government-sponsored enterprises (GSEs) into receivership by that time.[14] With the introduction of QE1, spreads collapsed over the first half of 2009, market functioning and liquidity improved notably, and mortgage rates fell.

This outcome was consistent with our intentions. Chairman Bernanke gave several speeches describing the asset purchase program as part of a broader package aimed at "credit easing." In October 2009, for example, he described asset purchases as part of a package (which included the numerous liquidity facilities that had been launched) "to address dysfunction in specific credit markets" and said that "the effectiveness of policy support is measured by indicators of market functioning, such as interest rate spreads, volatility, and market liquidity." Through the narrow lens of MBS market functioning, QE1 was a success.

The positive effects on market functioning, however, had largely played out by mid-2009, when the Desk was less than halfway through implementing the QE1 program. The simple narrative that QE1 was all about market functioning, and hence was entirely different from subsequent asset purchase programs, is not accurate. The FOMC had broader transmission channels in mind, especially when it expanded the program in March and included Treasury securities. Large-scale purchases, by taking duration risk out of the market, were intended to reduce the term premium, or the extra return demanded by investors for holding longer-term assets, illustrated in Figure 15.4. The resulting reduction in longer-term interest rates would cause other asset prices to rise as investors adjusted their portfolios to replace the purchased bonds and arbitrage across asset classes.[15]

14. Before the announcement of the asset purchase program in November, the Desk had already initiated a program to purchase agency discount notes to try to support that market. However, the initial announcement of QE1 brought considerably stronger support to the agency debt and agency-sponsored MBS markets.
15. It is also possible that asset purchases worked in part through the signals they provided for the path of the policy rate. Several considerations would seem to reduce the importance of that signaling—including that the FOMC was offering explicit policy rate guidance during much of the asset purchase programs, and that the FOMC repeatedly argued that large asset holdings would not prevent it from tightening policy when necessary. However, the response of market interest rates,

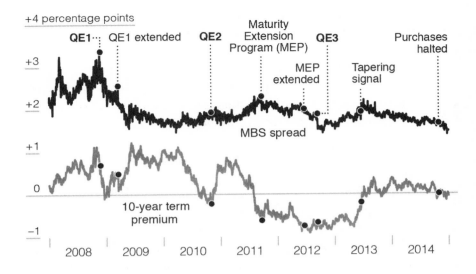

Figure 15.4 **Risk Premiums during Asset Purchase Programs**

Notes: (1) The term premium represents the excess return that investors expect to earn from purchasing a ten-year Treasury security relative to rolling over short-term Treasury investments. The estimate shown is from the Kim-Wright model. The tapering signal indicated in the figure refers to the chairman's press conference following the June 2013 FOMC meeting. (2) Acronyms used in this figure are defined in the list of abbreviations at the front of this book.

Sources: Bloomberg Finance L.P.; Federal Reserve Board of Governors (Kim-Wright model)

At the time that the decisions were being made on asset purchases, we faced substantial uncertainty about the size of their effects, given that we had little historical experience. The Committee was provided with repeated rounds of staff analysis, but that work necessarily had to draw on scant experience with this type of instrument.[16]

Looking now at the full experience with asset purchases, the consensus view in the literature seems to be that the asset purchase programs put meaningful down-

---

including at short- and intermediate-term maturities, to communications about the FOMC's intentions to taper purchases in 2013 suggest that some signaling effects were likely important.

16. It now appears that the Fed staff overestimated the effects of asset purchases to some degree at the beginning of QE1.

ward pressure on longer-term interest rates and created positive spillovers into other asset classes (see Gagnon [2016] and Kuttner [2018] for useful summaries).[17] These studies find that QE1 had the largest impact, but in addition they show that subsequent rounds in well-functioning markets also reduced longer-term interest rates. Achieving those effects in well-functioning markets, and particularly in ones with deep liquidity, required the asset purchases to be substantial.

The other major consideration was the potential costs associated with balance sheet expansion. Just as the FOMC would have to learn about the beneficial effects of asset purchases over time, it would also have to learn about undesirable side effects.

Some concerns that were forcefully voiced in the public debate were readily dismissed in internal policy discussions. The notion that a large expansion of the money base would, by itself, lead to considerable inflation and dollar weakness was largely rejected by the economic framework used by the staff and most of the Committee members.[18] In the event, undesirably low inflation persisted for years even after the extraordinary buildup in the Fed's balance sheet. Other concerns, however, were not easily dismissed at the time, including the potential consequences for market functioning should Fed purchases come to dominate transactions, and the potential complications of the Fed's eventual exit.

In general, the experience with asset purchase programs suggests that the potential costs involved were more limited than many on the FOMC feared. Treasury and MBS markets continued to function well even with relatively large holdings by the Fed, especially given the transparency around purchases implemented by the Desk and other operational steps aimed at mitigating shortages of particular securities. Inflation and inflation expectations remained low—often too low relative to the FOMC's objective—rather than rising and becoming unanchored by the balance sheet expansion. And some of the most important concerns about the exit strategy have been largely put to rest; in particular, the Desk has demonstrated that, with IOER and reverse repos with a broad set of counterparties in place, it has sufficient control of the federal funds rate even in an environment of abundant reserves. This control suggests that the sterilization of reserves, which received extensive focus

17. The research literature continues to debate the magnitude of these effects, as highlighted in Greenlaw et al. (2018) and Gagnon (2018).
18. Interestingly, this notion was the focus of much of the negative reaction by politicians, the media, and some academic economists to the asset purchase programs implemented by the Federal Reserve.

during the crisis, can be largely ignored in the future if the current framework is maintained.

On balance, concerns about the costs of balance sheet expansion did not prevent us from implementing the large asset purchase programs that were needed to support the recovery, but the sense of unease they fostered probably affected the magnitude and design of the programs. Now that we have evidence that such costs were limited, policymakers should take that into account in designing and implementing future programs, should they be needed. Of course, the asset holdings accumulated during the crisis have not been completely unwound at this point, hence we may continue to learn about the risks associated with this policy tool.[19]

SHAPING POLICY EXPECTATIONS WITH CENTRAL BANK COMMUNICATIONS

The final aspect of the FOMC's response to the financial crisis was its use of policy guidance. The initial use of guidance took place in the December 2008 statement, which said that the FOMC anticipated "exceptionally low levels of the federal funds rate for some time." That language was strengthened somewhat in the March 2009 FOMC statement, which said that the FOMC anticipated "exceptionally low levels of the federal funds rate for an extended period." Over the next several years, the FOMC engaged in a number of innovations in providing guidance to markets and the public, including the introduction of calendar-based guidance in August 2011, revisions to the calendar guidance in January 2012 and September 2012, and the introduction of economy-based guidance in December 2012. In early 2012 the FOMC also began to include the assumed path of "appropriate" monetary policy by FOMC participants in its Summary of Economic Projections.[20]

---

19. An additional concern that has been raised about QE is that it could distort asset prices and hence create financial stability problems as it is unwound. However, it is unclear whether this concern applies only to QE or also to conventional policy easing that leads to "low for long" outcomes for short rates, as those concerned about this risk often refer to "reaching for yield" as a primary channel for such distortions.
20. The Summary of Economic Projections includes projections of individual FOMC participants for key economic variables for the next several years and for the longer run. These projections are released quarterly.

The general purpose of this guidance was to flatten the path of the federal funds rate expected by financial markets, with the goal of lowering long-term interest rates and making broader financial conditions more supportive of growth. In this regard, guidance was intended to operate in the same direction as the asset purchase programs, but it would achieve those effects by altering expectations about short-term rates rather than by shifting the term premium.

The FOMC made clear it was not trying to implement a strategy of unconditional commitment where future decisions were set regardless of economic circumstances. We saw this approach as infeasible, as it both seemed too difficult to tie the hands of future policymakers and ran the risk that the committed path might prove inappropriate should economic developments fail to follow the FOMC's expectations. Nevertheless, the FOMC thought that it would be useful to use policy guidance to convey what it expected to happen, and perhaps to raise the threshold for deviating from that path.

The effectiveness of this type of communication depends on the information being conveyed. Indicating a more accommodative policy path can be counterproductive if it conveys a more pessimistic economic outlook. Alternatively, it can provide meaningful support to the economy if it conveys a more aggressive policy approach than is anticipated by market participants.[21]

When we first used the "extended period" guidance, the markets had a surprisingly hawkish view on the economic conditions that would be present at the time of liftoff from the ZLB. This can be seen in the uppermost point in Figure 15.5. Market participants at the time expected the Fed to lift off when the unemployment rate was still 5 percentage points above its equilibrium level and inflation was just below 1 percent. The most likely explanation for this perspective is that the policy stance was seen as unusual, so market participants thought that the FOMC would move away from it even when economic conditions were still challenging.

A typical policy reaction function that describes central bank behavior involves some trade-off between two variables, in that a central bank will usually be willing to wait for unemployment to fall closer to its full employment level if the level of inflation is running lower. This trade-off is captured in Figure 15.5 by the upward-sloping line, which is drawn to reflect the responsiveness found in the "balanced-approach rule" contained in the Fed's Monetary

21. See Woodford (2012) for an extensive discussion.

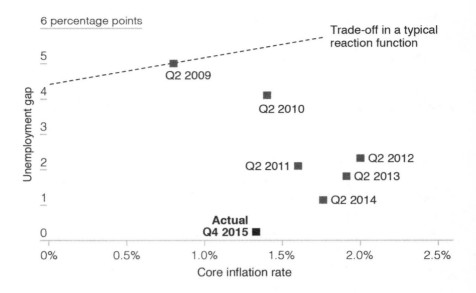

Figure 15.5 Market Expectations of Economic Conditions at Time of First Federal Funds Rate Hike

Note: The dashed line shows the set of outcomes for the two economic variables that would leave the timing of the rate hike unchanged under a typical monetary policy reaction function. A line with this slope could be drawn for each point in the chart, and shifts in the line would represent changes in the perceived reaction function.

Sources: Bloomberg Finance L.P.; Federal Reserve Bank of Philadelphia; authors' calculations

Policy Report (2018). Moving along the line reflects this trade-off under a given reaction function. Downward shifts in this line would instead convey a different, more accommodative reaction function.

The evolution of the points in the figure shows that there was an ongoing and meaningful shift of the perceived reaction function toward more accommodation—a process that was encouraged by the stronger use of guidance by the FOMC. These communication shifts were not taken as simple movements along a given reaction function, as would be the case if they simply conveyed pessimism about the state of the economy. Rather, the market was coming to the view that the reaction function itself was changing in a meaningful way.[22] That shift in perception could have been supported by a

22. The largest leg down came in 2011, likely reflecting the initial use of calendar-based guidance. The introduction of economy-based threshold guidance did not prompt

view that the guidance did involve some degree of commitment, as argued by Bernanke (2017).

In the event, the actual liftoff from the ZLB took place amid economic conditions consistent with a relatively dovish reaction function. Thus the communications helped move the perceived reaction function in the direction of what would ultimately be realized. This outcome implies that central bank communications over this period managed to make markets both more efficient (moving them toward the realized outcome) and more supportive of the economy (moving them lower) at a time that helped the FOMC meet its objectives.

The primary concern we had with the use of this tool was the possibility that market participants could misinterpret our statements as unconditional commitments. That concern was largely addressed by the language that was used, which made clear that the policy statements were conditional on the path of the economy. And though some were concerned that this conditionality might weaken the effects of the guidance, there still seemed to be considerable benefit.

The other issue widely discussed was the appropriate form of the guidance. Conditioning on economic variables rather than a calendar date was seen as a good practice, as it could make the policy information more consistent with how policy is formulated. It was not easy, however, to communicate about a complicated reaction function in a manner that was simple and easily understood.

Overall, the FOMC generally regarded any effects of guidance on the expected policy path as a powerful tool—and felt relatively comfortable with its usage, as shaping short-rate expectations is a part of policymaking during normal times as well. As a result, we were able to use policy guidance in a productive way throughout this period.

LESSONS FOR MONETARY POLICY DURING CRISIS PERIODS

The overriding theme of monetary policy through the financial crisis was one of innovation and aggressive action. We cut the federal funds rate at a rapid pace, to a lower bound that had not previously been reached in the United States. We created a new policy instrument by initiating the use of large-scale

---

any notable market response, in part because the FOMC was careful to communicate that it should be seen as consistent with the previous date-based guidance.

asset purchases. And we used policy guidance more extensively than at any time in the past. The FOMC was clearly in "uncharted waters." As a result, we learned a great deal that could help with monetary policy decisions during future periods of financial stress.

Lesson 1:
Recognize that financial developments can have substantial and highly uncertain effects on the economy during periods of financial stress.

- Central banks need to have information and expertise about a wide range of financial markets and institutions to evaluate financial developments and their effects on the economy. This point holds true at any time, but it becomes especially important during periods of financial stress, when problems can emerge in unexpected places and have more severe economic consequences.
- Policymakers must be aware of the potential for adverse feedback loops between financial developments and the economy. They should incorporate a broad range of financial effects into their economic models but should also be cognizant that models are not rich enough to incorporate all types of financial strains.
- Accordingly, policymakers have to be prepared to abandon those models and to make sizable adjustments to their forecasts, or at least take into account severe downside risks, as financial stress emerges.

Lesson 2:
Be sufficiently aggressive in cutting the federal funds rate as financial conditions deteriorate.

- Central banks may need to adjust their policy rates quickly and forcefully just to keep up with the changing outlook when severe financial strains emerge.
- Principles of risk management suggest the need for policymakers to be even bolder at times. The zero lower bound on rates presents a substantial hurdle to achieving employment and price stability objectives, and the odds of a severely negative outcome for the economy are elevated in times of financial stress. Cutting rates further and faster can provide critical support to the economy in those circumstances.

- Having inflation expectations anchored at a reasonable level in the precrisis period is critical, both for allowing aggressive actions to be taken without fear of creating persistent inflationary pressures and for having reductions in interest rates feed through to real interest rates.

Lesson 3:
Use asset purchases to achieve additional accommodation when the capacity to cut policy rates does not provide a sufficient response to economic conditions, and do so with less concern about the associated risks.

- Purchases of long-term assets do appear to reduce long-term interest rates to support economic recovery. The effects are especially large when the purchases can be used to restore the functioning of financial markets. But purchases also have beneficial effects in well-functioning markets.
- When operating in well-functioning markets, purchases of assets may need to be sizable to have meaningful effects.
- Asset purchases work through their effects on the prices of the assets acquired. The amount of high-powered money provided seems, by itself, to have little consequence for inflation or inflation expectations.
- The costs of implementing large-scale asset purchases were less severe than had been feared, and we can now be confident about the ability to raise the policy rate in a controlled manner even when the Fed's balance sheet is still large.
- Given the ability to control the policy rate, policymakers have the flexibility to design future asset purchase programs in the manner that will most effectively deliver the intended effects on financial conditions and the economy. Policymakers should not feel constrained by sterilization concerns.

Lesson 4:
Provide forward guidance on interest rates to signal a policy reaction function that differs from history or market expectations.

- Communication to shape market expectations is a natural aspect of central bank practices, and the expected path of the policy rate is a component of monetary policy transmission that is already embodied in central bank thinking and models.

- Communicating about the path of policy is especially critical when the scope to move the policy rate further is constrained by the zero lower bound.
- Because of the considerable uncertainty that surrounds periods of financial stress, significant misperceptions about the central bank's reaction function can emerge. Policy guidance can be effective at bringing market expectations more in line with central bank intentions.
- When possible, communications should focus on the policy reaction function—that is, on outcomes that are contingent on economic conditions. But experience suggests that date-based guidance can also be quite effective, especially if market expectations are stubbornly at odds with the intentions of policymakers.

Undoubtedly, the next financial crisis will differ in its origins, severity, and effects, and the policy response will have to differ in important dimensions. Still, we learned a great deal while implementing monetary policy through this crisis period, and those lessons should provide a useful compass when financial stresses emerge once again.

REFERENCES

Bernanke, B. S. 2017. "Monetary Policy in a New Era." Paper presented at Rethinking Macroeconomic Policy conference held at the Peterson Institute for International Economics, Washington, D.C., October 2, 2017.

Board of Governors of the Federal Reserve System. 2018. *Monetary Policy Report to the Congress*, July 13, 2018.

Gagnon, J. E. 2016. "Quantitative Easing: An Underappreciated Success." Policy Briefs PB16-4, Peterson Institute for International Economics.

Gagnon, J. E. 2018. "QE Skeptics Overstate Their Case." Realtime Economic Issues Watch, Peterson Institute for International Economics.

Greenlaw, D., J. D. Hamilton, E. Harris, and K. D. West. 2018. "A Skeptical View of the Impact of the Fed's Balance Sheet." U.S. Monetary Policy Forum 2018 Paper, University of Chicago Booth School of Business.

Kuttner, K. N. 2018. "Outside the Box: Unconventional Monetary Policy in the Great Recession and Beyond." Department of Economics Working Papers 2018–04, Department of Economics, Williams College.

Reifschneider, D., and J. C. Williams. 2000. "Three Lessons for Monetary Policy in a Low-Inflation Era." *Journal of Money, Credit and Banking* 32 (4): 936–66.

Woodford, M. 2012. "Methods of Policy Accommodation at the Interest-Rate Lower Bound." Economic Policy Symposium, Federal Reserve Bank of Kansas City.

CHAPTER SIXTEEN

The Fiscal Response to the Great Recession

Steps Taken, Paths Rejected, and Lessons for Next Time

JASON FURMAN

INTRODUCTION

The U.S. federal government's fiscal response to the Great Recession started when President Bush signed the Economic Stimulus Act of 2008 on February 13, 2008, and finished when the payroll tax cut enacted under President Obama expired at the end of 2012. Congress enacted at least 18 laws that explicitly included discretionary fiscal stimulus totaling more than $1.5 trillion during those five years, with about half of that coming from the American Recovery and Reinvestment Act (ARRA), which Obama signed into law on February 17, 2009.[1] The stimulus was 54 percent tax cuts, 19 percent individual transfers, 11 percent state and local fiscal relief, and 16 percent public investment—with nearly all of that public investment coming in the Recovery Act. The discretionary fiscal stimulus averaged 2.0 percent of GDP over those five years,

This chapter benefited from helpful conversations with and comments from Gabriel Chodorow-Reich, Timothy Geithner, Nellie Liang, Emi Nakamura, Henry Paulson, Christina Romer, Jay Shambaugh, Jón Steinsson, Lawrence Summers, and participants in the macroeconomic policy seminar at Harvard University. Tom Redburn made numerous excellent editorial suggestions. Roneal Desai and Wilson Powell III provided outstanding research assistance, and Deborah McClellan tried valiantly to keep me on track with this project. The fiscal response itself was designed and implemented by a large number of people in two administrations, dozens of agencies, and Congress.

1. This total does not include the Alternative Minimum Tax (AMT), Troubled Assets Relief Program (TARP), or support for the government-sponsored enterprises (GSEs).

boosting the level of economic activity from what it otherwise would have been by a maximum of 3.4 percent in the third quarter of 2010, with a smaller effect thereafter. In addition, automatic stabilizers brought the total magnitude of the countercyclical fiscal response to an average of 3.4 percent of GDP, the largest fiscal response to a recession in U.S. history.

The fiscal stimulus was an integral part of the overall macroeconomic response to the financial crisis. Absent these measures, the recession would have been much deeper and more prolonged—potentially even more so than conventional models indicate due to the possibilities of self-fulfilling vicious cycles and persistent losses in output. This stimulus acted in a synergistic manner with monetary and financial policy, helping the U.S. economy fare better than many historical precedents and outperform other countries in the wake of the Great Recession (Council of Economic Advisers [CEA] 2017).

As a result of the massive recession, incomes before taxes and transfers fell sharply for households across the income spectrum between 2007 and 2010. The combination of the preexisting automatic stabilizers and their expansion substantially cushioned this blow so that incomes after taxes and transfers rose for the bottom two quintiles and were relatively flat for the third and fourth quintiles. About half of the income gap closure for the bottom four quintiles was the result of provisions passed as part of the stimulus.

Nonetheless, the fiscal response suffered significant shortcomings, largely the result of the political difficulty of persuading Congress to sufficiently stimulate the economy in early 2009 and, later, because of the failure to win support for additional stimulus that was both large enough and more heavily weighted toward public investment.

Much of the stimulus was designed with reasonably good aggregate macroeconomic models, which have been further corroborated by the experience of 2008–2012. Knowledge of the different impacts of various types of measures, however, was much less certain than the point estimates published by macroeconomic forecasters might lead one to believe. We know only a little more today, and policymakers likely will still be flying blinder than should be the case when designing the specific composition of the next fiscal stimulus. The evidence for the overall importance of fiscal stimulus, however, is stronger than ever.[2]

2. This chapter is focused on the *macroeconomic* analysis of the fiscal response to the financial crisis and the extent to which it prevented a deeper recession and helped

THE THREE PHASES OF STIMULUS

The fiscal stimulus went through three phases: (1) an initial set of responses in 2008 that aimed to be "timely, targeted, and temporary"; (2) a large response in the Recovery Act in early 2009 that aimed to be "speedy, substantial, and sustained"; and (3) a number of laws passed in subsequent years that in retrospect could be described as opportunistic, extended, and under the radar.

THE 2008 STIMULUS: "TIMELY, TARGETED, AND TEMPORARY"

In 2007, the U.S. economy was deteriorating rapidly. Most notable was a rise in the unemployment rate from 4.4 percent in March 2007 to 5.0 percent in December 2007—a magnitude of increase that, based on historical precedent, signaled the coming of a recession that would cost many more jobs. Between September and December 2007, the Federal Reserve reduced its target federal funds rate from 5.25 percent to 4.25 percent, but because of lags in the effectiveness of monetary policy, this action was not expected to substantially bolster the economy until late 2008. In addition, the Fed took a number of other actions, such as expanding the discount window and establishing the Term Auction Facility (TAF), that had unknown efficacy and timing. As a result, many policymakers were concerned that the economy would become worse before monetary stimulus set in.

On December 5, 2007, Martin Feldstein (2007) became perhaps the first prominent economist to raise the possibility of fiscal stimulus. "The American economy is now very weak and could get substantially weaker," he wrote. "Current economic conditions call for lowering interest rates and for enacting a tax cut now that is conditioned on economic developments in 2008." Lawrence H. Summers (2007) went on to explicitly call for fiscal stimulus on December 19, 2007, saying it should aim to be timely, targeted, and temporary.

By this time, President Bush had already asked Secretary of the Treasury Henry M. Paulson, Jr., and his White House economics team to evaluate the need for a fiscal stimulus program. In January, Paulson and the White House

speed the economic recovery. It only briefly discusses other goals, like protecting the most vulnerable as well as improving infrastructure, health care, broadband, and energy efficiency. These are all very important topics but largely outside the scope of this work. See Grunwald (2012) for an excellent account of the Recovery Act and its longer-term structural legacy.

team reported back to Bush that a stimulus plan was needed urgently and could be devised in a manner that would receive broad bipartisan support and be quickly enacted. Bush wanted a package whose guiding motivation was to put money into consumers' hands quickly to provide a fast boost to the economy. On January 18, 2008, Paulson unveiled the broad parameters of a stimulus package, saying, "Our economy is growing slower than expected, and that means we need to act quickly to put together a package that is temporary, simple enough to get enacted quickly, effective at boosting growth and job creation this year, and large enough to make a difference" (Paulson 2008). This was enacted with strong cooperation by congressional Democrats in a matter of weeks and largely took the form of onetime refundable individual tax rebates. The first electronic payments were made in April 2008, and the first checks mailed out in May (Internal Revenue Service 2008).

Although the economic threat at the time appeared to be nothing worse than a typical recession, there were two prime rationales for the stimulus: (1) fiscal action could provide a faster boost to the economy than monetary policy, filling in some of the gap before the interest rate cuts started kicking in; and (2) given that the effectiveness of monetary stimulus was uncertain, it was best to diversify the response by using multiple instruments (Elmendorf and Furman 2008).

THE RECOVERY ACT: "SPEEDY, SUBSTANTIAL, AND SUSTAINED"

Despite the fiscal stimulus and further interest rate cuts, the economic and financial crisis intensified, particularly in the autumn after Lehman Brothers failed, with the unemployment rate rising from 5.0 percent to 7.3 percent over the course of 2008. By early January 2009, the numbers showed that the economy had lost an average of 510,000 jobs a month for the previous three months, a loss that was subsequently revised up to 647,000 jobs a month.

As the economy weakened, the target size of stimulus plans increased. Running for president, Obama originally proposed a fiscal stimulus in January 2008, proposed another one in April, and expanded the size of the proposed stimulus over the course of the year, including in June, August, and October. Fiscal stimulus was also motivated by the concern that the Fed, which had effectively cut its target rate to zero in December 2008, was running out of conventional monetary policy options and that all tools that relied on the financial sector for transmission to the real economy were of uncertain and potentially limited impact due to the crisis and associated breakdown of the financial system.

Building on these plans, the transition team, which included Jacob Lew, Daniel Tarullo, Jason Furman, and Austan Goolsbee, met with President-elect Obama on November 12 and presented him with the following rationale for a recommended $300 billion stimulus:

Broad expectation that economy will be anemic in 2009 and beyond: job losses are accelerating; consumption deteriorating; Blue Chip/WSJ Survey projecting negative GDP growth in the first quarter of 2009 while other analysts project negative growth for all of 2009; financially led recessions tend to last longer—Goldman Sachs projects unemployment to peak at more than 8 percent and remain high for most of 2009 and 2010.

Running out of other options: not clear where economic jump-start will come from given tight credit markets, tapped-out consumers, trading partners' following behind economic cycle and heading into recession, and a stronger dollar.

Appropriate tool in current environment: fiscal stimulus only real option since monetary tools are exhausted and there is room for monetary policy response if fiscal policy overshoots—recession risk much greater than fears of inflation and crowding out (though inflation concern will increase once a recovery is under way).

The question of whether the stimulus should be paid for was also debated during this meeting. Economically, there was no need to pay for a stimulus, and politically, the desire to move quickly and without complication to passing relief was compelling. On the other side of the argument, some were worried about the impact that rising debt would have on financial markets. Ultimately, Obama decided to advance a stimulus plan that could pass on a stand-alone basis but to make clear this was part of a longer-run budget that, taken as a whole, would make the debt sustainable.

At the time, even a $300 billion unpaid-for stimulus would have been considered large, pushing the bounds of what was possible in Congress. Any stimulus was expected to need the votes of the Blue Dog coalition, some 50 House Democrats concerned about the deficit and debt who had explicitly said they would not vote for another unpaid stimulus. House Democratic leaders had been considering a $150 billion stimulus, with some talking about packages of up to $300 billion. Leading progressive economists were advocating similar top-line numbers: A November 19 letter organized by the Center for Economic and Policy Research and signed by hundreds of economists, including George Akerlof, Dean Baker, James Galbraith, Lawrence Mishel, and Joseph E. Stiglitz, called for a $300 billion to $400 billion stimulus that would be "spent quickly" (Akerlof et al. 2008).

In an effort to create political space to pass a larger number through Congress, the transition team reached out to several signatories to encourage them to raise their public requests, advising one economist speaking to the House Democratic caucus in the late fall to call for $1 trillion in stimulus instead of the roughly $500 billion he had been planning to recommend.

The economic news and forecasts continued to deteriorate. Macroeconomic Advisers, a leading economic research and forecasting firm, made the largest negative revision to a forecast in its history on December 8. These developments plus the filling out of the Obama economic team—Christina Romer and Summers were both advocates of a much larger stimulus—led to a further upward revision of the number, with a memo to Obama stating: "We believe that $600 billion in stimulus over two years would create 2.5 million jobs relative to what would happen in the absence of stimulus. However, this falls well short of filling the job shortfall and would leave the unemployment rate at 8 percent two years from now. This has convinced the economic team that a considerably larger package is justified. . . . The memo outlines four alternative plan [*sic*] ranging from $550 billion to $890 billion with the difference between them being the state fiscal relief and tax proposals" (Summers 2008).

The upper end of this range was estimated to be sufficient to close half of the projected output gap of 7 percent of GDP. The stated rationale for not attempting to close the full output gap included the following: fiscal stimulus was not the only economic tool, concerns about spooking markets and raising interest rates with too large a fiscal package, and the view that adding to stimulus would always be possible but subtracting from it might not be.

At a meeting with the transition team on December 16, Obama decided to pursue the largest stimulus that his team thought was politically feasible, his view being that political constraints would be binding well before any economic concerns about market confidence would be relevant. This was agreed to be a stimulus in the $800 billion range, and Obama left it to his political and economic teams to develop a strategy to hit this target.

The teams decided that coming out with an explicit budget number this large would risk a backlash in Congress, slowing passage. In addition, they decided that proposing a full, explicit plan could slow passage given the limited resources of the transition team and the desire of Congress to put its stamp on the measure. Instead, publicly, Obama continued to push for the general concept of fiscal stimulus, using a job target instead of a cost target, which was originally 2.5 million jobs on November 22 but had been revised up to "at least" 3 million by December 20. Based on the economic team's analysis, this job target corresponded to at least $850 billion in stimulus. In addition, on January 8, 2009, Obama (2009a) listed a specific set of goals for these investments and framed the issue by saying: "It is not just another public works program. It's a plan that recognizes both the paradox and the promise of this moment— the fact that there are millions of Americans trying to find work, even as, all around the country, there is so much work to be done. That's why we'll invest in priorities like energy and education; health care and a new infrastructure that are necessary to keep us strong and competitive in the 21st century."

Behind the scenes, work was ongoing to have a bill well under way before the inauguration—with specific, detailed meetings with members and staff of Congress beginning immediately after the December 16 meeting. Originally, the transition team privately asked Congress for a smaller number because it was concerned about a negative reaction to a larger number, especially from the Blue Dogs, and expected that the total would increase in the legislative process. This expectation was initially justified as the House passed an $820 billion ten-year stimulus on January 28, 2009. The cost of the Senate bill passed on February 10, 2009, had a slightly higher headline number, $838 billion, although the effective stimulus was smaller than in the House bill because the Senate added an extension of a patch to the alternative minimum tax (AMT), a measure that didn't increase the effective magnitude of stimulus because it simply continued a long-standing practice that would have been included in other legislation anyway. But instead of the larger final deal the administration hoped and expected to get, the conference agreement was smaller than either the House or Senate bill, coming in at an originally estimated headline cost of $787 billion after three Senate Republicans insisted the cost come down. The effective stimulus was even smaller because of the inclusion of the AMT patch. Obama signed the Recovery Act into law on February 17.

The guiding philosophy for the Recovery Act was not "timely, targeted, and temporary" but instead "speedy, substantial, and sustained." The transition team evaluated a wide range of potential provisions against several criteria: (1) how quickly would they spend the stimulus money; (2) what was their expected multiplier for GDP; (3) how likely were they to be made permanent (which was generally viewed as a minus because of concern about the long-run deficit); and (4) how "transformative" would they be for various public purposes beyond immediately increasing GDP. The goal was to come up with a portfolio of provisions that would span short-run stimulus to long-run transformation.

Originally, the architects of the stimulus planned to have a limited set of areas for "transformative" provisions centered on health care, energy, education, and infrastructure. All of these areas were chosen to build on campaign proposals that were more long run and structural in nature but could be plausibly (or in some cases, less plausibly) separated from their broader context with a major down payment included in the Recovery Act. In some cases, these more transformative provisions were motivated less by their macroeconomic impact, instead heeding incoming White House chief of staff Rahm Emanuel's advice that you "never want a serious crisis to go to waste." For example, the campaign's health information technology spending program and energy investment program were put into the Recovery Act—while the fuller plans for health insurance coverage and cap-and-trade were left to be enacted later. Based on additional input from the transition team and Congress, more items were added to the list, including subsidies for broadband in underserved areas and funding for high-speed rail.

When Obama (2009b) signed the Recovery Act into law, he said: "Today does not mark the end of our economic troubles. Nor does it constitute all of what we must do to turn our economy around. But it does mark the beginning of the end—the beginning of what we need to do to create jobs for Americans scrambling in the wake of layoffs; to provide relief for families worried they won't be able to pay next month's bills; and to set our economy on a firmer foundation, paving the way to long-term growth and prosperity."

A *New York Times* (Stolberg 2009) headline read "Signing Stimulus, Obama Doesn't Rule Out More"—which turned out to be the case in the next phase.

POST–RECOVERY ACT: OPPORTUNISTIC, EXTENDED, AND UNDER THE RADAR

The unemployment rate continued to rise, hitting 9.4 percent in May 2009 (before the bulk of the Recovery Act had even kicked in), which was well above what forecasters had predicted as recently as early 2009. Many external and internal forecasting models used by the transition team insufficiently accounted for the role of the financial sector in exacerbating and, most importantly, perpetuating the downturn. The administration proposed more stimulus packages, including in December 2009, September 2010, and the $447 billion American Jobs Act in September 2011. All of these proposed a combination of tax cuts, relief for individuals and states, and public investment along the same lines as the Recovery Act. Congress, however, had lost its appetite for major additional legislation that was described as economic stimulus and did not enact another bill along these lines after February 2009—although the House did pass an infrastructure-oriented stimulus bill in December 2009, it was not taken up in the Senate.

Nevertheless, many of the different elements the administration proposed or Congress desired were still passed, attached to other legislation like defense appropriations bills or Federal Aviation Administration (FAA) reauthorizations. The largest opportunity came when the 2001 and 2003 tax cuts were expiring at the end of 2010. Obama had long called for the expiration of the provisions in the tax cuts that solely benefited high-income households. Republicans were in a stronger position after large gains in the midterm elections. Obama could still have pushed through the expiration of the tax cuts, but in that case, he would have had no leverage to get any additional priorities in the bill. Instead, he asked Vice President Joseph Biden to negotiate a deal with as much fiscal stimulus as possible—specifically, trading a two-year extension of the high-income tax provisions for a continuation of tax credits for low-income families with children, replacing the Making Work Pay ($58 billion annually) tax credit with a larger but less well-targeted payroll tax cut ($112 billion annually), and expanding bonus depreciation into 100 percent expensing for business investment.

This phase of stimulus was necessarily opportunistic. The administration generally wanted as much fiscal support as possible, including increased public investment and tax cuts. Congress generally wanted less stimulus but was more supportive of additional tax cuts than funding for infrastructure or other investments and more supportive of extending existing provisions than of devising new measures.

The net effect was a substantial additional stimulus: $657 billion above and beyond the Recovery Act by the end of 2012, resulting in an increase in total fiscal stimulus as a share of GDP in 2010, which was maintained at almost that level in 2011, and preventing a sharp falloff in 2012. But this funding was still well below the size Obama requested and did not have the composition the administration desired (public investment was almost entirely absent). The piecemeal nature of these additional provisions spread across at least 13 pieces of legislation, most of which were not explicitly marketed as stimulus, also sacrificed the potential benefit of clearly setting expectations and increasing confidence that a more visible stimulus package might have generated.

THE SIZE AND COMPOSITION OF THE FISCAL STIMULUS

Overall, the cumulative discretionary fiscal stimulus totaled $1.537 trillion through the end of calendar year (CY) 2012.[3] Nearly half of the fiscal stimulus came in the Recovery Act, which provided a net new $712 billion for the economy through the end of CY 2012.[4] The remainder came in at least 17 other laws that included the original 2008 rebate checks, the Cash for Clunkers program to encourage auto purchases, a tax credit for hiring the long-term unemployed, a tax credit for homebuyers, the payroll tax cut, and several additional provisions (Table 16.1).

As shown in Figure 16.1, the overall discretionary fiscal stimulus averaged 2.0 percent of GDP over the five years from 2008 through 2012, peaking at 2.7 percent of GDP in 2010. This was enhanced by automatic stabilizers that expanded unemployment insurance, means-tested programs, and reduced taxes—averaging an additional 1.4 percent of GDP in stimulus and bringing the total stimulus to as much as 4.6 percent of GDP in 2010 and an average of 3.4 percent over the entire period.

The largest category of stimulus was tax cuts for individuals, with total tax cuts making up 54 percent of the fiscal stimulus, as shown in Figure 16.2. (Most of these tax cuts are conceptually the same as expenditure increases.) An additional 30 percent of the stimulus went for relief, either directly to individuals or as fiscal relief for states. The remaining 16 percent of the stimulus was devoted to outlays on public investment. Some of the larger or more notable items in each of these categories, along with their costs from 2008 to 2012, are listed in the appendix.

---

3. The total was $1.456 trillion counting the budgetary impact through fiscal year 2019 because some provisions, like bonus depreciation and expensing, raised money in later years.
4. This differs from the headline $787 billion in that it reflects subsequent Congressional Budget Office (CBO) reestimates and subtracts items like AMT.

Table 16.1 Fiscal Support for the Economy during and after the 2007–2009 Recession

Stimulus phase	Legislation	Date of enactment	Stimulus through 2012 ($ in billions)[A]
Pre–Recovery Act	Economic Stimulus Act of 2008 (HR 5140)	Feb. 13, 2008	138
	Supplemental Appropriations Act, 2008 (HR 2642)	June 30, 2008	13
	Housing and Economic Recovery Act of 2008 (HR 3221)	July 30, 2008	11
	Unemployment Compensation Extension Act of 2008 (HR 6867)	Nov. 21, 2008	6
Recovery Act	American Recovery and Reinvestment Act of 2009	Feb. 17, 2009	712
Post–Recovery Act	Supplemental Appropriations Act, 2009 (HR 2346)	June 24, 2009	3
	Worker, Homeownership, and Business Assistance Act of 2009 (HR 3548)	Nov. 6, 2009	35
	Department of Defense Appropriations Act, 2010 (HR 3326)	Dec. 19, 2009	18
	Temporary Extension Act of 2010 (HR 4691)	March 2, 2010	9
	Hiring Incentives to Restore Employment Act (HR 2847)	March 18, 2010	13
	Continuing Extension Act of 2010 (HR 4851)	April 15, 2010	16
	Unemployment Compensation Extension Act of 2010 (HR 4213)	July 22, 2010	33
	FAA Air Transportation Modernization and Safety Improvement Act (HR 1586)	Aug. 10, 2010	26
	Small Business Jobs Act of 2010 (HR 5297)	Sept. 27, 2010	68

(continued)

Table 16.1 (continued)

Stimulus phase	Legislation	Date of enactment	Stimulus through 2012 ($ in billions)[A]
	Tax Relief, Unemployment Insurance Reauthorization, and Job Creation Act of 2010 (HR 4853)	Dec. 17, 2010	309
	VOW to Hire Heroes Act of 2011 (HR 674)	Nov. 21, 2011	0
	Temporary Payroll Tax Cut Continuation Act of 2011 (HR 3765)	Dec. 23, 2011	28
	Middle Class Tax Relief and Job Creation Act of 2012 (HR 3630)	Feb. 22, 2012	98
Total			**1,537**

[A] Calendar year basis. May not sum due to rounding.

Sources: Congressional Budget Office; Council of Economic Advisers (2014); author's calculations

EVIDENCE ON THE IMPACT OF THE FISCAL STIMULUS

The principal basis for evaluating the fiscal stimulus should match its primary purpose: raising GDP above what it otherwise would have been, thus preventing a deeper recession and speeding economic growth. In addition, analyzing the relative effectiveness of elements of the stimulus would be desirable, but evaluating individual provisions has proved nearly impossible, and the impacts that have been assessed are not necessarily comparable. Nevertheless, some general observations are possible.

EX ANTE PROJECTIONS OF THE MACROECONOMIC IMPACT

The fiscal stimulus was part of a broader response to the crisis that included monetary policy and policies affecting the financial, housing, and auto sectors. Evaluating the causal impact of the entire response, let alone any individual element, is not straightforward and may even be impossible because we cannot observe the baseline that reflects what would have happened absent the policy response. For example, observing that high unemployment rates follow

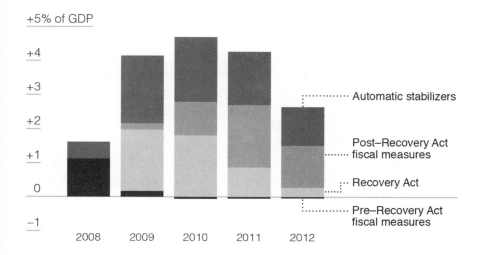

Figure 16.1 **Fiscal Expansion as a Percentage of GDP**

Notes: (1) Data are displayed in calendar year terms for all series. Data do not include AMT relief, TARP, GSE purchase of debt/equity, or certain other provisions included in pre–Recovery Act stimulus bills. (2) Acronyms are defined in the list of abbreviations at the front of this book.

Sources: U.S. Bureau of Economic Analysis; Congressional Budget Office; Council of Economic Advisers (2014); author's calculations

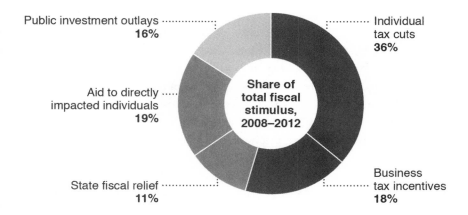

Figure 16.2 **Recovery Act and Prior and Subsequent Fiscal Measures, by Functional Category**

Notes: (1) Percentages may not sum to 100 due to rounding. Data are displayed in calendar year terms. Data do not include AMT relief, TARP, GSE purchase of debt/equity, or certain other provisions included in pre–Recovery Act stimulus bills. (2) Acronyms are defined in the list of abbreviations at the front of this book.

Sources: Council of Economic Advisers (2014); Congressional Budget Office; author's calculations

a stimulus may establish nothing more than that the stimulus was warranted in the first place. Conversely, observing the economy recovering may just be the natural self-equilibration of the economy and not the result of macroeconomic policy. Isolating the effect of fiscal policy produces additional issues arising from the circular impact of fiscal, monetary, and financial policies on each other.

Time series econometric methods have attempted to estimate the impact of fiscal expansions by separating out "endogenous" fiscal policy that is a response to where the economy is from "exogenous" fiscal policy that is done for reasons unrelated to the state of the economy. This method is impossible for the Recovery Act and subsequent stimulus measures, which effectively constitute a single data point. More importantly, the fiscal response was clearly an endogenous response to the widely held belief that the economy would weaken substantially in the future.

As a result, most of the estimates of the macroeconomic impact of the Recovery Act and other fiscal measures have been estimated ex ante. Specifically, they draw on research that was done before the Great Recession to predict the impact that a given fiscal policy would be expected to have on the economy. Generally, this is done by assigning a set of multipliers (spread out over time) to different types of fiscal measures. These multipliers are generally very imperfectly estimated from historical experience and may have changed over time or been different in the context of a massive financial crisis. The multipliers that the Council of Economic Advisers (CEA) used ranged from 1.5 for public investment outlays and for income and support payments, which were expected to generate more economic activity as the initial round of stimulus was spent and respent in the economy, to 0.1 for business tax incentives, reflecting the expectation that they would mostly be saved by businesses in the form of larger retained earnings. CEA's multipliers are shown in Table 16.2; they generally fall in about the middle of the range for the low and high multiplier estimates of the Congressional Budget Office (CBO).

Estimates for the macroeconomic impact of the Recovery Act alone provided in Table 16.3 are generally based on these types of multipliers, showing it adding between 0.7 percent and 4.1 percent to the level of GDP in 2010, when almost all forecasts predicted the legislation would have its peak impact. Blinder and Zandi (2015) used similar methods to estimate the impact of the broader set of fiscal expansions.

Table 16.2 **Estimated Output Multipliers for Different Types of Fiscal Support**

	Council of Economic Advisers (CEA)	Congressional Budget Office (CBO)	
		Low	High
Public investment outlays	1.5	0.5	2.5
State and local fiscal relief	1.1	0.4	1.8
Income and support payments	1.5	0.4	2.1
Onetime payments to retirees	0.4	0.2	1.0
Tax cuts to individuals	0.8	0.3	1.5
Business tax incentives	0.1	0.0	0.4

Source: Council of Economic Advisers (2014)

Table 16.3 **Estimates of the Effects of the Recovery Act on the Level of GDP**

	Percent				
	2009	2010	2011	2012	2013
CEA: Model approach	+1.1	+2.4	+1.8	+0.8	+0.3
CBO: Low	+0.4	+0.7	+0.4	+0.1	+0.1
CBO: High	+1.7	+4.1	+2.3	+0.8	+0.3
Goldman Sachs	+0.9	+2.3	+1.3	—	—
IHS Global Insight	+0.8	+2.2	+1.6	+0.6	—
James Glassman, JPMorgan Chase	+1.4	+3.4	+1.7	0.0	—
Macroeconomic Advisers	+0.7	+2.0	+2.1	+1.1	—
Mark Zandi, Moody's Economy.com	+1.1	+2.6	+1.7	+0.4	—

Source: Council of Economic Advisers (2014)

These same methods can be used to estimate the macroeconomic impact of the full set of fiscal stimulus legislation on GDP starting in 2008, which is shown in Figure 16.3.[5] Doing so implies that Q4-over-Q4 growth was substantially

5. The analysis combines the multipliers in Table 16.2 with the lag structure in CEA (2009). The lags are the reason the effect of the fiscal stimulus on output is maintained at a higher level even after the fiscal stimulus itself started to be withdrawn.

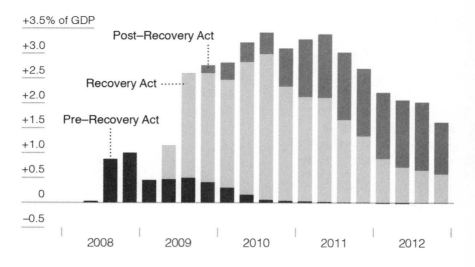

+3.5% of GDP

+3.0

+2.5

+2.0

+1.5

+1.0

+0.5

0

−0.5

Post–Recovery Act

Recovery Act ......

Pre–Recovery Act

2008   2009   2010   2011   2012

Figure 16.3 Quarterly Effect of Fiscal Stimulus Measures on GDP

Sources: U.S. Bureau of Economic Analysis; Congressional Budget Office; Council of Economic Advisers (2009, 2014); author's calculations

higher in 2008 and 2009, roughly unchanged in 2010 and 2011, and reduced in 2012 as the addition to the level wore off. This is equivalent to adding about 3 million jobs at the maximum point of the stimulus or a cumulative total of about 10 million job-years over the five-year period the stimulus was in effect.

EX POST CROSS-SECTIONAL EFFECTS

In general, evaluating the impact of any individual provision of the stimulus on GDP is difficult because numerous provisions were going into effect simultaneously. Nevertheless, research has exploited different types of variation to estimate the impacts of some of the individual provisions. These impacts, however, cannot easily be compared with each other because of differences in estimation strategies, noise, and the fact that many of the evaluations did not estimate national multipliers.

A number of papers have effectively used random cross-state variation in different components of the fiscal stimulus to estimate the state-level macroeconomic impact of these particular measures. Chodorow-Reich et al. (2012), for example, study the impact of higher Medicaid matches on state economies by looking at the portion of Medicaid matching that was based on prerecession Medicaid spending and thus not simply the result of the recession. They find a state-level multiplier of about 2. Conley and Dupor (2013) use a similar method for highway spending and find a much smaller multiplier. Dupor and McCrory (2018), Dupor and Mehkari (2016), and Wilson (2012) examined broader Recovery Act spending based on formula grants and find multipliers in between these two. The different estimated multipliers are probably an artifact of variations in modeling strategies and thus not comparable. Chodorow-Reich (2019) provides more harmonized estimates studying these three stimulus measures and finds multipliers of 1.53 to 2.29, with imprecise measurement meaning that none of them are statistically significantly different from each other at a 5 percent level. These estimates imply that increased federal transfers to states through a higher Federal Medical Assistance Percentage (FMAP) for Medicaid and other investments funded through state budgets were macroeconomically effective.

Feyrer and Sacerdote (2011) use state- and county-level spending of various federal stimulus grants (again, excluding tax cuts and some individual-level transfer payments) and find a smaller multiplier of 0.5 to 1.0, although this reflects heterogeneous estimates including a multiplier of −0.7 to −3.3 for education and police spending but much higher multipliers like 2 to 2.3 for low-income support and 1.8 for infrastructure and other grants. Dube et al. (2018) also use county-level stimulus spending, finding slightly larger effects than Feyrer and Sacerdote (2011).

Translating state-level multipliers into national multipliers is not straightforward because of many factors, most notably the spillovers from one state to another and other general equilibrium effects (Nakamura and Steinsson 2014; Farhi and Werning 2016). Chodorow-Reich (2019), however, argues that in many cases, the policy-relevant multiplier should assume no interest rate response and deficit financing, in which case he shows that state-level cross-sectional multipliers are a rough lower bound on what the relevant Keynesian national multiplier would be. He summarizes his analysis as finding that his own results and other cross-sectional results imply "a no-monetary-policy-response deficit-financed national multiplier of about 1.7 or above. This magnitude falls at the very upper end of the range found in a recent review article based mostly on time series evidence (Ramey 2011). Thus, cross-sectional multiplier studies suggest the national multiplier can be larger than often assumed."

A few other provisions of the stimulus have also been studied, although most of these estimates do not meaningfully change the ex ante parameters originally assumed when the stimulus passed.[6] The one case where the evidence suggests a substantially larger effect than originally assumed is for bonus depreciation. The CEA estimates assumed a multiplier of 0.1 for business tax provisions, similar to CBO's low estimates. Zwick and Mahon (2017), however, studied the actual data and find large effects of temporarily expanded equipment depreciation on investment, particularly for small and financially constrained firms. This finding is consistent with some of the thinking that originally went into designing these provisions, which were intended in part as an interest-free loan whose benefit would be related to the cash flow in the initial years but whose cost was the much lower present value to the government. The original bonus depreciation, for example, provided $50 billion of tax reductions in the first two fiscal years as firms shifted depreciation allowances earlier, but then most of this money was recouped in future years, leaving the ten-year cost at only $7 billion. If only 10 percent of the $50 billion was spent as additional investment, that would lead to a multiplier of nearly 1 evaluated against the entire fiscal cost of the measure.[7]

Overall, these results are not fully informative about how to design the composition of stimulus. But they do suggest that the multipliers used by CEA, CBO, and others may have been too low, especially for some items like business tax incentives and some forms of state fiscal relief, and that the actual aggregate impact of the Recovery Act and other stimulus programs may have been larger than previously estimated.

6. The 2008 rebate and Making Work Pay were studied by Parker et al. (2013), who looked at the impact on consumption, and Sahm, Shapiro, and Slemrod (2012), who relied on self-reported surveys. The former found larger impacts than the latter. The impact of the Cash for Clunkers program is debated with Mian and Sufi (2012) and Hoekstra, Puller, and West (2017) finding small to negative effects, while Green et al. (2018) find a larger effect. The resolution of this debate has little effect on the ex ante results reported earlier because Cash for Clunkers was only $3 billion of the overall $1.5 trillion stimulus. Other evaluations of specific programs include Berger, Turner, and Zwick (2018), who find large effects of the First-Time Homebuyer Credit, and Chodorow-Reich, Coglianese, and Karabarbounis (2019), who find smaller labor market effects of the unemployment insurance extensions.
7. The expansion of net operating losses (NOLs) was also based on a similar logic, but Dobridge (2016) finds that most of these additional payments were saved by firms rather than spent—although this does not rule out additional investment in future years.

EVALUATING OTHER GOALS FOR FISCAL STIMULUS: PROTECTING THE MOST VULNERABLE

In addition to their overall macroeconomic motivation, the Recovery Act and other fiscal stimulus measures were designed, in the terminology of their creators, to "protect the most vulnerable." This category included both the long-term poor, who were viewed as being more vulnerable to a downturn, and people who fell on hard times by losing their jobs. In total, $289 billion was spent on direct aid to individuals, including the unemployed and those receiving Supplemental Nutrition Assistance Program (SNAP) benefits. Additionally, much of the $836 billion in tax cuts and $167 billion in state and local fiscal relief disproportionately benefited these same households.

The labor market did indeed disproportionately inflict harm on more vulnerable populations. From the fourth quarter of 2007 through the fourth quarter of 2010, the overall unemployment rate rose 4.7 percentage points, while the unemployment rates for those with less education, African Americans, and Hispanics rose much more sharply, as shown in Figure 16.4.

The tax and transfer system, both the automatic measures in effect before the crisis and the additions in the Recovery Act and other legislation, did a remarkable job in protecting these more vulnerable households. Overall, the poverty rate would have risen by 4.8 percentage points from 2007 to 2010 absent these programs; but with them, it rose by 0.4 percentage points at most, and the increase may have been significantly less. Indeed, the results may have been even better because these estimates are based on surveys that undercount public programs (Furman 2017).[8]

A more comprehensive picture of how the Great Recession affected incomes from 2007 to 2010 is shown in Figure 16.5, which is based on CBO (2018) data for non-elderly-headed households.[9] The largest reductions to market in-

---

8. These estimates were from a November 2016 update of Wimer et al. (2013) provided for Furman (2017). These numbers use the Current Population Survey data on people's self-reporting of what public benefits, like SNAP, they received. As is widely understood (e.g., Meyer, Mok, and Sullivan 2009), these numbers substantially understate actual take-up of these programs and thus overstate the increase in poverty when these programs are expanded.
9. Technically, this is a combination of CBO's categories "households with children" (which includes a small number of elderly-headed households) and "nonelderly

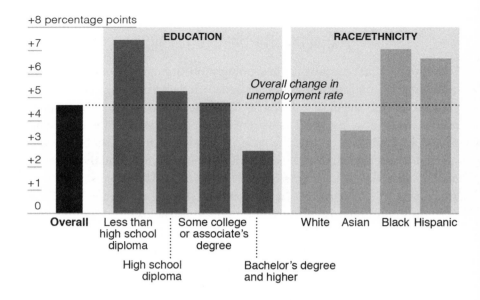

Figure 16.4 **Change in Unemployment Rate, Q4 2007–Q4 2010**

Sources: U.S. Bureau of Labor Statistics; Haver Analytics; author's calculations

comes were for the bottom two quintiles (due to the disproportionate job losses) and the top quintile (due to the large declines in capital income, although some of this is an artifact of the timing of capital gains). After taking account of taxes and transfers, non-elderly-headed households in the bottom quintile experienced substantial income gains even in the face of a massive recession. The second quintile also enjoyed small gains while taxes and transfers absorbed the bulk of the losses for the third and fourth quintiles. For the highest-quintile households, losses were similar both before and after taxes and transfers. In other words, from the perspective of the fiscal system, low- and moderate-income households got a bailout, not high-income ones.[10] Note that about half

households without children" (which includes a small number of households with secondary elderly persons). CBO's overall numbers, which include all elderly-headed households, tell a very similar story.

10. All of the estimates show only changes in income and do not reflect changes in wealth (e.g., the loss of home equity or stock market wealth). The specific estimate for the top quintile is dependent on the treatment of both the realization of capital gains income and the payment of capital gains taxes, but the finding of reductions in

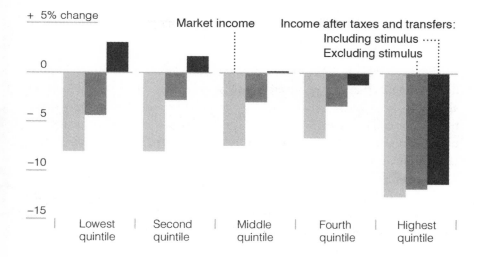

Figure 16.5 Change in Average Household Income by Quintile for Non-Elderly-Headed Households, 2007–2010

Note: Quintiles by household income after taxes and transfers.

Sources: U.S. Bureau of Labor Statistics; Congressional Research Service; Congressional Budget Office; Tax Policy Center; author's calculations

of the difference between before- and after-taxes-and-transfers incomes was due to existing automatic stabilizers, while the other half was due to new measures passed as part of the stimulus, like expanded unemployment insurance and the Making Work Pay tax credit.[11]

---

both market and after-tax income holds in any case. The other leading source for comprehensive income data—the World Inequality Database based on methods described in Piketty, Saez, and Zucman (2016)—has somewhat different findings overall, in part due to its exclusion of the income on capital gains but inclusion of the taxes on these gains.

11. The estimates excluding stimulus are based on using the actual distribution of Making Work Pay, the Earned Income Tax Credit (EITC) expansion, increased refundability of the child tax credit, and the American Opportunity Tax Credit (AOTC) combined with using average distributions to allocate the total legislatively induced increase in spending on unemployment insurance, supplemental nutrition assistance, and COBRA subsidies.

EVALUATING OTHER GOALS FOR FISCAL STIMULUS: PUBLIC INVESTMENT

As shown in Table 16.4, the Recovery Act included about $300 billion in public investments that were motivated not just by increasing short-run GDP but also by other goals like enhancing long-run growth through more infrastructure investment or increasing energy efficiency. The prior and subsequent stimulus was almost entirely tax cuts and relief for individuals and states. This chapter does not evaluate these goals.

One goal of the Recovery Act was to spend investment funding as quickly as possible through so-called shovel-ready projects. It was well understood that some measures, like high-speed rail and electronic medical records, would take some time to deliver their benefits, but the highway program was designed to spend out relatively quickly. In fact, the actual spendout for the highway pro-

Table 16.4 **Recovery Act Long-Term Growth Investment, by Category**

		Estimated cost, 2009–2019 ($ in billions)
Capital	Construction of transportation infrastructure	30.0
	Environmental cleanup and preservation	28.0
	Construction of buildings	23.9
	Public safety and defense	8.9
	Economic development	14.6
	Memo: business tax incentives	*11.7*
Labor	Pell Grants	17.3
	Special education	12.2
	Help for disadvantaged children	13.0
	Other human capital	10.3
Technology	Scientific research	18.3
	Clean energy	78.5
	Health and health information technology	32.0
	Broadband	6.9
Other		6.7
Total public investment[A]		**300.6**

[A] Total excludes business tax incentives.

Source: Council of Economic Advisers (2014)

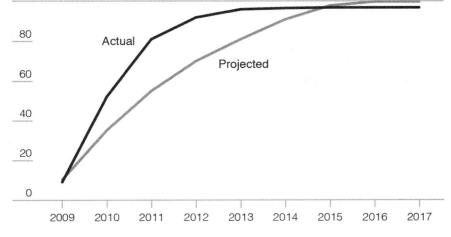

100% of projected outlays spent (cumulative)

80

Actual

60

Projected

40

20

0

2009   2010   2011   2012   2013   2014   2015   2016   2017

Figure 16.6   Recovery Act Highway Construction Outlays

Sources: Congressional Budget Office; Office of Management and Budget; author's calculations

gram was even faster than initially predicted: 80 percent of the funding was spent by 2011, well above the projection of 55 percent by that year (Figure 16.6).

ALTERNATIVES THAT WERE NOT TAKEN

The Obama administration consistently proposed a larger quantity of stimulus than Congress passed. In addition, a number of different alternative provisions were contemplated. Some were rejected by policymakers in the administration, while others failed to pass Congress. The following describes three of those alternatives, the thinking that went into them, and potential considerations for future fiscal stimulus.

NEW JOBS TAX CREDIT

During the campaign, Obama proposed a $3,000 tax credit for employers for each net new additional job added in 2009 and 2010 (Obama-Biden Campaign 2008). The transition team further refined the idea, and Obama signed off in late 2008 on proposing it as part of the Recovery Act. Congress rejected the idea because lawmakers were skeptical of the efficacy of a measure designed to *add* jobs at a time when firms were rapidly *shedding* jobs.

Obama proposed a retooled version in January 2010 that would have provided a tax credit of $5,000 per net new job along with a bonus for firms that raised total wages, with both capped at $500,000 in credits per firm (White House 2010). The credits would have been paid out quarterly and applied against payroll taxes so that even firms with tax losses would have been eligible. This proposal evolved into the Hiring Incentives to Restore Employment (HIRE) Act passed by Congress in March 2010; however, the final legislation was ultimately very different from the administration's original proposal as it was a tax credit for hiring the long-term unemployed rather than an incremental tax credit for net increases in new jobs.

The theory behind the new jobs tax credit was that it would have the same Keynesian boost as any tax cut while providing additional bang for the buck in terms of higher employment, effectively raising the number of jobs per unit of GDP. This theoretical intuition was bolstered by academic evaluations of the 1977–1978 New Jobs Tax Credit, which find that it was effective at promoting hiring (Perloff and Wachter 1979; Bishop 1981). Later in 2009, CEA and Treasury estimated that a new jobs tax credit would cost about $20,000 per net new job added. About 90 percent of the subsidy would go to jobs that would have been created anyway, but the other 10 percent would have provided a net increase in new jobs. Even with this unbalanced ratio, the cost per job created would have been considerably less than CEA's (2014) implied estimates of about $125,000 per job-year for the Recovery Act as a whole.

STATE SALES TAX HOLIDAY

In late 2008, the transition team considered a state sales tax holiday as a way to shift consumption forward by encouraging households to take advantage of temporarily lower prices. Specifically, the transition team contemplated proposing a fund of about $250 billion that would be available to states carrying out certain sales tax reductions. States without sales taxes would have been allowed to use the money for income tax cuts. The idea was ultimately not proposed to Congress.

The principal argument for the proposal was to take advantage of intertemporal substitution, effectively setting a very negative real interest rate for consumer purchases that would make it more attractive to pull forward consumption. This effect would have acted as an additional stimulus on top of the normal Keynesian expectation of increased demand associated with tax cuts. The federal role would have simply been to approve state plans and disburse money according to a specified formula. States' prior experience with sales tax holidays had demonstrated that such a plan would have been relatively straightforward to administer. Concerns with the proposal included worries that it could inhibit spending in the run-up to the tax holiday or hurt future demand by pulling spending forward. In retrospect, given how protracted the downturn was, it was probably economically wise that this proposal was left on the cutting-room floor. Nonetheless, it has a number of benefits that merit consideration by policymakers in future short, sharp downturns.

EXPIRING DEBIT CARDS

A final idea that received substantial consideration during the transition was delivering rebates on a debit card. The debit card could have been set with a use-it-or-lose-it feature so that any remaining balance would expire by the end of 2009. The goal of the proposal was to make the refund more salient than getting a check or having fewer taxes withheld while also ensuring that people spent the money quickly, raising the short-term multiplier relative to traditional tax credits. Extensive work was done with Treasury staff, who believed that it would have been administratively possible to provide such cards for all Americans at essentially no transaction cost to the federal government as card issuers would bid for a contract to earn the associated interchange fees and float interest. Ultimately, however, it was considered too administratively risky to design and launch a massive consumer-facing program in a short period of time. Further effort and contingency planning on this idea may be warranted given the potential advantages relative to conventional tax cuts.

LESSONS FOR THE FUTURE

The experience with the 2008–2012 fiscal stimulus and economic research that has been conducted in the years since then provide six lessons for future fiscal stimulus.

Lesson 1:
Discretionary fiscal stimulus can be particularly effective, especially when interest rates are at the lower bound.

Before 2008, economists were generally skeptical of discretionary fiscal stimulus, based on concerns about potentially large lags between recognizing the problem, passing a legislative response, implementing the legislation, and realizing the economic effect. In general, monetary policy was considered superior on all these counts and regarded as the best and potentially only line of defense in downturns.

The 2008–2012 experience suggests that these fears were overblown. Policymakers proposed a fiscal response in January 2008, essentially just after the recession began, according to subsequent analysis by the National Bureau of Economic Research (NBER) business cycle dating committee. Initial legislation was passed a month later, and as the situation became more severe at the end of 2008, the Recovery Act was passed within a month of Obama's inauguration. Many of the provisions were implemented quickly, with electronic refunds first sent out in April 2008, just two months after the first stimulus was passed. Similarly, the reductions in tax withholdings included in the Recovery Act were implemented within months. Moreover, the evidence suggests that fiscal measures impacted the economy more quickly than monetary policy.

Looking ahead, fiscal policy may become an even more important tool for aggregate demand management. Research following the Great Recession has helped build a "new view" of fiscal policy, which in many ways is a rediscovery of the old Keynesian liquidity trap framework (see Furman 2016 for a summary). In particular, the "new view" holds that if neutral interest rates have fallen, monetary policymakers will more often hit the effective lower bound for interest rates—thus limiting conventional monetary policy options and increasing the importance of fiscal policy.

Moreover, fiscal policy may be particularly effective when interest rates are at the lower bound. Traditional concerns about crowding out through higher interest rates may be superfluous when interest rates are stuck at the effective lower bound: Even with additional demand, the desired interest rate will not rise. Fiscal policy could also lead to "crowding in," either through an accelerator mechanism that increases growth rates and thus investment growth or by raising expected inflation and thus lowering real interest rates (Hall 2009; Christiano, Eichenbaum, and Rebelo 2011; Woodford 2011).

Concerns about fiscal space may be overstated in a highly depressed economy with interest rates at the effective lower bound because fiscal expansions may raise GDP by more than they raise debt—thus reducing the debt-to-GDP ratio. This result has been found in a variety of settings, including the Fed's main macroeconomic model, FRB/US (David Reifschneider and Summers as reported in DeLong, Summers, and Ball 2014); the Organisation for Economic Co-operation and Development's (2016) NiGEM and FM models; the International Monetary Fund's modeling (Gaspar, Obstfeld, and Sahay 2016); simulations by DeLong and Summers (2012); and regression-based estimates of past fiscal stimulus by Auerbach and Gorodnichenko (2017). On the other hand, there is still some reason for caution: Romer and Romer (2017) find that countries that go into financial crises with higher debt have smaller fiscal responses and worse macroeconomic outcomes. (It is not clear if their result reflects high-debt countries having little economic space for stimulus or making political mistakes about too little stimulus.)

Lesson 2:
Triggers and other automatic mechanisms should be expanded because policymakers can tire of fiscal stimulus prematurely.

The transition team thought that if the initial stimulus was too small or the economy worsened further, persuading Congress to provide more fiscal stimulus would not be very difficult. This view did not seem unreasonable at the time: In the face of a much milder recession in 2001, Congress passed bills it described as fiscal stimulus in 2001, 2002, 2003, and again in 2004, nearly three full years after the end of the recession. In the context of a widely accepted national economic emergency, it was reasonable to expect that garnering support for additional stimulus would have been easier, particularly in advance of the 2010 midterm elections.

This prediction was partially realized, considering the 13 subsequent bills, at least, that included additional stimulus. The size of these measures, however, still fell well short of the administration's requests, and in general, stimulus was removed well before it was economically sensible to do so. Congress repeatedly refused to pass more stimulus even when the unemployment rate was well above the levels that initially triggered action. This was also true of specific provisions: Extended unemployment insurance, for example, was initially passed when the unemployment rate was 5.6 percent, the long-term unemployment rate was 1.0 percent, and average duration of unemployment was 17 weeks—but was allowed to expire when these were 6.7 percent, 2.5 percent, and 37 weeks, respectively.

The difficulty in securing additional stimulus stemmed from three challenges. The first was that, paradoxically, the worse-than-expected macroeconomic outcomes reduced the desire in Congress to take more fiscal action. Even though the bulk of the unexpected deterioration of the economy happened by early to mid-2009, before the bulk of the Recovery Act went into effect, this was viewed by critics as evidence that the law had not worked, making future stimulus counterproductive. The second was concerns about the deficit—which nearly reached 10 percent of GDP in 2009, putting the debt on a course to eventually more than double as a share of GDP. The final reason was partisan politics, and in particular congressional Republicans not wanting to cooperate with the administration in passing more fiscal measures.

One way to overcome these political failures in the future would be to make the initial stimulus package contingent on economic outcomes. For example, the Recovery Act could have included an annual tax credit that would be in effect every year the unemployment rate was above 7 percent. Such a trigger would have delivered more consistent, predictable, and potentially larger fiscal support in subsequent years.[12]

Even better would be to expand the automatic stabilizers permanently. In general, the United States has smaller automatic stabilizers than most other advanced economies, largely because their magnitude is highly correlated with the size of government—and the United States has a generally smaller government as a share of GDP.

Automatic stabilizers could be measures that expand in response to falling demand, such as unemployment insurance and SNAP. In fact, the health insurance tax credits and Medicaid expansion in the Affordable Care Act (ACA) will increase automatic stabilizers in future years. Alternatively, automatic stabilizers could be contingent on national or state economic data, perhaps full federal funding for lengthening unemployment insurance benefits or higher Medicaid matching rates in states with elevated or rising unemployment rates.

12. An important caveat depending on the political context: If the Recovery Act had included such contingent measures while keeping within the $800 billion budgetary limit set by Congress, it would have actually been *smaller* up front. The reason is that CBO and the U.S. Congress Joint Committee on Taxation (JCT) score legislation probabilistically, and even a chance that such a trigger would still be in effect in, say, 2015 would count toward the cost, requiring other provisions to be smaller to fit in the $800 billion limit.

Lesson 3:
State and local fiscal relief can play an important role in ensuring that states and localities do not undercut the federal fiscal stimulus.

As the federal government was expanding fiscal support for the economy in the wake of the Great Recession, states and localities were cutting spending and thus undoing a meaningful portion of this stimulus. This was unusual. If state and local spending had followed the average procyclical pattern of six of the previous seven recoveries and everything else was the same, the GDP growth rate would have been 0.6 percentage points per year higher in the five years following the trough, according to my calculation of the counterfactual.[13]

The reductions in state and local purchases may have been specific to this recession because of the substantial and lagged effects of reduced housing prices on property tax revenue. Nevertheless, the causes of the large departure from previous experience are not fully understood. That the 2001 experience was also worse than the prior historical experience raises the concern that there could be a broader trend, and in the future, state and local fiscal policy could once again run against federal efforts or be insufficiently supportive of them. Moreover, even optimal subnational policy will be insufficiently fiscally supportive in a recession because states and localities do not take into account the substantial benefits of their stimulus measures on other states (Dupor and McCrory 2018).

This highlights the importance of supporting state and local spending in future recessions and their aftermaths. One approach would be to legislate discretionary fiscal relief, either general fiscal relief or labeled for a specific purpose with the understanding that it would be fungible. Another potentially superior approach would be to make state fiscal relief an automatic stabilizer that is triggered when the national and/or state unemployment rates rise.

Lesson 4:
Taxpayer confidence should be maintained when undertaking a large, rapid spendout of funds.

The Recovery Act included unprecedented transparency and accountability measures, including an independent Recovery Accountability and Transparency

---

13. Excludes the 1980 recession because of overlap with the 1981–1982 recession.

Board, regular and timely reporting of all contracts and other information, and an easily accessible website to share all of this public information. As a result, only a miniscule percentage of the contracts were considered fraudulent, and even Republican congressman Darrell Issa of California, a frequent critic of the administration, acknowledged that the new recipient reporting standards were "the key to the success of the Recovery Accountability and Transparency Board in catching and preventing fraud, waste, and abuse in stimulus spending" (House Oversight Committee 2011).

Lesson 5:
Tax cuts should potentially play a larger role, especially if targeted at lower-income households and at accelerating investment.

Beyond the specific evidence that has emerged from studying the Recovery Act itself, economic research focused on a longer period of time is finding growing evidence that tax cuts may have a higher multiplier than previously appreciated. Romer and Romer (2010) use a narrative method to identify exogenous tax shocks and find that the impact of a tax cut worth 1 percent of GDP grows over time to about 3 percent of GDP after ten quarters, an effect that may reflect expanded demand in a traditional Keynesian manner or increased supply through the incentives to work. Barro and Redlick (2011), Mertens and Ravn (2013), and Mertens and Montiel Olea (2017) find impulse responses from tax cuts that are similarly large. Zidar (2017) finds large responses as well but also finds substantial demographic heterogeneity, with a much larger multiplier for tax cuts for low-income households than high-income households.

Most of the literature following the crisis has focused on estimating the fiscal multiplier of either tax cuts or direct spending as isolated policies (for example, Ramey 2011; Ramey and Zubairy 2018). Although these studies have generally found higher tax multipliers than spending multipliers, the results are not directly comparable due to the differences in methodology. However, some recent studies that have estimated both tax and spending multipliers on a consistent basis (for example, Carlino and Inman 2016; Andrés, Boscá, and Ferri 2016; and Ramey 2019) find larger tax multipliers than spending multipliers—in some cases, by substantial magnitudes.

Zwick and Mahon (2017), discussed earlier, also find very large responses to accelerated depreciation relative to the cost to the government. These effects may be specific to a financial crisis, however, because the cash flow improvement was particularly material while the present value cost to the government was especially low as a result of low federal borrowing rates.

This evidence is about general tax changes that in many cases are permanent, not specifically about temporary tax cuts in a demand-constrained economy, so they may not be fully applicable to this case. Moreover, the general evidence on generic tax cuts—as with any macroeconomic evidence—is not definitive and in some cases is puzzlingly larger than one would expect based on the economic theory of either Keynesian multipliers or possible supply-side responses. Finally, it is possible that both spending multipliers and tax multipliers have been underestimated in the past.

Overall, however, the evidence suggests that some upward revision in estimated tax multipliers relative to what was believed in 2009 and 2010 may be warranted, particularly for tax cuts targeted at lower-income households and businesses.

Lesson 6:
Policy should aim to increase jobs for a given increase in GDP, not just to increase GDP.

Beyond the actual rise in the unemployment rate, the Great Recession had a particularly severe impact on the labor market, including sustained record-high long-term jobless rates, a spike in involuntarily part-time workers, and a large reduction in the labor force participation rate. Similar labor market dysfunctions followed the much shallower 2001 recession as well.

In many ways, the labor market experience was much worse in the United States relative to other advanced economies. For example, Germany experienced a larger decline in real GDP than the United States, yet its unemployment rate continued to fall while the unemployment rate more than doubled in the United States, as shown in Figure 16.7. The cause of this discrepancy is that hours worked, much more than jobs, were reduced in Germany, spreading the employment decline across a much larger number of people.

Although Germany had a different policy response and very different institutional arrangements than the United States, its experience highlights the potential for increasing the number of jobs conditional on a given amount of GDP—not just focusing on maximizing GDP. One way to do this is through a new jobs credit, described earlier, which CEA estimated would add one

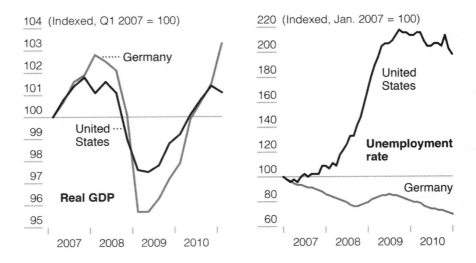

Figure 16.7 Real GDP and the Unemployment Rate in Germany and the United States

Sources: Real GDP: U.S. Bureau of Economic Analysis; Deutsche Bundesbank; Haver Analytics; author's calculations; unemployment rate: Organisation for Economic Co-operation and Development (2018), Harmonized Unemployment Rate (HUR) (indicator); author's calculations

job-year for each roughly $20,000 spent, giving it a considerably higher employment impact than generic stimulus. Another possibility would be to encourage more U.S. states to adopt the type of short-term compensation found in Germany that provides unemployment insurance not just for people fired from jobs but also for people who have their hours involuntarily reduced.

APPENDIX

Some of the larger or more notable items in each of the stimulus categories, along with their costs from 2008 through 2012, are as follows:

INDIVIDUAL TAX CUTS

- *Making Work Pay ($112 billion)*. A tax credit that was generally $400 for individuals and $800 for married couples, phased out for higher-income households. It was originally passed as part of the Recovery Act and lasted for 2009 and 2010.
- *Payroll tax cut ($207 billion)*. A 2-percentage-point reduction in Social Security payroll taxes, with the cost reimbursed to the Social Security Trust Fund. Originally passed for 2011 and extended through the end of 2012.
- *Tax credits for low- and moderate-income households with children ($41 billion)*. The Recovery Act expanded the Earned Income Tax Credit (EITC) for married couples and households with three or more children and increased the refundable portion of the child tax credit. These provisions were subsequently made permanent.

BUSINESS TAX INCENTIVES

- *Bonus depreciation and expensing ($180 billion)*. Originally allowed businesses to deduct 50 percent of the cost of their equipment investments up front and was expanded to 100 percent expensing of equipment investment from September 9, 2010, through the end of 2011.
- *Discharge of business indebtedness ($43 billion)*. Allows certain businesses repurchasing specific types of debt to pay taxes on the cancellation of that debt income over five years beginning in 2014.
- *Tax credits related to clean energy and energy efficiency ($12 billion)*. The Recovery Act included a number of tax credits for clean energy, including extending and expanding the energy tax credit.

AID TO DIRECTLY IMPACTED INDIVIDUALS

- *Unemployment insurance expansions ($240 billion)*. Full federal financing for benefits for up to 99 weeks of unemployment in high-unemployment states; initially also included temporarily increased benefit amounts. In addition, the Recovery Act and subsequent legislation included unemployment insurance reforms.

- *Increased Supplemental Nutrition Assistance Program (SNAP) ($38 billion)*. A temporary bump up to SNAP benefits that started in the Recovery Act was partially rescinded in two subsequent pieces of legislation and was phased out by November 2013.
- *Temporary Assistance for Needy Families (TANF) emergency fund ($5 billion)*. A temporary increase to TANF that could be used by states for purposes including public employment and hiring subsidies.

STATE FISCAL RELIEF
- *Increased Federal Medical Assistance Percentage (FMAP) ($100 billion)*. Increased federal matching for state Medicaid programs originally passed as part of the Recovery Act and extended in the summer of 2010.
- *State educational assistance ($63 billion)*. Federal subsidies for states and localities to fund efforts to prevent teacher layoffs. Included the Race to the Top program, a competitive grant for states undertaking major reforms.

PUBLIC INVESTMENT OUTLAYS
- *Increased investments in the highway and rail programs ($28 billion)*. Largely formula funding for the traditional surface transportation programs.
- *Transportation Investment Generating Economic Recovery (TIGER) grants ($3 billion)*. Competitive grants available to states and localities for a variety of transportation purposes.
- *High-speed rail ($2 billion)*. Grants to support state high-speed and intercity rail projects passed as part of the Recovery Act.
- *Health information technology ($15 billion)*. Included incentive payments to medical providers to adopt and meaningfully use electronic medical records, with penalties for those that took the subsidies without meaningfully using them.

REFERENCES

Akerlof, George, et al. 2008. "Economists' Letter to Congress." November 19, 2008. cepr
.net/documents/publications/Economists_letter_2008_11_19.pdf.
Andrés, Javier, José E. Boscá, and Javier Ferri. 2016. "Instruments, Rules, and Household
Debt: The Effects of Fiscal Policy." *Oxford Economic Papers* 68 (2): 419–43.

Auerbach, Alan J., and Yuriy Gorodnichenko. 2017. "Fiscal Stimulus and Fiscal Sustainability." NBER Working Paper, no. 23789, National Bureau of Economic Research, Cambridge, MA, September 2017.

Barro, Robert J., and Charles J. Redlick. 2011. "Macroeconomic Effects from Government Purchases and Taxes." *Quarterly Journal of Economics* 126 (1): 51–102.

Berger, David, Nicholas Turner, and Eric Zwick. 2019. "Stimulating Housing Markets." Working paper, January 2019. http://www.ericzwick.com/fthb/stim.pdf.

Bishop, John H. 1981. "Employment in Construction and Distribution Industries: The Impact of the New Jobs Tax Credit." In *Studies in Labor Markets*, edited by Sherwin Rosen, 209–49. Chicago: University of Chicago Press.

Blinder, Alan S., and Mark Zandi. 2015. "The Financial Crisis: Lessons for the Next One." Policy Futures Paper, Center on Budget and Policy Priorities, Washington, D.C., October 2015.

Carlino, Gerald, and Robert P. Inman. 2016. "Fiscal Stimulus in Economic Unions: What Role for States?" *Tax Policy and the Economy* 30 (1): 1–50.

Chodorow-Reich, Gabriel. 2019. "Geographic Cross-Sectional Fiscal Multipliers: What Have We Learned?" *American Economic Journal: Policy* 11 (2): 1–34.

Chodorow-Reich, Gabriel, John Coglianese, and Loukas Karabarbounis. 2019. "The Macro Effects of Unemployment Benefit Extensions: A Measurement Error Approach." *Quarterly Journal of Economics* 134 (1): 227–79.

Chodorow-Reich, Gabriel, Laura Feiveson, Zachary Liscow, and William Gui Woolston. 2012. "Does State Fiscal Relief during Recessions Increase Employment? Evidence from the American Recovery and Reinvestment Act." *American Economic Journal: Policy* 4 (3): 118–45.

Christiano, Lawrence, Martin Eichenbaum, and Sergio Rebelo. 2011. "When Is the Government Spending Multiplier Large?" *Journal of Political Economy* 119 (1): 78–121.

Congressional Budget Office (CBO). 2018. "The Distribution of Household Income, 2015." CBO Report No. 54646, November 2018.

Conley, Timothy G., and Bill Dupor. 2013. "The American Recovery and Reinvestment Act: Solely a Government Jobs Program?" *Journal of Monetary Economics* 60 (5): 535–49.

Council of Economic Advisers (CEA). 2009. *Estimates of Job Creation from the American Recovery and Reinvestment Act of 2009*. Report, May 2009.

Council of Economic Advisers (CEA). 2014. "Chapter 3: The Economic Impact of the American Recovery and Reinvestment Act Five Years Later." In *2014 Economic Report of the President*. Washington, D.C.: U.S. Government Printing Office.

Council of Economic Advisers (CEA). 2017. *2017 Economic Report of the President*. Washington, D.C.: U.S. Government Printing Office.

DeLong, J. Bradford, and Lawrence H. Summers. 2012. "Fiscal Policy in a Depressed Economy." *Brookings Papers on Economic Activity* 43 (1): 233–97.

DeLong, Brad, Larry Summers, and Laurence Ball. 2014. *Fiscal Policy and Full Employment*. Washington, D.C.: Center on Budget and Policy Priorities.

Dobridge, Christine. 2016. *Fiscal Stimulus and Firms: A Tale of Two Recessions.* Finance and Economics Discussion Series 2016-013. Washington, D.C.: Board of Governors of the Federal Reserve System.

Dube, Arindrajit, Thomas Hegland, Ethan Kaplan, and Ben Zipperer. 2018. "Excess Capacity and Heterogeneity in the Fiscal Multiplier: Evidence from the Recovery Act." Working paper, November 2018. http://econweb.umd.edu/~kaplan/stimulus_effects.pdf.

Dupor, Bill, and Peter B. McCrory. 2018. "A Cup Runneth Over: Fiscal Policy Spillovers from the 2009 Recovery Act." *Economic Journal* 128 (611): 1476–508.

Dupor, Bill, and M. Saif Mehkari. 2016. "The 2009 Recovery Act: Stimulus at the Extensive and Intensive Labor Margins." *European Economic Review* 85: 208–28.

Elmendorf, Douglas W., and Jason Furman. 2008. *If, When, How: A Primer on Fiscal Stimulus.* Washington, D.C.: Brookings Institution.

Farhi, Emmanuel, and Ivan Werning. 2016. "Chapter 31—Fiscal Multipliers: Liquidity Traps and Currency Unions." *Handbook of Macroeconomics* 2: 2417–92.

Feldstein, Martin. 2007. "How to Avert Recession." *Wall Street Journal,* December 5, 2007. https://www.wsj.com/articles/SB119682440917514075.

Feyrer, James, and Bruce Sacerdote. 2011. "Did the Stimulus Stimulate? Real Time Estimates of the Effects of the American Recovery and Reinvestment Act." NBER Working Paper, no. 16759, National Bureau of Economic Research, Cambridge, MA, December 2011.

Furman, Jason. 2016. "The New View of Fiscal Policy and Its Application." Remarks at Global Implications of Europe's Redesign Conference, New York, October 5, 2016.

Furman, Jason. 2017. "Reducing Poverty: The Progress We Have Made and the Path Forward." Remarks at the Center on Budget and Policy Priorities, Washington, D.C., January 17, 2017. https://obamawhitehouse.archives.gov/sites/default/files/page/files/20170117_furman_center_on_budget_poverty_cea.pdf.

Gaspar, Vitor, Maurice Obstfeld, and Ratna Sahay. 2016. "Macroeconomic Management When Policy Space Is Constrained: A Comprehensive, Consistent, and Coordinated Approach to Economic Policy." IMF Staff Discussion Note, September 2016.

Green, Daniel, Brian T. Melzer, Jonathan A. Parker, and Arcenis Rojas. 2018. "Accelerator or Brake? Cash for Clunkers, Household Liquidity, and Aggregate Demand." NBER Working Paper, no. 22878, National Bureau of Economic Research, Cambridge, MA, May 2018.

Grunwald, Michael. 2012. *The New New Deal: The Hidden Story of Change in the Obama Era.* New York: Simon & Schuster.

Hall, Robert E. 2009. "By How Much Does GDP Rise If the Government Buys More Output?" *Brookings Papers on Economic Activity* 40 (2): 183–249.

Hoekstra, Mark, Steven L. Puller, and Jeremy West. 2017. "Cash for Corollas: When Stimulus Reduces Spending." *American Economic Journal: Applied Economics* 9 (3): 1–35.

House Oversight Committee. 2011. "Issa Introduces Sweeping Open Government, Spending Transparency Reforms." Press release, June 13, 2011.

Internal Revenue Service. 2008. "Economic Stimulus Payments on the Way; Some People Will See Direct Deposit Payments Today." News release, April 28, 2008. https://www

.irs.gov/newsroom/economic-stimulus-payments-on-the-way-some-people-will-see
-direct-deposit-payments-today.

Mertens, Karel, and José L. Montiel Olea. 2017. "Marginal Tax Rates and Income: New Time Series Evidence." NBER Working Paper, no. 19171, National Bureau of Economic Research, Cambridge, MA, September 2017.

Mertens, Karel, and Morten O. Ravn. 2013. "The Dynamic Effects of Personal and Corporate Income Tax Changes in the United States." *American Economic Review* 103 (4): 1212–47.

Meyer, Bruce D., Wallace K. C. Mok, and James X. Sullivan. 2009. "The Under-Reporting of Transfers in Household Surveys: Its Nature and Consequences." NBER Working Paper, no. 15181, National Bureau of Economic Research, Cambridge, MA, July 2009.

Mian, Atif, and Amir Sufi. 2012. "The Effects of Fiscal Stimulus: Evidence from the 2009 Cash for Clunkers Program." *Quarterly Journal of Economics* 127 (3): 1107–42.

Nakamura, Emi, and Jón Steinsson. 2014. "Fiscal Stimulus in a Monetary Union: Evidence from US Regions." *American Economic Review* 104 (3): 753–92.

Obama, Barack. 2009a. "Address at George Mason University in Fairfax, Virginia." The American Presidency Project, January 8, 2009. https://www.presidency.ucsb.edu/node /286515.

Obama, Barack. 2009b. "Transcript: Obama Remarks at Stimulus Signing." Brian Montopoli, CBS News, February 17, 2009. https://www.cbsnews.com/news/transcript-obama -remarks-at-stimulus-signing.

Obama-Biden Campaign. 2008. "Barack Obama and Joe Biden: A Rescue Plan for the Middle Class." https://www.scribd.com/document/6523359/Barack-Obama-and-Joe -Biden-s-Rescue-Plan-for-the-Middle-Class.

Organisation for Economic Co-operation and Development (OECD). 2016. "Chapter 2: Using the Fiscal Levers to Escape the Low-Growth Trap." In *OECD Economic Outlook 2016*, no. 2. Paris: OECD Publishing.

Parker, Jonathan A., Nicholas S. Souleles, David S. Johnson, and Robert McClelland. 2013. "Consumer Spending and the Economic Stimulus Payments of 2008." *American Economic Review* 103 (6): 2530–53.

Paulson, Henry M. 2008. "Press Briefing by Treasury Secretary Henry Paulson and Chairman of the Council of Economic Advisors Ed Lazear." January 18, 2008. https:// georgewbush-whitehouse.archives.gov/news/releases/2008/01/20080118-6.html.

Perloff, Jeffrey M., and Michael L. Wachter. 1979. "The New Jobs Tax Credit: An Evaluation of the 1977–78 Wage Subsidy Program." *American Economic Review* 69 (2): 173–79.

Piketty, Thomas, Emmanuel Saez, and Gabriel Zucman. 2016. "Distributional National Accounts: Methods and Estimates for the United States Data Appendix." WID.world Working Paper Series No. 2016/4, December 2016. https://wid.world/document/t-piketty -e-saez-g-zucman-data-appendix-to-distributional-national-accounts-methods-and -estimates-for-the-united-states-2016.

Ramey, Valerie A. 2011. "Can Government Purchases Stimulate the Economy?" *Journal of Economic Literature* 49 (3): 673–85.

Ramey, Valerie A. 2019. "Ten Years after the Financial Crisis: What Have We Learned from the Renaissance in Fiscal Research?" *Journal of Economic Perspectives* 33 (2): 89–114.

Ramey, Valerie A., and Sarah Zubairy. 2018. "Government Spending Multipliers in Good Times and in Bad: Evidence from U.S. Historical Data." *Journal of Political Economy* 126 (2): 850–901.

Romer, Christina D., and David H. Romer. 2010. "The Macroeconomic Effects of Tax Changes: Estimates Based on a New Measure of Fiscal Shocks." *American Economic Review* 100 (3): 763–801.

Romer, Christina D., and David H. Romer. 2017. "Why Some Times Are Different: Macroeconomic Policy and the Aftermath of Financial Crises." NBER Working Paper, no. 23931, National Bureau of Economic Research, Cambridge, MA, October 2017.

Sahm, Claudia R., Matthew D. Shapiro, and Joel Slemrod. 2012. "Check in the Mail or More in the Paycheck: Does the Effectiveness of Fiscal Stimulus Depend on How It Is Delivered?" *American Economic Journal: Economic Policy* 4 (3): 216–50.

Stolberg, Sheryl Gay. 2009. "Signing Stimulus, Obama Doesn't Rule Out More." *New York Times,* February 17, 2009. https://www.nytimes.com/2009/02/18/us/politics/18web-stim.html.

Summers, Lawrence H. 2007. "Risks of Recession, Prospects for Policy." Remarks at the Brookings Institution, "State of the U.S. Economy," Washington, D.C., December 19, 2007. https://www.brookings.edu/wp-content/uploads/2012/04/20071219_summers.pdf.

Summers, Lawrence H. 2008. "Economic Policy Work, Executive Summary." Memo, December 15, 2008. https://delong.typepad.com/20091215-obama-economic-policy-memo.pdf.

White House. 2010. "Small Business Jobs and Wages Tax Cut." Fact Sheet. https://obamawhitehouse.archives.gov/sites/default/files/rss_viewer/fact_sheet_small_business_jobs_wages_tax_cut.pdf.

Wilson, Daniel J. 2012. "Fiscal Spending Jobs Multipliers: Evidence from the 2009 American Recovery and Reinvestment Act." *American Economic Journal: Economic Policy* 4 (3): 251–82.

Wimer, Christopher, Liana Fox, Irv Garfinkel, Neeraj Kaushal, and Jane Waldfogel. 2013. "Trends in Poverty with an Anchored Supplemental Poverty Measure." Working Paper 13–01, Columbia Population Research Center, New York.

Woodford, Michael. 2011. "Simple Analytics of the Government Expenditure Multiplier." *American Economic Journal: Macroeconomics* 3 (1): 1–35.

Zidar, Owen M. 2017. "Tax Cuts for Whom? Heterogeneous Effects of Income Tax Changes on Growth and Employment." NBER Working Paper, no. 21035, National Bureau of Economic Research, Cambridge, MA, February 2017.

Zwick, Eric, and James Mahon. 2017. "Tax Policy and Heterogeneous Investment Behavior." *American Economic Review* 107 (1): 217–48.

CHAPTER SEVENTEEN

International Coordination of Financial and Economic Policies

CLAY LOWERY, NATHAN SHEETS, AND EDWIN (TED) TRUMAN

The global financial crisis unfolded in fits and starts, noticeably spreading beyond the United States for the first time on August 9, 2007. On that date, BNP Paribas, a large French bank, suspended withdrawals from three of its affiliated investment funds because it could not value some of its U.S. subprime mortgage-backed securities (MBS) holdings. Although the action was dramatic, U.S. and foreign policymakers did not generally view it as the signal of what turned out to be an epic event on a scale not seen since the Great Depression of the 1930s. The economic downturn would touch every corner of the world and have consequences we are still living with today. This chapter outlines what American policymakers did, working with counterparts around

We thank Ben S. Bernanke, Jamie Franco, Timothy F. Geithner, Benjamin Henken, Zixuan Huang, George Jiranek, Karen Johnson, Michael Leahy, Nellie Liang, John Lipsky, Deborah McClellan, David McCormick, Patricia Mosser, Henry M. Paulson, Jr., Tom Redburn, Tara Rice, Ariel Smith, Mark Sobel, David Tam, Tracy Truman, Steve Tvardek, and David Wessel for comments and assistance on this project. None of them should be held responsible for the views expressed. Many of the actions and proposals we describe in this chapter came from U.S. officials, but we were not alone in developing crisis responses. Moreover, few of our proposals could have reached fruition without the cooperation and support of our counterparts around the world. It is impossible to calculate how many hours these individuals invested during the crisis. At home, the contributions of our dedicated colleagues at the U.S. Treasury and the Federal Reserve in both designing and implementing these proposals and addressing other pressing contemporary demands were crucial to the success of the collaborative global effort.

the world, to develop and orchestrate a response to the crisis that, in our view, helped mitigate its severity.

CONTEXT

The years before the crisis hit have been characterized as "the Great Moderation," but that period of spreading global prosperity masked many excesses that set the stage for what was to come. Low investment yields in advanced economies, combined with poor U.S. policies on housing finance, prompted global investors to chase returns and to misjudge and misprice risks in a global credit boom. Capital flows dwarfed the trade in goods, spreading hidden dangers far beyond their original sources. Lax financial regulation contributed to insufficient capital and liquidity in financial institutions as the risks were growing in most advanced countries.

Against this background, the global financial system was becoming far more dollar-dependent than we appreciated in August 2007. European banks were especially exposed. Between 2002 and 2007, European banks increased their cross-border dollar claims on the United States by 140 percent, to $2.1 trillion. The increase in claims by U.S. banks on European institutions rose by 230 percent, to $1.5 trillion.[1] In addition, European banks had extensive dollar-based operations in the United States.

Initially, the dominant narrative of the crisis in the international community was that it was born in the United States and most of the damage would likely remain there. But the crisis spread far beyond the United States, not just because of the relative importance of its economy or because of the direct exposure of many global financial institutions to its financial system, but also because there were substantial vulnerabilities in many other parts of the global economy as well.

In the early stage of the crisis, the perception that the United States was more at risk from the collapse of the housing bubble led to an appreciation of other major currencies, as well as those of emerging markets economies, against the U.S. dollar from late 2006 to mid-2008. But by mid-2008, as reality set in, the global scramble for U.S. dollar funding contributed to the depreciation of most

---

1. Stefan Avdjiev, Robert M. McCauley, and Hyun Song Shin, "Breaking Free of the Triple Coincidence in International Finance" (BIS Working Papers, no. 524, Oct. 2015).

Table 17.1 **Percent Change in Currency Values and International Reserves**

Time period	Currencies[A]					Reserves[C]	
			Emerging markets			Emerging markets less	
	All	Major	All[B]	Less China	China	China	China
Dec. 2006 to July 2008	11.9	14.3	9.5	8.4	14.4	51.8	73.1
July 2008 to March 2009	−15.1	−15.7	−14.5	−17.5	−0.0	−12.0	30.1
March 2009 to Dec. 2009	11.1	14.6	8.1	9.8	0.1	12.8	23.5
Total period Dec. 2006 to Dec. 2009	5.5	10.5	1.2	−1.7	14.6	50.7	127.1

[A] Currency movements are from Federal Reserve Board data on exchange rates and indexes for the foreign exchange value of the dollar from the perspective of the foreign countries, seven major currencies, and 19 currencies of emerging markets economies, as of August 2018.
[B] The index for all emerging markets currencies is "other important trading partners."
[C] Reserves are total excluding gold.

Sources: Board of Governors of the Federal Reserve System; IMF, *International Financial Statistics*

other currencies against the dollar, a decline that continued through March 2009 (see Table 17.1).[2]

The global financial interconnections to the U.S. housing market were evident in market apprehension about the condition of European banks, as measured by five-year credit default swap (CDS) spreads, which rose in the second half of 2007 and the first half of 2008. The rise was in line with that for U.S. banks (see Figure 17.1). This fear about European banks, coupled with financial vulnerabilities associated with their own domestic imbalances, affected the ability of European banks to continue to fund their dollar-denominated as-

2. The exception was China's renminbi (RMB), which was effectively pegged against the dollar for two years starting in July 2008.

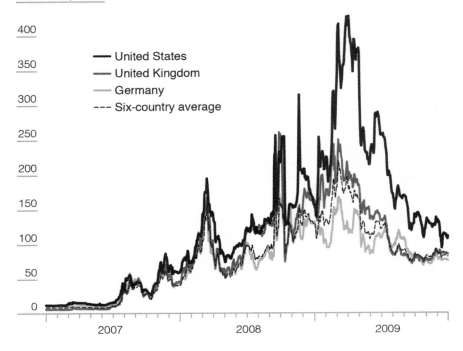

Figure 17.1 Five-Year Credit Default Swap Spreads for Major Banks, by Country

Note: Average of individual banks for countries listed. United States: JPMorgan Chase and Citigroup; Germany: Deutsche Bank; United Kingdom: Barclays Bank; six-country average: equal-weighted average of listed U.S., German, and U.K. banks, in addition to banks in Japan (Sumitomo Mitsui Banking Corp. and MUFG Bank), Italy (Intesa Sanpaolo and UniCredit), and France (BNP Paribas and Société Générale). Credit default swap spreads are shown in basis points but priced in local currencies.

Sources: Bloomberg Finance L.P.; IHS Markit

sets.[3] Equity indexes in other advanced economies started to decline as well in late 2007, along with U.S. equity prices (see Figure 17.2).[4]

3. Fourteen of the 23 advanced countries included in Carmen Reinhart's database (2011) experienced banking crises in 2007 to 2010. "Dates for Banking Crises, Currency Crashes, Sovereign Domestic or External Default (or Restructuring), Inflation Crises, and Stock Market Crashes (Varieties)," http://www.carmenreinhart.com/data/browse-by-topic/topics/7/.

4. Indexes for emerging markets economies did not start to decline until mid-2008.

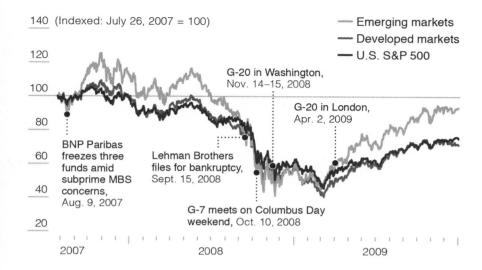

140 (Indexed: July 26, 2007 = 100)
120
100
80
60
40
20

— Emerging markets
— Developed markets
— U.S. S&P 500

G-20 in Washington,
Nov. 14–15, 2008

G-20 in London,
Apr. 2, 2009

BNP Paribas
freezes three
funds amid
subprime MBS
concerns,
Aug. 9, 2007

Lehman Brothers
files for bankruptcy,
Sept. 15, 2008

G-7 meets on Columbus Day
weekend, Oct. 10, 2008

2007   2008   2009

Figure 17.2 Selected Equity Indexes for the United States, Emerging Markets, and Developed Economies

Notes: (1) Emerging markets: iShares MSCI Emerging Markets ETF; developed markets: Vanguard FTSE Developed Markets ETF (U.S.); United States: S&P 500 Index. Equity indexes are scaled to July 26, 2007, because data for one or more of the series were not available for download before that date. (2) Acronyms used in this figure are defined in the list of abbreviations at the front of this book.

Source: Bloomberg Finance L.P.

Weakening economic activity in the advanced economies and contraction in cross-border financing contributed to a collapse in international trade, spreading the crisis to emerging markets and developing economies, especially in Eastern Europe. "All 104 nations on which the WTO reports data experienced a drop in both imports and exports during the second half of 2008 and the first half of 2009," the international economist Richard Baldwin found. "Imports and exports collapsed for the EU27 and 10 other nations that together account for three quarters of world trade; each of these trade flows dropped by more than 20% from 2008Q2 to 2009Q2; many fell 30% or more."[5]

5. Richard Baldwin, "Introduction," in *The Great Trade Collapse: Causes, Consequences and Prospects,* ed. Richard Baldwin (VoxEU e-book, Nov. 2009). WTO is the World Trade Organization.

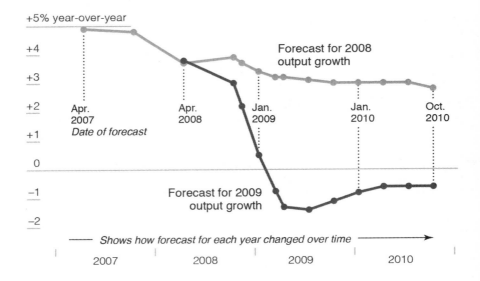

+5% year-over-year

Forecast for 2008
output growth

Apr.
2007
Apr.
2008
Jan.
2009
Jan.
2010
Oct.
2010

Date of forecast

Forecast for 2009
output growth

Shows how forecast for each year changed over time →

2007   2008   2009   2010

Figure 17.3 IMF Real GDP Growth Forecasts for the World

Note: March 2009 figures are the midpoint of ranges of projections made in "Global Economic Policies and Prospects," an IMF paper prepared for a meeting of G-20 ministers and governors in March 2009.

Source: IMF, *World Economic Outlook* and *Updates*, dates indicated

Forecasters did not initially recognize the full potential impact of these developments on the global economy. In April 2008, the official forecast of the International Monetary Fund (IMF) for year-over-year global economic growth in 2009 was 3.8 percent, the same as the forecast for 2008. As late as November 2008, it was 2.2 percent. It wasn't until March 2009 that the IMF predicted a small global decline, and not until April 2009, just as the crisis atmosphere was beginning to ease, that it cut its forecast for the year to −1.3 percent (see Figure 17.3).

The global crisis of the early twenty-first century presented a classic case for the need for effective international policy coordination. Though the positive impacts of policy actions by one country acting alone can spill over into other countries, each country can generate positive externalities for all other economies by acting in concert. In the end, in part because of the international policy response that began under the George W. Bush administration and continued after the inauguration of President Barack Obama, world economic activity in 2009 fell 0.6 percent, substantially less than the 1.3 percent expected in April.

PRINCIPAL INITIATIVES

From early on we recognized that the financial crisis was a global event requiring a global response. The challenge for the United States on the international front was to design policies in cooperation with its foreign counterparts to limit the global financial crisis and likely recession and prevent serious feedback effects to the United States. Although all countries faced similar problems of illiquid markets, fragile financial firms, and weakening economies, the economic and financial interconnections across countries made these problems especially challenging for policymakers because responses required global cooperation. A central element of the U.S. strategy was diplomacy—communication, development, and cooperation on policies—to build support for a more effective, multifaceted, global response to the crisis and to rebuild confidence among investors and the public.

DIPLOMACY

Diplomacy was a critical component of all the key U.S. international initiatives. These included the following:

1. Encouraging common supportive macroeconomic policies;
2. Avoiding beggar-thy-neighbor trade, currency, and financial intervention actions;
3. Supporting emerging economies with financial resources from international institutions.

At the same time, we pursued longer-range goals, such as designing programs to replenish the financial resources of those institutions and building global consensus on a new architecture for financial regulation. The Treasury utilized and expanded existing channels and organizations to foster cooperation, and the Federal Reserve utilized its multiple points of contact with other central banks to provide dollar funding to stressed banking systems.

Open lines of international communication were essential to establishing a consensus diagnosis as the basis for trust and international cooperation. We used existing multinational channels, including the Group of Seven (G-7),[6] the Group of Twenty (G-20)[7] finance ministers and central bank governors, the IMF's International Monetary and Financial Committee (IMFC),[8] and central bankers at the Bank for International Settlements (BIS). Treasury held weekly (and often daily) phone calls among the G-7 deputies. We also started holding G-20 phone calls. By being forthright with our partners and sharing our perspective on the highly connected financial system, we hoped to build trust to support joint actions or at least to avoid counterproductive actions.

We also used bilateral communications, not just with other advanced economies but with emerging markets economies as well. For instance, Treasury secretary Henry M. Paulson, Jr., had established a channel with China through the Strategic Economic Dialogue (SED)—particularly with then vice premier Wang Qishan and People's Bank of China governor Zhou Xiaochuan. These lines of communication helped build the trust that led China to support our financial rescue framework for Fannie Mae and Freddie Mac (see Chapter 6, on government-sponsored enterprises [GSEs]), to decline to collaborate with the Russians in selling Fannie and Freddie securities,[9] and to resist participating in the run on money market mutual funds after the Reserve Primary Fund "broke the buck" (see Chapter 7, on guaranteeing the money market funds).

Diplomatic initiatives with other countries also paid dividends at critical times. The central banks of Japan and South Korea, for example, had substantial holdings in Fannie Mae and Freddie Mac debt. Rather than join in a "fire sale" of those debt instruments, they responded positively to reassurances from the Treasury, echoed by the Federal Reserve, that U.S. rescue actions in the summer of 2008 would help put a floor under any losses on their bonds. Similarly, a series of communications between Secretary Paulson and Japanese finance minister Shoichi Nakagawa helped persuade the Japanese government

---

6. The G-7 consists of Canada, France, Germany, Italy, Japan, the United Kingdom, and the United States.

7. The G-20 is the G-7 plus Argentina, Australia, Brazil, China, India, Indonesia, Mexico, Russia, Saudi Arabia, South Africa, South Korea, Turkey, and the European Union.

8. The IMFC consists of 24 constituencies representing all 189 members (as of today) of the IMF.

9. Henry M. Paulson, Jr., *On the Brink: Inside the Race to Stop the Collapse of the Global Financial System* (New York: Business Plus, Hachette Book Group, 2010), 161.

not to oppose an injection of equity from Mitsubishi UFJ Financial Group into Morgan Stanley—the second-largest U.S. investment bank at the time.

At the G-7 meeting on October 10, 2008, policymakers emphasized their common resolve with an unusually short, blunt, and action-oriented statement. Almost all other G-7 statements are heavily negotiated documents that are several pages in length and read more like a laundry list of topics discussed. The purpose of the October 10 statement was to signal to the public that the world's largest economies were united to support the system, were rejecting beggarthy-neighbor approaches, and had agreed to back words with actions (see Appendix A). At its meeting the next day, the IMFC endorsed the G-7's plan of action word for word in its own communiqué. On Monday, October 13, U.S. authorities acted on their G-7 commitments; Secretary Paulson and Chairman Bernanke called together the heads of the major U.S. banks to accept capital injections (see Chapter 8, on recapitalizing the banking system) and the Federal Open Market Committee (FOMC) removed the caps on its liquidity swap lines with major central banks.

President Bush also endorsed the Treasury's proposal for a meeting of the G-20 heads of state to help mobilize support for a forceful international response to the crisis. It had become clear that the heads of state needed to be seen directing economic and financial experts dealing with a crisis that had clearly gone beyond technical issues. They could provide legitimacy for collective action as the crisis spread globally.

At the time, the only regular leaders' meeting of major countries that addressed international economic issues was the annual G-8 summit (the G-7 countries plus Russia at that time). The G-20—which had previously met only at the level of finance ministers and central bankers—was elevated to the national leaders' level as a vehicle to coordinate international economic policy. The inaugural meeting took place in Washington on November 14 and 15, 2008. With a little more than three weeks to prepare for the meeting, we obtained assurances from several countries, including China, that they would play a constructive role in the Washington gathering.[10] That meeting was followed by a second in London on April 1 and 2, 2009. These two meetings opened a new chapter in international cooperation—one that acknowledged that the G-7 no longer called all the international economic and financial policy shots and that widened the circle of international economic and financial decision-making.

10. For instance, before the summit, China announced a massive stimulus plan.

DOLLAR FUNDING FOR FOREIGN BANKS

As the financial crisis unfolded in the summer of 2007, term U.S. dollar funding markets deteriorated and became more expensive for financial institutions. The three-month Libor-OIS spread shot up in August and remained high (see Figure 17.4).[11] Access to foreign exchange swap markets to obtain dollars also tightened. These stresses prompted a scramble for dollars in U.S. financial markets.

One result was increased volatility in the federal funds market—transactions in reserves held at the Federal Reserve (see Chapters 2 and 15, on classic lender-of-last-resort programs and monetary policy, respectively). Each trading day, European institutions that had difficulty borrowing dollars piled into the federal funds market as it opened. The federal funds rate surged, only to fall sharply in the afternoon after the European trading day ended. In addition, foreign banks' difficulties in raising dollar funding prompted them to sell dollar-denominated mortgages and other assets, contributing to asset market pressures. Some of the foreign institutions had access to the Federal Reserve's discount window, but many did not or held collateral mainly in their home jurisdictions.

In part to address this source of unwanted financial volatility, the FOMC on December 6, 2007, authorized a $20 billion swap line with the European Central Bank (ECB) to provide it with dollar liquidity. This action was taken in tandem with authorization of the opening of the Term Auction Facility (TAF), under which the Fed auctioned fixed amounts of term discount window credit to eligible borrowers. On December 11, a $4 billion line with the Swiss National Bank (SNB) also was authorized.[12] The two lines were subse-

---

11. The Libor-OIS spread—a measure of the cost of short-term wholesale borrowing for banking firms—is an important metric of confidence in the banking system. The London Interbank Offered Rate (Libor) is the interest rate at which banks exchange deposits over a specified time period. The overnight indexed swap (OIS) rate is the policy rate, such as the federal funds rate, compounded over the specified time period.

12. The swap lines were approved with one FOMC member dissenting because he felt that both central banks had enough dollar-denominated foreign exchange reserves to meet the needs of their banks. This had been one of the alternatives considered along with the option of lending against cross-border collateral. See minutes of the Federal Open Market Committee (FOMC), Dec. 6 and 11, 2007. These actions were jointly announced on December 12, 2007, by the Fed, the BoE, and the SNB. Separately, the Bank of Canada and the Bank of England announced liquidity provision actions, and the Bank of Japan and the Swedish Riksbank issued supporting statements.

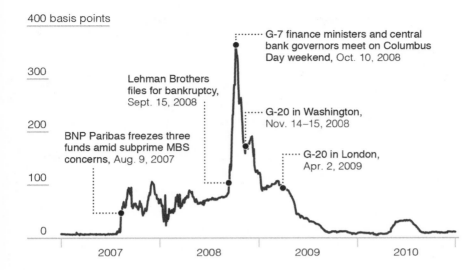

400 basis points

300

Lehman Brothers
files for bankruptcy,
Sept. 15, 2008

200

BNP Paribas freezes three
funds amid subprime MBS
concerns, Aug. 9, 2007

100

0

G-7 finance ministers and central
bank governors meet on Columbus
Day weekend, Oct. 10, 2008

G-20 in Washington,
Nov. 14–15, 2008

G-20 in London,
Apr. 2, 2009

2007   2008   2009   2010

Figure 17.4 **Three-Month Libor-OIS Spread**

Note: Acronyms used in this figure are defined in the list of abbreviations at the front of this book.

Source: Bloomberg Finance L.P.

quently expanded so that, by the time that Lehman Brothers filed for bankruptcy on September 15, 2008, they stood at $55 billion and $12 billion, respectively. The swaps involved an exchange of U.S. dollars and foreign currency between the Federal Reserve and the foreign central bank at the prevailing market exchange rate. The foreign central bank lent the dollars to its banks under its own lending terms. (See Appendix B for more detail on the structure of the liquidity swap lines.)

Under the terms of the swap arrangements, the foreign central bank passed back to the Fed all its earnings from the dollar auctions, typically 100 basis points over the OIS rate. This structure reflected the ECB's preference early in the crisis to act only as a pass-through agent in helping the Fed cope with dollar-funding pressures. The ECB initially sought to convey that it was just supporting the Fed's efforts to counter U.S.-centric and dollar-centric stresses, rather than embracing its role as the Fed's full partner in fighting a global crisis.[13]

13. This early divergence in perspectives on the crisis between the Fed and the ECB
    further manifested itself in July 2008 when the ECB hiked its policy interest rate out

After Lehman's collapse, global dollar funding markets became significantly more stressed. In response, the FOMC rapidly expanded its network of liquidity swap lines:

- On September 18, the Bank of Canada (BoC), the Bank of England (BoE), and the Bank of Japan (BoJ) were added as counterparties.
- On September 24, the central banks of Australia, Denmark, Norway, and Sweden were added.
- The drawing capacity on the lines was ramped up substantially further on September 29, to allow a total of $620 billion.
- Most consequentially, on October 13–14, following the G-7 meeting on October 10, the Fed announced that the caps on the swap lines with the BoE, the BoJ, the ECB, and the SNB would effectively be removed, allowing these central banks to supply as many dollars as their banks demanded.[14]
- New Zealand was added as the tenth advanced economy on October 28.

The rationale for this dramatic expansion of the swap network was the cascading financial stresses after Lehman's failure, further substantial upward pressure on the dollar Libor-OIS spread (see Figure 17.4), and the generalized withdrawal of financial institutions from term lending.

Following these decisions to greatly expand the program, drawings under the swap lines increased dramatically (see Figure 17.5), from $62 billion in mid-September 2008 to $500 billion by the end of October.

As the financial crisis escalated, contagion effects swept up many emerging markets economies, including some major countries that had track records of disciplined economic management. For example, the spread on five-year credit default swaps on the sovereign debt of Brazil, Mexico, and South Korea rose sharply after Lehman's collapse (see Figure 17.6). This contagion motivated the Fed's decision on October 29 to establish liquidity swap lines with the central banks of Brazil, Mexico, Singapore, and South Korea, each for $30 billion, on the same terms as those for the central banks of the advanced

---

of a stated concern over inflation. That action essentially signaled that the ECB believed the crisis was under control.

14. In early October 2008, Congress gave the Fed authority to pay interest on excess reserves. This gave the Fed increased scope to expand its balance sheet while still maintaining an effective target for the federal funds rate.

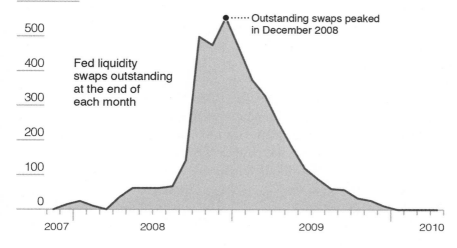

Figure 17.5 Federal Reserve Swaps Outstanding

Source: Federal Reserve Board

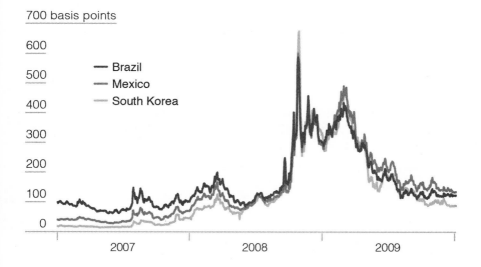

Figure 17.6 Five-Year Sovereign CDS Spreads for Selected Emerging Markets Economies

Note: CDS are credit default swaps.

Sources: Bloomberg Finance L.P.; IHS Markit

countries, except for size.[15] These four economies were chosen because of their relatively large size, their financial systems were more integrated into the global financial system than other candidate economies, and their relatively strong economic fundamentals. Swap lines were more likely to be effective in these cases than with other emerging economies facing greater economic challenges.

The reasoning behind these additional swap lines was twofold. First was the general seizing up of financial conditions that had motivated the swaps with the advanced countries. Second, though for many of the advanced economies the crisis in large measure reflected their own failures to adequately manage risks in their financial systems, these emerging markets countries were largely innocent bystanders.

Another consideration was articulated by Timothy F. Geithner, then president of the New York Fed: "The privilege of being the reserve currency of the world comes with some burdens."[16]

This observation was a core rationale for the overall swap line program. The financial crisis entailed an unprecedented seizing up of global, dollar funding markets. Only the Fed, as the issuer of the world's leading reserve currency, could supply enough dollars to help defuse intensifying funding stresses.

The Fed also had to consider its relationship with the IMF, the world's principal crisis-fighting institution, focusing primarily on programs to support emerging-markets-economy members. The Fed could have told the central banks of the four countries to go to the IMF even though at the time the Fund did not have a short-term lending facility in place. In proposing the swaps program, the staff argued that "meeting the potential liquidity needs of these large countries would strain the available resources of the Fund." Thus by "taking off the IMF's hands some of the largest potential liquidity needs . . . [this allows the IMF] to focus on a whole range of additional countries."[17] The Fed's efforts were seen as "broadly complementary" to those of the IMF, which es-

15. Transcript of the meeting of the FOMC on Oct. 28–29, 2008, 10.
16. Transcript of the meeting of the FOMC on Oct. 28–29, 2008, 21.
17. As discussed in this chapter, the G-20 leaders agreed in April 2009 to substantially increase the resources available to the IMF. But at the time, the Federal Reserve's commitment of potentially $120 billion in short-term liquidity assistance to these four countries freed up the IMF's balance sheet to make loans to a broader set of members when the IMF had only $250 billion in usable resources to lend.

tablished a short-term facility on the same date.[18] That facility was never drawn upon.

As part of its deliberations, the Fed informed the U.S. Treasury and State Department about the proposed additional liquidity swap lines. Secretaries Paulson and Condoleezza Rice supported the proposal.[19]

Although the FOMC found these arguments generally persuasive (the vote on the emerging markets lines was unanimous), there was concern that the program put the Fed in the position of being an "arbiter of the soundness of other countries' policies, the liquidity requirements of their banks, and their systemic importance."[20] For this reason, the FOMC made clear in its deliberations that the bar for additional emerging markets swap lines was high. The program was not expanded, notwithstanding inquiries from other potential central bank partners.[21]

In the end, only the line with South Korea was actively used. Its drawings reached about $16 billion during the first quarter of 2009. Mexico made one precautionary drawing on its line, of $3.2 billion in April 2009.

Overall, drawings peaked in mid-December 2008, at more than $580 billion. The ECB accounted for about $310 billion (exceeding the total foreign currency holdings of euro-area central banks of about $200 billion), the BoJ for about $125 billion, the BoE for $50 billion, and the SNB for $16 billion. At the same time, foreign banks borrowed $334 billion from the discount window, borrowed $208 billion from the TAF, and benefited from financing associated with the entities established using the emergency lending authority of Section 13(3) of the Federal Reserve Act (see Chapter 3, on novel lender-of-last-resort programs). Drawings fell off sharply during the first half of 2009, reflecting the initial stages of healing in global financial conditions. The lines

18. Transcript of the meeting of the FOMC on Oct. 28–29, 2008, 10, 11, and 37.
19. Transcript of the meeting of the FOMC on Oct. 28–29, 2008, 16.
20. Remarks delivered by Donald Kohn at a Federal Reserve Bank of Dallas conference on Sept. 18, 2014, and later released by the Brookings Institution (www.brookings .edu/on-the-record/the-feds-role-in-international-crises/).
21. An approach by Iceland had been turned down. Other potential applicants mentioned in the meeting were Chile, India, and South Africa; the names of some other countries mentioned were redacted. See transcript of the meeting of the FOMC on Oct. 28–29, 2008, 33, 17 and 29, and 30 and 32, respectively.

were closed on February 1, 2010, but were later reopened with major central banks in Europe and Asia.[22]

Fed policymakers were forced to make difficult judgments as they sought to balance their explicit domestic mandate, the constraints of historical precedent, and their commitment to the stability of the global financial system as the issuer of the world's premier reserve currency. The key connection between these considerations was inescapable evidence that, without Fed action, disruptions abroad would have negative feedbacks on the U.S. economy.

In addition to the substantial provision of dollar liquidity, the swap lines gave central banks a powerful, visible mechanism for collaboration and coordination. Communication by the individual central banks was carefully coordinated. Efforts were made to adopt common language in describing the problems that all the central banks faced and the policy actions that were being taken. In addition, these measures were typically announced in parallel. This communication approach, emphasizing the determination of central banks to work together, was a second important channel through which the swap lines helped soothe stresses in global markets. The general assessment of observers—including domestic and foreign policymakers, analysts, and academics—is that the swap lines were highly effective.[23]

The program was an example of the demands on the Fed to act as an international lender of last resort. Although its actions stirred controversy, the Fed primarily viewed its actions as being in the enlightened self-interest of the United States. It sought to satisfy its statutory, domestically focused, dual man-

22. The program was reinstated in response to the intensifying euro area debt crisis. These lines were made permanent in 2013.
23. See William Allen and Richhild Moessner, "Central Bank Cooperation and International Liquidity in the Financial Crisis of 2008–9" (BIS Working Papers, no. 310, May 2010); Joshua Aizenman and Gurnain Pasricha, "Selective Swap Arrangements and the Global Financial Crisis: Analysis and Interpretation" (NBER Working Paper, no. 14821, March 2009); Joshua Aizenman, Yothin Jinjarek, and Donghyun Park, "Evaluating Asian Swap Arrangements" (Asian Development Bank Institute Working Paper Series, no. 297, July 2011); Naohiko Baba and Frank Packer, "From Turmoil to Crisis: Dislocations in the FX Swap Market before and after the Failure of Lehman Brothers" (BIS Working Papers, no. 285, July 2009); Naohiko Baba and Ilhyock Shim, "Dislocations in the Won-Dollar Swap Markets during the Crisis of 2007–09" (BIS Working Papers, no. 344, April 2011); and Linda Goldberg, Craig Kennedy, and Jason Miu, "Central Bank Dollar Swap Lines and Overseas Dollar Funding Costs" (NBER Working Paper Series, no. 15763, Feb. 2010).

date regarding employment and inflation while contributing to stability in U.S. financial markets.

COORDINATION OF MACROECONOMIC POLICIES

As the financial dimensions of the global crisis intensified and the economic consequences became more severe, U.S. officials worked to mobilize a forceful macroeconomic policy response across the major economies. The monetary policy and fiscal policy responses differed in timing, intensity, and duration, in part because of the different conditions in each economy but also because of differences in views about the appropriate response, within countries and across countries.

Monetary Policy

The ECB responded to the BNP Paribas announcement on August 9, 2007, with a massive liquidity injection. But it did not alter its 4.0 percent policy interest rate until the following July—when the rate was raised by 25 basis points (see Figure 17.7).

The FOMC adopted a more aggressive trajectory. On August 10, it announced that reserves would be provided as necessary, but at the time its 5.25 percent target for the federal funds rate was not altered.[24] However, shortly after, on August 17, the Fed signaled an easing tilt in its future policy and a reduction in the spread between the discount rate and the target federal funds rate, from 100 to 50 basis points. On September 18, 2007, the FOMC's target was reduced to 4.75 percent. By early October 2008, the target was 2.0 percent.

Reflecting the view at the time in other countries that the problem was largely confined to the United States, the policy rates of other major central banks hardly budged over the first year of the crisis. The BoE had raised its bank rate to 5.75 percent in July 2007, then reduced it in December to 5.50 percent. By April 2008, the rate had declined to 5.0 percent but was still relatively high. The SNB raised its target for the Swiss franc three-month Libor to 3.25 percent in September 2007 and did not reduce it until October 2008.

24. At the September 18 FOMC meeting, some participants, in fact, criticized the Desk at the Federal Reserve Bank of New York (FRBNY) for allowing the funds rate to average less than 5.25 percent.

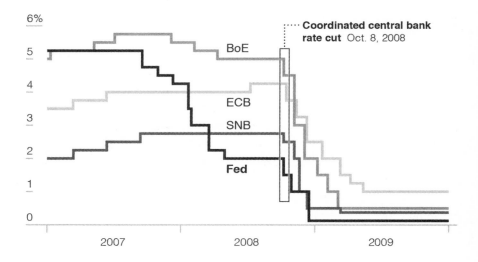

Figure 17.7 **Policy Interest Rates**

Note: Federal Reserve: midpoint of the range for the federal funds rate target; European Central Bank: main refinancing operations rate; Bank of England: official bank rate; Swiss National Bank: midpoint of the SNB target range.

Source: Bank for International Settlements

The ECB, as noted earlier, raised its refinancing tender rate to 4.25 percent in July 2008.

The watershed moment for global monetary policy cooperation came on October 8, 2008, when the FOMC acted in concert with the ECB, the BoE, the SNB, the BoC, and the Swedish Riksbank to cut policy rates.[25] A key motivation from the Fed perspective was to get the ECB out of the corner into which it had painted itself in July. The signal of coordination and cooperation was as important as the reduction itself.[26]

Soon after the G-7 meeting and the Washington G-20 leaders' meeting in November, all the major central banks moved more aggressively to ease policies.

25. Most of the rate cuts were 50 basis points, except for 25 basis points by the SNB. Cuts in policy interest rates of this size are unusual. The People's Bank of China cut rates the same day, but its move was not coordinated with the other central banks.
26. Transcript of conference call of the FOMC on Oct. 7, 2008, 14–15.

Fiscal Policy

Fiscal policy was less well agreed upon and coordinated. The Bush administration acted alone in implementing a moderate fiscal stimulus in early 2008, primarily in the form of onetime refundable individual tax rebates (see Chapter 16, on the fiscal response). The Washington G-20 declaration endorsed appropriate fiscal as well as monetary measures, but initially, only China responded with a major fiscal stimulus (organized around state-directed bank lending). IMF managing director Dominique Strauss-Kahn followed up on the Washington declaration by advocating a global fiscal stimulus of 2 percent of global GDP, equivalent to about $1.3 trillion.[27]

The Obama administration worked with the new Congress to pass a large fiscal stimulus, which began to take effect in early 2009. The logic underlying U.S. fiscal expansion was overwhelming. Monetary policy is less effective when deployed after a large boom in credit and when the engine of the financial system has broken down. Fiscal policy was essential to offset the collapse in demand. And the logic of joint action was compelling as well. If all major countries acted together, the leakage of one country's stimulus into another country would be reciprocated. But the IMF's proposal became trapped in technical and policy conflicts.

In London, the G-20 leaders endorsed a concerted fiscal stimulus of $5 trillion, intended to raise output in 2010 by 4 percent, but actions fell short of that mark. The IMF staff estimated that the cumulative change in the combined, overall fiscal balance for the G-20 countries in 2009 would increase only $2.7 trillion, but that figure compared favorably with Strauss-Kahn's original proposal. The IMF, however, correctly projected a withdrawal of stimulus in 2010.[28]

Although the global fiscal stimulus was smaller than advertised and its withdrawal was premature, policy actions by China and other emerging markets countries helped fill some of the gap left by advanced economies. Many of the emerging markets countries, along with smaller developing countries, were in

---

27. The estimate of the U.S. dollar amount of global GDP in 2008 is based on the IMF's April 2019 update of the *World Economic Outlook Database*.
28. "IMF Update on Fiscal Stimulus and Financial Sector Measures," International Monetary Fund, April 26, 2009, https://www.imf.org/external/np/fad/2009/042609 .htm.

sufficiently strong positions that they had the policy space to adopt counter-cyclical policies.

For all the difficulties, our central conclusion is that the coordinated response of fiscal and monetary policies to global economic weakness, agreed to in Washington and London and later implemented, ranks high in the annals of international economic cooperation in both country scope and broad scale.[29]

FINANCIAL SUPPORT FOR INTERNATIONAL FINANCIAL INSTITUTIONS

By the late summer and early fall of 2008, the crisis in the financial systems of advanced countries was clearly taking its toll on the economies of the emerging markets and developing economies (EMDEs). In April 2008, the IMF forecast for the global economy in 2009 was 3.8 percent—1.3 percent for the advanced countries and 6.6 percent for emerging markets and developing economies (see Figures 17.3 and 17.8). By October, the EMDEs were projected to be drawn significantly into the economic and financial maelstrom. Initially, the economic crisis primarily affected countries in Central and Eastern Europe and Latin America, but ultimately, countries in all regions were impacted.

The EMDEs also saw their currencies depreciating, driving up the cost of servicing their dollar-denominated debts as their international reserves were declining (see Table 17.1). Many EMDEs faced problems on both their current and financial accounts. In 2008, the combined current account positions of economies in Central and Eastern Europe, Latin America, and sub-Saharan Africa deteriorated by $82 billion, or about 1 percent of GDP, and portfolio investment inflows to all emerging and developing economies declined by more than $400 billion, to a mere $13 billion.[30]

The IMF and the multilateral development banks (MDBs) are the principal international institutions designed to address members' external financing

---

29. The previous, but controversial, high point, in the view of most analysts, was the 1978 Bonn economic summit.
30. IMF, Oct. 2018 update of the *World Economic Outlook Database*; and IMF, "Sovereigns, Funding, and Systemic Liquidity: Statistical Appendix," *Global Financial Stability Report,* Oct. 2010, 16.

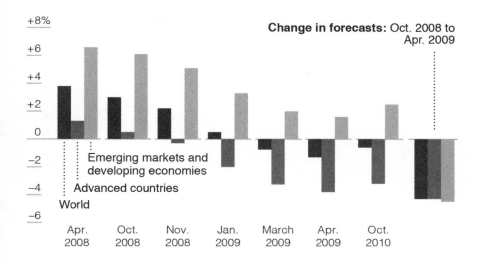

Figure 17.8 **Progression of World Economic Outlook Forecasts of Real GDP Growth for 2009**

Note: March 2009 figures are the midpoint of ranges of projections made in "Global Economic Policies and Prospects," an IMF paper prepared for a meeting of G-20 ministers and governors in March 2009. Forecasts reflect the predicted year-over-year change in real GDP growth.

Source: IMF, *World Economic Outlook* and *Updates,* dates indicated

problems.[31] At the Washington summit the G-20 committed to ensuring that these institutions had enough resources to play their traditional roles with adequate resources.

In the fall of 2008, the IMF began to approve programs to support countries that were affected by the spreading crisis. From September 2008 to February 2009, IMF lending commitments increased by $50 billion. This was the largest IMF financial intervention over a short interval in its history, even larger than during the Asian financial crisis in 1997 (see Figure 17.9). Member countries also turned to the MDBs. Their new nonconcessional lending, which had averaged $35 billion annually from 2005 to 2007, increased by 22 percent in 2008, to

31. The MDBs are the World Bank Group, the African Development Bank, the Asian Development Bank, the Inter-American Development Bank, and the European Bank for Reconstruction and Development.

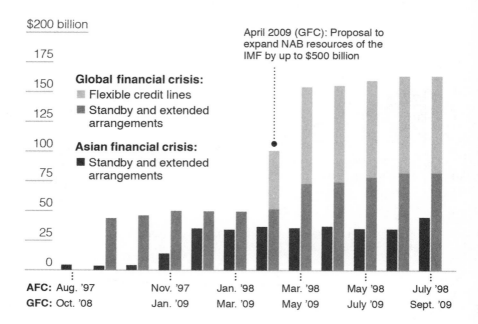

$200 billion

175

April 2009 (GFC): Proposal to
expand NAB resources of the
IMF by up to $500 billion

150   **Global financial crisis:**
        ▓ Flexible credit lines
125   ■ Standby and extended
        arrangements

100   **Asian financial crisis:**
        ■ Standby and extended
75   arrangements

50

25

0

AFC: Aug. '97   Nov. '97   Jan. '98   Mar. '98   May '98   July '98
GFC: Oct. '08   Jan. '09   Mar. '09   May '09   July '09   Sept. '09

Figure 17.9 **Increase in IMF Lending Commitments from Starts of Asian and Global Financial Crises**

Note: Start dates for new IMF lending are July 1997 for the Asian financial crisis (AFC)
and September 2008 for the global financial crisis (GFC). Special drawing right (SDR)
data were converted to U.S. dollars at $1.358620 per SDR (the rate on July 31, 1997) for
the AFC and $1.557220 per SDR (the rate on Sept. 30, 2008) for the GFC. NAB is the IMF's
New Arrangements to Borrow.

Sources: International Monetary Fund; authors' calculations

$43 billion.[32] By the start of 2009, the risk was that the demand for financial as-
sistance from the international institutions would outstrip prudent supply.

NEW ARRANGEMENTS TO BORROW

In September 2008, the IMF's effective lending capacity was about $250 bil-
lion. Following the commitment at the Washington G-20 summit to enhance
the resources of the IMF, the incoming Obama administration considered
three alternatives:

32. Rebecca M. Nelson, "Multilateral Development Banks: Overview and Issues for
Congress," Congressional Research Service, July 6, 2018.

1. Temporary bilateral lending to the IMF;
2. An increase in IMF quotas;[33]
3. Augmenting the new arrangements to borrow (NAB).[34]

We rejected the first, "tin cup" option because congressional approval would be required, which would be tough to obtain, would take time, and would not be available for the next crisis. We wanted something more multilateral and permanent.

We rejected the second option because the negotiation would take months, if not years. Not only would congressional approval be required, but a large majority of other IMF members would have to accept their quota increases before the new funds would be available.

U.S. policymakers settled on the third option: expanding the NAB, which is essentially a permanent reserve for the IMF.[35] Consistent with the doctrine of overwhelming force, Treasury secretary Geithner and U.S. Treasury staff developed a proposal to increase the NAB by as much as $500 billion, with an up-front U.S. commitment to provide a maximum of 20 percent of the total. At the time, the NAB had 26 IMF members with commitments of about $50 billion. We anticipated adding new participants such as China, India, Brazil, Mexico, and Russia.[36]

Leaders at the London G-20 summit agreed to the U.S. proposal. They also blessed the IMF management's ongoing effort to raise bilateral financing of $250 billion, which would be incorporated into the expanded NAB.[37]

The pledge of additional funds for the IMF helped release the pressure on its financial resources. Consequently, the Fund comfortably increased its com-

33. The IMF's financial resources for lending are pre-positioned primarily via quota subscriptions, which are based principally on the size of each member country's economy.
34. The NAB was a U.S. proposal in the mid-1990s, after the Mexican financial crisis, to increase the Fund's secondary source of financial resources.
35. Commitments to the NAB must be renewed every five years. Under then-existing U.S. law, the Treasury secretary could renew U.S. participation after notifying Congress.
36. In the end, 14 new participants were added.
37. We also agreed to an acceleration of the completion of the 14th review of IMF quotas by January 2011, a commitment that was kept. Unfortunately, the United States did not take the necessary steps to implement the agreement until December 2015. The 13th review of IMF quotas had been completed in January 2008, when the membership, including the United States, agreed that the IMF had adequate resources at the time. Events proved us wrong.

mitments to a record $164 billion by August 2009 while retaining a cushion for additional lending (see Figure 17.9).

SPECIAL DRAWING RIGHTS

The special drawing right (SDR) was an almost forgotten instrument in the IMF's toolkit.[38] On March 5, 2009, the *Financial Times* published an op-ed by Truman proposing that the G-20 leaders in London endorse a $250 billion allocation of SDR.[39] He argued that an SDR allocation would provide a boost to confidence, would signal concrete international cooperation, and could be implemented quickly. The allocation would provide $17 billion in potential low-cost aid to the poorest countries and a further $80 billion to other emerging markets and developing countries, helping to blunt subsequent demands to build up even larger holdings of international reserves. Developed countries, short on reserves, also could lend their SDR to other countries. But U.S. support of the proposal was crucial.[40]

Opponents of the proposal inside the U.S. government, in other advanced countries, and at the IMF argued that an SDR allocation would provide countries with unconditional financing (contributing to moral hazard), would not go to the right countries because allocations are based on quota shares and the large countries have the largest shares, would not respond to a long-term global need to add to international reserves (the official criterion for allocations), and would risk exacerbating inflation.

By contrast, many think tank experts and most representatives of EMDEs favored an SDR allocation. The latter kept the idea alive in the pre-summit meetings. The British authorities initially were noncommittal but were attracted by the proposal's novelty and size.

---

38. The instrument was established in 1969. It was envisioned as a supplement to international reserves that was both an asset for holders and a liability for countries that used their SDR allocation to acquire foreign currencies. Two allocations had been made, in 1970–1972 and in 1979–1981.
39. Edwin M. Truman, "How the Fund Can Help Save the World Economy," Peterson Institute for International Economics, op-ed in *Financial Times,* March 9, 2009. The *Financial Times* later endorsed the idea.
40. An SDR allocation requires an 85 percent weighted majority vote of IMF members; the United States held 16 percent of the votes. The United States could, without congressional authorization, support an SDR allocation in which the U.S. allocation of SDR was no larger than the U.S. quota in the IMF. This provision dictated the proposed $250 billion figure.

Shortly before the London summit, Secretary Geithner wrote to his G-20 colleagues outlining the U.S. position on the London agenda, including U.S. support for the SDR proposal.[41] The British subsequently lobbied successfully other European leaders for support. The allocation became effective on August 28, 2009, earlier than most other agreements from the London summit.

Twenty-one countries used their SDR allocations in the following year. Later analyses found only limited evidence that some of these countries may have delayed making needed adjustments.[42] In this context, the issue of moral hazard is a red herring. A few countries receiving SDR may have put off IMF-recommended policy adjustments, but the scope of these delays paled in comparison with the distorting effects on the global economy from countries that had acquired more than ample foreign exchange reserves to serve as self-insurance against adverse events and used them freely to postpone adjustment.

MULTILATERAL DEVELOPMENT BANKS

During the crisis, the World Bank and the other MDBs faced demands that they stretch their balance sheets to provide development finance to emerging markets and lower-income developing countries in need. They already had begun to respond in 2008; the London G-20 summit endorsed a further expansion, of $100 billion. Subsequently, nonconcessional MDB lending increased from 2009 to 2011 by a combined $126 billion relative to the 2005–2007 average.[43]

Understandably, the heads of the MDBs took the opportunity to press for commitments to augment the capital of their institutions. U.S. participation in these capital increases requires congressional approval. Before formally committing additional resources to the MDBs, the U.S. Treasury sought time to analyze the requests and to work with Congress on them.

The administration expressed caution on the eve of the London summit. On March 29, Secretary Geithner attended the annual meeting of the Inter-American Development Bank (IDB) and expressed positive though conditional

---

41. In retrospect, author Ted Truman is inclined to think that Secretary Geithner went along with his proposal to keep him happy. Geithner did not mention the SDR allocation in his memoir of the financial crisis, *Stress Test: Reflections on Financial Crises* (New York: Crown Publishers, 2014).
42. IMF, "Considerations on the Role of the SDR," April 11, 2018, 22, https://www.imf .org/en/Publications/Policy-Papers/Issues/2018/04/11/pp030618consideration-of-the -role-the-sdr.
43. Data supplied to authors by Rebecca M. Nelson of the Congressional Research Service.

support of IDB president Luis Alberto Moreno's request for a capital increase. Geithner committed the United States to beginning a formal review of the merits of the case but also laid down five principles to guide the review with respect to the IDB's operations and, implicitly, those of other MDBs.[44] At the time, the only institution to meet those criteria was the Asian Development Bank, which had been working with the Bush administration to meet similar conditions. In London, the United States supported a 200 percent capital increase for that institution.

TRADE PROTECTIONISM AND FINANCE

The global downturn had a devastating effect on international trade. The volume of world trade decreased by almost 20 percent between April 2008 and January 2009 before starting a slow recovery.[45] Responding in part to sharp contractions in global supply chains, the initial collapse in trade dramatically outpaced the decline during the early stages of the Great Depression.[46] Shrinking global trade spread the recession from the advanced countries to the

44. Timothy F. Geithner, "Prepared Statement by Treasury Secretary Tim Geithner at the Inter-American Development Bank's Annual Meeting of the Boards of Governors," March 29, 2009. "First, we need to re-examine the relative roles of the International Financial Institutions [IFIs] both in more normal economic conditions and in crisis. . . . [We] need a clearer division of labor. . . . Second, . . . we will evaluate whether each institution has shown its ability to demonstrate flexibility in its balance sheets under current resource constraints, as well as an ability to effectively leverage both public and private finance. . . . Third, we expect a commitment to good governance. This includes efforts to combat fraud and corruption and to strengthen the institution's risk management capacity and procedures to ensure sound investment of resources provided by the shareholders. . . . Fourth, we will look at the capacity of these institutions to adapt to change in the needs of their members, to demonstrate an ability to innovate and a capacity to achieve results with any increase in permanent capital, to continue to add value to the policy challenges of their members, and to deliver an ongoing commitment to reform. . . . Finally, for those institutions with concessional and grant windows, we want to see greater focus on the poorest countries."
45. Barry Eichengreen and Kevin O'Rourke, "A Tale of Two Depressions: What Do the New Data Tell Us?," Vox, March 8, 2010, https://voxeu.org/article/tale-two-depressions-what-do-new-data-tell-us-february-2010-update.
46. Miguel Almunia, Agustín Bénétrix, Barry Eichengreen, Kevin H. O'Rourke, and Gisela Rua, "From Great Depression to Great Credit Crisis: Similarities, Differences and Lessons," Economic Policy 25, no. 62 (April 1, 2010): 219–65.

EMDEs, especially low-income countries. For 2008, the growth of exports and imports by EMDEs was still positive, but well below the average increases of the previous four years. All regional groups experienced volume declines in 2009 relative to 2008. Sub-Saharan Africa recorded a collective current account surplus from 2004 to 2007. The surplus evaporated in 2008, and in 2009 turned into a deficit of 2.4 percent of GDP.[47] Something had to be done to support international trade.

With memories of the Great Depression revived, talk in the corridors at the Asia-Pacific Economic Cooperation (APEC) meeting of finance ministers on November 5 and 6, 2008, in Trujillo, Peru, focused on the risks of protectionism. The APEC statement at the end of the meeting, which reflected the views of many countries that were not members of the G-20, articulated those concerns. That view was echoed on November 9 by the G-20 ministers and governors after their meeting in São Paulo, Brazil. Six days later, the G-20 leaders issued their pledge to not raise new barriers to investment or trade for one year.[48] In London, the pledge was reiterated and extended until the end of 2010.

Unlike in the 1930s, any substantive descent into protectionism was largely contained. Trade protection measures were adopted, as they are in every economic downturn, but there were fewer than predicted by historical experience. Scholars attribute this record to the G-20's antiprotectionism pledge as well as close monitoring by the World Trade Organization, the World Bank, and such research organizations as Global Trade Alert.[49]

Nonetheless, it was clear in early 2009 that trade was shrinking beyond what was to be expected on the basis of the decline in economic activity.[50] The common interpretation was that trade finance had dried up. In advance of the London summit, the United States sought to do more to mobilize the interna-

---

47. IMF, *World Economic Outlook Database*, Oct. 2018.
48. The G-20 declaration also included a commitment that reforms should be based on a commitment to free-market principles.
49. For this positive view, see Chad P. Bown and Meredith A. Crowley, "Import Protection, Business Cycles, and Exchange Rates: Evidence from the Great Recession," *Journal of International Economics* 90 (2013): 50–64. For an early report on noncompliance, see Simon J. Evenett, "Broken Promises: A G-20 Summit Report by Global Trade Alert," Vox, Nov. 2009, https://voxeu.org/epubs/cepr-reports/broken -promises-g20-summit-report-global-trade-alert.
50. JaeBin Ahn, Mary Amiti, and David E. Weinstein, "Trade Finance and the Great Trade Collapse," *American Economic Review: Papers and Proceedings* 101, no. 3 (2011): 298–302.

tional financial institutions and national export credit agencies. The result was a G-20 commitment to ensure that at least $250 billion to support trade finance over the next two years would be available through various official mechanisms, international institutions, and regulatory relief.

The Trade Finance Experts Group met before and after the London summit to discuss implementation. This principally involved an agreement that export credit agencies should reverse their policies against support for short-term trade credit and use direct financing because banks were husbanding their liquidity and consequently were not attracted by traditional trade guarantees.

Subsequent analysis suggests that trade finance played only a minor role in the decline in global trade.[51] Nonetheless, the promise that $250 billion in trade finance would be available, along with the pledge to resist protectionism, sent a powerful message. The $250 billion commitment added to the increase in the NAB ($500 billion), to the SDR allocation ($250 billion), and to the increase in MDB lending ($100 billion) to produce a headline-grabbing figure of $1.1 trillion in new international financing committed at the London summit (see Appendix A, G-20 London Statement, paragraph 5).

INTERNATIONAL REFORM OF FINANCIAL REGULATION

In the early days of the crisis, the Treasury and the Federal Reserve initiated an international effort to strengthen regulation of financial institutions and markets. In September 2007, U.S. Treasury undersecretary for international affairs David McCormick and Federal Reserve Board vice chairman Donald Kohn wrote a letter to their G-7 counterparts proposing that the Financial Stability Forum (FSF) be tasked to study the causes of the stresses then rippling through financial markets.[52]

On September 12, 2007, the *Financial Times* published an op-ed by McCormick and U.S. Treasury undersecretary for domestic finance Robert Steel outlining the Bush administration's views on the ongoing market volatility. The administration's request was that the FSF examine four issues: financial

---

51. Irena Asmundson, Thomas Dorsey, Armine Khachatryan, Ioana Niculcea, and Mika Saito, "Trade and Trade Finance in the 2008–09 Financial Crisis" (IMF Working Paper WP/11/16, Jan. 2011).
52. The FSF was created by the G-7 ministers and governors in 1999 after the Asian crisis to coordinate cooperative work on international financial standards and related issues.

institutions' liquidity, market, and credit risk practices; accounting and valuation procedures for financial derivative instruments; supervisory principles for regulated financial entities' contingent claims; and the role of credit rating agencies in evaluating structured finance products.[53] The FSF work plan was endorsed by the G-7 ministers and governors on October 19, 2007.

The FSF established the Working Group on Market and Institutional Resilience, which reported regularly to subsequent meetings of the G-7 and the IMFC, and in April 2008 issued a final report containing 67 actions and recommendations. That report provided the framework for a set of principles for reforming financial markets, supervision, and standard-setting that was endorsed at the G-20 Washington summit. U.S. officials drafted a statement, based on the report, outlining 47 immediate (to be done by March 31, 2009) and medium-term actions in six areas: transparency and accountability, sound regulation, financial market integrity, international cooperation, risk management, and reform of international financial institutions. The last included a commitment to expand the membership of the FSF and other standard-setting bodies, which already had been endorsed by the G-20 ministers and governors meeting in São Paolo.

Immediately before the Washington summit, we also refereed a turf battle between the IMF and the FSF concerning their respective roles on financial system issues. The U.S. view was that international financial sector policies and standards should be the responsibility of the FSF, where the IMF would play a role as a member, because (1) regulations are implemented by national authorities that are members of the FSF, and (2) the regulators' experts worked through the various standard-setting bodies that were part of the FSF structure. With our encouragement, IMF managing director Dominique Strauss-Kahn and FSF chairman and Bank of Italy governor Mario Draghi wrote to the G-20 ministers and governors on November 13, 2008, outlining their concordat.[54]

Thus, work on international financial regulatory reform was well under way by the time the Obama administration came into office. By then, the global financial crisis had become a global recession. Some in the new administra-

---

53. David McCormick and Robert Steel, "A Framework to End the Market Volatility," op-ed in *Financial Times,* Sept. 12, 2007, https://www.ft.com/content/1eb92ef4-615c-11dc-bf25-0000779fd2ac.
54. Dominique Strauss-Kahn and Mario Draghi, "Joint Letter of the FSF Chairman and the IMF Managing Director to the G20 Ministers and Governors," Nov. 13, 2008, http://www.fsb.org/2008/11/r_081113/.

tion felt that dealing with the immediate economic situation should be the principal focus of the London summit. President Obama decided, however, that moving early on U.S. and global financial reform should receive as much emphasis as expanding crisis financing and coordinating macroeconomic policy. To demonstrate the U.S. commitment in this area, Secretary Geithner outlined the administration's framework for comprehensive U.S. regulatory reform on March 26, a week before the London summit.[55]

As negotiations for a new set of global standards began, a key issue was how many new countries should be added to the FSF.[56] Although not all G-20 countries had equal claim to membership in the expanded FSF, the U.S. view was that it would be best to include them all, and also to add Spain and the European Commission. In addition, the United States proposed, and the G-20 leaders accepted, broadening the mandate of the FSF and reconstituting it as the Financial Stability Board (FSB), with Mario Draghi continuing as chairman.

The work of the FSF and its various subgroups, beginning in the fall of 2007, had little immediate bearing on short-term crisis management challenges. But the United States believed that it was important to start the process of reform before memories of the crisis faded. These early actions accelerated the financial regulatory reform process, including agreement on the revised Basel III capital standards and a comprehensive set of other financial reforms. These helped lay the foundation for a dramatic increase in the level of capital in the major financial institutions of the largest economies. The agreements were reached in a fraction of the time it took to negotiate the earlier international accords on capital.[57]

55. For details, see "Treasury Outlines Framework for Regulatory Reform: Provides New Rules of the Road, Focuses First on Containing Systemic Risk," press release, U.S. Department of the Treasury, March 26, 2009, https://www.treasury.gov/press-center/press-releases/pages/tg72.aspx. This timing was somewhat controversial. Paul Volcker told Ted Truman that in meetings with President Obama, Volcker had counseled waiting to announce our plans until we knew more about the crisis and what regulatory weaknesses it revealed, but he received no support. Afterward, other advisers told Volcker that they agreed with him. So, he grumped, "why did they not speak up in the meeting?"

56. The FSF did include financial supervisors from some non–G-7 financial centers, such as Hong Kong, the Netherlands, Singapore, and Switzerland.

57. The last technical "t" was not crossed until December 7, 2017. "Governors and Heads of Supervision Finalise Basel III Reforms," BIS, Dec. 7, 2017, https://www.bis.org/press/p171207.htm.

OUTCOMES

Overall, our coordinated international actions were successful: Financial stresses moderated, and market conditions stabilized across the advanced industrial and the developing world. The fever broke in the spring and summer of 2009. Equity prices for advanced and emerging markets economies had bottomed out in early March 2009 (see Figure 17.2). As summarized in Chapter 18, on outcomes, U.S. real GDP per capita declined 5.25 percent over six quarters through June 2009 and recovered to its previous peak in less than six years. Carmen Reinhart and Kenneth Rogoff find that the U.S. economy fared far better than advanced economies in historical systemic banking crises from 1857 to 2013. Those crises were associated with an average peak-to-trough decline in real output per capita of 9.6 percent with an average duration of 2.9 years.[58] But the extent and speed of improvement differed across economies, reflecting the policy choices in those economics and the scale of the damage from the financial crisis. (Europe subsequently faced economic and financial crises that are beyond the purview of this volume.)

Forecasts for global economic performance in 2009 began to turn up within a few months of the London summit. In July, the IMF's year-over-year forecast for 2009 improved slightly on a fourth-quarter-over-fourth-quarter basis, but by October the improvement was more substantial.[59] The 2009 Greenbook forecast for real growth in foreign countries (fourth quarter over fourth quarter) for the meeting of April 28–29, 2009, was slightly less weak than the forecast for the previous meeting and then progressively improved (see Figure 17.10).

Exchange rates against the dollar bottomed out in early March 2009 for both the major currencies and the emerging markets currencies other than China's renminbi. By the end of the year, the currencies of the former group had appreciated by 10.5 percent from their average level in December 2006, whereas those of the latter group, on balance, were essentially unchanged. Aided by the allocation of SDRs, reserves of emerging markets countries increased substantially after March 2009 (see Table 17.1).

---

58. Carmen Reinhart and Kenneth Rogoff, "Recovery from Financial Crises: Evidence from 100 Episodes," *American Economic Association* 104, no. 5 (May 2014): 50–55.
59. Figure 17.3 shows the year-over-year forecast because we do not have data for Q4/Q4 IMF forecasts for all the crisis years.

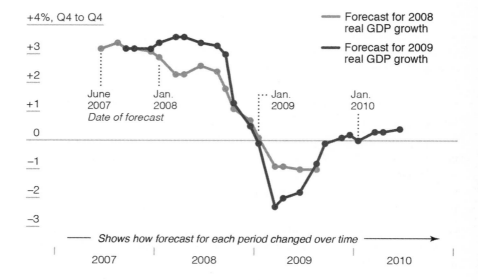

+4%, Q4 to Q4

— Forecast for 2008 real GDP growth

— Forecast for 2009 real GDP growth

+3

+2

+1

June 2007   Jan. 2008   ··· Jan. 2009   Jan. 2010

Date of forecast

0

−1

−2

−3

———→ *Shows how forecast for each period changed over time* ———→

2007   2008   2009   2010

Figure 17.10 Greenbook Forecasts for Growth of Real GDP in Foreign Countries

Source: Board of Governors of the Federal Reserve System, *Current Economic and Financial Conditions: Part 1 Summary and Outlook*

By the end of 2009, the rates on five-year CDS spreads for major international banks on average were less than 50 percent of their peaks in early March 2009, and most were down from where they were at the time of the London summit. The improvement for U.S. banks was most striking, relative to their peak, no doubt aided by the results of the U.S. stress tests (see Chapter 10, on reviving the banking system). But their average level at the end of the year matched Deutsche Bank's and the average for the four U.K. banks (see Figure 17.1).

CDS spreads for the sovereign debt of three of the emerging markets countries that had Fed swap lines—Brazil, Mexico, and South Korea—also continued to improve from their peaks in October 2008, especially for Mexican sovereign debt, which had been favorably impacted by Mexico's arranging a flexible credit line (FCL) from the IMF just before the London summit.[60] Still,

60. The FCL was a more attractive and less conditional successor to the short-term liquidity facility introduced in late October 2008.

at the end of the year, the CDS spreads for all three countries were more ele-vated than at the end of August 2007 (see Figure 17.6).

Capital flows to emerging markets economies also recovered. Their exter-nal bond issuance, which in 2008 was half as large ($78 billion) as in 2007, picked up starting in the second quarter of 2009. Total bond issuance for 2009 was essentially the same as in 2007 ($144 billion). Flows into mutual funds for emerging markets bonds and equities, which were negative in 2008, finished 2009 at record amounts.[61] No doubt this recovery was facilitated both by im-proving global economic and financial conditions and by low interest rates in the advanced economies.

We conclude that the comprehensive international treatments agreed to in Washington and London contributed importantly to the global economic and financial recovery. They built on coordinated steps that began haltingly after BNP Paribas stopped fund redemptions and were substantially deepened after the collapse of Lehman Brothers.

LESSONS LEARNED

The crisis of 2007–2009 was global because of the high degree of integration of the world economy and financial system. International coordination of eco-nomic policies in response was crucial to limiting the damage. No one action turned the tide. Crises have many dimensions, and global partners have many objectives. The challenge for U.S. policymakers was to expand the menu of co-operative actions, to recognize the complexity of the situation, and to satisfy the various subgoals of the key players.

Credible action is necessary during a financial crisis. The safest and, ulti-mately, most efficient course is often one that brings overwhelming economic and financial force into play, preferably at an early date. For the swap lines in 2007–2008, this meant finally uncapping the limits with major central banks in October 2008. Another example was the commitment to a package of more than $1 trillion in additional international financial resources at the London G-20 summit.

We draw seven key lessons from our review.

---

61. IMF, "Meeting New Challenges to Stability and Building a Safer System," *Global Financial Stability Report,* April 2010, 206.

Lesson 1:
Successful international economic and financial policy coordination depends on systematic and inclusive engagement that builds trust.

Trust is difficult to establish and to maintain. It requires years of patient nurturing through the tools of diplomacy, communication, and informal interchange in periods of calm. Engagement within the G-7 and G-20 often seems wasteful and bureaucratic, but the relationships and processes that result are necessary for an effective and rapid response in a crisis. Crucial to building trust is sharing information, listening to the concerns of others, and allowing those elements to sway collective thinking and actions. For all the differences in perspective that persisted among the G-7 countries, the succinct October 10, 2008, statement at the height of the crisis demonstrated a collective resolve to rescue the world economy and to support systemically important financial institutions. It follows that the clearest signal contains the fewest words.

Lesson 2:
All elements of the U.S. government need to work closely together.

The deep coordination between the Federal Reserve and the Treasury spanned the two administrations that served during the crisis and provided extensive benefits that served our interests in advancing the U.S. international agenda. The State Department during both the Bush and Obama eras was also updated regularly and helped advance our message around the world. And the leadership and coordination emanating from the White Houses of both administrations were vital. In a time of crisis, our integrated, coordinated response mattered.

Lesson 3:
International financial institutions should have enough resources to vigorously address emerging economic and financial crises. The United States should be prepared to play a leadership role in ensuring that condition is met.

As in the past, IMF members in 2008–2009 ultimately delivered additional resources so that the IMF could discharge its role as a lender and the MDBs could safely stretch their balance sheets. But it was touch and go. Actively managed, international institutions like the IMF can be a force multiplier in support of U.S. policies, but if U.S. leaders are not engaged with them, the institutions can take on a life of their own and could potentially cut against U.S. interests in the future.

Lesson 4:
Extraordinary times require the United States to lead and often propose extraordinary interventions.

The world, sometimes reluctantly, looks to the United States for leadership in a global crisis, economic and/or financial. Moreover, the international role of the U.S. dollar implies unique challenges and obligations for the United States. Extraordinary interventions in response to a crisis may include creating new mechanisms or expanding the menu of options for cooperation. Examples in the global financial crisis included providing direct financial support to emerging markets economies via Federal Reserve swap lines, lifting the G-20 to the leaders' level, supporting the U.S. takeover of Fannie Mae and Freddie Mac, and utilizing the rarely used IMF tool of SDR allocations. At the same time, U.S. officials should not shy away from making extraordinary diplomatic requests at senior government levels when necessary to avert disaster.

Lesson 5:
A shared diagnosis is only the first step in addressing a crisis. Successful international policy coordination also requires establishing a consensus on the appropriate policy responses.

The major central banks took many months, from August 2007 to the start of the fourth quarter of 2008, to reach consensus on the seriousness of the crisis and the need to act with common resolve. The reasons for the delays were numerous, varying from differences over the risk of renewed inflation to the proper use of unconventional monetary policy instruments. As a result, U.S. policymakers were unable to convince foreign counterparts of the need for synchronized monetary policy actions until the collapse of Lehman Brothers forced a coordinated response.

Consensus on fiscal policy was even more elusive. The Obama administration frequently ran into technical and philosophical differences with our European allies that delayed and limited joint stimulus and also contributed to disagreement over exit strategies. Nevertheless, the coordinated fiscal response, though short-lived, played an important role in containing the crisis.

Lesson 6:
The press of crisis management should not preclude looking ahead to improve crisis prevention.

In the global financial crisis, we responded to criticisms of U.S. financial regulation and supervision by proposing early on that the FSF, now the FSB, should analyze regulatory failures and make reform recommendations. This initiative not only laid the groundwork for faster implementation of reforms as the crisis was abating but also helped promote a policy buy-in by other countries in managing the ongoing crisis.

Lesson 7:
The Federal Reserve will continue to face demands to backstop global liquidity and should be prepared to respond.

Given the domestic orientation of the Federal Reserve's mandate, some critics argue that the Fed overstepped during the financial crisis and shouldn't repeat this pattern. They are mistaken. Until the international community builds a more efficient and effective global financial safety net, other nations will look to the Fed during crises for concrete evidence of financial leadership and resources. Responding to those demands enhances the ability of the Fed to serve both the immediate and the longer-term economic and financial interests of the United States. Central bankers and other U.S. financial statesmen should not be shy about encouraging the Fed to play this role in the future, perhaps even more promptly and on a greater scale than was initially the case in 2007–2008.

APPENDIX A: SELECTED STATEMENTS
FROM INTERNATIONAL MEETINGS

GROUP OF SEVEN (G-7) FINANCE MINISTERS
AND CENTRAL BANK GOVERNORS PLAN OF ACTION

Washington, D.C.
October 10, 2008

The G-7 agrees today that the current situation calls for urgent and exceptional action.[62] We commit to continue working together to stabilize financial markets and restore the flow of credit, to support global economic growth. We agree to:

1. Take decisive action and use all available tools to support systemically important financial institutions and prevent their failure.
2. Take all necessary steps to unfreeze credit and money markets and ensure that banks and other financial institutions have broad access to liquidity and funding.
3. Ensure that our banks and other major financial intermediaries, as needed, can raise capital from public as well as private sources, in sufficient amounts to re-establish confidence and permit them to continue lending to households and businesses.
4. Ensure that our respective national deposit insurance and guarantee programs are robust and consistent so that our retail depositors will continue to have confidence in the safety of their deposits.
5. Take action, where appropriate, to restart the secondary markets for mortgages and other securitized assets. Accurate valuation and transparent disclosure of assets and consistent implementation of high quality accounting standards are necessary.

The actions should be taken in ways that protect taxpayers and avoid potentially damaging effects on other countries. We will use macroeconomic policy tools as necessary and appropriate. We strongly support the IMF's critical role in assisting countries affected by this turmoil. We will accelerate full

---

62. G7 Information Centre, http://www.g7.utoronto.ca/finance/fm081010.htm.

implementation of the Financial Stability Forum recommendations and we are committed to the pressing need for reform of the financial system. We will strengthen further our cooperation and work with others to accomplish this plan.

EXCERPT FROM THE GROUP OF 20 (G-20) LEADERS' STATEMENT

London
April 2, 2009

5. The agreements we have reached today, to treble resources available to the IMF to $750 billion, to support a new SDR allocation of $250 billion, to support at least $100 billion of additional lending by the MDBs, to ensure $250 billion of support for trade finance, and to use the additional resources from agreed IMF gold sales for concessional finance for the poorest countries, constitute an additional $1.1 trillion programme of support to restore credit, growth, and jobs in the world economy.[63] Together with the measures we have each taken nationally, this constitutes a global plan for recovery on an unprecedented scale.

63. G20 Information Centre, http://www.g20.utoronto.ca/2009/2009communique0402 .pdf.

APPENDIX B: HOW WERE THE FED'S CRISIS-FIGHTING SWAP LINES STRUCTURED?

Swap lines have a long history in central banking. They were used in previous generations to fund intervention in foreign-exchange markets and to provide bridge financing to countries during times of stress. The important insight we gained during the financial crisis was that these lines, if scaled up sufficiently, could provide the liquidity needed to soothe dollar-funding pressures in global markets.

Under the swap lines put in place during the crisis, the Federal Reserve exchanged dollars with a foreign central bank for foreign currency at the prevailing market exchange rate. The two parties contractually agreed to reverse the transaction at some point in the future, ranging from one day to 90 days, at the same exchange rate. The foreign central bank, in turn, lent this dollar liquidity through a variety of mechanisms and against many different types of collateral (including both dollar-denominated and foreign-currency-denominated instruments).

This structure had numerous advantages for the Fed. First, the lines entailed essentially zero risk to the Fed's balance sheet. The Fed transacted at short tenure with foreign central banks, the safest possible counterparties. There was no foreign exchange risk because the exchange rate for unwinding the swap was predetermined. And the transaction was effectively collateralized by the foreign currency that the Fed received in exchange for the dollars. Second, the Fed's counterparty in the transaction was the foreign central bank, not the institutions that ultimately received the dollars. This structure served to minimize the Fed's exposure to credit risk, but more importantly, it acknowledged the jurisdiction-specific expertise of the foreign central banks.

Another notable feature of the swap lines was that the foreign central bank paid interest to the Fed on the dollars that it received, typically at 100 basis points over the overnight indexed swap (OIS) rate. From the time of the initial establishment of the swap lines in December 2007, the precedent was for the foreign central bank to pass back to the Fed all the earnings from the dollars it lent. The Fed did not pay interest on the foreign currency that it received in the swap. The Fed did agree to leave the foreign currency with its central bank counterpart; this sidestepped the sterilization operations, or other monetary management issues, that might have arisen for the foreign central bank if the Fed had withdrawn the reserves and employed them in the market.

Last, the emerging markets swap lines incorporated additional governance mechanisms to ensure that the resources were used to fight dollar-liquidity stresses as intended and to protect the Fed's balance sheet. All drawings under the lines required the approval of the Foreign Currency Subcommittee (which included the chairman) of the Federal Open Market Committee (FOMC).

CHAPTER EIGHTEEN

Evidence on the Outcomes from the Financial Crisis Response

J. NELLIE LIANG, MARGARET M. McCONNELL, AND PHILLIP SWAGEL

INTRODUCTION: ASSESSING OUTCOMES

From 2007 to 2009, the U.S. government faced extraordinary threats to the functioning of the financial system and the health of the economy. In response to these threats, the government took a series of steps—many unprecedented and hence untested in terms of their efficacy—to support economic activity and employment and to maintain the financial system's ability to provide essential services to the real economy.

This chapter summarizes the policy actions undertaken in response to the crisis and reviews the evidence on the outcomes of those actions. While the causes and manifestations of the next financial crisis will almost surely differ from those experienced in the United States at the end of the past decade, financial crises do have certain features in common. The purpose of this review is to inform the actions of decision-makers in future financial crises.

Given the wide range of policy actions taken during the crisis, and the variety of institutional authorities and objectives that shaped those actions, this chapter employs a simple organizing framework to explore the evidence. We sort policy actions into two broad categories. The first category—*macro policies*—includes actions designed to stimulate economic activity and spending. The second—*systemic policies*—includes actions designed to maintain the functioning of the financial system. The framework also identifies three phases of the crisis, each corresponding to an escalation in the nature and breadth of the concerns facing decision-makers in real time about conditions in the economy and financial system.

The complexity of the crisis, and of the broader economic and financial environment in which the crisis unfolded, makes it difficult—even with the benefit of hindsight—to identify clear cause-and-effect relationships between individual policy actions and observable outcomes. Moreover, much of what we now know about the outcomes we know *only* with the benefit of hindsight. This leaves our assessment of actions and outcomes vulnerable to hindsight bias—that is, the tendency to understate the degree of ambiguity and uncertainty that decision-makers faced in the moment, and to overstate the degree to which events were predictable in advance. It also leaves our assessment susceptible to outcome bias—that is, the tendency to treat decisions that yielded favorable outcomes as having been good (or appropriate) decisions and decisions that yielded unfavorable outcomes as having been bad or inappropriate.

These important challenges notwithstanding, our review suggests that the actions taken by the government prevented what might otherwise have been a second Great Depression. In fact, the evidence suggests that the U.S. recession was shorter and less steep, and the recovery more rapid, than might have been expected based on historical banking crises.

Nonetheless, the recession was severe and had lasting effects on the U.S. economy and on society. The unemployment rate rose to 10 percent, and millions lost their homes to foreclosure. Household net worth fell sharply. The recovery was lackluster, with the possibility of a decline in the growth of potential output compounding the harmful impact of the cyclical downturn. Contributing to the severity of economic outcomes may have been the fact that many of the extraordinary policy actions were undertaken only when conditions had eroded to the point at which financial markets and institutions were experiencing, or were extremely vulnerable to, runs, contagion, and panic. Indeed, it was not until the enactment of the Emergency Economic Stabilization Act (EESA) on October 3, 2008, that policymakers had the ability to take many of the systemic actions that would ultimately prove most consequential in restoring confidence in the capital adequacy of U.S. financial institutions.

Still, the timing of actions also was influenced by other factors, including policymakers' understanding of the situation as it was evolving in real time, and their concerns about moral hazard, political backlash, or even the possibility of creating panic with their actions. It is beyond the scope of this exercise to assess the appropriateness of the timing of actions from the perspective of these real-time considerations. And we cannot provide much insight into whether other actions would have yielded better outcomes. Nonetheless, we believe that policymakers' inability to undertake vital systemic actions until the fall of 2008 likely limited the range of more favorable economic outcomes that were achievable even with the subsequent extraordinary policy actions.

SETTING THE STAGE: THE U.S. RECESSION AND RECOVERY

The global financial crisis included a major recession in the United States that lasted from December 2007 to June 2009, with significant and evolving threats to financial system functioning. Although the downturn was mild in the first half of 2008—indeed, real GDP growth was positive in the second quarter— activity then plunged in the fall of 2008. (See Figure 18.1.) Real GDP declined by 4 percent from peak to trough, and the unemployment rate more than doubled, from 4.4 percent in May 2007 to 10.0 percent in October 2009. Most other advanced economies also had recessions around this time, including several that were deeper than in the United States, such as in the United Kingdom, where real GDP declined by more than 6 percent.

Real GDP in the United States recovered to its prerecession peak in 13 quarters. Ten years after the crisis, real GDP is 15 percent higher than the previous peak, slightly higher than in some other advanced economies, such as Germany, the United Kingdom, and France. On a per capita basis, U.S. real GDP did not recover until almost six years later, still a better performance than other advanced economies achieved, except for Germany.

Even so, the Great Recession was steeper and longer than any other post–World War II U.S. recession. (See Figure 18.2.) GDP per capita, unemployment, and bank credit growth were worse than in the 1990 recession following the S&L crisis, and the outcomes in both periods were worse than in the other post–World War II recessions in which there were no significant financial sector disruptions. The experience of the Great Depression is also shown in Figure 18.2, with a very large and prolonged decline in GDP and a steep rise in unemployment for four years as a reminder of a truly disastrous outcome, and as a possible counterfactual to the recent period. Of course, comparing recessions and recoveries across time does not control for all sorts of differences— the initial conditions of the financial sector, the precrisis trajectory of potential output growth, and the like—that might account for differences in outcomes.

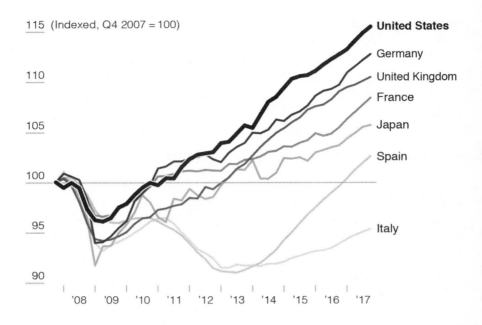

115 (Indexed, Q4 2007 = 100)

110

105

100

95

90

'08   '09   '10   '11   '12   '13   '14   '15   '16   '17

United States
Germany
United Kingdom
France
Japan
Spain
Italy

Figure 18.1 Global Financial Crisis: Real GDP Ten Years Later

Source: Organisation for Economic Co-operation and Development

An important challenge in evaluating the recovery in output after the crisis is that there appears to have been a decline in potential growth of U.S. output around the time of the crisis. There is no consensus on the cause of the decline. It is possible that it reflected forces already in place before the crisis—namely, a sharp decline in productivity growth beginning in 2004 after a period of high growth from 1995 to 2003, combined with a decades-long downward trend in labor force participation. John Fernald et al. (2017) adjust for these two factors and conclude that the more sluggish potential growth rate was in place before the crisis. Their adjustments imply that real GDP per capita returned to its precrisis potential in 2016 and that the disappointing economic performance since the crisis does not reflect the impact of actions taken during and after the crisis. Others argue that the financial crisis or subsequent policies may have led to a decline in potential output, mostly due to lower investment. For example, there were fewer business start-ups with high investment return opportunities after the crisis (Siemer 2014). This reduction in capital formation may have led to lower aggregate productivity growth because of the shift in the distribution of the capital stock away from high-return firms

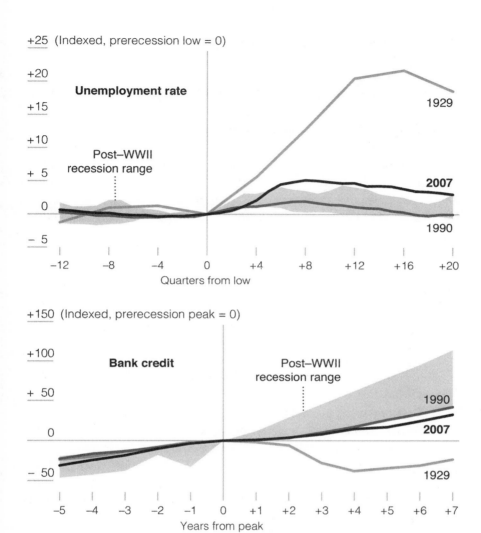

Figure 18.2 U.S. Economy: Unemployment Rate and Bank Credit

Note: Prerecession low (peak) is the previous business cycle low (peak). Post–World War II recession range is the range of outcomes in the post–World War II recessions before 2007.

Sources: Haver Analytics; Ahamed (2009); Federal Deposit Insurance Corp.; Federal Reserve Economic Data (FRED)

(Khan and Thomas 2013), suggesting the financial crisis and responses are causal factors.[1]

Nevertheless, studies of historical episodes of banking crises indicate that the U.S. economy performed better than might have been expected given the depth of financial sector problems. Carmen Reinhart and Kenneth Rogoff (2014) examine 100 systemic banking crises from 1857 to 2013, of which 63 were in advanced economies and 37 in emerging markets economies. They show for advanced economies that the average peak-to-trough decline in real per capita output was 9.6 percent, with a duration of 2.9 years, and that the average time for GDP per capita to recover to its prerecession peak was 7.3 years. (See Figure 18.3.) U.S. performance was better on all these dimensions: Real GDP per capita declined 5.25 percent over six quarters and recovered to its previous peak in less than six years.

Oscar Jorda, Moritz Schularick, and Alan Taylor (2013) and Christina Romer and David Romer (2017) control for the depth of financial distress when evaluating the recovery and find U.S. performance was better than their models would predict. Jorda, Schularick, and Taylor (2013) provide an interpretation of the postcrisis recovery based on the amount of excess credit in the run-up to the business cycle peak, drawing on a sample of 154 recessions, of which 35 were financial recessions, in 14 advanced economies since 1870. They find that the conditional path of U.S. real GDP per capita surpassed the expected recovery by more than 2 percent five years after the year-end 2007 peak.

Romer and Romer (2017) develop an index of financial distress based on narratives prepared by analysts from the Organisation for Economic Co-operation and Development (OECD) that focus on disruptions to credit supply (rather than on financial firm stresses) for a sample of 24 OECD countries from 1967 to 2012. The financial distress index for the United States reached the most extreme level for the entire sample in the second half of 2008 but then fell relatively rapidly compared with other countries, hitting zero in the first half of 2011. They attribute the rapid decline in distress to the large and

---

1. Studies of cross-country performance document the phenomenon that recessions, especially those associated with banking crises, lead to a downward shift in the path for potential output (Cerra and Saxena 2008, 2017). Blanchard, Cerutti, and Summers (2015) evaluate growth in the expansion relative to a trend line that removes the two years just ahead of the business cycle peak and adjust for rapid credit growth. They document that 83 percent of financial recessions are associated with a sustained negative output gap, of which one-third show a growing output gap.

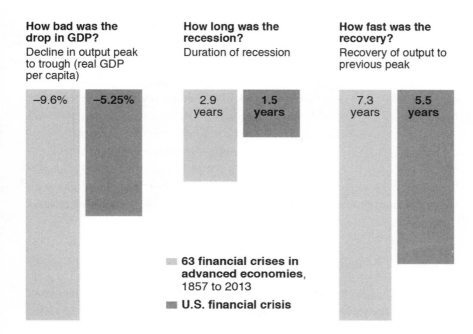

How bad was the drop in GDP?
Decline in output peak to trough (real GDP per capita)

−9.6%   −5.25%

How long was the recession?
Duration of recession

2.9 years   1.5 years

How fast was the recovery?
Recovery of output to previous peak

7.3 years   5.5 years

▨ **63 financial crises in advanced economies**, 1857 to 2013

▨ **U.S. financial crisis**

Figure 18.3   U.S. Financial Crisis Compared with Other Financial Crises

Sources: Reinhart and Rogoff (2014); Bureau of Economic Analysis via Federal Reserve Economic Data (FRED)

comprehensive set of macro and systemic policy responses taken by U.S. authorities to offset the shock to the financial system. They also use local projection estimation methods to predict real GDP growth based on previous growth and the distress index and show that the United States performed as expected within two years, and notably above expectations within four years.[2] In contrast, Romer and Romer document large negative errors for Iceland, Italy, Greece, Portugal, and Spain, even after accounting for the subsequent buildup in distress in 2011 after the emergence of problems in Greece. These errors were sizable, between −5 and −10 percent for Italy, Portugal, and Spain, and −30 percent for Greece, implying that the recoveries in these

2. They show that increases in financial distress are quite costly to real GDP growth, with a shock of half of what occurred in the United States from 2007 to 2010 (the average size shock in that period across the sample) leading to a decline of about 6 percent from the previous peak at about 3.5 years.

countries were worse than would have been expected from the historical experience.

Thus, our assessment is that while the macroeconomic costs were very high in absolute terms, the U.S. economy overall performed well relative to historical and contemporary benchmarks. Research that accounts for whether the financial sector was in distress, the amount of excess credit, or the size and duration of the financial shock indicates the U.S. recovery was in line with or better than expectations. This does not take away from the reality that the crisis caused severe hardship for millions of Americans. But we believe the outcomes were better than would have been expected from the experience with previous financial crises, implying that the U.S. policy responses made a difference.

A SIMPLE FRAMEWORK FOR ORGANIZING EVIDENCE ON OUTCOMES

Our organizing framework characterizes the policy actions that were taken in response to the evolving crisis as either "macro" policies or "systemic" policies, and recognizes that while the ultimate objective of both types of policies is to keep actual economic growth as close to potential as possible, the proximate objectives of the two types of policies differ. In addition, the desired outcomes associated with either macro or systemic policy actions can vary as conditions in the environment and concerns about potential future conditions evolve over time.

DISTINGUISHING BETWEEN DIFFERENT TYPES OF POLICY ACTIONS

Macro policies—essentially countercyclical monetary and fiscal policies—are intended to support economic activity and spending. Thus, the proximate objective of stimulative macro policies is to increase the *quantity* of economic activity as a way to minimize output and employment gaps. Fiscal policy includes increased government spending or tax cuts that boost private consumption or investment. Monetary policy stimulates aggregate spending by reducing the cost of credit, and through potential effects that flow through wealth, balance sheets, and net export channels.

In the case of systemic policies, the proximate objective is the *functioning* of the financial system—the system's ability to provide credit, payment, and risk transfer services to the real economy. Systemic policies are not themselves intended to generate new economic activity or spending. Instead, they are designed to restore the condition of the financial system such that it can provide the financial intermediation services necessary for an economy to grow at potential. The U.S. government deployed a variety of systemic policies during the crisis—provision of liquidity by the Fed secured by collateral, capital injections into financial firms, debt guarantees, resolution of failing firms, and support for mortgage modifications.[3]

Systemic and macro policies are complements rather than substitutes, in the sense that systemic policies are designed to mitigate a "supply" shock from the financial sector—which serves as a critical intermediary between saving and investment and between credit and economic growth—that would disrupt growth and employment. Recent research has found strong links between the functioning of the financial system and real economic activity, beyond the traditional effect of asset prices and lending through the balance sheet channel. Ben S. Bernanke (2018) shows that investor panic in the funding and securitization markets led to sharper declines in GDP, employment, and other broad economic outcomes through the disruption of the supply of credit. Mark Gertler and Simon Gilchrist (2018) show that the household balance sheet channel is important for regional variation in employment but that banking distress is central to the overall contraction in employment. Financial disruptions affect particular markets as well; for example, strains in the asset-backed commercial paper (ABCP) market reduced funding available to nonbank auto lenders, which provide financing for a large share of auto purchases, and there were fewer auto sales in areas in which nonbank lenders were especially important (Benmelech, Meisenzahl, and Ramcharan 2017).

Because the proximate objectives of the two types of policies differ, we identify different outcome measures for each. For macro policies, we look at real GDP, unemployment, and growth of bank credit for households and businesses. For systemic policies, we focus on Libor-OIS (overnight indexed swap) spreads, credit default swap (CDS) premiums for large financial firms, and mortgage spreads. The Libor-OIS spread captures the cost of short-term funds for banking firms, which reflects credit and liquidity risks and can often provide early indications of concerns about insolvency problems; CDS premiums reflect the

---

3. Mortgage modifications are sometimes viewed as structural policies (Andritzky 2014), but we group them with systemic policies as they work to allow households to reduce debt service and benefit more directly from lower interest rates or higher house prices brought about by macro policies.

risks to debt holders and market perceptions of the potential for insolvency of financial firms over longer horizons; and spreads between agency mortgage-backed securities (MBS) and Treasury securities reflect strains in the mortgage market.[4]

CAPTURING THE REAL-TIME EVOLUTION OF CONDITIONS AND CONCERNS

The severity of the situation was not generally apparent to policymakers from their vantage point in 2007. While the possibility of an episode on par with the Great Depression was possible from the start, such a scenario seemed remote until it became clear that the financial system was "on the brink of the abyss" in the late summer and early fall of 2008. In other words, when signs of financial stresses began emerging in 2007 after house prices had started to decline and many mortgage brokers had failed, there clearly were indications of an impending housing adjustment and concerns that it would present a headwind for the broad economy. A severe financial crisis, however, was generally not seen as being highly probable.

The evolution of the Federal Reserve's staff forecasts is illustrative. Figure 18.4 shows the forecast for real GDP provided to the Federal Open Market Committee (FOMC) in August 2007 and selected subsequent forecasts through June 2010. While strains in funding markets illustrated by the wider Libor-OIS spread prompted the Fed to encourage banks to use the discount window in August 2007 and then to cut the discount rate the following week, there was little sign of stress in the forecast for real GDP, which showed continued moderate growth. Indeed, the Fed's staff forecast in March 2008 showed only a shallow recession. The Congressional Budget Office (CBO) forecast released the second week of September 2008, just before the failure of Lehman Brothers and ensuing events, likewise did not see the collapse of activity. A more notable but still mild recession was in the Fed's staff forecast starting from October 2008, after the panic had taken hold, but not until the actual plunge in economic activity in late 2008 did the forecast show an unusually severe recession.

Similarly, the Libor-OIS spread rose substantially from less than 10 basis points in June 2007 to close to 100 basis points by September 2007 after inves-

---

4. Agency MBS are mortgage-backed securities issued and guaranteed by Fannie Mae and Freddie Mac.

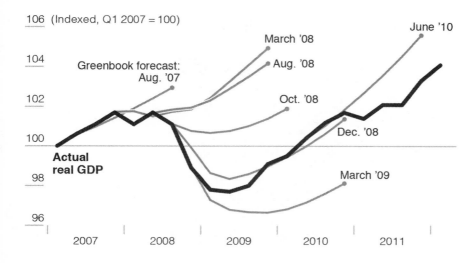

Figure 18.4 **Real GDP, Actual and Greenbook Forecasts**

Source: Federal Reserve Greenbook forecasts

tor runs on ABCP and on repurchase agreements (repos) backed by mortgage securities (see Covitz, Liang, and Suarez 2013; and Gorton and Metrick 2012). But we believe few policymakers would have assigned a high likelihood to the Libor-OIS spread spiking to more than 350 basis points and a shutdown in key funding markets such as commercial paper a year later. CDS premiums for large financial firms also were rising, but the initial stress was primarily in the investment banks (Bear Stearns, Lehman Brothers, Merrill Lynch) and depository institutions seen as relatively more exposed to real estate risk (Countrywide, Washington Mutual), suggesting the stresses remained mainly related to housing. Even the International Monetary Fund (IMF), which estimated headline losses of $2.7 trillion for the financial sector in April 2009, had more modest estimates of $945 billion in losses one year earlier. In its 2008 report on the United States, the IMF emphasized that appropriate policies would involve encouraging financial firms to raise private capital and increase transparency about their risks, and that authorities should minimize the use of public resources and avoid undermining market discipline.

To evaluate outcomes associated with the macro and systemic policies, we have broken the crisis down into three phases—Phase I: August 2007 to March 2008; Phase II: March 2008 to mid-September 2008; and Phase III: mid-September 2008 to December 2009.

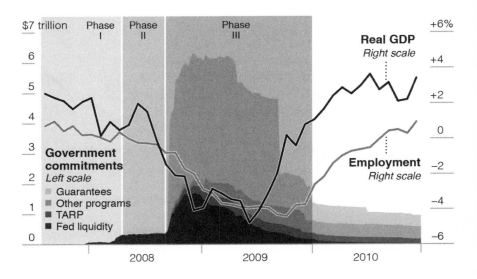

Figure 18.5 Government Commitments for Systemic Policies and GDP and Employment Growth

Note: Fed liquidity includes discount window credit, TAF, PDCF, AMLF, CPFF, TALF, TSLF, and currency swaps. TARP includes support to banks, auto companies, AIG, credit markets, and housing. Guarantees includes Treasury MMFs and the FDIC's TLGP. Other programs includes Fed lending to Maiden Lane LLCs, AGP, Treasury MBS purchases, and SPSPAs. Acronyms are defined in the list of abbreviations at the front of this book.

Sources: U.S. government exposures: Congressional Oversight Panel, "Guarantees and Contingent Payments in TARP and Related Programs" via Federal Reserve Bank of St. Louis, Federal Deposit Insurance Corp., Federal Reserve Board, Federal Housing Finance Agency, U.S. Treasury; employment: Bureau of Labor Statistics; real GDP: Macroeconomic Advisers via Haver Analytics

Figure 18.5 shows the total amount of government commitments for the systemic policy responses by the three phases, and monthly real GDP growth and employment growth. Government commitments began rising in the fall of 2007, escalated dramatically after panic took hold at the beginning of Phase III, but then moderated substantially in mid-to-late 2009 as financial market functioning began to be restored. In addition, event dates for key systemic policies are marked against daily Libor-OIS spreads, CDS premiums, and agency MBS spreads and are shown in Figures 18.5, 18.6, and 18.7. Although there are significant announcement effects for some policies, the impact of any particular policy is difficult to identify because of a substantial degree of interaction among them, especially after policymakers were showing a "whatever it takes" attitude to prevent the financial system and economy from collapsing.

Phase I, August 2007 to March 2008: Challenging but Manageable

Overview

Conditions in Phase I were generally viewed in real time as being characterized by economic weakness led by an adjustment in housing and exacerbated and spread by increasing incidence and severity of strains in financial markets, as many mortgage lenders failed and a few larger financial institutions heavily exposed to mortgages faced difficulties. Policy actions in this phase were consistent with the view that the drag from the financial sector would lead to a weak economy but not pose a significant risk of sparking a systemic crisis.

Macro policy actions consisted of traditional fiscal and monetary measures to support growth and credit in the face of an economic slowdown. Systemic policy actions took the form of extensions of the discount window to provide term funding rather than only overnight and to provide liquidity through auctions to help reduce the stigma associated with use of the discount window. The desired outcomes were to restore financial system functioning to support financial intermediation—that is, to limit the reduction in credit from financial market strains—and to address the increasing housing problem.

Details

Macro policies consisted of both monetary and fiscal actions. The FOMC cut interest rates from 5.25 percent before September 18, 2007, to 3 percent by January 30, 2008. The actions in January were notable for their size and speed: They cut the federal funds rate by 75 basis points on January 22, 2008, outside of a regularly scheduled FOMC meeting, followed by another cut of 50 basis points on January 30, 2008.

Fiscal stimulus was put in place with the Economic Stimulus Act (ESA), enacted in February 2008, which provided for about $100 billion of tax rebate checks to be sent to households in mid-2008 (mostly May to August) along with some investment incentives. The policy discussion at the time was for fiscal stimulus to be "temporary, targeted, timely"—that is, to focus narrowly on supporting near-term activity. This call is likewise consistent with the widespread belief in late 2007 and early 2008 that the slowdown would be temporary. The targeting of the tax rebate checks focused especially on lower-income families, who were viewed as having relatively high marginal propensities to consume. The 2008 stimulus appears to have offset headwinds from higher energy prices and the housing sector adjustment. Research suggests it had a positive impact on consumption and GDP (Parker et al. 2013; Broda and Parker 2014), though Valerie Ramey (2018) sees the estimated impact as overstated.

In terms of systemic policy responses, the Fed effectively extended its discount window liquidity in new ways. After cutting the discount rate from 100 to 50 basis points above the federal funds rate in August 2007 to encourage greater use, the Fed launched the Term Auction Facility (TAF) in December 2007. TAF was meant to provide longer-term funding for depository institutions through an auction mechanism with delayed receipt of funds that would help circumvent the stigma of the discount window. (See Figure 18.6.) Research such as that by James McAndrews, Asani Sarkar, and Zhenyu Wang (2017) has found that TAF achieved its aim of reducing liquidity strains in the interbank market, with statistically significant downward shifts of the Libor-OIS spread associated with TAF.

The Fed established foreign exchange (FX) swap lines with other central banks, starting in December 2007 with the European Central Bank (ECB) and the National Bank of Switzerland. It expanded the lines in March 2008 and again in the fall. Through these lines, the Fed provided dollar liquidity to counterpart central banks on a collateralized basis. This provision in turn enabled these central banks to lend in dollars to the banks in their jurisdictions. Research such as that of Naohiko Baba and Frank Packer (2009) found that the swap lines ameliorated foreign exchange dislocations that manifested as wider interest rate spreads between loans to European banks and U.S. Treasury securities. These strains reflected doubts about the safety of European banks, which made U.S. institutions less willing to lend to those in Europe.

TAF and FX swap lines were targeted at addressing particular financial market stresses affecting banks. Both were successful in reducing interest rate spreads for targeted classes of institutions, and Libor-OIS spreads fell. This impact in turn was expected to contribute to a positive impact for monetary policy by improving the transmission mechanism of lower interest rates to the economy.

Announced write-downs of assets by the largest financial firms for the second half of 2007 had already reached $100 billion, with about half at nonbank financial firms (for example, securities firms such as Merrill Lynch) and half at commercial banks (for example, Citigroup and banks specializing in mortgages). While some firms raised substantial new capital in late 2007 and early 2008, CDS premiums for investment banks and Citigroup rose notably, and

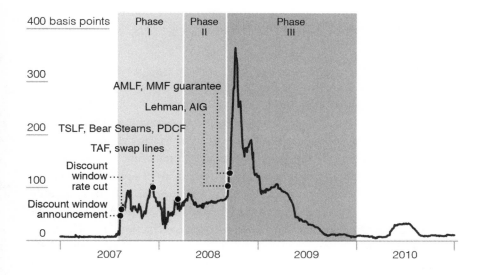

Figure 18.6 **Three-Month Libor-OIS Spread**

Note: Events shown are the following: discount window announcement, Aug. 10, 2007; discount window rate cut, Aug. 17, 2007; TAF announced and central bank liquidity swap lines, Dec. 12, 2007; TSLF announced, March 11, 2008; Bear Stearns rescue, March 14, 2008; PDCF announced, March 16, 2008; Lehman Brothers failure, Sept. 15, 2008; AIG rescue, Sept. 16, 2008; AMLF announced, Treasury's guarantee of the MMFs, Sept. 19, 2008. Acronyms are defined in the list of abbreviations at the front of this book.

Source: Federal Reserve Bank of New York, based on data from Bloomberg Finance L.P.

they were considerably higher than those for other large commercial banks still viewed to be more insulated from problem mortgages.

In addition, officials from the Treasury, banking agencies, and other agencies, including Housing and Urban Development (HUD), worked with banks and mortgage servicers to encourage mortgage modifications through the HOPE NOW coalition. A main effort in the early stage of the crisis was to persuade lenders to freeze interest rate resets for 1.8 million subprime borrowers who had taken out loans that would adjust after a two- and three-year initial period with a low teaser rate.

Phase I policy actions provided liquidity and moderate macro support, but financial conditions were deteriorating and the economy was slowing. Financial firms had not raised enough capital to provide investors assurance that they could absorb losses related to housing.

Phase II, March 2008 to Mid-September 2008: Broader Uncertainty, Deeper Concerns

Overview

We date Phase II as starting with the use of the Fed's emergency authority around the collapse of Bear Stearns in mid-March 2008. Conditions in this phase were characterized by growing concern about a continued deterioration in housing and the economy and by increasing uncertainty about the size and incidence of losses on mortgage-related assets, implicating a wider range of both U.S. and European financial institutions. During this phase, market participants and policymakers alike recognized the possibility of a negative feedback loop in which a weaker financial system and slower growth could feed on each other and precipitate a broad-based contraction in credit supply and materially harm growth. Policies undertaken in this phase included the Federal Reserve invoking its emergency authorities under Section 13(3) of the Federal Reserve Act (FRA) for the first time since the Great Depression, and actions taken to prevent destabilizing failures at key financial institutions such as Fannie Mae and Freddie Mac.

Details

We know in hindsight that the economy by early 2008 was in recession, but the first-quarter downturn was shallow and second-quarter growth was positive, so signals of economic strength at the time were mixed. Macro policies during this period involved 75 basis points of additional easing of monetary policy right after the collapse of Bear Stearns and then another cut, of 25 basis points, at the end of April. The federal funds rate was then unchanged until October, with some policymakers expressing concerns over the prospect of higher inflation after oil prices rose. The fiscal stimulus enacted in January 2008 took hold with the payment of tax rebates in the middle of the year. As noted earlier, most forecasts at the time expected only a mild downturn later in 2008.

In contrast, there was a significant escalation of systemic policies. Within the window of a week surrounding the collapse of Bear Stearns, the Fed used its emergency authorities to introduce new broad-based liquidity facilities for broker-dealers and funding to facilitate the acquisition of Bear Stearns to prevent a destabilizing failure. Reflecting the continued strains in funding markets, the Fed introduced the Term Securities Lending Facility (TSLF) to allow primary dealers to exchange illiquid assets for Treasury securities to improve their access to liquidity. This was followed days later with the Primary Dealer

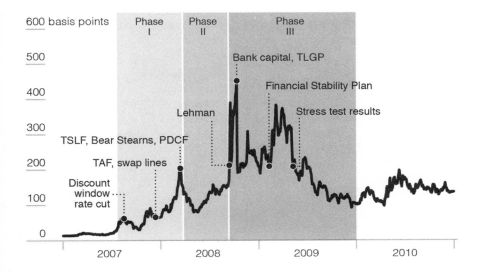

Figure 18.7 CDS Spreads for Financial Firms

Note: CDS spread shown is an equal-weighted average of Bank of America, Citigroup, Goldman Sachs, JPMorgan Chase, Morgan Stanley, and Wells Fargo. CDS spreads are on five-year senior debt. Events shown are the following: discount window rate cut, Aug. 17, 2007; TAF announced and central bank liquidity swap lines, Dec. 12, 2007; TSLF announced, March 11, 2008; Bear Stearns rescue, March 14, 2008; PDCF announced, March 16, 2008; Lehman Brothers failure, Sept. 15, 2008; bank recapitalization plan and FDIC TLGP announced, Oct. 14, 2008; Financial Stability Plan introduced, Feb. 10, 2009; Supervisory Capital Assessment Program results announced, May 7, 2009. Acronyms are defined in the list of abbreviations at the front of this book.

Source: Federal Reserve Bank of New York, based on data from Bloomberg Finance L.P.

Credit Facility (PDCF), in which the Fed lent to primary dealers against collateral accepted in the triparty repo market. That form of lending allowed the central bank to provide liquidity support for firms that might be facing strains like Bear Stearns experienced because investors perceived them to have similar funding models and asset holdings.

CDS premiums for large financial firms fell notably (see Figure 18.7), as the PDCF was widely seen by market participants as providing a respite from funding pressures, even for weak investment banks. Michael Fleming, Warren Hrung, and Frank Keane (2010) find that the PDCF was effective in reducing financial strains, with a significant narrowing of repurchase agreement (repo) spreads, between Treasury collateral and less liquid collateral such as

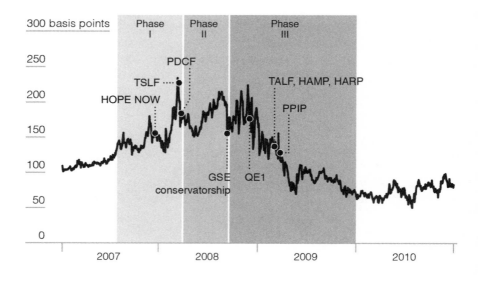

Figure 18.8 **Agency MBS-to-Treasury Spread**

Note: Spread shown is the Fannie Mae 30-year current coupon MBS to ten-year Treasury notes. Events shown are the following: HOPE NOW program announced, Oct. 10, 2007; TSLF announced, March 11, 2008; PDCF announced, March 16, 2008; GSE rescue, Sept. 7, 2008; quantitative easing (QE) announced, Nov. 25, 2008; TALF launch, March 3, 2009; Home Affordable Modification Program (HAMP) announced, March 4, 2009; Home Affordable Refinance Program (HARP) announced, March 4, 2009. Public-Private Investment Program (PPIP) announced, March 23, 2009. Acronyms are defined in the list of abbreviations at the front of this book.

Source: Federal Reserve Bank of New York, based on data from Bloomberg Finance L.P.

MBS. Another outcome of the PDCF was that the Fed required borrowers to provide information on their financial positions as a condition of access; the Fed had not had regular access to such information before because it was not a regulator for the dealers that were not parts of bank holding companies (BHCs).

Using authority granted by Congress in the Housing and Economic Recovery Act of 2008, the renamed and reconstituted regulator, the Federal Housing Finance Agency, placed Fannie Mae and Freddie Mac into conservatorship in early September. The Treasury made an initial pledge of $200 billion of taxpayer capital when the two government-sponsored enterprises (GSEs) were taken into conservatorship, a pledge that was later increased to $400 billion. Agency MBS-to-Treasury spreads declined sharply. (See Figure 18.8.) The actions with the two GSEs can be seen as working to ensure that mortgage financing remained available to creditworthy borrowers throughout the crisis even while many other parts of the mortgage market experienced serious strains (with Fed actions to purchase MBS later in the year then reducing mortgage interest rates).

Although the policy actions taken during Phase II were effective at alleviating certain areas of acute strain, the broader environment continued to deteriorate. CDS premiums moved higher, as investors remained especially concerned about insufficient capital at investment banks, as well as at commercial banks and large bank holding companies with substantial mortgage exposures. GDP and employment growth turned negative. The continued decline of the economy meant expected losses at financial firms were also continuing to increase.

Phase III, Mid-September 2008 to December 2009: Panic

Overview

The third phase of the crisis—the start of which we mark by the bankruptcy of Lehman Brothers on September 15, 2008—was characterized by conditions of panic and contagion across a wide range of financial markets, a broad loss of confidence in the adequacy of capital held by many types of financial institutions, a sharp economic contraction, and deepening concerns that a collapse in financial system functioning would lead to a depression. Although the threat of widespread contagion and loss of confidence in financial institutions had been present during the earlier phases of the crisis, the realization of this threat in the wake of Lehman's failure ultimately led to the creation of the Troubled Assets Relief Program (TARP) under EESA, enacted on October 3. TARP added a critical systemic element to the policymakers' tool kit—notably the ability to purchase assets from financial institutions. This additional tool not only provided a mechanism for directly addressing concerns about the capital adequacy of these institutions—it also created a powerful complement to the authority of the Federal Deposit Insurance Corporation (FDIC) to guarantee liabilities. The use of these two tools, along with a range of other systemic policy actions during this phase, was aimed at alleviating fire sale dynamics, preventing or minimizing contagion from both wholesale and retail funding runs, and restoring investor and creditor confidence in the capital adequacy of financial institutions.

The macro actions taken during this phase included the Fed initiating its first round of quantitative easing (QE), the provision of assistance to two large car companies, and the enactment of the American Recovery and Reinvestment Act (ARRA).

Details

Although Lehman was widely regarded as the weakest of the investment banks and market participants had been significantly reducing their exposure to the firm since Bear Stearns' failure in March, its bankruptcy filing set off events that were much more disruptive than expected by policymakers. In the aftermath, many new responses were launched in a coordinated effort by government agencies:

- The Fed significantly expanded liquidity facilities and lending by providing liquidity to new types of firms—such as insurance companies, in the case of AIG—to new central bank counterparties through the currency swap lines, and to new markets. These included the commercial paper market, with the Asset-Backed Commercial Paper Money Market Mutual Fund Liquidity Facility (AMLF) and the Commercial Paper Funding Facility (CPFF), and later the asset-backed securities (ABS) markets, with the Term Asset-Backed Securities Loan Facility (TALF).
- The Treasury guaranteed money market mutual fund shares under the Temporary Guarantee Program for Money Market Funds, using the exchange stabilization fund.
- The FDIC guaranteed certain newly issued bank debt and non-interest-bearing transaction accounts through the Temporary Liquidity Guarantee Program (TLGP), which the FDIC put in place after the complementary tool of TARP capital became available.
- While a few weakened financial institutions either raised private capital on their own (Goldman Sachs and Morgan Stanley) or were acquired by firms that seemed stronger (the acquisition of Merrill Lynch by Bank of America), the Treasury also injected $205 billion into 707 financial institutions across 48 states, starting with capital injections into the nine largest financial institutions on October 13, 2008, Columbus Day.

The economy weakened sharply with the financial market panic—the problems on Wall Street now resounded on Main Street, with real GDP declining by 8.4 percent at an annual rate in the fourth quarter. The weaker economy and housing market meant further uncertainty about the size and scope of losses in the financial system, with measures of stress remaining elevated well after the initial panic in money markets and commercial paper markets sparked by Lehman's failure had subsided.

More responses had to be made. In the wake of the Lehman failure, the government implemented an insurance program to prevent a destabilizing failure of Citigroup, with the Treasury (using TARP), the FDIC (invoking its systemic risk exemption authority), and the Fed coming together to provide a ring-fenced guarantee for troubled assets spun off into a separate subsidiary. And the Fed announced it would purchase agency debt and agency MBS (QE1) in November 2008 and lowered the federal funds rate to zero in December. Yields on agency MBS fell substantially on QE1 as the spread to Treasury yields narrowed and continued to decline, providing support to the mortgage market and house prices.

These measures helped stabilize the financial system, yet the economy remained weak, with real GDP declining by 4.4 percent at an annual rate in the first quarter of 2009 and still modestly negative in the second quarter. Financial strains widened again in February and March, as market participants grew concerned about what seemed like a lack of clarity regarding the Financial Stability Plan announced by the new administration on February 10, 2009, a core element of which was the unprecedented execution of a stress test on a cross-section of major U.S. financial institutions.

The strains during this period stemmed from both generalized uncertainty about the condition of financial institutions and speculation from official quarters suggesting that the government might seek to nationalize some large banks. The Fed's release of the supervisory stress test results in May 2009 helped resolve some of this uncertainty by giving market participants insight into the expected losses at the largest BHCs under the stress test scenario. The credibility of this exercise played a significant role in restoring the flow of private-sector capital into the financial sector. This was due both to the stringency of the requirement that firms meet any shortfall relative to the test's prescribed capital ratios by raising capital rather than shrinking assets, and to the unprecedented degree of transparency surrounding the results. TALF and the Public-Private Investment Program (PPIP) helped restart the securitization markets with a combination of private and government capital, working to boost asset prices. The recession ended in June 2009; GDP growth (monthly year-over-year) turned positive in the third quarter of that year.

Expansionary fiscal policy in Phase III included assistance to two large car companies in late 2008 and then enactment of the American Recovery and Reinvestment Act on February 17, 2009. ARRA provided $712 billion in net new spending for the economy through the end of 2012, with the discretionary fiscal stimulus peaking in 2010 at 2.7 percent of GDP. The fiscal stimulus phased down, however, giving way to a fiscal drag on GDP as early as 2011. Research surveyed by Ramey (2018) finds that the fiscal stimulus was effective in supporting output, even while concluding that many of the research papers to date overstate the fiscal multiplier. Fiscal policy was expected to be especially effective with monetary policy at the zero lower bound, but Ramey (2018) sees the evidence for this in the postcrisis research literature as tentative rather than conclusive.

Discerning the impacts of particular Phase III policy actions is particularly challenging because of the number of actions that were taken as well as the significant degree of interaction among them. Still, research has evaluated the outcomes of some of the responses by evaluating differences in prices or issuance of securities that were eligible and ineligible for the programs.

For example, Burcu Duygan-Bump et al. (2013) find that ABCP eligible for the AMLF had lower spreads than similar securities that were not eligible, and that money market funds (MMFs) with larger amounts of eligible securities had lower outflows than other MMFs. Tobias Adrian, Karin Kimbrough, and Dina Marchioni (2011) find that spreads on eligible commercial paper and ABCP declined sharply relative to ineligible paper and that the maturity of new commercial paper increased notably from overnight, adding to stability. Naohiko Baba, Robert McCauley, and Srichander Ramaswamy (2009) document that central bank swap lines were available to replace the substantial dollar funding to non-U.S. banks previously provided by money market funds, and William Allen and Richhild Moessner (2010) show that foreign-exchange risk indicators, such as covered interest differentials and cross-currency basis swap spreads, narrowed substantially. Joshua Aizenman and Gurnain Pasricha (2010) document that the CDS spreads of the emerging markets countries that received the swap arrangements fell, and by more than the CDS of other emerging markets countries, suggesting perhaps that the announcement of the swap lines supported a general boost to confidence across all emerging markets.

Combined, the AMLF, CPFF, money market fund guarantee, and currency swap lines worked to reduce significant pressures in money markets by stabilizing money market fund assets, reducing the costs for nonfinancial companies to issue commercial paper and the costs for non-U.S. banks to access dollar funding. In addition, Tobias Adrian, Christopher Burke, and James McAndrews (2009) show that the PDCF eased funding strains faced by primary dealers when, following Lehman's failure, counterparties began demanding higher haircuts on repo and less risky collateral. Marco Del Negro et al. (2017) argue that liquidity facilities that exchanged liquid paper for illiquid private paper in the third phase of the crisis (TAF, TSLF, PDCF, and currency swap lines) played a key role in supporting GDP. Without the extraordinary liquidity facilities, the authors estimate that the decline in GDP would have been about 30 percent larger than it was during the crisis and the decline in inflation even larger.

TALF had a positive effect on ABS markets, which rebounded from near-zero issuance in the months following the Lehman failure. Adam Ashcraft, Allan Malz, and Zoltan Pozsar (2012) show that TALF led to declines in spreads of asset-backed securities by improving market liquidity, including for certain legacy commercial mortgage-backed securities (CMBS) that were eligible for the TALF program (Ashcraft, Gârleanu, and Pedersen 2011). Sean Campbell et al. (2011) show that TALF's effect on spreads was more evident for categories of asset-backed securities than for securities funded by the program, suggesting that TALF improved investor sentiment regarding securitizations in general.

The Columbus Day action to inject capital into the nine largest financial institutions and to guarantee bank debt led to a significant decline in Libor-OIS and CDS premiums. Pietro Veronesi and Luigi Zingales (2010) find a positive net impact on the economy from the TARP capital injections and the FDIC debt guarantee. Assessing the ex ante cost of the insurance and the impact on banks, they find that these actions together resulted in a benefit to the economy of about $84 billion to $107 billion, calculated as the net of the increased value of banks of $131 billion and an ex ante cost to taxpayers of $25 billion to $47 billion, where the cost reflects the riskiness of the guarantee provided by the government.

The announcement of the stress test results in May 2009 had similar effects on these broad indicators, reducing the Libor-OIS spreads and CDS premiums that had increased again starting in February 2009. Studies of the effects of the announcement of the results suggest the stress tests provided information to investors, with banks that had identified capital gaps having more negative abnormal stock returns after accounting for the gaps the market had expected (Morgan, Peristiani, and Savino 2014). By the end of 2009, these firms (with the exception of GMAC) had raised the capital required by the stress tests, largely by issuing new common equity to private investors. Large BHCs raised $120 billion of new equity in 2009 following the stress tests to increase their risk-weighted ratios by more than 3 percent.

In addition to injecting capital into the largest institutions in October 2008, government capital was made available to other depository institutions to promote lending through the Capital Purchase Program (CPP), and 707 firms participated, drawing a total of $205 billion. Charles Calomiris and Urooj Kahn (2015) find that the program was effective, even while asserting that the appearance of political interventions into application approvals tainted the program. Allen Berger and Raluca Roman (2017) and Lei Li (2013) compare outcomes in areas where banks received more TARP funds against markets where fewer or no banks received TARP support. They find that TARP capital led to increased bank lending, stronger bank balance sheets, increased job creation, and lower business and personal bankruptcies. On average, they find that banks employed about one-third of TARP funds for new loans.

Other research suggests that bank credit growth in the United States, while still weak coming out of the crisis even after turning positive in late 2010, recovered relatively quickly compared with the experiences of other financial crises. It seems likely that the aggressive responses to inject capital and guarantee liabilities once the panic hit likely contributed to credit growth, and that credit growth in turn supported more rapid GDP growth. Abdul Abiad, Giovanni Dell'Ariccia, and Bin Li (2011) study "creditless" recoveries, which they define as when the growth in real bank credit is still negative in the first three years after a recession. For a sample of 48 countries with 388 recoveries from 1970 to 2004, they document that 1 in 5 recoveries is creditless and that these recoveries are weaker, with average output growth of 4.5 percent per year, compared with about 6.3 percent in recoveries in which credit rebounded. They find that most creditless recoveries are associated with an impaired banking sector, consistent with the view that the lower growth reflected impaired provision of credit rather than weak demand for credit. This evidence suggests that efforts to quickly recapitalize the banking system to restore credit were important to the recovery.

Actions to help homeowners were initiated early on a modest scale but were escalated as the crisis intensified. Mortgage delinquencies were rising as problems spread from subprime borrowers to other borrowers as the economy weakened and house prices continued to fall. A broad set of initiatives discussed in Chapter 12, on housing programs, aimed to stabilize and improve housing markets, seeking to reduce the number of foreclosures while reducing financial market strains and supporting the overall economy. The actions taken were especially notable starting in 2009, with an estimated lifetime cost of $33 billion to TARP on programs to reduce foreclosures and related housing initiatives.

The efforts implemented from 2009 onward together led to 8.2 million mortgage modifications, 9.5 million loans being refinanced, and 5.3 million other mortgage assistance actions. Although millions of families nonetheless faced foreclosure, the housing-related programs together contributed to the housing market and macroeconomic recovery. Research suggests that these programs were beneficial. Sumit Agarwal et al. (2017) estimate that through 2012, the Home Affordable Modification Program (HAMP) induced an additional 1 million permanent modifications than otherwise would have taken place and reduced the number of foreclosures by 600,000. Some other studies estimate that refinancing under the Home Affordable Refinance Program (HARP) roughly halved the probability of default (see, for example, Karamon, McManus, and Zhu [2017]). In addition, a broader set of policies—including lowering the federal funds rate to near zero, purchasing agency MBS, and putting Fannie Mae and Freddie Mac into conservatorship—also contributed importantly to reducing defaults and foreclosures. Moreover, Fed purchases of agency MBS resulted in significant refinancings and lower interest expenses (Di Maggio, Kermani, and Palmer 2016).

These studies on the effects of modifications cannot inform us about whether more aggressive programs would have been more effective. But the mortgage modification policy responses, combined with broader policy responses to reduce mortgage rates and support the mortgage market, were more effective and consequential than commonly thought, and together they contributed to the housing market and macroeconomic recovery.

Looking at the broader range of outcomes, Alan Blinder and Mark Zandi (2010) estimate the economic impacts of the government's responses to the financial panic and recession and conclude that the effects probably averted what could have been a second Great Depression. They use a large-scale macro model to simulate the effects of the government's total policy response and estimate that the effects on real GDP, jobs saved, and inflation were substantial. They report that without the policies, the peak-to-trough decline in real GDP through 2010 would have been about 11.5 percent, compared with an actual decline of 4 percent, an enormous difference. They also attribute the bulk of the effects to financial policies, which include the full array of actions from monetary policy to TARP, but find that fiscal policies also were important and that the two types of policies reinforced one another.

The aggressive actions taken after Lehman's failure—which escalated from liquidity measures to broad debt guarantees and the injection of capital into financial institutions—broke the escalating panic. CDS premiums for the two remaining investment banks fell sharply after the capital injections, though they remained elevated. The Fed's announcement that it would purchase agency MBS and agency debt in November 2008 led to sharp declines in agency MBS spreads and CDS premiums. Additional policies announced in February 2009 to improve transparency about the health of individual financial firms with the stress tests and to restart securitization markets contributed to the continued improvement. GDP growth turned positive in the second half of 2009, marking the end of the recession, and employment growth started to turn up by the end of 2009. Indicators of stress in the financial sector were much improved, though house prices continued to decline through early 2012. The decline in bank credit slowed, and positive growth returned in mid-2010. Only two investment banks survived as stand-alone entities, and they had become bank holding companies. The banking industry as a whole was raising private capital again, much of it in the form of common equity.

Finally, there are a few outcome measures that sit outside our framework but are nonetheless important to understanding the impact of the actions taken during the crisis. The first such measure is the cost to taxpayers of the systemic actions that were taken with TARP. We do not view whether the government made money on TARP investments as a reasonable measure of whether the systemic actions were successful, but instead believe that success is better measured by whether the financial system and the economy recovered as a result of the actions. That said, despite a popular view to the contrary, the TARP money invested in financial firms during the crisis was more than repaid, with the government earning $29.5 billion from its commitments of $269.6 billion to financial firms and the credit market programs.

The second measure is the impact of extraordinary systemic actions on risk-taking behavior and expectations of future public support on the part of financial-sector entities—that is, moral hazard. We consider the moral hazard issue through the admittedly narrow lens of whether banks or their investors are generally behaving as if banks will get bailed out again. We think the balance of evidence leans toward not.

The postcrisis regulatory regime is substantially stricter, with tougher capital and liquidity regulations, living wills, and a new resolution authority for financial firms if bankruptcy is not viable. BHCs are now also required to fund themselves with a layer of debt that is meant to absorb losses in the event of bankruptcy or resolution. This regime is meant to ensure that shareholders and unsecured bondholders, not taxpayers, would bear losses in the event of failure. In addition, in evaluating the postcrisis regulatory regime, including the greater limits on the Fed's authority as lender of last resort, credit rating agencies no longer ascribe increased safety to bank bonds from an implicit too-big-to-fail subsidy.

Still, some studies have interpreted the fact that CDS premiums and market betas for the largest banks are higher now than they were just before the crisis as evidence that banks now are riskier and more vulnerable to shocks (Sarin and Summers 2016). However, given the degree to which investors were likely underpricing risk in the years leading up to the crisis, other studies argue that simple comparisons of CDS premiums and market betas are difficult to interpret as evidence of changes in actual risk-taking behavior. Disentangling risk from risk-taking behavior is the subject of active research (see Atkeson et al. 2018).

The final outcome measure we consider is the degree to which the policy actions taken during the crisis affected the level of public trust in governmental authorities and institutions. Research since the financial crisis suggests that some amount of increased distrust and dissatisfaction with authorities may be virtually inevitable in these circumstances. Within the United States, states and localities with deeper recessions experienced larger increases in political polarization (Mian, Sufi, and Trebbi 2014). Based on cross-country experience of 20 advanced economies and more than 800 general elections since the late 1870s, policy uncertainty increases and extremist political parties gain voting shares after financial crises but not normal recessions (Funke, Schularick, and Trebesch 2016).

The sentiment outcomes associated with the policy actions undertaken during this crisis seem consistent with these findings. The slogan "where's my bailout?" succinctly conveyed the sentiment of many in late 2008 who felt unease at seeing government support go to banks that had been so deeply involved in the crisis through their lending and securitization, among other activities. Evidence from polls taken in the years after the crisis demonstrates the generally negative sentiment that surrounded many of the actions taken in response to the crisis. The negative sentiment surrounding these actions has likely contributed to what has been identified as a longer-term erosion of trust in government and a diminished belief in government fairness.[5]

---

5. For example, see Pew Research Center for the People and the Press, *Mixed Views of Regulation, Support for Keystone Pipeline: Auto Bailout Now Backed, Stimulus Divisive*, Feb. 23, 2012, https://www.pewresearch.org/wp-content/uploads/sites/4/legacy-pdf/2

More generally, it is likely that because of the way they are implemented, systemic policy actions are particularly vulnerable to the perception that they are being taken to support specific firms or groups of firms, rather than to support economic activity and employment, let alone ordinary individuals. There were indeed programs targeted directly to homeowners, with $33 billion of TARP funding spent on efforts to avoid foreclosures and related housing initiatives, but the number of families receiving assistance did not peak until 2012 and 2013, years after policy efforts to stabilize large banks, and the time lag contributed to a sense of unfairness. And even then, many people who were not behind on their mortgages felt disquiet at the idea of taxpayer money for foreclosure relief going to those who, for example, might have bought a bigger house than they could afford.

LESSONS LEARNED

The review conducted in this chapter suggests that the policy actions taken by the U.S. government over the course of the crisis served to prevent what might otherwise have been a second Great Depression. Research on individual policy actions taken provides evidence that many were effective in that they moved key indicators—such as risk spreads, credit, output, and employment—in the desired direction. However, even though the economy performed better than might be expected based on benchmarks from previous financial crises, the actions were not able to prevent a severe recession and a weak recovery.

As the crisis escalated, the response of the U.S. authorities also escalated from a set of relatively traditional macro and systemic policies to a more powerful mix of extraordinary measures. On the systemic front, a number of combined actions were crucial to breaking the panic and restoring financial system functioning. These actions included injecting government capital into private financial firms, issuing government guarantees on the debt of private financial firms, and conducting supervisory stress tests on large banking organ-

-23-12-Regulation-release.pdf; Pew Research Center, *Household Incomes, Jobs Seen as Lagging: Five Years after Market Crash, U.S. Economy Seen as "No More Secure,"* Sept. 12, 2013, https://www.pewresearch.org/wp-content/uploads/sites/4/legacy-pdf/9-12-13 -Econ-Release.pdf; and Pew Research Center, *Beyond Distrust: How Americans View Their Government,* Nov. 23, 2015, https://www.pewresearch.org/wp-content/uploads /sites/4/2015/11/11-23-2015-Governance-release.pdf.

izations in the presence of a government capital backstop. But many of the extraordinary actions were undertaken and only possible after conditions in the financial system had eroded significantly and TARP was made available, at which point the groundwork for a deeper and more protracted economic downturn had already been laid.

We do not mean to suggest that the timing of the extraordinary measures was inappropriate when viewed from the perspective of decision-makers' real-time understanding and constraints. Nor do we mean to suggest that other policies might not have yielded better outcomes. Instead, we have in mind the following hypothetical: The same set of policy actions, had they been taken before the panic conditions of Phase III had set in, likely would have generated better economic outcomes than those that actually occurred during this period. To be sure, this is not just a hypothetical but a counterfactual in the sense that policymakers did not have the legal authority to take important actions such as capital investments in banks until after the panic had started and EESA was enacted.[6] And there were many other factors influencing decision-making in real time, including uncertainty, concerns about potential consequences such as moral hazard, signaling of information, and political ramifications. But this hypothetical serves to highlight one key point: Waiting until conditions have eroded sufficiently as to clearly warrant extraordinary actions will almost inevitably generate a cost in terms of foregone economic growth owing to the reduction in financial sector functioning during the period of stress.

From this and other insights coming out of this review, we offer eight lessons for future crisis fighters to help reduce the damage to growth and employment stemming from a financial crisis.

---

6. For example, there was no legal authority to make capital investments in financial institutions until enactment of the EESA on October 3, 2008, and even then the regulators could not force banking firms to accept capital if they met their minimum regulatory capital requirements and other standards. In addition, there was no legal authority to resolve nonbank financial institutions outside of bankruptcy, such as by imposing debt-for-equity swaps or otherwise imposing losses on creditors. This authority was made available only in 2010 in the Dodd-Frank financial regulatory reform legislation. See Swagel (2009, 2015) for discussions of legal and other constraints on policymaking during the crisis.

Lesson 1:
A strong regulatory and supervisory structure is necessary to reduce the expected costs of a crisis on the real economy.

The U.S. regulatory and supervisory structure was weak and not well matched to the risks in the financial system, which had grown rapidly outside of commercial banks prior to the crisis. It also did not have a viable bankruptcy or resolution process that would allow large and complex financial firms to fail in an orderly way that would minimize damage to the economy. The regulatory and supervisory structure needs to be kept up to date with changes in the financial system and to be made more resilient to a wider range of shocks.

Lesson 2:
A strong regulatory and supervisory structure is not a substitute for strong crisis management capabilities.

A more stringent regime is now in place in the United States and in many other jurisdictions; however, no regime, no matter how well designed, will be able to prevent a financial crisis from ever occurring again. By reflecting on the lessons from the responses to past crises, governments will be better prepared to respond more effectively when faced with the next crisis.

Lesson 3:
Prepare (at least) for what is likely.

Understand that the causes and manifestations of future crises will likely differ from those of this crisis, but prepare for a few conditions that are likely to be present in any financial crisis. These include sudden and sustained reductions in liquidity in financial markets, widespread loss of confidence in the adequacy of financial institution capital even if the institutions comply with regulatory standards, and the potential for abrupt failures of financial entities that could seriously disrupt credit and growth. Authorities should practice responses to manifestations of these common types of conditions.

Lesson 4:
Prepare to be surprised.

Recognize the limits of real-time information and the inherent ambiguity and unpredictability associated with navigating effectively in crisis situations. Organizations should develop the capacity for rapid innovation, experimentation, and learning.

Lesson 5:
Communicate before, during, and after periods of financial crisis.

Communicate with the public on an ongoing basis about the role that the financial system plays in the economy and the principles that will guide policy actions in a crisis. Communication alone cannot deliver concrete outcomes in terms of economic performance or financial system functioning, but it can help increase the public's understanding of the rationale for the types of policy actions taken in a crisis.

Lesson 6:
There will always be forces that push against early intervention.

Accept that there will always be a variety of forces—including uncertainty, valid concerns about triggering unintended consequences, and gaps in legal authority—that will come together to favor inaction over action until conditions become sufficiently dire. In other words, many of the actions we judge in hindsight as having come too late will have been seen by many decision-makers in real time as having come precisely when, and not before, conditions warranted.

Lesson 7:
Late intervention limits the potential for good outcomes.

Recognize that once conditions become sufficiently extreme or dire, even good decisions and well-executed actions may not yield good outcomes, particularly on the macro front, because the extreme conditions themselves have often already laid the groundwork for a deeper economic downturn. One of the hallmarks of decision-making in a financial crisis may be that even the best decisions are likely to yield outcomes that would be viewed as weak or lack-luster during normal times.

Lesson 8:
Late intervention may raise rather than lower the potential for unintended consequences.

Recognize that once conditions have eroded sufficiently, the range of policy options shrinks. Late intervention may necessitate more extreme actions and more substantial deviation from the public's expectations. These actions may also engender in the public a greater sense of unfairness.

REFERENCES

Abiad, Abdul, Giovanni Dell'Ariccia, and Bin Li. 2011. "Creditless Recoveries." IMF Working Paper WP/11/58.

Adrian, Tobias, Christopher R. Burke, and James J. McAndrews. 2009. "The Federal Reserve's Primary Dealer Credit Facility." *Current Issues in Economics and Finance* 15 (August).

Adrian, Tobias, Karin Kimbrough, and Dina Marchioni. 2011. "The Federal Reserve's Commercial Paper Funding Facility." *Federal Reserve Bank of New York Economic Policy Review*: 25–39.

Agarwal, Sumit, Gene Amromin, Itzhak Ben-David, Souphala Chomsisengphet, Tomasz Piskorski, and Amit Seru. 2017. "Policy Intervention in Debt Renegotiation: Evidence from the Home Affordable Modification Program." *Journal of Political Economy* 125 (3): 654–712.

Ahamed, Liaquat. 2009. *Lords of Finance: The Bankers Who Broke the World.* New York: Penguin Press.

Aizenman, Joshua, and Gurnain Pasricha. 2010. "Selective Swap Arrangements and the Global Financial Crisis: Analysis and Interpretation." *International Review of Economics and Finance* 19 (3): 353–65.

Allen, William, and Richhild Moessner. 2010. "Central Bank Cooperation and International Liquidity in the Financial Crisis of 2008–09." BIS Working Papers, no. 310.

Andritzky, Jochen. 2014. "Resolving Residential Mortgage Distress: Time to Modify?" IMF Working Paper WP/14/226, December.

Ashcraft, Adam, Nicolae Gârleanu, and Lasse Heje Pedersen. 2011. "Two Monetary Tools: Interest Rates and Haircuts." *NBER Macroeconomics Annual* 25 (1): 143–80.

Ashcraft, Adam B., Allan M. Malz, and Zoltan Pozsar. 2012. "The Federal Reserve's Term Asset-Backed Securities Loan Facility." *Economic Policy Review* 18 (3): 29–66.

Atkeson, Andrew G., Adrien d'Avernas, Andrea L. Eisfeldt, and Pierre-Olivier Weill. 2018. "Government Guarantees and the Valuation of American Banks." *NBER Macroeconomics Annual* 33.

Baba, Naohiko, Robert N. McCauley, and Srichander Ramaswamy. 2009. "U.S. Dollar Money Market Funds and Non-U.S. Banks." *BIS Quarterly Review* (March): 65–81.

Baba, Naohiko, and Frank Packer. 2009. "From Turmoil to Crisis: Dislocations in the FX Swap Market before and after the Failure of Lehman Brothers." *Journal of International Money and Finance* 28 (8): 1350–74.

Benmelech, Efraim, Ralf Meisenzahl, and Rodney Ramcharan. 2017. "The Real Effects of Liquidity during the Financial Crisis: Evidence from Automobiles." *Quarterly Journal of Economics* 132 (1): 317–65.

Berger, Allen N., and Raluca Roman. 2017. "Did Saving Wall Street Really Save Main Street? The Real Effects of TARP on Local Economic Conditions." *Journal of Financial and Quantitative Analysis* 52 (5): 1827–67.

Bernanke, Ben S. 2018. "The Real Effects of Disrupted Credit: Evidence from the Global Financial Crisis." *Brookings Papers on Economic Activity,* September.

Blanchard, Olivier, Eugenio Cerutti, and Larry Summers. 2015. "Inflation and Activity—Two Explorations and Their Monetary Policy Implications." IMF Working Paper, 15/230.

Blinder, Alan, and Mark Zandi. 2010. "How the Great Recession Was Brought to an End." Moody's Corporation.

Broda, Christian, and Jonathan A. Parker. 2014. "The Economic Stimulus Payments of 2008 and the Aggregate Demand for Consumption." *Journal of Monetary Economics* 68: S20–S36.

Calomiris, Charles W., and Urooj Khan. 2015. "An Assessment of TARP Assistance to Financial Institutions." *Journal of Economic Perspectives* 29 (2): 53–80.

Campbell, Sean, Daniel Covitz, William Nelson, and Karen Pence. 2011. "Securitization Markets and Central Banking: An Evaluation of the Term Asset Backed Securities Loan Facility." *Journal of Monetary Economics* 58 (5): 518–31.

Cerra, Valerie, and Sweta Saxena. 2008. "Growth Dynamics: The Myth of Economic Recovery." *American Economic Review* 98 (1): 439–57.

Cerra, Valerie, and Sweta Saxena. 2017. "Booms, Crises, and Recoveries: A New Paradigm of the Business Cycle and Its Policy Implications." IMF Working Paper, 17/250, November.

Covitz, Daniel, Nellie Liang, and Gustavo Suarez. 2013. "The Evolution of a Financial Crisis: Collapse of the Asset-Backed Commercial Paper Market." *Journal of Finance* 68 (3): 815–48.

Del Negro, Marco, Gauti Eggertsson, Andrea Ferrero, and Nobuhiro Kiyotaki. 2017. "The Great Escape? A Quantitative Evaluation of the Fed's Liquidity Facilities." *American Economic Review* 107 (3): 824–57.

Di Maggio, Marco, Amir Kermani, and Christopher Palmer. 2016. "How Quantitative Easing Works: Evidence on the Refinancing Channel," MIT Sloan Working Paper, December.

Duygan-Bump, Burcu, Patrick Parkinson, Eric Rosengren, Gustavo A. Suarez, and Paul Willen. 2013. "How Effective Were the Federal Reserve Emergency Liquidity Facilities? Evidence from the Asset-Backed Commercial Paper Money Market Mutual Fund Liquidity Facility." *Journal of Finance* 68 (2): 715–37.

Fernald, John, Robert Hall, James Stock, and Mark Watson. 2017. "The Disappointing Recovery of Output after 2009." Brookings Papers on Economic Activity, Spring.

Fleming, Michael J., Warren B. Hrung, and Frank M. Keane. 2010. "Repo Market Effects of the Term Securities Lending Facility." *American Economic Review* 100 (2): 591–96.

Funke, Manuel, Moritz Schularick, and Christoph Trebesch. 2016. "Going to Extremes: Politics after Financial Crises, 1870–2014." *European Economic Review* 88: 227–60.

Gertler, Mark, and Simon Gilchrist. 2018. "What Happened: Financial Factors in the Great Recession." *Journal of Economic Perspectives* 32 (3): 3–30.

Gorton, Gary, and Andrew Metrick. 2012. "Securitized Banking and the Run on Repo." *Journal of Financial Economics* 104 (3): 425–51.

Jorda, Oscar, Moritz Schularick, and Alan Taylor. 2013. "When Credit Bites Back." *Journal of Money, Credit and Banking* 45 (2): 3–28.

Karamon, Kadiri, Douglas McManus, and Jun Zhu. 2017. "Refinance and Mortgage Default: A Regression Discontinuity Analysis of HARP's Impact on Default Rates." *Journal of Real Estate Finance and Economics* 55 (4): 457–75.

Khan, Aubhik, and Julia Thomas. 2013. "Credit Shocks and Aggregate Fluctuations in an Economy with Production Heterogeneity." *Journal of Political Economy* 121 (6): 1055–107.

Li, Lei. 2013. "TARP Funds Distribution and Bank Loan Supply." *Journal of Banking & Finance* 37 (12): 4777–92.

McAndrews, James, Asani Sarkar, and Zhenyu Wang. 2017. "The Effect of the Term Auction Facility on the London Interbank Offered Rate." *Journal of Banking & Finance* 83: 135–52. https://doi.org/10.1016/j.jbankfin.2016.12.011.

Mian, Atif, Amir Sufi, and Francesco Trebbi. 2014. "Resolving Debt Overhang: Political Constraints in the Aftermath of Financial Crises." *American Economic Journal: Macroeconomics* 6 (2): 1–28.

Morgan, Donald P., Stavros Peristiani, and Vanessa Savino. 2014. "The Information Value of the Stress Test." *Journal of Money, Credit and Banking* 46 (7): 1479–500.

Parker, Jonathan A., Nicholas S. Souleles, David S. Johnson, and Robert McClelland. 2013. "Consumer Spending and the Economic Stimulus Payments of 2008." *American Economic Review* 103 (6): 2530–53.

Ramey, Valerie A. 2018. "Ten Years after the Financial Crisis: What Have We Learned from the Renaissance in Fiscal Research?" Prepared for the NBER Conference, "Global Financial Crisis @10," July 3, 2018.

Reinhart, Carmen M., and Kenneth S. Rogoff. 2014. "Recovery from Financial Crises: Evidence from 100 Episodes." *American Economic Review* 104 (5): 50–55.

Romer, Christina, and David Romer. 2017. "New Evidence on the Aftermath of Financial Crises in Advanced Countries." *American Economic Review* 107 (10): 3072–118.

Sarin, Natasha, and Lawrence Summers. 2016. "Have Big Banks Gotten Safer?" *Brookings Papers on Economic Activity,* September.

Siemer, Michael. 2014. "Firm Entry and Employment Dynamics in the Great Recession." FEDS 2014-56, Federal Reserve Board, Washington, D.C.

Swagel, Phillip. 2009. "The Financial Crisis: An Inside View." *Brookings Papers on Economic Activity,* Spring.

Swagel, Phillip. 2015. "Legal, Political, and Institutional Constraints on the Financial Crisis Policy Response." *Journal of Economic Perspectives* 29 (2): 107–22.

Veronesi, Pietro, and Luigi Zingales. 2010. "Paulson's Gift." *Journal of Financial Economics* 97 (3): 339–68.

| ACKNOWLEDGMENTS |

This book began with the simple conviction that we owed the crisis fighters of the future the manual that we were never given. None of us was especially eager to look back in great depth at such a painful time in our nation's history, so we weren't sure we'd be able to persuade anyone to join us in revisiting the choices we made in fighting the global financial crisis of 2007–2009. We extend our heartfelt thanks to the authors whose essays are collected in this volume, for both their tireless efforts to help save and revive the U.S. economy during the crisis and their willingness to return to those difficult days in these pages.

More broadly, we owe an enormous debt of gratitude to all those who served the United States during the crisis—in particular the men and women who worked at the Board of Governors of the Federal Reserve System and the Federal Reserve Banks, the Federal Deposit Insurance Corporation, the U.S. Department of Treasury, and the White House. Special thanks are due to Presidents George W. Bush and Barack Obama for their leadership, and to the members of Congress who worked for bipartisan solutions to the crisis.

This project started with a conference at the Yale Program on Financial Stability (YPFS) at the Yale School of Management in March 2018, evolved into a symposium at the Brookings Institution's Hutchins Center on Fiscal & Monetary Policy in September 2018, and coalesced into the book you are holding in your hands today. None of this would have been possible without the support of Brookings/Hutchins, led by director David Wessel, and YPFS, led by program director Andrew Metrick. Wessel and Metrick collaborated with us on the design of the project and provided significant institutional support along the way. The presentations and panel discussions at the Yale and Brookings events allowed the authors a chance to test their ideas and to interact with other authors, scholars, the editors, and the public.

For her outstanding leadership on this project we are deeply indebted to Nellie Liang. In addition to cowriting two chapters and delivering presentations at the conference and symposium, Liang was our unflappable scholar-leader and content and quality control overseer, helping to shape the vision of the project, editing countless drafts, guiding the presentations at both events, and weighing in with her extensive expertise. Her efforts improved this book greatly, making it more authoritative.

Project manager Deborah McClellan kept track of all the moving parts to keep a complex enterprise on schedule. She pushed a volunteer army of more than 30 writers and three busy principals to deliver their chapters and then continue revising them; served, with Liang, as an editorial first line of defense to ensure that the delivered manuscripts met our criteria; coordinated the efforts of the research team; and, in leading the chart crew, ensured that we produced some 150 financial crisis charts. It was a remarkable feat of organization and management.

Andrew Metrick's indispensable team at YPFS played a pivotal role—it's hard to thank them enough for all they did. For hosting the March 2018 conference and handling a host of administrative challenges throughout the project, we are grateful to Metrick, Ashley Cumberledge, Kyra Baum, and Katie Hunsberger. For their outstanding research support, we thank the YPFS New Bagehot Project team, led by Christian McNamara, June Rhee, and Rosalind Z. Wiggins. Research associates Julia Arnous, Alec Buchholtz, Lily Engbith, Ben Henken, Aidan Lawson, Manuel Leon Hoyos, Riki Matsumoto, Alexander Nye, Kaleb B. Nygaard, Keni Sabath, Claire Simon, Ariel Smith, Daniel Thompson, and David Tam were responsible for the daunting task of providing research and fact-checking this volume under tight deadlines. Buchholtz and Tam deserve special thanks for coordinating the fact-checking effort. Greg Feldberg added his expertise, weighing in with valuable suggestions on content.

For helping to frame many of the questions in this project and reading early drafts of the manuscript, we thank Brookings/Hutchins's David Wessel. We extend our appreciation to Wessel and Brookings/Hutchins for hosting the September 11–12, 2018, anniversary symposium at Brookings in Washington, D.C., which included public presentations by the authors of this book and an interview with us by Andrew Ross Sorkin. Stephanie Cencula, Anna Dawson, Delaney Parrish, and Kevin Thibodeaux deserve recognition for their help in organizing the symposium, as do Brookings research staff members Sage Belz, Haowen Chen, Jeffrey Cheng, Vivien Lee, and Michael Ng for providing research support and help with data on the project.

We are grateful to Eric Dash, founder and principal of Golden Triangle Strategies, for helping to organize our approach to the content of this book. Dash, along with Barry Adler, Bob Goetz, and Tom Redburn, provided top-notch editorial guidance and support. Dash also played a critical leadership role on our chart project.

The charts and tables in this book reflect a team effort. We thank Seth W. Feaster for his data visualization mastery and YPFS's Ben Henken and Aidan Lawson for their willingness to dig for the right data and ensure their accuracy. The chart team worked long hours to deliver the charts for this project, many of which were first generated as part of *Charting the Financial Crisis,* available at http://ypfs.som.yale.edu/sites/default/files/Charting%20The%20Financial%20Crisis.pdf. The authors of the chapters also provided chart data, as did YPFS's Daniel Thompson and Yale University's Chase Ross.

For their help in securing data for the charts and tables and gaining necessary permissions, we wish to thank the following individuals and institutions: Bloomberg Finance L.P. (Jeff Levy, Josh Steiner); CoreLogic, Inc. (Alyson Austin); Federal Deposit Insurance Corporation (Diane Ellis); Federal Reserve Bank of New York (Tony Baer, Francis Mahoney); Federal Reserve Bank of St. Louis; Federal Reserve Board (Alex Martin); Haver Analytics (Ryan Sherlock); IHS Markit (Daniel Yergin); iMoneyNet (Kevin Grist); George Jiranek; Annabel Jouard; Vivek Manjunath; Wilson Powell III; Lorenzo Rasetti; Securities Industry and Financial Markets Association (Research Department); Ernie Tedeschi; U.S. Department of Housing and Urban Development (Carolyn Lynch); and Wharton Research Data Services.

Members of the Golden Triangle Strategies team also deserve recognition: Monica Boyer for production, fact-checking, and copy editing; Ingrid Accardi and Melissa Wohlgemuth for copy editing; and Emily Cincebeaux, Bill Marsh, and Debrah Kaiser for data visualization.

Michael Grunwald provided us with invaluable editorial guidance. For their highly professional logistical and administrative support and help with publicity and communications, we thank Mary King, Katherine Korsak, Missy Lajka, Andrew Morimoto, Rebecca Neale, and Claire Buchan Parker.

Finally, we are grateful to Robert Barnett and Michael O'Connor of Williams & Connelly, Seth Ditchik and his team at Yale University Press, and Melody Negron and Westchester Publishing Services for their efforts in bringing this volume to fruition.

Ben Bernanke, Tim Geithner, Hank Paulson
Spring 2019

| INDEX |

Note: Information found in footnotes is indicated by an n and the note number following the page number.

266–270, 272–273, 288; systemic
surcharge of, 40; tangible common
equity and, 260, 270, 272, 281; uncertainty and, 281–282. *See also* Banking
system recapitalization
Bank credit, 531–533; effect of capital on,
552; outcome measure of macro policies
on, 537, 554
Bank failures, 289–319; asset disposition
with, 292–293, 301–311, 313; bank runs
leading to, 4–5; capital infusion to
avert, 303, 304–306, 311, 313; cascade of,
289–293; contingent-loss reserves for
future, 294–295; Deposit Insurance
Fund management with, 292, 293–300,
311–312; equity partnerships from,
309–311; expanding potential acquirer
pool for, 304–306; FDIC impacted by,
290, 292–314; legal authorities to
address, 293; lessons learned from,
311–314; loss-share proposition with,
306–309, 313; minimizing payouts for,
300; overview of, 4; resolution with,
293–294, 300, 304, 309, 313, 317–319;
risk-sharing programs for, 306–311, 313;
savings and loan crisis comparison
with, 297, 301, 314–317; supervisory
coordination for, 302–304. *See also*
specific banks
Bank for International Settlements (BIS),
496
Bank holding companies, 132–134, 140,
213, 263, 369
Banking system recapitalization, 208–225;
allocation for, 220, 221, 222; Asset
Guarantee Program and, 222–223; bank
capital status after, 259–260; "Break the
Glass" Bank Recapitalization Plan,
211–212; broad participation in, 216,
217, 218, 220–222; Capital Purchase
Program for, 139, 215–225, 228, 229–230,
270, 390–392, 395, 399–401, 408–409,
411, 552; context for, 208, 209–214; debt

guarantees with, 219–220; dividends
with, 217, 218, 260; evaluation of,
223–225, 548, 551–552; executive
compensation and, 218, 260, 392–393;
incentivizing, 216–218; international
policy coordination on, 497; legal
authorities for, 216, 557; lessons learned
from, 223–225; overview of, 208–209;
preferred stock for, 216–218, 221, 260,
270, 391; repayment of and profits from,
209, 218–219, 223–224, 260; rollout of,
220; stigma avoidance with, 216; TARP
role in, 29, 31, 33, 209, 213–215, 390–393,
399–401, 408–410, 551–552; Temporary
Liquidity Guarantee Program strengthening, 219–220, 228, 229–230; warrants
with, 218, 219, 391–392. *See also* Bank
capital
Bank of America (BoA): Asset Guarantee
Program for, 222n8, 263; Countrywide
Financial acquisition by, 16, 41, 122;
Lehman potential acquisition by, 22,
130; Merrill Lynch acquisition by, 4, 22,
41, 132, 548; nonbank affiliates of, 121;
recapitalization of, 220–221, 222n8, 263;
rescue/stabilization of, 32, 139, 169,
220–221, 222n8, 263; stress test results
for, 273; Super-SIV role of, 211; Temporary Liquidity Guarantee Program
eligibility, 239–240, 246–247
Bank of Canada (BoC): liquidity provision
actions of, 498n12; monetary policy of,
506; swap lines with, 59n17, 500
Bank of England (BoE): liquidity
provision actions of, 74n38, 106, 498n12;
monetary policy of, 505–506; swap lines
with, 59n17, 500, 503
Bank of Japan (BoJ): asset purchases by,
440; international policy coordination
with, 496, 498n12; swap lines with,
500, 503
Bank of New York Mellon, 194, 220–221,
412

Bankruptcy laws: AIG resolution under, 135; bank recapitalization programs and, 261, 264, 274; General Motors and Chrysler restructuring under, 32, 359–361, 364, 365, 368, 372–376; housing programs and filings under, 323–324, 329, 343, 358 (*see also* Foreclosures); legal authorities beyond, 164; Lehman Brothers subject to (*see* Lehman Brothers); orderly liquidation authority and, 43–44, 141, 143, 293; prepackaged bankruptcies under, 373, 374; Temporary Liquidity Guarantee Program triggered by, 231, 243; 363 sales under, 373–376

BankUnited, 305

Barclays, 22, 130–131, 158–159

Basel III, 39

Bayh, Evan, 339

Bear Stearns: capital insufficiency of, 122, 124, 210; conventional liquidity tools affected by failure of, 57, 63; executive leadership removal at, 25; JPMorgan Chase acquisition of, 18, 19, 41, 124–128, 152, 195; legal authorities for emergency credit to, 152–153, 156–158, 161–162; monetary policy in response to collapse of, 425; as nonbank financial institution, 9, 17, 40, 122, 124–128, 152–153, 156–158, 161–162; special purpose vehicle facilitating credit for, 156–158; weakening and averted collapse of, 16–19, 43, 124–128, 152–153, 156–158, 161–162, 195, 544

Bernanke, Ben S.: banking system recapitalization role of, 213–214, 395; on Capital Assistance Program, 270; on conventional liquidity tools, 55, 60, 64n29; financial crisis response role of, generally, 2–3, 15, 18, 19–21, 23, 27, 32, 33, 35; General Motors and Chrysler rescue/restructure role of, 364–365; on housing programs, 339–340, 355;

international policy coordination role of, 497; monetary policy role of, 427, 430, 438n12, 441, 447; on money market funds, 196; on nonbank financial institutions, 122, 131–132n13; on novel lender-of-last-resort programs, 82, 104; on Supervisory Capital Assessment Program, 268; Temporary Liquidity Guarantee Program role of, 228

Biden, Joseph, 459

BIS. *See* Bank for International Settlements

BlackRock, 194

Bluebook, 428, 438–439

BNP Paribas, 12, 49–50, 195, 423, 489

BoA. *See* Bank of America

Board of directors. *See* Executive leadership

BoC. *See* Bank of Canada

BoE. *See* Bank of England

BoJ. *See* Bank of Japan

Brazil: International Monetary Fund participation, 511; swap lines with, 501–502, 520–521

"Break the Glass" Bank Recapitalization Plan, 211–212

Broker-dealers: growth of credit from, 115–116, 118 (*see also* Investment banks; Nonbank financial institutions); legal authorities to address, 159; novel lender-of-last-resort programs for, 90, 99n11, 106; regulatory system reforms applicable to, 40, 141; securities firms and market-wide liquidity facilities, 124–134

Budget deficits, 45, 455, 478, 515

Buffett, Warren, 133, 213n6, 217, 277

Bush, George W./Bush administration: banking system recapitalization under, 214, 270, 392; fiscal policy response under, 451, 453–454, 507; General Motors and Chrysler rescue/restructure under, 32, 359–361, 363–372, 383–384;

housing programs under, 37, 321–322, 330–332, 354–355; international policy coordination under, 494, 497, 516–517; TARP under, 32, 214, 365–372, 384, 392, 393, 397

CAMELS rating, 245, 291n10, 399
Canada, central bank of. *See* Bank of Canada
Capital Assistance Program (CAP), 269–273, 274, 400
Capital Purchase Program (CPP), 139, 215–225, 228, 229–230, 270, 390–392, 395, 399–401, 408–409, 411, 552
Cash for Clunkers program, 460, 468n6
CBO. *See* Congressional Budget Office
CDCI. *See* Community Development Capital Initiative
CDFIs. *See* Community Development Financial Institutions
CDOs. *See* Collateralized debt obligations
CDS. *See* Credit default swaps
Center for Economic and Policy Research, 455–456
Central banks: Federal Reserve as (*see* Federal Reserve); international policy coordination with foreign (*see* International policy coordination); monetary policy communication by, 444–447, 449–450; nonbank financial institution limitations of, 120; swap lines with foreign (*see* Swap lines with foreign central banks); unique role of, for emergency liquidity, 73. *See also specific central banks*
CEOs. *See* Executive leadership
Cerberus Capital Management, 363, 377
Chile: swap line request by, 503n21
China: currency values in, 491, 519; Financial Stability Forum membership of, 518n56; fiscal policy in, 507; International Monetary Fund participation, 511; international policy coordina-

tion with, 496, 497, 507; monetary policy of, 506; People's Bank of China, 496, 506
China Investment Corporation, 211n3
Chrysler Financial, 368–370
Chrysler rescue/restructure. *See* General Motors and Chrysler rescue/restructure
CITIC Securities, 210n3
Citigroup: Asset Guarantee Program for, 222–223, 263; capital raised by, 122, 210; Citi Holdings troubled asset transfer by, 274; executive leadership removal at, 25; nonbank affiliates of, 121; preferred stock conversion at, 217, 221, 272; recapitalization of, 220–223, 263, 272; rescue/stabilization of, 32, 139, 169, 220–223, 549; stress test results for, 273; Super-SIV role of, 211; Temporary Liquidity Guarantee Program eligibility, 239–240, 246–247
Coca-Cola, 25–26, 196, 197
Colgate-Palmolive, 196
Collateralized debt obligations (CDOs), 115, 120, 326
Colonial Bank, 249n48
Commerce, Department of, 363–364
Commercial banks: capital requirements for, 10; conventional liquidity tools applicable to (*see* Conventional liquidity tools); investment bank separation from, erosion of, 118; nonbank affiliates of, 9, 62n25, 118, 119n2, 121; regulatory system oversight of, 9–10, 47, 118; securities role of, 118, 119n2. *See also specific banks*
Commercial Paper Funding Facility (CPFF): coordinated response including, 228, 239; evaluation of, 101, 110, 548, 550; legal authorities for, 167–168; as novel lender-of-last-resort program, 30, 83, 92–94, 101, 107–108, 110, 140, 167–168, 228, 239, 548, 550; summary of, 107–108, 167–168; TARP and, 93, 140, 167–168

Goldman Sachs: bank holding company transition, 132–134; capital raised by, 133, 213, 548; Paulson at, 209; recapitalization of, 220–221; stress tests of, 284, 286; Temporary Liquidity Guarantee Program eligibility, 240

Gold Reserve Act, 163

Gonzalez, Arthur J., 374, 376

Goolsbee, Austan, 378, 455

Government Accountability Office (GAO): on bank failures, 292; financial crisis-era reports, 41; on novel lender-of-last-resort programs, 109; on savings and loan (S&L) crisis, 297n20; TARP oversight by, 414–415, 418–419; on Temporary Liquidity Guarantee Program, 236

Government of Singapore Investment Corporation, 210–211n3

Government-sponsored enterprises (GSEs): conservatorship for, 4, 20–21, 129, 147, 178–189, 191–192, 195, 212, 264, 331, 546–547, 553; conventional liquidity tools affected by, 57; executive leadership removal and compensation constraint at, 25, 183; financial condition assessment of, 176–178, 180, 187; financial crisis response hinging on, 185, 190–191; flawed structure of, 190; foreign investors in, 172; housing programs intertwined with, 183, 321, 323, 330, 331, 332–333, 334–335, 336, 339, 345–346, 348, 351–352, 355, 401n23; international policy coordination on, 496; legal authorities to avert failure of, 147; lessons learned from, 190–192; lobbying by, 183; money market fund investment in, 197; nonbank financial institutions and, 9, 119, 129; obtaining ownership in, 182; outcomes of policies on, 546–547, 553; overview of, 171–173; portfolio limit raises for, 186–187; preferred stock purchase agreement for, 181–182,

185–190; proposals for lifeline to, 173–176; quantitative easing buying securities of, 275; recapitalization of, 37, 174, 186–190; receivership of, 174, 176, 178–180; reform of, 183; regulatory system oversight of, 9, 11, 20, 40, 174–180, 184, 187, 190, 321, 331, 334–335, 339, 546; structuring investment in, 180–181. *See also* Fannie Mae; Freddie Mac

Gramm-Leach-Bliley Act (1999), 118

Great Depression: bank failures in, 41, 146, 301; FDIC creation in, 226; Home Owners' Loan Corporation in, 341–342, 347, 350, 357; international trade decline in, 514; legal authorities in, 82, 120, 126–127, 145, 146, 151; loan losses in, 34, 266, 288; outcomes in comparison to, 531, 533, 538; unemployment and bank credit in, 531, 533

Great Recession, 15, 325, 531; economic contraction during, 31, 95, 166, 254–257, 424, 427–428, 531; economic recovery after, 35–38, 257, 323, 360, 381, 422, 519, 531–532, 534

Greece: real GDP in, 535

Greenbook, 424, 425, 431, 434–438, 519

Gross domestic product. *See* GDP

Group of Eight (G-8), 497

Group of Seven (G-7), 496, 497, 506, 516–517, 522, 525–526

Group of Twenty (G-20), 496, 497, 506, 507, 509–516, 517–518, 522, 526

GSEs. *See* Government-sponsored enterprises

Gutierrez, Carlos, 364

HAMP. *See* Home Affordable Modification Program

Hardest Hit Fund, 335, 336, 348, 403–404

HARP. *See* Home Affordable Refinance Program

Health care, fiscal stimulus for, 457, 458, 466–467, 472–473, 484

327–329, 342; loan modification programs as, 37, 322, 323, 327–329, 331, 333–352, 401–404, 553; moral hazard concerns with, 341, 355–356; mortgage servicers' role in, 337–339, 402–403; outcomes of, 543, 552–553, 555; payment reduction in, 329–330, 333–334, 335, 350–351; principal reduction in, 329–330, 331, 334, 335; private-sector initiatives for, 330, 346, 355; problems and constraints shaping, 323–330; quantitative easing and, 35–36, 321, 332, 336; re-default rates with, 350–352; TARP funds for, 400, 401–404, 416–417, 419n32, 552, 555; timeline and evolution of, 322, 335; "undeserving homeowner" bailout concerns with, 329, 337, 339–340, 343, 355–356, 403, 555

Iceland: real GDP in, 535; swap line request by, 503n21
IMF. *See* International Monetary Fund
Immelt, Jeffrey, 239
India: International Monetary Fund participation, 511; swap line request by, 503n21
IndyMac, 292, 294, 297n19, 305, 334
Infrastructure, fiscal stimulus for, 457, 458, 472–473, 484
Inter-American Development Bank, 509n31, 513–514
Internal Revenue Service (IRS), 182, 396
International Monetary Fund (IMF): flexible credit line of, 520; international policy coordination with, 496, 497, 502–503, 507, 508–513, 517, 520, 522–523, 525–526; new borrowing arrangements for, 510–512; real GDP growth forecasts by, 494, 508–509, 519, 539; special drawing rights of, 512–513, 526; TARP predictions by, 34, 256
International policy coordination, 489–528; on banking system recapital-

ization, 497; consensus on appropriate, 523–524; context for, 490–495; for crisis prevention, 524; currency values and, 490–491, 519; diplomacy for, 495–497; emerging and developing economies in, 490–491, 492n4, 493, 495–496, 500–503, 504–505, 508–510, 512–515, 519–521, 550; on financial support for international financial institutions, 508–510; on fiscal policy, 507–508, 523–524; G-7 role in, 496, 497, 506, 516–517, 522, 525–526; G-20 role in, 496, 497, 506, 507, 509–516, 517–518, 522, 526; IMF role in, 496, 497, 502–503, 507, 508–513, 517, 520, 522–523, 525–526; international trade decline prompting, 493, 514–515; lessons learned from, 521–524; macroeconomic, 505–508; on monetary policy, 505–506, 523; on multilateral development banks, 508–509, 513–514, 522, 526; on new borrowing arrangements, 510–512; outcomes of, 519–521, 550; overview of, 489–490; principal initiatives of, 495–518; on regulatory reform, 39, 516–518, 526; on special drawing rights, 512–513, 526; on swap lines with foreign central banks, 15, 497, 498–505, 520–521, 527, 550; systematic and inclusive engagement for, 522; on trade protectionism and finance, 514–516; trust-building for, 522; U.S. inter-agency coordination for, 522; U.S. leadership in, 523
Investment banks: bank holding company transition, 132–134, 140, 213; Bear Stearns as example (*see* Bear Stearns); commercial bank separation from, erosion of, 118; context for vulnerabilities of, 114; Goldman Sachs as example (*see* Goldman Sachs); legal authorities to address, 263; Lehman Brothers as example (*see* Lehman Brothers); Morgan Stanley as example (*see* Morgan Stanley); post-crisis status of, 140–141;

Investment banks (cont.)
Primary Dealer Credit Facility for, 128; regulatory system oversight of, 9. *See also* Broker-dealers; Nonbank financial institutions; *specific banks*
IRS (Internal Revenue Service), 182, 396
Irwin Union Bank and Trust, 249n48
Issa, Darrell, 480
Italy, real GDP in, 532, 535

Jackson, Mike, 370
Japan: asset purchases in, 440; Bank of Japan, 440, 496, 498n12, 500, 503; international policy coordination with, 496–497, 498n12, 500; real GDP in, 532; swap lines with, 500, 503
Job losses. *See* Unemployment
JPMorgan Chase: Bear Stearns acquisition, 18, 19, 41, 124–128, 152, 195; recapitalization of, 220–221; special purpose vehicle facilitating credit for, 156–157; stress tests of, 284; Super-SIV role of, 211; Temporary Liquidity Guarantee Program eligibility, 240; Washington Mutual acquisition by, 27, 41

Keepwell agreements, 181
KeyCorp, 273
Kohn, Donald, 89, 503, 516
Korea Development Bank, 129
Korean Investment Corporation, 211n3
Kuwait Investment Authority, 211n3

Lacker, Jeffrey, 54, 430
Legacy Loan Program, 273–275
Legal authorities, 144–170; for asset-based lending, 157–158; for bank capital requirement changes, 268; for banking system recapitalization, 216, 557; for broad-based lending facilities, 165–169; conclusions about, 169–170; for conventional liquidity tools, 51–53,

148–149; for depository institution credit, 148–150; for discount for individuals, partnerships, or corporations, 153–154; emergency lending powers (*see* Emergency lending powers); evolving need for, 144–146; existing, in early financial crisis, 146–147; of FDIC, 144, 146–147, 169–170, 229, 235–237, 261, 274, 293; Fed *vs.* Treasury, clarification of, 104–105; future applications of, 161–162, 164, 169–170; for General Motors and Chrysler rescue, 365–366, 371, 384; for housing programs, 323, 342, 356–357; legal challenges to, 159–161; for money market funds support, 163–164, 166–167nn46–47, 200; for mortgage giants' rescue, 183; for nonbank financial institutions, 146–147, 150–154, 156–162, 165–169, 263; for novel lender-of-last-resort programs, 165–169; orderly liquidation authority as, 43–44, 141, 143, 293; regulatory reform and constraints of, 43, 46–48, 145–146, 162; for resolution, 261, 263, 274; satisfactory securitization with, 154–156, 167–168; for special purpose vehicles, 156–158; for TARP, 147, 159, 164–165, 167–168, 169, 389–394; for Temporary Liquidity Guarantee Program, 169, 229, 235–237; for Term Asset-Backed Securities Loan Facility, 166–167nn46–47, 167, 276; timing of authorization for, 557
Lehman Brothers: capital insufficiency of, 129; executive leadership removal at, 25; failure of, 4, 18, 21–24, 88, 128–132, 158–159, 162, 193, 195, 227, 427, 548; legal authorities exceptions with, 158–159, 162; monetary policy in response to collapse of, 427; as nonbank financial institution, 9, 40, 128–132, 158–159, 162; regulatory limited options to rescue, 19, 22–23

Northern Trust, 194

Norway: international policy coordination with, 500

Novel lender-of-last-resort programs, 81–110; AMLF as (*see* Asset-Backed Commercial Paper Money Market Mutual Fund Liquidity Facility); conclusions about, 106; context for, 81–83; coordination and role clarification for, 104–105; CPFF as (*see* Commercial Paper Funding Facility); evaluation of, 100–102, 109–110, 544–546, 548–551; legal authorities for, 165–169; lessons learned from, 102–106; outcomes of, 544–546, 548–551; PDCF as (*see* Primary Dealer Credit Facility); preparedness for, 102–103; stigma avoidance with, 105, 109; summary of, 107–108, 114; TALF as (*see* Term Asset-Backed Securities Loan Facility); TSLF as (*see* Term Securities Lending Facility)

NUMMI. *See* New United Motor Manufacturing Inc.

Obama, Barack/Obama administration: bank capital stabilization under, 254–261; banking system recapitalization under, 33, 392–393; fiscal policy response under, 36, 451, 454–460, 473–475, 507, 523–524; Geithner nomination by, 32; General Motors and Chrysler rescue/restructure under, 359–361, 364, 366–367, 372–380, 383–384; housing programs under, 36–38, 321–322, 332–333, 339, 343, 355, 401n23; international policy coordination under, 494, 510–511, 517–518, 523–524; monetary policy under, 431; mortgage giants' rescue under, 182, 185–186, 188, 331; TARP under, 32–33, 36, 366–367, 384, 389, 392–393, 397–398, 405

OCC. *See* Office of the Comptroller of the Currency

Office of Federal Housing Enterprise Oversight (OFHEO), 174–176

Office of Financial Stability (OFS), 386, 394–399, 418–420

Office of the Comptroller of the Currency (OCC): bank charters from, 304–305; mortgage giants' financial review by, 176, 180; regulatory system role of, 9, 232; stress test development role, 286; TARP support from, 396

Office of Thrift Supervision (OTS): abolishment of, 41; bank charters from, 304–305; regulatory system role of, 9, 41, 120, 134n16, 232; TARP support from, 396

OFHEO. *See* Office of Federal Housing Enterprise Oversight

OFS. *See* Office of Financial Stability

OIS rate. *See* Overnight indexed swap (OIS) rate

Open bank resolution, 264, 271–272

Oppenheimer Group, 272

Orderly liquidation authority, 43–44, 141, 143, 293

OTS. *See* Office of Thrift Supervision

Outcomes, 529–560; context for, 531–536, 538–556; economic reinvigoration and, 38; evidence organization framework for, 536–556; hindsight bias on, 530; historical comparisons for, 531, 533–536, 538; lessons learned from, 556–560; of macro policies, 529, 536–538, 541–542, 544, 547–554; moral hazard and, 554–555; overview of assessing, 529–531; for Phase I (Aug. 2007 to March 2008), 540, 541–543; for Phase II (March 2008 to Sept. 2008), 540, 544–547; for Phase III (Sept. 2008 to Dec. 2009), 540, 547–556; public trust in government decline as, 555; real GDP as reflection of, 519, 531–532, 534–535, 537–540, 542, 549–554;

Regulatory system: bank capital requirements in, 39, 40–41, 223, 281; Congressional negotiations to modify, 26–28; coordination of entities in, 142, 232–233; crisis management and, 558; financial crisis and weaknesses of, 2, 9–11, 16–19, 26–28, 40–41; international policy coordination on reform of, 39, 516–518, 526; legal authority under (*see* Legal authorities); money market funds under, 197; mortgage giants under, 9, 11, 20, 40, 174–180, 184, 187, 190, 321, 331, 334–335, 339, 546; nonbank financial institutions under, 9–10, 16–19, 40–41, 117–118, 119–121, 134, 140–141, 142, 143, 162; reform of, 11, 39–48, 140–141, 143, 145–146, 169–170, 223, 251, 312, 314, 389n5, 516–518, 526, 558; TARP coordination with, 413; TARP oversight under, 418–420. *See also specific laws and regulations*

Reich, John, 270

Reinhart, Carmen, 126n6, 492n3, 519, 534

REMIC. *See* Real Estate Mortgage Investment Conduit

Repayment of government funds. *See* Profit from government initiatives

Repurchase (repo) market: financial crisis in relation to, 8, 16–17, 26, 40; financial system vulnerability with, 8; nonbank financial institutions in, 115–117, 128; reverse repos, 52n5, 56n12, 65, 105n14, 443; runs in, 539; single-tranche repo program, 51, 52–53, 63–65, 66–67, 68–72, 76, 169; term repos, 59; triparty repo market, 63, 83–88, 128

Reserve Primary Fund, 25, 88, 193–194, 197–198, 227

Resolution: for bank recapitalization, 260–261, 261–263, 264, 271–272, 274; by FDIC, 261, 263, 274, 293–294, 300, 304, 309, 313, 317–319; of government-sponsored enterprises, 4, 20–21, 129, 147,

178–189, 191–192, 195, 212, 264, 331; open bank, 264, 271–272; for savings and loan failures, 314–317

Resolution Trust Corporation (RTC), 278, 297n20, 306, 315–317, 386

Resource Bancshares Mortgage Group, 289

Rice, Condoleezza, 502

Rogoff, Kenneth, 126n6, 492n3, 519, 534

Romer, Christina, 378, 456

RTC Completion Act (1993), 314n69

Runnable short-term financing, 5, 8, 42; as commercial paper, 92, 92n7; in money market funds, 89, 194–195; nonbank financial institutions in, 115–117, 141; preventing runs on, 16, 24, 26, 30–31, 32, 225; run on ABCP, 50, 539; run on repo, 63, 539; runs at depository institutions, 147, 226, 237. *See also* Money market funds; Novel lender-of-last-resort programs; Temporary Liquidity Guarantee Program

Runs: in asset-backed commercial paper, 75, 539; on bank debt and deposits, 147, 219, 226–228, 237, 265, 270, 318; as cause of panic, 4, 5, 8, 14, 26, 89, 122, 196, 203–205, 262n5; intervention to prevent, 17, 19, 23, 92–93, 123, 226, 227; investor runs on secured financing of dealers 101, 539; lending into, 23, 24, 131; on money market funds, 83, 92, 163, 166–167n47, 219, 496; on specific institutions, 21, 28, 124, 128, 129, 131–132n13, 158, 194, 318; in triparty repo markets, 63, 83

Russia: International Monetary Fund participation, 511

Salvatore, Tony, 412

Savings and loan (S&L) crisis: cost of cleanup of, 297n20; financial crisis comparison to, 297, 301, 314–317, 386, 531; lessons learned from, 306, 314–317;

Treasury, Department of the (cont.)
400; Exchange Stabilization Fund of, 26,
43, 146, 163–164, 199–207, 548; FDIC
borrowing from, 297n20, 298, 311, 313;
Fed role distinction from, 104–105; fiscal
policy of (*see* Fiscal policy response);
international policy coordination with
(*see* International policy coordination);
legal authorities of, 42–43, 104–105, 144,
146, 159, 163–165, 169–170, 200; money
market fund guarantees by, 4, 26,
163–164, 199–207, 227, 548, 550;
mortgage giants' rescue role of (*see*
Fannie Mae; Freddie Mac); nonbank
financial institutions and, 113, 124–134,
136–140, 391; Public-Private Investment
Program of, 96n10, 139, 278–279, 391,
401, 549; regulatory system role of, 17,
233; Supplementary Financing Program
of, 103–104nn12–13, 427, 429; TARP
under (*see* Troubled Assets Relief
Program); Term Asset-Backed Securities Loan Facility role of, 95–97, 100,
370–371
Treasury Securities Lending Facility,
426n3
Triparty repo market, 63, 83–88, 128
Troubled Assets Relief Program (TARP),
385–420; accountability for, 414–415;
administrative implementation of, 29,
386–388, 393–394, 399–404; AIG rescue
under, 401, 410–411, 412, 417n30; allocation
for, 216, 254; Automotive Industry
Financing Program of, 400; banking
system recapitalization with, 29, 31, 33,
209, 213–215, 390–393, 399–401, 408–410,
551–552; Capital Assistance Program
and, 270, 400; Capital Purchase Program
of, 139, 215–225, 228, 229–230, 270,
390–392, 395, 399–401, 408–409, 411, 552;
Commercial Paper Funding Facility and,
93, 140, 167–168; Community Development Capital Initiative of, 400; Congres-

sional negotiations on, 27–28;
deployment of, 28–35; effect on credit
supply, 101–102; Emergency Economic
Stabilization Act authorizing, 147,
164–165, 214, 332, 385n1, 386, 390, 397n18,
415, 547; evaluation of, 419–420, 547,
551–552, 554; executive compensation
provisions of, 392–393; executive
leadership recruitment under, 406;
exercising voting rights with, 405–406;
exiting investments in, 408–414;
financial controls and reporting for,
414–415; General Motors and Chrysler
rescue with, 32, 36, 365–372, 381–382,
384, 400, 411–413; government shutdown not affecting, 399; housing
programs under, 400, 401–404, 416–417,
419n32, 552, 555; investment exiting in,
408–414; investment management in,
404–408; legal authority for, 147, 159,
164–165, 167–168, 169, 389–394; lessons
learned from, 399, 400–401, 418;
minority ownership issues with, 407;
mortgage debt purchased under, 27–35,
213–215, 321, 332, 385–420; name of,
385n1; net cost of, 417; nonbank financial
institutions under, 134, 137, 139–140, 159,
160n33, 391; outcomes of, 547, 551–552,
554; overview of, 385–389; Public-Private
Investment Program matched by, 278,
391, 401; regulatory and policy interference avoided under, 406; regulatory
system coordination with, 413; regulatory system oversight of, 418–420;
regulatory system reform constraints on,
389n5, 408; repayment of, 34, 272–273,
381–382, 387–388, 393, 408–409, 411, 417,
554; reporting to Congress and public
on, 415–418; restructuring process
under, 406–407, 409; scope of authority
for, 390–391; securities law challenges
for, 413–414; Special Inspector General
for, 328, 337, 341, 414, 418–420; staffing

for, 394–399, 420; summary of programs, 388; Temporary Liquidity Guarantee Program and, 30, 140, 229, 230, 239; Term Asset-Backed Securities Loan Facility funding from, 95, 97, 139, 277, 370–371, 401; third-party advisers for, 404; trading prohibitions under, 407–408; transferring investments to separate entity in, 404–405; transparency of, 387, 397n18, 414–415; troubled assets, defined, 214, 390, 391; use of funds requirements under, 407; warrants and guarantee provisions of, 391–392

TSLF. *See* Term Securities Lending Facility

Underwriting standards: erosion of, and financial crisis, 6, 290, 324–325; stringent, with quantitative easing, 336

Unemployment: early crisis-level, 423–424; economic trends and, 533; financial crisis effects on, 3, 34, 38, 41, 284n14, 285, 321, 324, 329, 360, 423–425, 428, 431, 435, 437, 453, 454–455, 458–459, 530, 531; financial crisis response lowering, 1, 38 (*see also specific programs*); fiscal policy response to, 36, 454–458, 460–464, 468n6, 469–471, 473–474, 477–478, 481–482, 483; forecasts for, 433–437, 458–459; General Motors and Chrysler failure affecting, 376, 381; housing program aid *vs.* aid for, 37; monetary policy to ease, 425, 428, 432, 440, 445, 448; mortgage debt paid with insurance for, 333; outcomes reflected in changes in, 540; stress tests estimating, 284n14

Unemployment Compensation Extension Act (2008, 2010), 461

United Kingdom: Bank of England, 59n17, 74n38, 106, 498n12, 500, 503, 505–506; Barclays-Lehman potential acquisition under regulations of, 22, 130–131; credit default swap spreads in, 492; equity injections in, 264; financial crisis in, 531; international policy coordination with, 498n12, 500, 513; legal authorities in, 146; liquidity provision actions and guarantees of, 30, 74n38, 106, 219, 233, 243, 498n12; monetary policy of, 505–506; nonbank financial institutions growth in, 117; real GDP in, 531–532; swap lines with, 59n17, 500, 503

U.S. Bancorp, 240

Volcker, Paul, 518n55

VOW to Hire Heroes Act (2011), 462

Vulnerable population, fiscal policy response to protect, 469–471

Wachovia: capital raised by, 122; executive leadership removal at, 25; failure of, 4, 28, 41, 213, 319; Wells Fargo acquisition of, 28, 41

Wachtell, Lipton, Rosen & Katz, 177

Wagoner, Rick, 363–364, 379

Wang Qishan, 496

Washington Mutual (WaMu): capital raised by, 122; failure of, 4, 27–28, 41, 213, 227, 292, 317–319; JPMorgan Chase acquisition of, 27, 41; regulatory oversight of, 41; resolution of, 317–319

Wells Fargo: recapitalization of, 220–221; stress test results for, 273; Temporary Liquidity Guarantee Program eligibility, 240; Wachovia acquisition by, 28, 41

Wilson, Ken, 194

Worker, Homeownership, and Business Assistance Act (2009), 461

World Bank Group, 509n31, 513, 515

World Trade Organization, 515

Yellen, Janet, 45

Zhou Xiaochuan, 496